The Taste of Scotland Guide

Introduction

Scotland's landscape and climate are ideally suited to producing raw materials for the food and drinks industries that thrive within its borders.

The lush pastures of the west coast, warmed by the Gulf Stream and watered by Atlantic rain, provide the ideal feeding conditions for the grazing herds of cattle and sheep that produce Scotland's top quality beef and lamb.

Offshore, favourable climatic conditions provide the perfect environment for shellfish, which are exported throughout Europe. The sea lochs along the west coast have tidal current flows and sheltered environments, making them ideal sites for fish farms producing salmon and trout. Inland, rivers such as the Tweed and the Tay are natural breeding grounds for these two prize catches, and are where some of the best wild salmon in the world can be caught with rod and line.

Herds of red deer roaming wooded glens and grouse on heather moors not only add to the spectacular natural beauty of the Highlands, but also supply game meats to markets across the world.

This lush land and seascape is harvested by indigenous producers of high quality raw materials - such as fish, meat and milk - which are readily available to the processing industry. The food and drink that carry Scotland's name around the world, such as salmon, game, whisky and fancy foods, are high value premium products.

Quality is the hallmark of Scottish products whether they be bought in retail shops or served in restaurants and hotels. Scottish farmers have led the world in putting in place a number of farm assurance schemes and linking these to quality initiatives. Each year an increasingly wider range of product categories in Scotland is subject to rigorous independent procedures, which stress quality from conception to consumption, increasing consumer confidence in the true and honest quality of Scottish food and drink.

Nevertheless, quality is more than product and price. The processing and preparation of food must be handled by people whose skills, care and attention in their work are of a standard to complement the quality of the produce they are handling. Scotland proudly possesses some of the best and most innovative chefs in the world today, whose success in last year's Culinary Olympics in Frankfurt far exceeded any other country.

Scotland has the natural resources, the right environment, and the quality products, which, with the unequalled culinary skills to be found in the country's best hotels and restaurants, result in not only simple, good food, but also innovative mouth-watering dishes to be enjoyed and remembered.

Contents

Taste of Scotland

current members are identified by the 1994 Certificate of Membership which should be on display.

THE TASTE OF
SCOTLAND
1994

This is to certify that

The Haven Hotel

has been selected for membership of

The Taste of Scotland Scheme

in recognition of its commitment to the pursuit of
excellence in food preparation and service

The Taste of Scotland Scheme Ltd is sponsored by:

Scottish Tourist Board
Scottish Enterprise
Highlands & Islands Enterprise
Scotch Quality Beef & Lamb Association
Scottish Salmon Board

How to use this Guide

Appin

Map Reference

Map

Address & Tel. No. etc ▶

INVERCRERAN COUNTRY HOUSE HOTEL
Glen Creran, Appin
Argyll PA38 4BJ
Tel: 063 173 414/456
Fax: 063 173 532

Just off A828 Oban-Fort William at head of Loch Creran, 14 miles north of Connel Bridge.

◀ How to find it

Description ▶ The first thing that strikes one about Invercreran is the superb site. It is perched on a hillside with really magnificent panoramic views over glens and hills. The house itself is strikingly different, a stylish modern mansion house, yet not in the slightest out of place in this remote and lovely glen. Splendid public rooms with spacious terraces, and large comfortable bedrooms, contribute to the overall feeling of luxury. John and Marie Kersley with their family have created a really special place which offers total relaxation and enjoyment. There are lots of interesting walks locally – and don't be surprised if you come across the odd herd of red deer. The food lives up to the high standards that mark this place and is served with courtesy and charm in the delightful dining room. Children over five years are welcome.

Any seasonal limitations ▶ *Open 1 Mar to 31 Oct*
Rooms: 9 with private facilities ◀ Accommodation
Dining Room/Restaurant Lunch 12.15 – 1.30 pm except Mon (c) ◀ Meal times & prices
Dinner 7 – 8 pm (e)
No dogs
No smoking in dining room

Specimen inclusive terms quoted on per person per night basis ▶ *Bed & breakfast £44 – £69*
Dinner B & B £71 – £96
Pan-fried scallops with white wine and chive butter sauce. Collops of Highland venison with a cranberry and Port sauce. Poached fillet of turbot with a tarragon and mint cream. Collops of fillet of beef sauté with brandy and wild mushroom sauce.
◀ Specimen food specialities

STB ratings ▶ *STB Deluxe 4 Crowns*
Credit cards: 1, 3 ◀ Credit cards accepted
Proprietor: John Kersley

Entries

- Establishments selected by Taste of Scotland are listed in this Guide in alphabetical order under the nearest town or village.

- Island entries are shown alphabetically by island or island group, e.g. Skye, Orkney.

- A full list of hotels, restaurants etc is given in alphabetical order in the Index at the end of the Guide.

Special diets or requirements

- Although vegetarian meals are more readily available nowadays, we would advise that you mention this requirement when making your booking.

- Other special needs, such as diet or facilities for disabled guests, should also be arranged in advance.

Wines and spirits

- Except where otherwise stated, all hotels and restaurants are licensed for the service of wines, spirits, beers etc.

- Most unlicensed establishments - which tend to be small guest houses or farmhouses - will welcome your taking your own wine, but again please enquire in advance.

- Where an establishment is shown to have a 'restricted licence' it generally means that residents and diners may be served alcoholic beverages, but members of the public may not call in for a drink.

Lunches

- Nowadays lunchtime eating has become much less formal except in city centre hotels and restaurants. Bar snacks are more usual in some smaller establishments and rural hotels.

- To simplify the choice available, we specify Bar Lunch or Dining Room/Restaurant Lunch in this Guide.

Restrictions on smoking

- Within the information on each establishment, we have noted where there is no smoking permitted in the dining room or restaurant.

- Where an area is set aside for non-smokers, the entry will show 'No smoking area in dining room/restaurant'.

- In addition we have highlighted where no smoking is permitted throughout an establishment or where there are restrictions on smoking in guest bedrooms.

- Entries which do not give any such information are taken to have no restriction on smoking.

Pets

- Pets are accepted in some hotels by arrangement. It is wise, however, to confirm this when booking as there may be a small charge and sometimes there is a restriction on the areas within the establishment where pets are permitted.

- Restaurants generally do not accept dogs.

Foreign Languages

- Where establishments have provided us with information on any foreign languages spoken, this has been incorporated within the descriptive paragraph about the establishment.

Prices

- Prices are quoted as a **guideline only** and Guide readers are advised to check prevailing prices when making their reservation.

- These estimated prices for 1994 were provided by the establishments, based on a three course meal, excluding drinks.

Key

(a)	under £10
(b)	£10 - £15
(c)	£15 - £20
(d)	£20 - £25
(e)	£25 - £30
(f)	over £30

- Specimen inclusive terms are listed, once again as a **guideline**.

- Where a price range is given, the **lower price** normally indicates the rate **per person sharing** a double room, and the higher price the rate for **single occupancy** or **per person** in a **higher quality room**.

- Where a **room rate** is offered, this information is shown in the entry.

- Times of food service are listed to show **first and last orders**, unless otherwise indicated.

Credit/Charge Cards

- Where an establishment accepts credit/charge cards, those taken are listed under the following codes:

Key

1	Access/Mastercard/Eurocard
2	American Express
3	Visa
4	Carte Bleu
5	Diners Club
6	Mastercharge
	SWITCH and DELTA cards are also listed where appropriate.

How to avoid disappointment

- Make an **advance reservation** whenever possible.

- Mention you are using the **Taste of Scotland Guide**.

- **Remember!** Many food items are seasonal and that the specialities listed have been selected as examples of the style of food on offer, but there is no guarantee of availability on any particular day.

- **Check** if any **price changes** have taken place since the publication of this Guide.

- Confirm that **credit cards** are accepted.

Comments

- Taste of Scotland welcomes comments – both good and bad.

- However, **if you have an unsatisfactory meal**, we would always advise that you **speak to the restaurant or hotel manager or proprietor _at the time_**.

- It gives an immediate opportunity for the situation to be rectified or explained.

- If this fails to solve the problem, do write to the Taste of Scotland Scheme about your experience. While we do not have operational control of any establishment listed, we will pass on your comments for investigation.

- But do let us hear of your good experiences too!

- We like to give our members feedback on comments from the public, so we provide a comment slip at the end of this Guide for your use.

STB *Grading and Classification Scheme*

Since 1985, the Scottish Tourist Board has been systematically inspecting hotels, bed and breakfasts, and self catering accommodation, defining the standards that visitors expect and helping owners and operators meet those standards.

In a two-tier scheme, accommodation all over the country – from the simplest to the most sophisticated – is GRADED for quality and CLASSIFIED for its facilities.

Every establishment which is a member of the STB Grading and Classification Scheme – and there are over 4,000 – is visited each year. Grading and classification covers both serviced accommodation (hotels, guest houses, bed and breakfast) and self catering accommodation.

Members display blue oval plaques, to tell you whether they are approved, commended, highly commended or deluxe.

The centre panel of the plaque tells you whether the establishment is

APPROVED (offering an acceptable standard)

COMMENDED (offering a good standard)

HIGHLY COMMENDED (offering a very good standard)

or

DELUXE (offering an excellent standard)

These GRADINGS are awarded by the STB inspectors once they have checked all the important factors that contribute to quality in an establishment. Just as you would, they look for clean, attractive surroundings, well furnished and heated. They sample meals, sleep in the beds, and talk to the staff. Like you, they appreciate atmosphere and a friendly smile of welcome.

Each type of establishment is assessed on its own merits, so that any type of accommodation can achieve the highest grading – and many do, in all categories.

The second section of the plaque displays the CROWN CLASSIFICATION, denoting the range of facilities on offer – things such as private bathrooms, lounges, meal provision and so on. From a basic LISTED classification up to FIVE CROWNS can be added. So more crowns on the plaque mean more facilities.

"The Taste of Scotland Island Experience"

Taste of Scotland and Scotsell, the Scottish Islands Holiday specialist, are pleased to introduce this unique car touring island holiday to the west coast and Hebridean Islands of Scotland.

Enjoy the splendid coastal scenery of Wester Ross with your first night at the Dundonnell Hotel near Ullapool, before sailing from Ullapool to Stornoway on the Isle of Lewis, where three nights evening meal, bed and breakfast is arranged for you at one of the comfortable Taste of Scotland guest houses.

Collectively known as the 'Long Island', remarkable examples of stone antiquity are to be found in Lewis, while in its more mountainous neighbour of Harris, the ancient crafts of hand spinning and weaving are still practised.

Sail from Tarbert to Lochmaddy in North Uist, drive over the causeway to Benbecula and enjoy sampling the extensive menu at the Dark Island Hotel during your two nights here.

Discover the contrasting scenery of the Uists, from a crofting and machair landscape, home to many wild flowers, to the magnificent beaches of the west.

From Lochmaddy, sail over the sea to the magical island of Skye, where two nights of comfortable hotel accommodation and fine dining complement your explorations of this fascinating island.

Be enchanted by the dramatic scenery and legends of the Cuillin Mountains, the castles of the Clans MacDonald and MacLeod, visitor centres and croft house museums, with even a distillery to tempt you!

In such magnificent surroundings, this is a wonderful way in which to sample a 'Taste of Scotland'.

Details of this unique holiday will be found in Scotsell's Scottish Island Brochure. Friendly and knowledgeable experts arrange your ferries and accommodation, leaving you peace of mind to look forward to and enjoy your 'Taste of Scotland' Island Holiday.

Discover the Western Isles the easy way this year!

For your Scottish Islands brochure, please telephone Scotsell on 041 772 5928, or send the coupon below to:

SCOTSELL,
SUITE 2D CHURCHILL WAY,
BISHOPBRIGGS,
GLASGOW G64 2RH
TEL (041) 772 5928   FAX (041) 762 0297

NAME ....

ADDRESS ....

....

....

POSTCODE...

REF. TOFS94

Caithness Glass

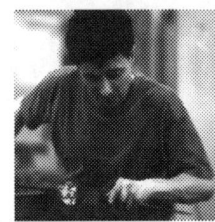

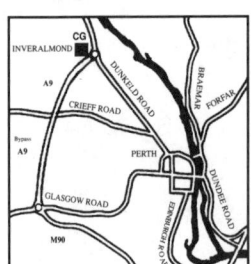

Taste Of Scotland Prestige Awards

The Prestige Award scheme - now in its seventh year - was set up to give recognition to existing high standards in the hotel and catering trade in Scotland and by so doing to encourage others to emulate the winners.

The awards are restricted to establishments which are members of the Taste of Scotland Scheme and thus already identified as leaders in their particular category.

Each year the public is invited to help the judging panel by nominating hotels and restaurants in which they have experienced particularly good standards of food and service.

Taste of Scotland is pleased to record and congratulate the award winners in the 1993 awards sponsored by Caithness Glass plc:

Hotel of the Year	***Sheraton Grand Hotel, Edinburgh***
Restaurant of the Year	***The Cellar, Anstruther***
Country House Hotel of the Year	***Balgonie Country House, Ballater***
Special Merit Awards	***Creelers Seafood Restaurant, Isle of Arran***
	The Haven Hotel, Plockton
	The Kirroughtree Hotel, Newton Stewart

These winners' entries have been highlighted in the listings for ease of identification.

During 1994, the judges will be considering nominations under the same categories as 1993.

In the light of your experience in Taste of Scotland establishments, we would welcome your nominations.

You can do so by sending in the coupons on pages 197 and 199 of this Guide, nomination cards available at Taste of Scotland establishments, or by letter or postcard.

Closing date for entries: 31 August 1994

Past Winners

1992

Moat House International, Glasgow
Pompadour Restaurant, Caledonian Hotel, Edinburgh
Greywalls, Gullane
Harding's Restaurant, North Berwick
Three Chimneys Restaurant, Isle of Skye
The Gean House, Alloa

1991

Cameron House Hotel, Loch Lomond
Arisaig House, by Arisaig
The Anchorage, Tarbert, Loch Fyne
Crinan Hotel, Crinan, Argyll
Balbirnie House Hotel, Markinch, by Glenrothes
Summer Isles Hotel, Achiltibuie

1990

Turnberry Hotel, Turnberry
Knockie Lodge, Whitebridge
The Triangle, Glasgow
Ardanaiseig Hotel, Kilchrenan
The Gleneagles Hotel, Auchterarder
Shieldhill Country House, nr Biggar

1989

Cromlix House, Dunblane
North West Castle Hotel, Stranraer
The Cross, Kingussie
Ostlers Close, Cupar
Smugglers Restaurant, Crieff
Auchterarder House, Auchterarder

1988

Caledonian Hotel, Edinburgh
Murrayshall Country House Hotel, nr Perth
Tiroran House, Isle of Mull
Taste of Speyside, Dufftown
Martins Restaurant, Edinburgh
Broughton's Restaurant, Blair Drummond

Achray House Hotel

Stunning Lochside position in St Fillans – an area of outstanding natural beauty.

Well established, family run hotel, known for its wide selection of good food, service & a caring attitude that brings people back year after year.

The perfect base for sightseeing, golf, walking, field & watersports.

From £28.00/night, en-suite, B & B per night.

Contact: Tony or Jane Ross
Achray House Hotel
St Fillans, Crieff PH6 2NF
Tel 0764 685231
Fax 0764 685320

EGON RONAY'S **GUIDES**

 AA ★★ ❀

see entry page 112
see entry page 48

AUCHTERARDER
H O U S E

One of Scotland's finest country mansions, set in 17½ acres of scenic grounds, Auchterarder House reflects the elegance & splendour of the Victorian era. The house is ideal for parties to use exclusively. Guests are offered the highest standards of personal service, comfort & cuisine, in magnificent surroundings. All 15 bedrooms including three suites have en-suite bathrooms. Shooting, fishing & golf can be arranged.

Only one hours drive from Edinburgh & Glasgow.

Caithness Glass/Taste of Scotland Award 1989
for Best Overall Excellence
Member of Small Luxury Hotels of the World Consortium

Owned & managed by two generations of the Brown family, Auchterarder House is not just a hotel, it is an experience in gracious living. Experience the pleasure of a real Scottish country house - experience the magic of Auchterarder House.

For brochure, tariff & reservation write, telephone or fax...

Auchterarder, Perthshire PH3 1DZ
Tel 0764-663646 • Fax 0764-662939

see entry page 46
see entry page 127

RAC ★★ AA ★★ **Aultbea Hotel** *On the shores of Loch Ewe* S T B COMMENDED

ASHLEY COURTENAY
HIGHLY RECOMMENDED HOTEL

Family run hotel with friendly atmosphere, all bedrooms are en-suite and have colour TV, tea/coffee maker, radio, direct dial telephone, hair drier etc.

Restaurant with suberb Table d'Hote and a la Carte menus specialising in Local Sea Food and Venison also including our Carvery Trolley. 7pm - 9pm(last orders)

Bistro serving tea, coffee, grills, steaks, seafood, curries, vegetarian dishes, home baking. Open 9am to 9pm daily. Inverewe Gardens 6 miles, ideal centre for walking, climbing or touring the Highlands. Fishing Arranged.

Fully Licensed Bars Open All Day
Aultbea, Ross-shire. Tel 0445 731201, Fax 0445 731214

Ballathie
HOUSE HOTEL

An outstanding Country House Hotel and Restaurant situated within its own estate in an idyllic setting overlooking the Tay.

Public rooms which are bright and spacious; bedrooms of individual character and style; the renowned Ballathie cuisine; service which is cheerful and attentive, yet discreet - all this and more make up **The Ballathie Experience.**

Phone for details of 2 nights inclusive breaks.

Egon Ronay Hotel & Restaurant
Member of Scotland's Heritage Hotels Association
STB *Deluxe*

AA  ❀ ❀ **Food Award**

Kinclaven, by Stanley, nr Perth, Perthshire PH1 4QN
Tel 0250-883268 • Fax 0250-883396

Spirit of Scotland

"Inspiring bold John Barleycorn!
What dangers thou canst make us scorn!
Wi tipenny, we fear nae evil!
Wi usquaebae, we'll face the devil!"

[Robert Burns]

Whisky is the national spirit of Scotland, celebrated in song, literature and legend, but its ancient origins lost in the mists of time. It is a natural accompaniment to Scotland's cuisine and, perhaps, Scotland's greatest gift to the world. Your trip to Scotland will not be complete without at least one visit to a distillery (most hospitably open their doors to the public) and, ideally, more than one taste of the 'water of life'.

Made from malted barley and pure Scottish water, there are three types of whisky - grain, blended and single malt. All have their adherents, though the majority of whisky sold is blended, that is to say a mixture of grain and single malt. Widely available blended whiskies include such favourites as The Famous Grouse, Bells, Teachers and Black Bottle, though many hundreds of different blends are produced to suit every taste.

A single malt whisky is the original expression of Scotch. It is the output of a single distillery, produced in distinctively shaped swan-necked stills, and bottled after 10 or more years storage in oak barrels. Every aspect of its production alters the flavour, and the contribution made by wood, water, barley, still shape, warehouse conditions and location and length of storage is different for every single malt. By the way, the age that you will see prominently displayed on the bottle is not an average age or the age of the oldest whisky, but the age of the youngest spirit!

Amongst the most famous single malt distilleries are Glenfiddich, The Glenlivet, and Glengoyne, all of which are open to the public and well worth visiting. However, a visit to Scotland is a perfect time to try some of the less well-known but excellent malts such as the gentle Bruichladdich, salty Springbank from Campbeltown on the Mull of Kintyre, or the fiery Talisker from Skye. Advice will be freely given by any good barman!

Having made your choice - and there are well over 100 malts to choose from - you face the great water debate. To add a splash of water or not? It may help to know that professional tasters and blenders add water to their dram to release the distinctive aromas and free the complex range of flavours, without blunting the palate. The 'nose' of a great French perfume house was once asked to analyse the aromas of a malt whisky, and gave up after detecting 21 distinct notes, so it is well worth persisting with your research.

As you savour, reflect that Scotch whisky in all its forms is vitally important to Britain's economy. It provides employment in remote rural locations, without which the local economy would be badly hit; it contributes to the balance of payments, through its continued export success; and it provides a steady and very large source of revenue to the exchequer, through the taxes on production and consumption levied by the Government.

It has been copied throughout the world but never equalled. It remains a success story to this day; a distinctive Scottish industry that is a true world leader. Make sure you finish your meal with a mellow dram, and reflect on the true Taste of Scotland that you can carry away with you.

Slainte! Cheers!

Ian Buxton

Local Tourist Information

For specific information on a particular part of Scotland contact the following:

Angus Tourist Board
Tel: Arbroath (0241) 72609/
76680

Aviemore & Spey Valley Tourist
Board
Tel: Aviemore (0479) 810363

Ayrshire Tourist Board
Tel: Ayr (0292) 79000

Banff & Buchan Tourist Board
Tel: Banff (0261) 812419

Bute & Cowal Tourist Board
Tel: Dunoon (0369) 3785

Caithness Tourist Board
Tel: Wick (0955) 2596

City of Aberdeen Tourist Board
Tel: Aberdeen (0224) 632727

City of Dundee Tourist Board
Tel: Dundee (0382) 27723

Clyde Valley Tourist Board
Tel: Lanark (0555) 662544

Dunfermline District Council
Tel: Dunfermline (0383) 726262

Dumfries & Galloway Tourist Board
Tel: Dumfries (0387) 50434

East Lothian Tourist Board
Tel: Dunbar (0368) 63353

Edinburgh Tourist Board
Tel: Edinburgh (031) 557 1700

Fort William & Lochaber Tourist
Board
Tel: Fort William (0397) 70 3781

Forth Valley Tourist Board
Tel: Linlithgow (0506) 84 4600

Gordon District Tourist Board
Tel: Aberdeen (0224) 276276

Greater Glasgow Tourist Board
Tel: Glasgow (041) 204 4400

Inverness, Loch Ness & Nairn
Tourist Board
Tel: Inverness (0463) 234353

Isle of Arran Tourist Board
Tel: Brodick (0770) 302140

Isle of Skye & South West Ross
Tourist Board
Tel: Portree (0478) 612137

Kincardine & Deeside Tourist
Board
Tel: Banchory (033 02) 2066

Kirkcaldy District Council
Tel: Leven (0333) 429464

Loch Lomond, Stirling & Trossachs
Tourist Board
Tel: Stirling (0786) 475019

Midlothian Tourism Association
Tel: (031) 440 2210 (Roslin)

Moray Tourist Board
Tel: Elgin (0343) 543388

Orkney Tourist Board
Tel: Kirkwall (0856) 872856

Perthshire Tourist Board
Tel: Perth (0738) 27958

Ross & Cromarty Tourist Board
Tel: Kessock (0463 73) 505

St Andrews & North East Fife
Tourist Board
Tel: St Andrews (0334) 72021

Scottish Borders Tourist Board
Tel: Jedburgh (0835) 63435/
63688

Shetland Islands Tourism
Tel: Lerwick (0595) 3434

Sutherland Tourist Board
Tel: Dornoch (0862) 810400

Western Isles Tourist Board
Tel: Stornoway (0851) 70 3088

West Highlands & Islands of Argyll
Tourist Board
Tel: Oban (0631) 63122

Map Areas

Map 1 - The South West

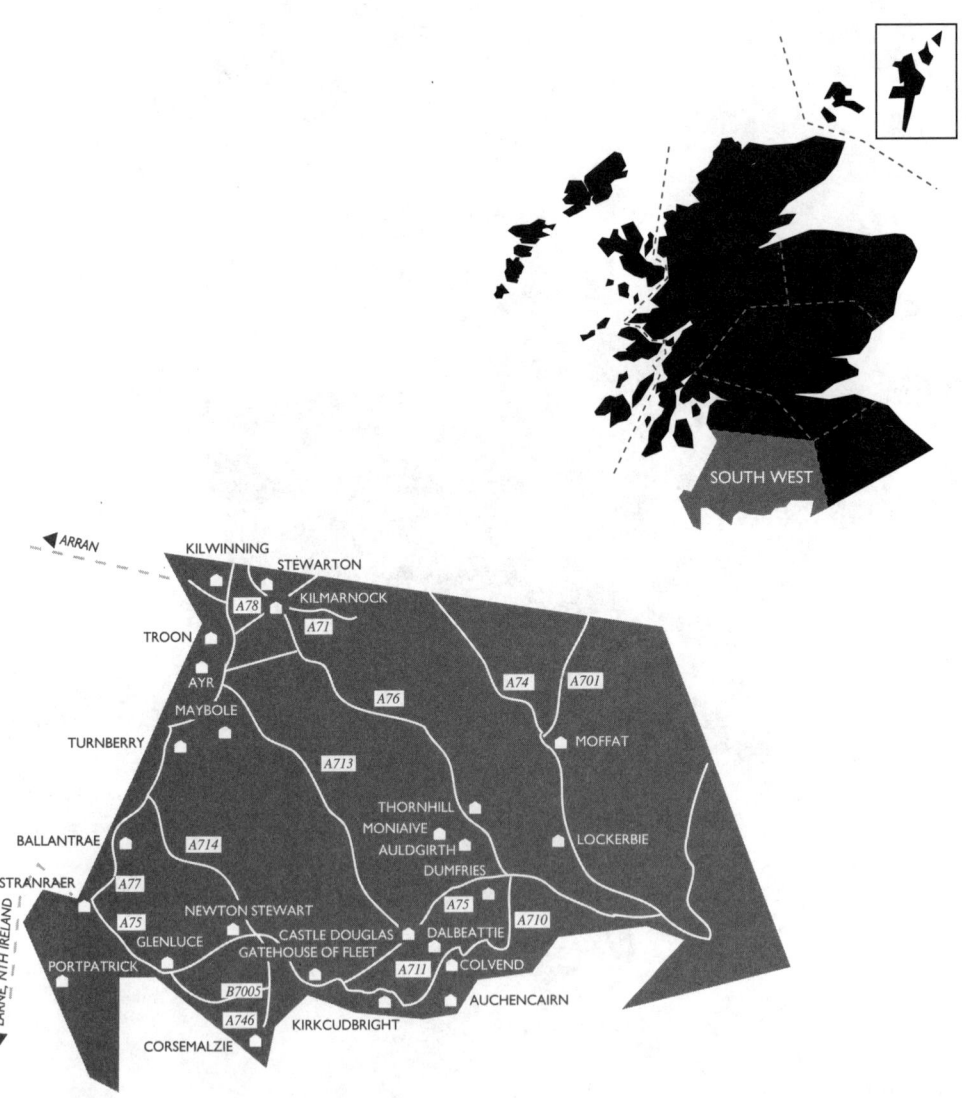

Map 2 - The Borders

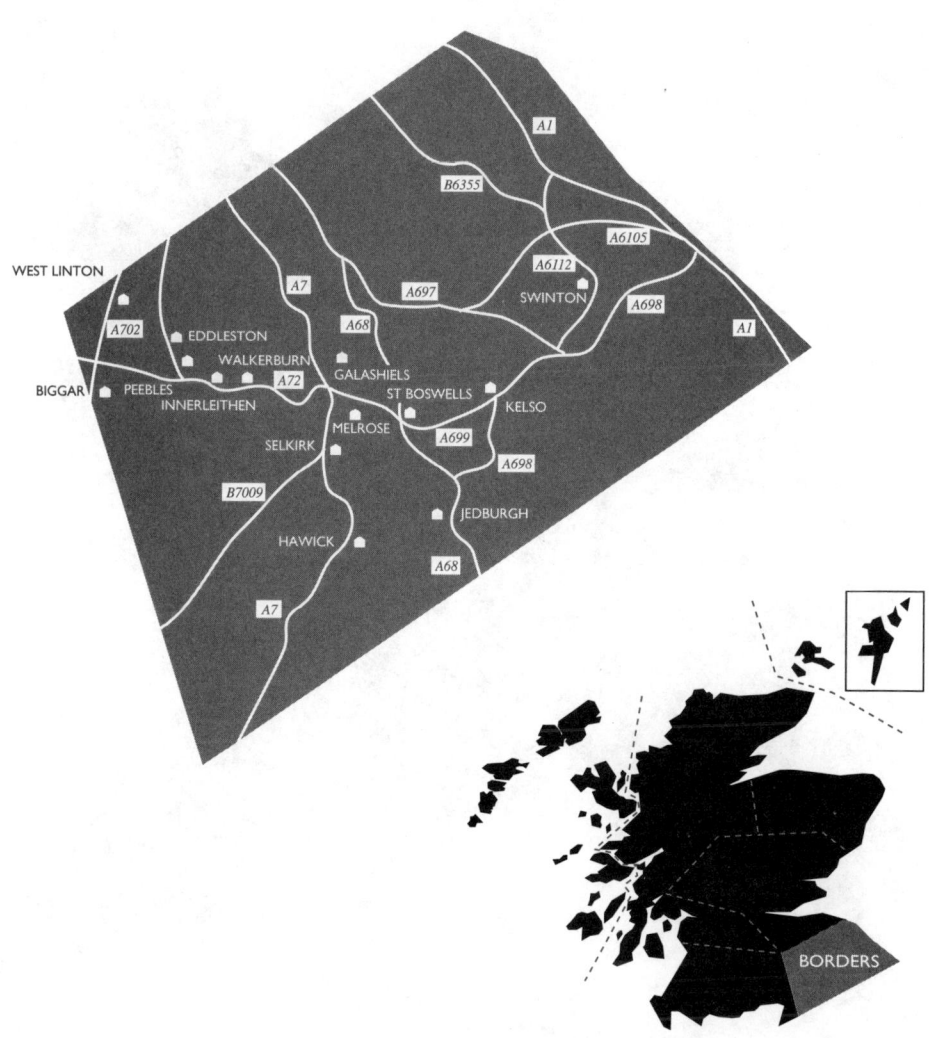

Map 3 - The Clyde

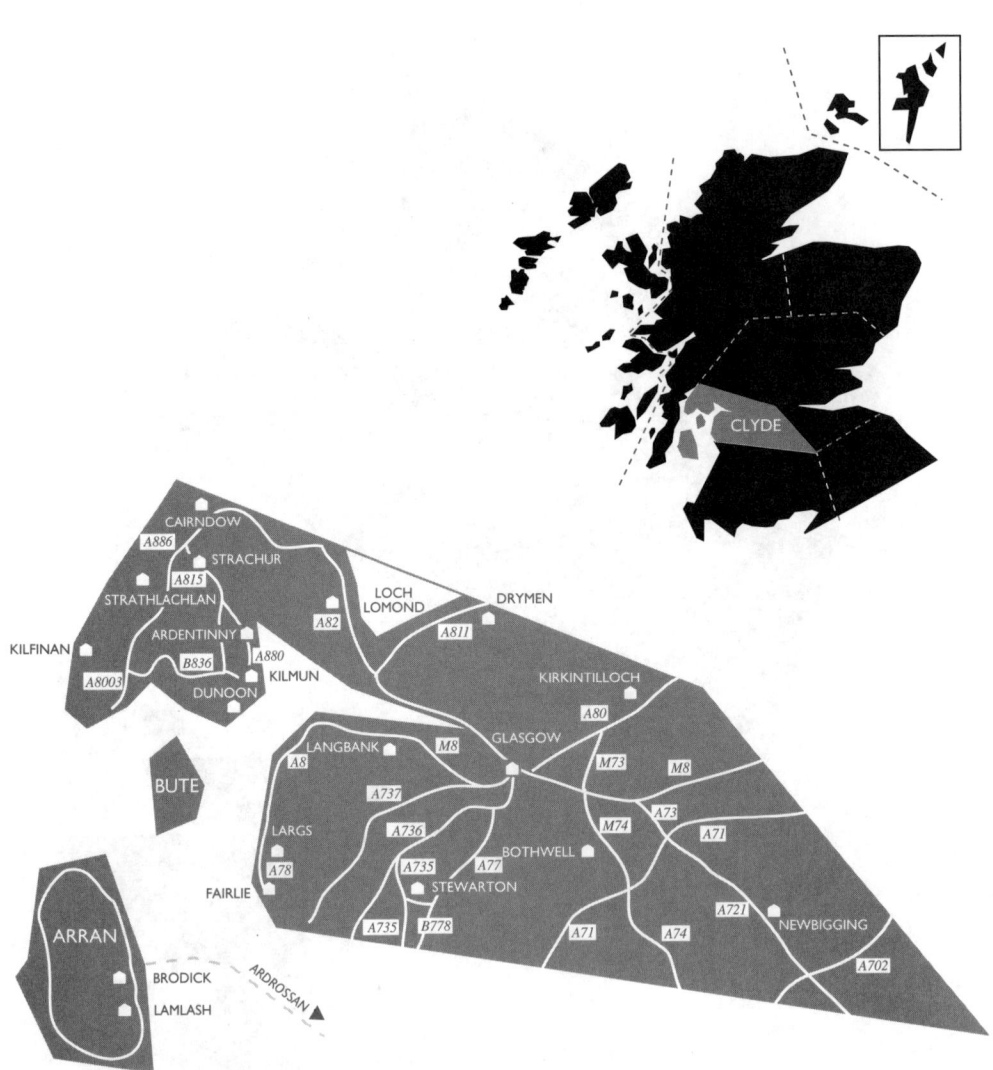

Map 4 - Central and Eastern

Map 5 - The North East

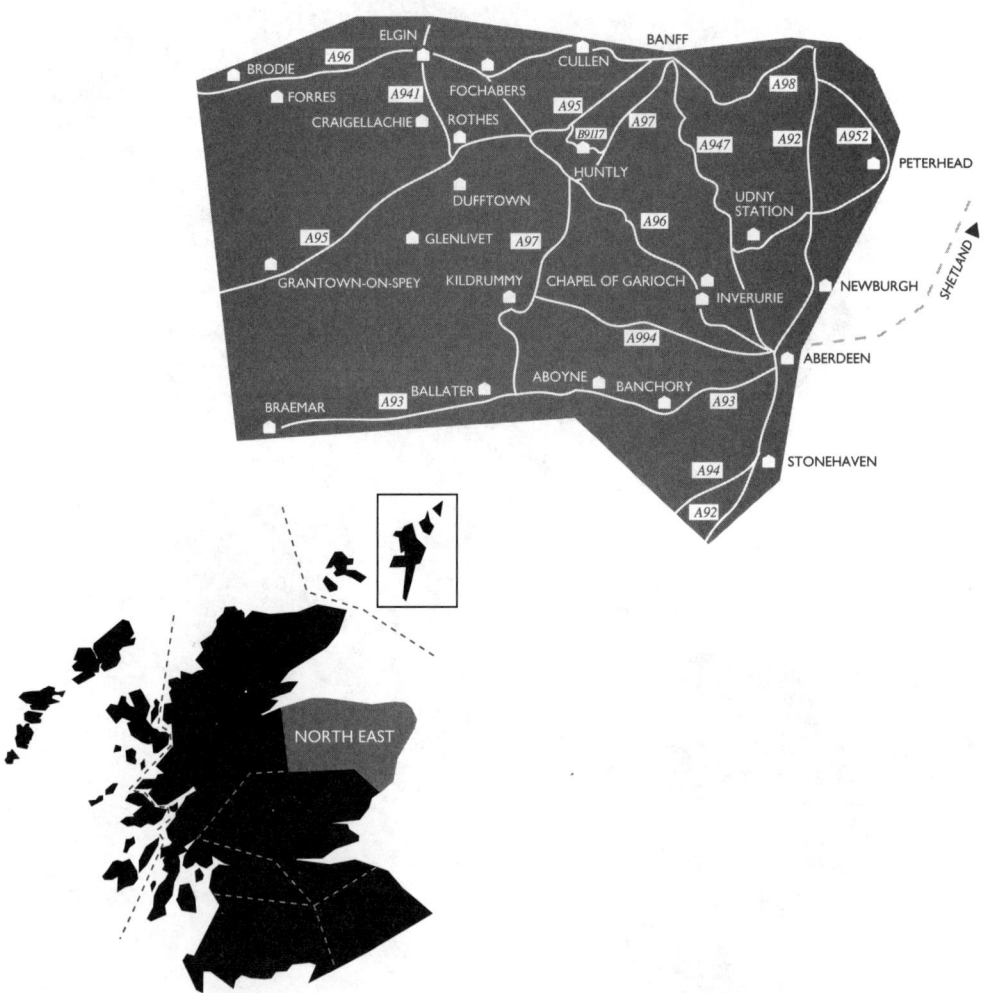

Map 6 - The Highlands

Map 7
~ The Hebrides, Orkney and Shetland

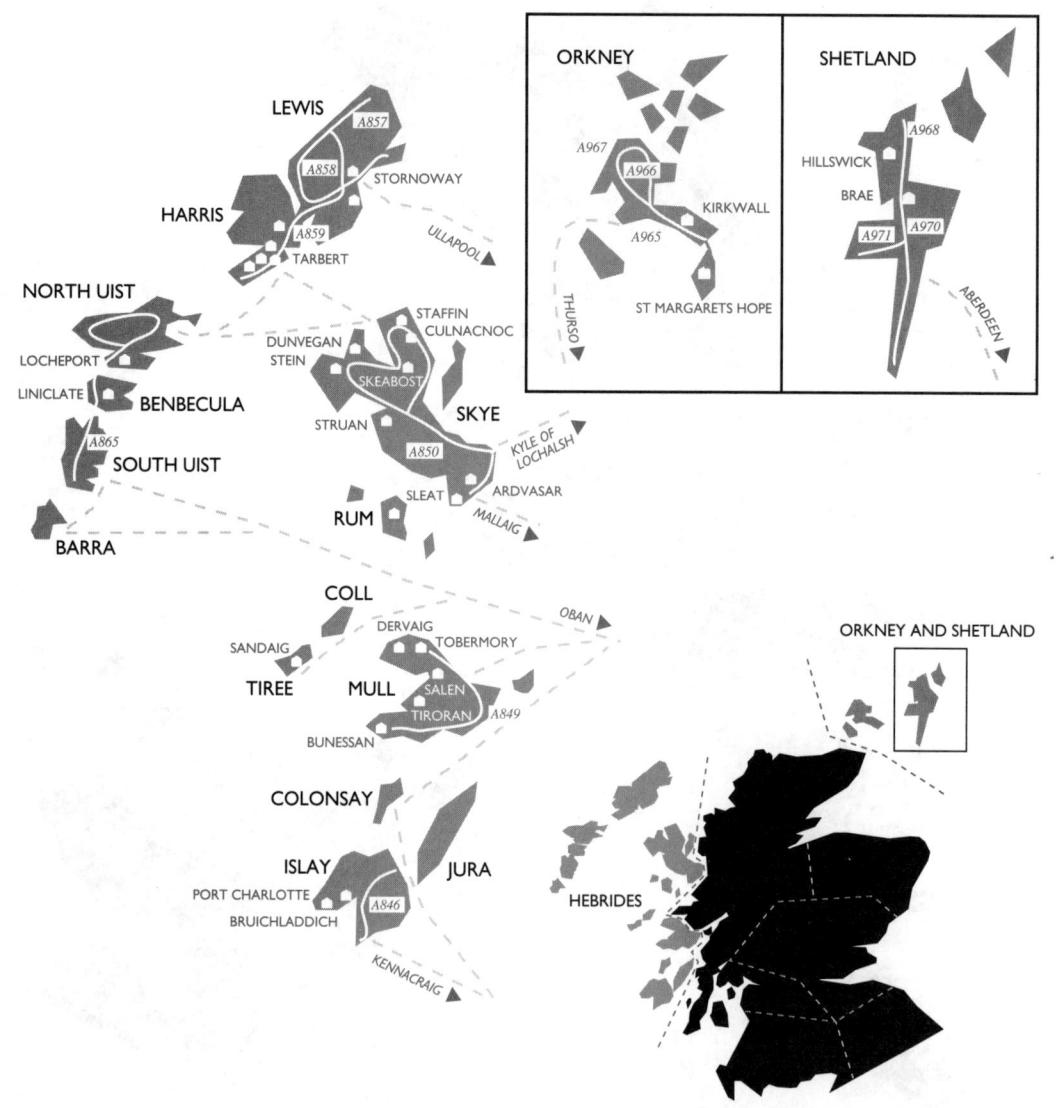

 **N**

OLD FRIEND INVITES

YOU TO DINNER.

It's not often you get to eat out at a landmark. Stonehenge may have many attractions, but a Loch Fyne Oyster Soup isn't one of them. Nor is St. Paul's famed for its Prime Fillet of Angus Beef. Yet, you can get both these dishes at The Grill, No 1 Princes Street at another national treasure, The Balmoral Hotel. Enjoy Chef Porciani's daily changing 5-course dinner menu or choose from an extensive à la Carte menu.

THE GRILL

No. 1 Princes Street

For a copy of our menu please call 031 556 2414

THE **BALMORAL** EDINBURGH

FORTE GRAND

THE BUTTERY

Join us in
OUR 10th ANNIVERSARY YEAR
for an old-fashioned style
WELCOME
with modern, award-winning
Scottish cuisine

652 ARGYLL STREET, GLASGOW G3 8UT
TELEPHONE 041-221 8188

see entry page 73

see entry page 86
see entry page 51

The Coach House Hotel

*"A warm hearted welcome
in the heart of Royal Deeside"*

3 Twin & 3 Double Bedrooms all
with private facilities.

Our Lounge Bar & Restaurant are open to
Non-Residents every day serving Lunches & Suppers
from a varied Bar Menu comprising of Scottish,
European & Oriental dishes & Dinners from a very
extensive A La Carte Menu.

Children welcome • Open all year

**Netherley Place, Ballater,
Aberdeenshire AB35 5QE
Tel 03397-55462
Fax 03397-55462**

BURTS HOTEL

Melrose   Roxburghshire

Distinguished family-run town Hotel built in 1722. Tastefully furnished with 21 en suite bedrooms all with modern facilities including colour televisions, direct-dial telephones, Tea/Coffee facilities, etc.

Elegant restaurant offering both à la carte and table d'hôte menus where the emphasise is on the abundance of local game and fresh fish imaginatively prepared and beautifully presented by our chef, Gary Moore, who was a regional finalist in the recent Taste of Scotland Scotch Lamb Challenge. Lounge bar serving light lunches and suppers daily, billiards room, two lounges, private carpark and extensive gardens.

Burts Hotel is the ideal centre for touring the beautiful Border country and enjoying traditional Scottish hospitality. Several golf courses are within easy reach and salmon and trout fishing can be arranged. Game shooting on local estates also available with prior notice.

AA ★★★   RAC★★★   ♕♕♕ STB Commended   EGON RONAY'S GUIDES   Michelin   Les Routiers   THE TASTE OF SCOTLAND recommended
                                                            Johansens

For brochure write to Graham and Ann Henderson, Proprietors. Tel 089682-2285 Fax 089682-2870

see entry page 115

see entry page 112

Sample Menu.

ﱠ

Smoked Mackerel & Whisky Pate
served with toasted oatcakes.
Mushrooms Braemar
rich haggis, whisky & sour cream sauce.
Pheasant & Chive Terrine
crusty bread, hot mustard sauce.

ﱠ

Fillet of Aberdeen Angus Steak Bears Heid
topped with pate, red wine & cummin sauce.
Escalopes of Veal Hunters Choice
breaded, sauted in basil & garlic Butter.
Fillets of Lemon Sole Lorna Doone
*wrapped with Loch Fyne smoked salmon & tarragon leaf,
shellfish sauce with grapes.*

ﱠ

MacCallums Shortbread Pudding.
Local Strawberries & Clotted Cream.
Homemade Peach Cheesecake.

ﱠ

Clachan Cottage Hotel

Lochside, Lochearnhead, Perthshire FK19 8PU
Tel (Lochearnhead) 0567-830247

see entry page 72

CHATTERS RESTAURANT

Centrally situated in the Clyde Resort of Dunoon, 'Chatters' has rapidly become the place to 'eat out'.

The tasteful decor and friendly welcome complements food of the highest standard exquisitely presented.

A visit to the Cowal Peninsula would not be complete without experiencing the culinary delights of Chatters.

Open for Morning Coffee, Lunch, Afternoon Tea and Dinner.

58 John Street (opp. Cinema), Dunoon PA23 8BJ
Tel 0369-6402

Cheese from Scotland

The geography and climate of Scotland are well suited to cheese-making, with numerous breeds of cattle and sheep raised on terrain ranging from fertile lowlands and straths to exposed highland moorland.

At one time nearly every county in Scotland had its own cheese, but dairy industrialisation in the last century and wartime and post-war restrictions and rationalisation took a heavy toll on farmhouse cheese-making.

However, the handful of cheddar cheese-makers remaining nurtured Scotland's reputation for excellent quality cheddar, and in recent years there has been an encouraging re-awakening of interest in a diversity of cheeses by independent cheese-makers in a dozen small dairies and farms across the country.

The earlier scepticism regarding the output of these small dairies has disappeared and been replaced by an upsurge in demand, particularly for the finer examples, such as the St Andrews washed rind soft cheese from Howgate Dairy near Dundee which gained a first prize at the 1993 London International Cheese Show.

For the first time there are now available genuinely Scottish speciality cheeses and superb adaptations of internationally popular fine cheeses, such as brie and camembert (also from Howgate Dairy).

Scottish cheddar still accounts for over 90% of the total output and the main creameries are located in the milk producing areas of Galloway, Lockerbie, Mull of Kintyre (Campbeltown), and on the islands of Bute, Arran, Islay and, of course, Orkney with its own distinctive and popular variety of cheddar.

Production of Dunlop, probably Scotland's most important indigenous cheese, takes place in Ayrshire, Arran and Islay, and production of Mozzarella has been introduced near Edinburgh and in Fife. The longer established speciality cheese-makers are located near Dundee, Lanark and Inverness, and on Orkney and Mull.

Scottish cheddar is widely available but the farmhouse and speciality cheeses are sometimes available only locally. However, these are often well featured by "Taste of Scotland" members throughout Scotland and in retail outlets in the main "tourist trail" from Edinburgh to St Andrews, Perth and Pitlochry. There are several excellent cheese-mongers in and around Edinburgh and Perth, and both Safeway and main branches of Wm Low feature a good selection of Scottish cheeses.

Some of the varieties and names to look out for include:

Bonchester	:	small coulommier-style cheese from unpasteurised Jersey milk. Suitable for vegetarians. Available Mar to Dec.
Bonnet	:	mild, pressed goatsmilk cheese from small Ayrshire dairy. Similar types - Inverloch (Isle of Gigha) and Sanday (Orkney).
Brie	:	(see Howgate) traditionally made, pasteurised farmhouse-style brie.
Brodick Blue	:	ewes milk blue cheese from Brodick, Arran.
Caboc	:	(see cream cheese)
Camembert	:	(see Howgate) traditionally made farmhouse-style camembert.
Cream Cheese	:	several varieties, mostly based on revived traditional Highland recipes and rolled in oatmeal, e.g. Caboc (Ross-shire), Howgate (Tayside), Lochaber-smoked (Glenuig) and St Finan (Aberdeenshire). Also available with peppercorns, garlic or herbs.
Crowdie	:	(see fresh cheese)
Dunlop	:	resembles Scottish cheddar with soft texture. Mostly creamery-made on Arran and Islay; also traditionally in Ayrshire (Burns), near Dumfries and at Perth (Gowrie).

- *Continued overleaf*

Dunsyre Blue : Cows milk farmhouse blue cheese made with vegetarian rennet and unpasteurised milk.

Ettrick : traditional Borders pressed cheese mould ripened and made at Howgate. Similar in style is Teviotdale (Borders).

Fresh Cheeses : several varieties of soft fresh cheeses, including Crowdie - an ancient Highland crofters cheese (originally made using milk left after the cream had separated naturally). Also available with oatmeal, peppercorns, garlic or herbs.

Howgate : established innovative cheese-maker, originally from Howgate near Edinburgh, now located near Dundee. Pioneered the making in Scotland of continental cheeses including Howgate Brie, Camembert and Pentland.

Inverloch : pasteurised cheddar-type goats cheese from Isle of Gigha, coated in red wax.

Isle of Mull : traditional unpasteurised matured farmhouse cheddar from Tobermory, cloth-bound.

Kelsae : unpasteurised pressed cheese made near Kelso (Borders) from Jersey milk. Similar to Wensleydale but creamier in texture and taste.

Lanark Blue : unpasteurised ewes milk cheese with blue-green veins, in style of Roquefort. From same Lanarkshire farm as Dunsyre Blue.

Mull of Kintyre : small truckle of mature Scottish cheddar coated in black wax.

Orkney : Scottish cheddar made in two creameries in the Orkney Islands, the history of which history goes back nearly two centuries.

Pentland : traditional unpasteurised versions of Howgate Brie and Howgate Camembert, made in small quantities and not widely available.

St Andrews : award winning full fat, washed rind soft cheese made by Howgate. Mild creamy full flavoured soft cheese with characteristic golden rind, eaten with the cheese.

Scottish Cheddar : creamery produced cheddar now made in Galloway (Stranraer), Lockerbie, Rothesay and Campbeltown.

Stichill : unpasteurised creamy Jersey milk Cheshire-style cheese from the Scottish Borders.

Swinzie : pasteurised, pressed, scalded ewes milk cheese from Ayrshire.

Teviotdate : (see Ettrick)

HOWGATE

Scottish Cheeses of Distinction

Skara Brae, Orkney

Rackwick, Hoy, Orkney

Small Boat Harbour, Lerwick, Shetland Islands

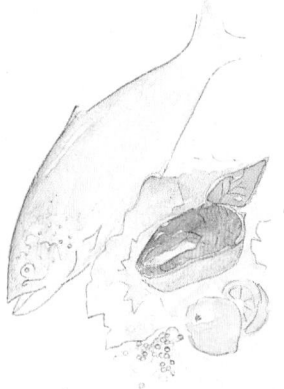

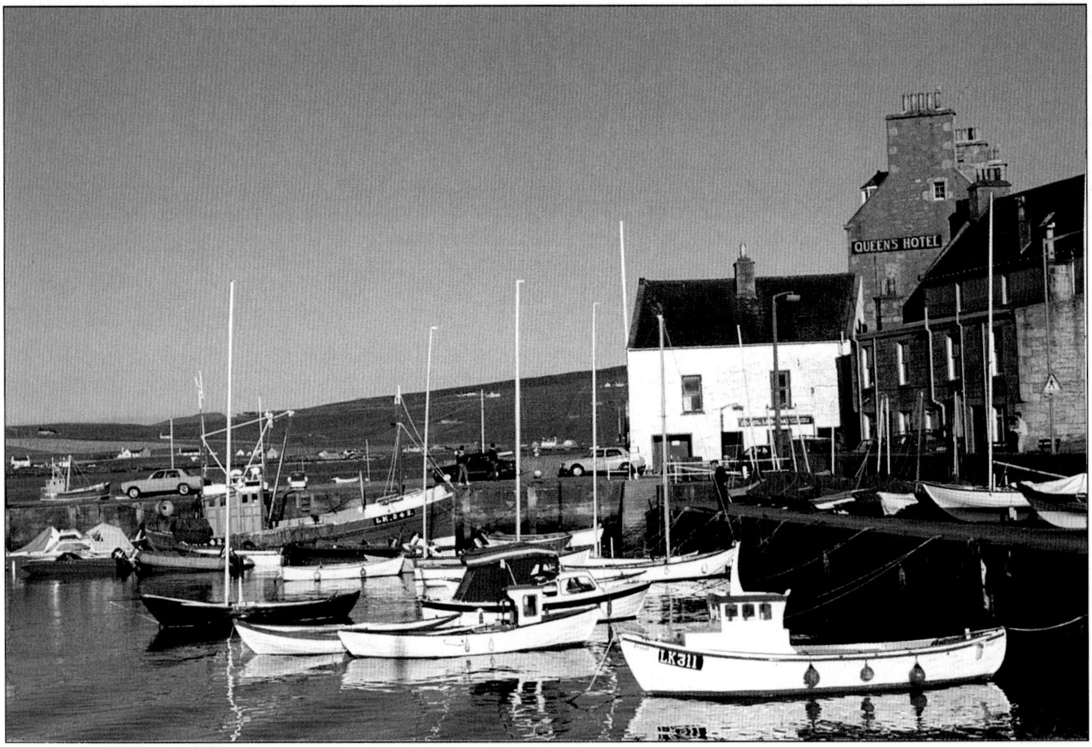

SHETLAND ISLANDS TOURISM

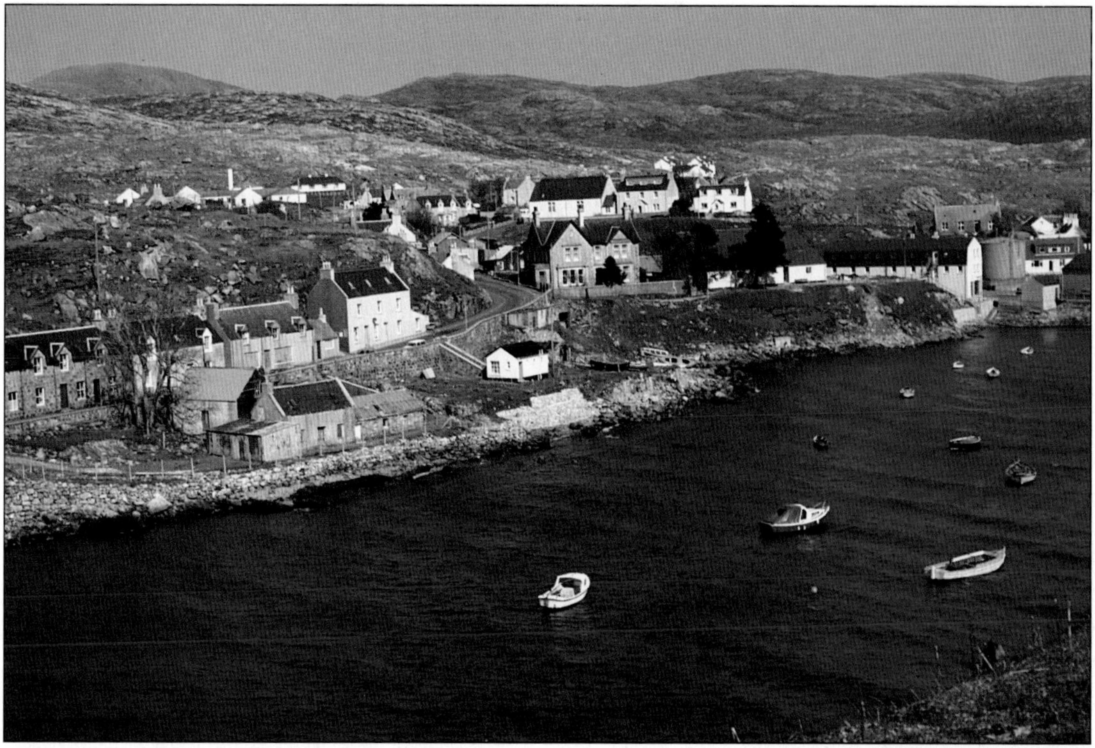
WESTERN ISLES TOURIST BOARD

Tarbert, Harris

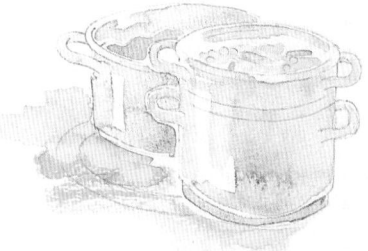

Fort Augustus

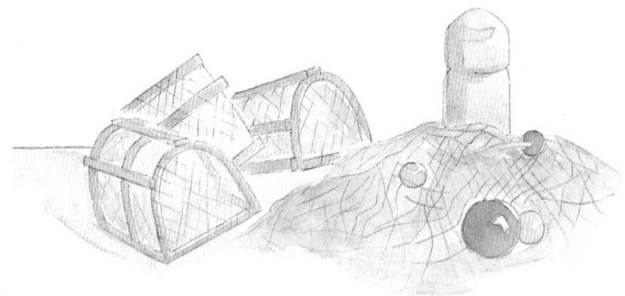

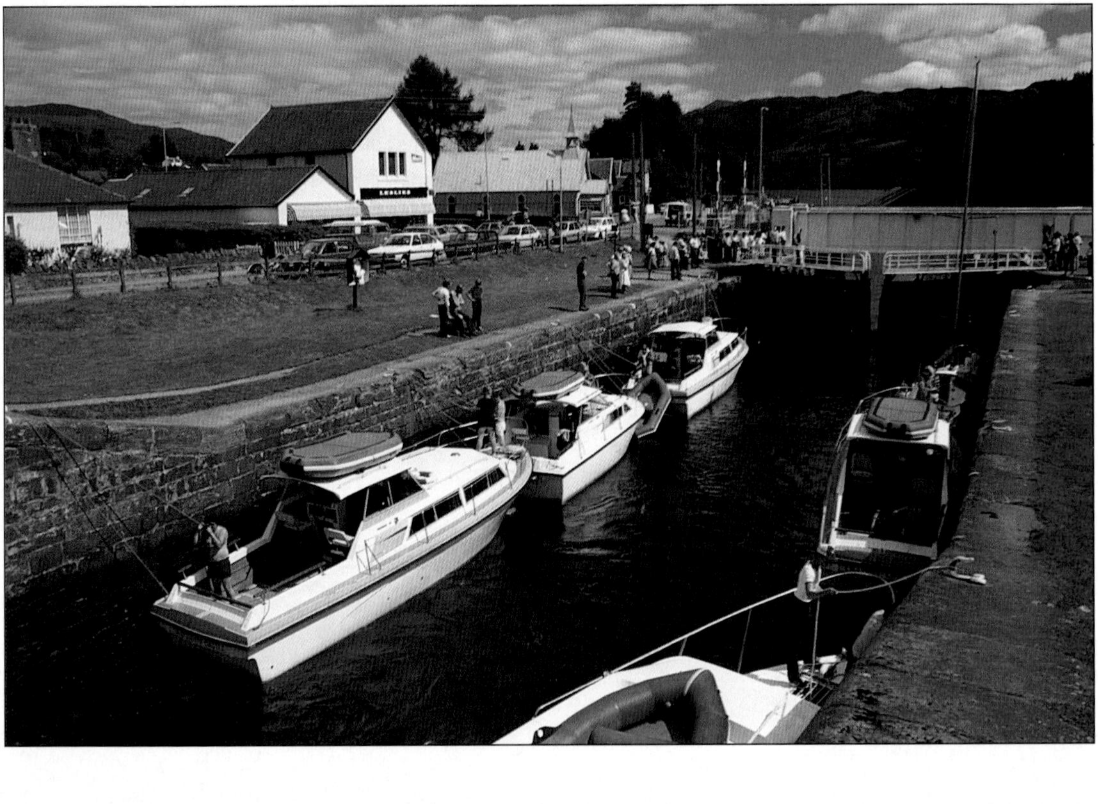

Inverness, Loch Ness & Nairn Tourist Board

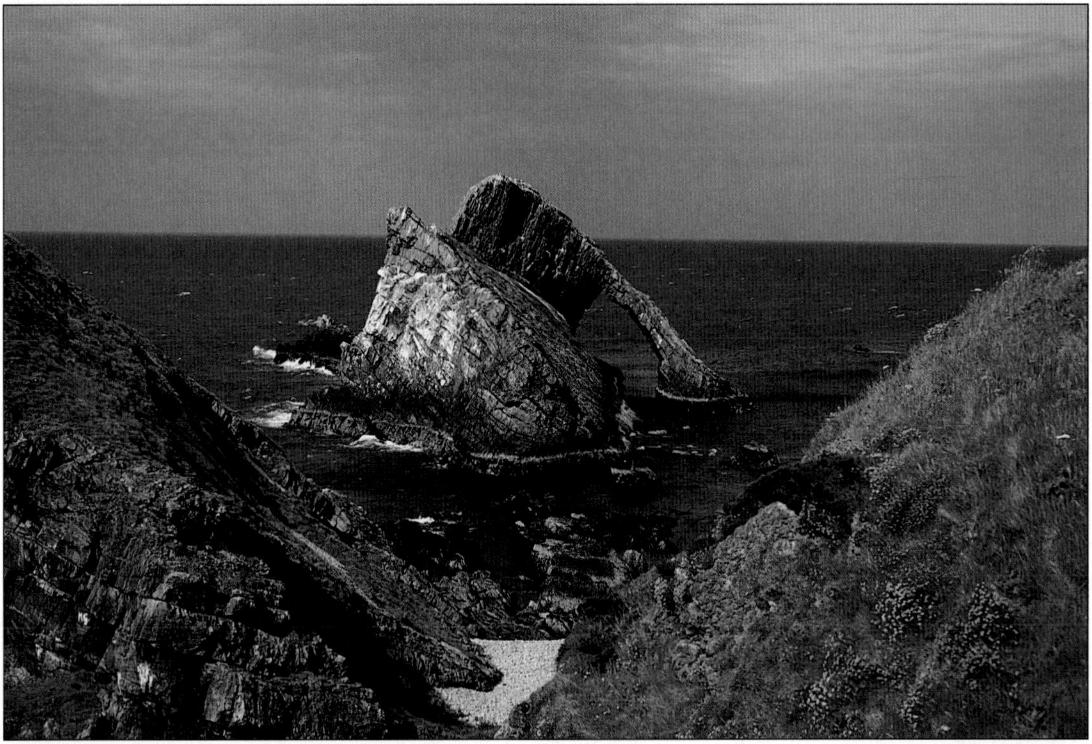

Moray Tourist Board/Anne Burgess

Bow Fiddle, Portknockie

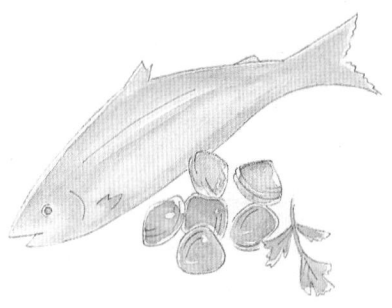

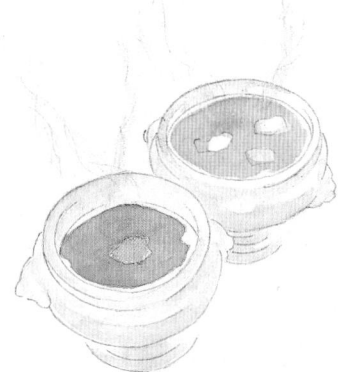

Cullen

Aberdeen Tourist Board

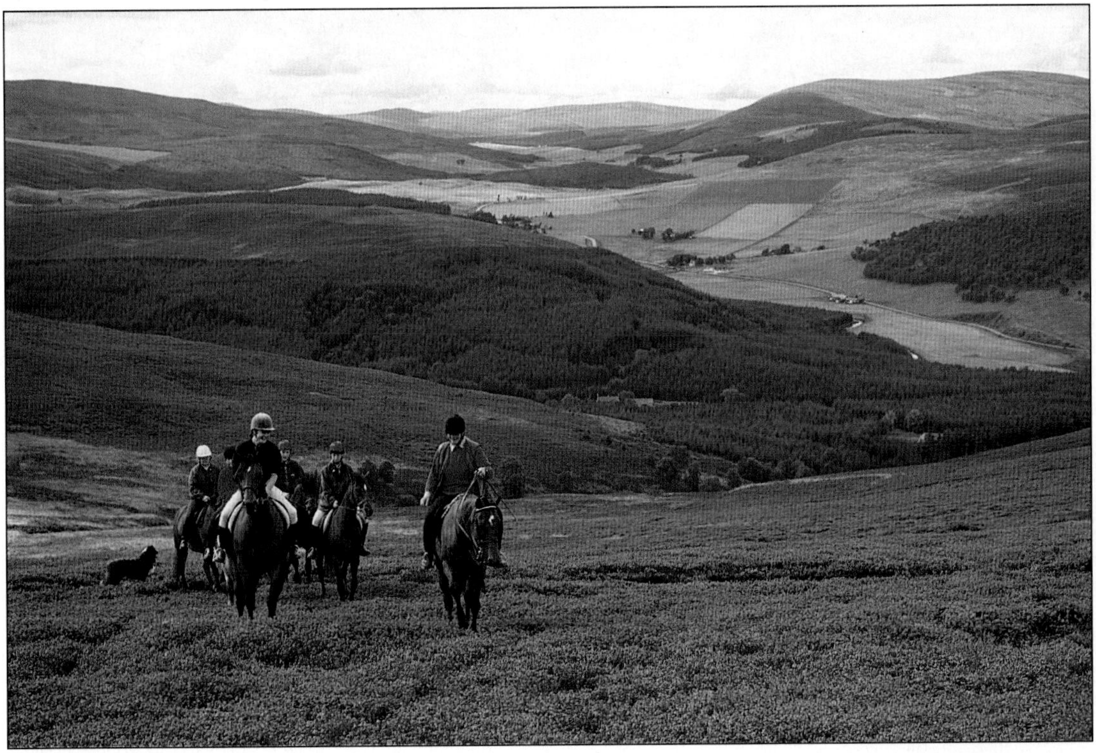

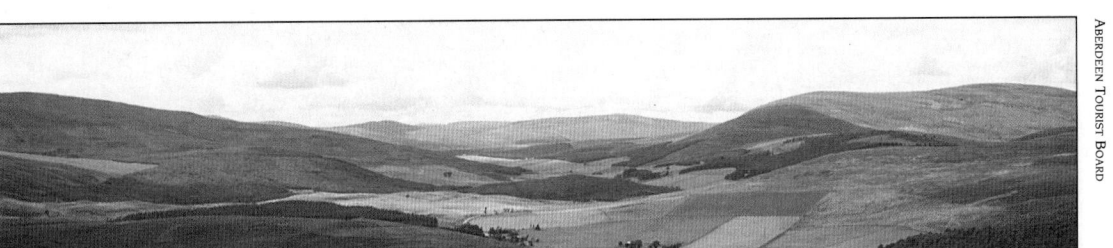

Upper Donside,
Highland Tourist Route

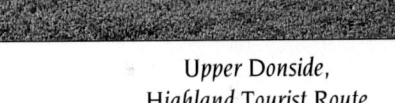

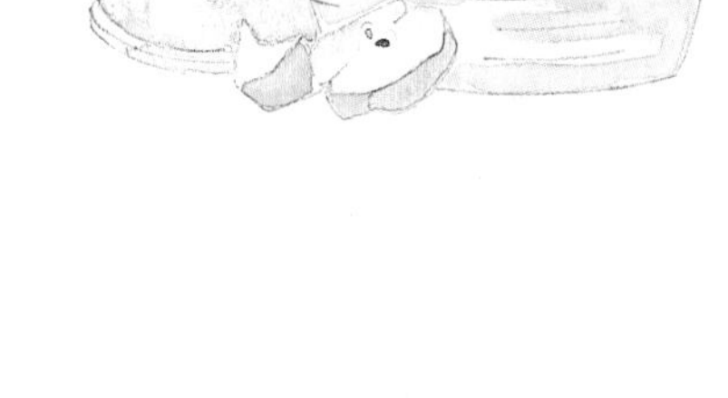

CLYDE VALLEY TOURIST BOARD

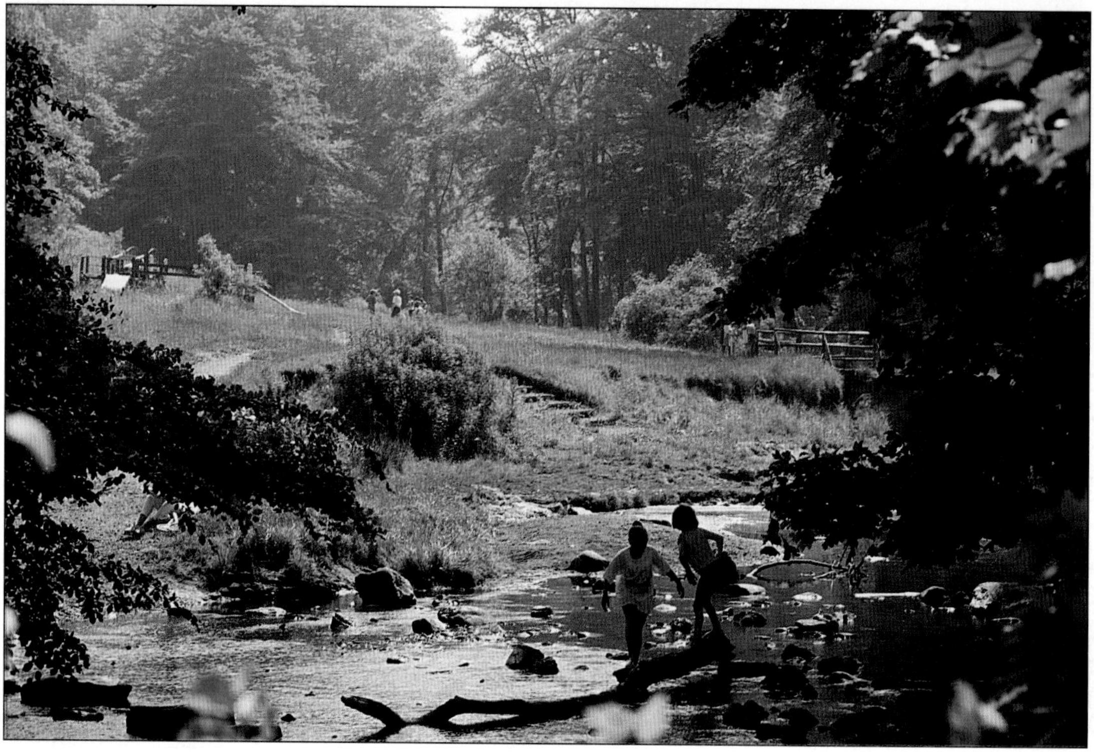

Calderglen, East Kilbride

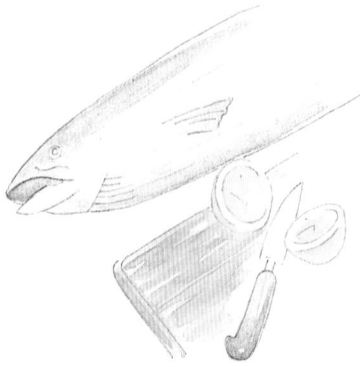

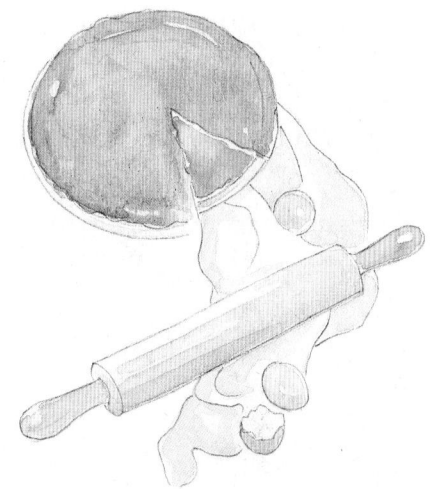

Glasgow University

On holiday in the Highlands and Islands of Scotland, you can be as shellfish as you like.

Some of the finest seafood in the world can be found in our beautifully clear waters. Some of the country's most discerning connoisseurs can be found in our restaurants. Do you think the two could be related, by any chance? The only way to find out is to come here yourself and sample some of the most exquisite cuisine (not to mention breathtaking scenery) that Europe has to offer. What a drag.

Highlands & Islands
OF SCOTLAND

The Scottish Highlands and Islands
- where all the signs point to peace and contentment

Starting with Argyll and the Isles...

From the Mull of Kintyre to Oban and beyond, Argyll stretches serenely across mountains, forests, glens and lochs. Like a necklace around it lie the Isles: Mull, Coll, Tiree, Iona, Colonsay, Jura, Islay, Gigha, Arran, Cumbrae and Bute.

Here you can visit some of Britain's most beautiful gardens: all kinds of flowers flourish in the gentle Gulf Stream climate. You can play golf amid some of the finest scenery in Europe; visit prehistoric standing stones; go cruising in waters Saints and Vikings have sailed; walk wooded mountain trails; and enjoy unrivalled hospitality.

... moving into the centre of the Highlands

embraces Mallaig, Fort William, Inverness, Nairn and the Spey Valley. It's a region of superlatives: Britain's highest mountain, Ben Nevis; Britain's deepest loch, Loch Morar; Britain's oldest monster, Nessie (she may also be the shyest but could well pop out to see you); and Britain's biggest inland waterway, the Caledonian Canal. Here, naturally, you'll have a superlative holiday, whether you're visiting castles, beaches, wildlife centres or the sites of ancient battlefields.

... and then to the Northern Highlands and Islands

Within the broad scope of the Northern Highlands and Islands you'll find far-flung islands; Skye and the Inner and Outer Hebrides. On the mainland you'll discover the dramatically varied scenery of Ross and Cromarty, Caithness and Sutherland.

This is a land of remarkable contrasts. In the course of a day you can come across towering mountains, gentle moors, quiet beaches, stone-age remains and magnificent castles. You can enjoy boat trips, visit bird sanctuaries, go hill-walking or fish for record-breaking skate and halibut. And at the end of the day, you can frequently enjoy a Ceilidh, where the music and dancing continue into the wee small hours.

...and finally to Orkney and Shetland

Just about where ancient mariners thought the world ended, the Orkney Isles start. And beyond the Orkney Isles, only 200 miles from the coast of Norway, lie the Shetland Isles. The nearness of Scandinavia has influenced life in these islands down the centuries. Listen carefully to the locals: you'll find their accents owe more to the Viking than the Pict.

Explore the countryside, the ragged cliffs and sandy beaches: you'll see the work of the wild Atlantic and the North Sea everywhere. (You'll also find the work of early man in the ancient forts and burial mounds that dot the landscape.)

Above all be ready to make new friends. If you were expecting to find these islands peopled by inward-looking folk, wrapped in splendid isolation, you'd be wrong. Orcadians and Shetlanders have been welcoming visitors from over the seas since time immemorial. Make this the year they welcome you.

How do you get here?

Easily - by road, rail or air. Excellent roads bring you into the Highlands, some leading you to drive-on, drive-off ferries which connect you to the main islands. For train-lovers, the Inter-City service goes to Inverness, and the tracks in the Highlands lead you along some of the most beautiful rail journeys in the world.

Information

For a brochure on the Scottish Highlands and Islands contact

Highlands & Islands of Scotland
FREEPOST
Dunoon
Argyll   PA23 8BR

Aberdeen

Map 5

ARDOE HOUSE HOTEL
Blairs, South Deeside Road
Aberdeen AB1 5YP
Tel: 0224 867355 • Telex: 739413
Fax: 0224 861283

B9077, 3 miles west of Aberdeen.
A very impressive-looking granite mansion with lofty turrets and inscriptions of heraldry and now a high class country house hotel, which is constantly being upgraded and improved. It stands in its own grounds and wooded parkland on the south Deeside road, just five minutes out of Aberdeen. The public rooms are particularly impressive with beautiful carved wood panelling and magnificent fireplaces, and the staircase with its stained glass windows at landing level is especially grand. There is a modern function room with superb views across the Dee. Food in the dining room lives up to the quality image of the hotel: it is imaginative in concept and is presented with the same care and attention that is given to its preparation. There is also the delightful Garden Room in which breakfast is served.
Open all year
Rooms: 71 with private facilities
Bar Lunch 12 – 2.30 pm (a)
Dining Room/Restaurant Lunch 12 – 2.30 pm (a)
Bar Supper 6.30 – 10.30 pm (a)
Dinner 6.30 – 9.30 pm (d)
Dogs accepted at Manager's discretion
Bed & breakfast £37 – £117.25
Dinner B & B £53 – £143
Room Rate £55 – £140
Fresh fish from the market daily. Local seasonal game.
STB Highly Commended 5 Crowns
Credit cards: 1, 2, 3, 5

CALEDONIAN THISTLE HOTEL
Union Terrace
Aberdeen AB9 1HE
Tel: 0224 640233 • Telex: 73758
Fax: 0224 641627

City centre.
This large traditional city centre hotel is right in the heart of Aberdeen, overlooking Union Terrace Gardens and just a hundred yards or so from Union Street, the main shopping street of the Granite City. The Restaurant on the Terrace with its adjacent cocktail bar offers good standards of food and service. For less formal eating there is Elrond's Cafe, a spacious bar and restaurant with an interesting range of light meals representing excellent value for money.
Open all year
Rooms: 80 with private facilities
Bar Lunch 11 – 2 pm (a)
Dining Room/Restaurant Lunch 12 – 2 pm except Sun Sat (b)
Dinner 6.30 – 10 pm (c)
Bed & breakfast £40 – £113 (weekend special)
Dinner B & B £48 – £87
Room Rate £95 – £120
Roulade of fresh salmon and sole on a pool of fresh herbs and crème fraiche. Skate wings pan-fried and deglazed with Beaujolais, tarragon and lemon grass. Aberdeen Angus steak grilled with king prawns and glazed with bearnaise sauce.
STB Commended 5 Crowns
Credit cards: 1, 2, 3, 5

THE COURTYARD RESTAURANT
Aberdeen
Tel: 0224 742540

The Courtyard Restaurant, which earned such renown when based at the Broadstraik Inn at Elrick, was being re-located within Aberdeen at the time this Guide was going to press but all the necessary details had not been finalised at that stage. Its many devoted customers will be delighted that it is continuing under the ownership of Tony Heath and Shona Drysdale who did so much to establish its reputation for excellent food and service. Though there will be a change of address, to make life easy the original telephone number (0224 742540) is being retained so bookings can be made, opening times checked and directions given. It won't be too far away and it was always worth the journey!
Open all year except Christmas Day
Dining Room/Restaurant Lunch 12 – 2 pm except Mon Tue Sat (b)
Dinner 6.30 – 9.45 pm except Mon Tue (d)
Closed Mon Tue
Loin of local venison with cherry tomato compote. Ravioli of langoustine with lemon oil dressing. Caramelised pear tart with toffee sauce.
Credit cards: 1, 2, 3, 6
Proprietor: Tony Heath & Shona Drysdale

CRAIGHAAR HOTEL
Waterton Road, Bucksburn
Aberdeen AB2 9HS
Tel: 0224 712275
Fax: 0224 716362

Turn off A96 at Greenburn Drive. Follow to end then turn left up Waterton Road.
The Craighaar Hotel is set in a quiet wooded residential area, five minutes from Aberdeen Airport and ten minutes from the city centre. It is not only the convenience of its situation that appeals to guests of this popular privately run hotel, which enjoys a good reputation with both the business community and local residents. It boasts a number of distinctive features, not the least of which are its attractive gallery suites with comfortable sitting room and an upstairs bedroom, providing ideal business or family accommodation. The traditional lounge bar has an open log fire and there are function rooms for conferences, seminars or private dining. There is a choice of restaurants and the menus are created around the prime local produce and excellent seafood for which Aberdeen is renowned.
Open all year except Christmas Day
Rooms: 55 with private facilities
Bar Lunch 12 – 2 pm except Sun Sat (a)
Dining Room/Restaurant Lunch 12 – 2 pm Mon to Fri: Carvery Lunch 12 – 2.30 pm Sun only (a-b)
Bar Supper 6.30 – 10 pm (a-b)
Dinner 7 – 9.30 pm except Sun (b-d)
No dogs
Bed & breakfast £25 – £95
Dinner B & B from £40
Note: Christmas Day accommodation available on request
Steamed queenie scallops in a puff pastry shell with a tomato, white wine and fresh dill sauce. Best end of lamb roasted with a herb crust, served with a rich red wine sauce. Marinated medallions of venison pan-fried with shallots, with a redcurrant jelly sauce and wild mushrooms.
STB Highly Commended 3 Crowns
Credit cards: 1, 2, 3, 5, 6

CRAIGLYNN HOTEL
36 Fonthill Road
Aberdeen AB1 2UJ
Tel: 0224 584050
Fax: 0224 584050

On corner of Fonthill Road and Bon Accord Street, midway between Union Street and King George VI Bridge. Car park access from Bon Accord Street.

Craiglynn is an impressive granite building, formerly owned by an Aberdeen merchant and now a very comfortable small hotel. The dining room, originally the billiard room of this fine house, features rosewood panelling and a corniced ceiling. The hotel is run in a relaxed yet efficient manner – the theme being "Victorian elegance with modern comforts". The bedrooms are tastefully furnished and decorated, all having direct dial telephones and colour TVs. No smoking in the bedrooms or dining room. There are two elegant lounges to relax in, one of which has an open fire burning during the Winter evenings. Dinner menus are decided upon daily and offer an interesting choice of dishes carefully cooked.

Open all year except Christmas + Boxing Days
Rooms: 9, 7 with private facilities
Dinner at 7 pm (c)
Reservations required for non-residents
No smoking in dining room + bedrooms
Restricted Licence
No dogs
Bed & breakfast £30 – £52
Dinner B & B £45.80 – £66.80
Home-made soups. Lemon sole in prawn and whisky cream sauce. Carbonnade of beef. Pear and cinnamon crumble.
STB Commended 3 Crowns
Credit cards: 1, 2, 3, 5
Proprietors: Chris & Hazel Mann

FARADAY'S RESTAURANT
2 Kirk Brae, Cults
Aberdeen AB1 9SQ
Tel: 0224 869666

4 miles from city centre on north Deeside road. On reaching Cults, turn right at traffic lights – Faraday's 100 yards on right.

This restaurant takes its name from a Victorian engineer, Michael Faraday who is now considered to be the father of electrical engineering. The building, which has been carefully restored, used to be an electric pump station for the area of Cults. A minstrel's gallery overlooks the wood-panelled restaurant,

which is decorated in dusky pink and grape colours. The cuisine is prepared by John Inches and his food reflects his background of traditional Scottish cooking, combined with extensive travel through France.

Open all year except Boxing Day to 10 Jan
Restaurant Lunch 12 – 1.15 pm except Sun Mon (b)
Dinner 7.30 – 9.30 pm except Sun (c-d)
Closed Sun
Facilities for the disabled
Crispy filo pancake of scallops, leeks, beansprouts and fresh ginger served with a lemon cream sauce and a mirepoix of peppers. Rosemary roasted rack of Spring lamb with fresh cranberries and rich sauce Madeira. Millefeuille of caramelised bananas with rich toffee sauce and crisp almond pralines. Brandy and noisette frangipane cake with orange sugared red fruits.
Credit cards: 1, 3
Proprietor: John Inches

THE MARCLIFFE AT PITFODELS
North Deeside Road, Pitfodels
Aberdeen AB1 9PN
Tel: 0224 861000
Fax: 0224 868860

At the west end of Aberdeen, 2 miles from city centre.

The luxurious Marcliffe at Pitfodels is a splendid addition to the hotel scene in Aberdeen. A great deal of detailed planning, based on extensive experience, has gone into creating a special and eminent hotel with every conceivable comfort and facility. Elegant reception and conference rooms, banqueting suites and tastefully furnished bedrooms, set the tone of the hotel. As would be expected, the same attention to detail and aspiration to perfection is reflected in the Conservatory Restaurant and Invery Room Restaurant, where only the best of Scottish and local produce is used by the team of chefs, with a choice of 200 wines and 100 malt whiskies.

Open all year
Rooms: 46 with private facilities
Bar Lunch 12.15 – 2.15 pm (b)
Dining Room/Restaurant Lunch 12.15 – 2.15 pm (b)
Bar Supper 6 – 10 pm (b)
Dinner 6 – 10 pm (c)
No smoking area in restaurant
Bed & breakfast £60 – £125
Dinner B & B £80 – £145

Room Rate £70 – £145
Grilled lobster, halibut, turbot, whole sole. Aberdeen Angus beef, venison, pheasant, grouse.
Credit cards: 1, 2, 3, 5, 6
Proprietors: Stewart & Sheila Spence

MARYCULTER HOUSE HOTEL
South Deeside Road
Aberdeen AB1 0BB
Tel: 0224 732124
Fax: 0224 733510

Take South Deeside road out of Aberdeen for 5 miles then take signposted turning to right.

The origins of Maryculter House go back to the 13th century so it is not surprising that there is a lot of character about this appealing country hotel. Just a few miles out of Aberdeen, it is set in five acres of private grounds and has been furnished and decorated to high standards. Some of the bedrooms have glorious views and all of them are comfortable and well equipped with those little extras that pamper the guest. The food shows imagination and skilled hands in the kitchen, and is served by smart attentive staff.

Open all year except 26 + 27 Dec
Rooms: 22 with private facilities
Bar Lunch 12.30 – 2 pm (b)
Bar Supper 6.30 – 9.30 pm (b)
Dinner 7 – 9.30 pm except Sun (e)
Facilities for the disabled
No smoking in restaurant
Bed & breakfast from £90
Dinner B & B from £65 weekend rate
Roast rack of Scottish lamb with a Drambuie and thyme essence. Layers of Scottish salmon filled with strips of seasonal vegetables, with a saffron cream sauce. Dried fruits soaked in whisky blended with cream, honey and toasted oatmeal served in a chocolate cup.
STB Commended 4 Crowns
Credit cards: 1, 2, 3, 5

Aberdour

Map 4

HAWKCRAIG HOUSE

Hawkcraig Point, Aberdour
Fife KY3 0TZ
Tel: 0383 860335

From centre of Aberdour, take Hawkcraig road, through large car park, then down very steep access to Hawkcraig Point.
Elma Barrie has earned a fine reputation for the high standard of food, hospitality and comfort she offers in her whitewashed old ferryman's house. Situated at the water's edge, next to the harbour, the views across Aberdour bay to the golf course and Inchcolm's 12th century abbey are superb. Seals and seabirds abound, yet the village is only 30 minutes from Edinburgh by road or rail (best by train to avoid the city's traffic and parking problems). The East Neuk of Fife, Gleneagles and St Andrews are all within a pleasant hour's drive and there is much to see and enjoy on the way. Children over eight years welcome.
Open 1 Mar to 31 Oct
Rooms: 2 with private facilities
Dinner 7 – 8.30 pm (c)
Open to non-residents – booked meals only
Unlicensed – guests welcome to take own wine
No smoking throughout
No dogs
Bed & breakfast £18 – £25
Dinner B & B £35 – £42
Home cooking par excellence, using prime Scottish produce.
STB Highly Commended 2 Crowns
No credit cards
Proprietor: Elma Barrie

Aberfeldy

Map 4

GUINACH HOUSE

by The Birks, Aberfeldy
Perthshire PH15 2ET
Tel: 0887 820251
Fax: 0887 829607

On A826, south-west outskirts of Aberfeldy, on road to 'The Birks', Guinach is signposted from Urlar Road.
Guinach House is situated in three acres of secluded garden grounds with magnificent views across the valley. It was built at the turn of the century as a private country house and is now the home of Bert and Marian MacKay who are attentive hosts, helping create a relaxed friendly atmosphere for their guests. Bert is a Master Chef and makes full use of local produce to create interesting and imaginative four course dinner menus.
Open all year except Christmas Day
Rooms: 7 with private facilities
Dining Room/Restaurant Lunch 12 – 1.30 pm (b)
Dinner 7 – 9.30 pm (c)
No smoking in dining room
Bed & breakfast from £25
Dinner B & B from £53.50
Timbale of crab mousse wrapped in smoked salmon served with a lemon and chive mayonnaise. Poached monkfish tails in a light Noilly Prat cream sauce with mushrooms. Rosettes of new season Spring lamb flavoured with garden herbs on a ragoût of wild mushrooms, in a red wine and redcurrant jus.
STB Highly Commended 3 Crowns
Credit cards: 1, 3
Proprietor: Albert Mackay

Aboyne

Map 5

HAZLEHURST LODGE

Ballater Road, Aboyne
Aberdeenshire AB34 5HY
Tel: 03398 86921

On A93 on western side of Aboyne.
Imaginative, highly regarded cooking by Chef Anne Strachan in the intimate atmosphere of this attractive rose granite former coachman's lodge to Aboyne Castle. With creative use of herbs and fresh vegetables Anne brings traditional cooking to today's table. Wines are personally selected from top growers and the prices are friendly. The accommodation in three individually designed bedrooms, all with full private facilities, is of a high standard reflecting the owners' artistic background. The specially commissioned furniture exemplifies the best of Scottish craft design. Hazlehurst makes an ideal base for a relaxing stay on beautiful unspoilt Royal Deeside.
Open Feb to Dec
Rooms: 3 with private facilities
Dining Room Lunch available for special bookings
Dinner 7.30 – 9.30 pm (d)
No smoking in dining room + bedrooms
Bed & breakfast from £25
Fish and seafood straight from the sea, wild river salmon, game from the ancient Caledonian forests, home-cured meats. Creative use of herbs and fresh vegetables bringing traditional cooking to today's table.
STB Deluxe 3 Crowns
Credit cards: 1, 2, 3, 5
Proprietors: Anne & Eddie Strachan

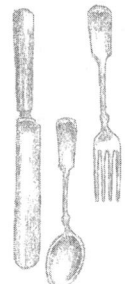

Achiltibuie

Map 6

SUMMER ISLES HOTEL

Achiltibuie
Ross-shire IV26 2YG
Tel: 085 482 282
Fax: 085 482 251

Prestige Award Winner 1991

Ten miles north of Ullapool turn west off A835 and continue for 15 miles along single track road.
Leaving the main road is like leaving one world and moving into another, and the terrain to Achiltibuie is primitive, enchanting and hauntingly beautiful. The village itself is a haphazard layout of cottages, but its pièce de résistance is the Summer Isles Hotel, a haven of civilised comfort and culinary standards of astonishingly high level. Mark and Geraldine Irvine are utterly charming hosts, bent on ensuring that in this remote corner of Ross-shire you will want for nothing – and indeed you won't. There is everything here, and overlying it is the sheer tranquillity and beauty of the place. You will feed on the finest harvest of seafish, shellfish and the freshest of fresh locally grown vegetables, fruit and farm produce all prepared with skill and

presented with flair. Like everyone else who has been there, you will leave reluctantly, determined to return.

Open 29 Mar to 9 Oct
Rooms: 11 with private facilities
Bar Meals (Achiltibuie Cafe) 12 – 9 pm (a-b)
Dinner at 8 pm (f) 5 course set menu – booking essential for non-residents
Note: Lunch is not served in the hotel, but is available in the adjoining Achiltibuie Cafe
No smoking in restaurant
Bed & breakfast £31 – £59
Dinner B & B £62 – £90
Mushroom and Meaux mustard soup served with a fresh buckwheat loaf. Fresh Summer Isles Prawns and spiney lobsters with a Hollandaise sauce. Haunch of roe deer venison, roasted with bacon and juniper, served with a Port gravy.
STB Award Pending
No credit cards
Proprietors: Mark & Geraldine Irvine

Airth

Map 4

AIRTH CASTLE HOTEL
Airth, by Falkirk
Stirlingshire FK2 8JF
Tel: 0324 831411 • Telex: 777975
Fax: 0324 831419

Junction 7 of M9/A905 from Kincardine Bridge.

Airth Castle stands on a small hill and looks out over the lush grazing of the Forth Valley. It has been part of Scotland's history since the 14th century. The public rooms are spacious and elegant enjoying fine views over the surrounding countryside and designed for guests to make themselves at home in. There is a splendid air of permanence about this building which has several interesting features both externally and internally and has earned a good reputation for its food and service. There is also a leisure club. The hotel has

been further extended and improved during the past couple of years.

Open all year
Rooms: 75 with private facilities
Bar Lunch 12 – 2 pm (a)
Dining Room/Restaurant Lunch 12.30 – 2 pm (b)
Bar Supper 6 – 8 pm (a)
Dinner 7 – 9.45 pm (c)
No dogs
Facilities for the disabled
Bed & breakfast from £70
Dinner B & B from £85
Credit cards: 1, 2, 3, 5, 6

Alloa

Map 4

THE GEAN HOUSE
Gean Park, Tullibody Road
Alloa
Clackmannanshire FK10 2HS
Tel: 0259 219275
Fax: 0259 213827

Prestige Award Winner 1992

A907 from Kincardine Bridge or Stirling. Park entrance on B9096 Tullibody, less than 5 minutes from Alloa Town Hall roundabout.

Almost as soon as it opened, the Gean House attracted attention and earned a high reputation, and it is pleasing that the standards so evident then are being maintained. This luxurious country house hotel stands in its own grounds with parks, woodlands, lawns and a rose garden. The interior decor and furnishings exude elegance and impeccable good taste. Ranking high in the many architectural features are the minstrel gallery and the inglenook fireplace in the oak-panelled reception hall. The bedrooms are superb and beautifully furnished with many delightful personal touches. Everything about this magnificent house is outstanding and the food is of the same standard of excellence and perfection so obvious throughout the building.

Open 4 Jan to 31 Dec
Rooms: 7 with private facilities
Dining Room/Restaurant Lunch 12.30 – 2 pm (c)
Dinner 7 – 9.30 pm (e)
No dogs
Facilities for the disabled
No smoking in dining room
Bed & breakfast from £70
Dinner B & B from £99
Terrine of game and young asparagus served with seasonal leaves and a rowanberry jelly. Fillets of trout layered with a salmon and spinach mousse and baked in a filo pastry. Gean House bread and butter pudding.
STB Deluxe 4 Crowns
Credit cards: 1, 2, 3, 5, 6
Proprietors: Sandra & Paul Frost

Altnaharra
by Lairg

Map 6

ALTNAHARRA HOTEL
Altnaharra
Sutherland IV27 4UE
Tel: 054 981 222
Fax: 054 981 222

A836, 21 miles north of Lairg.

Splendid isolation and tranquillity could be the theme of this famous fishing hotel, located deep in the heart of beautiful Sutherland and well remote from the hurly burly of the modern world and main traffic routes. This is a hotel for lovers of outdoor pursuits, and though anglers form a fair proportion of its clientele there are lots of other things to do. The accommodation is comfortable and the cuisine will satisfy the hungriest of hunters returning from the hills.

Open 1 Mar to 15 Oct
Rooms: 20 with private facilities
Bar Lunch 12 – 2.15 pm (b)
Bar Supper 6 – 7.30 pm (b)
Dinner 7.30 – 8.30 pm: cold buffet Sun (c)
No smoking in dining room
Bed & breakfast £35 – £42
Dinner B & B £49 – £59
Home-made soups. Seafood platter in a lobster sauce. Roast leg of Sutherland lamb with mint sauce. Tiger prawns sautéd with onions, peppers, mushrooms and Drambuie in a rich cream sauce. Loch Awe rainbow trout with lemon butter and flaked almonds.
Credit cards: 1, 3

Credit Card Code		Meal Price Code	
1.	Access/Mastercard/Eurocard	(a)	under £10
2.	American Express	(b)	£10 – £15
3.	Visa	(c)	£15 – £20
4.	Carte Bleu	(d)	£20 – £25
5.	Diners Club	(e)	£25 – £30
6.	Mastercharge	(f)	over £30

Alyth

Map 4

DRUMNACREE HOUSE
St Ninians Road, Alyth
Perthshire PH11 8AP
Tel: 082 83 2194

Turn off A926 Blairgowrie-Kirriemuir to Alyth. Take first turning on left after Clydesdale Bank – 300 yards on right.

A traditional stone-built country house of character at the foot of Glenisla in the old market town of Alyth. High standards are obvious throughout and the proprietors, Allan and Eleanor Cull, pay particular attention to making their guests feel welcome and comfortable. Eleanor takes care of the front of the house while Allan is chef and calls on his wide experience of overseas travel and international cuisine to produce imaginative menus with that little bit of extra in flavour and presentation. Many of the organic vegetables and herbs come from the hotel's own garden and dinner in the relaxed atmosphere of the candlelit dining room can be a splendid way to round off the day.

Open 1 Mar to 23 Dec
Rooms: 6 with private facilities
Dining Room/Restaurant Lunch 12 – 1.30 pm (b) – by arrangement
Dinner 7 – 9.30 pm (b-c)
Restricted Licence
Facilities for the disabled
No smoking in dining room + bedrooms
Bed & breakfast £30 – £41
Dinner B & B £46.50 – £56.50
Home-cured beef, lamb, duck, ham. Tay salmon with beurre blanc and dill sauce. Roast best end of lamb with a herb crust. Steamed gingerbread pudding. Home-made truffles.
STB Highly Commended 3 Crowns
Credit cards: 1, 3
Proprietors: Allan & Eleanor Cull

Anstruther

Map 4

Restaurant of the Year Award 1993

THE CELLAR RESTAURANT

24 East Green, Anstruther
Fife KY10 3AA
Tel: 0333 310378

Peter Jukes, who owns the Cellar, has long had a reputation as one of the country's leading chefs and his skills are demonstrated at their finest in his masterly treatment of seafood. It is little wonder that he attracts discerning diners from all over the country. The Cellar is full of character with an interior of stone walls, beamed ceilings and open fires, and approached through a walled courtyard that helps to prepare the atmosphere of the place. Though fish and shellfish are the specialities there is almost always excellent lamb and beef on the menu, prepared and presented with the same care and attention that is the hallmark of the proprietor. There is a distinguished wine list to complement the food. You shouldn't miss a chance to visit the Cellar – but do book in advance. It is deservedly popular.

Open all year except 1 wk Christmas/New Year + 1 wk May
Dining Room/Restaurant Lunch 12.30 – 1.30 pm Tue to Sat (a-c)
Dinner 7 – 9.30 pm except Sun (d)
Closed Sun: also Mon in Winter
Facilities for the disabled
No smoking in restaurant
Fish soups, langoustine, scallops, crab, lobster, turbot, monkfish etc. Rosettes of lamb with rosemary. Fillet of Scotch beef.
Credit cards: 1, 2, 3, 6
Proprietors: Peter & Vivien Jukes

Appin

Map 6

INVERCRERAN COUNTRY HOUSE HOTEL
Glen Creran, Appin
Argyll PA38 4BJ
Tel: 063 173 414/456
Fax: 063 173 532

Just off A828 Oban-Fort William at head of Loch Creran, 14 miles north of Connel Bridge.

The first thing that strikes one about Invercreran is the superb site. It is perched on a hillside with really magnificent panoramic views over glens and hills. The house itself is strikingly different, a stylish modern mansion house, yet not in the slightest out of place in this remote and lovely glen. Splendid public rooms with spacious terraces, and large comfortable bedrooms, contribute to the overall feeling of luxury. John and Marie Kersley with their family have created a really special place which offers total relaxation and enjoyment. There are lots of interesting walks locally – and don't be surprised if you come across the odd herd of red deer. The food lives up to the high standards that mark this place and is served with courtesy and charm in the delightful dining room. Children over five years are welcome.

Open 1 Mar to 31 Oct
Rooms: 9 with private facilities
Dining Room/Restaurant Lunch 12.15 – 1.30 pm except Mon (c)
Dinner 7 – 8 pm (e)
No dogs
No smoking in dining room
Bed & breakfast £44 – £69
Dinner B & B £71 – £96
Pan-fried scallops with white wine and chive butter sauce. Collops of Highland venison with a cranberry and Port sauce. Poached fillet of turbot with a tarragon and mint cream. Collops of fillet of beef sauté with brandy and wild mushroom sauce.
STB Deluxe 4 Crowns
Credit cards: 1, 3
Proprietor: John Kersley

THE STEWART HOTEL
Glen Duror, Appin
Argyll PA38 4BW
Tel: 063 174 268/220
Fax: 063 174 328

A828 – Fort William 17 miles; Glencoe 10 miles; Oban 30 miles.
In a delightful setting of five acres of tranquil landscaped gardens overlooking Loch Linnhe, and a mere ten miles from Glencoe, The Stewart Hotel makes a very good base for touring this spectacular area of the country. The original building goes back over a century and was designed as as hunting lodge with the generous internal proportions associated with the period. The dining room, bar and public rooms are in this part while the modern well equipped bedrooms are in a newer wing. With ready access to plentiful supplies of the delicious fish and shellfish for which the west coast is renowned, the chefs create well balanced menus which change daily and are presented with finesse.
Open 1 Apr to 15 Oct
Rooms: 19 with private facilities
Bar Lunch 12 – 2 pm (a)
Bar Supper 6 – 7.30 pm (a)
Dinner 7.30 – 9 pm (d)
No smoking in dining room
Bed & breakfast £40 - £50
Dinner B & B £65 – £75
Warm salad of pheasant and mango with a walnut dressing. Oven roasted rack of lamb served on a bed of onion confit with a garlic and rosemary jus. Pan-fried fillet of salmon with three pimento sauces.
STB Commended 4 Crowns
Credit cards: 1, 2, 3, 5
Proprietors: The Lacy Family

Arbroath
Map 4

BYRE FARM RESTAURANT
Redford, Carmyllie
Arbroath DD11 2QZ
Tel: 02416 245

On B961 Dundee-Brechin. From Forfar, take Carnoustie road to turn off for Redford. From Arbroath, turn off at Condor and follow Redford sign.
This old stone building constructed from local stone and slates used to be a cottage with a byre at the end. It is now a popular venue for people passing through the area as well as for locals who go to enjoy the home-baking and wholesome cooking in a peaceful rustic atmosphere. The food is straightforward and unpretentious yet introduces some interesting speciality dishes and makes provision for vegetarians.
Open all year
Meals available 12 – 2.30 pm: 4.30 – 6.30 pm (a)
Dining Room/Restaurant Lunch 12 – 2.30 pm (a)
Dinner 6.30 – 8 pm (b) – reservations only
Facilities for the disabled
No smoking in restaurant
Roast chicken with oatmeal stuffing. Smokie pie with cheese and potato topping. Angus Glen venison in rich gravy. Clootie dumpling with fresh cream.
Credit card: 1
Proprietor: Anne Law

Ardelve
Map 6

LOCH DUICH HOTEL
Ardelve
by Kyle of Lochalsh IV40 8DY
Tel: 059 985 213
Fax: 059 985 214

Off A87 from Fort William and Inverness (via Loch Ness), 7 miles from Kyle of Lochalsh/Skye ferry.
One of the most photographed ancient monuments in the country marks the spot – or almost does. The Loch Duich Hotel looks out towards Eilean Donan Castle and is well located at the junction of three sea lochs and only 12 minutes or so from the Skye ferry at Kyle of Lochalsh. The new owners have done much to improve standards and upgrade the hotel. Menus are well thought out and food is carefully prepared and presented. Naturally enough there is a leaning towards the splendid fish and shellfish for which the west coast is so renowned.
Open all year
Rooms: 18, 5 with private facilities
Bar Lunch 12.30 – 2 pm (a)
Dinner 7 – 9 pm (c)
No smoking in dining room
Bed & breakfast from £22

Dinner B & B from £37
Smoked haddock loaf, queenie scallop crumble, oysters and mussels, wild salmon, local langoustines, lobster, crab. Wild duck, pigeon, venison, heather lamb.
STB Commended 2 Crowns
Credit cards: 1, 3
Proprietors: Iain Fraser & Sonia Moore

Ardentinny
Map 3

ARDENTINNY HOTEL
Ardentinny
Loch Long, nr Dunoon
Argyll PA23 8TR
Tel: 036 981 209
Fax: 036 981 345

By ferry Gourock-Dunoon, then A815 and A880 – or drive round Loch Lomond.
This is a delightful old coaching inn established almost 300 years ago on the shores of Loch Long, 12 miles north of Dunoon. Situated on the edge of the mountainous Argyll Forest Park which is a delightful place through which to drive or walk, the hotel has lovely gardens down to the sea loch. There are moorings available to diners arriving by yacht. Fishermen and other lovers of outdoor pursuits make Ardentinny their base, enjoying the buttery and hotel dining room with their sound reputation for good food. The hotel still retains many distinctive features but offers every modern comfort to its guests with well equipped en suite bedrooms which have good views out over loch and mountain.
Open 15 Mar to 1 Nov
Rooms: 11 with private facilities
Sunday Brunch 12 – 3 pm
Bar Lunch 12 – 2.30 pm Mon to Sat: 12 – 3.30 pm Sun (a)
Bar Supper 6 – 9.30 pm (b)
Dinner 7.30 – 9 pm (d)
No smoking in dining room
Bed & breakfast £25 – £39
Dinner B & B £49 – £69
West coast seafood and ratatouille tartlets. Freshly landed langoustine with garlic butter served on a bed of rice. Aberdeen Angus roast beef with Yorkshire pudding. Roast quail with Cumberland sauce.
STB Commended 4 Crowns
Credit cards: 1, 2, 3, 5, 6
Proprietors: John & Thyrza Horn, Hazel Hall

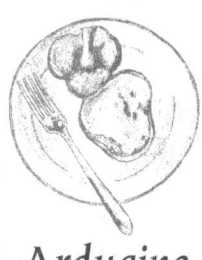

Arduaine

Map 6

LOCH MELFORT HOTEL
Arduaine, by Oban
Argyll PA34 4XG
Tel: 08522 233
Fax: 08522 214

On A816, 19 miles south of Oban.
The reputation of the Loch Melfort continues to grow as Philip and Rosalind Lewis keep improving standards. The location is quite outstanding with dramatic views to the islands across Asknish Bay. Originally the home of the Campbells of Arduaine it has been extended to take full advantage of the outlook and give bedrooms and dining room the maximum opportunity to enjoy landscape and seascape. Adjacent to the hotel and with access directly from it are Arduaine Gardens which are superbly maintained by The National Trust for Scotland and are open all year. There are few who will not revel in a morning or afternoon wandering through these delightful grounds.
Open all year except 4 Jan to 26 Feb
Rooms: 26 with private facilities
Morning coffee + afternoon teas 10 am – 6 pm
Bar Lunch 12 – 2.30 pm (a)
Bar Supper 6 – 9 pm (a)
Dinner 7.30 – 9 pm (d)
No smoking in dining room
Facilities for the disabled
Bed & breakfast £35 – £57
Dinner B & B £55 – £75
Terrine of fish layered with asparagus and crawfish served warm with a sweet tomato vinaigrette. Smoked haddock roulade with diced mushroom and langoustine. Sautéed medallions of loin of venison with a Port and orange sauce. Roast best end of lamb with a herb and green peppercorn crust and a red wine sauce.
STB Commended 4 Crowns
Credit cards: 1, 3 + SWITCH
Proprietors: Philip & Rosalind Lewis

Arisaig

Map 6

THE ARISAIG HOTEL
Arisaig
Inverness-shire PH39 4NH
Tel: 06875 210
Fax: 06875 310

At edge of Arisaig village on A830 Fort William-Mallaig, 10 miles before Mallaig on Loch Nan Ceall.
This splendid old coaching inn has its roots in the early 18th century. Through Victorian times to more recent years additions have been made and it became a comfortable country hotel. The hotel occupies a splendid site on the sea shore at the edge of the village, with some marvellous views. Nearby there are some good beaches. The Stewarts run the hotel almost as a large family home and it is furnished in keeping with the style of the building. There are open fires in the public rooms and comfortably equipped bedrooms. Janice Stewart shows much flair and imagination in the presentation of meals, with a heavy reliance on the daily changing menus on the excellent seafood and shellfish so abundant locally.
Open 15 Mar to 31 Oct
Rooms: 15, 6 with private facilities
Bar Lunch 12.30 – 2 pm (b)
Bar Supper 6.30 – 9 pm (b)
Dinner 7.30 – 8.30 pm (c)
No smoking in main dining room
Bed & breakfast £24 - £39
Dinner B & B £36 – £59
Room Rate £19 – £30
Local seafood, lobster, prawns, clams, halibut, turbot etc. Home-made soups and puddings. Traditional breakfast with Mallaig kippers.
Credit cards: 1, 3
Proprietors: George & Janice Stewart

ARISAIG HOUSE
Beasdale, by Arisaig
Inverness-shire PH39 4NR
Tel: 06875 622
Fax: 06875 626

Prestige Award Winner 1991

Just off A830 Fort William-Mallaig, 3 miles east of Arisaig
Arisaig House continues to attract the attention and earn the plaudits of connoisseurs – and rightly so. This fine old building stands on a commanding site surrounded by lovely gardens and woodlands through which you can wander down to the seashore and enjoy the beaches or rock cliffs. It is one of those special country houses emanating an immediate air of elegant and luxurious living. The high standards of Ruth and John Smither and their family are apparent throughout the building. Public rooms and bedrooms are furnished with good taste, and the staff are trained to a high degree and polite well mannered service comes naturally. The chefs make full use of the excellent fresh seafood so readily available but menus are carefully compiled to ensure sufficient variety of choice. Arisaig House is an experience to be savoured and one to which you will want to return. Children over 10 years welcome.
Open 31 Mar to 5 Nov
Rooms: 11 + 2 suites with private facilities
Bar Lunch 12.30 – 2 pm (b)
Dining Room/Restaurant Lunch 12.30 – 2 pm (e)
Dinner 7.30 – 8.30 pm (e)
Restricted Licence
No dogs
Bed & breakfast £70 – £102.50
STB Deluxe 3 Crowns
Credit cards: 1, 2, 3
Proprietors: Ruth, John & Andrew Smither

THE OLD LIBRARY LODGE & RESTAURANT
High Street, Arisaig
Inverness-shire PH39 4NH
Tel: 06875 651

In centre of village on seafront.
Overlooking the sea, with views to the small isles, The Old Library Lodge is a 200 year old stone built stable which has been tastefully converted into a charming restaurant with good accommodation. Alan Broadhurst's creative cooking makes full use of local shellfish, fish and meat and he has built up a fine reputation for his restaurant with both locals and visitors. A carefully selected wine list complements the food which includes garden produce from the village and herbs from the Broadhursts' own herb garden.
Open 1 Apr to 31 Oct
Rooms: 6 with private facilities
Restaurant Lunch 11.30 am – 2.30 pm (a)
Dinner 6.30 – 9.30 pm (c)
Restricted Licence
Bed & breakfast £29.50 – £40

Dinner B & B £48.50 – £59.50
Crab bisque with home-made bread.
Grilled Mallaig scallops on a leek purée.
Monkfish with a cream and mustard
sauce. Pot roast shoulder of lamb
provençale.
STB Commended 3 Crowns
Credit cards: 1, 3 + SWITCH, DELTA
Proprietors: Alan & Angela Broadhurst

Arran
Isle of

Map 3

AUCHRANNIE COUNTRY HOUSE HOTEL
Auchrannie Road, Brodick
Isle of Arran KA27 8BZ
Tel: 0770 302234
Fax: 0770 302812
One mile north of Brodick Ferry Terminal
and 400 yards from Brodick Golf Club.
Auchrannie is a red sandstone old
Scottish mansion, once the home of the
Dowager Duchess of Hamilton, now a
comfortable hotel with a leisure centre,
indoor swimming pool and a popular
Bistro. However it is the renowned
Garden Restaurant which is
recommended by Taste of Scotland,
where varied menus are presented with
particular emphasis on fresh local
produce including seafood. The hotel
enjoys a unique situation from which to
explore Arran's magnificent scenery – 56
miles of varied coastline and its seven
golf courses. In addition to the
luxuriously appointed bedrooms and
family suites, there are spacious lodges
sleeping up to six persons.
Open all year
Rooms: 28 with private facilities
Bistro Lunch 12.30 – 2.30 pm (a):
Dinner 5 – 9.30 pm (b)
Dinner (Garden Restaurant) 6.30 –
9.30 pm (d)
No smoking in Garden Restaurant
No dogs, except in lodges
Bed & breakfast £27.50 – £57
Dinner B & B £39 – £74.50
Ragoût of mushroom and prawns in a
light puff pastry case. Roast haunch of
Highland venison with a Port and orange
sauce. Poached supreme of salmon on a
delicate saffron and vermouth cream
sauce. Prime Scottish fillet steak with a
red wine sauce and straw potatoes.
STB Highly Commended 5 Crowns
Credit cards: 1, 3
Proprietor: Iain Johnston

CREELERS SEAFOOD RESTAURANT
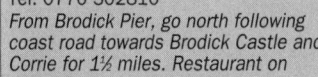
The Home Farm, Brodick
Isle of Arran KA27 8DD
Tel: 0770 302810
From Brodick Pier, go north following
coast road towards Brodick Castle and
Corrie for 1½ miles. Restaurant on
right.
Set in the Arran Visitors Centre, the
restaurant, formerly the bothy to the
old home farm of Brodick Castle, has
been established by Tim and Fran
James as a seafood bistro. The decor
like the food is simple, but colourful,
the atmosphere almost continental
and the service is quite charming. Tim,
formerly a trawlerman on the west
coast, still creels for a majority of the
shellfish and catches the wild salmon
and sea trout. The remainder of the
fish is bought fresh off the quays of
Kintyre. However the meat and
vegetarian dishes are an excellent
alternative to eating fish. There is an
extensive starter choice to accompany
both the lunch and dinner menus. The
seafood shop and smokehouse
attached to the restaurant enables you
to purchase some of the produce you
may have sampled in the restaurant. A
mail order service is also available.
Open 15 Mar to 31 Oct
Dining Room/Restaurant Lunch 12 –
2.30 pm except Mon (b)
Dinner 7 – 10 pm except Mon (d)
Closed Mon, except during Jul + Aug
Facilities for the disabled
Fresh local fish and shellfish, both
simply and elaborately presented.
Seasonal game. Vegetarian dishes. All
home-made.
Credit cards: 1, 3
Proprietors: Tim & Fran James

GLEN CLOY FARMHOUSE
Glencloy, Brodick
Isle of Arran KA27 8DA
Tel: 0770 302351
1½ miles from Brodick Pier on road
towards Brodick Castle. Sign at post box
in wall.
Glen Cloy Farmhouse is a beautiful
century old sandstone house, situated in
a peaceful glen just outside Brodick. The
bedrooms are individually furnished and
are cosy and warm. Two of the five
bedrooms have en suite facilities and

there are two other bathrooms. The
chef/proprietor and his wife bake their
own bread, and vegetables and herbs
come from the kitchen garden. The
farmhouse is ideally located to explore
the island's attractions, being close to
golf, castle, and the mountains.
Open 1 Mar to 7 Nov
Rooms: 5, 2 with private facilities
Dinner 7 – 7.30 pm (b)
Residents only
Unlicensed – guests welcome to take
own wine
No smoking in dining room
Bed & breakfast £19 – £27
Dinner B & B £30 – £36
Home-made bread, soups and desserts.
Roast Arran duckling with apple and
sage sauce. Arran cheeses.
STB Commended 2 Crowns
No credit cards
Proprietors: Mark & Vicki Padfield

GLENISLE HOTEL
Shore Road, Lamlash
Isle of Arran KA27 8LS
Tel: 0770 600 559/258
On main street of Lamlash.
The Glenisle is a white painted country
village hotel situated in the centre of
Lamlash overlooking the sea. A good
selection of Scottish and local produce
is offered in the restaurant, the cocktail
lounge of which features wooden
carvings from the famous Clyde steamer,
the Talisman. The hotel has been taken
over by Fred Wood, who was manager
under the previous owner, and he plans
to continue to run the Glenisle on similar
lines so guests can be assured of the
standards being maintained.
Open all year
Rooms: 13 with private facilities
Bar Lunch: 12 – 2 pm (a)
Dining Room/Restaurant Lunch 12 –
2 pm (a)
Dinner 7 – 9 pm (b)
Bed & breakfast £22.50 – £32.50
Dinner B & B £32 – £42
Haggis with a creamy onion and whisky
sauce. Courgette roulade. Strips of fillet
steak in an onion, mushroom and wine
sauce. Grilled halibut with parsley sauce.
Fillet of lamb with a crème de menthe
sauce.
STB Commended 4 Crowns
Credit cards: 1, 3
Proprietor: Fred Wood

KILMICHAEL COUNTRY HOUSE HOTEL

Glen Cloy, by Brodick
Isle of Arran KA27 8BY
Tel: 0770 302219

1½ miles from Brodick Pier, turning inland up golf course (signposted). In own grounds at end of long private drive.
Kilmichael is believed to be the oldest house on Arran and it has been lovingly transformed to a splendour it could never have known in the past. This is a small country house of a special standard enriched with antique furniture, oriental rugs, Chinese porcelain and objets d'art, and the only hotel on Arran graded 'Deluxe' by the Scottish Tourist Board. Elegance is sometimes an over-worked word, but not here. The decor, furnishings, style and quality of the place demonstrate impeccable good taste and the same care and attention go into the planning of meals. The rich harvest of the island's seas together with its game and agricultural produce are incorporated in appealing menus and complemented by a well chosen wine list. This is a wonderful restful hideaway from the hustle and bustle of ordinary life.
Open all year except Nov, Christmas + Feb
Rooms: 6 with private facilities
Dinner 7.30 – 8.30 pm (d)
Dinner for non-residents by arrangement
Children over 8 years welcome
No smoking in dining room + bedrooms
Bed & breakfast £30 – £50
Dinner B & B £51 – £71
Salad of mixed leaves with fresh Arran crab. Mushroom and walnut soup. Red mullet served with fennel and chives. Rhubarb and elderflower crumble.
STB Deluxe 3 Crowns
Credit card: 3
Proprietors: Geoffrey Botterill & Antony Butterworth

Auchencairn

Map 1

BALCARY BAY HOTEL

Auchencairn, nr Castle Douglas
Kirkcudbrightshire DG7 1QZ
Tel: 055664 217/311
Fax: 055664 272

Off A711 Dalbeattie-Kirkcudbright, along single track road from Auchencairn.
A lovely old country house dating back to 1625 which stands in over three acres of garden in a secluded and enchanting

situation on the shores of the bay. This former smugglers' haunt provides a wonderful retreat away from it all. The present day family run hotel has been tastefully decorated, providing every modern amenity and comfort for its guests, yet it still retains much of the old character and charm. The restaurant menus give prominence to the variety of local delicacies available, for example prime Galloway beef and lamb, seafood, salmon and lobster. Excellent hospitality, good food and a superb setting combine to make this an ideal holiday hotel.
Open 4 Mar to 12 Nov
Rooms: 17 with private facilities
Bar Lunch 12 – 2 pm (a)
Dining Room/Restaurant Lunch 12 – 1.45 pm Sun only (a): à la carte lunch by reservation only Mon to Sat (b)
Dinner 7 – 9 pm high season: 7 – 8.30 pm low season (c)
Bed & breakfast £40 – £48
Dinner B & B £45 – £65
Note: early/late season breaks and 3 or 7 day reductions available
Halibut cooked in a dill and lemon butter. Queen scallops in white wine with basil, bacon and julienne of vegetables. Lamb fillet coated in walnuts, cooked in filo pastry and glazed with honey and rosemary. Mignons of fillet of beef served with a cream sauce flavoured with coarse grain mustard.
STB Highly Commended 4 Crowns
Credit cards: 1, 3
Proprietors: Ronald & Joan Lamb, Graeme & Clare Lamb

Auchterarder

Map 4

AUCHTERARDER HOUSE

Auchterarder
Perthshire PH3 1DZ
Tel: 0764 663646/7
Fax: 0764 662939

Prestige Award Winner 1989

Off B8062 Auchterarder-Crieff, 1 mile from village.
Country house hotels don't come much better than this. Auchterarder House is superb in every way and Ian and Audrey Brown are constantly striving to raise standards even higher. This fine old red sandstone mansion house is set in 17½ acres of beautifully manicured lawns and mature trees. Public rooms are quite exceptional and sumptuously furnished,

and the conservatory is a particularly attractive feature. The master bedrooms are so grand in scale that they might have come straight off a Hollywood set which may be one reason why ex-President Ronald Reagan and his wife chose to stay there on a visit to Scotland. Food in the elegant dining room is cooked and presented with the same imagination and flair that is so evident throughout. The Browns are charming and attentive hosts and make everyone feel like a personal guest.
Open all year
Rooms: 15 with private facilities
Dining Room/Restaurant Lunch 12 – 3 pm Sun only (c) – other days by arrangement
Victorian teas in Winter Garden Conservatory 3 – 5 pm
Dinner 7 – 10 pm (f)
Reservations essential
No children
Bed & breakfast £65 - £100
Salmon tartare and chilled roulade of smoked salmon and sole, scented with chives, on a cucumber and sherry vinegar sauce. Medallion of Angus beef with a bone marrow herb crumble and a red wine and grain mustard sauce. Baked syrup pudding with a vanilla sauce.
Credit cards: 1, 2, 3, 5, 6
Proprietors: Ian & Audrey Brown

DUCHALLY HOUSE HOTEL

Duchally, by Auchterarder
Perthshire PH3 1PN
Tel: 0764 663071
Fax: 0764 662464

Just off A823 Crieff-Dunfermline, 2 miles south of Auchterarder.
A fine old Victorian country manor house set in sweeping lawns and woodland. The proprietors have carried out tasteful and stylish refurbishments. The dining room and drawing room are particularly elegant and there is an attractive bar, a beautifully panelled billiard room and a lovely staircase. There are beautiful views of the Ochil Hills from both restaurants, and open log fires throughout the public areas. Menus are interesting with a clear concentration on fresh local produce, and food is very well presented. A lovely place to stay.
Open all year except 23 to 30 Dec
Rooms: 15 with private facilities
Bar Lunch 12 – 2.15 pm (a)
Dining Room/Restaurant Lunch 12 – 2.15 pm (b)

Bar Supper 6 – 9.30 pm (a)
Dinner 7 – 9.30 pm (c)
Facilities for the disabled
No smoking area in restaurant
Bed & breakfast £37.50 – £55
Dinner B & B £50 – £70
Wild salmon with mousseline of sole.
Poached turbot with a whole grain
mustard sauce. Fillet of Scotch beef with
a Stilton sauce. Baked duck breast with
peach or pink peppercorn sauce.
STB Commended 4 Crowns
Credit cards: 1, 2, 3, 5, 6
Proprietor: Maureen Raeder

THE GLENEAGLES HOTEL
Auchterarder
Perthshire PH3 1NF
Tel: 0764 662231
Telex: 76105
Fax: 0764 662134

Prestige Award Winner 1990

½ mile west of A9, 10 miles north of
Dunblane, 1 mile south of Auchterarder.
A magnificent hotel of international
reputation and a resort in itself with an
exceptional range of leisure and sporting
facilities. A spectacular Scottish 'palace'
in rolling Perthshire countryside built in
grand style in the early part of this
century and immaculately restored. Food
and accommodation are of the highest
standard as would be expected from the
first hotel in Scotland to have been
awarded the AA's highest accolade
of five red stars, and they are richly
deserved. In the restaurants, the best of
local produce is used to create dishes
with a uniquely Scottish flavour, cooked
and presented to standards of
international excellence. Few will
experience Gleneagles without full
enjoyment of the occasion and a wish to
return as soon as possible. French and
German spoken.
Open all year
Rooms: 236 with private facilities
Bar Lunch 12.30 – 2.30 pm (c)
Dining Room/Restaurant Lunch 12.30 –
2.30 pm (d)
Bar Supper 5 – 10 pm (c)
Dinner 7.30 – 10 pm (f)
Note: please telephone in advance for
non-residential dining
Country Club Brasserie and Equestrian
Centre Restaurant & Bar – residents/
members only
No smoking area in restaurants
Bed & breakfast £102.50 – £140
Dinner B & B £142.50 – £180

Rich smoked salmon consommé with
mussels, leek and curry sabayon.
Supreme of Gressingham duck with
smoked bacon and broad bean stew.
Cherries flambéd in Kirsch and served
with honey ice cream.
Credit cards: 1, 2, 3, 5

Auchtermuchty

Map 4

ARDCHOILLE FARM GUEST HOUSE
Dunshalt
Auchtermuchty KY14 7EY
Tel: 0337 828414
Fax: 0337 828414
On B936 just outside Dunshalt village,
1½ miles south of Auchtermuchty.
Donald and Isobel Steven welcome you
to Ardchoille – a spacious, well
appointed farmhouse, with superb views
of the Lomond hills. The accommodation
is in twin-bedded rooms with en suite or
private facilities, colour TV and
tea/coffee trays with home-made butter
shortbread. Large comfortable lounge.
Attractive dining room with elegant china
and crystal where delicious freshly
prepared meals are presented with flair
and imagination. Just an hour's drive
from Edinburgh and 20 minutes from St
Andrews or Perth, Ardchoille makes an
excellent base for touring, golfing – or
just relaxing.
Open all year
Rooms: 3 with private facilities
Dinner 7 – 8 pm (d) 4 course set menu
Dinner for non-residents by prior
arrangement only
Unlicensed – guests welcome to take
own wine
No dogs
No smoking in dining room + bedrooms
Bed & breakfast £25 – £35
Dinner B & B £40 – £50
Fresh salmon soufflé topped with

cucumber and basil. Home-made chicken
broth. Roast leg of new season's Scotch
lamb with home-made garden mint and
apple sauce, and a creamed swede and
carrot tartlet. Apricot roulade with
toasted flaked almonds and home-made
vanilla ice cream.
STB Highly Commended 3 Crowns
Credit card: 3
Proprietors: Donald & Isobel Steven

Auldgirth
by Dumfries

Map 1

LOW KIRKBRIDE FARMHOUSE
Auldgirth
Dumfries DG2 0SP
Tel: 038 782 258
From Dumfries take A76 Kilmarnock for
2 miles, then B729 to Dunscore. Beyond
Dunscore at crossroads go right. After
1½ miles take first left. Farm first on left.
This is a working farm with a prize-
winning herd of Friesian cattle and lots
of sheep, so there is much of interest for
those who love the country and farm
animals. It is located in splendidly
remote, rolling cultivated countryside
with fine views in all directions, and here
you are genuinely away from it all. The
traditional farmhouse building is
surrounded by out-buildings and a
colourful garden to the front. Guest
rooms are attractively decorated with
pretty duvet covers and pillow cases,
with matching curtains. Electric blankets
are provided and there is a tea/coffee
making tray with a jug of fresh farm milk.
Dinner is provided for residents if
booked in advance and there are
plentiful helpings of good wholesome
food which you take in the family kitchen
while Zan chats, cooks and serves. A
real atmosphere of family living.
Open all year
Rooms: 2
Dinner 6 – 9 pm (a)
Residents only
Unlicensed
No dogs
No smoking in bedrooms ·
Bed & breakfast from £15
Dinner B & B from £22
Home-made soup. Roast leg of Low
Kirkbride lamb. Bramble and apple pie.
STB Award Pending
No credit cards
Proprietors: Joe & Zan Kirk

Aultbea

Map 6

AULTBEA HOTEL & RESTAURANT
Seafront, Aultbea
Ross-shire IV22 2HX
Tel: 0445 731201
Fax: 0445 731214
Off A832, on the shores of Loch Ewe.
The Aultbea Hotel is situated in an
exceptionally beautiful location at the
waterside of Loch Ewe and has
magnificent views over the Isle of Ewe to
the Torridon Mountains. It is believed to
have been built for Lord Zetland in the
early 1800s. The hotel has been run by
Peter and Avril Nieto for the past seven
years and its reputation for comfort and
cuisine has continued to grow. There is a
choice of eating styles – the Waterside
Bistro which is open all day and where a
varied menu from teas and coffees with
home-baking to local fish and grills is
available; and the more formal Zetland
Restaurant, overlooking the loch, where
three or four course daily changing table
d'hôte menus are offered which feature
local seafood, game and a carvery, as
well as an à la carte option.
Open all year except Christmas Day
Rooms: 8 with private facilities
Waterside Bistro 9 am – 9 pm (a)
Bar Meals 11 am – 9 pm (a)
Dinner 7 – 9 pm (c)
Bed & breakfast £25 (Winter) – £38
Dinner B & B £44 (Winter) - £58
Home-made soups. Prime Highland
venison steak cooked in red wine and
onions and finished with cream. Fillet of
locally landed cod poached in wine with
herbs and topped with black grapes.
Collops of prime Highland beef cooked
with walnuts and red wine. Fresh local
scallops lightly poached, served with a
cheese sauce.
STB Commended 4 Crowns
Credit cards: 1, 3
Proprietors: Peter & Avril Nieto

Aviemore

Map 6

LYNWILG HOUSE
Lynwilg, by Aviemore
Inverness-shire PH22 1PZ
Tel: 0479 811685
Fax: 0479 811685
A9 Perth-Inverness, take Lynwilg road 1
mile south of Aviemore.
This impressive country house was built
by the Duke of Richmond and is set on
high ground commanding beautiful views
across to the Cairngorms. Four acres of
landscaped gardens include a kitchen
garden contributing fresh fruit,
vegetables and herbs for the house.
Although only a mile from Aviemore, the
beauty of the surroundings and the
elegance of the house interior set it
worlds apart. Fishing on a private loch,
croquet on the lawn, log fires and
comfort, confirm the best features of
country house living. The food lives up to
the same high standards, with
imaginative menus, excellent presentation and efficient attentive service.
Open 27 Dec to 31 Oct
Rooms: 4 with private facilities
Dinner 7 – 8 pm (b)
Unlicensed – guests welcome to take
own wine
Dogs by arrangement
No smoking in restaurant
Bed & breakfast £17 – £22
Dinner B & B £29 – £36
Cream of watercress soup. Carrot and
lovage soup. Smoked trout and salmon
timbales. Salmon, venison, game in
season. Home-made pâtés, terrines, ice
creams, bread. Summer desserts with
Lynwilg fruits.
STB Award Pending
Credit cards: 1, 3
Proprietor: Marjory Cleary

Ayr

Map 1

BURNS MONUMENT HOTEL
Alloway
Ayr KA7 4PQ
Tel: 0292 442466
Fax: 0292 443174
In Alloway village on B7024, 2 miles
south of Ayr town centre.
An elegant and charming historic hotel
located in the famous Alloway village.
Splendidly situated in its own grounds
with landscaped gardens along the
banks of the River Doon with the back-
drop of Burns Monument and Auld Brig
of Doon. Locally renowned restaurant
using only the best of fresh local
produce. French and German spoken.
Open all year
Rooms: 9, 8 with private facilities
Bar Lunch 12 – 2.15 pm (a)
Dining Room/Restaurant Lunch 12 –
2.15 pm (b)
Bar Supper 5 – 9.45 pm (a)
Dinner 5 – 9.45 pm (c)
No smoking area in restaurant
Bed & breakfast £35 – £45
Dinner B & B £51 – £61
Room Rate £30 – £40
Imaginative cuisine featuring locally
caught seafood, with meat, game and
poultry from the hotel's farm; poached
fresh local salmon, medallions of
Aberdeen Angus fillet steak. Home-made
sweets and cheeses.
STB Commended 3 Crowns
Credit cards: 1, 2, 3, 5, 6
Proprietor: Robert Gilmour

DUNURE ANCHORAGE
Harbour View, Dunure
nr Ayr KA7 4LN
Tel: 0292 50 295
In Dunure village, off A719 (coast road)
about 6 miles south of Ayr.
This corner of the Ayrshire coastline is
positively steeped in history and
nowhere does it come more alive than in
the charming harbourside hostelry of
Dunure Anchorage. There is a distinctly
old world appeal about the place from
the moment you find yourself in the
welcoming reception area which leads to
the bar and restaurant. Walls
half-panelled in wood, stucco and stone,
with pretty pictures, old brass ornaments
and fishing paraphernalia, set the tone.
The dining room is warm and cosy with
beamed ceiling, thick carpet and
comfortable chairs, and little windows
overlooking the harbour. There is a good
menu of interesting dishes which
indicate a talented chef behind the
scenes. The food is sensibly priced and
good, served in a relaxed and friendly
atmosphere by caring staff who seem
keen to protect the restaurant's
reputation.
Open all year
Meals available from 12 – 2 pm (a): 6 –
9 pm (b)
A selection of pan-fried seafood in lemon

and chive butter on bed of salad leaves. Venison in a rich Port, redcurrant and Claret sauce. Grilled sirloin steak on bed of haggis with cream, peppercorn and Highland whisky sauce.
Credit cards: 1, 3
Proprietors: The Smith Family

FOUTERS BISTRO RESTAURANT
2A Academy Street, Ayr
Ayrshire KA7 1HS
Tel: 0292 261391
Town centre, opposite Town Hall and Tourist Information Centre.
Following a meal at Fouters a satisfied guest wrote to the Editor of this guide saying "Delicious...... superb...... it is time this wonderful establishment got the recognition it deserves". That seems to sum up the general reaction to Ayr's premier bistro. Laurie and Fran Black have made a great success of this cosy little restaurant in what were once the vaults of an old bank. Full use has been made of the unusual architectural features and the result is a warm, friendly and relaxing atmosphere. Interesting as that may be, it is the food that is the prime concern of most patrons and they are not disappointed with a carefully constructed menu that offers remarkable value for money. The chef draws heavily on the rich agricultural produce of Ayrshire and a surfeit of good local seafood, and presents it tastefully and appetisingly. Fouters is naturally busy so do take time to book in advance if possible.
Open all year except Christmas Day, 26 Dec, 1 to 3 Jan
Bistro Menu 12 – 2 pm except Sun Mon (a)
Restaurant Lunch 12 – 2 pm except Sun Mon (a)
Bistro Menu 6.30 – 10.30 pm Sun, Tue to Fri (b)
Dinner 6.30 – 10.30 pm Tue to Sat: 7 – 10.30 pm Sun (d)
Closed Mon
Taste of Scotland platter: smoked salmon, smoked Summer Isles chicken and venison, pâtés, shrimps, gravadlax cured salmon – served with a little salad. Roast Spring Ayrshire lamb with Arran honey mustard and ginger wine sauce. Fillet of Scottish salmon on a cream and vermouth sauce flavoured with fresh basil. Chargrilled prime Scottish beef.
Credit cards: 1, 2, 3, 5, 6 + SWITCH
Proprietors: Laurie & Fran Black

THE HUNNY POT
37 Beresford Terrace
Ayr KA7 2EU
Tel: 0292 263239
In the town centre of Ayr, close to Burns' Statue Square.
This small but popular and attractive coffee shop is run personally by Felicity Thomson. It has a cosy intimate atmosphere and the pine furniture and teddy bear theme give the place character. There is a range of eating available all day – from morning coffee and afternoon tea with home-baking, to more substantial snacks and meals.
Open all year except Christmas + Boxing Days, 1 Jan
Meals served all day from 10 am – 10 pm (a)
Traditional afternoon teas served 2 – 5.30 pm Sun
Unlicensed
No smoking area in restaurant
All home-made soups, scones, brown sugar meringues, cakes and dish of the day. Puddings include seasonal fruit crumbles, hazelnut meringue cake. Scottish cheeses with oatcakes.
No credit cards
Proprietor: Felicity Thomson

THE STABLES RESTAURANT & COFFEE HOUSE
Queen's Court, Sandgate
Ayr KA7 1BD
Tel: 0292 283704
Immediately behind the Tourist Information Centre in the Sandgate.
In the centre of Ayr is a tiny Georgian courtyard which is a haven of little shops with a tea garden. The Stables were built of local stone probably in the late 1760s. The menu leans heavily towards ethnic Scots dishes, predominantly 'kail yard' rather than 'castle'. You may

choose just tea and a scone or have a full meal. Children are welcome and there is a range of toys and books available, but burgers, beans and chips don't feature on the menu!
Open all year except Christmas + Boxing Days, 1 + 2 Jan
Coffee House open 10 am – 5 pm Mon to Sat: 1 – 5 pm Sun (a)
No smoking area in restaurant
Tweed kettle, stovies, ham and haddie pie. Clootie dumpling. Local cheeses. Wines from Moniack Castle and English vineyards. Family owned smokehouse (Craigrossie) provides smoked fish and meats.
No credit cards
Proprietor: Ed Baines

Ballachulish

Map 6

THE BALLACHULISH HOTEL
Ballachulish, nr Fort William
Argyll PA39 4JY
Tel: 08552 606
Fax: 08552 629
On A828 at the Ballachulish Bridge.
The Ballachulish Hotel commands an inspiring panorama over Loch Linnhe to the peaks of Morvern and Ardgour. In this friendly family owned hotel, careful restoration and refurbishment have ensured a skilful blend of traditional style with modern, international standards. Gracious baronial lounges lead to the welcoming Cocktail Bar and the Loch View Restaurant. Guests enjoy the complimentary use of a heated swimming pool nearby. French and German spoken.
Open all year
Rooms: 30 with private facilities
Bar Meals 10 am – 10 pm (a-b)
Dining Room/Restaurant Lunch 1 – 2.30 pm (a)
Dinner 7 – 10 pm (d)
Bed & breakfast £34 – £44
Dinner B & B £37 – £65
Smoked Highland goose breast in lemon and lime essence. Roast saddle of venison with juniper berry and Scottish wine sauce. Pheasant Glenarthur filled with asparagus forcemeat. Highlander's toffee pudding with whisky butterscotch sauce.
STB Highly Commended 4 Crowns
Credit cards: 1, 3, 6
Proprietors: The Young Family

Ballantrae

Map 1

BALKISSOCK LODGE
Ballantrae
Ayrshire KA26 0LP
Tel: 046 583 537
Fax: 046 583 537

Take first inland road off A77, south of River Stinchar at Ballantrae (signed to Laggan caravans) and follow for 2¼ miles. Turn right at T-junction and continue along single track 'no through road' to its end.

Leaving the A77 immediately south of Ballantrae takes you at once into another world of gentle rolling hills, total peace and quiet and wonderful panoramic views. It also takes you to Balkissock Lodge, which dates from around 1800. The Lodge has recently been refurbished and takes full advantage of its location to provide a thoroughly relaxing atmosphere. Janet and Adrian Beale are thoughtful hosts and Janet's skill in the kitchen is evident in her imaginative menus and the degree to which she makes use of the fine supply of local produce for which Ayrshire is famous. Occasional speciality and gourmet events are held for serious lovers of good food. Vegetarians and vegans can make their requirements known in advance and be well looked after. There is a wealth of sporting and recreational activities in the locality.

Open all year except 1 Nov to 15 Dec
Rooms: 3 with private facilities
Dinner 7 – 9 pm (c-d)
Non-residents by prior arrangement
Unlicensed – guests welcome to take own wine
No dogs
No smoking in dining room
Bed & breakfast £25 – £45
Dinner B & B £37.50 – £60
Local salmon with a Champagne and herb sauce. Supreme of chicken with lemon and fresh ginger. Pheasant with Madeira and pecan nuts. Roast Gressingham duckling with a honey and lemon sauce, perfumed with cloves. Ballantrae Bay lobster, bound with a light wine sauce dusted with breadcrumbs and cheese, and baked in the shell. Savoy cabbage leaves stuffed with minced mushrooms and nuts, served with a saffron and cider coulis.
STB Commended 3 Crowns
Credit cards: 1, 3 + DELTA
Proprietors: Adrian & Janet Beale

COSSES
Ballantrae
Ayrshire KA26 0LR
Tel: 046 583 363
Fax: 046 583 598

From A77 at southern end of Ballantrae, take inland road signed to Laggan. Cosses is c. 2 miles on right.

Cosses is one of those special places that one loves to discover – converted farm buildings tucked away in a remote and secluded valley of lovely garden and woodlands. It is only a couple of miles from the well travelled A77 but it is in a different world. The accommodation is limited – two double bedrooms each with private bathroom – but the larger, in an out-building, is really a delightful little suite of sitting room, large bedroom and large bathroom. The sitting room can be converted into another bedroom if required, making a compact family unit. Robin and Susan Crosthwaite are charming hosts and invite you into their own sitting room for a complimentary aperitif before dinner. Susan is an accomplished Cordon Bleu cook and her meals are exquisite testimony to the fact. Though she may only be cooking for two or four people she goes to much trouble to prepare an inviting and well balanced menu and to make you feel like her own personal dinner guests. Seasonal vegetables, herbs and fruit are from the kitchen garden. In this lovely part of south west Scotland this is a place you would not want to miss.

Open all year except Christmas Day, 31 Dec + 1 Jan
Rooms: 2 with private facilities
Dinner 7 – 9.30 pm (c)
Residents only
Unlicensed – guests welcome to take own wine
Bed & breakfast £26 - £40
Dinner B & B £44 - £60
Dunsyre Blue crêpes with a tomato sauce. Lemon and tarragon baked chicken breast served with a creamy tarragon sauce. Rhubarb and ginger syllabub with florentines. Ballantrae Bay
lobster. Selection of Scottish cheeses.
STB Deluxe 3 Crowns
No credit cards
Proprietors: Susan & Robin Crosthwaite

Ballater

Map 5

Country House Hotel of the Year Award 1993

BALGONIE COUNTRY HOUSE
Braemar Place
Ballater AB35 5RQ
Tel: 03397 55482
Fax: 03397 55482

Off Braemar Road (A93), a few hundred yards west of Church Green.

Built in 1899 in the heart of Royal Deeside, Balgonie is now a small country house hotel set in tranquil mature gardens overlooking the golf course towards the hills of Glenmuick. There is much to appeal to the visitor to this area, ranging from hill-walking, golf and fishing, touring castles and distilleries, or simply relaxing in peaceful surroundings. Balgonie makes an ideal home from which to explore the many facets of the area. The menu is well balanced and interesting, reflecting the wealth of local produce such as game, salmon, beef and lamb with seafood fresh from the coast, and herbs and soft fruits from Balgonie's own garden. French and German spoken.

Open all year
Rooms: 9 with private facilities
Dining Room/Restaurant Lunch 12.30 – 2 pm (b)
Dinner 7 – 9 pm (e)
Facilities for the disabled
No smoking in dining room
Bed & breakfast £30 – £50
Dinner B & B £45 – £75
Terrine of salmon and halibut with a chive mayonnaise sauce. Roast local pheasant on a nest of honey braised red cabbage, with poached apricots and redcurrants and a Port wine game jus. A light pastry filled with bananas and sultanas on a warm toffee sauce. Warm treacle tart with a Grand Marnier crème anglaise.
STB Deluxe 4 Crowns
Credit cards: 1, 2, 3
Proprietors: John & Priscilla Finnie

THE COACH HOUSE HOTEL
Netherley Place, Ballater
Aberdeenshire AB35 5QE
Tel: 03397 55462
Fax: 03397 55462

Beside church green in centre of Ballater.

The Coach House is conveniently situated in central Ballater beside the village green. Ballater is probably the heart of Royal Deeside and an ideal base from which to explore the many castles, stately homes and whisky distilleries so plentiful in the area. There is a cosy lounge bar where locals and visitors alike assemble to chat and the restaurant offers good seasonal produce, carefully presented and served with courtesy.

Open all year
Rooms: 6 with private facilities
Bar Lunch 12 – 2.15 pm (b)
Dining Room/Restaurant Lunch 12 – 2.15 pm (b)
Bar Supper 5 – 9 pm (b)
Dinner 7 – 9 pm (c)
Bed & breakfast £24 - £30
Dinner B & B £40 - £46
Deeside smoked salmon with dill mustard. Guinea fowl in white wine, mushroom and shallot cream sauce. Venison Macduff. Trio of lamb cutlets in a ginger sauce. Aberdeen Angus steaks.
STB Commended 3 Crowns
Credit cards: 1, 2, 3, 5
Proprietor: Gena Campbell

CRAIGENDARROCH HOTEL & COUNTRY CLUB
Braemar Road, Ballater
Royal Deeside AB35 5XA
Tel: 03397 55858 • Telex: 739952
Fax: 03397 55447

On A93 western end of Ballater, near Balmoral.

There was a time when this Victorian red sandstone building was the Highland retreat of the Keiller family of Dundee. Greatly expanded it is now a first class hotel and country club with spectacular indoor swimming pools, squash courts, sauna, trimnasium, solarium etc. Outdoors there is a dry ski slope and an all weather tennis court. If even the mere thought of all that exercise gives you an appetite you will be able to indulge it in any one of three restaurants. The Oaks, at the top of the range, has a fine reputation for excellent cuisine and impeccable service and the Master Chef demonstrates his skills with flair and

imagination. Here you may expect a special occasion and a memorable meal. At a slightly different level, the Lochnagar with its splendid views of the mountain of that name concentrates on grills, seafood and the superb Aberdeen Angus beef for which the region is famed. Around the pool area is the rather Parisian looking Cafe Jardin, specialising in everything from light snacks to substantial meals, which is open to residents and club members only.

Open all year
Rooms: 50 with private facilities
Dinner (The Oaks) 7 – 10 pm (c-f)
Dinner (Lochnagar) 7 – 10 pm Thu to Sat (b-c)
Cafe Jardin (members and residents only) Lunch 12 – 2.30 pm (a-b): Dinner 5 – 10 pm (a-b)
Bed & breakfast £99 – £175
Pan-fried rack of lamb. Confit of wild duck and sautéed sweetbreads. Crayfish tails with strips of fennel, shallots, fine tomato, Pernod and saffron rice. Hot apple and black cherry pancakes.
STB Highly Commended 5 Crowns
Credit cards: 1, 2, 3, 5, 6

DARROCH LEARG HOTEL
Braemar Road, Ballater
Aberdeenshire AB35 5UX
Tel: 03397 55443
Fax: 03397 55443

On A93 at western edge of Ballater on road to Braemar.

Originally a Victorian country house, the Darroch Learg is now a family owned hotel of 20 bedrooms. There are log fires in the drawing room and a separate smoke room where pre-dinner drinks can be enjoyed in a relaxing and welcoming atmosphere. The dining room is a conservatory with a bright and airy feeling and a wonderful outlook into the Grampian Hills. The head chef and his team use the best of Scottish beef, lamb, game and fish to prepare the interesting and daily changing menu.

Open Feb to Dec (incl)
Rooms: 20 with private facilities
Bar Lunch 12.30 – 2 pm except Sun (a)
Dining Room/Restaurant Lunch 12.30 – 2 pm Sun only (b)
Dinner 7 – 8.30 pm (c-d)
No smoking in dining room
Bed & breakfast £35 – £45
Dinner B & B £48 – £64.75
Duck rillette and potato gâteau crowned with candied parsnips. Wild Dee sea trout with local chanterelles and salsa.

Saddle of roe deer on a pear and thyme pancake with apricots and shallot confit. Iced praline parfait with fresh bramble sauce.
STB Highly Commended 4 Crowns
Credit cards: 1, 3, 5
Proprietors: Nigel & Fiona Franks

THE GLEN LUI HOTEL
Invercauld Road, Ballater
Aberdeenshire AB35 5RP
Tel: 03397 55402
Fax: 03397 55545

Off A93 in Ballater.

The picturesque little village of Ballater is, of course, the very heart of Royal Deeside, an area in which there is so much to see and do. The Glen Lui Hotel is therefore well placed for those who wish to explore and enjoy the area. It is a small friendly country house, with modern bedroom and restaurant extensions, in a quiet corner of the village with delightful views over the golf course and Lochnagar. Bedrooms are very comfortable and well equipped and there are a number of executive suites. A great deal of imagination goes into the preparation of the restaurant menus and food is first class with a suitably supportive and extensive wine list. Conference facilities available.

Open 15 Mar to 30 Nov
Rooms: 19 with private facilities
Bar Lunch 12 – 2 pm Mon to Sat: 12.30 – 2.30 pm Sun (a)
Bar Supper 6 – 9.30 pm (b-c)
No smoking in restaurant + conference room
Bed & breakfast £25 – £40
Room Rate £40 – £60
Fresh hill venison pan-fried with tarragon and finished with a red wine game sauce. Poached supreme of salmon with a dill and lemon butter sauce. Deeside lamb cutlets grilled with honey and thyme and set on a ruby Port jus. Chocolate and orange millefeuille on a fresh fruit sauce.
STB Highly Commended 4 Crowns
Credit cards: 1, 2, 3
Proprietors: Serge & Lorraine Geraud

THE GREEN INN
9 Victoria Road
Ballater AB35 5QQ
Tel: 03397 55701

In centre of Ballater on village green.
A granite-built former temperance hotel overlooking the village green, which is now a small licensed restaurant with three letting bedrooms. Chef/proprietor Jeffrey Purves has a creative flair with food, his emphasis being on maximum use of fresh local produce. His 'Chef's specials' change every night reflecting the best of what is available to him.
Open all year except Christmas Day, 2 wks Oct
Rooms: 3 with private facilities
Dining Room/Restaurant Lunch 12.30 – 1.30 pm Sun Sat (b)
Dinner 7 – 9 pm (c)
No smoking in dining room
Bed & breakfast £20 – £35
Dinner B & B £39.50 – £55
St Andrews cheese tart. Supreme of salmon on a bed of watercress, spinach and sorrel, served with a tomato and basil butter sauce. Medley of venison on a compote of braised red cabbage and a bramble sauce. Lemon and crowdie tart with a fig sauce. Sticky toffee pudding with date and Armagnac ice cream.
STB Commended 3 Crowns
Credit cards: 1, 3, 6
Proprietors: Carol & Jeffrey Purves

Balquhidder

Map 4

MONACHYLE MHOR FARMHOUSE/HOTEL
Balquhidder, Lochearnhead
Perthshire FK19 8PQ
Tel: 0877 384 622
Fax: 0877 384 305

North of Callander A84 to Balquhidder. 7 miles beyond village at end of lochside.
In a land of mountains and lochs, Monachyle Mhor sits in its own 2,000 acres of farmland in the heart of The Braes o' Balquhidder. It is a small family run farmhouse/hotel of great character and offers a unique blend of modern comfort and country living. All bedrooms are en suite, and in the restaurant and cosy bar you will find good food and a wealth of hospitality. For those who like to go as they please, the hotel has three luxury cottages each of which sleeps six people.

Open all year
Rooms: 4 with private facilities
Bar Lunch 12 – 2.30 pm (a)
Dining Room/Restaurant Lunch 12 – 2.30 pm (b)
Bar Supper 6.30 – 10 pm (a)
Dinner 7.30 – 10 pm (c)
No dogs
Bed & breakfast £23 – £25
Dinner B & B £38 – £45
Squid ink tagliatelle with lightly poached queenies, in saffron, white wine and fish stock decorated with samphire. Mousseline of lemon sole with fresh herbs. Breast of Monachyle grouse with juniper and Madeira, lightly pan-fried. Terrine of Summer fruits. Bread home-baked daily.
STB Commended 3 Crowns
Credit cards: 1, 3
Proprietors: Rob & Jean Lewis

Banchory

Map 5

HORSE MILL RESTAURANT (NATIONAL TRUST FOR SCOTLAND)
Crathes Castle, Banchory
Kincardineshire AB31 3QJ
Tel: 033044 634
(out of season: 033044 525)
Fax: 033044 797

Royal Deeside (A93) 3 miles east of Banchory.
An attractive and unusual restaurant with helpful staff and a friendly atmosphere. Situated in a converted circular horse mill it is in the grounds of the picturesque 16th century Crathes Castle famous for its painted ceilings, fine furniture and interesting decorations. The walled garden of almost four acres is considered to be among the finest in Britain: it includes a notable collection of unusual plants and has its own plant sales centre. A visitor centre contains permanent exhibitions and a gift shop. The grounds extend to 600 acres, with some 15 miles of well marked woodland trails. Frequent events add to the attraction of this charming property.
Open Apr to Oct
Food service 12 – 5.30 pm (a)
Dinner – booked parties as arranged (b)
Private room available
Facilities for the disabled
No smoking in restaurant
Coffee or tea with home-baked scones and cakes. Lunch from an à la carte menu with a Scottish flavour includes soup, traditional dishes and desserts, or freshly made sandwiches and salads – all home-made.
Credit cards: 1, 3

RAEMOIR HOUSE HOTEL
Banchory
Kincardineshire AB31 4ED
Tel: 0330 824884 • Telex: 73315
Fax: 0330 822171

Off A980, Royal Deeside.
A really beautiful old mansion house set in open parkland in an 3,500 acre estate. Many of the bedrooms have fine period furniture and furnishings but also incorporate all the conveniences of modern living like direct dial telephones and TV. For those who enjoy outdoor pursuits there is a tennis court, mini nine hole golf course and a croquet lawn, not to mention shooting, fishing and stalking in season. For those who take their leisure more gently there is a sauna, sunbed and trimnasium in the house. Kit Sabin has presided over Raemoir with great distinction and energy for many years. In fact in 1993 Raemoir celebrated its 50th year as an hotel and still under the same ownership. Kit's daughter and son-in-law, Judy and Mike Ollis, have a very active role in continuing a policy of gracious living, good food and caring attentive service. With their daughter Nikki Chivers now in place as the manager it marks the third generation of the family at Raemoir.
Open all year except first 2 wks Jan
Rooms: 28 with private facilities
Bar Lunch 12.30 – 2 pm except Sun (a)
Dining Room/Restaurant Lunch 12.30 – 2 pm Sun only (b)
Dinner 7.30 – 9 pm (c-f)
Bed & breakfast £52.50 – £79
Dinner B & B £77 to £97.50
Pheasant consommé with sherry. Cream of avocado pear and mint soup. West coast lobster with poached smoked Dee salmon bound in a Champagne and dill

sauce, presented in a filo pastry basket.
Roast haunch of venison set on a black
cherry and Port sauce.
STB Highly Commended 4 Crowns
Credit cards: 1, 2, 3, 5
Proprietors: Kit Sabin, Judy & Mike Ollis

Beauly

Map 6

CHRIALDON HOTEL
Station Road, Beauly
Inverness-shire IV4 7EH
Tel: 0463 782336
On A862 main road through Beauly, 12
miles from Inverness.
Step through the entrance of this
detached red sandstone Victorian villa
into a timbered hallway of Highland
charm. The Chrialdon is elegant, yet
informal, small yet spacious, where
comfort and enjoyment of good food are
of the utmost importance. Jennifer Bond
creates interesting menus for the small
dining room overlooking the garden and
offers exceptionally good value for
money. The hotel provides an ideal base
for touring the Highlands.
Open 1 Mar to 31 Nov
Rooms: 8, 6 with private facilities
Dinner 7 – 8.15 pm (b)
No smoking in dining room
Bed & breakfast £19 - £26
Dinner B & B £34 - £39
Residents only
Cheese and broccoli soup. Poached
fillets of lemon sole in a light sauce of
coarse grain mustard and tomato. Fillet
of Scottish salmon with sorrel sauce.
Pan-fried venison steak with a sauce of
juniper berries and redcurrant jelly.
STB Commended 3 Crowns
Credit cards: 1, 3
Proprietor: Jennifer Bond

PRIORY HOTEL
The Square, Beauly
Inverness-shire IV4 7BX
Tel: 0463 782309
Fax: 0463 782531
A862, 12 miles north-west of Inverness.
The Priory is a bustling local hotel with
an excellent reputation for good food and
friendly efficient service. It is situated in
the main square in Beauly, close to the
ancient Priory ruins. The hotel has all the
facilities required for an enjoyable stay
and is an ideal base for touring the
beautiful north and west of Scotland.

Families with children welcome.
Open all year
Rooms: 24 with private facilities
Selection of food available all day
Bar Lunch 12 – 2 pm (a)
Dining Room/Restaurant Lunch 12 –
2 pm (a)
Bar Supper 5.30 – 9 pm (a)
Dinner 7.15 – 9 pm (b)
Bed & breakfast £30 - £39.50
Traditional haggis enhanced with whisky
flavoured cream and onion sauce.
Selection of seafood in a white wine and
cream sauce encased in pastry. Roast
breast of duck with black cherry sauce
laced with Kirsch.
STB Highly Commended 4 Crowns
Credit cards: 1, 2, 3, 5, 6
Proprietors: Stuart & Eveline Hutton

Benbecula
Isle of

Map 7

DARK ISLAND HOTEL
Liniclate, Isle of Benbecula
Western Isles PA88 5PJ
Tel: 0870 2414/2283
Benbecula lies between North and South
Uist (Western Isles). A865 to Liniclate.
Hotel is c. 6 miles from the airport.
A large low ranch-style hotel with a large
welcome as is the nature of the
islanders. This unusually named hotel is
acclaimed as one of the best hotels in
the Hebrides. The finest of fresh local
produce is presented in the Carriages
Restaurant, where the menus offer a
wide choice of locally caught fish and
shellfish all carefully selected by the
chef. The restaurant caters for everything
from intimate dinners to major functions.
There is also a comfortable and
spacious residents' lounge. The hotel is
an ideal spot from which to explore the
adjacent islands, or for fishing, golf, bird-
watching and visiting interesting
archaeological sites.
Open all year except 1 Jan
Rooms: 42, 35 with private facilities
Bar Meals 12 – 5 pm (a)
Dining Room/Restaurant Lunch 12 –
2.30 pm (a)
Dinner 6.30 – 9.30 pm (c)
Bed & breakfast £24 – £60
Dinner B & B £30 – £90
Small whole squat rock lobsters gently
cooked in garlic butter and white wine,
served with fresh baked bread. Local
king scallops lightly cooked in butter.

Local lobster in a variety of sauces.
Crisply roasted duckling with a raspberry
sauce flavoured with honey mead.
STB Commended 4 Crowns
Credit cards: 1, 3

Biggar

Map 2

HARTREE COUNTRY HOUSE HOTEL
Biggar
Lanarkshire ML12 6JJ
Tel: 0899 21027
Fax: 0899 21259
Just off A702 on western outskirts of
Biggar.
A fine old baronial building dating back
to the 15th century, and now a delightful
country house hotel in peaceful and
pleasant Lanarkshire countryside. It has
been extensively refurbished to provide
modern standards of comfort in elegant
public rooms and bedrooms. The menu
includes many Scottish specialities and
there is a wide range of choice from bar
lunches to à la carte dinners. Almost
equidistant (about 40 minutes) from
both Edinburgh and Glasgow, Hartree
House makes a very convenient and
central base.
Open all year except Christmas Day
Rooms: 14 with private facilities
Bar Lunch 12 – 2 pm Sun only (b)
Dining Room/Restaurant Lunch 12 –
2 pm Sun only (c)
Bar Supper 6 – 9 pm (b)
Dinner 6 – 9 pm (c)
No dogs
Bed & breakfast £30 – £45
Dinner B & B £47 – £62
Local smoked venison with a malt whisky
vinaigrette. Scottish salmon pan-fried
with fennel, peppers and onion served
with a rich crab sauce. Home-made
honey and Drambuie ice cream.
STB Commended 3 Crowns
Credit cards: 1, 2, 3, 6
Proprietors: John & Anne Charlton,
Robert & Susan Reed

SHIELDHILL COUNTRY HOUSE HOTEL

Quothquan, Biggar
Lanarkshire ML12 6NA
Tel: 0899 20035
Fax: 0899 21092

Prestige Award Winner 1990

Signposted off main street (A702) in Biggar, 4 miles west taking B7016 for 2 miles then follow signs to hotel.
This splendid old country house, the roots of which go back to 1199, is a delightful away-from-it-all retreat, well off the beaten track yet only about 40 minutes by car from both Edinburgh and Glasgow. Christine Dunstan and Jack Greenwald have exercised great care and good taste in transforming it into an excellent country house hotel. Laura Ashley fabrics and wallpapers are much in evidence and the furniture and fittings are entirely appropriate to their surroundings. Bedrooms are sumptuous, some with jacuzzi and four posters and all with private bathrooms. A new team took charge in the kitchen in 1993 and have given an uplift to the already high standards of cuisine.
Open all year
Rooms: 11 with private facilities
Dinner 7 – 9 pm (d)
No children
No dogs
No smoking in restaurant
Bed & breakfast £49 – £82.50
Dinner B & B £71 – £104.50
Fillet of west coast halibut with a salmon and Arran mustard crust, on a mixed pepper, basil and samphire dressing. Honey glazed breast of Gressingham duck with a caramelised orange and soy sauce. Pan-fried fillet of Aberdeen Angus beef with a duxelle of field mushrooms on a red wine and Arran mustard sauce. STB Highly Commended 4 Crowns
Credit cards: 1, 2, 3, 5, 6
Proprietors: Christine Dunstan
*   & Jack Greenwald*

Blair Atholl

Map 4

THE LOFT RESTAURANT

Invertilt Road, Blair Atholl
Perthshire PH18 5TE
Tel: 0796 481377

6 miles north of Pitlochry in the heart of Blair Atholl.
In a world where restaurants are often lookalikes it is refreshing to come across places like this. The Loft has been splendidly converted from a former hayloft and retains all the genuine characteristics of twisted oak beams, stone walls and oak floors. Chef/patron Martin Hollis is an award winning chef and, with his wife Stella, does his utmost to ensure that customers leave satisfied. Menus are compiled from available fresh local produce and are imaginative. The Loft is popular and advance booking, especially for evening meals, is strongly advised.
Open 21 Mar to 1 Nov
Light all day menu available 10 am – 5.30 pm except Sun (a)
Restaurant Lunch 12.30 – 4 pm Sun only (b)
Light bistro menu 6.30 – 9.30 pm except Sat (a)
Dinner 7.30 – 9.30 pm Sat only (b) .
Table Licence
Children welcome – lunchtime only
A chicken and smoked salmon roulade filled with scampi tails on a lime and pink peppercorn cream. Fresh Oban mussels with herbs, shallots, wine and cream. Fillet of Scotch lamb with a morel and chanterelle mousse on a rosemary and red wine essence.
No credit cards
Proprietor: Martin Hollis

WOODLANDS

St Andrews Crescent, Blair Atholl
Perthshire PH18 5SX
Tel: 0796 481 403

A9, 7 miles north of Pitlochry.
Woodlands was built in 1903 and maintains most original features including service bells. The house is situated down a quiet lane off the main road in Blair Atholl and has a sheltered garden. While Dolina MacLennan is taking a year out, this comfortable guest house is in the capable hands of Bim Atkinson from Australia. He is an enthusiastic chef and offers three course daily changing dinner menus based on fresh local produce. Everything including the bread is made on the premises. Woodlands will run on the same lines as when Dolina is there. The tranquil atmosphere still prevails.
Open all year
Rooms: 4
Dinner 5 – 12 pm (c)
Dinner for non-residents by arrangement
Unlicensed – guests welcome to take own wine
Dinner B & B £35 – £40
Game soups. Lewis mussels with scampi in a seafood bisque. Pheasant. Lewis salmon and lobster. Jugged Buckie undyed kippers. Fresh salads and vegetables from the garden.
No credit cards
Proprietor: Dolina MacLennan

Blairgowrie

Map 4

DUAN VILLA GUEST HOUSE

Perth Road, Blairgowrie
Perthshire PH10 6EQ
Tel: 0250 873053

On A93 Perth – Braemar road.
An attractive Victorian villa with many of its original features intact and providing a homely relaxing atmosphere in which to enjoy a satisfying meal after the day's activities. Blairgowrie is very central to the many things to do and see in Perthshire and there are numerous golf courses and other recreational facilities nearby. Adele and Ken Barrie really do strive to maintain a home from home feel about this modest villa.
Open all year
Rooms: 5
Dinner 6 – 7.30 pm (b)
Residents only
Unlicensed
Dogs by arrangement
No smoking in restaurant
Bed & breakfast £17 – £20
Dinner B & B £30.50 – £33.50
Old fashioned Scotch broth. Tay salmon steaks with lemon and tarragon. Chicken with bacon in a rich tomato sauce. Scottish roast beef. Lamb with onion sauce. Bread and butter pudding. Cloutie dumpling.
No credit cards
Proprietor: Adele Barrie

Boat of Garten

Map 6

HEATHBANK – THE VICTORIAN HOUSE
Boat of Garten
Inverness-shire PH24 3BD
Tel: 0479 83 234

Situated in village of Boat of Garten.
Heathbank House was built around 1900 and is set in gardens primarily of heathers – hence the name – and herbs. Each room is decorated in a different colour theme and filled with Victoriana – lace, tapestries, fans, prints, mirrors. The overall effect is very turn of the century, with lots of interesting junk to discover! One of the bedrooms has a four poster bed. The dining room is bright with flowers and candle lamps and there is a large comfortable lounge with a log fire and an excellent selection of books. Food is varied, interesting, of unusually high standard and excellent value. There is a strong commitment to Scottish dishes and produce. There is an obvious anxiety to satisfy guests' every need.
Open 26 Dec to 31 Oct
Rooms: 7 with private facilities
Dinner at 7 pm (b) four course menu
Restricted Licence
No smoking in dining room + bedrooms
Bed & breakfast £18 – £30
Dinner B & B £32 – £44
Leek and ginger soup. Fillets of Spey trout with turmeric and cream. Scottish lamb steak with mint Hollandaise. Ice cream eclair with hot butterscotch sauce. Home made ice creams e.g. banana and cinnamon, honey and Stag's Breath liqueur.
STB Highly Commended 3 Crowns
No credit cards
Proprietors: Graham & Lindsay Burge

Bothwell

Map 3

THE GRAPE VINE RESTAURANT & CAFE BAR
27 Main Street, Bothwell
Lanarkshire G71 8RW
Tel: 0698 852014

½ mile off M74 (East Kilbride turn-off). The Grape Vine is situated in the centre of the picturesque conservation village of Bothwell, yet is within easy access of the motorway. Whether you are looking for a light meal in the bar, or a more leisurely experience in the restaurant, both are available all day, with the emphasis on fresh local produce, carefully and creatively prepared under the guidance of the owner, Colin Morrison.
Open all year except Christmas + Boxing Days, 1 + 2 Jan
Food Service 10 am – 10 pm (a-c)
Noisettes of lamb pan-fried and coated with a rich Madeira sauce. Fillets of sole poached in white wine with shallots, tomato, herbs and cream.
Credit cards: 1, 2, 3
Proprietor: Colin Morrison

Braemar

Map 5

BRAEMAR LODGE
Glenshee Road, Braemar
Aberdeenshire AB35 5YQ
Tel: 03397 41627
Fax: 03397 41627

On main A93 Perth-Aberdeen road, on the outskirts of Braemar.
Braemar Lodge is a restored Victorian shooting lodge, set amidst spectacular Highland scenery. Alex and Caroline Smith are welcoming hosts to this small friendly hotel. Cosy wood panelling and roaring log fires all add to the atmosphere. All bedrooms are spacious, individually decorated, en suite and with many personal touches. Dining is a relaxed affair in the candlelit restaurant. Caroline prepares the daily changing menus and has recently been awarded two AA Rosettes for her dedicated approach to cooking. The emphasis is on quality and imaginative use of fresh local ingredients.
Open 14 Mar to 31 Oct, Christmas + New Year
Rooms: 5 with private facilities
Dining Room/Restaurant Lunch – parties by reservation (c)
Dinner 7 – 8.45 pm (c)
No smoking except in bar
Bed & breakfast £34 – £40
Dinner B & B £50 – £60
Salad of Orkney queen scallops and bacon tossed in warm hazelnut oil. Grilled Isle of Gigha goats cheese served on a basil toast with pear salad. Smoked leg of lamb with bramble and rosemary sauce. Casseroled venison with juniper, cranberries, Port and mushrooms. Shortcake with raspberries and Glayva cream.
STB Commended 3 Crowns
Credit cards: 1, 3
Proprietors: Alex Smith & Caroline Hadley-Smith

Brig O' Turk

Map 4

THE BYRE INN
Brig O' Turk, The Trossachs
Perthshire FK17 8HT
Tel: 08776 292

North of Callander on A84, turn onto A821 at Kilmahog: Brig O' Turk 5 miles.
A mellow old farm building in a wooded area, just off the main road, which has been converted into a most attractive timbered bar full of rusticity and charm. A more modern design of dining room leads off from it and the whole effect is restful and pleasing. Good quality country cooking and presentation of wholesome dishes from a fairly extensive menu. A daily vegetarian dish is also available. This is a delightful and popular stopping-off place for people touring The Trossachs.
Open all year
Bar Lunch 12 – 2.30 pm: 12 – 5 pm Sun (a)
Dining Room/Restaurant Lunch 12 – 2.30 pm: 12 – 5 pm Sun (a)
Dinner 6 – 9.30 pm (c)
Facilities for the disabled
No smoking in restaurant
Seafood chowder. Red mullet with citrus fruits. Escalope of venison with a redcurrant sauce. Lamb cutlets on a rosemary sauce. Pan-fried monkfish with an orange sauce.
Credit cards: 1, 3
Proprietor: John Park

Credit Card Code		*Meal Price Code*	
1.	Access/Mastercard/Eurocard	(a)	under £10
2.	American Express	(b)	£10 – £15
3.	Visa	(c)	£15 – £20
4.	Carte Bleu	(d)	£20 – £25
5.	Diners Club	(e)	£25 – £30
6.	Mastercharge	(f)	over £30

Brodie

Map 5

BRODIE COUNTRYFARE
Brodie, by Forres
Morayshire IV36 0TD
Tel: 03094 555

On A96 between Forres and Nairn.
This is a very popular self-service restaurant which seats over 100 people and has a reputation for good food. It is furnished in country style with traditional decor and farmhouse-style dining furniture indoors, and pine picnic benches outdoors. A conservatory extends and enhances the main dining area. Brodie Countryfare forms part of a shopping complex and diners can find crafts, produce, exclusive fashions and designer knitwear all under the same roof.
Open all year except Christmas + Boxing Days, 1 + 2 Jan
Food service 12 – 5 pm (a)
Facilities for the disabled
Restaurant is non-smoking with small smoking area
Salad bar a speciality. Home-cooked dishes using local produce. Home-made soups. Seasonal soft fruit. Selection of home-baking and desserts.
No credit cards
Proprietor: Kathleen Duncan

Brora

Map 6

ROYAL MARINE HOTEL
Golf Road, Brora
Sutherland KW9 6QS
Tel: 0408 621252
Fax: 0408 621181

Leave A9 Inverness-Wick at bridge in Brora, heading towards beach and golf course.
A most attractive country mansion built by Sir Robert Lorimer in 1913 and converted into a hotel in 1939. Leaded windows, magnificent woodwork, log fires, a gracious ambience of yesteryear, allied to courteous service justify its claim to be the North's favourite golfing and fishing hotel. Adjacent to Brora's 18 hole James Braid links golf course and overlooking the mouth of the famous salmon river, the site has much to commend it. The food is exactly what the hungry sportsman or traveller would

want. Good quality, generous portions of fresh traditional fare, nicely presented and served with charm.
Open all year
Rooms: 11 with private facilities
Bar Lunch 12 – 2 pm (a)
Dining Room/Restaurant Lunch 12.30 – 2.30 pm Sun (b)
Bar Supper 6.30 – 9 pm (b)
Dinner 7 – 9 pm (c)
Bed & breakfast £40 – £50
Dinner B & B £55 – £65
Grilled halibut with lobster sauce. Barbary duck breast served with dark blackberry sauce. Medallions of beef fillet set on a bed of noodles with Madeira sauce.
STB Commended 4 Crowns
Credit cards: 1, 2, 3, 5

Cairndow

Map 3

LOCH FYNE OYSTER BAR
Cairndow
Argyll PA26 8BH
Tel: 04996 217/264

Head of Loch Fyne A83.
The name is a slight misnomer because in addition to excellent local and really fresh oysters you can enjoy just about every other popular shellfish you can name. The place has been a tearaway success since first it opened and the concept has already been extended to England. The building is a conversion of old farm buildings transformed simply in rustic style so that you know you are not wasting money on elaborate decor themes. It makes an excellent stopping place on the long sweep round the north of Loch Fyne and you can indulge yourself with some of the finest and freshest fish and shellfish in the 80-seat restaurant. The wine list is short but carefully selected to complement the menu and there is a busy shop from which you can see and smell the

smokehouse busy at work providing smoked salmon, trout, eel and mussels etc to buy and take home with you for your refrigerator or deep freeze.
Open all year except Christmas + Boxing Days, 1 Jan
Menu available throughout the day 9 am – 9 pm (b)
Note: closes 6 pm Nov to Feb
Oysters on crushed ice in half shell, baked oysters in parsley and garlic butter, langoustines, poached salmon, sea fish platter, Finnan haddock in milk, Loch Fyne kippers.
Credit cards: 1, 2, 3
Proprietors: Andrew Lane & John Noble

Callander

Map 4

BRIDGEND HOUSE HOTEL
Bridgend, Callander
Perthshire FK17 8AH
Tel: 0877 30130
Fax: 0877 31512

On A81 – 250 yards from Callander main street, just over the bridge.
There is a hint of Tudor architecture in the style of this timbered 17th century building, so conveniently located just off the centre of the town. It is a rambling old building but bright, clean and welcoming with a pleasing and restful garden from which there are lovely views of Ben Ledi. Bedrooms are en suite with TVs and tea-makers. Bar lunches are popular and in the evening there is a choice of a bar supper or a more extensive menu in the restaurant which often includes traditional Scottish dishes and game in season. Children and pets welcome.
Open all year except Christmas + Boxing Days, 1 Jan
Rooms: 7, 5 with private facilities
Bar Lunch 12 – 2 pm (a)
Dining Room/Restaurant Lunch 12.30 – 2 pm Sun only (b)
Bar Supper 6 – 8.30 pm (a)
Dinner 6.30 – 8.45 pm (b)
Note: pipe and cigars only after 9 pm
Bed & breakfast £25 – £39.50
Dinner B & B £37.50 – £52.50
A wide range of food – traditional home-made Scottish soup, sizzle platter steaks, local salmon, Scottish pancakes with ice cream and syrup.
STB Commended 3 Crowns
Credit cards: 1, 2, 3, 5
Proprietors: Sandy & Maria Park

HIGHLAND HOUSE HOTEL

South Church Street, Callander
Perthshire FK17 8BN
Tel: 0877 30269

Just off A84 in town centre.
Roses round the door of the neat
Georgian frontage of Highland House
almost suggest that it will be cosy and
comfortable inside – and it is. It is no
surprise therefore that it was voted the
winner of the "Best Place to Stay"
category in the Antartex Tourism Awards
co-sponsored by the Loch Lomond,
Stirling and Trossachs Tourist Board.
Dee Shirley's home cooking is a major
contributor to the fine reputation that
she and her husband have established
in this popular tourist town. There is a
good range of malt whiskies in the
intimate bar, and the dining room and
lounge have been furnished with good
taste and the comfort of guests in mind.
Colour TV, en suite facilities and full
central heating in all rooms.
Open 1 Mar to 5 Nov
Rooms: 9, 8 with private facilities
Bar Supper 6.30 – 8 pm (a)
Dinner 7 – 8 pm (b)
No smoking in dining room + bedrooms
Dogs accepted at proprietors'
discretion
Bed & breakfast £17 – £29
Dinner B & B £29 – £43
Home-made soups and pâtés. Fresh
local produce including salmon, trout,
venison. Delicious desserts. Children's
menu available.
STB Commended 3 Crowns
Credit cards: 1, 2, 3
Proprietors: David & Dee Shirley

ROMAN CAMP HOTEL

Callander
Perthshire FK17 8BG
Tel: 0877 30003
Fax: 0877 31533

Signposted off main route through
Callander (A84).
Look out for the hotel sign at the east
end of the long main street through
Callander and follow the drive down to
the banks of the River Teith where this
fine old house has been standing for
almost 400 years. It is set in 20 acres
of beautiful gardens and has gracious
public rooms and an atmosphere of
unhurried dignity and relaxation. The
dining room service is quietly efficient
and the food is of the high standard one
would expect in such a charming old
country house. As a base from which to
explore the Trossachs it is ideally
situated.
Open all year
Rooms: 14 with private facilities
Dining Room/Restaurant Lunch 12 –
2 pm (c)
Dinner 7 – 9 pm (e) 4 course menu
Facilities for the disabled
No smoking in restaurant
Bed & breakfast £35 – £65
Dinner B & B £65 – £95
Strips of beef fillet with apple and
peppercorns in a Port and tarragon
sauce. Fillet of salmon roasted with
leeks on a grain mustard sauce with a
light mushroom timbale. Best end of
lamb with a wild mushroom and
redcurrant sauce. Chilled terrine of
chocolate with a vanilla custard sauce.
STB Highly Commended 4 Crowns
Credit cards: 1, 2, 3, 5
Proprietors: Eric & Marion Brown

Campbeltown

Map 6

SEAFIELD HOTEL

Kilkerran Road, Campbeltown
Argyll PA28 6JL
Tel: 0586 554385

On the shores of Campbeltown Loch – 4
minutes walk from town centre.
The external appearance of this Victorian
villa is deceptive. Originally built by the
founders of the Springbank Distillery, it
has a pleasing site overlooking the shore
and is reputed to be the first home in
Campbeltown fitted with a bath! There is
an attractive dining room with well

spaced tables and a menu offering a
good range and balance of choice. A
garden court annexe in the walled
garden at the rear of the hotel offers
quiet peaceful accommodation.
Open all year
Rooms: 9 with private facilities
Snacks available in restaurant
Dining Room/Restaurant Lunch 12 –
2 pm: buffet Sun (b)
Bar Supper 5.30 – 8.30 pm (a)
Dinner 7 – 8.30 pm (c)
Bed & breakfast from £32.95
Room Rate £50 – £55.50
Local fresh seafoods and salmon.
Scottish beef, lamb and game.
STB Commended 3 Crowns
Credit cards: 1, 3
Proprietors: Alastair & Elizabeth Gilchrist

WHITE HART HOTEL

Main Street, Campbeltown
Argyll PA28 6AN
Tel: 0586 552440/553356
Fax: 0586 554972

On main street in centre of town.
An eye-catching building on a corner site
right in the centre of town emphasises
that this attractive white painted old
world hotel is a well established and
prominent feature of this busy fishing
port and market town. Perhaps the
relative remoteness of Campbeltown on
the Mull of Kintyre is a factor in the
prominence of excellent local seafood
and lamb in the hotel's menus. The Mull
of Kintyre and Campbeltown Loch have
inspired quite a few song writers in the
past and the nearby famous
Machrihanish golf links are another
reason for the White Hart's popularity as
a base.
Open all year except Christmas Day +
1 Jan
Rooms: 17 with private facilities
Bar Lunch 12 – 2 pm except Sun (a)
Dining Room/Restaurant Lunch 12 –
2 pm except Sun (a)
Bar Supper 7 – 9 pm except Sun Sat (a)
Dinner 7 – 9.30 pm except Sun: 5.30 –
8.30 pm Easter Sun to 1 Nov (b)
Bed & breakfast £32.50 – £34.50
Dinner B & B £45 – £48
Serving the best of local fresh seafood,
game and meat products.
Credit cards: 1, 3
Proprietors: P Stogdale & B Kennedy

Carradale

Map 6

CARRADALE HOTEL

Carradale
Argyll PA28 6RY
Tel: 058 33 223
Fax: 058 33 223

From Tarbert (Loch Fyne) 26 miles via A83, B8001 and B842. From Campbeltown about 17 miles on B842.
Quite the most prominent feature of the village, the Carradale Hotel occupies a splendid location above the harbour in its own grounds and gardens, overlooking Kilbrannan Sound and the Isle of Arran. Comfortable accommodation and a reputation for high quality Scottish cooking make it an ideal centre for fishing, golfing or exploring the Kintyre peninsula. Mountain bikes, squash courts, sauna and the adjacent nine hole golf course are all part of the facilities.
Open all year except 20 to 27 Dec
Rooms: 14 with private facilities, 3 children's rooms (adjacent to parents' rooms) + 1 family suite
Bar Lunch 12 – 2 pm (a)
Bar Supper 6 – 7.30 pm (a)
Dinner 7.30 – 9 pm (c)
No smoking area in restaurant
Bed & breakfast £33 – £43
Dinner B & B £49 – £59
Special 3 + 5 day breaks available
Mousseline of Kilbrannan seafood wrapped in Loch Fyne smoked salmon with a shellfish dressing. Medallions of duck and Carradale venison served with buttered noodles, bound in a Port and red berry sauce. Home-made toffee and banana ice cream.
Credit cards: 1, 3
Proprietors: Marcus & Morag Adams

Carrbridge

Map 6

DALRACHNEY LODGE HOTEL

Carrbridge
Inverness-shire PH23 3AT
Tel: 047 984 252
Fax: 047 984 382

On A938 to Dulnain Bridge, c. 400 yards from Carrbridge.
A former Victorian shooting lodge set in 16 acres of peaceful grounds on the banks of the Dulnain River on the outskirts of the village. Internally there is much that is old and much that is new but they have been blended with skill and the hotel now offers 11 tastefully furnished and generously proportioned bedrooms. A further five comfortable rooms are in the adjacent Keeper's House. The Lodge Restaurant has a pleasant outlook on to the garden. There is a fairly wide choice on the four course table d'hôte menu which is inexpensively priced, and a much more ambitious à l carte menu is also available. Provision is made for anyone with food allergies or special needs. The log fire in the cosy Stalkers Bar makes it popular for a pre-prandial drink or an after dinner malt whisky from a large selection.
Open all year
Rooms: 16 with private facilities
Bar Lunch 12 – 2 pm (a)
Dining Room/Restaurant Lunch 12 – 2 pm (a)
Bar Supper 5.30 – 9.30 pm (a)
Dinner 7 – 8.30 pm (c)
No smoking area in restaurant
Bed & breakfast £23 – £35
Dinner B & B £39 – £53
Baked rainbow trout filled with spinach, white wine and currants. Escalope of venison with a crushed juniper berry sauce. Lamb cutlets with a red wine and herb sauce.
STB Highly Commended 4 Crowns
Credit cards: 1, 2, 3, 6, + SWITCH, DELTA
Proprietor: Helen Swanney

ECCLEFECHAN BISTRO

Main Street, Carrbridge
Inverness-shire PH23 3AJ
Tel: 047 984 374

Main road Carrbridge, on Carrbridge by-pass off A9 north of Aviemore.
A pleasant wayside stopping place on the way through Carrbridge, this scrupulously clean and attractive family run bistro concentrates on the best of straightforward Scottish food with a slight touch of French influence. At coffee and teatime you can enjoy delicious scones and doughnuts – and coffee that tastes like coffee. For lunch or dinner there is a frequently changing menu ranging from Hebridean soups and scallops to steaks and venison, and an interesting variety of speciality desserts like Ecclefechan tart.
Open all year except Nov, Christmas + Boxing Days
Lunch 12 – 3 pm except Tue (a)
Dinner 6.30 – 9.30 pm except Tue (c)
Closed Tue
Facilities for the disabled
Venison in claret, Hebridean skink, haggis and clapshot, local smoked salmon, Scottish prawns with dill. Ecclefechan tart, Blairgowrie raspberry trifle.
Credit cards: 1, 3
Proprietors: Duncan & Anne Hilditch

FEITH MHOR COUNTRY HOUSE

Station Road, Carrbridge
Inverness-shire PH23 3AP
Tel: 0479 841621

One mile west of village of Carrbridge on road signed to Dalnahaitnach.
Feith Mhor is a charming 19th century country house set in an acre of delightful gardens and surrounded by peaceful unspoilt countryside. The comfortable well appointed en suite bedrooms enjoy beautiful views. There is an attractive dining room and comfortable lounge. Here you will experience the best of home-cooked fare, simply presented, based on local and garden produce in season. Vegetarian dishes are available by arrangement. This is a wonderful area for those who enjoy walking, bird-watching or touring.
Open 20 Dec to 10 Nov
Rooms: 6 with private facilities
Dinner at 7 pm (b)
It is requested that guests select their menu by 6 pm
No smoking in dining room + lounge
No children under 14 years
Bed & breakfast £20 – £22
Dinner B & B £30 – £32
Fruity spiced gammon, roast Scotch lamb and beef, poached fresh salmon. Vegetarian lentil bake, leek and dumpling casserole. Desserts include meringue sunrise, pavlova with raspberries, fresh fruit crumbles.
STB Commended 3 Crowns
No credit cards
Proprietor: Penny Rawson

Castle Douglas

Map 1

LONGACRE MANOR

Ernespie Road, Castle Douglas
Kirkcudbrightshire DG7 1LE
Tel: 0556 3576

*Off A75 Dumfries-Stranraer (eastern exit)
to Castle Douglas, c. ¾ mile.*
A small but charming country house on
the outskirts of the town set in a
beautiful woodland garden and having
fine views to Screel and the Galloway
Hills. All four bedrooms have been
delightfully furnished – one features a
king-size four poster and another twin
four poster beds – and each has en
suite facilities. There is thoughtful
attention to every aspect of a guest's
comfort, and TV, radio, tea/coffee-
making equipment, direct dial telephone,
hairdryer and trouser press are standard.
Meals are planned on a daily basis
consistent with the availability of fresh
produce, are well presented and good
value. Castle Douglas, of course, is
close to the famous Threave Gardens
and there are lots of other interesting
things to see locally plus a full range of
sporting and recreational activities.
Open all year
Rooms: 4 with private facilities
Dinner at 7.30 pm (b)
Bed & breakfast £25 – £30
Dinner B & B £40 – £45
*Dinner for non-residents by prior
arrangement*
Restricted Licence
No children
No smoking in dining room
*Cock-a-Leekie soup. Trout terrine. Solway
salmon. Galloway lamb and beef. Solway
scallops. Cranachan, sticky toffee
pudding, coffee and Tia Maria syllabub.*
STB Highly Commended 3 Crowns
No credit cards
Proprietors: Charles & Elma Ball

Chapel of Garioch

Map 5

PITTODRIE HOUSE HOTEL

Chapel of Garioch, nr Pitcaple
Aberdeenshire AB51 9HS
Tel: 0467 681444 • Telex: 739935
Fax: 0467 681648

*Off A96 just north of Pitcaple, 21 miles
north of Aberdeen, 17 miles north of
airport.*

This is a beautiful turreted Scottish
baronial style mansion which stands in
its own extensive grounds at the foot of
Bennachie and was originally the home
of the owner, Theo Smith. Although the
hotel was extended in 1990 to give
additional bedrooms and a function
room, this was done skilfully and
sympathetically. The original character of
the public rooms with their antiques and
family portraits has been maintained.
There is a beautifully kept three acre
walled garden.
Open all year
Rooms: 27 with private facilities
Bar Lunch 12 – 2 pm except Sun (a)
*Dining Room/Restaurant Lunch 12.30 –
2 pm (c)*
Dinner 7.30 – 8.45 pm (e)
Bed & breakfast £55 – £89
Dinner B & B £49 – £64
Room Rate £89 – £110
*Roast gigot of Spring lamb with fresh
mint sauce. Fillet steak with green
peppercorn sauce. Poached rock turbot
with cucumber sauce. Baked halibut with
vermouth and herbs. Summer pudding
with crème anglaise. Treacle tart with
chestnut ice cream.*
STB Approved 4 Crowns
Credit cards: 1, 2, 3, 5, 6 + SWITCH

Cleish
nr Kinross

Map 4

NIVINGSTON HOUSE

Cleish
Kinross-shire KY13 7LS
Tel: 0577 850216
Fax: 0577 850238

*In country, 2 miles from Junction 5 on
M90.*
The phrase "an oasis of tranquillity" is
sometimes overdone, but not here. The
commanding site has superb views over
the rolling countryside and with its 12
acres of pleasant garden this Victorian
mansion really is a peaceful haven, yet
only a couple of miles from the M90. It
has been comfortably furnished and the
relaxed and friendly country house
atmosphere is apparent as soon as you
enter. Allied to this is a reputation for
fine food, interestingly prepared and
presented, with regularly changing
menus showing a sound degree of
creativity. Sitting outside with a cool
drink on a Summer's evening can be

very pleasant, but so too are the iog
fires and flickering candles on the table
in Winter.
*Open all year except Boxing Day + first
2 wks Jan*
Rooms: 17 with private facilities
Bar Lunch 12 – 2 pm (a)
*Dining Room/Restaurant Lunch 12 –
2 pm (c)*
Dinner 7 – 9 pm (e)
Bed & breakfast £40 – £80
Dinner B & B £65 – £105
*Guinea fowl roasted with a sultana and
rum sauce. Roasted whole Spring
chicken with a mushroom, apple and
lemon sauce. Fillet steak served with a
green peppercorn sauce laced with
brandy. Raspberry brûlée.*
STB Highly Commended 4 Crowns
Credit cards: 1, 2, 3 + SWITCH
Proprietors: Allan & Pat Deeson

Colvend

Map 1

CLONYARD HOUSE HOTEL

Colvend, Dalbeattie
Dumfriesshire DG5 4QW
Tel: 055 663 372
Fax: 055 663 422

*4½ miles south of Dalbeattie on A710
Solway coast road. 18 miles west of
Dumfries.*
Victorian country house hotel in six acres
of wooded grounds. Typical 19th century
dining room overlooking lawns. Also
pleasant large cocktail bar for informal
meals. Ground floor bedroom wing with
full facilities. One room fitted for
disabled guests. Safe grounds for
children. French and some German
spoken. Dogs welcome (small charge).
*Open all year except Christmas Day
Note: Accommodation closed 24 to
26 Dec*
Rooms: 15 with private facilities
Bar Lunch 12 – 2 pm (a)
Bar Supper 6 – 9.30 pm (a)
Dinner 7 – 9 pm (b)
Facilities for the disabled
Bed & breakfast £28 – £38
Dinner B & B £42 – £53
Room Rate £56 – £66
*Solway salmon, Kirkcudbrightshire
scallops, Galloway beef and lamb,
venison.*
STB Commended 4 Crowns
Credit cards: 1, 2, 3
*Proprietors: N M Thompson
& D Thompson*

Comrie

Map 4

THE DEIL'S CAULDRON LOUNGE BAR & RESTAURANT

27 Dundas Street, Comrie
Perthshire PH6 2LN
Tel: 0764 670352

On A85 west end of Comrie.
Don't let the name put you off! This is an attractive looking bar restaurant taking its name from a well known beauty spot. It has been created from a 200 year old Listed building. Internally the place has lots of character and a good atmosphere, with original stone walls and furniture and fittings of a very high standard, interesting paintings, prints and old photographs. The menu is carefully constructed and reasonably priced, with everything freshly produced on a daily basis. The garden with its well stocked ponds and heathers is a delightful and pleasant place to stroll. A popular place so reservations are advisable.
Open all year except Christmas Day, 31 Dec to 2 Jan
Bar Lunch 12 – 2.30 pm except Tue (a)
Dining Room/Restaurant Lunch 12 – 2 pm except Tue (b)
Bar Supper 6 – 10 pm except Tue (b)
Dinner 7 – 9 pm except Tue (c)
Closed Tue
Separate dining room for non-smokers
The menu features local beef, lamb, fish, home-grown vegetables and game in season. Auld Alliance cooking.
Credit cards: 1, 2, 3
Proprietors: Robert & Judith Shepherd

TULLYBANNOCHER FARM FOOD BAR

Comrie
Perthshire PH6 2JY
Tel: 0764 670827

Just outside Comrie on A85 Lochearnhead road.
This is a very popular stopping place for people enjoying the drive along Loch Earn. A solid timber construction, it stands on a prominent knoll among trees and lawns just outside the pretty village of Comrie and with plenty of parking alongside. The self-service restaurant offers a wide choice of freshly prepared meats, fish and quiche with simple but varied salads. There is a refreshing aura of healthy eating and home-baking about the place. Freshly brewed coffee and tea and a selection of wines, beers and soft drinks are available. In fine weather people enjoy eating outside on the rustic tables on the lawns, but there is lots of dining space inside for those who prefer it.
Open 28 Mar to mid Oct
Meals available 10 am – 7 pm (a)
Table Licence
Dogs allowed outside only
Home-baked ham. Local smoked trout. Scottish salmon. Home-made quiches. Spit roasted chicken. Meat pies. Coronation chicken. Hot dishes of the day. Fresh strawberry flan. A large selection of home-baking.
No credit cards
Proprietor: Peter Davenport

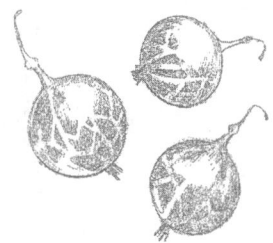

Contin
by Strathpeffer

Map 6

CONTIN HOUSE

Contin, by Strathpeffer
Ross-shire IV14 9EB
Tel: 0997 421920
Fax: 0997 421851

On A853 at eastern end of Contin village – follow sign to Contin Church.
Formerly a substantial manse dating from 1794, Contin House is situated in its own gardens surrounded by the grandeur of the Highlands. David and Daphne Du Boulay offer the friendly welcome which won them the Scotcom Award in 1993 (the most welcoming hotel) together with great comfort, really good food and an excellent selection of wine. Traditional furniture and family things allow you to relax in front of log fires as though staying with friends. In the dining room, silver and crystal sparkle in the candlelight, setting the scene for a menu which is changed daily and is created from the best of local produce, including fresh vegetables from the garden.
Open Mar to Nov
Rooms: 5 with private facilities
Dinner at 7.30 pm (d-e)
Dinner for non-residents by arrangement
Restricted Licence
Children over 8 years welcome
Dogs by arrangement
No smoking in dining room + bedrooms
Bed & breakfast £33 – £42.50
Dinner B & B £58 – £67.50
Quails eggs in a nest of smoked salmon and cucumber. Halibut marinated in Greek yoghurt, topped with toasted sesame seeds. Breast of Gressingham duck with raspberry sauce.
STB Deluxe 3 Crowns
Credit cards: 1, 3
Proprietors: David & Daphne Du Boulay

COUL HOUSE HOTEL

Contin, by Strathpeffer
Ross-shire IV14 9EY
Tel: 0997 421487
Fax: 0997 421945

On A835 to Ullapool, 17 miles north-west of Inverness.
This country house hotel commands fine views over the area and the Mackenzies of Coul, whose secluded country mansion it was, obviously had this in mind when they chose the site. There are log fires and spacious public rooms, and all bedrooms are en suite with colour tele-text TV, radio, direct dial telephone, hospitality tray, hairdryer and trouser press. Bar lunches get a high rating and there is an extensive à la carte menu majoring in seafood and steaks to complement the daily changing dinner menu in Mackenzie's Taste of Scotland Restaurant. The hotel has some salmon and trout fishing rights and there is a choice of five golf courses within easy reach.
Open all year
Rooms: 21 with private facilities
Bar Lunch 12 – 2 pm Mon to Sat: 12.30 – 2 pm Sun (a)
Dining Room/Restaurant Lunch 12 – 2 pm (b) by arrangement only
Bar Supper 5.30 – 9 pm (a)
Dinner 7 – 9 pm (d)
Bed & breakfast £32 – £54
Dinner B & B £49 – £76.50
Sauté of Summer Isles scallops. Seafood terrine with layers of salmon, lemon sole, prawns and mussels. Roast

pheasant on a Port and rowanberry coulis. Fillet of fresh salmon with chive butter. Roast rack of lamb served with pan juices and mint sauce.
STB Highly Commended 4 Crowns
Credit cards: 2, 5
Proprietor: Martyn Hill

Corsemalzie

Map 1

CORSEMALZIE HOUSE HOTEL
Corsemalzie, Port William
Newton Stewart
Wigtownshire DG8 9RL
Tel: 098 886 254

Halfway along B7005 Glenluce-Wigtown, off A714 Newton Stewart-Port William or A747 Glenluce-Port William.
There are 40 acres of woodland and gardens surrounding this 19th century Scottish mansion house and it is not uncommon to see a few gamebirds strutting about the lawns together with the domestic peacocks. Whilst primarily a sporting country house hotel with its own extensive game, fishing and shooting rights, it has a much wider appeal as a base from which to explore the many interesting corners of this largely unknown part of the country. The menu is broadly based and much of the excellent local game finds its way to the hotel kitchen.
Open 5 Mar to 15 Jan except Christmas + Boxing Days
Rooms: 15, 14 with private facilities
Bar Lunch 12.15 – 2 pm (a)
Dining Room/Restaurant Lunch 12.30 – 2 pm (b)
Bar Supper 7.15 – 9.15 pm (a)
Dinner 7.30 – 9.30 pm (c)
Dogs accepted (small charge)
Bed & breakfast £29.50 – £49.50
Dinner B & B £39.50 – £67
Solway seafood chowder. Local venison with Port and redcurrant sauce. Baked fillet of lemon sole stuffed with smoked salmon. Queenies with lime and ginger butter. Poached fresh salmon with Hollandaise sauce. Local pheasant with honey and chestnut sauce.
STB Commended 4 Crowns
Credit cards: 1, 3
Proprietor: Peter McDougall

Coupar Angus

Map 4

BURRELTON PARK INN
High Street, Burrelton
Perthshire PH13 9NX
Tel: 08287 206

On A94 Perth-Coupar Angus, 3 miles south of Coupar Angus, within 10 minutes of Perth or 25 minutes of Dundee.
The colourful hanging baskets of flowers along the frontage make it easy to locate this popular inn on the main street of the village. Burrelton is at the heart of one of Europe's best soft fruit growing areas and there are rich surrounding farmlands. The inn concentrates on satisfying the demanding and exacting palates of the agricultural community and it does so with first class personal service and good food. But there is more to it than that: it is equally popular with tourists on their way north or south and its proximity to golfing, fishing, shooting and skiing facilities makes it a desirable centre for sports enthusiasts.
Open all year except 1 Jan
Rooms: 6 with private facilities
All day menu served 12 – 10.30 pm (a)
Dinner 6.30 – 10.30 pm (b)
No smoking area in restaurant
Bed & breakfast £22.50 – £30
Dinner B & B £30 – £37.50
Daily specials highlighted on blackboard. Gravadlax – home-cured salmon, steak Diane, mixed grill – a small selection of items from the extensive menu.
STB Commended 3 Crowns
Credit cards: 1, 3
Proprietors: Malcolm & Karen Weaving

Craigellachie

Map 5

CRAIGELLACHIE HOTEL
Craigellachie
Banffshire AB3 9SS
Tel: 0340 881204
Fax: 0340 881253

On A941, 12 miles south of Elgin.
An imposing hotel in its own grounds just off the main square of the village and with the famous Spey walk at the foot of the garden. It is decorated and furnished to a very high standard and in excellent taste. The same care and attention that is so evident in the furnishing of the hotel is also reflected in the quality of

the food. The high reputation it enjoys is well earned. Craigellachie of course is very much fishing and shooting country but it is also on the whisky trail and there are several distinguished distilleries nearby. French, Swedish and Danish spoken.
Open all year
Rooms: 30 with private facilities
Bar Lunch 12 – 2 pm (a)
Dining Room/Restaurant Lunch 12.30 – 2 pm (b)
Bar Supper 6.15 – 7 pm (b)
Dinner 7.30 – 9.30 pm (e)
No smoking in dining room
Bed & breakfast £45.50 – £78.50
Dinner B & B £71 – £104
Locally made haggis with a dram. Smoked pheasant terrine with redcurrant sauce. Grilled Spey salmon with a sesame crust and Spring onion sauce. Ben Aigan hot butterscotch pudding.
STB Deluxe 4 Crowns
Credit cards: 1, 2, 3, 5, 6
Proprietor: Tomas Gronager

Crail

Map 4

CAIPLIE GUEST HOUSE
53 High Street, Crail
Fife KY10 3RA
Tel: 0333 50564

High Street, Crail.
A three storey villa that was at one time the village bakery but is now a well maintained and comfortable guest house, right in the centre of this historic and quaint little fishing village. Guests are invited to select their evening meal by 4 pm to enable it to be prepared to order and there is usually a choice of fish, poultry or meat for the main courses. Good value, good home cooking.
Open 1 Mar to 30 Oct
Rooms: 7
Dinner at 7 pm (b)
It is requested that guests select their menu by 4 pm
Residents only
No smoking area in dining room
Bed & breakfast £15 – £16.50
Dinner B & B £27 – £28.50
Scottish and continental dishes prepared from fresh local produce. Cloutie dumpling, cranachan.
STB Commended 1 Crown
No credit cards
Proprietor: Jayne Hudson

HAZELTON GUEST HOUSE
29 Marketgate, Crail
Fife KY10 3TH
Tel: 0333 50250

In town centre opposite tourist office and Tolbooth.

The Hazelton is one of an impressive terrace of Victorian merchants houses in the centre of Crail. It has high standards of comfort, all rooms having central heating, colour television, tea-making facilities etc and wash-hand basin. Elsewhere in this Guide you will read that Rita Brown came second in the national Taste of Scotland Scotch Lamb Challenge competition and this speaks well for the standard of her cooking. Alan and Rita Brown are charming hosts and care for the comfort of their guests. The relaxed and friendly atmosphere in this lovely little guest house allied to the Browns' attention to detail ensures that most guests want to come back for more.

Open 1 Jan to 31 Oct
Rooms: 7
Dinner at 7 pm (b) except Mon Tue – unless by prior arrangement
It is requested that guests select their menu by 4 pm
Residents only
No dogs
Bed & breakfast £15 – £17
Dinner B & B £28 – £30
Daily changing menu using local produce. Fish, seafood and game featured. Home-smoked specialities. Vegetarians catered for by arrangement.
STB Commended Listed
No credit cards
Proprietors: Alan & Rita Brown

Crianlarich

Map 4

ALLT-CHAORAIN COUNTRY HOUSE
Crianlarich
Perthshire FK20 8RU
Tel: 08383 283
(0838 300283 from 1/94)
Fax: 08383 238
(0838 300238 from 1/94)

Off A82, 1 mile north-west of Crianlarich.

Perched on a hill in its own grounds, Allt-Chaorain is sited so that it looks out over the picturesque countryside of Benmore and Strathfillan from the south facing sun lounge. Although compact there is a quiet quality feel to the place. The wood-panelled dining room seats 18

at three tables of six. There is usually a log fire burning in the lounge throughout the year.

Open 20 Mar to 28 Oct
Rooms: 8 with private facilities
Dinner 7 – 8 pm (c)
Residents only
No smoking in dining room, bedrooms + main lounge
A sun lounge is set aside for those who wish to smoke
Bed & breakfast £27 – £33
Dinner B & B £42 – £48
Home-made soups e.g. spicy parsnip, carrot and orange. Local salmon and trout. Lamb steaks with a haggis crust. Traditional steak and kidney pie. Home-made desserts – orange meringue pie, bread and butter pudding, cranachan, Ecclefechan tart.
STB Commended 3 Crowns
Credit cards: 1, 3
Proprietor: Roger McDonald

Crieff

Map 4

CRIEFF VISITORS CENTRE
Muthill Road, Crieff
Perthshire PH7 4AZ
Tel: 0764 654014

On A822 leading out of Crieff to the south.

The self-service restaurant is part of a visitor complex of showroom, shops, audio-visual presentation and garden centre beside two rural factories producing thistle pattern Buchan pottery and high quality Perthshire Paperweights. Open seven days a week, it is within an hour's drive of Glasgow, Edinburgh or St Andrews, and close by Gleneagles. The restaurant itself is spacious and smooth running and the intelligent use of wood, brick and glass gives it a light open atmosphere. The large self-service area is clearly laid out with good displays of food and an impressive home-baking section. The standard menu is augmented with daily dishes to incorporate a wide range of good interesting food. There are children's menus with reduced portions available, and in good weather there is al fresco eating in a large patio area.

Open all year except Christmas + Boxing Days, 1 + 2 Jan
Food served 9 am – 5.30 pm: 9 am – 4.30 pm Winter (b)
Facilities for the disabled
Credit cards: 1, 2, 3

MURRAYPARK HOTEL
Connaught Terrace, Crieff
Perthshire PH7 3DJ
Tel: 0764 653731
Fax: 0764 655311

Turn off A85 at Connaught Terrace, uphill to residential part of town.

Pink-stoned large Victorian house set in its own gardens in the residential part of the town. The comfortable restaurant has an uncrowded atmosphere and overlooks the pleasant garden. Menus are based on established Scottish foods with many interesting variations. French is spoken. Children and dogs welcome.

Open all year except Christmas Day
Rooms: 21 with private facilities
Bar Lunch 12 – 2 pm (a)
Dining Room/Restaurant Lunch 12 – 2 pm (b)
Bar Supper 7.30 – 9.30 pm (b)
Dinner 7.30 – 9.30 pm (c)
No smoking in restaurant
Bed & breakfast £32.50 – £45
Dinner B & B £52 – £66
Scampi wrapped in bacon and grilled on a skewer. Chicken in a light curry cream with banana and pineapple served on rice. Mushrooms with Stilton, cream and Port.
STB Commended 4 Crowns
Credit cards: 1, 2, 3, 5, 6
Proprietors: Ann & Noel Scott

SMUGGLERS RESTAURANT
Glenturret Distillery
The Hosh, Crieff
Perthshire PH7 4HA
Tel: 0764 656565
Fax: 0764 654366

Prestige Award Winner 1989

A85 north-west of Crieff.

Glenturret is Scotland's oldest Highland malt distillery and its award winning visitors centre is an immensely popular tourist attraction. There are audio-visual presentations, the Spirit of the Glen Exhibition and a whisky tasting bar to sample 8 to 21 year old Glenturret and The Glenturret Original Malt Liqueur. Restaurant facilities are on site, within a converted 18th century whisky

warehouse. Smugglers is a self-service operation of an unusually high standard, cleverly constructed and adaptable for functions of different sizes, and the Pagoda Room is an upmarket restaurant with waitress service. As one would expect, the menus feature local venison, salmon and trout in a wholesome cooking style, and there is always a vegetarian dish and a good choice of sweets or cheeses. Morning coffees and afternoon teas with home-baking are also available. The whole complex attracts much favourable comment from visitors. Children welcome. New disabled access.
Open all year except Christmas + Boxing Days, 1 + 2 Jan
Note: closed weekends Jan + Feb
Bar Lunch (Smugglers) 12 – 2.30 pm (a)
Dining Room/Restaurant Lunch (Pagoda Room) 12 – 2.30 pm (b)
Dinner – by private arrangement only
Complete facilities are no smoking but a smoking area is provided in Smugglers Restaurant
Glenturret flavoured pâté and hot oatcakes. Home-made soups. Venison in illicit whisky sauce. Highland beef in red wine sauce. Tay salmon. Hosh haggis. Glenturret ice cream. Cranachan and gâteaux.
Credit cards: 1, 2, 3

Crinan

Map 6

CRINAN HOTEL
Crinan, Lochgilphead
Argyll PA31 8SR
Tel: 054 683 261
Fax: 054 683 292

Prestige Award Winner 1991

A82 Glasgow-Inveraray, then A83 to Lochgilphead. Follow A816 (Oban) for c. 5 miles, then B841 to Crinan.
Magnificent scenery is part of the Scottish heritage, but for genuinely stunning views and breathtaking sunsets, dine in the renowned Lock 16 roof top restaurant. The Crinan Hotel has the best of both worlds. The yachting enthusiasts who use the Crinan Canal invariably want to eat here as do the many visitors who have heard of its reputation. Seafood, but particularly shellfish, is a speciality. It is landed daily at the Canal entrance and is so fresh

that it may be 5 pm before the chef knows what will be available for dinner that night. The ground floor Westward Restaurant is less seafood based than the specialised Lock 16, but enjoys an equally fine reputation. The bedrooms have been individually designed by Frances Ryan, an artist of repute, some have their own private balconies and each has a sea view.
Open all year except 5 days at Christmas
Rooms: 22 with private facilities
Bar Lunch 12.30 – 2 pm (a)
Dinner (Westward Restaurant) 7 – 9 pm (e)
Dinner (Lock 16 mid Apr to Sep only) at 8 pm except Sun Mon (f) -booking essential
Bed & breakfast £55 - £65
Jumbo Prawns Corryvreckan, Scottish beef, local wild salmon.
STB Highly Commended 4 Crowns
Credit cards: 1, 2, 3, 6
Proprietors: Nick & Frances Ryan

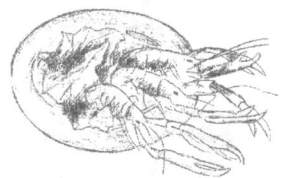

SEALGAIR
c/o Wave Yacht Charters
1 Hazel Drive
Dundee DD2 1QQ
Tel: 0382 68501
Fax: 0382 68501

Yacht based at Bellanoch, by Crinan, Argyll

Beauty and craftsmanship combine in this 46 foot wooden ketch "Sealgair". The only cruising yacht in the Taste of Scotland Guide, she offers you a great holiday experience. Equipped to the highest standards for comfort, performance and safety, she can take you from her base on the Crinan Canal to meander round secluded bays, or taste adventure on a trip to St Kilda. The skipper ensures that you can relax without worry, while from the galley the

cook offers an imaginative menu based on fresh ingredients. French spoken.
Open 1 May to mid Sep
Cabins: 4
Unlicensed – guests welcome to take own wine
No dogs
No smoking in dining area + cabins
Daily rate (all meals + accommodation) per person £48 – £65
Tasty soups, Scottish lamb, venison and fresh fish. Vegetarian dishes. Home-baking.
No credit cards
Proprietor: Wave Yacht Management Ltd

Cromarty

Map 6

ROYAL HOTEL
Marine Terrace, Cromarty
Ross-shire IV11 8YN
Tel: 0381 600217
Fax: 0381 600217
On A832, 20 miles north-east of Inverness.
Welcoming coal fires are a prominent feature of this white-painted hotel situated overlooking the beach and harbour in the ancient and historic village of Cromarty. The furnishing and decor are of a high standard throughout and all the rooms have views of the sea and Ross-shire mountains. The bright sunny dining room looks out over the Cromarty Firth and there is a comfortable bar with an interesting bar lunch and supper menu. The hotel has a good reputation for traditional Scottish hospitality, excellent food and sound value for money.
Open all year except Christmas + Boxing Days, 1 to 3 Jan
Rooms: 10 with private facilities
Bar Lunch 12 – 2 pm (a)
Dining Room/Restaurant Lunch 12 – 2 pm (b)
Bar Supper 5.30 – 9 pm (a)
Dinner 6 – 8.30 pm except Sun (c)
No smoking in dining room
Bed & breakfast £28 – £32
Mussel and onion stew. Crêpe with fresh and smoked seafood in a light cheese sauce. Cromarty crab salad. Prime steaks and lamb. Wide range of traditional Scottish fare.
STB Commended 3 Crowns
Credit cards: 1, 2, 3
Proprietors: Yvonne & Stewart Morrison

Cullen

Map 5

BAYVIEW HOTEL

Seafield Street, Cullen
Banffshire AB56 2SU
Tel: 0542 41031
(0542 841031 from Autumn 93)

*A98 between Banff and Fochabers –
overlooking Cullen Harbour.*

Cullen is a pleasant little harbour town on the Moray Firth and the Bayview is a splendid place to stay when you are there. A really charming little hotel, it has been cleverly converted to provide interesting public rooms and well equipped bedrooms. On a fine day there is a view to Caithness from the top floor breakfast room. The hotel makes good use of its harbour location by specialising in some of the excellent fish soups and fish dishes for which this part of the north-east is noted.

Open all year except Christmas
Rooms: 6 with private facilities
Bar Lunch 12 – 1.45 pm (a)
*Dining Room/Restaurant Lunch 12.30 –
1.45 pm Sun only (b)*
Bar Supper 6.30 – 9 pm (b)
Dinner 6.30 – 9 pm (c)
No dogs
Bed & breakfast £27.50 – £35
Cullen skink. Poached fillet of salmon, garnished with fresh mussels. Fillet steak stuffed with game pâté served with a Cognac and cream sauce.
STB Commended 4 Crowns
Credit cards: 1, 3
Proprietor: David Evans

THE SEAFIELD ARMS HOTEL

Seafield Street, Cullen
Moray AB56 2SG
Tel: 0542 40791
(0542 840791 from Autumn 93)
Fax: 0542 40736
(0542 840736 from Autumn 93)

*Situated on A98 (main road through
Cullen) up from town square.*

A fine old coaching inn, built in 1822 by the Earl of Seafield, and described in the statistical account of Scotland 1845 as having "no superior between Aberdeen and Inverness". In keeping with that inherited reputation, the staff of the Seafield Arms work hard to maintain the tradition of courtesy and caring attention. A very extensive menu caters for a wide range of diners of all age groups and does so successfully judging by the level of activity. The proprietors are much in evidence, supervising the smooth running of the dining room, ably supported by a team of smart, well-trained local staff.

Open all year
Rooms: 25, 23 with private facilities
*Dining Room/Restaurant Lunch 12 –
2 pm (a-b)*
Dinner 6 – 9 pm (b)
No dogs
Facilities for the disabled
Bed & breakfast £25 – £30
Dinner B & B £38 – £45
Cullen skink – a local traditional smoked haddock soup. Locally caught prawns cooked with garlic. Fillet of salmon served with a shrimp and wine sauce.
STB Award Pending
Credit cards: 1, 2, 3, 6 + SWITCH
Proprietors: Herbert & Alison Cox

Cupar

Map 4

OSTLERS CLOSE

Bonnygate, Cupar
Fife KY15 4BU
Tel: 0334 55574

Prestige Award Winner 1989

A92 in Cupar town centre.

It hardly seemed possible that Ostlers Close could improve on the excellent standards that first established its reputation, but it has done so. This small intimate and unpretentious restaurant really is a gem. It is situated in a small lane, or 'close' from which it gets its name, off the main street in Fife's main market town, and Jimmy Graham, the chef/proprietor, produces some of the best food in the county. Fish and shellfish are naturally emphasised but the same deft and imaginative touch of the chef can be seen in his treatment of game and meat dishes. His wife Amanda presides over the dining room with much friendliness and charm, and the combination of the two is irresistible.

*Open all year except first 2 wks Jun,
Christmas + Boxing Days, 1 Jan*
*Dining Room/Restaurant Lunch 12.15 –
2 pm except Sun Mon (b)*
Dinner 7 – 9.30 pm except Sun Mon (d)
Closed Sun Mon
Local seafood broth scented with saffron. Roast saddle of roe venison with wild mushrooms. Fillet of halibut topped with lobster on a herb butter sauce. Honey, Drambuie and oatmeal ice cream. Apricot and almond tart with cream custard.
Credit cards: 1, 3 + SWITCH, DELTA
Proprietors: Jimmy & Amanda Graham

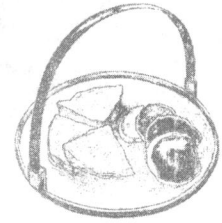

Dalbeattie

Map 1

AUCHENSKEOCH LODGE

by Dalbeattie
Kirkcudbrightshire DG5 4PG
Tel: 038 778 277

*5 miles south-east of Dalbeattie on
B793.*

Former Victorian shooting lodge personally run by the proprietors. Period furnishings throughout ensure a genuine country house atmosphere, whilst woodlands, formal gardens and rhododendron walks provide privacy and tranquillity. Facilities include fishing on own loch, billiard room, croquet lawn and turf and gravel maze. Great emphasis is put on the quality and freshness of the food. To this end the menu is kept small with a choice of two dishes at each course; it changes daily and makes full use of the excellent meat and fish available locally. Wherever possible the vegetables, salads, herbs and soft fruit are fresh from the garden.

Open Easter to 31 Oct
Rooms: 5 with private facilities
Dinner 7.30 – 8 pm (b)
Booking essential for non-residents
Facilities for the disabled
Bed & breakfast £22 – £32
Dinner B & B £34 – £44
Small menu, changing daily. Emphasis on fresh local produce.
STB Commended 3 Crowns
Credit cards: 1, 3
*Proprietors: Christopher & Mary
Broom-Smith*

Daviot
nr Inverness

Map 6

DAVIOT MAINS FARM
Daviot
Inverness IV1 2ER
Tel: 0463 772215
Fax: 0463 772215

On B851 (B9006) to Culloden/Croy, 5 miles south of Inverness.
A comfortable early 19th century Listed farmhouse in a quiet situation five miles from Inverness, under the personal supervision of Margaret and Alex Hutcheson. Relax in the warm atmosphere of this friendly home where delicious meals are thoughtfully prepared and where log fires burn in both sitting room and dining room. A light supper of tea and home-baking is offered around 9.30 pm. Dogs accepted by arrangement.
Open all year
Rooms: 3, 2 with private facilities
Dinner at 6.30 pm except Sun Sat (7 May to 17 Sep): except Sun rest of year (b)
Unlicensed – guests welcome to take own wine
No smoking in dining room + bedrooms
Bed & breakfast £15 – £21
Dinner B & B £24.50 – £31
According to season – home-made soups, fresh local salmon and trout, Scottish meats, vegetables and cheeses. Local fruits and home-made puddings.
STB Highly Commended 2 Crowns
Credit cards: 1, 3
Proprietors: Margaret & Alex Hutcheson

Dirleton

Map 4

OPEN ARMS HOTEL
Dirleton
East Lothian EH39 5EG
Tel: 0620 850241
Fax: 0620 850570

Off A198 to Dirleton village, between Gullane and North Berwick.
Some families are now into their third generation as guests of the Open Arms, a much loved up market inn set in the charming East Lothian coastal village of Dirleton, overlooking the 13th century castle and the village green and only about half an hour's drive from Edinburgh. Arthur Neil is a host par excellence and a much respected figure in the hotel and catering business. It follows almost automatically that he knows and understands his customers' requirements. The menus take full advantage of the excellent seafood and agricultural produce so readily available and food is both prepared and presented with the panache one would expect from a successful operation which has been in the same family's hands for over 40 years. French, German and Gaelic spoken.
Open all year
Rooms: 7 with private facilities
Bar Lunch 12.30 – 2.30 pm except Sun (a)
Dining Room/Restaurant Lunch 12.30 – 2.30 pm Sun only (b)
Dinner 7 – 9.30 pm (d)
Bed & breakfast £50 – £75
Dinner B & B £60 – £100
Smoked salmon parcels filled with avocado mousse served with a pink peppercorn sauce. Mussel and onion stew. Roast supreme of duck with a Port and orange sauce. Pan-fried medallions of lamb served with a timbale of courgettes and mint on a sherry sauce. Trio of fish with a light shellfish sauce.
STB Highly Commended 4 Crowns
Credit cards: 1, 3
Proprietor: Arthur Neil

Dornoch

Map 6

DORNOCH CASTLE HOTEL
Castle Street
Dornoch IV25 3SD
Tel: 0862 810216
Fax: 0862 810981

In the centre of the cathedral town of Dornoch, 2 miles off A9.
Dornoch is a peaceful little town but, as the 13th century cathedral testifies, it is not without historic significance. At about the same time the cathedral was being built so was the Bishop's Palace and parts of it are still incorporated in Dornoch Castle Hotel in the centre of the town. The majority of the comfortable bedrooms overlook the sheltered garden and there is a coffee lounge opening on to the terrace. The Bishop's Room restaurant was once the palace kitchen and now offers diners a good selection of fine food based on local specialities and the abundance of excellent game, fish, shellfish so easily available.
Open 1 Apr to 30 Oct
Rooms: 17 with private facilities
Bar Lunch 12.15 – 2 pm (a)
Dining Room/Restaurant Lunch 12.15 – 2 pm (a)
Bar Supper 6 – 9 pm (a)
Dinner 7.30 – 8.30 pm (c)
No smoking in restaurant
Bed & breakfast £30.50 - £39
Dinner B & B £47.50 – £56
Local venison, salmon, trout and lobster. Aberdeen Angus steaks. Home-made soups, e.g. Brochan Buidhe, and chef's pâtés.
STB Commended 4 Crowns
Credit cards: 1, 2, 3
Proprietor: Michael Ketchin

THE MALLIN HOUSE HOTEL
Church Street, Dornoch
Sutherland IV25 3LP
Tel: 0862 810335
Fax: 0862 810810

Down to centre of town, turn right.
The Mallin House is a family run hotel with a popular bar where there is an exceptionally good range of bar meals (which even include lobster!) and a special 'malt of the month' feature. The restaurant itself is spacious and has magnificent views of the Dornoch Firth and Struie Hills. It has a well balanced à la carte menu which changes quarterly and features local fish, shellfish and game, and excellent steaks.
Open all year
Rooms: 11 with private facilities
Bar Lunch 12.30 – 2.30 pm (b)
Dining Room/Restaurant Lunch 12.30 – 2.30 pm (b)
Bar Supper 6.30 – 9 pm (b)
Dinner 6.30 – 9 pm (c)
Kennel for dogs
Facilities for the disabled: wheelchair ramp
Bed & breakfast £22 – £28
Dinner B & B £40 – £46
Breast of duck studded with peppercorns, roasted and served in a rich sauce of brambles and Drambuie. Partridge with courgette and red wine sauce. Escalope of salmon with fresh herbs, prawns and caviar sauce.
Credit cards: 1, 2, 3
Proprietors: Malcolm & Linda Holden

THE ROYAL GOLF HOTEL
1st Tee, Dornoch
Sutherland IV25 3LG
Tel: 0862 810283
Fax: 0862 810923

From A9, 2 miles into Dornoch town square.

This aptly named hotel is virtually on the golf course; indeed you can almost lie in bed and watch the players on the first tee, or look beyond that to the sandy beaches of the Dornoch Firth. Comfortable bedrooms and suites have all the usual facilities and the restaurant offers high class cuisine with an appropriate inclusion of local regional produce. Bar lunches and suppers are served in the sun lounge in which there is usually entertainment on Saturday evenings. Golf may well be the pre-eminent activity of many of the guests but there is also a fine range of other recreational pursuits in the vicinity.

Open Apr to mid Oct
Rooms: 30 with private facilities
Bar Lunch 12 – 2 pm (a)
Dining Room/Restaurant Lunch 12.30 – 2 pm (a)
Bar Supper 6.30 – 9 pm (a)
Dinner 7 – 9 pm (c)
Bed & breakfast £24 - £39.50
Dinner B & B £32.50 - £49.50
Fresh vegetables and wild mushrooms stir-fried and simmered in cream and saffron, served with a timbale of rice. Smoked salmon parcel filled with prawns.
STB Commended 4 Crowns
Credit cards: 1, 2, 3, 5

Drymen
by Loch Lomond

Map 3

BUCHANAN HIGHLAND HOTEL
Main Street, Drymen
by Loch Lomond
Stirlingshire G63 0BQ
Tel: 0360 60588
Fax: 0360 60943

A811 Balloch (Loch Lomond)/Stirling. Drymen is c. 7½ miles east of Balloch.

This has long been a favourite hotel for those who enjoy the lovely scenery of the Trossachs and Loch Lomond, and when you have finished seeing the countryside there is so much to return to. This attractive old 18th century building has a fully equipped leisure club with

swimming pool, sauna, solarium, gymnasium and squash courts. It also has a bowling green and can arrange tennis, golf or fishing for those so inclined. Public rooms are spacious and comfortably furnished, and there are two good restaurants; Tapestries, with an excellent menu of well presented food, and the Granary, for less formal eating. The staff have been well trained and it shows in polite, attentive and informed service. Breakfasts are quite something, with a great range of choice.

Open all year
Rooms: 50 with private facilities
Bar Lunch (Granary) 12 – 2.30 pm Fri Sat Sun only (a)
Dining Room/Restaurant Lunch (Tapestries) 12.30 – 2.30 pm (a)
Bar Supper (Granary) 6 – 9.30 pm Fri Sat Sun only (a)
Dinner (Tapestries) 7 – 9.30 pm (c)
Facilities for the disabled
Bed & breakfast £64 - £80
Dinner B & B £50 - £66 (min 2 nights stay)
Roast monkfish with bacon, thyme and Noilly Prat. Venison with celeriac and a Glayva cream.
STB Commended 4 Crowns
Credit cards: 1, 2, 3, 5, 6 + SWITCH

Dufftown

Map 5

A TASTE OF SPEYSIDE
10 Balvenie Street, Dufftown
Banffshire AB5 4AB
Tel: 0340 20860

Prestige Award Winner 1988

50 yards from Tourist Information Centre on Elgin road (A941).

This is real malt whisky territory and A Taste of Speyside bases its business on that. Originally set up primarily as a whisky tasting centre and restaurant, it has earned a fine reputation as an inexpensive good quality restaurant promoting the best of Speyside food and Speyside malts of which it has an

unrivalled selection. This is home-cooking at its best, and the Taste of Speyside Platter is something special and wonderful value for money. There are no pretentious frills just honest to goodness food. Group bookings out of season can be arranged.

Open 1 Mar to 31 Oct
Bar Meals 11 am – 5.30 pm (a)
Restaurant Lunch 11 am – 5.30 pm (a)
Dinner 6 – 9 pm (b)
Taste of Speyside Platter, roast loin of Scottish lamb, venison and red wine pie, home-made pâtés, soups, bread. Whisky cake. Heather honey and malt whisky cheese cake.
Credit cards: 1, 2, 3
Proprietors: J Thompson & R McLean

Dulnain Bridge

Map 6

AUCHENDEAN LODGE HOTEL
Dulnain Bridge, Grantown-on-Spey
Morayshire PH26 3LU
Tel: 047 985 347

On A95, 1 mile south of Dulnain Bridge.

A comfortable country house hotel on a knoll commanding some of the finest views across the River Spey and Abernethy Forest towards the Cairngorm Mountains. At one time an Edwardian hunting lodge, it has been furnished with good taste and retains much of its Edwardian elegance. The welcome is genuine, the log fires are cheerful, and the award winning home-cooked dinners are something special with many specialities from the local countryside. An

Credit Card Code	**Meal Price Code**	
1. Access/Mastercard/Eurocard	(a)	under £10
2. American Express	(b)	£10 – £15
3. Visa	(c)	£15 – £20
4. Carte Bleu	(d)	£20 – £25
5. Diners Club	(e)	£25 – £30
6. Mastercharge	(f)	over £30

extensive wine cellar and a wide choice of malt whiskies will add to your enjoyment. Numerous walks in the woods behind the hotel. Pets welcome. French spoken.
Open all year
Rooms: 7, 5 with private facilities
Dinner 7.30 – 9 pm (d) 4 course menu with choices
No smoking in dining room + one of the lounges
Bed & breakfast £22.50 – £39
Dinner B & B £45 – £61.50
Carrot and lovage soup. Arbroath smokie baked in ale and cream. Poached sea trout with Hollandaise sauce. Venison steak in rowan jelly sauce. Apple-stuffed pheasant breast with Calvados sauce. Black and white chocolate truffle cake. Banana baked pudding with a rum and caramel sauce.
STB Highly Commended 3 Crowns
Credit cards: 1, 2, 3, 5
Proprietors: Eric Hart & Ian Kirk

MUCKRACH LODGE HOTEL
Dulnain Bridge, Grantown-on-Spey
Morayshire PH26 3LY
Tel: 047 985 257
Fax: 047 985 325
On A938, ½ mile west of Dulnain Bridge.
Former shooting lodge located in ten secluded acres; the Dulnain River is adjacent to the hotel. This tastefully furnished lodge has a warm friendly atmosphere. You may relax with a drink by the log fire in the elegantly furnished cocktail bar before dining in the extended and refurbished restaurant, where the emphasis is on the best of local produce and friendly efficient service. Muckrach Lodge offers both table d'hôte and à la carte dinners and an extensive wine list. All rooms have colour TV, telephone, tea/coffee-making facilities and are fully centrally heated. There is also a special suite for accompanied disabled persons.
Open all year except Nov
Rooms: 12 with private facilities
Bar Lunch 12 – 2 pm (a)
Dining Room/Restaurant Lunch 12 – 2 pm (b)
Dinner 7.30 – 9 pm (d)
Facilities for the disabled
Bed & breakfast £39 – £49
Special weekly rates for Dinner B & B available
Roast sirloin of Aberdeen Angus beef in a mushroom, red wine and walnut sauce. Darne of fresh wild Spey salmon with caper and fresh lime sauce. Medallions of Rannoch venison in Drambuie

and pink peppercorn sauce. Lunchtime – Muckrach 'substantial' sandwiches.
STB Highly Commended 4 Crowns
Credit cards: 1, 2, 3, 5, 6
Proprietors: Roy & Pat Watson

Dumfries

Map 1

CAIRNDALE HOTEL
English Street, Dumfries
Dumfriesshire DG1 2DF
Tel: 0387 54111
Fax: 0387 50555
Situated opposite the Regional Council offices, on old A75 route running through the centre of Dumfries.
This well established family run hotel has a prime location in the centre of the town. It has grown in size and reputation recently and now offers all the facilities and services to be expected of one of the region's leading three star hotels. All rooms have private bathrooms, TV, radio, direct dial telephone, hairdryer and hospitality tray as standard, while the executive rooms and suites have queen size double beds, mini-bars, trouser presses and jacuzzi spa baths. To top all that there is a leisure centre with heated indoor swimming pool, sauna, steam room, gymnasium and health and beauty salon. Either before or after the exercise, the Forum continental cafe bar within the Club or the hotel's Sawney Beans Carvery restaurant will tempt you with an interesting array of local produce and delicacies.
Open all year
Rooms: 76 with private facilities
Bar Lunch 12 – 2 pm (a)

Dining Room/Restaurant Lunch 12 – 2 pm (a)
Bar Supper 7 – 9 pm (a)
Dinner 7 – 9.30 pm (c): Carvery 7 – 10 pm (b)
Bed & breakfast £40 – £69
Dinner B & B £55 – £70
Special Bargain Breaks from £55
Salmon and haddock roulade with elderflower wine sauce. Asparagus feuilleté. Fillet steak with crayfish sauce. Poached pear with Cassis.
STB Commended 5 Crowns
Credit cards: 1, 2, 3, 5
Proprietors: The Wallace Family

STATION HOTEL
Lovers Walk, Dumfries
Dumfriesshire DG1 1LT
Tel: 0387 54316
Fax: 0387 50388
Just outside town centre opposite railway station.
This imposing old red sandstone building has recently been refurbished whilst retaining the lofty proportions of some of its public rooms and the ornate cornices and ceilings. The lounge bar is a comfortable meeting place at any time of day for a drink or a snack but there are alternative eating places. The dining room is a spacious and elegant room, tastefully decorated and 'Somewhere Else' is an informal bistro with stone floor tiles, patio style tables and beamed ceilings. The dining room menu has some very enterprising dishes in the à la carte version with enough choice for everyone, while the cafe bar bistro restricts itself to popular demand snacks and pastas. Between the two even the most fastidious palate should find something to satisfy it.
Open all year except Boxing Day, 1 + 2 Jan
Rooms: 32 with private facilities
Bar Lunch 12 – 2 pm (a)
Bar Supper 5 – 10 pm (a)
Dinner 7 – 9.30 pm (b)
Taste of Scotland applies to main restaurant only
No smoking area in restaurant
Bed & breakfast £30 – £58
Dinner B & B £37.50 – £47.50
Tartlet of prawns in a creamy ginger sauce. Smoked salmon on a bed of smoked mussels with marinated melon. Sirloin steak in a sauce with mushrooms flavoured with Drambuie. Sea bass and salmon plait on a fennel and asparagus sauce. Selection of Scottish cheeses.
STB Commended 4 Crowns
Credit cards: 1, 2, 3, 5, 6

Dunbar

Map 4

THE COURTYARD HOTEL & RESTAURANT

Woodbush Brae, Dunbar
East Lothian EH42 1HB
Tel: 0368 64169

A1 to Dunbar, 28 miles east of Edinburgh. Take road off south end of town's main street towards seashore.

The water washes against the walls of these fishermen's cottages which have been sympathetically converted to a small hotel and restaurant. Superb views from the first floor restaurant over the North Sea. The Courtyard is set in the heart of golf country and is also ideal for touring the Border country with its wild and beautiful coastline – yet only 28 miles from the Edinburgh city lights. The proprietor has built up a good regular clientele and a sound reputation for interesting, imaginative – and inexpensive – food.

Open all year except Christmas Day night
Rooms: 7, 2 with private facilities
Dining Room/Restaurant Lunch 12 – 2 pm (a)
Dinner 7 – 9.30 pm (b)
Bed & breakfast £24.50 – £42
Dinner B & B £39 – £56.50
Home-made pâtés and soups. Locally landed fish and shellfish e.g scallops with a light white wine and tomato sauce, dressed crab, monkfish with garlic, haddock with spiced cream sauce. Steaks with home-made sauces, chicken with wild mushroom sauce. Home-made desserts.
STB Commended 2 Crowns
Credit cards: 1, 2, 3, 5
Proprietor: Peter W Bramley

Dunblane

Map 4

CROMLIX HOUSE

Kinbuck, by Dunblane
Perthshire FK15 9JT
Tel: 0786 822125
Fax: 0786 825450

Off A9, B8033 to Kinbuck, through village, cross narrow bridge, drive is second on left. From Crieff A822 to Braco, then B8033 Kinbuck.

One of Scotland's finest country houses, Cromlix stands within its own 5000 acre estate and is easily accessible from Perth, Edinburgh, Glasgow. Built in 1874, the house is steeped in history and full of antiques. It retains the informal welcome and atmosphere of a well loved home, making it a comfortable house in which to relax. The six rooms and eight spacious suites are all delightfully individual. There is a feeling of space and comfort throughout, with three public rooms, three dining rooms, and a conservatory. Cromlix even has its own private chapel which is available for weddings. David and Ailsa Assenti came to Cromlix from Ballathie House, bringing Head Chef Stephen Robertson with them. His young kitchen team produce delicious and imaginative meals for the daily changing menus which feature the best of fresh produce for the discriminating palate. Cromlix is a uniquely pleasurable experience!

Open 1 Mar to 10 Jan
Rooms: 14 with private facilities
Light Lunch & Snacks 12.30 – 1.45 pm (a-b)
Dining Room Lunch 12.30 – 1.45 pm (c-d)
Note: Nov to Mar full Lunch available Sun Sat only
Dinner 7 – 9 pm (f) 5 course menu
No smoking in dining rooms
Bed & breakfast £40 – £90 Oct to Mar: £60 – £110 Apr to Oct
Dinner B & B £72 – £112 Oct to Mar: £94 – £145 Apr to Oct
Special rates for 3 or more nights
STB Deluxe 4 Crowns
Credit cards: 1, 2, 3, 5, 6 + SWITCH
Proprietors: David & Ailsa Assenti

STAKIS DUNBLANE HYDRO

Perth Road, Dunblane
Perthshire FK15 0HG
Tel: 0786 822551 • Telex: 776284
Fax: 0786 825403

At northern exit (B8033) from Dunblane.
Built in 1878 as a hydropathic, this splendid Victorian hotel has been extended, modernised and refurbished to a high standard. High on a hill on the fringe of the town, it commands wonderful views across the countryside and has some 44 acres of private mature policies. It is a popular conference centre but also attracts much family trade. There are extensive leisure facilities, both indoors and outdoors, and regular entertainment.
Open all year
Rooms: 219 with private facilities

Dining Room/Restaurant Lunch 12.30 – 2 pm (a-b)
Dinner 6.30 – 9.30 pm (c)
No smoking area in restaurant
Bed & breakfast £31.50 – £39.50
Dinner B & B £41.50 – £49.50
Terrine of Perthshire pheasant, pigeon and pistachio. Steamed fillet of Tay salmon with fresh spinach and pine kernels.
STB Award Pending
Credit cards: 1, 2, 3, 5

Dundee

Map 4

THE OLD MANSION HOUSE HOTEL

Auchterhouse
by Dundee DD3 0QN
Tel: 082 626 366

On A923, 7 miles west of Dundee, then B954 past Muirhead.
A most attractive 16th century baronial house which has been tastefully converted into a delightful small luxury hotel, whilst retaining its historic features. The hotel is set in 10 acres of beautiful gardens and woodland, and the lands around it are steeped in Scottish history having, at different times, been in the hands of the Ogilvies, the Strathmores and the Earls of Buchan. The restaurant has an incredibly ornate ceiling and a huge old fireplace, and good quality table linen, crystal and china enhance the atmosphere. Menus are reasonably priced and indicative of locally procured produce with interesting sauces.
Open all year except Christmas + Boxing Days, 31 Dec + first wk Jan
Rooms: 6 with private facilities
Bar Lunch 12 – 2 pm (a)

*Dining Room/Restaurant Lunch 12 –
1.45 pm (b)
Bar Supper 7 – 9.30 pm Mon to Sat:
Sun 7 – 9 pm (a)
Dinner 7 – 9.15 pm Mon to Sat: Sun 7 –
9 pm (e)
No smoking in restaurant
Bed & breakfast £47.50 – £69
Cullen skink. Mussel and herb chowder
with garlic croutons. Fillets of sole
stuffed with prawns in a Chablis cream
sauce with dill and tomato. Medallions
of lamb with an aromatic savoury butter.
Poached salmon on a bed of spinach
with chive butter. Raspberry crème
brûlée with a nut and sugar crust.
STB Highly Commended 4 Crowns
Credit cards: 1, 2, 3, 5, 6
Proprietors: Nigel & Eva Bell*

THE SANDFORD COUNTRY HOUSE HOTEL

Newton Hill, Wormit
nr Dundee
Fife DD6 8RG
Tel: 0382 541802
Fax: 0382 542136

*Near to B946 junction with A914 route
which links Forth Road Bridge,
Edinburgh, with Tay Bridge, Dundee.*
Undoubtedly one of Fife's most picturesque venues for a leisurely meal. The
fine architecture of the Listed country
house has an ambience of its own and
the gardens are worthy of a pre- or after-
dining stroll to appreciate them fully. An
attractively presented menu tempts the
palate with a balanced variety of tastes,
colours and textures. There are seasonal
dishes a-plenty and the chef clearly
relies on good local ingredients. A
comprehensive wine list has been
carefully selected to complement the
menu. The hotel is close to Dundee and
St Andrews and makes an ideal venue
for those touring in the region, or golfing,
fishing or shooting. German, Italian and
some Japanese spoken.
*Open all year
Rooms: 16 with private facilities
Bar Lunch 12 – 2 pm (b)
Dining Room/Restaurant Lunch 12 –
2 pm (c)
Bar Supper 6 – 9 pm Sun to Thu: 6 –
8 pm Fri Sat (b)
Dinner 6 – 9.30 pm (c-d)
No smoking in restaurant
Facilities for the disabled
Bed & breakfast from £47.50
Dinner B & B £69 – £101.50
Fricasée of local pigeon and woodland*

*mushrooms. Gâteau of East Neuk
lobster and crab with smoked salmon,
cucumber, saffron and olive oil. Double
loin of Perthshire lamb, roasted with
garlic and rosemary in a Port essence
with potato and celeriac. Fillet of wild
salmon with monkfish, fennel ravioli and
orange butter. Parfait of bitter chocolate
with crystal-lised hazelnuts and coffee
custard.
STB Highly Commended 4 Crowns
Credit cards: 1, 2, 3, 5*

SOUTH KINGENNIE HOUSE RESTAURANT

Kellas, by Broughty Ferry
Dundee DD5 1BJ
Tel: 082 625 562

*From A92 Dundee-Arbroath, take B978
to Kellas then road to Drumsturdy to
signpost for South Kingennie, 2 miles.*
A converted Scottish farmhouse now
operating as a lounge bar and licensed
restaurant. It is owned and run by Peter
and Jill Robinson whose high standards
are demonstrated in the elegance of the
restaurant with its fine linen and fresh
flowers. Menus are well balanced and
imaginative and utilise to the full the
pick of fresh market and local produce,
to give value for money meals in a
friendly relaxed atmosphere. Peter's

skills in the kitchen are well matched by
his wife's caring supervision of the front
of the house.
*Open all year except last wk Jan + first
wk Feb
Dining Room/Restaurant Lunch 12 –
2 pm except Mon (b)
Dinner 7 – 9 pm except Mon (c)
Closed Mon
Facilities for the disabled
Sauté loin of lamb with rosemary sauce
and mint Hollandaise. Fillets of wild
salmon poached with vermouth and
prawn tails. Medallions of Angus beef
with red wine and roasted shallots.
Credit cards: 1, 3, 6 + SWITCH
Proprietors: Peter & Jill Robinson*

STAKIS DUNDEE EARL GREY HOTEL

Earl Grey Place
Dundee DD1 4DE
Tel: 0382 29271 • Telex: 76569
Fax: 0382 200072

City location on the waterfront.
Right on the waterfront and adjacent to
the new Discovery Berth overlooking the
Tay estuary, the hotel is nevertheless
virtually in the city centre. Its proximity to
the business hub makes it a popular
rendezvous for the business community,
but leisure interests are well catered for
too – the leisure suite incorporates a
swimming pool, exercise area, whirlpool
and sauna. The whole length of the
dining room on one side has full height
windows and most diners have
magnificent views of the Tay estuary and
road bridge. Light lunches are
inexpensive while the evening menu is
more varied and serious with something
for all tastes.
*Open all year
Rooms: 104 with private facilities
Bar Lunch 12.30 – 2 pm Sat only (b)
Dining Room/Restaurant Lunch 12.30 –
2.30 pm except Sat (b)
Dinner 6.30 – 10 pm (c)
Bed & breakfast £64 – £94
Dinner B & B £80.50 – £110.50
Room Rate £87 – £112
Smoked Highland venison with
gooseberry relish and toasted bannocks.
Pan-fried medallion of beef served on a
potato pancake topped with haggis,
coated in wild mushroom and Madeira
sauce. Iced Drambuie soufflé with
raspberry sauce.
STB Commended 5 Crowns
Credit cards: 1, 2, 3, 5*

STRATHDON HOTEL
277 Perth Road, Dundee
Tayside DD2 1JS
Tel: 0382 65648

On main Perth road, in Dundee's west end – close to Ninewells Hospital, Dundee Airport and the University.
The Strathdon Hotel is an attractive Edwardian terrace and many of its rooms enjoy delightful views over the River Tay. It is personally run by chef/proprietor Ian Hornsby and his wife, Carole, who take pride in ensuring their guests are made to feel welcome and at home during their stay. The Strathdon's popular restaurant is steadily gaining a reputation for exceptional cuisine using fresh local produce, complemented by a fine selection of wines. The hotel now has two further bedrooms and has added a lounge for guests.
Open all year except Christmas Day + 1 Jan
Rooms: 10 with private facilities
Dinner 7 – 8.30 pm except Sun (b-c)
Restricted Hotel Licence
No dogs
No smoking in restaurant
Bed & breakfast £20 – £32
Dinner B & B £30 – £50
Lemon sole and Tay salmon pleated together, lightly grilled with tarragon and served with a creamy watercress sauce. Duo of lamb fillet and venison, pan-fried with a garnish of cinnamon pear and served with a rich Port wine and bramble sauce. Ginger and honey pudding served with a creamy vanilla custard.
Credit cards: 1, 3
Proprietors: Ian & Carole Hornsby

Dundonnell

Map 6

DUNDONNELL HOTEL
Dundonnell, by Garve
Ross-shire IV23 2QR
Tel: 085 483 204

On A832 south of Ullapool.
The Florence family have been running this acclaimed hotel for the last 30 years and during that time it has grown both in size and in reputation. It is set by the shores of Little Loch Broom, right on the roadside midway between Ullapool and Gairloch, on a splendidly remote and spectacular route. The hotel is very comfortably equipped with pleasing decor in bedrooms and sitting rooms, and is an ideal place from which to explore and enjoy the local hills and glens as well as better known attractions such as Inverewe Gardens. The menus offer an excellent selection of of dishes, are well balanced with a lot of original touches, and represent good value. This is a hotel that attracts lots of repeat business from satisfied guests.
Open 1 Mar to 22 Nov + Christmas/New Year
Rooms: 24 with private facilities
Bar Lunch 12 – 2.15 pm (b)
Bar Supper 6 – 8.15 pm (b)
Dinner 7 – 8.30 pm (d)
Bed & breakfast £29.50 – £42.50
Dinner B & B £39.50 – £62.50
Special rates for 2 or more nights
Home-made soups and pâtés. Savoury choux pastry with a creamy smoked haddock filling. Roast rack of Highland lamb with Port and orange. Pot-roast Aberdeenshire beef in a red wine sauce. Lemon sole grilled with a hazelnut butter.
STB Highly Commended 4 Crowns
Credit cards: 1, 3, 6
Proprietors: Selbie & Flora Florence

Dunfermline

Map 4

DAVAAR HOUSE HOTEL & RESTAURANT
126 Grieve Street, Dunfermline
Fife KY12 8DW
Tel: 0383 721886/735365

From M90 Junction 3 to Dunfermline, follow A907 Kincardine into Carnegie Drive. Right into Chalmers Street, then

second left to Grieve Street.
This fine old house has just passed its one hundredth birthday and retains the splendid oak staircase and elaborate ornate ceiling cornices that were such a feature of the period. Now comfortably furnished and tastefully decorated it has eight en suite bedrooms and a pleasingly relaxed and informal atmosphere. Doreen Jarvis' skill in the kitchen is demonstrated in the excellent variety and style of her cooking and is augmented by having a husband who is a local greengrocer and florist and ensures that she is supplied with really fresh produce from the market and local growers.
Open mid Jan to 24 Dec
Rooms: 8 with private facilities
Dining Room/Restaurant Lunch (b) private party bookings only
Supper 6 – 8 pm except Sun Fri Sat (b)
Dinner 6 – 9 pm except Sun (c)
Restricted Licence
No dogs
Facilities for the disabled
No smoking in restaurant
Bed & breakfast £24 – £34
Dinner B & B £36 – £48
Home-made soups, broths and pâté. Stuffed rainbow trout. Grilled salmon steak with Arran mustard and dill sauce. Roast duck with brandy and orange sauce. Roast pheasant with oatmeal stuffing.
STB Commended 3 Crowns
Credit cards: 1, 3
Proprietors: Jim & Doreen Jarvis

PITFIRRANE ARMS HOTEL
Main Street, Crossford
nr Dunfermline KY12 8NJ
Tel: 0383 736132 • Telex: 728255
Fax: 0383 621760

A994 west of Dunfermline, i.e. Glasgow road.
The Pitfirrane Arms Hotel is one of the few original coaching inns left in the country which has been restored and extended to meet the modern demand for excellent cuisine and high standards. Situated in the pleasant village of Crossford, on the main Dunfermline-Glasgow road (A994), the hotel is within easy access of M90.
Open all year
Rooms: 38 with private facilities
Bar Lunch 12 – 2.15 pm (a)
Dining Room/Restaurant Lunch 12 – 2.15 pm (b)
Bar Supper 5.30 – 9.15 pm (a)

Dinner 7 – 9.15 pm (b)
Bed & breakfast £20 – £53
Dinner B & B £23.75 – £68
Locally available fresh produce.
Credit cards: 1, 2, 3
Proprietor: M McVicars

Dunkeld

Map 4

ROYAL DUNKELD HOTEL
Atholl Street, Dunkeld
Perthshire PH8 0AR
Tel: 0350 727322
Fax: 0350 728989

From A9 follow signs for Dunkeld. Over Telford's Bridge, hotel in prominent position on Atholl Street.
The famous Telford Bridge spanning the river at Dunkeld was completed in 1809 and so was the Royal Dunkeld Hotel. A former coaching inn, it is now a comfortable hotel which has recently undertaken a refurbishment of all its bedrooms which are attractive, comfortable and well equipped. An enthusiastic and innovative chef produces some excellent food and is constantly striving to keep his menus interesting and inviting. In addition to the restaurant there is the informal Gargoyles bistro lounge. The little cathedral town of Dunkeld is a haven for golf enthusiasts with numerous courses within easy reach, and is also a splendidly central point for many of the other attractions of Perthshire.
Open all year
Rooms: 35 with private facilities
Bar Lunch 12 – 2.30 pm (a)

Dining Room/Restaurant Lunch 12 – 2 pm (b)
Bar Supper 5 – 9.30 pm (a)
Dinner 7 – 9.30 pm (c)
No pipes or cigars in restaurant
Facilities for the disabled
Bed & breakfast £32.50 – £50
Dinner B & B £45 – £60
Arbroath smokie mousse in a savoury case. Pheasant with turnip cake. Venison and salmon dishes. Home-made bread and ice cream. Freshly prepared sweets.
STB Approved 3 Crowns
Credit cards: 1, 2, 3, 5, 6 + SWITCH
Proprietors: Graham & Ann Rees

STAKIS DUNKELD HOUSE HOTEL
Dunkeld
Perthshire PH8 0HX
Tel: 0350 727771 • Telex: 76657
Fax: 0350 728924

A9 to Dunkeld, hotel lies c. 1 mile east of village.
The first glimpse of Dunkeld House suggests Edwardian elegance. It is approached through the old gatehouse and a mile along an immaculately kept drive through wooded countryside and is set in its own 280 acre estate on the banks of the River Tay, one of Scotland's finest salmon rivers. Built originally for the seventh Duke of Atholl, Dunkeld House is now a combination of luxury hotel and country house with a touch of originality and individuality. There is a much better than usual bar lunch menu and the dining room choice, particularly in the evening – as it is not always open for lunch in the quiet season – meets the requirement of most discerning diners. This is a haven for bird-watchers and walkers but the hotel also has a private two mile salmon beat, a world class shooting academy and first class leisure facilities.
Open all year
Rooms: 92 with private facilities
Bar Lunch 12 – 2 pm (b)
Dining Room/Restaurant Lunch 12 – 2 pm (b)
Dinner 7 – 9.30 pm (d)

Bed & breakfast £54 – £82.50
Dinner B & B £67 – £95.50
Room Rate £89 – £139
Breast of Perthshire wood pigeon served on pickled red cabbage with a lime and redcurrant sauce. Medallion of beef topped with a herb crust and served with a red wine and shallot sauce. Rich orange chocolate mousse with chocolate shortbread. Raspberry crème brûlée.
STB Highly Commended 5 Crowns
Credit cards: 1, 2, 3, 5, 6

Dunoon

Map 3

ARDFILLAYNE HOTEL
BEVERLEY'S RESTAURANT
Bullwood Road, Dunoon
Argyll PA23 7QJ
Tel: 0369 2267
Fax: 0369 2501

At west end of Dunoon (A815).
A visit to this lovely country house set in beautifully kept gardens is a trip down memory lane to Victorian splendour. The proprietors have gathered around them a treasure trove of antique furniture and clocks, and Beverley's Restaurant with its fresh flowers, lace tablecloths, candlelight and silver, exudes an atmosphere of the sophistication and style of days gone by. The à la carte menu presents a good combination of classical French and traditional Scottish dishes, with extensive reliance on Scotland's prime seafood and game. The high standard of food supported by a good wine list and a comforting range of old Ports, brandies and malts, altogether makes it a very pleasant experience.
Open all year
Rooms: 8 with private facilities
Dinner 6.30 – 9.30 pm (d)
Restaurant closed Sun evening in Winter
No smoking in restaurant
Bed & breakfast £35 – £55
Dinner B & B £57.50 – £67
Venison with spices, claret, lemons, butter and walnut ketchup. Prime steak grilled with smoked Orkney cheese and flamed with Glengoyne whisky. Halibut steak poached in milk with a light lemon and cream sauce. Scallops St Veronique. Cream of mussel soup. Loch Fyne oyster and champagne soup. Baked Loch Fyne crab.
STB Deluxe 4 Crowns
Credit cards: 1, 2, 3, 5
Proprietors: Bill & Beverley McCaffrey

Credit Card Code		Meal Price Code	
1. Access/Mastercard/Eurocard	(a)	under £10
2. American Express	(b)	£10 – £15
3. Visa	(c)	£15 – £20
4. Carte Bleu	(d)	£20 – £25
5. Diners Club	(e)	£25 – £30
6. Mastercharge	(f)	over £30

CHATTERS

58 John Street, Dunoon
Argyll PA23 8BJ
Tel: 0369 6402

On John Street, Dunoon, opposite the cinema.

The conversion of this traditional cottage into a warm and welcoming restaurant has been very well done and, in its second year of operation, Chatters has consolidated its position and strengthened its reputation in the town – and beyond. David Craig and his keen young chefs in the kitchen have presentation of food down to an art form. There are some excellent dishes on offer in the well planned à la carte menu with a good range of choice, and a leisurely evening meal here can be quite memorable. Chatters is also deservedly popular for lunches and people drop in for a light snack or coffee etc during the day. Rosemary MacInnes presides over it all with all the gracious qualities of a good hostess intent on ensuring that her guests leave contentedly and cannot wait to go back. In good weather there is a delightful little patio to the rear where you may eat al fresco.

Open mid Feb to 23 Dec
Bar Lunch 11.30 am – 2.30 pm except Sun (a)
Dining Room/Restaurant Lunch 11.30 am – 2.30 pm except Sun (a-b)
Bar Supper 6 – 9.30 pm except Sun (a)
Dinner 6 – 9.30 pm except Sun (c)
Closed Sun
Table Licence
Smoking discouraged
Loch Fyne shellfish including langoustines, mussels, oysters and scallops etc. Hot roulade of red pepper and wild mushrooms on a sauce of Stilton and spinach. Fillet of Scotch lamb in a natural jus with a timbale of cream and parsley. Local salmon with tiger prawns and a sauce of fresh herbs. Wide selection of home-made desserts and petit fours.
Credit cards: 1, 3
Proprietor: Rosemary Anne MacInnes

ENMORE HOTEL

Marine Parade, Kirn
Dunoon
Argyll PA23 8HH
Tel: 0369 2230
Fax: 0369 2148

On seafront near Hunters Quay ferry, on road to Dunoon.

Originally built as a Summer house for a rich cotton merchant, Enmore occupies a splendid location with commanding views across the Firth of Clyde. It has all the charm of a Georgian country house and has been beautifully furnished by Angela and David Wilson. The Victorian dining room is light and airy, with original ceilings and features. It is attractively laid out with fine linen, china, crystal and silver. There is not a wide choice on the menu but that is no bad thing. Too many extensive menus indicate an extensive deep-freeze. What is offered here is changed daily, gives every evidence of being prepared with great skill and is presented with professional flair. The hotel's own garden contributes to the fresh herbs and vegetables, and the fine produce for which Argyll and Loch Fyne are noted feature regularly on the menu.

Open all year except Christmas
Rooms: 11 with private facilities
Bar Meals served all day from 12 noon (a)
Dining Room/Restaurant Lunch 12 – 3 pm (b)
Dinner 7.30 – 9.30 pm (d)
Bed & breakfast £29 – £55
Dinner B & B £50 – £75
Home-made bread and soups. Croustade filled with prawns and whisky cream. Fillet of turbot served with chive-scented juices. Loch Fyne fish dishes, local venison and salmon.
STB Highly Commended 4 Crowns
Credit cards: 1, 3
Proprietors: David & Angela Wilson

Eddleston

Map 2

BARONY CASTLE HOTEL

Blackbarony, Eddleston
Peebles EH45 8QW
Tel: 0721 730395
Fax: 0721 730275

12 miles south of Edinburgh, 4 miles north of Peebles.

The Barony Castle has a truly impressive appearance – so reminiscent of a French château that one almost looks for the vineyards. The building goes back to the early 16th century and it is claimed that King James VI and Sir Walter Scott have stayed there. Bedrooms are large and comfortable with all the modern accessories one expects. There are 65 acres of grounds, an indoor heated swimming pool, sauna and jacuzzi.

Open all year
Rooms: 30 with private facilities
Bar Lunch 12 – 2.30 pm (a)
Dining Room/Restaurant Lunch 12 – 2.30 pm (a)
Bar Supper 7 – 9.30 pm (a)
Dinner 7 – 9.30 pm (c)
Facilities for the disabled
No smoking area in restaurant
Bed & breakfast £33 – £83
Dinner B & B £49 – £99
Pan-fried breast of quail on a bed of savoy cabbage. Roast rack of Border lamb.
STB Commended 4 Crowns
Credit cards: 1, 2, 3, 5

Edinburgh

Map 4

ABBOTSFORD RESTAURANT & BAR

3 Rose Street
Edinburgh EH2 2PR
Tel: 031 225 5276

Rose Street, behind Jenners.

The Abbotsford is a good example of a traditional pub. It has a separate restaurant upstairs, where, in an atmosphere of Victorian charm, good honest inexpensive meals are served. It has been acclaimed in the United States as one of the best hostelries in Scotland. Small parties are catered for, by arrangement, in the restaurant.

Open all year except Christmas Day + 1 Jan
Bar Lunch 12 – 2 pm except Sun (a)
Dining Room/Restaurant Lunch 12 – 2.15 pm except Sun (a)
Dinner 6.30 – 10 pm except Sun (b)
Closed Sun
Seafood platter with a light lemon vinaigrette. Baked supreme of salmon with Hollandaise sauce. Steaks with a choice of sauces, e.g. smoked cheese, whisky and cream; pickled walnut; wild mushroom.
Credit cards: 1, 3, 6
Proprietor: Colin Grant

ATRIUM

10 Cambridge Street
Edinburgh EH1 2ED
Tel: 031 228 8882

It is Edinburgh's good fortune that Andrew Radford has now established his own restaurant in the city. The Atrium in the Saltire Court, Traverse Theatre building, is decidedly different. There is a theatrical flair to the character of the restaurant but that is of little relevance to those who patronise it to enjoy Andrew Radford's distinctive, unusual and quite excellent style of cooking. The maestro has gained even more skill over the years and his devoted followers expect, and get, the exceptional. For a light lunch, a gourmet meal or a special occasion the Atrium will rise to the event and meet the demand. This is one show that will run and run – but it is popular and busy so do book in advance.

Open all year except 2 wks Christmas
Dining Room/Restaurant Lunch 12 –
3 pm except Sun (c)
Dinner 6 – 10.30 pm except Sun (e-f)
Closed Sun
Fresh Scottish produce, in particular game and fish.
Credit cards: 1, 2, 3 + SWITCH
Proprietors: Andrew & Lisa Radford

THE BALMORAL HOTEL EDINBURGH

1 Princes Street
Edinburgh EH2 2EQ
Tel: 031 556 2414 • Telex: 727282
Fax: 031 557 3747

East end of Princes Street at corner of North Bridge.

No 1 Princes Street must rank as one of the most impressive addresses in Europe. It is an imposing and impressive building with magnificent public rooms and function suites. Many bedrooms have uninterrupted views along the entire mile length of Princes Street and across the gardens to Edinburgh Castle perched on its volcanic cone. No 1 Princes Street Restaurant is a sumptuous and elegant hideaway – an oasis of dignity and calm that makes a wonderful retreat from the bustle of the city. Menus are impressive and imaginative and whether table d'hôte or à la carte represent good value for money. For those who want an informal style of eating the continental-style brasserie, The Bridges, on the ground floor has a wide range of excellent quick meals and snacks, while the comfortable

Palm Court is much enjoyed by those for whom a restful morning coffee or afternoon tea makes their day. A well equipped leisure centre provides the opportunity to lose some of those ounces it is so enjoyable to put on!

Open all year
Rooms: 189 with private facilities
Bar Lunch (NB's Bar) 12 – 2.30 pm (b)
Brasserie Lunch (Bridges) from
12 noon (c)
Dining Room/Restaurant Lunch (No 1
Princes St) 12 – 2.30 pm except Sun
Sat (d)
Bar Supper (NB's Bar) 7 – 11 pm (b)
Dinner (Bridges) 7 – 11 pm (d)
Dinner (No 1 Princes St) 7 –
10.30 pm (f)
No dogs
Facilities for the disabled
No smoking area in restaurants
Bed & breakfast from £135 per room
Dinner B & B from £99
Room Rate from £120
NB's Bar: roast rib of Angus beef served in a bap. Bridges: duo of smoked halibut and salmon on a scallion and lime crème fraiche. No 1 Princes St: fresh langoustines, scallops and dill flavoured smoked salmon in a vegetable nage with bell peppers; noisette of Perthshire lamb with a tartlet of vegetables, in a natural jus with tomato and basil; redcurrant and yoghurt mousse with a Blairgowrie raspberry coulis and fresh berries.
STB Deluxe 5 Crowns
Credit cards: 1, 2, 3, 5

CALEDONIAN HOTEL

Princes Street
Edinburgh EH1 2AB
Tel: 031 225 2433 • Telex: 72179
Fax: 031 225 6632

Prestige Award Winner 1988 + 1992

West end of Princes Street.

This magnificent five star deluxe hotel has dominated the Edinburgh scene for most of this century and is truly the 'Grand Dame' of the city, known to and loved by people from all over the world. It is constantly being improved and upgraded in some sector. The dignified and gracious Pompadour Restaurant offers the very best experience in elegant eating with superb menus featuring Scottish specialities and reflecting the high culinary skills of a well

trained and experienced kitchen brigade. The Carriages Restaurant on the ground floor offers a simpler menu than that in The Pompadour, but nevertheless carries a fine range of classic dishes with a leavening of international cuisine both at lunchtime and in the evening. For those in a desperate hurry, or a restful hour to spare, there is also an all day long service of coffee, sandwiches, afternoon tea etc in the foyer lounge. This is a hotel with it all and an Edinburgh without the Caley, as it is affectionately known, is unthinkable.

Open all year
Rooms: 240 with private facilities
Bar Lunch (Platform 1) 12 – 2 pm except Sun (a)
Lunch (Carriages) 12 – 2.30 pm Mon to Fri: 12.30 – 2.30 Sun Sat (b-c)
Lunch (Pompadour) 12.30 – 2 pm except Sun Sat (e)
Afternoon Tea (Lounge) 3 – 5.30 pm
Dinner (Carriages) 6.30 – 10 pm (d)
Dinner (Pompadour) 7.30 – 10.30 pm except Sun: 7.30 – 10 pm Sun (Summer only) (f)
No smoking area in restaurants
Room Rate £145 – £240
Carriages: baked supreme of salmon with herb mousse and puff pastry. Lamb hotpot with leeks and sliced potatoes. Pompadour: grilled medallions of monkfish and Dublin Bay prawns with braised bacon and spinach ravioli.
STB Deluxe 5 Crowns
Credit cards: 1, 2, 3, 5, 6

CARLTON HIGHLAND HOTEL

North Bridge
Edinburgh EH1 1SD
Tel: 031 556 7277 • Telex: 727001
Fax: 031 556 2691

City centre – North Bridge links the east end of Princes Street with the Royal Mile.

The Carlton Highland Hotel is a handsome Victorian building standing proud against the Edinburgh skyline, overlooking Princes Street and the historical Royal Mile. It prides itself on offering traditional Scottish hospitality, courtesy and a friendly welcome to all its guests. Its excellent facilities include 197 bedrooms and suites, each with every modern comfort, superb leisure centre, gift shop, hair and beauty salon, patisserie, tapas bar and nightclub. Fine Scottish cuisine with seasonal specialities is enjoyed in the hotel's two restaurants, Quills and Carlton Court.

Open all year
Rooms: 197 with private facilities
Bar Lunch 12 – 2.30 pm (a)
Dining Room/Restaurant Lunch 12 – 5 pm (b)
Dinner 5 – 10.30 pm (c)
Facilities for the disabled
Bed & breakfast £118 – £128
Dinner B & B £51 – £98 (min 2 nights stay)
Avocado mousse with smoked Scottish salmon on a cucumber dressing. Crab and lobster soup with caviar. Rib of beef chargrilled with garden herbs, served with a woodland mushroom and sherry jus. Casserole of monkfish, crayfish and scallops on a lime and spinach cream sauce. Rack of lamb roasted with herbs, served with garlic flavoured potatoes and sorrel sauce.
STB Highly Commended 5 Crowns
Credit cards: 1, 2, 3, 5, 6

CHANNINGS

South Learmonth Gardens
Edinburgh EH4 1EZ
Tel: 031 315 2226
Fax: 031 332 9631

South Learmonth Gardens is parallel to Queensferry Road, a few minutes walk from the west end of Edinburgh city centre.

Channings is something rare today, a privately owned hotel, originally five Edwardian town-houses, where a cosy club-like atmosphere can be found. Considerable restoration of traditional features has been undertaken and the

bedrooms have been individually designed. Peaceful lounges provide a retreat from the busy city. Menu selections in Channings Brasserie range from a light lunch to a full evening dinner, all prepared from fresh local produce, emphasising an honest and natural cuisine with both a traditional Scottish and French flavour. The bustling bar offers an interesting range of malt whiskies.

Open all year
Rooms: 48 with private facilities
Bar Lunch 12 – 2 pm except Sun (a)
Dining Room/Restaurant Lunch 12 – 2 pm except Sat (a-b)
Dinner 6.30 – 9.30 pm (a-d)
Bed & breakfast £51.50 – £88
Dinner B & B £69 – £105.50
Haggis wrapped in a parcel of carrageen and served on a bed of creamed leeks. Escalope of Scottish salmon with mussels and chopped dill in a light cream sauce.
STB Commended 4 Crowns
Credit cards: 1, 2, 3, 5, 6 + SWITCH
Proprietor: Peter Taylor

CRAMOND GALLERY BISTRO

4 Riverside Cramond, Cramond Village
Edinburgh EH4 6NY
Tel: 031 312 6555

Follow Cramond Glebe Road down to harbour front.

With its narrow wynds, steep steps and huddle of cottages, Cramond still looks the lovely little fishing village it had been for centuries and it is difficult to believe that one is still within the city of Edinburgh. There are even the foundations of a Roman fort clearly visible alongside Cramond Kirk. This is, therefore, a clever spot for Alan and Evelyn Bogue to have established a charming little bistro, right on the quayside, within one of the traditional old 16th century buildings which was built on the foundation of a 4th century Roman boatshed. Yachts nod gaily on the tide outside and there are glorious views across the Firth of Forth. Cramond Bistro, with its low timbered ceilings and lace tablecloths, exudes an entirely appropriate and relaxed atmosphere. Sensibly, the menu changes frequently depending on the availability of fresh produce, and concentrates on excellent local fish, shellfish and steaks. As the premises are unlicensed, guests are welcome to take their own wine.

Open all year except Christmas Day,

1 Jan, 2 wks Apr + last 2 wks Sep
Dining Room/Restaurant Lunch 12 – 2.30 pm (a-b)
Afternoon Tea
Dinner 6.30 – 9.30 pm except Mon Tue (c)
Note: closed Mon Tue from Oct to Jun
Unlicensed – guests welcome to take own wine
No smoking in restaurant
Baked turbot. Halibut topped with prawns in a dill cream sauce with mussels. Lemon sole with a smoked salmon coulis.
No credit cards
Proprietors: Alan & Evelyn Bogue

DALMAHOY HOTEL, GOLF & COUNTRY CLUB

Kirknewton
nr Edinburgh EH27 8EB
Tel: 031 333 1845
Fax: 031 335 3203

On A71 Edinburgh-Kilmarnock, 7 miles from Edinburgh city centre.

Little more than 15 minutes from the city centre, this first class country club is equally convenient for local citizens and visitors to the city. Dalmahoy has had a distinguished past and in its new form is heading for a successful future. It is set in rolling acres of beautiful little lochs, burns and trees with views of Edinburgh Castle and the city. There is a first class leisure club and two challenging golf courses, one of which is of championship standards. The Pentland Restaurant, which is on two levels, has stately regency columns and is given over to elegant dining from menus which have obviously been drawn up by a chef who really knows his job. Food is markedly good, interestingly different and very well presented.

Open all year

Rooms: 115 with private facilities
Bar Meals 9.30 am – 9.45 pm (a)
Dining Room/Restaurant Lunch 12.30 –
2 pm except Sun Sat (b)
Dinner 7 – 9.45 pm (d)
No dogs
Facilities for the disabled
Bed & breakfast £55 - £150
Dariole of west coast lobster served on a
bed of fine vegetables with juices of the
lobster scented with sweet basil. Pot
roast of corn-fed chicken cooked with
champagne, shallots and mushrooms.
Tuille basket of local strawberries with
vanilla pod ice cream and champagne
sabayon.
STB Commended 5 Crowns
Credit cards: 1, 2, 3, 6

DUBH PRAIS RESTAURANT
123B High Street
Edinburgh EH1 1SG
Tel: 031 557 5732
Fax: 031 557 5732
Edinburgh Royal Mile.
The Scandic Crown Hotel in the High
Street is sufficiently prominent to be
used as a marker and it is important to
have one because Dubh Prais, directly
opposite the hotel, has a frontage of
only three feet – the width of a door –
and you can walk past it without being
aware of it. That would be a pity because
here is a warm cosy and intimate little
cellar restaurant with good food and
good atmosphere. James McWilliams,
the chef/proprietor, has built up a very
successful restaurant based on good
produce from the pick of the market,
cooked with a light and skilled touch.
The menu is sufficiently extensive to
provide adequate choice without being
overdone. The restaurant is rightly
popular with locals and visitors alike but
it is small so do book in advance,
especially during the Summer season.
Open all year except 2 wks Christmas +
2 wks Easter
Dining Room/Restaurant Lunch 12 –
2 pm Tue to Fri (a)
Dinner 6.30 – 10.30 pm Tue to Sat (c)
Closed Sun Mon

Light pheasant and watercress mousse,
saddle of hare, duck and bramble sauce,
poached wild salmon, Mallaig scallops
and Aberdeen Angus steak – just a few
of the dishes you could expect to find on
the menu.
Credit cards: 1, 2, 3
Proprietors: James & Heather
McWilliams

GEORGE INTER-CONTINENTAL EDINBURGH
George Street
Edinburgh EH3 2PB
Tel: 031 225 1251
Fax: 031 226 5644
City centre of Edinburgh.
One of Edinburgh's premier hotels the
George Inter-Continental is a long
established prestigious hotel with a high
reputation. Its central location in the
New Town gives it a convenient proximity
to the main attractions of the capital. Le
Chambertin Restaurant serves the finest
of good food in a comfortable and
relaxed atmosphere and is a favourite of
the business community while the
Carvers Table in its lofty pillared
grandeur concentrates primarily on
traditional roasts. The Clans Bar has a
predominantly Scottish theme and
exhibits artifacts and curios of the
whisky trade. Many of the 195
comfortable bedrooms have superb
views over the city.
Open all year
Rooms: 195 with private facilities
Bar Meals 11 am – 10 pm (a)
Dining Room/Restaurant Lunch
(Chambertin) 12.30 – 2.30 pm except
Sun Sat (b)
Dining Room/Restaurant Lunch (Carvers
Table) 12.30 – 2.30 pm (b)
Dinner (Chambertin) 6.30 – 10.30 pm
except Sun (b)

Dinner (Carvers Table) 6.30 –
10.30 pm (b)
Note: Chambertin closed Sun
No smoking area in restaurant
Bed & breakfast £87 – £137
Dinner B & B £103 – £153
Room Rate £125 – £150
Baked tartlet of Lanark Blue cheese with
a poached pear and garden fresh herbs.
Tenderloin of lamb with roast shallots
and garlic on a light rosemary glaze.
Poached fillet of salmon in a pink
grapefruit butter sauce. Chargrilled king
scallops on a bed of tomatoes with
warm balsamic vinaigrette and soy
sauce.
STB Commended 5 Crowns
Credit cards: 1, 2, 3, 5, 6

GRINDLAYS RESTAURANT
8-10 Grindlay Street
Edinburgh EH3 9AS
Tel: 031 229 5405
Adjacent to Royal Lyceum Theatre and
Usher Hall.
In its second year, Grindlays has had
some refurbishment and behind the red
canopies and astragalled windows is a
small quality restaurant. The location
has everything going for it – a few yards
from Saltire Court, the financial heart of
the city, adjacent to the Lyceum Theatre
and Usher Hall, a few hundred yards
from the Lothian Road cinemas on one
side and Castle Terrace multi-storey car
park on the other. The restaurant itself
is tastefully decorated and skilfully laid
out to create the impression of small
and intimate dining rooms rather than a
large impersonal one. The menu is
interestingly different with some
traditional favourites alongside a good
range of well prepared but not over-fussy
dishes created from good daily fresh
market produce. Grindlays opens from
6 pm so that you may eat before a
theatre show or concert – or even have
one or two courses and come back after
the show for a dessert or cheese and
coffee.
Open all year except Boxing Day + 1 Jan
Dining Room/Restaurant Lunch 12 –
2.30 pm except Sun (a)
Dinner 6 – 10.30 pm except Sun (b)
Closed Sun
Smoked salmon pâté. Breast of duck in
tarragon sauce. Salmon with julienne of
vegetables en papillote. Chicken in a
basil and mustard sauce.
Credit cards: 1, 3, 5 + SWITCH
Proprietor: Lady Peta Linlithgow

Credit Card Code		Meal Price Code	
1.	Access/Mastercard/Eurocard	(a)	under £10
2.	American Express	(b)	£10 – £15
3.	Visa	(c)	£15 – £20
4.	Carte Bleu	(d)	£20 – £25
5.	Diners Club	(e)	£25 – £30
6.	Mastercharge	(f)	over £30

HENDERSON'S SALAD TABLE

94 Hanover Street
Edinburgh EH2 1DR
Tel: 031 225 2131

2 minutes from Princes Street under Henderson's wholefood shop.

Henderson's has graced the Edinburgh scene for 30 years and was a pioneer of healthy eating in the city. It has a devoted clientele and it is not unusual to almost queue to get in. Henderson's features a continuous buffet of fresh salads, quiches, savouries and sweets, all prepared with care and served in an informal atmosphere. It specialises in wholefood, vegetarian and vegan dishes and seats up to 200! Live music in the evenings. Several have tried to imitate the Henderson formula but none has succeeded to beat the original and the best.

Open all year except Christmas + Boxing Days, 1 + 2 Jan
Meals served all day from 11.30 am; open from 8 am
Breakfast 8 – 11.30 am except Sun (a)
Lunch 11.30 am – 3 pm except Sun (a)
Dinner 4.30 – 10.15 pm except Sun (a)
Closed Sun except during Edinburgh Festival
Main restaurant areas non smoking
Wide selection of herb teas, wines from growers using organic methods, hand-made bakery items made with stoneground flour, free range eggs.
Credit cards: 1, 2, 3
Proprietors: The Henderson Family

THE HOWARD

32/36 Great King Street
Edinburgh EH3 6QH
Tel: 031 557 3500
Fax: 031 557 6515

Great King Street is off Dundas Street, the continuation of Hanover Street – 5 minutes from Princes Street.

Surprisingly perhaps, Edinburgh does not have many town house hotels though its quiet Georgian terraces in the New Town lend themselves to the concept. The elegant and luxurious Howard Hotel therefore has its own place in the market. Within comfortable walking distance of Princes Street – though most of it uphill! – it is centrally located yet remote from the bustle of the main traffic routes. The hotel has been beautifully furnished and the high standards of the public areas are carried through to the kitchen from which skilful and creative young chefs present an

interesting menu which should satisfy the most exacting diner. The Number Thirty Six Restaurant is not normally open at lunchtime, but by prior arrangement lunch can be provided there.

Open all year
Rooms: 16 with private facilities
Dining Room/Restaurant Lunch – by prior arrangement only
Dinner 7.30 – 9.30 pm (e)
Dogs by arrangement
Bed & breakfast £90 – £127.50
Dinner B & B rates on application
Platter of oak smoked salmon and quails eggs and caviar. Roast saddle of Rannoch Moor venison served with a juniper berry and cranberry jus. Fillet of Aberdeen Angus beef with a wild mushroom and Scotch whisky sauce, on a bed of wild rice. Rendezvous of Scottish seafood and shellfish with a lime and herb cream sauce.
STB Commended 4 Crowns
Credit cards: 1, 2, 3, 5, 6

IGG'S RESTAURANT

15 Jeffrey Street
Edinburgh EH1 1DR
Tel: 031 557 8184

Off the Royal Mile.

This is a very interesting restaurant in a street just off the Royal Mile which has a reputation for its small interesting shops. The unusual name is derived from the first name of the proprietor, Ignacio Campos, who runs the restaurant personally. He has a wealth of catering experience behind him and this is a dignified yet relatively relaxed restaurant,

with a bright interior and good standards of food preparation and presentation. "Specials" on the menu change daily dependent on the availability of produce in the market. Spanish and French spoken.

Open all year
Dining Room/Restaurant Lunch 12 – 2 pm except Sun Mon (a)
Dinner 6 – 10.30 pm except Sun Mon (b-d)
Closed Sun Mon
No smoking area in restaurant
Roulade of smoked salmon and crab mousse with a watercress and lemon purée. Fillets of lemon sole and queenie scallops poached in white wine with a pink peppercorn and grapefruit sauce. Tournedos of Scottish beef brushed with chopped rosemary and mustard, served on a sweet pimento sauce.
Credit cards: 1, 2, 3, 5
Proprietor: Ignacio Campos

JACKSON'S RESTAURANT

209-213 High Street
2 Jackson Close, Royal Mile
Edinburgh EH1 1PL
Tel: 031 225 1793
Fax: 031 220 0620

On the Royal Mile.

An interesting cellar restaurant on the Royal Mile that bustles from noon till late at night. Its location attracts a great many tourists and locals who enjoy the Scottish emphasis in a number of dishes. The lunchtime menu is remarkably inexpensive but there is more serious eating and more realistic pricing in the evenings. A private dining room is available for parties of up to 45. The ambience of the place and the cheerful friendly service give Jackson's a special cachet.

Open all year except Christmas + Boxing Days, 1 + 2 Jan
Dining Room/Restaurant Lunch 12 – 2 pm except Sun Sat (a)
Dinner 6 – 11 pm (d)
Extended hours during Edinburgh Festival
Fillet of Scotch lamb coated with a truffle and yellow chanterelle duxelle, wrapped in strudel leaves and garnished with roasted pear. Prime Aberdeen Angus steaks with speciality sauces. Rack of Scotch lamb baked pink with a garlic and pine kernel crust, on an elderflower and rosemary sauce. Fillet of Tay salmon baked in Crabbies green ginger wine and finished with a delicate lime sauce.
Credit cards: 1, 2, 3
Proprietor: Lyn MacKinnon

KEEPERS RESTAURANT
13B Dundas Street
Edinburgh EH3 6QG
Tel: 031 556 5707/0831 185792

Dundas Street (continuation of Hanover Street) is to north of Princes Street.
This is an unusual cellar restaurant in a Georgian basement in the New Town. There are three cellar rooms with their original stone floors and walls so there is always a pleasing element of intimacy and lack of distracting bustle. The menu is fairly straightforward with good wholesome cooking the order of the day rather than extravagant frills. Individual rooms or indeed the whole restaurant can be reserved for business or private functions.
Open all year except Boxing Day + 1 Jan
Dining Room/Restaurant Lunch 12 – 2 pm (b-c)
Dinner 6 – 10 pm (b-c)
Pre-theatre meals 6 – 7 pm (a)
No smoking area in restaurant
Haggis and leek parcels. Quail filled with pink peppercorn mousse on a pepper sauce. Fillet of salmon with squat lobsters in a citrus sauce. Venison steak in a sauce of cranberry, Port and mustard. Fillet of Scotch lamb with an elderberry and orange sauce.
Credit cards: 1, 2, 3, 5
Proprietor: Sheena Marshall

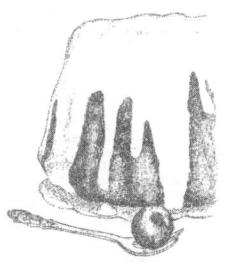

KELLY'S RESTAURANT
46 West Richmond Street
Edinburgh EH6 9DZ
Tel: 031 668 3847

West Richmond Street is off Clerk Street (continuation of North Bridge from east end of Princes Street) convenient for the Queen's Hall and the new Festival Theatre.
A really delightful and friendly little restaurant which has established itself very firmly as a favourite eating place for discerning diners looking for something special in the way of food, and a warm comfortable atmosphere in which to enjoy it. The Kellys are a charming couple, very much in evidence, and exercising close personal supervision of their restaurant. Jacque Kelly, sensibly, operates a limited but well balanced menu emphasising prime Scottish produce and the fact that it is almost impossible to get a table without booking in advance, speaks for itself. A place to which you will almost certainly want to return.
Open all year except 1 to 3 Jan + 1 to 18 Oct
Dinner 6.30 – 9.30 pm except Sun Mon (d)
Closed Sun Mon
Diners requested not to smoke until after 9 pm
Smoked Scottish salmon with mushrooms in Pernod sauce. Border lamb cutlets with orange Grand Marnier and rosemary glaze. Scallops poached in cream, Spring onion and whisky sauce. Chocolate box surprise.
Credit cards: 1, 2, 3
Proprietor: Jacque Kelly

LIGHTBODY'S RESTAURANT & BAR
23 Glasgow Road
Edinburgh EH12 8HW
Tel: 031 334 2300

On main Corstorphine road out of Edinburgh towards the airport and Glasgow.
A family run bar restaurant on the busy road out through Corstorphine towards Glasgow. It is a popular rendezvous for the local business community and for special evening-out groups. The dining area is cheerfully set out with fresh flowers and colourful napkins and many pictures on the walls. A special three course businessman's lunch is very good value and portions are generous. A much broader à la carte menu is also available and offers a wide range of choice.
Open all year except Christmas Day, 26 Dec, 1 + 2 Jan
Bar Lunch 12 – 2 pm except Sun (a)
Dining Room/Restaurant Lunch 12 – 2 pm except Sun (a-b)
Bar Supper 6 – 9.30 pm except Sun Sat (a)
Dinner 6 – 10 pm except Sun (c)
Closed Sun
Mussel and onion soup with sherry and cream. Pan-fried fillet of trout with mushrooms, tomato, onion, capers and cream. Steak with crushed peppercorns flamed in brandy and cream. Haunch of venison in red wine with onions, mushroom and orange. Fresh lobster, salmon, mussels in season.
Credit cards: 1, 2, 3
Proprietors: Malcolm & Norman Lightbody

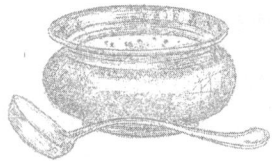

MARTINS RESTAURANT
70 Rose Street North Lane
Edinburgh EH2 3DX
Tel: 031 225 3106

In the north lane off Rose Street between Frederick Street and Castle Street.
This is one of Edinburgh's best kept secrets. Martins is not a place you stumble upon; it is tucked away in a service lane in the city centre and you have to know where it is to find it. It is most certainly worth doing so for Martins is one of the very best restaurants in the capital. When you do find it you will experience a charming well appointed little restaurant where the welcome will be so warm and genuine that you will immediately feel special. Chef Forbes Stott's menus change daily, use only the very best ingredients and present food of the highest calibre which has recently earned three Rosettes from the Automobile Association. Martin Irons and his wife Gay run this delightful restaurant with style yet in an easy relaxed way, and make it a special place to eat.
Open all year except 24 Dec to 24 Jan, 28 Jun to 2 Jul, 24 Sep to 3 Oct
Dining Room Lunch 12 – 2 pm except Sun Mon Sat (c-e)
Dinner 7 – 10 pm except Sun Mon (e)
Closed Sun Mon
No smoking in dining areas
Menus are based on the availability of fresh local produce, are regularly changed and specialise in fresh Scottish seafish, shellfish and game.
Credit cards: 1, 2, 3, 5, 6
Proprietors: Martin & Gay Irons

NORTON HOUSE HOTEL
Ingliston, Edinburgh
Midlothian EH28 8LX
Tel: 031 333 1275
Fax: 031 333 5305

Just off A8, 6 miles from Edinburgh city centre, on the road to Glasgow.
On the outskirts of Edinburgh, only minutes from the airport and the central Scotland motorway network, Norton House is set in acres of secluded parkland. The original house retains much of the original character and air of quiet luxury. The Conservatory Restaurant is one of the city's top eating venues, has two Rosettes for its food and service, and exemplifies the creative skills of the team of Scottish chefs. The Tavern has a much more informal style and features a walled garden and barbecue area. Bedrooms are excellently furnished and equipped. The whole house exudes an air of gracious living and the high standards that so distinguish Richard Branson's Virgin Group of which this is a part.
Open all year
Rooms: 47 with private facilities
Bar Lunch 12 – 2.30 pm (a)
Dining Room/Restaurant Lunch 12 – 2.30 pm except Sat (b)
Bar Supper 5.30 – 9.30 pm (a)
Dinner 7 – 9.30 pm (c)
Facilities for the disabled
No smoking area in restaurant
Bed & breakfast £60 – £80
Dinner B & B £52.50 – £67.50
Warm oak smoked Scottish salmon with caviar and cucumber butter. Mallaig scallops with a hot potato salad. Saddle of Scottish venison with raspberry sauce.
STB Highly Commended 5 Crowns
Credit cards: 1, 2, 3, 5, 6 + SWITCH

OLD BORDEAUX COACH HOUSE
47 Old Burdiehouse Road
Edinburgh EH17 8BJ
Tel: 031 664 1734

Just off A720 city bypass (Straiton junction), on A701 heading into Edinburgh.
This district of Edinburgh developed at the time when Mary Queen of Scots arrived from the French Court with her retinue. Burdiehouse is a corruption of 'Bordeaux House'. The Old Bordeaux Coach House was at one time the abode of exiled French silk weavers. Today it is a warm welcoming old world inn of character. There is indeed a fine old world feel to it and it has been furnished in appropriate style with attention to traditional comforts. This is a popular venue for citizens of Edinburgh, set in well kept gardens. You can enjoy eating by the log fire in the cosy lounge, or watching the world go by from the conservatory. French and German spoken.
Open all year except Christmas + Boxing Days, 1 + 2 Jan
Food service 9.30 am – 10 pm (a-b)
Facilities for the disabled
Baked catfish in oatmeal. Oxtails with sage dumplings. Cod stuffed with scallops and prawns. Steak and kidney pie. Roast beef and Yorkshire pudding.
Credit cards: 1, 2, 3, 5
Proprietors: Alan & Linda Thomson, Adrian Dempsey

ROCK CAFE RESTAURANT
18 Howe Street
Edinburgh EH3 6TG
Tel: 031 225 7225

Howe Street (continuation of Frederick Street) is to north of Princes Street.
The Rock Cafe's decor may be reminiscent of the '60s and '70s with its huge murals of rock stars past and present, but this is a serious eating place which will appeal to all age groups. There is a marked tendency towards modern day eating styles in some of the dishes on offer, but there are also excellent steaks served in a variety of interesting ways, specialities such as salmon en croûte and dishes of the day listed on the blackboard. Our inspector "thought this place was great. The food may be American style but it was all cooked superbly."
Open all year
Open 12 – 11 pm Sat only
Dinner 5 – 11 pm except Sun (b–c)
Closed Sun

Aberdeen Angus steaks and burgers. Scottish salmon fillet with a prawn sauce. Chicken supreme filled with spinach, Gruyere and garlic. Fish of the day. Fresh pasta.
Credit cards: 1, 3
Proprietor: John Mackay

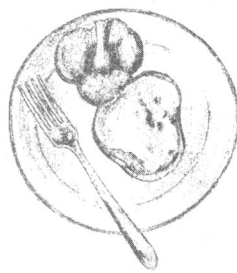

THE ROUND TABLE
31 Jeffrey Street
Edinburgh EH1 1DH
Tel: 031 557 3032

Off the Royal Mile and less than five minutes walk from Waverley Station.
The Round Table has the appearance and many of the attributes of a traditional cafe bistro. Money has not been wasted attempting to create a trendy theme or a pseudo atmosphere. The restaurant probably takes its name from the many round tables which seem to be a feature of it and these, with the assortment of stout wooden chairs on polished wooden floors, provide a simple but effective enough ambience. The menu leans heavily towards seafood but meat-eaters are not forgotten and there are some good value for money dishes. An inexpensive "shoppers lunch" and a modestly priced dinner menu will appeal to many.
Open all year except Christmas + New Year's Days
Open from 10 am
Dining Room/Restaurant Lunch 12 – 5.30 pm except Sun (a)
Dinner 6 – 10 pm Tue to Sat (a)
Closed Sun except during Edinburgh Festival
Fillets of beef with pickled walnut and a rich sauce. Smoked haddock in a cream leek sauce. Raspberry cranachan with malt whisky.
Credit card: 1
Proprietors: Anne & Robert Winter

SCANDIC CROWN HOTEL

80 High Street, Royal Mile
Edinburgh EH1 1TH
Tel: 031 557 9797 • Telex: 727298
Fax: 031 557 9789

Centre of the Royal Mile tourist area.
Edinburgh's newest luxury four star hotel is situated right on the Royal Mile in the heart of the city, ideal for exploring the Old Town. The traditional exterior gives way to a spacious modern interior which combines the best of Scotland and Scandinavia to good effect. Food in The Jewel Restaurant is of high standard, specialising in produce of distinctly Scottish origin, but of course as befits the name of the hotel there is another restaurant where you can ring the changes and indulge in traditional Smorgasbord. There is a well equipped leisure centre and – exceptional in a city centre hotel – a large undercover and on site car park, giving direct access to the hotel.
Open all year except 3 + 4 Jan
Rooms: 238 with private facilities
Dining Room/Restaurant Lunch 12 – 2.30 pm (b)
Dinner 6.30 – 10.30 pm (c-d)
Facilities for the disabled
No smoking area in restaurant
Bed & breakfast from £74
Room Rate £89 – £155
Pockets of finest smoked Scottish salmon filled with marinated salmon, dill, capers and shallots accompanied by a light mustard dressing. Prime fillet of Angus beef, pan-fried with whole shallots and surrounded by a truffle sauce, topped with a garlic cream. Poached loin of Border lamb with crispy savoy cabbage served with creamy horseradish sauce and studded with redcurrants.
Credit cards: 1, 2, 3, 5, 6

SHERATON GRAND HOTEL

1 Festival Square
Edinburgh EH3 9SR
Tel: 031 229 9131
Telex: 72398
Fax: 031 229 6254

Lothian Road opposite Usher Hall and only 5 minutes from Princes Street.
The Sheraton has emerged from its major refurbishment with its grandeur and its stature enhanced. The functional aspects of the original building have been replaced with fine traditional materials and a warmth and richness that confirm its position as one of the leading hotels of the city. It is of course superbly sited opposite the Usher Hall, The Royal Lyceum and Traverse Theatres, and only a few minutes walk from the King's Theatre in one direction and from Princes Street in the other. Edinburgh's new international conference centre is being built adjacent to the hotel which also has its own splendid conference suites. The superb new Grill Room Restaurant is elegant and sumptuous and offers a fine selection of choice food based on the best of Scotland's prime produce, while the Terrace Restaurant looks out on to the fountains of Festival Square and has an all-day service of light meals and snacks with the same dedication to quality as the neighbouring Grill Room. This new-look Sheraton is surely a winner. Children are welcome. French, Italian, German and Spanish spoken.
Open all year
Rooms: 263 with private facilities
Food served in the Terrace 11 am – 11 pm (b)
Lunch (Grill) 12 – 2.30 pm except Sun Sat (d)
Dinner (Grill) 7 – 10.30 pm except Sun (e)
No smoking areas in restaurants + lounge
Room Rate £130 – £170
Weekend rates on application
Home-smoked Scottish salmon with nettles and bacon. Loin of Ayrshire lamb with stovies and garden vegetables.
STB Deluxe 5 Crowns
Credit cards: 1, 2, 3, 5, 6

THE TATTLER

23 Commercial Street, Leith
Edinburgh EH6 6JA
Tel: 031 554 9999

On corner of main road in Leith port area (north Edinburgh).
A cosy Victorian style pub and restaurant, in an area now enjoying a resurgence of bustle and interest and in which some highly acclaimed eating places have become established. The Tattler's menu is extensive, covering a wide range of seafood, meat, poultry and vegetarian dishes. Dessert items have not always been a strong point but more attention is now being given to these. The Tattler enjoys a good reputation locally and is a popular lunchtime rendezvous for Leith business people while in the evening it attracts clientele from a much wider area.
Open all year except Christmas Day + 1 Jan
Bar Lunch 12 – 2.30 pm Sun to Fri (a-b)
Dining Room/Restaurant Lunch 12 – 2.30 pm Sun to Fri (b-c)
Bar Supper 6 – 10 pm Sun to Fri (a-b)
Dinner 6 – 10 pm Sun to Fri (b-c)
Note: meals available all day Sat
Venison, duck, scallops and monkfish etc, as well as traditional dishes such as steak pie, liver and bacon, mince and oatmeal potatoes.
Credit cards: 1, 2, 3, 5, 6
Proprietors: Alan & Linda Thomson

THE WITCHERY BY THE CASTLE

Castlehill, Royal Mile
Edinburgh EH1 1NE
Tel: 031 225 5613
Fax: 031 220 4392

Situated at the entrance to Edinburgh Castle.
The Witchery survives the tourist crush to remain intimate, friendly and quite unique. Already steeped in eight centuries of history, it claims once to have been the very centre of witchcraft in the Old Town and the Witchery restaurant captivates this atmosphere. The Secret Garden restaurant was formerly a school playground which has been carefully converted to retain the atmosphere of bygone days, but is fully contemporary in regard to style and presentation of food.
Open all year except Christmas Day
Bar Lunch 12 – 3 pm (a)
Dining Room/Restaurant Lunch 12 – 4 pm (a)
Dinner 4 – 11 pm (c)

Reservations advisable
Warm salad of wild mushrooms and toasted pine kernels with a honey dressing. Collops of venison in a red berry sauce.
Credit cards: 1, 2, 3, 5, 6
Proprietor: James Thomson

Elgin

Map 5

MANSEFIELD HOUSE HOTEL
Mayne Road, Elgin
Moray IV30 1NY
Tel: 0343 540883
Fax: 0343 552491

Just off A96 in Elgin. From Inverness, drive towards town centre and turn right at first roundabout. At mini-roundabout, hotel on right.
A gracious old Georgian town house which has been tastefully converted to its present role and stands amid beautifully kept flower beds and garden. There is a gymnasium and sauna room and everywhere a high standard of decor and comfort. The dining room is quite sumptuous and a delightful place in which to relax and enjoy some of Chef Robin Murray's renowned cooking. There is a very extensive menu but, rightly, a concentration on the abundance of excellent fish for which the north east is noted. En suite bedrooms have all the little accessories that are a feature of good hotels nowadays. There are facilities for conferences and private parties.
Open all year
Rooms: 17 with private facilities
Dining Room/Restaurant Lunch 12 – 2.30 pm except Sun: 12.30 -2.30 pm Sun (a)
Dinner 6.30 – 9.30 pm Sun to Thu: 6.30 – 10.30 pm Fri Sat (c)
No dogs
Facilities for the disabled
No smoking in restaurant
Bed & breakfast from £45
Dinner B & B from £62.50
Fresh lobster, scallops and oysters from own tank. Fresh shellfish and fish daily from Lossiemouth and Buckie harbour.
STB Highly Commended 4 Crowns
Credit cards: 1, 2, 3 + SWITCH
Proprietors: Ross & Kathleen Murray

THE MANSION HOUSE HOTEL
The Haugh, Elgin
Moray IV30 1AN
Tel: 0343 548811

Located ¼ mile from main road, on north east side of Elgin.
This old 19th century baronial type mansion is really in the centre of the town yet the parkland and beautiful grounds around it suggest it is in the country. It has some lovely architectural features and the furnishings and decor are of a high standard throughout. Bedrooms have every modern comfort and there is a leisure centre and swimming pool. The Mansion House enjoys a good reputation locally for food and service, and its function suite is much in demand. The menu is priced in an unusual way but it gives clear evidence of having been carefully planned with some very interesting combinations of flavour. Elgin is a pleasing old town from which to visit the many castles in the north-east or follow the whisky trails.
Open all year
Rooms: 22 with private facilities
Bar Lunch 12 – 2 pm (a)
Dining Room/Restaurant Lunch 12 – 2 pm (b)
Dinner 7.30 – 9 pm (d)
Bed & breakfast £55 – £75
Dinner B & B £70 – £90
Pastry chest overflowing with seafood. Poached salmon garnished with fresh scampi. Baked venison with forest fruits. Roast prime fillets of beef. Noisettes of lamb with walnuts and grapes.
STB Highly Commended 5 Crowns
Credit cards: 1, 2, 3, 5
Proprietor: Fernando de Oliveira

Elie

Map 4

BOUQUET GARNI RESTAURANT
51 High Street, Elie
Fife KY9 1BZ
Tel: 0333 330374

A delightful little restaurant in the centre of this charming East Neuk town. With ample supplies of fresh fish and seafood on its doorstep the Bouquet Garni naturally specialises in high quality fish dishes but with a complementary range of other typical Scottish fare. The intimate and cosy candlelit dining room is almost certain to appeal to the connoisseur of good food. Well worth a

detour. A little French spoken.
Open all year except Christmas + Boxing Days, 1 + 2 Jan also first 2 wks Jan + 14 to 19 Nov
Bar Lunch 12 – 2 pm (a)
Dining Room/Restaurant Lunch 12 – 1.30 pm except Tue: open for Lunch 7 days in Summer (b)
Dinner 7 – 9.30 pm except Sun (b-c)
Note: Nov to Feb closed all day Sun
No smoking area in restaurant
Rich langoustine and tomato flavoured bisque. Fillet of salmon with langoustine mousse and creamed leeks, on a Muscadet sauce of potato, chives and cheese. Strawberry shortcake with Glayva liqueur cream and sweet butterscotch sauce.
Credit cards: 1, 2, 3
Proprietors: Andrew & Norah Keracher

Erbusaig
by Kyle of Lochalsh

Map 6

THE OLD SCHOOLHOUSE RESTAURANT
"Tigh Fasgaidh"
Erbusaig, Kyle
Ross-shire IV40 8BB
Tel: 0599 4369

Outskirts of Erbusaig on Kyle-Plockton road.
A charming old 19th century schoolhouse in its own grounds, retaining all of its atmosphere of the past yet comfortably converted to satisfy the high standards of today. Imaginative cuisine makes full use of all the wonderful shellfish and fish so readily available locally. The menu is reasonably priced and well balanced, and there is obviously culinary skill in its execution. Booking advisable.
Open 1 Apr to 31 Oct
Rooms: 2 with private facilities
Dinner 7 – 10.30 pm (b-d)
Bed & breakfast £18 – £30
Fresh whole prawns from local creels. Scallops wrapped in bacon and grilled,

served with a Glayva sauce. Roast rack of lamb served with a mint and white wine sauce. Monkfish tail with a herb and tomato sauce. Wine-poached salmon with a Hollandaise dill sauce.
STB Award Pending
Credit cards: 1, 3
Proprietors: Calum & Joanne Cumine

Fairlie

Map 3

FINS RESTAURANT
Fencefoot Farm, Fairlie
Ayrshire KA29 0EG
Tel: 0475 568989
Fax: 0475 568921

On A78, 1 mile south of Fairlie near Largs.
A pretty selection of terracotta planters filled with fuchsias and geraniums brighten the outside of this tastefully converted barn, and inside there are beamed ceilings, whitewashed walls and a cheerful dining room atmosphere. Fish dominates the menu and rightly so because the seafish and shellfish are something special. Bernard and Jill Thain also have their own fish farms and smokery and you can be assured that everything is absolutely fresh. Indeed the whole philosophy of this venture is that fish and shellfish are the most wonderful foods in the world so long as they are fresh. There are, of course, some non-fish items and vegetarian dishes are also featured. This is a busy place so do book in advance.
Open all year
Dining Room/Restaurant Lunch 12 – 2.30 pm except Mon (a)
Dinner 6.45 – 10 pm except Sun Mon (c)
Closed Mon
Facilities for the disabled
Seafood is the order of the day....Pacific oysters, smoked salmon and trout, salmon gravadlax, fish pâtés and marinades. Lobster and squat lobster. Mussels and crab.
Credit cards: 1, 2, 3, 5
Proprietors: Bernard & Jill Thain

Falkirk

Map 4

INCHYRA GRANGE HOTEL
Grange Road, Polmont
Falkirk FK2 0YB
Tel: 0324 711911 • Telex: 777693
Fax: 0324 716134

Junction 4 or 5, M9 motorway. Situated on border of Polmont/Grangemouth.
A fine Scottish country house set in eight acres of private grounds. It has been extended and modernised to a high degree of comfort and modern amenity. There is a leisure club available to residents with swimming pool, spa bath, sauna, snooker room and solarium. The restaurant has a very comprehensive menu with some interesting and unusual dishes, including a vegetarian option. Prices are modest.
Open all year
Rooms: 43 with private facilities
Bar Lunch 12 – 2 pm (a)
Dining Room/Restaurant Lunch 12.30 – 2 pm except Sat (a)
Bar Supper 6 – 10 pm (a)
Dinner 7 – 9.30 pm (c)
Bed & breakfast £30 – £80
Dinner B & B £40 – £50
Lobster and bacon chowder. Scottish seafood served in a pancake with a creamy cheese sauce. Oven roasted fillet of lamb with a honey and rosemary glaze. Poached fillet of salmon with a sauce of fresh dill, cream, onions and white wine.
STB Commended 4 Crowns
Credit cards: 1, 2, 3, 5, 6

STAKIS FALKIRK PARK HOTEL
Camelon Road
Falkirk FK1 5RY
Tel: 0324 28331 • Telex: 776502
Fax: 0324 611593

On A803 west of town centre.
Set back from the road on a hill overlooking a quiet park, is the Stakis Falkirk Park Hotel. It is ideally located less than one hour from Glasgow and Edinburgh. The well appointed bedrooms all include private facilities, radio, TV, telephone and hospitality tray. For the business user, function facilities from five to 200. The hotel's restaurant boasts à la carte menus specialising in 'Taste of Scotland' dishes.
Open all year
Rooms: 55 with private facilities

Bar Lunch 12.30 – 2 pm except Sun (a)
Dining Room/Restaurant Lunch 12.30 – 2.30 pm except Sat (a)
Dinner 7 – 10 pm (b)
Bed & breakfast £48 – £77.50
Dinner B & B £61.95 – £91.45 (min 2 nights stay)
Room Rate £39.50 – £69
STB Commended 4 Crowns
Credit cards: 1, 2, 3, 5, 6

Falkland

Map 4

COVENANTER HOTEL
The Square, Falkland
Fife KY7 7BU
Tel: 0337 857542/857224

Centre of Falkland.
George and Margaret Menzies are well established hosts at this 17th century coaching inn almost opposite Falkland Palace. They have been running the Covenanter for 15 years during which time it has steadily increased its profile and its reputation for good honest food, good service and warm hospitality. There is a choice of eating styles, either in the traditional restaurant or the informal bistro. In addition to the hotel accommodation, there is also a selection of self-catering cottages available in the village.
Open all year
Rooms: 4 with private facilities
Bar Lunch 12 – 2 pm except Mon (a)
Dining Room/Restaurant Lunch 12 – 2 pm except Mon (a)
Bar Supper 5.30 – 9.30 pm except Mon (a)
Dinner 7 – 9 pm except Mon (b)
(table d'hôte + à la carte dinner menus available)
Closed Mon
No dogs
Bed & breakfast £25 – £37.50
Dinner B & B £37.50 – £50
A selection of made to order dishes with emphasis on home produce. Scampi Falkland, Tay salmon, and Scottish beef dishes.
STB Commended 3 Crowns
Credit cards: 1, 2, 3, 5
Proprietors: George & Margaret Menzies

KIND KYTTOCK'S KITCHEN
Cross Wynd, Falkland
Fife KY7 7BE
Tel: 0337 857477

Off main street in village.
Falkland must be one of Fife's most charming villages. Not only is it steeped in history but it has fascinating architecture and also seems to be a frequent winner of Best Kept Village Awards. It is a place to walk around and enjoy, and when you do so you will come across Kind Kyttock's Kitchen. This delightful little restaurant and tearoom is something special, dedicated to delicious home-baking in the traditional Scottish manner. It is one of a vanishing breed, and you should not visit Falkland without enjoying the ambience of the place and the good things it has to offer. Kind Kyttock's was winner of The Tea Council's Award for Excellence two years running.
Open all year except Christmas Day to 5 Jan
Food service 12 – 5.30 pm except Mon (a)
Closed Mon
No smoking throughout
Home-baked pancakes, scones, fruit squares, shortbread, wholemeal bread, stovies, cloutie dumpling. Locally grown vegetables used in Scotch broth and at salad table. Selection of teas available.
Credit cards: 1, 3
Proprietor: Bert Dalrymple

Fintry

Map 4

CULCREUCH CASTLE
Culcreuch Castle Country Park, Fintry
Stirlingshire G63 0LW
Tel: 036 086 228/555 • Telex: 557299
Fax: 036 086 555

From Stirling, take A811 west for 10 miles to junction with B822. Turn left to Fintry – 6 miles. From Glasgow, take A81 to Killearn then turn right on B818 to Fintry – 6 miles.
There are castles aplenty in Scotland and while some may lay claim to individual distinction, here is one with it all! Culcreuch has romance – in its close proximity to that most romantic of lochs, Loch Lomond; history – in its 700 years of existence as a fortress home for the Clan Galbraith; ghosts – human, animal and musical – but be re-assured, they are benevolent; and grace, beauty and

dignity in the way in which it has been restored to the elegant country house hotel it is today. Set in a tranquil 1600 acre estate, there are log fires, a cosy dungeon bar, four poster beds and candlelit dinner; and the chef responds to the atmosphere by basing his menus on traditional Scottish fare.
Open all year except 1 Jan (Residents only 1 Jan)
Rooms: 8 with private facilities + 16 lodges
Bar Lunch 12.30 – 2.30 pm (a-c)
Bar Supper 5 – 9 pm (a-c)
Dinner 7 – 8.30 pm (c)
Bed & breakfast £32 – £60
Dinner B & B £52 – £80
Smoked trout fillet with citrus cream. Salmon steak oven-baked with white wine, prawns and capers.
STB Commended 3 Crowns
Credit cards: 1, 2, 3, 5

Fochabers

Map 5

GORDON ARMS HOTEL
80 High Street, Fochabers
Morayshire IV32 7DH
Tel: 0343 820508
Fax: 0343 820300

A96 between Inverness and Aberdeen.
A lovely old coaching inn with roots going back over 200 years. It is conveniently located for all the activities for which Speyside is famous – whisky trails, golf, fishing on the Spey. The hotel retains a lot of the character and atmosphere of bygone days. It offers warm hospitality and good food. There is an interesting à la carte menu complemented by a well balanced wine list.
Open all year
Rooms: 12 with private facilities
Bar Lunch 12 – 2.15 pm (a)
Dining Room/Restaurant Lunch 12 – 2.15 pm (a)
Bar Supper 5 – 9.15 pm (a)
Dinner 7 – 9.15 pm (b)
Facilities for the disabled
Bed & breakfast from £30
Dinner B & B from £37.50
Special rates available
Cornets of smoked salmon with a lime sauce. Langoustines. Noisettes of lamb served with a purée of mint cream sauce. Fillets of venison filled with prunes.
Credit cards: 1, 2, 3, 6

Forfar

Map 4

IDVIES HOUSE
Letham, by Forfar
Angus DD8 2QJ
Tel: 0307 818787
Fax: 0307 818933

B9128 Forfar-Carnoustie, 4 miles east of Forfar towards Craichie/Letham. Hotel is signposted.
First impression of this fine country mansion is of acres of magnificent grounds, impressive mature trees and flowering shrubs. Bedrooms are all en suite and are comfortable and well appointed. The main dining room is bright and cheerful, with large windows overlooking the well kept lawn. The menus are quite extensive with a number of regional speciality dishes and – almost uniquely – offer "granny portions" for senior citizens who may not wish to tackle a large meal. The bar features 150 Scottish malt whiskies. Idvies is personally run by the resident owners who are much in evidence and are assisted by friendly local staff.
Open all year except Christmas Eve Night + Christmas Day Night, 26 to 28 Dec + 1 Jan
Rooms: 10 with private facilities
Bar Lunch 12 – 2 pm (a)
Dining Room/Restaurant Lunch 12 – 2 pm (b)
Bar Supper 6.30 – 9.30 pm except Sun Sat (a)
Dinner 7 – 9.30 pm Mon to Sat: 7 – 8 pm Sun (c)
Bed & breakfast £30 – £50
Dinner B & B £40 – £65
Home-smoked Tay salmon and home-cured gravadlax. Arbroath smokie mousse. Local crab and lobster. Sliced breast of duckling with orange and Drambuie sauce. Collops of Angus venison in a sauce of rowanberry, herbs, celery, shallots and malt whisky.
STB Commended 4 Crowns
Credit cards: 1, 2, 3, 5
Proprietors: Pat & Fay Slingsby, Judy Hill

Forres

Map 5

KNOCKOMIE HOTEL

Grantown Road, Forres
Moray IV36 0SG
Tel: 0309 673146
Fax: 0309 673290

On A940 just south of Forres on Grantown road.

Just on the outskirts of the Royal Burgh of Forres, Knockomie Hotel is set back half a mile from the main road and commands lovely views over the Moray Firth. There is some fine wood panelling in the foyer and a beamed ceiling in the dining room. Bedrooms are very pleasingly furnished and the addition of a further seven en suite bedrooms in 1993 gives the hotel considerably more substance. The new extension includes one ground floor bedroom for disabled guests. Both table d'hôte and à la carte menus are normally available in the dining room and offer a fine choice of some classic and regional dishes. Food is well prepared and presented, of a high standard, and served by smart well trained and polite staff.

Open all year except Christmas
Rooms: 14 with private facilities
Bar Lunch 12 – 2 pm (a)
Dining Room/Restaurant Lunch 12 – 2 pm (b)
Dinner 7 – 9 pm (d)
Bed & breakfast £35 – £69
Dinner B & B £57 – £90
Scottish salmon steak cooked and served in a papillote of buttered vegetables. Pan-fried medallions of lamb with a redcurrant sauce. Fillet of Aberdeen Angus with a brandy and green peppercorn sauce.
STB Commended 4 Crowns
Credit cards: 1, 2, 3, 5
Proprietor: Gavin Ellis

RAMNEE HOTEL

Victoria Road, Forres
Moray IV36 0BN
Tel: 0309 672410
Fax: 0309 673392

A96 Inverness-Aberdeen, off bypass at roundabout at eastern side of Forres – 500 yards on right.

The Royal Burgh of Forres is famous for its award winning gardens in Grant Park, and just across from the park is the Ramnee Hotel set in its own two acres of well manicured lawns and garden. Ramnee was built in 1907 as a private house for Richard Hamblin on his retirement from the Indian Civil Service. It retains much of the opulence and grandeur of that period but has been completely and sensitively refurbished. The en suite bedrooms have all the little extras to be found in a quality hotel and the food is of an extremely high standard, with excellent value table d'hôte lunch and dinner menus augmented by an imaginative à la carte menu. Lighter and more informal meals are also served in Tipplings cocktail lounge. An impressive hotel with smart well trained staff.

Open all year except Christmas Day + 1 to 3 Jan
Rooms: 18 with private facilities
Bar Lunch 12 – 2 pm (a)
Dining Room/Restaurant Lunch 12 – 2 pm (a)
Bar Supper 6 – 9 pm (a)
Dinner 7 – 9 pm (c)
Bed & breakfast £33.50 - £40
Dinner B & B £49 – £56.50
Poached Findhorn salmon flamed in Drambuie. Rack of Scotch lamb with shallots, red wine and redcurrants. Medallion of beef fillet with pickled walnut sauce. Prime Aberdeen Angus steaks.
STB Commended 4 Crowns
Credit cards: 1, 2, 3, 5 + SWITCH

Fort Augustus

Map 6

LOVAT ARMS HOTEL

Fort William Road, Fort Augustus
Inverness-shire PH32 4DU
Tel: 0320 6204/6
Fax: 0320 6677

Set back from the main Fort William-Inverness road (A82), almost exactly half way between these two famous Highland towns.

Only those in a tremendous hurry will resist the temptation to tarry a while in Fort Augustus when travelling between Fort William and Inverness, and those who do will no doubt repair to the Lovat Arms – the dominant hotel in the village. The original 18th century Fort Augustus barracks were erected in what are now the grounds of the hotel and remnants remain in the huge wall alongside the car park. This spacious Victorian hotel in 2½ acres of beautifully kept grounds is redolent of a more leisurely age and is relaxed, comfortable and welcoming. The restaurant relies heavily, and rightly, on a wide range of west coast fish and shellfish together with local game and beef. Food is prepared to a high standard by an award winning chef and bar meals are available in the spacious lounge bar.

Open all year except Christmas Day + mid Jan to mid Feb
Rooms: 21 with private facilities
Bar Lunch 12.30 – 2 pm (a-b)
Dining Room/Restaurant Lunch – parties by arrangement only
Bar Supper 6.30 – 8.30 pm: 6.30 – 9 pm Jun to Sep (a-b)
Dinner 7 – 8.30 pm: 7 – 9 pm Jun to Sep (c)
Bed & breakfast £29.50 – £36.50
Dinner B & B £46 – £56
Mussels, langoustines, pan-fried scallops. Wild Scottish mushrooms in sherry. Own gravadlax, game terrines and pâtés. Medallions of beef. Saddle of lamb. Salmon and seafood. Vegetarian dishes.
STB Commended 3 Crowns
Credit cards: 1, 3
Proprietors: Hector & Mary MacLean

Credit Card Code	Meal Price Code	
1. Access/Mastercard/Eurocard	(a)	under £10
2. American Express	(b)	£10 – £15
3. Visa	(c)	£15 – £20
4. Carte Bleu	(d)	£20 – £25
5. Diners Club	(e)	£25 – £30
6. Mastercharge	(f)	over £30

Fort William

Map 6

CRANNOG SEAFOOD RESTAURANT
Town Pier, Fort William
Inverness-shire PH33 7NG
Tel: 0397 705589/703919
Fax: 0397 705026

Fort William town pier – off A82 Fort William town centre bypass.
It would be lovely to think that every city had a Crannog Seafood Restaurant, but then much of the magic would be lost. This is a really special little restaurant and one that Fort William has long needed. It is located on the town pier and its bright red roofs make it starkly visible on the main road running along the waterfront. A wonderfully integrated business where you can watch the catch being off-loaded directly into the kitchen and shortly afterwards enjoy some of the finest and freshest shellfish you have ever tasted. From the same pier you can then set off on a cruise to Seal Island. This is a speciality restaurant concentrating on wonderfully good seafood; the decor is simple if not spartan so you do not pay for frills but get splendid value for money.
Open all year except Christmas + Boxing Days, 1 + 2 Jan
Dining Room/Restaurant Lunch 12 – 2.30 pm (b)
Dinner 6 – 9.30 pm: 6 – 10.30 pm Jun to Sep (c)
Note: opening times may vary in Winter months
No smoking area in restaurant
Crannog bouillabaisse. Smoked mussels and aioli. Langoustine with hot garlic butter. Salmon en croûte with spinach sauce. Walnut tart and cream.
Credit cards: 1, 3

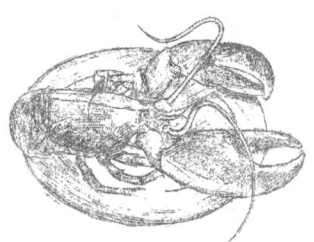

THE MOORINGS HOTEL
Banavie, Fort William
Inverness-shire PH33 7LY
Tel: 0397 772 797
Fax: 0397 772 441

Situated off A830, 3 miles from Fort William, by the Caledonian Canal at Neptune's Staircase.
The Moorings has been quietly improving over recent years and has now been awarded two AA Rosettes, the RAC Merit award and highly commended four crowns by the Scottish Tourist Board. There have been changes too in the comfortable elegant Jacobean Restaurant with its rich colourful ambience. Menus are well balanced, carefully compiled and, in such a location, concentrate rightly on the best of local west coast seafood, Highland game and other prime produce. There is much evidence of skill and expertise in the kitchen with careful combinations of flavour and pleasing presentation. The Head Chef was a finalist in the Taste of Scotland Scotch Lamb Challenge 1993. Smart well trained young staff add to the enjoyment of the dining experience.
Open all year except Christmas + Boxing Days
Rooms: 24 with private facilities
Bar Lunch 12 – 2 pm (a)
Bar Supper 6 – 9.30 pm (a)
Dinner 7 – 9.30 pm (d)
Bed & breakfast £25 – £45
Dinner B & B £48 – £68
Hot platter of west coast seafood in a puff pastry shell with a tarragon cream sauce. Pan-fried fillet of lamb with fresh herbs and spinach accompanied by a lamb sauce. Fillet of salmon with a white wine and chive sauce.
STB Highly Commended 4 Crowns
Credit cards: 1, 2, 3, 5, 6
Proprietor: Norman Sinclair

Gairloch

Map 6

CREAG MOR HOTEL
Charleston, Gairloch
Ross-shire IV21 2AH
Tel: 0445 2068
Fax: 0445 2044

A9 north from Inverness, then A835 and A832 through Garve and Achnasheen and on via Loch Maree to Gairloch. First hotel on right.
An impressive looking hotel with a large conservatory perched high on the outskirts of Gairloch in landscaped gardens and with fine views of old Gairloch Harbour and the Isle of Skye. Bedrooms have recently been refurbished to a high standard of comfort and all have en suite facilities. The public rooms exhibit a range of interesting paintings by a local artist. A carefully compiled menu offers a good range of well prepared and presented food in the main dining room, the Mackenzie Room, with an emphasis on seafood straight from Gairloch pier. Alternatively, in the less formal Buttery there is an all day service of light snacks, coffees, etc.
Open all year
Rooms: 19 with private facilities
All day menu 8 am – 10 pm (a)
Dinner 6.30 – 9.30 pm (d)
Bed & breakfast £38 – £42
Dinner B & B £59 – £63
Local prawns grilled with garlic and lemon. Grilled turbot served with ginger, coriander and white wine sauce. Pan-seared Gairloch salmon glazed with a tarragon bearnaise. Loin of local lamb roasted with garlic and rosemary, deglazed with Port and nutmeg.
STB Commended 5 Crowns
Credit cards: 1, 3, 6
Proprietors: Larry & Betty Nieto

LITTLE LODGE
North Erradale, Gairloch
Wester Ross IV21 2DS
Tel: 0445 85 237

Take B8021 from Gairloch towards Melvaig, situated ¼ mile beyond turning to North Erradale.
The charm of Little Lodge starts with its stone and pine-lined walls, tasteful furnishings, burning logs and gracious hospitality, but there is much more to it than that. The rest of the special atmosphere of the place is created by its proprietors, Di Johnson and Inge Ford, whose personal charm, interest in their guests and superb cuisine have earned much praise. This white-washed crofthouse with its domestic hens and sheep is set on a moorland peninsula north of Gairloch, with fine views to the Torridon Mountains and Skye, and is an idyllic retreat. Di's imaginative marinades and sauces enhance excellent local produce, fish from the harbour and vegetables from the garden, while Inge's home-made bread, oatcakes, yoghurt and preserves, make the Scottish breakfast memorable and

put the crowning seal on the excellent food and service.
Open Feb to Dec
Rooms: 3 with private facilities
Dinner at 7 pm (b)
Residents only
Unlicensed – guests welcome to take own wine + spirits
No children
No dogs
Facilities for the disabled
No smoking throughout
Bed & breakfast £22.50 – £29.50
Dinner B & B £32.50 – £39.50
Menus planned each day to suit guests' preferences, from a repertoire of traditional Scottish, cosmopolitan and vegetarian recipes.
STB Highly Commended 3 Crowns
No credit cards
Proprietors: Di Johnson & Inge Ford

THE STEADING RESTAURANT
Achtercairn, Gairloch
Ross-shire IV21 2BP
Tel: 0445 2449
On A832 at junction with B802 in Gairloch.
Coffee shop/restaurant adjoining the prize winning Gairloch Museum of West Highland Life and located in converted 19th century farm buildings and retaining their old world atmosphere, with stone floors, white-washed walls and open rafters. Local produce, seafood fresh from the loch, home-baked cakes and scones are on offer and there are special dishes for children. Self-service by day and waitress service in evenings. As the complete menu is available all day it is possible to choose what is wanted when it is wanted. The price ranges shown are therefore what a smaller (lunch) or a larger (dinner) meal might cost. Some French and German spoken. Dogs not allowed in restaurant but may be tied up outside in courtyard with water and shade.
Open Easter to 30 Sep
Food service all day 9.30 am – 9 pm except Sun (b)
Dinner 6 – 9 pm except Sun (c)
Closed Sun
Seafood platter – at least six varied seafoods presented with salad and a variety of dressings. Venison casseroled with red wine, mushrooms and spices. Haddock thermidor, baked in squat lobster sauce. Sirloin steak with herb and garlic, lemon, or prawn butter.
No credit cards

Galashiels

Map 2

WOODLANDS HOUSE HOTEL & RESTAURANTS
Windyknowe Road, Galashiels
Selkirkshire TD1 1RQ
Tel: 0896 4722
Fax: 0896 4722
Just off A7, take A72 towards Peebles. Turn left up Hall Street – Windyknowe Road is second on right.
The Scottish Border countryside is, of course, quite beautiful: full of stately homes, old abbeys and gentle rolling hills and woodland. Perhaps that is why Woodlands is so named, but whatever the origin, here is a lovely Victorian Gothic mansion in two acres of picturesque garden and splendidly situated for the entire Borders area yet within an hour of Edinburgh. Kevin and Nicki Winsland are caring hosts, keen to ensure that their guests every comfort is looked after. They have been careful to preserve the original ambience and character of the building which has several fine architectural features. The dining room is elegant and comfortable and has a good reputation for fine food and interesting menus. There is more informal dining in the recently opened Sanderson's steak-house which specialises in Scotch beef, lamb and pork.
Open all year except Boxing Day
Rooms: 9 with private facilities
Bar Lunch 12 – 2 pm except Sun (a)
Dining Room/Restaurant Lunch 12 – 2 pm except Sun Mon (b)
Carvery 12 – 7 pm Sun (a-b)
Bar Supper 6 – 9.30 pm (a)
Dinner 6 – 9.30 pm (c)
Bed & breakfast £34 – £40
Prawns cooked with hot pilaff rice served with a brandy and lobster sauce. Poached salmon steak served on a prawn and cream sauce. Charcoal grilled prime steaks.
STB Commended 4 Crowns
Credit cards: 1, 3
Proprietors: Kevin & Nicki Winsland

Garve

Map 6

INCHBAE LODGE HOTEL
by Garve
Ross-shire IV23 2PH
Tel: 09975 269
On A835 Inverness-Ullapool, 6 miles west of Garve village.
In the very heart of the northern Highlands, Inchbae Lodge is ideally located for exploring this beautiful unspoilt part of Scotland. A former Victorian hunting lodge on the banks of the River Blackwater, it is surrounded by forests and mountains but while secluded it is only six miles from Garve village and gives easy access to all areas north of Inverness. The resident proprietors, Les and Charlotte Mitchell, have established a good reputation for the variety and high standard of their food, and show imagination in the treatment of locally procured produce. Menus are very reasonably priced for the composition, preparation and care with which they are presented. There is free trout fishing at the bottom of the garden and clay pigeon shooting in the grounds – and a special deal for families, children are welcomed and accommodated free.
Open all year except Christmas + Boxing Days
Rooms: 12 with private facilities
Bar Lunch 12 – 2 pm Mon to Sat: 12.30 – 2 pm Sun (a)
Bar Supper 5 – 8.30 pm Mon to Sat: 6.30 – 8.30 pm Sun (a)
Dinner 7.30 – 8.30 pm (d)
No smoking in restaurant
Bed & breakfast £28 – £33
Dinner B & B £49 – £54
Interesting home-made soups – cream of lettuce, carrot and lemon etc. Monkfish baked with black peppercorns and served with a Port and cream sauce. Gressingham duck slowly cooked with Puy lentils. Sirloin of Scotch beef with a Beaujolais juice. Strawberries with a hot brandy citrus sauce. Clootie dumpling with whisky marmalade sauce.
STB Commended 3 Crowns
No credit cards
Proprietors: Les & Charlotte Mitchell

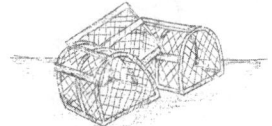

Gatehouse-of-Fleet

Map 1

CALLY PALACE HOTEL
Gatehouse-of-Fleet
Dumfries & Galloway DG7 2DL
Tel: 0557 814341
Fax: 0557 814522

1 mile from Gatehouse-of-Fleet exit off A75 Dumfries-Stranraer, 30 miles west of Dumfries.

Drive through magnificent grounds to reach this palatial four star hotel. Marble pillars, floors and tables reflect the grandeur of this former 18th century mansion, in an idyllic setting of 100 acres of forest, parkland and loch. Probably few other hotels attract quite as much repeat business as does the Cally Palace from its ever-expanding list of satisfied guests. The 56 rooms, suites and family rooms are tastefully furnished, all with private facilities, colour TV, trouser press, hairdryer etc, and the public rooms are spacious and grand in every sense of the word. There is a splendid traditional dining room with flowers and candles on the tables and silver service. Huge windows look out over the lawns and a grand piano provides music each evening. There are excellent indoor leisure facilities of swimming pool etc, and outdoors there is putting, tennis and croquet with the hotel's own 18 hole golf course opening in time for Summer 1994. The restaurant concentrates on selecting and presenting good local produce and does so with style, offering a daily changing table d'hôte menu as well as à la carte. The hotel is superbly managed by Jennifer Adams who selects and trains staff to be alert and responsive to guests' every need.
Open 4 Mar to 3 Jan
Rooms: 56 with private facilities
Dining Room/Restaurant Lunch 12.30 – 2 pm (b)
Dinner 6.30 – 9.30 pm (d)
No smoking in dining room
Dinner B & B £52 – £70

Grilled escalope of salmon with Hollandaise sauce. Pan-fried venison coated with a rich vegetable gravy. Supreme of chicken filled with a layer of smoked salmon then poached with a lemon sauce. Two small fillet steaks coated in oatmeal, stuffed with chestnuts and mushrooms, with a tarragon and Madeira gravy.
STB Deluxe 4 Crowns
Credit cards: 1, 3

Gigha
Isle of

Map 6

GIGHA HOTEL
Isle of Gigha
Argyll PA41 7AA
Tel: 05835 254
Fax: 05835 254/244

From Glasgow take A82/83 Campbeltown. Before reaching Campbeltown turn right into Tayinloan. Gigha ferry slip to north of village.

The island of Gigha may be only a 20 minute ferry trip from the Mull of Kintyre but in some respects it is a century or two distant. Here life is gentle and unhurried and flows at a pace that holidaymakers can adjust to their needs whether they be walking, fishing, golfing, bird-watching or enjoying Achamore Gardens. Island life seems to revolve round the Gigha Hotel, a traditional white-painted building with a character and charm of its own. Bedrooms are well appointed and the restaurant takes full advantage of freshly delivered seafood from the local fishing boats. Sailing and fishing yarns are swapped by locals and visitors in the hotel bar.
Open Mar to mid Oct
Rooms: 13, 11 with private facilities
Bar Lunch 12 – 2.30 pm (a)
Bar Supper 6 – 8.30 pm (a)
Dinner 7 – 9 pm (c)
Bed & breakfast £30 – £36
Dinner B & B £44.50 – £49.50
Seafood chowder. Lamb roasted with rosemary and thyme served with mint and onion sauce. Poached Gigha clams in a white wine and creamy fennel sauce. Venison in a redcurrant and pink peppercorn sauce. Gigha salmon and lobster.
STB Award Pending
Credit cards: 1, 3
Proprietors: William & Sandra Howden

Glasgow

Map 3

THE BRASSERIE
176 West Regent Street
Glasgow G2 4RL
Tel: 041 248 3801

Approach via Bath Street from city centre; turn left into Blythswood Street then left into West Regent Street. From outwith city, follow one way systems via Blythswood Square to West Regent Street.

The Brasserie exudes an instant air of quality. An imposing pillared entrance leads in to a dining area that gives the impression of an exclusive club. The food is first class with some unusual items on the menu, and skill and flair demonstrated in its presentation. A courteous and quickly attentive staff have established the Brasserie as a lunchtime favourite for the business community while in the evening it appeals to a wider section of the population looking for a good destination restaurant.
Open all year except public holidays
Bar Lunch 12 – 3 pm except Sun (a)
Dining Room/Restaurant Meals 12 – 11 pm except Sun (b-c)
Bar Supper 5 – 11 pm except Sun (a)
Closed Sun
Oysters. Baked salmon with a herb crust. Chocolate mousse with a white chocolate sauce.
Credit cards: 1, 2, 3, 5

THE BUTTERY
652 Argyle Street
Glasgow G3 8UF
Tel: 041 221 8188
Fax: 041 204 4639

Junction 19, M8 – approach by St Vincent Street and Elderslie Street.

The Buttery continues to be one of Glasgow's best restaurants and Jim Wilson, its manager, is determined to keep it that way. The external appearance give no hint of the delight within and the transformation from the grim old tenement facade to the unique character inside has to be experienced to be believed. There are lots of touches of Victoriana, and bits and pieces of church furniture create an excellent atmosphere and a quiet oasis of comfort and elegance. The food is first class: interesting menus and beautifully

presented food reflect much credit on the kitchen brigade and – combined with the polite and unobtrusive service that characterise The Buttery – confirm its place in the rankings. For less formal dining, there is the Belfry which has its own entranceway from the car park and – unlike its name – it is in the basement!
Open all year except Bank Holidays
Bar Lunch 12 – 2.30 pm except Sun Sat (a)
Dining Room/Restaurant Lunch 12 – 2.30 pm except Sun Sat (c)
Dinner 7 – 10.30 pm except Sun (e)
Closed Sun
Crêpe with Finnan haddock, potato, turnip and dill on a smokie cream. Feuilleté of pastry with seafood in a snowpea mustard sauce. Roast loin of venison with red lentil and celery rissoles on an orange and Cointreau jus. Carved rack of lamb with minted farce vine leaves and feta cheese on cardamom seed jus.
Credit cards: 1, 2, 3, 5 + SWITCH, DELTA

CRANNOG SEAFOOD RESTAURANT
28 Cheapside Street
Glasgow G3 8BH
Tel: 041 221 1727
Fax: 041 221 1727
Off Broomielaw by River Clyde. At north end of Kingston Bridge. Accessible from Clydeside expressway.
Tucked away inconspicuously in Cheapside Street, Finnieston, the Crannog is not a restaurant that you chance upon or one that is dependent on passing trade. This is one you mark and remember. The simple, almost spartan, decor reassures you straight away that you will not be paying for an extravagant 'theme' and expensive furnishings. Time and money is not wasted on frills, yet the restaurant is comfortable enough and the ambience appropriate and pleasing. This is an establishment where seafood is king. The menu is built around really fresh fish and shellfish cooked to perfection in straightforward traditional style so that it agitates the tastebuds the moment it is set before you. The Crannog formula started in Fort William where it has been a tearaway success, and has been introduced to Glasgow with the same care for quality that marks the original. Smoked salmon, mussels, trout etc are smoked in Crannog's own smokehouse in Fort William.
Open all year except Christmas Day

Dining Room/Restaurant Lunch 12 – 2.30 pm except Sun Mon (a-d)
Dinner 6 – 9.30 pm Tue to Thu: 6 – 10.30 pm Fri Sat (b-d)
Note: Pre-theatre meals available 5.30 – 7 pm
Closed Sun Mon
Crannog bouillabaisse. Fresh langoustines in hot garlic butter. Salmon fillet in filo pastry with a rich prawn sauce. Wing of skate in foamed lemon butter with capers. Fresh trout with Spring onions baked in a ginger sauce.
Credit cards: 1, 3 + SWITCH

GLASGOW HILTON INTERNATIONAL CAMERONS RESTAURANT
1 William Street
Glasgow G3 8HT
Tel: 041 204 5555
Fax: 041 204 5004
City centre.
Camerons Restaurant is the fine dining room within the new five star Glasgow Hilton International. The theme is that of a Highland hunting lodge and the menu echoes this in its concentration on the very best of Scottish produce prepared and presented with the style and panache that one would expect from one of the country's leading chefs. Ferrier Richardson has been a tireless advocate of excellence in the culinary field, has led the Scottish Culinary Olympics Team in overseas competitions and invariably returns with even more gold medals to add to the Team's collection. Clad in their traditional Cameron tartan trews, the waiting staff have the attentive confidence that goes with the knowledge that they are offering the best of good food.
Open all year
Rooms: 319 with private facilities
Dining Room/Restaurant Lunch 12 – 2.30 pm except Sun Sat (c)
Dinner 7 – 11 pm (f)
No dogs
Facilities for the disabled
No smoking area in restaurant
Bed & breakfast £127.50 – £362
Dinner B & B £132 – £367
Room Rate £115 – £350
Terrine of Perthshire game with beetroot dressing. Loch Fyne oysters. Saddle of Highland venison with elderberry jelly. Camerons Grand Desserts.
STB Deluxe 5 Crowns
Credit cards: 1, 2, 3, 5, 6 + SWITCH

THE GLASGOW MARRIOTT
Argyle Street
Glasgow G3 8RR
Tel: 041 226 5577
Fax: 041 221 9202
At Junction 19 of M8 in centre of city, close to Central Station, Bus and Air Terminal, main shopping/commercial areas, and only 10 minutes by road from Glasgow Airport.
The Glasgow Marriott, so conveniently and centrally located, has consolidated its position as a focal point in the city's business and social life. It is constantly being improved and its near 300 bedrooms are of the excellent standard to be expected from the Marriott name. There are three levels of eating, top of the range being L'Academie, a superb up market restaurant of the highest international standards but as an alternative you may eat in The Terrace or have a light meal or snack throughout the day in the Cafe Rendezvous. A courtesy coach service is provided to and from Glasgow Airport for hotel guests.
Open all year
Rooms: 298 with private facilities
Cafe Rendezvous 10 am – 6 pm (a)
Restaurant Lunch (Terrace) 12 – 2.30 pm (b)
Dinner (Terrace) 7 – 10.30 pm (b)
Dinner (L'Academie) 7 – 10.30 pm except Sun (c)
Note: L'Academie closed 23 Dec to 10 Jan
No smoking area in restaurant
Bed & breakfast £43 – £120
Dinner B & B £55 – £150
Room Rate £60 – £110
Terrace: warm salmon and lobster terrine with watercress and dill sauce. Grilled rock lobster tails and asparagus spears with fresh continental leaves and new potatoes. L'Academie: individual fillet of beef Wellington with a truffle and Madeira sauce. Medallions of venison with a peppered sauce and chestnuts. Scallops in fish stock flavoured with Pernod.
Credit cards: 1, 2, 3, 5, 6

MOAT HOUSE INTERNATIONAL
Congress Road
Glasgow G3 8QT
Tel: 041 204 0733 • Telex: 776244
Fax: 041 221 2022

Situated on the banks of the River Clyde, next to the SECC.

The award winning Moat House International has one of Glasgow's most desirable sites right on the banks of the River Clyde, adjacent to the Scottish Exhibition Centre, and with generous parking. The interior layout is dramatically different from normal with a huge open court area featuring a magnificent mural of Clydeside Glasgow. Bedrooms are luxuriously equipped and have splendid panoramic views. There are two restaurants and the principal – The Mariner – is outstanding with food of exceptional quality and style. A leisurely meal here is a special occasion. For those in more of a hurry, the Pointhouse Restaurant adjacent to The Mariner gives adequate choice and excellent value of equally high standard. The Moat House is very well managed and deserves its prominence as one of the city's very best hotels.

Open all year
Rooms: 300 with private facilities
All day dining 6.30 am – 10.45 pm (Pointhouse)
Bar Meals 11 am – 10.45 pm (Quarterdeck) (a)
Dining Room/Restaurant Lunch 12 – 2 pm (Mariner) except Sun (c)
Dinner (Mariner) 7 – 10.45 pm except Sun (c)
No dogs
Facilities for the disabled
No smoking in restaurant
Bed & breakfast £45 – £107
Dinner B & B rates on application
Peppered lamb fillet with a Winter salad, fennel and honey dressing. Seared sea scallops wrapped in cured ham with a warm tarragon and saffron essence. Medallions of beef on a wild mushroom rosti with lentils and red onion jus. Nage of west coast seafood flavoured with fresh garden herbs and a lobster tortelloni. Best end of lamb with savoury potato and a lavender jus.
STB Highly Commended 5 Crowns
Credit cards: 1, 2, 3, 5, 6

ROGANO RESTAURANT & CAFE ROGANO
11 Exchange Place
Glasgow G1 3AN
Tel: 041 248 4055
Fax: 041 248 2608

Glasgow city centre, near Buchanan Street precinct and Queen Street/ George Square.

Restaurants come and go but those that are really good survive and Rogano has been around the Glasgow scene for as long as anyone can remember. It was re-modelled in 1935 in "art deco" style and retains the appeal, the ambience and the high standards on which its reputation was founded. It concentrates primarily on serving superb fish and shellfish for which it has always been noted and it does so with style, but there are several other interesting alternatives to fish for those who prefer them. The main restaurant on the ground floor has an air of unchanging class and elegance, and downstairs the Cafe Rogano is much more liberal with a busy bistro atmosphere and equally good food.

Open all year except public holidays
Bar Lunch 12 – 2.30 pm except Sun (a)
Cafe Rogano 12 – 11 pm Mon to Thu: 12 – 12 midnight Fri Sat: 6 – 10 pm Sun (c)
Dining Room/Restaurant Lunch 12 – 2.30 pm except Sun (c-f)
Dinner 6.30 – 10.30 pm Mon to Sat: 6 – 10 pm Sun (f)
No smoking requested before 2 pm (Lunch) and 9 pm (Dinner)
Warm sole mousse with lobster on a crab sauce. Steamed John Dory in a tomato and vermouth sauce. Scallops and monkfish with ginger, Spring onions and lemon grass, en papillote. Rack of Borders lamb with sweet roast garlic and peppers. Strudel of sweet potato, chestnuts and spinach.
Credit cards: 1, 2, 3, 5 + SWITCH

THE UBIQUITOUS CHIP
12 Ashton Lane
Glasgow G12 8SJ
Tel: 041 334 5007

A secluded lane in the heart of Glasgow's West End.

The Ubiquitous Chip is more than a restaurant, it is almost an institution in Glasgow which everyone seems to know and of which everyone has heard. The setting is unlikely, a white-washed Victorian mews stable down an old fashioned cobbled street, but a

restaurant with a style all of its own. The menu really does emphasise and concentrate on the wealth of good regional produce and the chef presents his meals with inspired originality and combination of flavour. 'Upstairs at the Chip' serves light inexpensive lunches and evening meals. Dinner downstairs is something to be taken seriously and prices reflect this though they are still good value for money. 'The Chip' boasts one of the UK's most celebrated, extensive and modestly priced wine lists.

Open all year except Christmas Day, 31 Dec, 1 Jan
Upstairs Restaurant 12 – 11 pm (a)
Dining Room Lunch 12 – 2.30 pm (b-c)
Dinner 5.30 – 11 pm (d)
Shellfish bisque with cream and fresh ginger. Warm salad of west coast seafood with bacon and tarragon vinaigrette. Marinaded haunch of Inverness-shire venison with baked porridge cakes and a compote of fresh fruit. Oban landed monkfish tails in a lightly spiced creamy Sautérnes sauce on a bed of cracked wheat flavoured with saffron and ginger.
Credit cards: 1, 2, 3, 5
Proprietor: Ron Clydesdale

VICTORIA & ALBERT
159 Buchanan Street
Glasgow G1 2JX
Tel: 041 248 6329

Approach via Buchanan Street pedestrian precinct towards St Vincent Street or from West George Street, short distance from George Square.

A much patronised and very popular establishment with the business community of Glasgow city centre, the Victoria and Albert is primarily an up market bar restaurant, situated beneath Glasgow's Stock Exchange. There is a Victorian charm and elegance about it which is very appealing and the dining areas are entirely harmonious. Its central location near the Royal Concert Hall and the Theatre Royal, make it a suitable rendezvous for dining before or after performances, but you can enjoy morning coffee or light meals throughout the day. For more serious eating there are first class fixed price menus of two or three courses representing good value for money, and the à la carte menu is served both in the restaurant and bar.

Open all year except Christmas + Boxing Days, 1 + 2 Jan, Glasgow Holiday Mondays

*Bar Meals 11.30 am – 10.30 pm except
Sun (b)
Restaurant Lunch/Dinner 11.30 am –
10.30 pm except Sun (b)
Closed Sun
Children welcome in restaurant only
Smoked chicken and orange salad.
Halibut steak en papillote. Fresh fruit
sabayon.
Credit cards: 1, 2, 3, 5*

WESTERWOOD HOTEL, GOLF & COUNTRY CLUB
St Andrews Drive
Cumbernauld G68 0EW
Tel: 0236 457171
Fax: 0236 738478

*A80 Cumbernauld, 13 miles north-east
of Glasgow. Take Wardpark exit. Follow
to roundabout, take Dullatur exit. At mini
roundabout, turn right – road leads to
hotel entrance.*

This spacious and luxurious hotel is
maintained in immaculate condition and
has established a high reputation for the
excellence of its food. The 18 hole golf
course was designed by Seve
Ballesteros and Dave Thomas and is of
course the principal recreational feature
of the hotel, but tennis, squash,
snooker, swimming and a gymnasium
are also available. The young kitchen
brigade seem to be constantly aspiring
to even higher standards and whether
you eat in the Club House or the
upmarket Old Masters Restaurant in the
hotel, you can expect to experience and
enjoy well prepared well presented food,
and an interesting wine list to
complement it. French, German and
Spanish spoken.
*Open all year
Note: accommodation closed 23 to 28
Dec*

*Rooms: 49 with private facilities
Bar Lunch 12 – 2.30 pm (a)
Dining Room/Restaurant Lunch (Club
House) 12 – 2.30 pm (b)
Bar Supper (Club House) 7 – 10 pm (c)
Dinner (Old Masters) 7 – 9.30 pm except
Sun Mon (d)
Facilities for the disabled
Bed & breakfast £50 – £60
Room Rate £55 – £95
West coast scallops with a lemon butter
sauce. Loin of Scottish lamb with
maize-fed chicken parfait and tarragon
essence. Seasonal berries with Drambuie
sabayon. Home-made chocolates.
STB Highly Commended 5 Crowns
Credit cards: 1, 2, 3, 5, 6*

Glenborrodale

Map 6

GLENBORRODALE CASTLE
Glenborrodale, Acharacle
Argyll PH36 4JP
Tel: 09724 266
Fax: 09724 224

*Take A82 south of Fort William and
cross by Corran Ferry. Follow A861 from
Ardgour to Salen, then B8007 to
Glenborrodale.*

Poised on the northern shores of Loch
Sunart, overlooking the Isle of Mull, is
Glenborrodale Castle – a magnificent
château built at the turn of the century
by a Victorian mining magnate. Being
one of Scotland's finest private houses
the furnishings are suitably stately with
well chosen antiques, paintings and
tapestries indicative of the dignified
sense of luxury which characterises this
superb hotel. Local salmon, trout,
shellfish and game all feature
prominently on the menus whether the
choice be a light lunch or a full five
course dinner. An excellent wine list
complements the fine cuisine.
*Open Easter to 31 Oct
Rooms: 16 with private facilities
Bar Lunch 12 – 2 pm (b)
Dining Room/Restaurant Lunch 12 –
2 pm (d)
Dinner 7 – 9 pm (f)
No smoking in dining room
Bed & breakfast £80 – £130
Dinner B & B £112.50 – £162.50
Salad of prawns and scallops flavoured
with chives. Fillet of Scotch beef with
wild mushrooms and Madeira sauce.
Pear and ginger soufflé.
Credit cards: 1, 2, 3, 6*

Glenelg

Map 6

GLENELG INN
Glenelg Bay, Glenelg, nr Shiel Bridge
Ross-shire IV40 8AG
Tel: 059 982 273
Fax: 059 982 373

*Access to Glenelg via unclassified road
west of A87 at Sheil Bridge, 1 mile from
Kylerhea-Skye ferry which runs April to
October.*

The Glenelg Inn has been recently
refurbished to a high standard from an
old coaching mews with cobbled
courtyard, on the shores of Glenelg Bay.
It has six bedrooms offering the best in
comfort. There is a bar where guest,
crofter and fisherman alike may relax in
the genuine atmosphere of the ceilidh.
The restaurant offers fine Scottish
cuisine using local seafood, game and
other fresh produce. It is several miles
along a single track road to get to the
Glenelg Inn, but most people find it well
worth the effort. Boat trips available.
*Open Easter to Oct
Rooms: 6 with private facilities
Bar Lunch 12.30 – 2.15 pm (a)
Dining Room/Restaurant Lunch 12.30 –
2.15 pm (a)
Bar Supper 7 – 9 pm except Sun (a)
Dinner 7.30 – 9 pm (c)
Facilities for the disabled
Dinner B & B £55 – £85
Kylerhea oysters and mussels. Local
lamb with lentil and cardamom purée.
Wild salmon. Organic strawberries.
Walnut and rum tart.
No credit cards
Proprietor: Christopher Main*

Glenfinnan

Map 6

THE STAGE HOUSE
Glenfinnan
Inverness-shire PH37 4LT
Tel: 0397 722 246
Fax: 0397 722 307

15 miles west of Fort William on A830 'Road to the Isles' ½ mile on right past Glenfinnan Monument.
Glenfinnan is almost a "must" stopping place for those on the Road to the Isles. It is a historic location – the place at which Bonnie Prince Charlie landed from France in 1745 to claim the Scottish throne. Just half a mile west of the Glenfinnan Monument, The Stage House is an old coaching inn dating back to the 17th century which has been thoroughly modernised and provides comfortable accommodation and a peaceful relaxed atmosphere. Chef/proprietor Carole Hawkes has established an enviable reputation for providing an excellent menu making extensive use of fresh and smoked local produce, in particular game and shellfish. Log fires in Winter add to the appeal of The Stage House which is a good base for lots of outdoor pursuits like fishing and walking. Boats and mountain bikes may be hired, and there are beaches nearby.
Open 1 Apr to 31 Oct + New Year
Rooms: 9 with private facilities
Bar Lunch 12.30 – 2.30 pm (b)
Bar Supper 5 – 9 pm (b)
Dinner 6.30 – 8.30 pm (c)
No smoking in restaurant or rooms
Bed & breakfast £27.95 – £34.95
Dinner B & B £39.95 – £47.95
Home-made soups. Grilled Loch Linnhe langoustines with garlic, herbs and lemon. Roasted pheasant served with a sauce of Calvados, cream and apples. Grilled Minch plaice with fresh scallops, prawns and mussels in a white wine sauce.
STB Commended 3 Crowns
Credit cards: 1, 2, 3
Proprietors: Robert & Carole Hawkes

Glenisla

Map 4

GLENISLA HOTEL
Glenisla, nr Blairgowrie
Perthshire PH11 8PH
Tel: 057 582 223

From Blairgowrie, A93 for 9 miles then B951 into Glenisla – c. 6 miles. From Alyth, B954 – 9 miles to Glenisla.
There is a lot of atmosphere in this old coaching inn that dates back to the late 17th century. The bar with its oak beams and log fires prides itself on hand-pumped real ales and is a splendid place for a chat with the locals over a drink or a good bar meal. The restaurant menu is refreshingly straightforward and unpretentious, yet offering a good choice for each course and real value for money. The place itself is steeped in history and the proprietors, Michael and Kirsten Bartholomew, are intent on retaining all that is best of it. An excellent base or stopping place in the picturesque valley of Glenisla.
Open all year except Christmas + Boxing Days
Rooms: 6 with private facilities
Bar Lunch 12 – 2.30 pm (a)
Dining Room/Restaurant Lunch 12 – 2.30 pm (b)
Bar Supper 6.30 – 9 pm (b)
Dinner 6.30 – 9 pm (b)
Facilities for the disabled
No smoking area in restaurant
Bed & breakfast £23 - £25
Whole prawns sauté in garlic butter. Local lamb cutlets, grilled and served with Cumberland jelly. Fillet of local salmon, grilled and served with Hollandaise sauce.
STB Commended 3 Crowns
Credit cards: 1, 3
Proprietors: Michael & Kirsten Bartholomew

Glenlivet

Map 5

MINMORE HOUSE
Glenlivet, Ballindalloch
Banffshire AB37 9DB
Tel: 0807 590 378
Fax: 0807 590 472

On B9136, off B9008, 9 miles from Tomintoul. Adjacent to The Glenlivet Distillery.
Originally the home of the founder of the nearby Glenlivet Distillery, Minmore House has four acres of landscaped gardens, is situated above the River Livet and has glorious open views. The Crown Estate has thoughtfully provided some well maintained local walks and a light pedestrian bridge over the river. The nine en suite bedrooms are comfortably furnished with appropriate period furniture. In the oak-panelled bar with its log fires you will find nearly 100 malts from which to choose. There is a spacious drawing room in which afternoon tea is a joy. Belinda Luxmoore's cooking is delicious and the menu changes daily. This is really a rather special place for all who enjoy the peace of remote countryside and the satisfaction of wholesome good food – and remarkably good value.
Open 1 May to 25 Oct
Rooms: 9 with private facilities
Bar and Picnic Lunches can be arranged for residents
Dinner at 8 pm (d) – 5 course set menu
No smoking in dining room
Bed & breakfast £32 – £35
Dinner B & B £44 – £50
Fresh Lossiemouth langoustine, roast Highland rack of lamb with fresh mint and honey glaze, Cullen skink, venison and game, Lochin Ora burnt cream.
STB Commended 4 Crowns
Credit cards: 1, 3
Proprietor: Belinda Luxmoore

Glenluce

Map 1

KELVIN HOUSE HOTEL
53 Main Street, Glenluce
Wigtownshire DG8 0PP
Tel: 05813 303

Just off A75, 10 minutes from Stranraer ferry terminals.
Kelvin House is the centre of social life in the pleasant and tranquil little village of Glenluce, not so far from the shores

of Luce Bay. The hotel is an unpretentious traditional two storey building on the main street, dating back to c. 1785. An interesting bar menu is available all day in the lounge or public bar with a wider than normal choice. It is in the Cranachan Restaurant that chef/proprietor Gary Conlan is able to demonstrate his skills. A good choice of local fish such as Luce Bay scallops or lobster is usually available together with a selection of seasonal game or meat courses. Provision is also made for vegetarians. There is lots in the way of outdoor pursuits to do in this out of the way corner of south-west Scotland .
Open all year
Rooms: 6 , 5 with private facilities
Food served all day Jun to end Sep
Bar Lunch 12 – 3 pm (a)
Dining Room/Restaurant Lunch 12 – 3 pm Sun only (a)
Bar Supper 6 – 10 pm (b)
Dinner 7 – 10 pm (c)
Bed & breakfast £18 – £28
Home-made soup and pâté. Poached Cree salmon fillet in a dill and dry vermouth cream sauce. Lamb cutlets flamed in whisky with woodland mushrooms and pan gravy. Marinated haunch of local venison cooked in apples, redcurrants, Port and juniper berries. STB Commended 3 Crowns
No credit cards
Proprietors: Gary Conlan &
Karen Howden

Glenrothes

Map 4

BALBIRNIE HOUSE HOTEL
Balbirnie Park, Markinch
by Glenrothes
Fife KY7 6NE
Tel: 0592 610066
Fax: 0592 610529

Prestige Award Winner 1991

Off A92 on B9130, follow directions to village of Markinch and Balbirnie Park. Balbirnie is a delightful Georgian country house dating from 1777, now Listed Grade 'A' – of architectural and historical importance. Privately owned, the house has now been caringly restored and converted to a quite magnificent small luxury hotel which is situated in a beautiful landscaped estate and country park of 400 acres. Internally it is superb, the unique long gallery, old library and drawing room being noteworthy. The restaurant looks over formal gardens and ancient yew hedges. This is an establishment of which the entire staff seem to be proud and anxious to maintain standards. Chef Ian MacDonald presides in the kitchen and upholds the hotel's reputation for fine food and interesting dishes that use, whenever possible, the natural larder that is Scotland. Geographically the hotel is ideally situated in the heart of the Kingdom of Fife, within easy reach of St Andrews, the quaint fishing villages and countryside of Fife, as well as Edinburgh, the capital, which is about 30 minutes drive away.
Open all year
Rooms: 30 with private facilities
Bar Lunch 12 – 2.30 pm (a-b)
Dining Room/Restaurant Lunch 12.30 – 2.30 pm (a-b)
Dinner 7 – 9.30 pm (d)
Bed & breakfast £62.50 – £95
Dinner B & B from £75 (special breaks)
A light Arbroath smokie quiche with a chive butter sauce. Rack of lamb roasted with a herb crust, with honey and orange roasted celeriac, served with a rich rosemary and garlic flavoured essence. Hot oak-roasted Loch Fyne salmon served warm with an olive oil dressing, garnished with mushroom filled tartlets topped with quails egg and Hollandaise sauce.
STB Deluxe 5 Crowns
Credit cards: 1, 2, 3, 5
Proprietors: The Russell Family

RESCOBIE HOTEL & RESTAURANT
Valley Drive, Leslie
Glenrothes
Fife KY6 3BQ
Tel: 0592 742143
Fax: 0592 620231
8 miles from M90 – just off A911 at west end of the village of Leslie.
"What a nice place" our inspector wrote of Rescobie. "It should have the value for money award of the year." This is a warm and friendly little country house hotel of the 1930s, with many original features and appropriate period furniture, and set in immaculate grounds. There are two comfortable and uncrowded dining rooms and a lovely lounge with deep armchairs and a log fire. The table d'hôte menu changes daily and there is a supplementary à la carte extending the choice, and always a full vegetarian menu. The food is excellent, of a far higher standard than is normally associated with a two star hotel, and has been recognised by the award of a Rosette from the Automobile Association. Perhaps because it is off the beaten tourist track Rescobie has to try harder and it certainly seems to do so, attracting much repeat business from the business community in Glenrothes as well as local residents. Children are very welcome with appropriate reductions. French and German spoken.
Open all year except Christmas + Boxing Days
Rooms: 10 with private facilities
Bar Lunch 12 – 2 pm (a)
Dining Room/Restaurant Lunch 12 – 2 pm (b)
Dinner 7 – 9 pm (c)
No dogs
Bed & breakfast £30 – £52
Dinner B & B £43 – £56 (min 3 nights stay)
Cullen skink. Game terrine. Fillets of sole stuffed with crab and shrimps. Grilled fillet of salmon with cream and fresh ginger sauce. Scottish steak cooked with mushrooms and onions, flamed with whisky and finished with cream. Venison with home-made rowanberry jelly. Strawberry shortcake, bramble brûlée, hot flavoured soufflés.
STB Commended 4 Crowns
Credit cards: 1, 2, 3
Proprietors: Tony & Wendy Hughes-Lewis

Grange
by Errol

Map 4

WATERYBUTTS LODGE
Grange, by Errol
Perthshire PH2 7SZ
Tel: 0821 642894
Fax: 0821 642523

A85 Perth-Dundee, 9 miles out of Perth take road for Grange. Then after 1½ miles turn left, immediately before railway crossing.

The original building was a 15th century friary attached to Coupar Angus Abbey though the lectern style doocot and small turreted stone stair is all that remains. The main Georgian building was erected in 1802 and later added to in the Victorian era. Today it is now a beautiful Georgian lodge set in lovely grounds, and with en suite accommodation. A unique herb garden, which provides fresh herbs for the kitchen, was formed originally from Dutch soil shipped as ballast on boats returning from Holland after delivering potatoes. The atmosphere at Waterybutts is distinctly 'house party' and guests wine and dine in style around a 16 foot Charles I refectory table, enjoying good conversation, good food, and an ambience of yesteryear.
Open all year
Rooms: 7 with private facilities
Dinner 7 – 10 pm (b)
Non-residents – by prior arrangement
Restricted Licence
No children
Bed & breakfast £25 – £33
Dinner B & B £40 – £50
Fresh trout pâté. Moules marinière. Haunch of roe venison. Tay salmon poached in herbs. All game in season.
STB Highly Commended 3 Crowns
Credit cards: 1, 2, 3
Proprietors: Barry & Rachael Allenby-Wilcox

Grantown-on-Spey

Map 5

THE ANVIL
16 Castle Road, Grantown-on-Spey
Moray PH26 3HL
Tel: 0479 873371

Off main square of town.
The Anvil is a Listed building dating back to 1741, reputedly the oldest house in Grantown-on-Spey, and – as the large horse-shoe on the front door testifies – was once the blacksmith's cottage. It is now a comfortable family house in which Olwen and Irvine Powell work hard at making their guests feel at home, providing a homely atmosphere with a splendid open fire, board games and a piano around which it is not unknown for impromptu ceilidhs to be held. Good wholesome cooking is attractively presented, and special provision is made for vegetarians and vegans.
Open all year except Nov
Rooms: 3, 1 with private facilities
Car park nearby
Dinner 6.30 – 7.30 pm (b)
Non-residents by arrangement
Unlicensed – guests welcome to take own wine
Dogs by arrangement
Facilities for the disabled
No smoking in dining room + bedrooms
Bed & breakfast £14 – £16
Dinner B & B £24 – £32
Room Rate £28 – £32
Christmas + New Year breaks available
Home-made soups. Local wild salmon in a buttery herb dressing. Scotch lamb with onion sauce. Aberdeen Angus beef. Mushroom sauce on a bed of stir-fried vegetables, served in a nest of Yorkshire pudding. Scottish raspberries with home-made rich shortbread.
STB Commended 2 Crowns
No credit cards
Proprietor: Olwen Powell

ARDCONNEL HOUSE
Woodlands Terrace, Grantown-on-Spey
Moray PH26 3JU
Tel: 0479 872104
Fax: 0479 872104

On A95, south-west entry to town.
Well kept gardens and neatly trimmed lawns round this splendid Victorian villa on the southern edge of Grantown-on-Spey, give an immediate indication that here is a well tended property in which high standards prevail. The interior lives up to expectation and is pleasingly furnished and attractive, with all bedrooms having en suite facilities. Menus change daily in order to utilise the best available produce and the standard of food is high and of interesting variety. James and Barbara Casey express their philosophy as providing quality food and accommodation in a relaxed and friendly atmosphere – and at realistic prices.
Open Jan to Oct + New Year
Rooms: 7 with private facilities
Dinner at 7 pm (b)
Residents only
Restricted Licence
Children over 10 years welcome
Dogs by arrangement
No smoking throughout
Bed & breakfast £23 – £28.50
Dinner B & B £35.50 – £41
Menu changes daily in order to utilise the best fresh local produce – lamb, salmon, venison, beef.
STB Highly Commended 3 Crowns
Credit cards: 1, 3
Proprietors: James & Barbara Casey

THE ARDLARIG
Woodlands Terrace, Grantown-on-Spey
Moray PH26 3JU
Tel: 0479 873245

From A9 Perth-Inverness follow signs for Grantown-on-Spey. On entry to town, one of first houses on left.
The Ardlarig is an imposing blue whinstone villa set in its own gardens. Before conversion to a guest house, it was the private residence of Sir Thomas Shankland – a notable local figure who was Britain's Commissioner to Nigeria. Mike and Sue Greer are proud of their standards of food and every dish is home-made, using local produce whenever possible, and presented with care in a pleasantly furbished dining room. The entire operation is based on offering affordable accommodation and food in a relaxed comfortable

atmosphere where the emphasis is on friendly, courteous service. Children welcome.
Open all year except 23 to 28 Dec
Rooms: 7, 1 with private facilities
Dinner at 7 pm (b)
Residents only
Restricted Licence
No smoking in dining room
Bed & breakfast £18.50 – £22.50
Dinner B & B £29 – £33
Home-made soups and pâté. Venison in a red wine casserole. Supreme of Scottish chicken in a cream and tarragon sauce.
STB Commended 2 Crowns
No credit cards
Proprietors: Sue & Mike Greer

CULDEARN HOUSE
Woodlands Terrace, Grantown-on-Spey
Moray PH26 3JU
Tel: 0479 872106
Fax: 0479 873641
On A95, south-west entry to Grantown-on-Spey.
A detached Victorian house on the outskirts of the town, surrounded by a very well kept garden of lawns and mature trees. There is a distinctly Scottish feel to it and a high standard of decor throughout, bedrooms having recently been refurbished. Alasdair Little and his wife Isobel are genuinely interested in people and their guests are immediately made to feel welcome and at home. The menu changes daily offering a limited but reasonable choice of fresh local produce, and including some old favourites and some regional specialities. Grantown-on-Spey is ideally situated for touring the Highlands and with lots of appeal to walkers, anglers, bird-watchers and golfers.
Open 1 Mar to 31 Oct
Rooms: 9 with private facilities
Picnic Lunches to order
Dinner 6.45 – 7.30 pm (b)
Residents only
Restricted Licence
No dogs
No smoking in dining room
Dinner B & B £38 – £50
Traditional Scottish fare using lamb, beef, venison and trout, is complemented by a modestly priced wine list and range of malt whiskies.
STB Highly Commended 3 Crowns
Credit cards: 1, 3, 6
Proprietors: Alasdair & Isobel Little

GARTH HOTEL
The Square, Grantown-on-Spey
Moray PH26 3HN
Tel: 0479 872836/872162
On the Square of Grantown-on-Spey.
The Garth Hotel commands a view of the picturesque Square of Grantown-on-Spey and sits amidst four acres of landscaped gardens. This three star hotel dates from the 17th century and offers old world charm with every modern comfort and convenience. Seventeen individually furnished bedrooms – all en suite – with direct dial telephone, colour TV and tea/coffee-making facilities. Extensive and selective menu with an accent on fresh local produce. French and German spoken.
Open all year
Rooms: 14 with private facilities
Bar Lunch 12 – 2 pm (a)
Dining Room/Restaurant Lunch 12 – 1.30 pm (a)
Dinner 7.30 – 8.30 pm (d)
No dogs
No smoking in restaurant
Bed & breakfast £42 – £49
Dinner B & B from £56.65
Highland game pâté. Salmon soup. Monkfish tails flamed with brandy served with a fresh cream and peppercorn sauce. Local venison pan-fried and served with Port and bramble sauce.
STB Highly Commended 4 Crowns
Credit cards: 1, 2, 3, 5
Proprietor: Gordon McLaughlan

KINROSS HOUSE
Woodside Avenue, Grantown-on-Spey
Moray PH26 3JR
Tel: 0479 872042
Proceeding up High Street from south on A95 turn right at traffic lights, then right at first crossroads – 200 yards on left.
An attractive Victorian villa in a quiet residential area of the town with a tidy garden in front and car parking at the side. Bedrooms are bright, cheerful and spacious, with welcome tray and colour TV. A no smoking rule applies throughout the house. The set menu of good

wholesome fare changes daily, is well balanced and good value and attracts favourable guest comments. Mr Elder dons his kilt for the occasion and is an attentive and caring host. Children over seven years welcome.
Open 1 Apr to 31 Oct
Rooms: 6 , 5 with private facilities
Dinner at 7 pm (b)
Residents only
No dogs
Facilities for the disabled
No smoking throughout
Bed & breakfast £18 – £23
Dinner B & B £29 – £34
Daily changing menu using local produce. Speyside smoked salmon. Fresh fish, venison, beef, lamb. Rumbledethumps. Home-made desserts. Scottish cheeseboard.
STB Commended 3 Crowns
No credit cards
Proprietors: David & Katherine Elder

RAVENSCOURT HOUSE HOTEL
Seafield Avenue, Grantown-on-Spey
Moray PH26 3JG
Tel: 0479 872286
Fax: 0479 873260
Just off main Square.
A country house hotel which exudes an atmosphere of quality and elegance. Dining is in the conservatory with tasteful decor and beautiful table appointments. The drawing rooms, where there are fine original oil paintings and water colours, have been furnished sumptuously. Menus are well balanced, the standard of cooking and presentation is high and the service faultless. Judging by the remarks in the visitors book there is a very satisfied clientele. There are excellent value house wines and generally a wine list catering for all tastes and pockets.
Open 1 Mar to 31 Oct
Rooms: 9 with private facilities
Dinner 7 – 9.30 pm except Sun Mon (d)
4 course set menu
Dinner residents only Sun Mon
No dogs
No smoking area in conservatory
Bed & breakfast £35 – £39
Dinner B & B £56 – £60
Fresh fish daily. Scottish and French dishes feature equally. Menu changes every third day, with a traditional roast meal on Sunday. Sirloin steaks 'New York' cut. Rack of lamb for two.
STB Deluxe 3 Crowns
No credit cards

Gullane

Map 4

GOLF INN HOTEL
Main Street, Gullane
East Lothian EH31 2AB
Tel: 0620 843259
Fax: 0620 842066

18 miles east of Edinburgh, 4 miles west of North Berwick.
Originally an old coaching house, the Golf Inn Hotel is now an established family run business, catering both for the golfer and non-golfer. The emphasis is on personal and friendly service coupled with excellent food and good beer! The hotel has been refurbished to a high standard and offers facilities for weddings, conferences, dinner dances etc. For the resident, golf packages can be tailored to requirement. The Carriage Lounge has an interesting range of light snack dishes and the Saddlers Restaurant menu, for the serious diner, has just the right touch of choice and quality.
Open all year except Christmas Day
Rooms: 18, 11 with private facilities
Bar Meals 12 – 10 pm (b)
Dining Room/Restaurant Lunch 12 – 2.30 pm (b)
Dinner 6.30 – 9.45 pm (c)
Dogs by arrangement
Restricted parking
Bed & breakfast £32 – £42
Dinner B & B £45 – £55
Noisettes of Scotch lamb with a raspberry and redcurrant coulis. Selection of prawns, scampi and halibut served in a puff pastry with a rich creamy sauce. Fillet steak served with a Drambuie and mushroom sauce.
Credit cards: 1, 3, 5, 6
Proprietors: Tom & Kathleen Saddler

GREYWALLS
Muirfield, Gullane
East Lothian EH31 2EG
Tel: 0620 842144
Fax: 0620 842241

Prestige Award Winner 1992

Signposted off A198 in Gullane – a few miles from A1.
This exquisitely proportioned country house was designed at the turn of the century by the renowned architect Sir Edwin Lutyens and retains all of the grace and grandeur of the times. Its gardens are equally magnificent and look out over the famous Muirfield Golf Course. The house is almost a time capsule, but incorporating the elegance of the Edwardian era with modern comfort and amenities. The cuisine is outstanding and Chef Paul Baron's deft touch makes every meal a special occasion. The whole atmosphere of Greywalls is of luxury and relaxation.
Open 14 Apr to 31 Oct
Rooms: 23 with private facilities
Bar Lunch 12.30 – 2 pm except Sun (b)
Dining Room/Restaurant Lunch 12.30 – 2 pm (b)
Dinner 7.30 – 9.15 pm (f)
No smoking in dining room
Facilities for the disabled
Room Rate £90 – £150
Finest Highland smoked salmon and home-cured gravadlax. Pan-fried king scallops served in a puff pastry case with a saffron and dill sauce. Best end of lamb roasted in oven served with a timbale of ratatouille and Madeira sauce. Poached fillet of turbot with steamed mussels and a lemon butter sauce. Rich bitter chocolate torte with strawberry sauce.
STB Highly Commended 4 Crowns
Credit cards: 1, 2, 3, 5
Proprietors: Giles & Ros Weaver

Harris
Isle of

Map 7

ALLAN COTTAGE GUEST HOUSE
Tarbert
Isle of Harris PA85 3DJ
Tel: 0859 2146

Upper road overlooking ferry road, c. 600 yards from ferry.
An attractive old building at the side of the road which was formerly a telephone exchange and which has preserved some of the best features. It has been extended to form a house of unusual charm and character, quiet, homely and welcoming. Rooms are all beautifully furnished in cottage style and all bedrooms will have private facilities by the start of 1994. Bill and Evelyn Reed look after their guests well and their likes and dislikes in food are noted when the daily changing dinner menu is discussed each morning. For such a small place the food is interesting and imaginative and attracts favourable comment.
Open 1 Apr to 22 Oct
Rooms: 3 with private facilities
Dinner 7 – 7.30 pm (b)
Residents only
Unlicensed
No smoking in dining room
Bed & breakfast from £20
Dinner B & B from £33.50
Harris venison with walnuts, Port and Guinness. Local lamb with apricots, orange and walnut stuffing. Aberdeen Angus steak with fresh ginger and horseradish. Wild salmon in season.
STB Highly Commended 3 Crowns
No credit cards
Proprietors: Bill & Evelyn Reed

ARDVOURLIE CASTLE
Aird A Mhulaidh
Isle of Harris PA85 3AB
Tel: 0859 50 2307

On A859 10 miles north of Tarbert.
A memorable castle that stands prominently in the splendid countryside on the shores of Loch Seaforth. It was carefully restored by the present owner and has an atmosphere of its own. Excellent home-cooking is a particular feature of Ardvourlie, even bread comes straight from the oven to the table and there are other painstaking culinary delights. Derek Martin, who has now been joined by his sister Pam, has created a guest house of unusual distinction.
Open all year except over Christmas period
Rooms: 4
Dinner by arrangement (d)
Residents only
Restricted Licence
Bed & breakfast £35 – £40
Dinner B & B £60 – £65
Food based on blend of traditional Scottish and innovation, using local and free-range ingredients when available. Home-made bread.
No credit cards
Proprietor: Derek Martin

SCARISTA HOUSE
Isle of Harris PA85 3HX
Tel: 0859 550 238
Fax: 0859 550 277

*On A859, 15 miles south-west of Tarbert
(Western Isles).*

Scarista House is a charming Georgian dwelling and occupies an imposing position overlooking a three mile long shell-sand beach on the magnificent Atlantic coast of Harris. The eight bedrooms, all with views over the sea, are comfortably and traditionally furnished, with bathrooms en suite. There are two lawned gardens, a walled herb garden and a vegetable garden. With no television or radio, but an extensive library, the hotel offers an atmosphere of complete tranquillity, complemented by excellent cuisine – noted in guides worldwide – in which local fish and shellfish feature prominently, and a carefully selected wine list. Children over eight years welcome.

Open Apr to mid Oct
Rooms: 8 with private facilities
Dinner at 8.15 pm (d)
Residents Licence
No smoking in dining room
Bed & breakfast £42 – £57
Dinner B & B £67 – £82
Razor-shell clams. Prawn soufflés. Fillet of wild venison with a blackcurrant and Cassis sauce. Vegetables from the garden. Praline ice cream with raspberry and almond biscuits. Various Scottish cheeses. Home-made oatcakes, bread, scones etc.
No credit cards
Proprietors: Ian & Jane Callaghan

SIAMARA GUEST HOUSE
6 Leacklee
Isle of Harris PA85 3EH
Tel: 085 983 314

South of Tarbert (c. 5 miles) take fourth road on left, signposted for Roghadal (Rodel) via east. After c. 1½ miles take first left for Stockinish, second house on right.

Siamara is a small cosy guest house on the shores of Loch Stockinish where herons, buzzards, seals and otters are frequently to be seen from guest rooms. If your interest is sea fishing, Tony Dolby will arrange to take you out in his 16 foot boat at a nominal cost. For those who just want to enjoy peace and quiet there is plenty of it available and Tony and his wife, Penny, are trying to develop the

concept of a word 'Harris-ed' as being exactly the opposite to 'harassed'. This is a place where you can enjoy good company, high quality food and accommodation and revel in the tranquillity.

Open all year except Christmas Day
Rooms: 3 with private facilities
Dinner at 7 pm (b)
Residents only
Unlicensed
Children over 12 years welcome
Bed & breakfast £26
Dinner B & B £36
Local salmon and beef. Lamb with rosemary. Venison with Port and walnuts. Steamed puddings. Home-made meringues etc.
STB Highly Commended 3 Crowns
No credit cards
Proprietors: Penny & Tony Dolby

TWO WATERS GUEST HOUSE
Lickisto
Isle of Harris PA85 3EL
Tel: 085 983 246

From Tarbert take road signed to Roghadal (Rodel), then fourth road on left C79 single track. Between Stockinish and Geocrab.

A modern comfortable bungalow situated just 15 yards from the sea in wild mountainous scenery. If you are lucky you may well spot otters and seals nearby. John and Jill Barber have concentrated on making this a home from home and guests look forward eagerly to the imaginative evening meals which feature local seafoods and some of John's own smoked products. The choice of fish for breakfast is quite exceptional but standard normal breakfast fare is of course also available. All rooms are en suite with tea/coffee-making facilities and thoughtful little touches like home-made biscuits. There is free trout fishing and a sea boat is available. A lovely spot from which to indulge in some hill-walking, angling, sailing or bird-watching.

Open 1 May to 30 Sep
Rooms: 4 with private facilities
Dinner at 7 pm (b) 4 course menu
Residents only
Unlicensed
No children
No smoking in dining room
Bed & breakfast £24 – £29
Dinner B & B £37 – £42
Hot smoked salmon and trout. Shellfish. Scottish beef, venison and pheasant.

Home-made soups and sweets. Fresh vegetables from garden.
STB Highly Commended 3 Crowns
No credit cards
Proprietors: Jill & John Barber

Hawick

Map 2

MANSFIELD HOUSE HOTEL
Weensland Road, Hawick
Roxburghshire TD9 9EL
Tel: 0450 73988
Fax: 0450 72007

On A698 approximately 1 mile from centre of Hawick.

The Scottish Borders are famed for their knitwear and Hawick is probably the centre of the area's textile industry. It is not clear whether Mansfield House was built for a textile baron or not, but certainly it is a distinguished house perched on a hill in 10 acres of gardens overlooking the town. The large public rooms are splendidly ornate and the dining room is particularly well proportioned with well spaced tables. All bedrooms are en suite with TV and tea-making facilities. The Mansfield enjoys a good reputation locally for its food and wines.

Open 3 Jan to 25 Dec
Rooms: 12 with private facilities
Bar Lunch 12 – 2 pm (a)
Dining Room/Restaurant Lunch 12 – 2 pm except Sun Sat (b)
Bar Supper 5.30 – 8.30 pm except Sat (a)
Dinner 7 – 9 pm except Sun (c)
No smoking area in restaurant
Bed & breakfast £30 – £52
Dinner B & B £45 – £70
Room Rate £46 – £66
All meals individually prepared by prize winning chef using the best local produce. Home-made desserts a speciality. Extensive range of Scottish cheeses, malt whiskies and liqueurs.
STB Commended 3 Crowns
Credit cards: 1, 2, 3, 5
Proprietors: Sheila & Ian MacKinnon

THE OLD FORGE RESTAURANT
Newmill-on-Teviot, by Hawick
Roxburghshire TD9 0JU
Tel: 0450 85 298

A7, 4 miles south of Hawick, 18 miles north of Langholm. (Edinburgh 54 miles)
This attractive roadside licensed restaurant on the A7 was once the local blacksmith's and all the character of the old 19th century buildings have been retained. Exposed brick walls, beamed ceilings, genuine working bellows and even the original anvil, give the place special appeal. Chef/proprietor Simon Findlay is an award winning chef and it shows in excellent menus, drawing extensively on local produce and representing good value for money. Deservedly he has earned a high reputation for fine food which his wife Judith serves with great charm and courtesy. Our inspector was moved to describe The Old Forge as "a little gem hidden in the rolling Border hills." It is very popular so do book in advance if possible.
Open 11 Jan to 24 Dec except 1 to 8 Nov
Dining Room/Restaurant Lunch 12 – 2 pm Tue to Sat: 12.30 – 2 pm Sun (a)
Dinner 7 – 9 pm Tue to Sat: High Tea 4 – 6 pm Sun (b-c)
Closed Mon
Facilities for the disabled
No smoking area in restaurant
Chicken liver paté with home made granary bread and rhubarb chutney. Loch Fyne mussels with a curry and apricot Hollandaise. Chicken fillet stuffed with Bonchester cheese and banana. Noisettes of Border lamb with an orange and mint sauce. Fillet of beef with haggis and Leith Port.
Credit card: 1
Proprietors: Simon and Judith Findlay

WHITCHESTER CHRISTIAN GUEST HOUSE
Borthaugh, Hawick
Roxburghshire TD9 7LN
Tel: 0450 77477
Fax: 0450 371080

¼ mile off A7, 2 miles south of Hawick on B711 to Roberton.
A former Dower House of the Buccleuch Estate set in 3½ acres of garden. David and Doreen Maybury relocated from Duns to this quiet beautiful spot. The house has been refurbished in a comfortable and relaxing style. All food including the bread is cooked on the

premises and local produce is widely used. Full board includes a traditional Scottish afternoon tea. A wide range of soups are made such as carrot and coriander and lemon and yoghurt, sweets include brûlées, pavlovas, sorbet concoctions and many others, a large Scottish cheese board is kept.
Open 1 Feb to 29 Dec
Rooms: 8 , 4 with private facilities
Dining Room/Restaurant Lunch 12.30 – 1.30 pm (a)
Tea 4.30 – 5 pm
Dinner 7 – 8.30 pm (c)
Unlicensed
No smoking in dining room, bedrooms + conservatory
Bed & breakfast £20.50 – £25
Dinner B & B £30 – £35.50
Home-made soups and bread. Rowan poached trout. Grouse, pheasant, venison, local lamb. Nut meringue gâteau, cranachan, syllabubs.
STB Commended 3 Crowns
No credit cards
Proprietors: David & Doreen Maybury

Helmsdale

Map 6

NAVIDALE HOUSE HOTEL
Helmsdale
Sutherland KW8 6JS
Tel: 043 12 258

½ mile north of Helmsdale on A9.
A former Victorian shooting lodge of the Dukes of Sutherland, Navidale is now a comfortable country house hotel. It stands in seven acres of garden on a cliff top overlooking the North Sea. There is an air of spacious elegance about the public rooms which have superb panoramic views and open fires. There are fine sea views from most of the bedrooms. The kitchen makes good use of the fine supply of local seafish and shellfish.
Open 15 Jan to 15 Nov
Rooms: 15 with private facilities
Bar lunch 12 – 2 pm (a)
Dinner 7 – 9 pm (c)
No smoking in restaurant
Bed & breakfast £25 – £45
Dinner B & B £45 – £52
Fresh Skye oysters. Steamed mussels with garlic butter. Wing of skate with prawn and caper butter. Caithness rack of lamb with garlic and red wine sauce.
Credit cards: 1, 3
Proprietor: Marcus Blackwell

Humbie
nr Edinburgh

Map 4

JOHNSTOUNBURN HOUSE HOTEL
Humbie
East Lothian EH36 5PL
Tel: 0875 833696
Fax: 0875 833626

From A68 Edinburgh-Jedburgh 2 miles south of Pathhead, turn at Fala (hotel is signposted) – 2 miles on right.
A beautifully kept large country mansion, approached by a long tree-lined drive and surrounded by acres of lawns, gardens and picturesque farmland at the foot of the Lammermuir Hills. The visitor to Johnstounburn would hardly imagine that he or she is only 15 miles away from bustling Edinburgh. And once inside the 17th century stone walls, warmed by the open fires and treated to an outstanding menu made with fresh local produce, one begins to appreciate the depth of Scotland's heritage. Johnstounburn has 20 well appointed bedrooms, conference rooms for as many delegates, an exquisite pine-panelled dining room, and a singularly relaxing wood-panelled lounge.
Open all year
Rooms: 20 with private facilities
Bar Lunch 12 – 2 pm (a)
Dining Room/Restaurant Lunch 12 – 2 pm (b)
Dinner 7 – 9 pm (e)
Bed & breakfast £47.50 – £90
Dinner B & B £67.50 – £126
Noisettes of Border lamb with a redcurrant and rosemary sauce. Grilled salmon with prawn and dill butter. Medallions of beef fillet with a coarse grain mustard sauce.
STB Commended 4 Crowns
Credit cards: 1, 2, 3, 5, 6

by
Huntly

Map 5

THE OLD MANSE OF MARNOCH
Bridge of Marnoch
by Huntly AB54 5RS
Tel: 0466 780873

On B9117, 1 mile off A97 midway between Huntly and Banff.
A secluded Georgian country house set in three acres of splendid gardens on the River Deveron. Well appointed en suite bedrooms, elegant lounges, and dining room set with silver and crystal, combine to provide an experience of true Scottish hospitality. The set four course dinner changes daily and everything is prepared in The Old Manse kitchen, whilst the herb parterre and walled kitchen garden supply organic produce in season. A destination for the discerning traveller. Fluent German spoken. Dogs welcome, but not in the dining room.
Open all year except 2 wks Nov
Rooms: 5 with private facilities
Packed lunch – as requested (a)
Dining Room/Restaurant Lunch – residents only, by request (b)
Afternoon tea – as requested (a)
Dinner 7.30 for 8 pm (d) 4 course menu
Reservations essential for non-residents
No smoking in dining room + one of two lounges
Bed & breakfast from £35
Dinner B & B from £52.50
Fine Scots cooking, traditional and contemporary. Award winning breakfast menu includes three different sausages, Scotch woodcock, devilled ham, home-baked breads, home-made preserves.
STB Deluxe 3 Crowns
No credit cards
Proprietors: Patrick & Keren Carter

Innerleithen

Map 2

TRAQUAIR ARMS HOTEL
Traquair Road, Innerleithen
Peeblesshire EH44 6PD
Tel: 0896 830229
Fax: 0896 830260

On A72 midway between Peebles and Galashiels. Turn off Innerleithen High Street on B709, Traquair Road 150 yards.
An attractive traditional 19th century Scottish inn, just a half hour from Edinburgh and ten minutes from

Peebles, in a delightful Borders valley. Hugh and Marian Anderson run it as a relaxing, friendly, family run hotel with genuine concern for the comfort of their guests. Imaginative menus utilise the best local produce and, in appropriate weather, can be enjoyed beside a blazing log fire in the dining room or al fresco in the secluded garden. The bar prides itself on its real ales.
Open all year except Christmas + Boxing Days
Rooms: 10 with private facilities
Bar Meals 12 – 9 pm (a)
Dinner 7 – 9 pm (b-c)
Bed & breakfast £27 – £35
Dinner B & B £40 – £51
Lemon sole with hazelnut butter. Wedges of Dunsyre cheese coated in wholemeal breadcrumbs, with sloeberry jelly. Border lamb cutlets with a sauce of fresh ginger, lemon juice and cream. Grilled Border trout with prawn butter. Vegetarian dishes.
STB Commended 3 Crowns
Credit cards: 1, 3
Proprietors: Hugh & Marian Anderson

Inverkeilor
by Arbroath

Map 4

GORDON'S RESTAURANT
Homewood House, Main Street
Inverkeilor, by Arbroath
Angus DD11 5RN
Tel: 02413 364

Just off A92 Arbroath-Montrose, at north end of Main Street.
A cosy little village restaurant, Gordon's occupies the end of a row of terraced properties forming Main Street and dates back to 1850. The restaurant is attractively decorated in a traditional cottage style and the two bedrooms are tastefully appointed and have en suite showers. Chef/proprietor Gordon Watson's cooking is imaginative and unpretentious making full use of quality fresh ingredients from the locality and fresh herbs from their own garden. His wife, Maria, looks after the customers and sets a tone of friendly and efficient service. Booking is advisable.
Open all year except last 2 wks Jan
Rooms: 2 with private facilities
Bar Lunch 12 – 2.30 pm except Mon (a)
Bar Supper 6 – 9.15 pm except Mon Sat (a)
Dinner 7 – 9.15 pm except Mon (c)

Closed Mon
Facilities for the disabled
No smoking area in restaurant
Bed & breakfast £20 – £25
Dinner B & B from £30
Seafood bisque with Cognac. Smoked wild venison with a warm salad. Pan-fried prime fillet of Aberdeen Angus beef flamed in brandy, served with a sauce of sherry, woodland mushrooms, onions, tomatoes and cream. Marinated noisettes of Scotch lamb, pan-fried and served with a plum sauce. Home-made desserts.
STB Commended 2 Crowns
Credit cards: 1, 3
Proprietors: Gordon & Maria Watson

Invermoriston

Map 6

GLENMORISTON ARMS HOTEL
Invermoriston, Glenmoriston
Inverness-shire IV3 6YA
Tel: 0320 51206

At junction of A82 and A887 in Invermoriston.
The junction of the A82 and the A887 to Kyle of Lochalsh makes a prime site for the 200 year old coaching inn which nestles at the foot of Glenmoriston, a few minutes from world famous Loch Ness. It is typically Scottish, furnished and decorated pleasingly, and with a restaurant serving an impressive menu of national and regional specialities. There is a superb range of malt whiskies to complement your meal. An ideal base for touring the West Highlands and Skye.
Open all year except Christmas Day
Rooms: 8 with private facilities
Bar Lunch 12 – 2 pm (a)
Bar Supper 5.30 – 9 pm (a)
Dinner 6.30 – 8.30 pm (c)
Bed & breakfast £30 – £45
Dinner B & B £49 – £60
Home-made soup. Haggis with a whisky and chive sauce. Fillet steak with a sauce of mushrooms, onions, Drambuie and cream. Medallions of prime venison cooked with mushrooms and green ginger. Local salmon wrapped in sole fillets and gently poached in white wine and cream.
STB Commended 4 Crowns
Credit cards: 1, 3
Proprietor: Alan Draper

Inverness

Map 6

ANCHOR & CHAIN RESTAURANT

Coulmore Bay, North Kessock
Ross-shire IV1 1XB
Tel: 0463 73313

Off A9, 5 miles north of Inverness.
Superb location on the water edge with magnificent views of the Beauly Firth. Fresh local produce is used in the preparation of meals and the same care and attention is taken be it for a bar meal or an à la carte dinner. The site of the restaurant is such that there is not too much "passing traffic", and for survival it is necessary to ensure that customers go away completely satisfied and willing to recommend it to their friends. What better basis for a successful restaurant.
Open Apr to Oct
Bar Lunch 12 – 2 pm except Sun (a)
Dining Room/Restaurant Lunch 12.30 – 2.30 pm Sun only (b)
Bar Supper 6 – 7.30 pm (a)
Dinner 6 – 9 pm (d)
Deep-fried mushrooms stuffed with haggis, with a whisky chive and cream sauce. Lightly poached fillet of sole with a lobster and Pernod sauce.
Credit cards: 1, 3
Proprietor: Iain MacPherson

BUNCHREW HOUSE HOTEL

Bunchrew
Inverness IV3 6TA
Tel: 0463 234917
Fax: 0463 710620

On A862 Inverness-Beauly, c. 10 minutes from centre of Inverness.
Bunchrew House changed ownership early in 1993 but many of the staff remain and early reports indicate that Stuart and Lesley Dykes will continue to maintain and improve the high standards that have distinguished this fine old country house. With foundations going back to 1621 it is set within 18 acres of landscaped gardens and woodlands right on the shores of the Beauly Firth. The public rooms are first class, spacious and comfortable, and meals can be enjoyed in leisurely fashion in the dining room while watching the changing scene out over the Firth.
Open all year
Rooms: 11 with private facilities
Bar Lunch 12 – 2 pm (a)

Dining Room/Restaurant Lunch 12 – 2 pm (b)
Dinner 7 – 9 pm (d)
Facilities for the disabled
No smoking in dining room
Bed & breakfast £30 – £60
Dinner B & B £50 – £80
Avocado and prawn mousse with dill mayonnaise. Smoked salmon with quenelles of cream cheese. Assorted seafood in a cream sauce, served in a hot croissant. Baked gigot of lamb. Roast Highland grouse in a redcurrant and honey sauce. Grape crème brulée.
STB Award Pending
Credit cards: 1, 2, 3
Proprietors: Stuart & Lesley Dykes

CULLODEN HOUSE HOTEL

Culloden
nr Inverness IV1 2NZ
Tel: 0463 790461

A96, 3 miles south of Inverness, take road signed to Culloden. 5 miles from Inverness Airport.
Culloden House must surely be Inverness's most magnificent building, an architectural gem with an historic and romantic association with Bonnie Prince Charlie and the Battle of Culloden which was fought nearby. It has acres of parkland, fine lawns and trees and is an oasis of exceptional quiet. Discerning guests choose Culloden for its comfort, dignity and luxury. The public rooms are magnificent and bedrooms and bathrooms are spacious and splendidly equipped and furnished. The food is of exceptionally high standard, served by attentive staff in an imposing dining room. Adjacent to the main building in a discreet area of wooded grounds, there has been built a most impressive Palladian mansion with four suites which represent the ultimate in luxury and will serve as an additional facility to the main house.
Open all year
Rooms: 23 with private facilities + 4 Garden Suites

Dining Room/Restaurant Lunch 12.30 – 2 pm (d)
Dinner 7 – 9 pm (e)
Room Rate £150 – £190
Mousse of Scottish blue cheese served with salad and a hazelnut vinaigrette. Terrine of duck liver and venison served with an apple compote and rich Madeira sauce. Marinated loin of venison wrapped in pastry with spinach and mushrooms, served with a rich game sauce.
STB Deluxe 5 Crowns
Credit cards: 1, 2, 3, 5, 6
Proprietors: Ian & Marjory McKenzie

DUNAIN PARK HOTEL

Dunain Park
Inverness IV3 6JN
Tel: 0463 230512
Fax: 0463 224532

A82, 1 mile west of Inverness.
Dunain Park seems to grow in stature every year. Ann and Edward Nicoll have established a very high reputation for their delightful country house hotel secluded in six acres of garden and woodland just a mile out of Inverness. As one would expect, the public rooms, bedrooms and suites are extremely well furnished and equipped; the suites particularly being the last word in comfort and elegant living. But it is for the food that Dunain is renowned. Ann Nicoll's cooking is something special and has earned high praise from discerning food writers and brings guests back time and time again. There is a hint of French influence in her deft light touch, especially with fish, but her prowess is also displayed in fine home-cooking and a mouth watering range of desserts. There is an indoor heated swimming pool and a sauna in a log cabin in the grounds and two delightful family suites in the coach house. And fresh herbs and vegetables for the kitchen come from a two acred walled garden.
Open all year except Christmas Day + 3 wks Jan
Rooms: 14 with private facilities
Dinner 7 – 9 pm (c)
No smoking in dining room
Bed & breakfast £45 – £75
Dinner B & B £65 – £95
Special low season rates available
Sun-dried tomato soufflé with grain mustard cream sauce. Fillet of John Dory with brown lentils and a warm vinaigrette. Loin of lamb in pastry, topped with a nutmeg flavoured duxelle

and served with a mint bearnaise sauce. Millefeuille of monkfish served with Noilly Prat sauce. Breast of duck with citric sauce.
STB Deluxe 4 Crowns
Credit cards: 1, 2, 3, 6
Proprietors: Ann & Edward Nicoll

GLEN MHOR HOTEL & RESTAURANT
Ness Bank
Inverness IV2 4SG
Tel: 0463 234308
Fax: 0463 713170
On river bank below castle.
As locations go Glen Mhor could not do much better – a prime site on the south bank of the River Ness near the town centre. There are two levels of eating. The spacious Riverside Restaurant, which is usually open for lunch only on Sundays, concentrates on good value four course table d'hôte dinner meals in the evenings. The menu emphasises the local origin of fish and game and features a "Modern Taste of Scotland". Alternative eating is in Nico's Bistro Bar where Highland specialities are served in addition to a range of char-grills, pasta and snacks both at lunchtime and till late in the evening.
Open all year except 31 Dec to 2 Jan
Rooms: 30 with private facilities
Bar Lunch 12 – 2.15 pm (a)
Bar Supper 5 – 9.30 pm Sun to Thu: 5 – 10.30 pm Fri Sat (a-c)
Dinner 6.30 – 9 pm (d)
Note: Restaurant closed Sun from Oct to Apr
Bed & breakfast £35 – £60
Salmon in various styles. Langoustines, oysters, mussels, fresh fish, beef, lamb.
STB Commended 4 Crowns
Credit cards: 1, 2, 3, 5, 6 + SWITCH
Proprietor: J Nicol Manson

WHINPARK HOTEL
17 Ardross Street
Inverness IV3 5NS
Tel: 0463 232549
By Eden Court Theatre.
Whinpark describes itself as a restaurant with rooms so it is on its food that the main emphasis is to be expected. It is fairly central in the town in a quiet locality near the Eden Court Theatre and the River Ness, in a two storey Victorian terrace. Food is taken seriously and there is enlightened treatment of salmon and beef. New

menus are being developed which will extend the range of choice.
Open all year except Christmas + Boxing Days, 1 Jan
Rooms: 8, 4 with private facilities
Dining Room/Restaurant Lunch 12 – 2 pm except Sun Sat (a-b)
Pre/After Theatre Suppers by arrangement
Dinner 6.30 – 9 pm (c-d)
Bed & breakfast £15 – £27.50
Dinner B & B £32 – £45
Tartlet of flaked crab and smoked chicken baked with diced cheese and apple, served with fresh basil and tomato dressing. Fillet of beef flamed in Madeira and finished in a rich mushroom sauce. Ness salmon with a creamy mussel and shellfish sauce.
STB 3 Crowns
Credit cards: 1, 3
Proprietor: Jackie McIntosh

WHITECROSS RESTAURANT
Ivy Cottage
Muirtown Locks, off Telford St
Inverness IV3 6LS
Tel: 0463 240386
From town centre take A 862 (old Beauly road) for ½ mile. Restaurant just off Telford Street before crossing Caledonian Canal on left.
Once a lock-keeper's cottage this small intimate restaurant beside the Caledonian Canal has established a high reputation for fresh Scottish food cooked with flair and imagination to tempt the dullest of appetites but enough of it to satisfy the fresh air enthusiasts of the boating world. The food is light and natural with flavours and textures nicely blended. Paul and Glynis Whitecross deservedly have a winner on their hands here with standards that are difficult to fault.
Open all year except first 2 wks Nov + first 2 wks Jan
Dining Room/Restaurant Lunch 12.30 – 2 pm except Sat Sun Mon (c)
Dinner 7 – 9.30 pm (early/later by request) except Sun Mon (c-d)
Closed Sun Mon (but available to party bookings by arrangement)
No smoking restaurant but smoking area provided
Lasagne of leeks, Scottish mussels and monkfish. Tartlet of vegetable fricassee, chervil sabayon. Theme of Drambuie (ice cream, soufflé, mousse, gâteau).
Credit cards: 1, 3, 5
Proprietors: Glynis & Paul Whitecross

Inverurie

Map 5

THAINSTONE HOUSE HOTEL
Thainstone Estate, Inverurie
Aberdeenshire AB51 5NT
Tel: 0467 21643
Fax: 0467 25084
On A96 north of Aberdeen (8 miles from airport).
The impressive facade of Thainstone House remains unchanged, but behind it has been completely transformed and has become a sumptuous and luxurious hotel and leisure centre. Architects and designers have done a wonderful job in retaining the character of the old palladian building whilst introducing gracious new public rooms and well equipped bedrooms. International award winning chef Bill Gibb won the Taste of Scotland Scotch Lamb Challenge in 1992 and his sous-chef Garry Rendall won first place in his category in the 1993 competition. The food presented at Thainstone is of an exceptional standard of excellence, contributing to the hotel's high ranking within the quality country house hotels of Scotland.
Open all year
Rooms: 48 with private facilities
Bar Lunch 12 – 2 pm except Sun (b)
Dining Room/Restaurant Lunch (Simpsons) 12 – 2 pm (b)
Bar Supper 6 – 9.30 pm (b)
Dinner (Simpsons) 7 – 9.30 pm (c)
No smoking in restaurant
No dogs
Bed & breakfast £33.50 – £91.95
Dinner B & B £53 – £119.50
Room Rate £67 – £125
Special weekend rates available
Fillet of beef with mushroom duxelle glazed in tarragon butter on a balsamic vinegar sauce with lardons and rosti potato. Loin of lamb with a herb crust on an Arran mustard sauce, with a tartlet of baby vegetables. Collops of venison with young spinach leaves, nutmeg quenelles and red wine pears on a game essence. Pan-fried salmon with fennel, cucumber, langoustine and dill cream.
STB Highly Commended 5 Crowns
Credit cards: 1, 2, 3, 5, 6

Islay
Isle of

Map 7

KILCHOMAN HOUSE RESTAURANT
by Bruichladdich, Isle of Islay
Argyll PA49 7UY
Tel: 049 685 382

*At end of B8018, off A847 Bridgend-
Bruichladdich. Beyond Kilchoman
Church, on the Atlantic side of the
Rhinns of Islay, 6 miles from
Bruichladdich.*

A Listed Georgian building, formerly a manse, Kilchoman House sits in a little hollow, overlooked by majestic crags and open farmland, and is the Taylor family's home. Their attractive and relaxed 20 seat dining room is admirably hosted by Stuart whilst Lesley applies imagination in creating daily changing menus with the help of superior local produce. A very pleasant way to spend an evening. The five self-catering cottages are open all year, minimum three nights stay, early booking advised.

*Open Apr to Oct + booked parties by
arrangement
Dinner 7.30 – 9 pm except Sun Mon (c)
Reservations essential
Closed Sun Mon
Drunken bullock. Venison McHarrie.
Lobster Thermidor (pre-ordered). Stir-
fried Islay scallops. Vegetarian and
special diets by request.
No credit cards
Proprietors: Stuart & Lesley Taylor*

TAIGH-NA-CREAG
7 Shore Street, Port Charlotte
Isle of Islay
Argyll PA48 7TR
Tel: 049 685 261

*Loch side, Port Charlotte village almost
opposite pier.*

Not everyone goes off to the islands in search of peace and quiet. But that is what you will find in Islay. Little more than the soft murmur of the sea in a place where 'getting away from it all' really means that. There are no five star hotels here but what there is may well be preferable; unpretentious, scrupulously clean little B & Bs such as Carole and David Harris operate in tiny Port Charlotte getting on for 200 years old but architecturally virtually unchanged. In the little private dining room overlooking Loch Indaal the Harrises serve good breakfasts and interesting dinners using only fresh meat, fish and vegetables and if you are having a day out walking or bird-watching they will pack you a generous lunch and look after your special needs if you are a vegetarian. This is the real way to live in the islands.

*Open all year
Rooms: 2
Dinner at 7 pm (b)
Residents only
Unlicensed – guests welcome to take
own wine
Dogs – by arrangement
No smoking throughout
Bed & breakfast £17 – £19.50
Dinner B & B £28 – £31
Lobster bisque. Smoked fish chowder.
Cock-a-leekie soup. Mussels in white
wine and garlic. Islay oysters. Venison
pie with red wine, cream and
mushrooms. Islay lamb with apricots.
Fresh fish always available. Carrot and
cashew nut pie (vegetarian). Home-made
bread, chocolates and Islay cream ice
cream.
No credit cards
Proprietors: Carole & David Harris*

Jedburgh

Map 2

WILLOW COURT
The Friars, Jedburgh
Roxburghshire TD8 6BN
Tel: 0835 63702

*From Market Place, Jedburgh, take
Exchange Street – The Friars is first road
on right.*

This charming guest house overlooks the town of Jedburgh and diners have a panoramic view from the bright dining conservatory. Bedrooms are pleasingly decorated with a cheerful airy feel to them. Jane McGovern and her husband put a lot of effort into ensuring the comfort and satisfaction of their guests and to establishing a personal rapport with them. Jane's cooking is much acclaimed; her menus change regularly and include some enterprising dishes. The garden provides much of the fruit and vegetables needed in the kitchen, and fresh flowers for the house.

*Open all year
Rooms: 4 with private facilities
Dinner 5.30 – 6.30 pm (a)
Restricted Licence
Facilities for the disabled
No smoking in restaurant + bedrooms
Bed & breakfast £13 – £25
Dinner B & B £21.50 – £33.50
Grilled Jedburgh haggis with orange and
whisky sauce. Mervinshaw venison
braised in red wine and juniper berries.
Border lamb chops with elderberry jelly.
Trout baked in butter with fresh garden
herbs. Home-grown fruit and vegetables.
Local cheeses and speciality home-made
ice creams.
STB Highly Commended 3 Crowns
No credit cards
Proprietor: Jane McGovern*

Keiss

Map 6

SINCLAIR BAY HOTEL
Main Street, Keiss
Caithness KW1 4XA
Tel: 0955 83 233

*On main A9, 7 miles from John o'
Groats.*

Sinclair Bay Hotel is situated just seven miles south of John o' Groats and eight miles north of Wick on the A9. The hotel is fully licensed and is well appointed and pleasingly decorated throughout. Most bedrooms have views over sea and cliffs, and all have wash basins with continuous hot water, tea and coffee-making facilities and television. There is also a comfortable lounge with television. For those who enjoy eating – farm-reared fowls, roasts and grills (only the finest of Scotland's beef) and fresh seafood are your choice from a daily changing menu. Free golf for all residents. Fishing and sea angling by arrangement.

*Open all year
Rooms: 7, 1 with private facilities
Dining Room/Restaurant Lunch 12.30 –
2 pm (a)
Bar Supper 6.30 – 9 pm (b)
No smoking in dining room
Dinner B & B £17 – £22*

Home-made soup. Fillet steak with pâté in a puff pastry case. Noisettes of lamb with a mint cream sauce. Lemon sole in a mushroom and prawn sauce. Haddock baked with onion, tomatoes and cheese. Prawn and crab salad. Vegetarian dishes.
STB Award Pending
Credit cards: 1, 3
Proprietors: David & Margaret Angus

Kelso

Map 2

FLOORS CASTLE
Kelso
Roxburghshire TD5 7RW
Tel: 0573 223333

A699 west of Kelso.
Floors is the magnificent and imposing Border home of the Duke of Roxburghe much of which is open to the public. The self-service restaurant which caters for visitors is plainly but comfortably furnished and has a well sheltered open courtyard in which you may eat out in good weather. The restaurant makes good use of available fresh produce from the castle gardens, salmon from the River Tweed, and there is some good home-baking.
Open May to Oct
Food service/Restaurant Lunch 11 am – 4.30 pm Sun to Thu: Jul + Aug open 7 days (a)
No smoking area in restaurant
Floors kitchen pheasant pâté, Tweed salmon, smoked Tweed salmon, home-baking from Floors Castle kitchens.
Credit cards: 1, 3

SUNLAWS HOUSE HOTEL
Heiton, Kelso
Roxburghshire TD5 8JZ
Tel: 0573 450331
Fax: 0573 450611

On A698 Kelso-Jedburgh in the village of Heiton.
The origins of Sunlaws go back many hundreds of years and the present 18th century mansion, owned by the Duke of Roxburghe, is magnificent both inside and out. It is surrounded by lovely grounds and gardens, totally secluded and utterly delightful. The current management have continued to improve standards, and food is excellent both in quality and in value; indeed the bar lunch is quite exceptional. Care has been

taken to produce interesting and well balanced menus for more formal meals in the dining room and the abundance of good Borders produce is highlighted. This is a luxurious country house with charm, comfort and style, and with plenty of outdoor recreational activities readily available.
Open all year
Rooms: 22 with private facilities
Bar Lunch 12.30 – 2 pm (a)
Dining Room/Restaurant Lunch 12.30 – 2 pm except Sun Sat (b)
Dinner 7.30 – 9.30 pm (d)
No smoking in restaurant
Bed & breakfast £65 – £85
Dinner B & B £78 – £95
Pan-fried collops of beef fillet topped with oyster mushrooms on a red wine and thyme sauce. Roasted wild salmon on a bed of samphire and spinach beurre blanc. Oven-roasted rack of Border lamb with a light rosemary and garlic jus. Grilled fillet of halibut with a Spring onion and ginger butter sauce.
STB Highly Commended 4 Crowns
Credit cards: 1, 2, 3, 5, 6

Kenmore

Map 4

CROFT-NA-CABER
Garden Restaurant, Kenmore
Perthshire PH15 2HW
Tel: 0887 830 236
Fax: 0887 830 649

A827 to Kenmore, then take unclassified road along south shore of the loch for ½ mile.
An attractive old stone building originally a manse which has been extended and improved to provide a new dining room still in keeping with the original building. It overlooks Loch Tay and a busy water sports complex. All bedrooms have en suite facilities. The Swiss trained chef introduces an intriguing element of conti-nental cooking and combines this with the best of traditional and modern Scottish fare to present interesting menus.
Open all year
Rooms: 5 with private facilities plus 17 chalets
Bar Meals 12 – 10 pm (b)
Dining Room/Restaurant Lunch 12 – 2.30 pm (c)
Dinner 7 – 9 pm (c)
Taste of Scotland applies to Garden Restaurant
Facilities for the disabled

No smoking in restaurant
Bed & breakfast £29 – £35.50
Home-made soup and pâté. Baked rainbow trout with brown butter and almonds. Poached salmon in a white wine and herb sauce. A rich stew of venison, mushrooms and bacon. Pheasant in a cream sauce garnished with grapes. Grilled lamb cutlets with a savoury butter.
Credit cards: 1, 3
Proprietor: A C Barratt

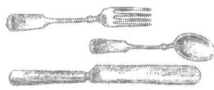

KENMORE HOTEL
Kenmore
Perthshire PH15 2NU
Tel: 0887 830 205
Fax: 0887 830 262

Off A9 on A827, 16 miles west of Ballinluig, 17 miles east of Killin.
Kenmore at the head of Loch Tay is designated as one of Scotland's prettiest villages and it also boasts Scotland's oldest inn. Built in 1572 the Kenmore Hotel is the focal point in the village and has a splendid reputation for the excellence of its facilities and the courteous good manners of an attentive staff. Bedrooms are comfortable, very well equipped and en suite, and the restaurant offers lovely panoramic views over the River Tay. Golfers and fishermen enjoy 50% reduced rates at Taymouth Castle Golf Course and a two mile stretch of the River Tay, but if your preference is for a quietly luxurious and relaxing stay, this would be the place for you.
Open all year
Rooms: 38 with private facilities
Bar Lunch 12 – 2.30 pm (a)
Bar Supper 7.30 – 9.30 pm (b)
Dinner 7.30 – 9.30 pm (d)
Dogs by arrangement
No smoking in restaurant
Bed & breakfast £28 – £49
Dinner B & B £40.25 – £70
Roast loin of lamb filled with apricot seasoning and served on a sherry sauce. Pan-fried julienne of Aberdeen Angus fillet with cream, paprika and onion. Poached Scottish salmon with a wine sauce.
STB Commended 4 Crowns
Credit cards: 1, 2, 3
Proprietor: Andrew MacTaggart

Kentallen of Appin

Map 6

ARDSHEAL HOUSE
Kentallen of Appin
Argyll PA38 4BX
Tel: 063 174 227
Fax: 063 174 342

On A828, 4 miles south of Ballachulish Bridge.
There are some lovely features in this old house once the home of the Stewarts of Appin and set in 900 acres of woods and meadows overlooking Loch Linnhe. The impressive oak staircase and the oak-panelled reception lounge with its unique barrel window are especially noteworthy. The dining room with its conservatory area is a pleasant place to enjoy some really first class food cooked to perfection and well presented. Local game and seafood feature strongly on the menu, bread is baked fresh each day and herbs and fruits come from the hotel's two acre garden. An excellent wine list and wide choice of malt whiskies add to the enjoyment of a meal. There are beautiful gardens, a billiard room and a tennis court.
Open all year except last 3 wks Jan
Rooms: 13 with private facilities
Dining Room/Restaurant Lunch 12 – 2 pm (a-c)
Dinner 8.15 – 8.30 pm (f)
No smoking in restaurant
Dinner B & B £64 – £90
Filo purses of scallops and leeks with saffron cream sauce. Roast saddle of venison with lentil and tarragon mousse. Pressed terrine of duck, black pudding and new potatoes with fresh dill dressing. Warm carrot and plum cake with ginger crème anglaise.
Credit cards: 1, 2, 3
Proprietors: Bob & Jane Taylor

Kilchrenan

Map 6

ARDANAISEIG HOTEL
Kilchrenan, by Taynuilt
Argyll PA35 1HE
Tel: 086 63 333
Fax: 086 63 222

Prestige Award Winner 1990

3½ miles off B845 at Kilchrenan.
It is easy to fall in love with a place like Ardanaiseig. Everything about it seems just right. It is set in a renowned shrub and woodland garden on the shores of Loch Awe with really magnificent views. This is a country house hotel that is beautifully appointed. The kitchen reflects the same high standards that prevail throughout this peaceful haven, food is imaginative and prepared and presented with panache.
Open Easter to 21 Oct
Rooms: 14 with private facilities
Bar Lunch 12.30 – 2 pm (a)
Dining Room/Restaurant Lunch 12.30 – 2 pm (b-c)
Dinner 7.30 – 9 pm (e-f)
No smoking in dining room
Dinner B & B £68 – £135
Chicken liver parfait with toasted brioche and lavender jelly. Ravioli of lobster. Roasted monkfish tail on a bed of leeks, with a light mussel stew. Millefeuille of caramelised pears and ginger served with vanilla ice cream.
Credit cards: 1, 3, 5
Proprietor: James Smith

TAYCHREGGAN HOTEL
Kilchrenan, by Taynuilt
Argyll PA35 1HQ
Tel: 086 63 211

Leave A85 at Taynuilt on to B845 on loch side past Kilchrenan.
In a relatively short time at Taychreggan, Annie Paul has worked wonders in establishing new and higher standards of comfort and cuisine in this delightful small hotel. The location has everything going for it – a secluded site with splendid views across the loch and the spot at which sturdy Highland cattle going to market came to shore after being made to swim across the loch. The cobbled courtyard is a pleasant place in which to sit out on a Summer's evening and enjoy a cool drink and there are comfortable and well equipped public rooms and a delightful dining room. The resident chefs prove their mettle and take great pride, rightly, in their presentation of fresh seasonal and local produce. Even the cheeseboard has a distinctly Scottish theme. The wine list is comprehensive with flair and includes several half bottles. One of the house wines has been personally selected by the owners on one of their many visits to Provence and is first class value.
Open all year
Rooms: 15 with private facilities
Bar Lunch 12.30 – 2 pm (b)
Dinner 7.30 – 9 pm (e) 5 course menu
Bed & breakfast £34 – £46.50
Dinner B & B £60 – £72.50
Special Christmas + New Year Breaks
Local fresh fish, prawns, turbot, halibut, salmon, venison, beef, etc – served in a purist and innovative manner.
Credit cards: 1, 2, 3
Proprietors: Euan & Annie Paul

Kildrummy

Map 5

KILDRUMMY CASTLE HOTEL
Kildrummy, by Alford
Aberdeenshire AB33 8RA
Tel: 09755 71288
Fax: 09755 71345

On A97 Ballater-Huntly, 35 miles west of Aberdeen.
A grand and impressive mansion house overlooking the ruins of the original 13th century castle nearby. It has superb grounds – acres of beautiful gardens and woodland on which it is a joy to meander. The interior is very imposing with a grand staircase, what looks like acres of wood panelling, and tapestries dating from the turn of the century. The whole building abounds in character and atmosphere and Tom Hanna the proprietor maintains the highest of standards in all aspects of the hotel. Bedrooms are spacious and have every modern comfort and convenience, and the food is of the same high level of excellence that is demonstrated throughout. There is a superb wine list including – and full marks to Kildrummy – about 40 different half bottles.
Open Feb to Dec
Rooms: 16 with private facilities
Dining Room/Restaurant Lunch 12.30 – 1.45 pm (b)
Dinner 7 – 9 pm (e)
No smoking in dining room

Bed & breakfast £55 – £70
Dinner B & B £57 – £95
Filo pastry case of chicken and mushrooms in a paprika and brandy sauce. Poached fillet of sole with a mango and ginger sauce. Peppered rack of lamb cutlets with a four peppercorn and brandy sauce. Pan-fried medallions of venison with a sweet apple and blackcurrant sauce. Poached salmon with a white wine sauce and julienne of vegetables.
STB Deluxe 4 Crowns
Credit cards: 1, 2, 3, 6
Proprietor: Thomas Hanna

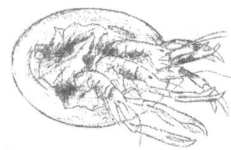

Kilfinan

Map 3

KILFINAN HOTEL
Kilfinan, nr Tighnabruaich
Argyll PA21 2EP
Tel: 070 082 201
Fax: 070 082 205

On B8000, between Tighnabruaich and Otter Ferry, on the eastern side of Loch Fyne.
A truly delightful old coaching inn dating back to the 17th century and most tastefully and comfortably modernised. It is set in lovely countryside on the eastern shore of Loch Fyne and is a real haven of relaxation. Lynne and Rolf Mueller make their guests feel specially welcome and their attitude of caring attention is reflected in other members of staff. The dining room is a timeless characterful room of dark wood and low ceilings set out with fine china, glassware, fresh flowers and good table linen. The food is first class as one would expect from Chef Mueller who is a member of the Master Chefs of Great Britain. Perhaps our inspector summed it up succinctly by saying "this was just a joy, I can't wait to go back".
Open 1 Mar to 31 Jan
Rooms: 11 with private facilities
Bar Lunch 12 – 2 pm (a)
Dining Room/Restaurant Lunch 12 – 2 pm (b)

Bar Supper 6 – 7.30 pm (a)
Dinner 7.30 – 9.30 pm (d) 4 course menu
Bed & breakfast £34 – £44
Dinner B & B £56 – £66
Grilled fillet of brill in a tarragon and tomato sauce. Medallion of Kilfinan red deer with grain mustard. Noisettes of lamb served with a thyme jus. Fillet of halibut in a vermouth and dill sauce. Entrecote marinated in Guinness and served with herb butter. Supreme of duck with passion fruit.
STB Highly Commended 3 Crowns
Credit cards: 1, 2, 3

Killiecrankie

Map 4

KILLIECRANKIE HOTEL
Killiecrankie, by Pitlochry
Perthshire PH16 5LG
Tel: 0796 473220
Fax: 0796 472451

On old A9, 3 miles north of Pitlochry.
This former Dower House is set in four acres of well kept gardens and wooded grounds overlooking the River Garry and the historic Pass of Killiecrankie. The hotel is furnished to a high standard and conveys the atmosphere expected of a small country house. Bedrooms are individually and tastefully decorated and provide every comfort requirement for the most fastidious guest. The restaurant is renowned for its high standard of food, presenting the best of local produce in an interesting and imaginative way.
Open to 3 Jan, then 4 Mar to early Jan
Rooms: 11 with private facilities
Bar Lunch 12.30 – 2 pm (b)
Bar Supper 6.30 – 9.30 pm (b)
Dinner 7 – 8.30 pm (d)
No smoking in dining room
Bed & breakfast £39 – £46
Dinner B & B £64 – £69
Darne of sea trout grilled in lemon oil, coated with a citrus Hollandaise and served with a warm salad of marinaded sea scallops. Prime fillet of Scotch beef served on a crouton of walnut bread with a duxelle of bacon, mushrooms, garlic and red onions, with a rich Madeira and rosemary sauce. Breast of Guinea fowl en croûte with orange and pineapple sauce.
STB Commended 4 Crowns
Credit cards: 1, 3
Proprietors: Colin & Carole Anderson

Kilmarnock

Map 1

THE COFFEE CLUB
30 Bank Street, Kilmarnock
Ayrshire KA1 1HA
Tel: 0563 22048

In town centre.
Situated in one of the oldest streets in Kilmarnock opposite the Laigh Kirk. Offering something for everyone – quick service, snack meals and a large varied menu including grills and vegetarian dishes. In addition there is the new Executive Room menu. All food is produced to order using fresh produce where practicable and bakery items are a speciality. The ambience is relaxed and friendly, and you may take your own wine.
Open all year except Christmas + Boxing Days, 1 + 2 Jan
Coffee and meals served from 9.30 am – 10 pm except Sun (a-b)
Closed Sun for meals but coffee lounge open 12 – 5.30 pm
Unlicensed – guests welcome to take own wine
No smoking area in air-conditioned restaurant
Sandwiches, salads, omelettes etc. Children's menu. Vegetarian dishes. Grilled salmon steak with Hollandaise sauce. Sole with almonds in a rich cream sauce. Duck breast fillet served with a hot cherry compote. Steaks with a variety of sauces.
Credit cards: 1, 2, 3
Proprietors: Svend Kamming & William MacDonald

Kilmelford

Map 6

CUILFAIL HOTEL
Kilmelford
Argyll PA34 4XA
Tel: 085 22 274
Fax: 085 22 264

A816 midway between Oban and Lochgilphead, at top of Loch Melfort.
An old drovers inn and now a very comfortable traditional Scottish country hotel with a good west of Scotland atmosphere. It is a very popular overnight or meal time stopping place on the Oban-Lochgilphead road. A good base for touring or exploring the Firth of Lorn and well known to hill-walkers, fishermen and sailors. There is lots of character about the place and a recent major refurbishment and renovation programme did much to improve the standard of bedrooms and public rooms. It has delightful gardens just across the road – splendid for a relaxing Summer evening's cool drink as you watch the world go by.
Open all year
Rooms: 12 with private facilities
Bar Lunch 12 – 2.30 pm (a)
Bar Supper 6.30 – 9.30 pm (a-b)
Dinner 6.30 – 9.30 pm (b)
Bed & breakfast £27.50 – £32.50
Dinner B & B £40 – £47.50
Home-made pies with crisp puff pastry. Chicken in pastry with various fillings and sauces. Pork and beef en croûte. Local salmon. Prawns and lobster. All dishes freshly prepared.
STB Commended 3 Crowns
Credit cards: 1, 3 + DELTA
Proprietor: David Birrell

Kilmun

Map 3

FERN GROVE
Kilmun
Argyll PA23 8SB
Tel: 0369 84 334
Fax: 0369 84 424

6 miles from Dunoon on A880 on the side of the Holy Loch.
The former family home of the 'Campbells of Kilmun' is on a site overlooking the Holy Loch. The welcoming warm hospitality of hosts Ian and Estralita Murray creates a very comforting and friendly atmosphere in this attractive Victorian house. It is not a large building and it emanates an air of relaxation and cosy family living. Estralita presides in the kitchen and prepares daily menus using only fresh local and home-grown produce and creates interesting and appealing meals. There is a sensibly priced wine list.
Open Apr to Oct + weekends only Nov to Mar
Rooms: 4 with private facilities
Dining Room/Restaurant Lunch – by prior arrangement
Dinner 7 – 9.30 pm except Tue (c)
No dogs
No smoking in restaurant + bedrooms
Bed & breakfast £20 – £25
Dinner B & B £35 – £43
Special Winter rates on application
Home-baked assorted breads. Unusual soups and patés. Best of home-produced beef and lamb. Imaginative vegetarian dishes (by request). No rules 'sweetaholics' dessert trolley! Only the best of Scottish cheeses.
Credit cards: 1, 3
Proprietors: Ian & Estralita Murray

Kilwinning

Map 1

MONTGREENAN MANSION HOUSE HOTEL
Montgreenan Estate, Torranyard
Kilwinning
Ayrshire KA13 7QZ
Tel: 0294 57733 • Telex: 778525
Fax: 0294 85397

Off A736 Glasgow-Irvine near Torranyard, c. 5 miles north of Irvine.
A stay at this lovely old mansion house is a journey back in time to an age of elegance and gracious living. Although its origins go back to the 14th century the present building is primarily 18th century and attractive features from that time have been retained. Stately rooms, decorative ceilings, marble and brass fireplaces spell out the inherited character of the place, yet outside is a heliport facility for those whose schedules are much more exciting than was the case when Montgreenan was first built. Bedrooms are excellent and the newly refurbished sitting room is ultra comfortable. In the kitchen Chef Alan McCall creates an exciting menu based on the best raw materials. The overall experience is very satisfying.
Open all year
Rooms: 21 with private facilities
Bar Lunch 12 – 2.30 pm (a-b)
Dining Room/Restaurant Lunch 12 – 2.30 pm (b)
Dinner 7 – 9.30 pm (d)
Bed & breakfast £46 – £77
Dinner B & B £56 – £96
Room Rate £60 – £146
Poached fillet of sole with Guinness and crab sauce. Lamb cutlets with Arran mustard and rosemary jus-lie. Roast breast of duck with orange and black cherries. Roast salmon with sun-dried tomatoes and fresh mango. Escalope of venison in a whisky and sweet chestnut sauce.
STB Commended 4 Crowns
Credit cards: 1, 2, 3, 5, 6
Proprietors: The Dobson Family

Kincraig

Map 6

MARCH HOUSE GUEST HOUSE
Feshiebridge, Kincraig
Kingussie
Inverness-shire PH21 1NG
Tel: 0540 651 388
Fax: 0540 651 388

Off A9 at Kincraig. Follow B970 for 2 miles to Feshiebridge. Past red telephone box, turn right. Half mile on left down gravel drive.
This very comfortable family run guest house is situated in the tranquillity of beautiful unspoilt Glenfeshie. Surrounded by mature pine trees it enjoys outstanding views of the Cairngorm Mountains. Perfect for all outdoor pursuits including skiing, gliding, watersports and golf (six courses within easy reach) and a naturalist and bird-watcher's paradise. Mountain bike hire available. Local attractions include the Wildlife Park, Highland Folk Museum and Inchriach Alpine Nursery. All rooms have private facilities and tea/coffee etc. Home-baking and cooking with imagination using the best of local produce including salmon, trout, lamb, Angus beef and venison, and fresh herbs from the garden. Friendly relaxed atmosphere.
Open 27 Dec to 30 Oct except 17 Apr to 14 May
Rooms: 6 with private facilities
Dinner at 7 pm (b)
Reservations essential for non-residents
Unlicensed – guests welcome to take own wine

Bed & breakfast £18 – £24
Dinner B & B £30 – £36
Special weekly rate available
Broccoli and asparagus soup.
Wholemeal soda bread rolls with
walnuts. Venison with pickled walnuts
and red wine. Local trout, grilled and
served with cucumber and yoghurt.
Carbonnade of beef. Raspberry and
apple pie. Hot light lemon sponge
pudding served with cream.
STB Commended 2 Crowns
No credit cards
Proprietors: Caroline & Ernie Hayes

Kingussie

Map 6

THE CROSS
Tweed Mill Brae, Ardbroilach Road
Kingussie PH21 1TC
Tel: 0540 661166
Fax: 0540 661080

Prestige Award Winner 1989

From traffic lights in centre of village,
travel uphill along Ardbroilach Road for
c. 200 yards, then turn left down private
drive.
Having made such a huge success of
their restaurant in the High Street,
Kingussie, it was inevitable that Tony
and Ruth Hadley would relocate to
somewhere more worthy of their
standards and they have found this in an
old tweed mill in the town. The site is
superb, on a hillside overlooking the
river, and the mill has been converted
with imagination and flair into a first

class facility. Because they put food first
in their planning, the Hadleys may well
describe this as a restaurant with
rooms. But it is more than that – it is
really a delightful small country hotel
with beautifully furnished bedrooms, a
restaurant full of character and a
pleasant terrace to sit out on and enjoy
a drink. As for the food...... Ruth Hadley
is still masterminding it personally and
that is a guarantee of something special.
Everything about the new Cross augurs
well and it will almost certainly be
another resounding success.
Open 1 Mar to 31 Nov
Rooms: 9 with private facilities
Dining Room/Restaurant Lunch 12.30 –
2 pm except Tue Wed (b)
Dinner 7 – 9 pm except Tue (e-f)
Closed Tue
Dinner B & B £65 – £75
Roast Gressingham duck with a sauce of
cranberries and ginger. Fillet of local wild
red deer, lightly sauté with a Port wine
and redcurrant sauce. Breast of Guinea
fowl lightly roasted with tarragon, sherry
and crème fraiche. Pan-fried fillet of
Aberdeen Angus beef with a Madeira
sauce scented with ceps.
Credit cards: 1, 3
Proprietors: Tony & Ruth Hadley

THE OSPREY HOTEL
Ruthven Road, Kingussie
Inverness-shire PH21 1EN
Tel: 0540 661510
Fax: 0540 661510
In Kingussie village, on corner of main
road.
An attractive small Highland hotel in the
middle of the village, where the owners,
Robert and Aileen Burrow, put great
emphasis on personal service and
providing a relaxing and informal
atmosphere for their guests. The
imaginative menu features the best of
local produce, home-baking and
interesting vegetarian dishes, and
earned The Osprey a Rosette from the
Automobile Association in 1993. An
ideal base from which to tour, or for
those wishing to take advantage of the

numerous sporting and outdoor pursuits
in the area.
Open all year except first 2 wks Nov
Rooms: 8 with private facilities
Dinner 7.30 – 8 pm (c)
No smoking in dining room
Bed & breakfast £22 – £36
Dinner B & B £39 – £54
Broccoli cream cheese soup. Baked
salmon and spinach creams. Guinea
fowl with mushrooms and mustard
cream. Woven sole with sweet and sour
sauce. Raspberry and almond tart.
Hazelnut shortbread with Summer fruits.
STB Commended 3 Crowns
Credit cards: 1, 3
Proprietors: Robert & Aileen Burrow

Kinlochbervie

Map 6

THE KINLOCHBERVIE HOTEL
Kinlochbervie, by Lairg
Sutherland IV27 4RP
Tel: 0971 521275
Fax: 0971 521438
On B801, via A838 from Lairg.
In the remoteness of Sutherland this is a
surprisingly modern hotel set on top of a
hill with superb views of Kinlochbervie
harbour and Loch Clash. Kinlochbervie is
a major fishing port and the hotel takes
full advantage of this by featuring really
fresh locally caught seafood on its menu
in the candlelit dining room. There is
also a bistro for informal eating. The
hotel is well appointed with comfortable
bedrooms and good standards.
Open 1 Apr to 31 Oct
Rooms: 14 with private facilities
Bar Lunch 12 – 1.45 pm (a)
Bar Supper 6.30 – 8.30 pm (b)
Dinner 7.30 – 8.30 pm (d)
No smoking in dining room
Bed & breakfast £42 – £52
Dinner B & B £68 – £78
Roulade of smoked salmon with cottage
cheese and dill. Cream of courgette
soup. Pan-fried breast of duck with bitter
orange sauce. Steamed fillet of halibut
with lemon butter sauce.
STB Highly Commended 4 Crowns
Credit cards: 1, 2, 3, 5
Proprietors: Rex & Kate Neame

Credit Card Code		Meal Price Code	
1. Access/Mastercard/Eurocard		(a)	under £10
2. American Express		(b)	£10 – £15
3. Visa		(c)	£15 – £20
4. Carte Bleu		(d)	£20 – £25
5. Diners Club		(e)	£25 – £30
6. Mastercharge		(f)	over £30

Kinloch Rannoch

Map 4

BUNRANNOCH HOUSE

Kinloch Rannoch
Perthshire PH16 5QB
Tel: 0882 632407

Turn right after 500 yards on Schiehallion road, just outside Kinloch Rannoch off B846.

Bunrannoch is a family run former hunting lodge nestled at the foot of the 'sleeping giant' mountain close by Loch Rannoch. The cosy lounge, log fires and uninterrupted Highland views complement the delicious aromas from the kitchen. Walk the mountain glens, ramble on Rannoch Moor or catch a trout in the loch, then return to Bunrannoch House to relax and savour the delights of Highland cooking.

Open all year except Christmas + New Year
Rooms: 7, 5 with private facilities
Dinner 7 – 9 pm (c)
No smoking in dining room
Bed & breakfast £16 – £18
Dinner B & B £28 – £30
Fillet of venison in redcurrant and Port. Salmon cooked in foil with nutmeg and rosemary and served with an orange sauce. Best Scotch fillet in whisky cream sauce. Apple and raspberry cake with Drambuie cream. Oat baskets with heather honey cream and strawberries.
STB Approved 2 Crowns
Credit cards: 1, 3
Proprietor: Jennifer Skeaping

CUILMORE COTTAGE

Kinloch Rannoch
Perthshire PH16 5QB
Tel: 0882 632218

Small is Beautiful Award 1990

100 yards from east corner of Loch Rannoch.

Anita Steffen has made a tremendous success of this cosy little 18th century croft and the standard and style of her food has been lauded and publicised to a degree that is remarkable for such a small establishment. Much of the produce is grown in the cottage garden and the rest is carefully sourced to ensure freshness and quality. Thereafter Anita displays her own skill and flair to the great satisfaction of her diners. Cuilmore is delightfully secluded and

guests have the complimentary use of mountain bikes, dinghy and canoe to explore the locality.
Open 1 Feb to 30 Oct
Rooms: 2 with private facilities
Dinner 7 – 9 pm (d)
Prior booking essential for non-residents
Unlicensed – guests welcome to take own wine
No children
No smoking in dining room
Bed & breakfast from £20
Dinner B & B from £40
Local smoked loin of lamb dressed with redcurrant jelly. Ballotine of game with select salad leaves. Casseroled saddle of rabbit with herby dumplings. Baby Guinea fowl on a ragoût of mushrooms. Chocolate and Cointreau delice with orange chantilly cream. Baked rum and raisin cheesecake.
STB Deluxe 3 Crowns
No credit cards
Proprietor: Anita Steffen

Kinnesswood

Map 4

THE LOMOND COUNTRY INN

Kinnesswood, by Loch Leven
Perthshire KY13 7HN
Tel: 0592 84 253
Fax: 0592 84 693

4 miles from Kinross. From south, M90 Junction 5, B9097 via Scotlandwell. From north, M90 Junction 7, A911 via Milnathort.

Situated in the historic village of Kinnesswood, by the Lomond Hills, this cosy family run hotel offers magnificent views over Loch Leven. Only fresh food is served – simply prepared and very tasty – good wines and real ale. Twelve en suite bedrooms all with colour TV, telephones, tea and coffee-making facilities. Only 45 minutes from Edinburgh, Perth and St Andrews, and at the hub of all the sporting, leisure and cultural opportunities that abound in the area.

Open all year except Christmas Night
Rooms: 12 with private facilities
Light snacks (scones, sandwiches and tea) served all day
Bar Lunch 12 – 2 pm (a)
Dining Room/Restaurant Lunch 12 – 2.30 pm (a)
Bar Supper 6 – 9 pm (a)
Dinner 7 – 9 pm (b)
Bed & breakfast £24.50 – £30.50

Dinner B & B £34.50 – £40.50
Scottish menu includes Cullen skink, local grilled goats cheese, baked fillet of Tay salmon wrapped in puff pastry and served in vermouth sauce, Athol brose or Scottish cheeses.
STB Commended 3 Crowns
Credit cards: 1, 2, 3, 5 + SWITCH
Proprietors: David Adams & Neil Hunter

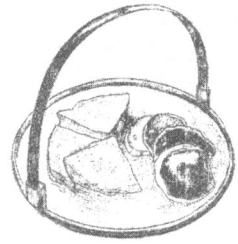

Kinross

Map 4

CROFTBANK HOUSE HOTEL

30 Station Road, Kinross
Fife KY13 7TG
Tel: 0577 863819

Junction 6, M90 on approach to Kinross.

This old Victorian mansion house is a popular friendly hotel and restaurant not more than half a mile off the motorway. Bill Kerr is a chef of distinction and serves up really imaginative and creative dishes while his wife Diane looks after the front of the house with great charm and attention. Kinross is well placed for Fife's famous golf courses or for fishing, shooting or just sight-seeing as it is very convenient for Edinburgh, Perth, St Andrews or Stirling.

Open all year except Christmas/New Year period
Rooms: 3 with private facilities
Bar Lunch 12 – 2 pm except Mon (b)
Dining Room/Restaurant Lunch 12 – 2 pm except Mon (b)
Supper 6.30 – 9 pm except Mon (b)
Dinner 6.30 – 9 pm except Mon (c)
Closed Mon
No smoking in restaurant
Bed & breakfast £20 – £24
Dinner B & B £40 – £45
Room Rate £20 – £24

Stuffed warm courgette flower with salmon mousse and a tomato and basil vinaigrette. Breast of Guinea fowl with wild chanterelle mushrooms and Madeira wine jus-lie. Fresh apricot parfait. Whole poached peach with a fresh strawberry coulis and Glayva ice cream.
STB Commended 2 Crowns
Credit cards: 1, 3
Proprietors: Bill & Diane Kerr

THE GROUSE & CLARET RESTAURANT
Heatheryford
Kinross KY13 7NQ
Tel: 0577 864212
Fax: 0577 864212

Junction 6, M90, opposite the Granada Services.
Within sight of, but not sound of, the M90 at Exit 6 with its entrance drive exactly opposite the motorway service area yet a world apart in style and standard. Taking its unusual name from a fishing fly this really is a special place with a peaceful atmosphere, serving delightful food and wine. The decor is charming and the old sandstone buildings are filled with unusual antique furniture, old rugs and lovely pictures. The new dining room overlooks the fishing lochans. There are many examples of fine local craftwork for sale in the art gallery, which also caters for special parties of up to 70 guests and is popular for birthdays, anniversaries and business meetings. Meriel Cairns takes pride in floral table decorations and garlands the beams with flowers and ivy for special occasions. The delicious home-made food is beautifully presented with lots of fresh herbs and garnished with tiny wild flowers. It is a bit like dining with a good friend and one who is an exceptional cook. The accommodation is in a modern annexe with comfortable ground floor rooms overlooking the water. Good fly-fishing for trout is available for the enthusiastic fisherman.
Open all year except Feb
Rooms: 3 with private facilities
Bar Lunch 11.30 am – 3 pm (a)
Dining Room/Restaurant Lunch 12 – 2.30 pm (b)
Dinner 7 – 9 pm (b-c)
Table Licence
Facilities for the disabled
No smoking in restaurant
Bed & breakfast £18.50 – £24
Grilled Heatheryford trout with fresh

garden herbs and lemon. Rack of lamb coated in mustard and puff pastry with rosemary sauce. Braised breast of duck garnished with avocado and orange. Pan-fried fillet of beef on a tomato and courgette provençale sauce.
STB Approved 3 Crowns
Credit cards: 1, 3
Proprietors: John & Meriel Cairns

THE MUIRS INN KINROSS
49 Muirs, Kinross
Perthshire KY13 7AU
Tel: 0577 862270

M90 exit Junction 6 (Milnathort). At 'T' junction, Inn is diagonally opposite to right.
A delightful Scottish country Inn, close to the shores of Loch Leven and its historical connection with Mary, Queen of Scots, who was imprisoned on an island in the loch in 1567. There is marked attention to detail and to the comfort of guests in the attractively furnished en suite bedrooms, and the 'old world' atmosphere of the Inn proper is well carried through in the Maltings Restaurant with its interesting historical pictures and prints, and dark beams overhead. The Muirs Inn aims to offer good wholesome food at sensible prices and succeeds in doing so, while for the connoisseur there are nearly 100 malt whiskies and a choice of eight predominantly Scottish Real Ales in addition to the Inn's own branded beers and lagers.
Open all year
Rooms: 5 with private facilities

Bar Lunch 12 – 2.30 pm (a)
Dining Room/Restaurant Lunch 12 – 2.30 pm (a)
Bar Supper 5 – 9 pm (a)
Dinner 5 – 9 pm (b)
No dogs
Smoking discouraged
Bed & breakfast £27.50 – £35
Dinner B & B £40 – £47.50
Potted hough with toast. Muirs fish brose – a creamy smoked haddock soup. Prime Scottish venison with a bitter-sweet honey and hazelnut sauce. Smoked trout served with a Mull whisky dressing. Prime Scottish steaks.
STB Commended 3 Crowns
Credit cards: 1, 3, 6
Proprietors: Gordon Westwood & Graham Philip

Kippen

Map 4

CROSS KEYS HOTEL
Main Street, Kippen
by Stirling FK8 3DN
Tel: 0786 870293

On B822 Callander-Fintry and just off A811 Stirling-Erskine Bridge, only 8 miles west of Stirling.
An attractive old 18th century village inn, now a small family run hotel, set in the peaceful and picturesque village of Kippen, near Stirling. The hotel has retained its old world character which is enhanced by log fires in the bars during Winter. In addition to informal meals in the bar and family room, there is a small restaurant where the interesting menu offers a good selection of freshly prepared dishes.
Open all year except Christmas Night + 1 Jan
Rooms: 3
Bar Lunch 12 – 2 pm Mon to Sat: 12.30 – 2 pm Sun (a)
Dining Room/Restaurant Lunch 12 – 2 pm Mon to Sat: 12.30 – 2 pm Sun (a)
Bar Supper 5.30 – 9.30 pm (a)
Dinner 7 – 8.45 pm (c)
Bed & breakfast from £21
Home-made soups and patés. Breast of chicken with a lemon and tarragon sauce. Scottish salmon en croûte. Roast haunch of venison with a raspberry and red wine sauce. Medallions of fillet of beef with a peppered brandy and cream sauce. Athole brose with Kippen honey.
Credit cards: 1, 3
Proprietors: Angus & Sandra Watt

Kirkcudbright

Map 1

AULD ALLIANCE RESTAURANT
5 Castle Street
Kirkcudbright DG6 4JA
Tel: 0557 30569

Kirkcudbright town, opposite the castle.
A Listed building constructed of old castle stones and formerly a tradesman's cottage. There are very few airs and graces about the decoration of this little restaurant but the food says it all. Alistair Crawford's cooking is of a very high order combining the best of French and Scottish cuisine in menus of unusual scope for such a relatively small county town and featuring prominently the excellent local seafood and Galloway beef.
Open Easter to 31 Oct + Christmas wk
Dining Room/Restaurant Lunch 12.30 – 2 pm Sun only (a)
Dinner 6.30 – 9.30 pm (c)
Smoked Scottish salmon wrapped around lightly sauté Kirkcudbright queen scallops and salmon mousse, with apple and mint jelly and a hint of Pernod. Prime Scotch sirloin steak, pan-fried with crushed black peppercorns, finished in brandy and Galloway cream. Kirkcudbright queen scallops fried in garlic butter with smoked Ayrshire bacon, finished in Galloway cream.
No credit cards
Proprietors: Alistair & Anne Crawford

SELKIRK ARMS HOTEL
High Street, Kirkcudbright
Kirkcudbrightshire DG6 4JG
Tel: 0557 30402
Fax: 0557 31639

Off A75, 27 miles west of Dumfries.
Historic 18th century hotel with Burns connection in the picturesque harbour town of Kirkcudbright, with its own large secluded garden. Although recently refurbished the hotel still manages to retain its character. There are extensive à la carte and daily changing table d'hôte menus. Marvellous walking, fishing, bird-watching and beaches nearby.
Open all year
Rooms: 15 with private facilities
Bar Lunch 12 – 2 pm (a)
Dining Room/Restaurant Lunch 12 – 2 pm (a) – booking essential
Bar Supper 6 – 9.30 pm (b)

Dinner 7 – 9.30 pm (c)
Bed & breakfast £34.50 – £44
Dinner B & B £31 – £61.50
Queen scallops in white wine, bacon and tomato served in a filo pastry basket. Fillets of plaice rolled with smoked salmon and spinach, poached in dry vermouth and served with a light dill sauce. Pan-fried Barbary duck breast with Calvados and apples. Venison cooked with red wine and black cherries in a rich brown sauce. Fillet steak flamed with dry sherry and brandy with a sauce of onions, mushrooms, tomatoes and cream.
STB Highly Commended 4 Crowns
Credit cards: 1, 2, 3, 5
Proprietor: John Morris

Kirkintilloch

Map 3

THE LADY MARGARET CANALBOAT
Scotland in View Ltd
c/o 22 Main Street, The Village
Cumbernauld G67 2RS
Tel: 0836 607755/041 776 6996/0236 723523

> **Canalboat based at Glasgow Road Bridge Jetty, on A803 between Bishopbriggs and Kirkintilloch, near The Stables.**

Calm water canal cruises on the northern outskirts of Glasgow, in country scenery, with floodlights and central heating for all year round operation. The purpose-built canalboat is tastefully appointed. Crystal glasses and Wedgwood crockery enhance attractive table settings, with pink linen and fresh flowers. A relaxing experience, unrivalled in Scotland. Available for group bookings at any time, any day. The boat provides a quality venue which is especially suitable for business entertainment, family gatherings and weddings any day – as well as for individual table bookings on weekend cruises for that special occasion.
Operates all year except Christmas Day + 1 Jan
Lunch (Sun only) sailing at 1 pm (c)
Dinner sailing at 7.30 pm Thu Fri Sat (e)
Advance booking essential
Imaginative set menus incorporating the best in fresh Scottish produce and dishes with an emphasis on quality and presentation. Dinner menus incorporate

an exceptional range of Scottish cheeses.
Credit cards: 1, 2, 3, 5
Contact: Andrew Flockhart

Kirkmichael

Map 4

THE LOG CABIN HOTEL
Kirkmichael, by Blairgowrie
Perthshire PH10 7NB
Tel: 0250 881288
Fax: 0250 881402

Signposted off A924 in Kirkmichael.
Uniquely built of whole Norwegian pine logs, the Log Cabin Hotel nestles high in Glen Derby with some wonderful panoramic views. The hotel is centrally heated and double glazed so guests are assured of a warm welcome. Lovely views from the restaurant where the menus change each evening to reflect the availability of local produce. An ideal centre for touring Perthshire. Also popular with hill-walkers and convenient for skiing in Glenshee.
Open all year except Christmas + Boxing Days
Rooms: 13 with private facilities
Bar Lunch 12 – 1.45 pm (a-b)
Bar Supper 6 – 8.45 pm (a-b)
Dinner 7.30 – 8.45 pm (c)
Bed & breakfast £25.50 – £27.80
Dinner B & B £40.55 – £42.75
Home-produced dishes using tender game and local produce including salmon and trout. Delicious desserts for those on and off diets(!) with a selection of home-made ice creams.
STB Commended 3 Crowns
Credit cards: 1, 2, 3, 5, 6
Proprietor: A F Finch

Kyle of Lochalsh

Map 6

BIADH MATH RESTAURANT
Railway Platform, Kyle of Lochalsh
Ross-shire IV40 8XX
Tel: 0599 4813

At Kyle of Lochalsh railway station on platform 1. Parking on slipway to station.
You have to know exactly where you are going to find Biadh Math the good food cafe which is right on the railway platform, but do not be deterred by that. For holiday-makers on a budget and lovers of good homely food this is a find.

It specialises in the abundance of fresh local seafood, langoustine, scallops and monkfish, served up in interesting ways, but for those who prefer red meat there are usually good lamb and steak alternatives. Jams, chutneys and cakes are home-made as is the fudge with your coffee. On cold nights a coal fire burns bright and creates a snug little haven overlooking the harbour, the Cuillin Hills and the ferry to Skye. In the peak season, the restaurant is open for breakfast and for light snacks all day.
Open Easter to Oct
Note: please telephone to check opening times during off-peak season
Breakfast served 10 – 11.30 am
Dining Room/Restaurant Lunch 12 – 2.45 pm Thu Fri only (a)
Dinner 6.30 – 9 pm (b)
Table Licence
Langoustines in garlic butter. Seafood crêpes in a tarragon sauce. Queen scallops in a white wine sauce. Seafood platter. Lamb marinated in garlic, lemon, mint and oil, skewered with pepper, mushroom, tomato and onion, served on cous cous with yoghurt dressing. Pan-fried steaks with onions and mushrooms, flamed in whisky and finished with cream. Raspberry cranachan. Traditional bread and butter pudding.
Credit cards: 1, 3
Proprietors: Andrea Matheson & Jann MacRae

WHOLEFOOD CAFE, HIGHLAND DESIGNWORKS
Plockton Road
Kyle of Lochalsh IV40 8DA
Tel: 0599 4388
North of Kyle of Lochalsh, on road to Plockton.
There is an inviting range of home-baking and unusual salads on display in this popular cafe situated in what was the old village school which is on the outskirts of Kyle of Lochalsh facing the sea. Fiona Begg's food is varied, good, interesting – and healthy. It is all prepared and cooked on the premises from prime products. You are equally welcome whether you drop in for a coffee or for the full meals which are available all day. There is an outside terrace and garden.
Open Easter to Oct
Lunch (Spring & Autumn) 12 – 2.30 pm except Mon Sat (a)
Lunch (Summer) 12 – 6 pm (a)

Dinner (Spring & Autumn) 6.30 – 8.30 pm (b) – reservations essential
Dinner (Summer) 7 – 9 pm (b)
No smoking in restaurant
Smoked seafood platter of salmon, mussels and mackerel with home-made granary bread. Fresh spinach and crowdie cheese lasagne. Oat pancakes filled with smoked haddock and fennel, with fresh tarragon sauce. Wild Loch Duich salmon. Organic salad vegetables with a spicey peanut dip. Leek, cream cheese and sweetcorn roulade with yoghurt and dill sauce. Meringues filled with Atholl brose and local raspberries. Local cheeses and oatcakes. Rhubarb and banana pie.
Credit cards: 1, 3
Proprietor: Fiona Begg

Kylesku

Map 6

LINNE MHUIRICH
Unapool Croft Road, Kylesku
by Lairg, Sutherland
IV27 4HW
Tel: 0971 502227
¾ mile south of the new Kylesku Bridge on A894, last house in a cul-de-sac road.
Fiona and Diarmid MacAulay welcome non-smokers to their modern family home which is peacefully situated overlooking Loch Glencoul with panoramic views of hills and lochs. The Handa Island Nature/Bird Reserve and lovely, lonely sandy beaches are nearby. Directions and maps for many local walks are provided. The dinner menus change daily and are discussed with guests after breakfast. Vegetarian dishes are enthusiastically prepared. Guests are welcome to take their own wine as the premises are not licensed to provide alcoholic beverages. In the evening at 10 pm guests are offered a choice of hot drink and something tasty to eat. French spoken.
Open 11 Apr to 30 Nov except 1 wk mid Oct
Rooms: 3 , 1 with private facilities
Dinner at 7.30 pm except Sun Sat (a)
Residents only

No smoking throughout
Bed & breakfast £17.50 – £20.50
Dinner B & B £27.50 – £30.50
Local fish and seafood – Kylesku prawn vol au vents; smoked haddock au gratin; salmon baked with lemon and herbs. Home-made quiches and pâtés. Casseroles. Vegetarian dishes. Unusual salads. Tempting desserts and home-baking. Filter coffee. Scottish honey and cheeses.
STB Commended 2 Crowns
No credit cards
Proprietors: Fiona & Diarmid MacAulay

Laggan
nr Newtonmore

Map 6

THE GASKMORE HOUSE HOTEL
Laggan, nr Newtonmore
Inverness-shire PH20 1BS
Tel: 05284 250 or via 0540 673884
Fax: 05284 350
On A86 Newtonmore-Fort William: 8 miles from Newtonmore, 10 minutes from A9.
The Gaskmore House Hotel is situated in a beautiful historical part of the Spey Valley. Set amidst some of the most splendid scenery in the Highlands and with a wide range of sporting activities practically on the doorstep. If all you want to do is get away from it all and relax in comfort with the peace and tranquillity Gaskmore offers, then this could be an excellent hideaway. This is a family run country house hotel distinguished by exceptional cuisine and offering friendly efficient service.
Open all year
Rooms: 24 with private facilities
Light Lunch 12.30 – 2 pm (a)
Dining Room/Restaurant Lunch 12.30 – 2 pm (b)
Dinner 7 – 9.30 pm (e)
Facilities for the disabled
No smoking in restaurant
Bed & breakfast £41 – £52
Dinner B & B £59 – £70
Escalope of salmon with a saffron cream. Scottish Spring lamb with an apricot flan, served with a pearl barley and thyme sauce. Warm puff pastry box of berries with a blackberry sorbet. Hand-made chocolates.
STB Highly Commended 3 Crowns
Credit cards: 1, 3
Proprietors: John & Janet Grover

Langbank

Map 3

GLEDDOCH HOUSE
Langbank
Renfrewshire PA14 6YE
Tel: 0475 54 711
Fax: 0475 54 201

Off M8 Glasgow-Greenock at Langbank (B789).
A wonderful site high on a hill looking across the River Clyde to the Loch Lomond hills and with 360 acres of grounds around it including such facilities as an 18 hole golf course, horse-riding, clay pigeon shooting and off-road driving. The building itself epitomises gracious living with beautiful and spacious public rooms. It was once a private home and the finest characteristics have been retained. Bedrooms are tastefully furnished and comfortable and the standard and presentation of food has always been of the highest order with well planned and well balanced menus.
Open all year
Rooms: 33 with private facilities
Bar Lunch (Clubhouse) 12 – 2.30 pm except Sun Sat (a)
Dining Room/Restaurant Lunch 12.30 – 2 pm (c)
Bar Supper (Clubhouse) 6 – 9.30 pm except Sun Sat (a)
Dinner 7.30 – 9 pm (e)
Bed & breakfast £90 – £130
Dinner B & B £70 – £80 (weekend break)
Room Rate £81.50 – £96.50
Roast loin of Lanarkshire lamb resting on a sweet sherry, shallot and nutmeg cream sauce with a crisp feuilleté of buttered spinach leaves. Pan-fried whole lemon sole with a lime, rosemary and prawn butter sauce.
STB Highly Commended 4 Crowns
Credit cards: 1, 2, 3, 5

Largs

Map 3

MANOR PARK HOTEL
Skelmorlie, nr Largs
Ayrshire PA17 5HE
Tel: 0475 520832
Fax: 0475 520832

Off A78, c. 2 miles north of Largs.
Gracious Victorian manor situated in its own grounds on a hillside overlooking Firth of Clyde. Beautiful gardens with acres of lawns, shrubs, trees and a water garden. Panoramic views from all public rooms towards the islands and mountains of Argyll, with glorious sunsets. Family run hotel with first class cuisine and service. Bedrooms well appointed, with tea-making facilities and hairdryers. Unique cocktail bar with renowned malt whisky collection.
Open all year
Rooms: 23, 22 with private facilities
Bar Lunch 12.30 – 3 pm (a)
Dining Room/Restaurant Lunch 12.30 – 2.30 pm (b-c)
Bar Supper 5.30 – 8.30 pm (b)
Dinner 7 – 9.15 pm (c-d)
Bed & breakfast £35 – £65
Dinner B & B £50 – £80
Rainbow trout pan-fried in butter with capers, tomatoes and mushrooms. Escalope of venison in a mushroom and herb sauce flavoured with Macallan whisky. Scottish salmon served with a white wine sauce. Scampi in a cream sauce flavoured with rosemary and Laphroaig whisky.
STB Commended 4 Crowns
Credit cards: 1, 2, 3, 5

Letham

Map 4

FERNIE CASTLE HOTEL
Letham, Cupar
Fife KY7 7RU
Tel: 0337 810381
Fax: 0337 810422

Off A914 Glenrothes-Tay Bridge/Dundee, 1 mile north of A91/A914 Melville roundabout.
The origins of Fernie Castle go back to the 14th century when it was a fortified hunting tower and, with the estate, went the titles of Constable of Cupar and Forester of Falkland. It has seen many changes since but retains an impressive appearance and has been comfortably converted internally. There is an excellently preserved Ice House to the rear of the hotel, one of the finest of the few that still remain in the country and in which blocks of ice were stored from the frozen lochan and used throughout the Summer as refrigeration. Menus show a commendable reliance on local produce, and a degree of original thinking and professional skill by the chef.
Open all year
Rooms: 15 with private facilities
Bar Lunch 12 – 3 pm (b)
Dining Room/Restaurant Lunch 12 – 2.30 pm Sun Sat only (c)
Bar Supper 6 – 9.30 pm (b)
Dinner 6.30 – 9.30 pm (d)
Bed & breakfast £35 – £55
Dinner B & B £55 – £70
Poached fillet of Tay salmon. Rack of lamb. Steamed Orkney mussels. Fernie creel – seafood in a wine stock. Grand dessert selection.
STB Commended 3 Crowns
Credit cards: 1, 2, 3, 6
Proprietors: Norman & Zoe Smith

Lewis
Isle of

Map 7

ESHCOL GUEST HOUSE
Breasclete, Callanish
Isle of Lewis PA86 9ED
Tel: 0851 72 357

On A858, 17 miles from Stornoway, 40 miles from Tarbert.
Isobel and Neil Macarthur run this modern little guest house on a small croft in Breasclete, a weaving village on the west coast of Lewis within walking distance of the famous Callanish Stones. There are wonderful views across Loch Roag to the island of Great Bernera and beyond, with the hills of Uig and Harris in the distance. Bedrooms are en suite with tea-making facilities etc and are attractively furnished. A small establishment where you will be made welcome and comfortable, and from which you can go walking, fishing, sightseeing and exploring the splendid shoreline of West Lewis. Gaelic spoken.
Open mid Mar to mid Oct
Rooms: 3 with private facilities
Dinner 6.30 – 7 pm (b)
Residents only
Unlicensed
No smoking in dining room
Bed & breakfast £18 – £20

Dinner B & B £29 – £34
Home-made soups. Local smoked salmon. Lamb with rosemary. Cranachan (Eshcol-style). Fresh vegetables from garden.
STB Highly Commended 3 Crowns
No credit cards
Proprietors: Neil & Isobel Macarthur

HANDA
18 Keose Glebe (Ceos), Lochs
Isle of Lewis PA86 9JX
Tel: 0851 83334
1½ miles off A859, 12 miles south of Stornoway: last house in village of 'Ceos'.
This is a delightful modern home on a hilltop which seems hundreds of miles from anywhere but of course is not. It is a convenient spot for exploring Lewis and Harris but much nearer at hand – virtually on the doorstep – there is hill-walking, bird-watching, fishing, and otter sighting if you are lucky. In this small comfortable haven, island hospitality and personal attention are very much to the fore. Alongside traditional recipes there is innovative home-cooking using fresh herbs and vegetables from the kitchen garden. Vegetarian and individual dietary requirements are catered for. There is brown trout fishing on the private loch 100 yards from the house and a boat and equipment can be hired.
Open 1 Apr to 1 Oct
Rooms: 3, 1 with private facilities
Dinner 6.30 – 7.30 pm (b)
Unlicensed – guests welcome to take own wine
No smoking in dining room
Bed & breakfast £16 – £22
Dinner B & B £28 – £34
Home-made breads, soups. Lamb and dill hotpot. Lemon sole with walnut stuffed mushrooms. Shellfish platter. Salmon in orange and vermouth. Wild brown trout with mint. Fillet steak in Port and mushrooms.
STB Highly Commended 2 Crowns
No credit cards
Proprietors: Murdo & Christine Morrison

PARK GUEST HOUSE & RESTAURANT
30 James Street, Stornoway
Isle of Lewis PA87 2QN
Tel: 0851 70 2485
½ mile from ferry terminal. At junction of Matheson Road, James Street and A866 to airport and Eye peninsula.
A substantial stone built house dating to around 1883, centrally located in the town of Stornoway. The old wood of the interior has been refurbished and the public rooms and bedrooms are tastefully decorated. The dining room, featuring a Glasgow style fireplace, has a warm, homely atmosphere. Fresh local produce – shellfish, game, venison, Lewis lamb – feature on the menu prepared with care and presented by Chef/Proprietor Roddy Afrin. Ideal base for touring, golf, bird-watching, fishing etc, or just exploring some of the lunar-like landscapes of Lewis and Harris.
Open all year except 24 Dec to 5 Jan
Rooms: 5
Packed Lunches available (a)
Dining Room/Restaurant Lunch 12 – 1.45 pm Tue to Fri (a)
Dinner at 6 pm (table d'hôte) (b) – residents only
Dinner 7.30 – 8.30 pm (à la carte) except Sun Mon (c-d)
Note: Dinner Sun Mon – residents only
No dogs
Bed & breakfast from £19
Dinner B & B from £30
Home-made soups, patés, desserts. Smoked trout mousse wrapped in oak-smoked salmon. Hebridean scallops and crowdie in puff pastry. Noisettes of local venison in Port wine sauce with blackcurrants.
STB Commended 1 Crown
No credit cards
Proprietors: Catherine & Roddy Afrin

Lochcarron

Map 6

LOCHCARRON HOTEL
Lochcarron
Ross-shire IV54 8YS
Tel: 05202 226
At east end of village, facing the loch.
This 19th century Highland hostelry has been modernised to provide the facilities expected of an AA two star hotel. The majority of the accommodation, which includes two suites with their own small sitting rooms, overlook the sea loch. This view is also shared by the lounge

bar and restaurant, where fish and shellfish from local boats and game from nearby sporting estates feature highly on both à la carte and table d'hôte menus which cater for every taste.
Open all year except Christmas Day + 1 Jan
Rooms: 10 with private facilities
Bar Lunch 12 – 2 pm (a-b)
Dining Room/Restaurant Lunch 12 – 2 pm (a-b)
Bar Supper 6 – 9 pm (a-c)
Dinner 7 – 9 pm (b-c)
Bed & breakfast £26 – £35
Dinner B & B £41.50 – £50.50
Platter of seafood. Poached salmon with prawns and lemon butter. Breast of duck in red wine. Beef and venison steaks.
STB Commended 4 Crowns
Credit cards: 1, 3
Proprietors: Pam & Tony Wilkinson

ROCKVILLA HOTEL & RESTAURANT
Main Street, Lochcarron
Ross-shire IV54 8YB
Tel: 05202 379
Situated in centre of village, c. 20 miles north of Kyle of Lochalsh.
A small family run hotel in the main street of this lochside village with a cheerful air of informality which should appeal to guests. The dining room has a relaxing bistro feel and marvellous views of the loch. A substantial breakfast is a good start to a day of walking, touring around some of the local scenery or visiting Gairloch, the Applecross Peninsula or the Skye Ferry terminal. On return in the evening there is a fairly wide choice menu of local specialities and some traditional favourites. Bedrooms are simply but adequately furnished and are immaculate.
Open all year except Christmas Day + 1 Jan
Rooms: 4, 2 with private facilities
Bar Lunch 12 – 2 pm (a)
Dining Room/Restaurant Lunch 12 – 2 pm Jun to Sep only (b)
Bar Supper 6 – 9.30 pm (a)
Dinner 6.30 – 9.30 pm (c)
No dogs
No smoking in restaurant
Bed & breakfast £22 – £27
Dinner B & B rates on application
Poached Lochcarron salmon steak with dill sauce. Pan-fried fillet of rainbow trout with almonds and cream sauce. Grilled halibut steak with Hollandaise sauce. Prime Scottish beef steak with fresh prawns sauté in butter and served with bernaise sauce and salad.
STB Commended 3 Crowns
Credit cards: 1, 3
Proprietors: Lorna & Ken Wheelan

Loch Earn

St Fillans

Map 4

ACHRAY HOUSE HOTEL

St Fillans, Loch Earn
Perthshire PH6 2NF
Tel: 0764 685 231
Fax: 0764 685 320

A85, 12 miles west of Crieff.
This popular and well established family run hotel has a stunning lochside position in this area of outstanding natural beauty. The proprietors set themselves impressively high standards and it is little wonder that their guests keep coming back for more. The food, for which the hotel has been awarded an AA Rosette, is particularly good and remarkably inexpensive for the quality and variety offered. Mrs Ross's puddings are renowned. The dining room was recently extended and is very tastefully appointed. A good base for the many outdoor activities of the area.
Open 1 Mar to 1 Nov
Rooms: 10, 7 with private facilities
Bar Lunch 12 – 2 pm Mon-Sat: 12.30 – 2 pm Sun (a)
Bar Supper 6.30 – 9.30 pm (a)
Dinner 7 – 9.30 pm (b-c)
Bed & breakfast £22 – £29
Dinner B & B £36 – £43
Room Rate £44 – £58
Wide choice of Scottish produce – pheasant, grouse, steaks, salmon, venison, trout, lamb, pork and seafood. Good choice of vegetarian dishes always available. Large selection of freshly made desserts (the house speciality).
STB Highly Commended 3 Crowns
Credit cards: 1, 3 + SWITCH
Proprietors: Tony & Jane Ross

THE FOUR SEASONS HOTEL

St Fillans, Loch Earn
Perthshire PH6 2NF
Tel: 0764 685 333
Fax: 0764 685 333

On A85, 12 miles west of Crieff, at west end of St Fillans overlooking Loch Earn.
There are few lovelier locations than that of the Four Seasons at the east end of Loch Earn in the charming little village of St Fillans. Huge picture windows in all the public rooms and most of the bedrooms offer stunning views across and down the loch, and there are six chalets on the wooded hillside behind the hotel. The Scott family are anxious to ensure the comfort of their guests and Chef Andrew Scott has some really interesting and imaginative dishes on his menu. There are not too many places where the bar lunch menu runs to large bowls of Skye mussels cooked in white wine, or Guinea fowl terrine, or Arbroath smokies and poached eggs. That, however, should whet the appetite for a leisurely dinner in the attractive dining room where regularly changing menus emphasise the abundance of game and seafood, but the chef is willing to prepare any special requests, given appropriate notice.
Open 1 Mar to mid Dec
Rooms: 18 with private facilities
Bar Lunch 12.15 – 2.15 pm (a)
Dining Room/Restaurant Lunch – reservations only (b)
Bar Supper 6.30 – 9.30 pm (b)
Dinner 7 – 9.30 pm (d)
Facilities for the disabled
No smoking in dining room
Bed & breakfast £28 – £45
Dinner B & B £49 – £66
Baked halibut with oatmeal crust, horseradish and mustard sauce. Steamed west coast shellfish – lobster, scallops, mussels – with a langoustine saffron cream. Local wild mushrooms with pink wood pigeon and juniper.
STB Award Pending
Credit cards: 1, 2, 3
Proprietors: Allan & Barbara Scott

Lochearnhead

Map 4

CLACHAN COTTAGE RESTAURANT

Clachan Cottage Hotel
Lochside, Lochearnhead
Perthshire FK19 8PU
Tel: 0567 830247
Fax: 0567 830300

Lochearnhead is on A85 Crieff-Crianlarich.
Clachan Cottage Hotel enjoys a spectacular lochside setting on the east side of the village of Lochearnhead. It is well placed for touring central Scotland including the Trossachs, Glencoe, Oban and Scone Palace. For the energetic there are 26 golf courses within an hour, and a good choice of walking, fishing and watersports. The restaurant which is upstairs has good views across the loch. It offers freshly prepared meals using Scottish produce. All rooms have private facilities and tea and coffee-making equipment. Open fires – range of malts, and friendly service in a relaxed atmosphere. Frequent live entertainment. Special breaks available throughout year.
Open 31 Mar to 3 Jan
Rooms: 21 with private facilities
Bar Lunch 12 – 2.30 pm (a)
Bar Supper 6 – 9.30 pm (a)
Dinner 7 – 9 pm (c)
Taste of Scotland applies to restaurant only
Smoking not encouraged in restaurant
Bed & breakfast £25 – £35
Dinner B & B £38 – £50
Fillets of sole lightly poached, in a leek, potato and carrot sauce topped with toasted oats. Supreme of chicken filled with a rich haggis, cooked in fresh basil with button mushrooms. Trio of lamb cutlets served pink with a little rosemary, glazed with wild honey and brown sugar.
STB Approved 3 Crowns
No credit cards
Proprietor: Andrew Low

Lochinver

Map 6

THE ALBANNACH

Baddidarroch, Lochinver
Sutherland IV27 4LP
Tel: 05714 407

From Lochinver follow signs for Baddidarroch. After ½ mile, pass turning for Highland Stoneware, turn left for the Albannach.

There have been some changes at this fine old 19th century house with its spectacular views across Lochinver Bay towards Suilven and Canisp. There are now four bedrooms all with en suite facilities and plans for two more suites are underway. A licence has been granted and there is now no need for guests to take their own wine. Good reports have come in from satisfied guests so it is clear that those factors and standards which established Albannach's reputation are being maintained. The Albannach presents an original style of cooking, without shortcuts, emphasising the best of game and seafood. Using home-grown herbs, vegetables, mushrooms and fruit in season, meals are served before an open log fire in the wood-panelled dining room. There is a daily changing set menu and vegetarian meals are willingly provided with prior notification. French spoken. Children over five years welcome.

Open all year
Rooms: 4 with private facilities
Dinner at 7.30 pm (b-c)
Non-residents welcome by prior arrangement
Table Licence
No dogs
Facilities for the disabled
No smoking throughout
Bed & breakfast £25 – £27
Dinner B & B £40 – £42
Lochinver oysters, langoustines, halibut, Dover sole. Home-made bread. Local lamb and game with fresh herbs and sauces. Wild salmon, oak-smoked or fresh. Lobster by arrangement. Puddings with seasonal soft fruits and nuts.
STB Commended 3 Crowns
Credit cards: 1, 3
Proprietors: Colin Craig & Lesley Crosfield

LOCHINVER LARDER'S RIVERSIDE BISTRO

Main Street, Lochinver
Sutherland IV27 4JY
Tel: 05714 356

A837 to Lochinver, second property on right as enter village.

Polished wooden tables and chairs, Highland stoneware, good glassware and attractive table settings, give a pleasing appearance to this 44 seat restaurant which you enter through the delicatessen shop. It is situated on the bank of the River Inver as it flows into the sea and a large bay window provides pleasant panoramic views of the bay and its activities. With a plentiful supply of seafood landed directly at the village harbour, the menu majors on this and on really good steaks, but there are sufficient other items to provide adequate choice. Presentation is good and the service is pleasant and unhurried. Very popular and very busy in the season.

Open 1 Apr to 31 Oct + weekends only Nov to Mar except Christmas /New Year
Food service 9 am – 9 pm Mon to Sat: 10.30 am – 9 pm Sun
Dining Room/Restaurant Lunch 12 – 2 pm (a)
Dinner 6.30 – 8 pm Apr/May Sep/Oct: 6.30 – 8.30 pm May Jun: 6.30 – 9.30 pm Jul Aug (c)
Facilities for the disabled
No smoking in restaurant
Freshly landed seafood and fish from village harbour. Beef steaks from Highland cattle.
Credit cards: 1, 3, 6 + DELTA
Proprietors: Ian & Debra Stewart

MACPHAILS'

216 Clashmore, Stoer
by Lochinver
Sutherland IV27 4JQ
Tel: 057 15 295

B869 (single track), 10 miles north of Lochinver, West Sutherland, beyond Stoer on road to lighthouse.

A traditional croft house, modernised to a high standard, but retaining much of the original character, including roof beams and peat/log fire. The atmosphere is welcoming, warm and friendly. A lochside situation overlooking the sea to the Hebrides. Sandy beaches nearby. Peaceful with no passing traffic. French spoken.

Open 1 May to 22 Oct
Rooms: 3, 1 with private facilities
Dinner at 7 pm (b)
No dogs
Facilities for the disabled
No smoking area in dining room
Unlicensed – guests welcome to take own wine
Bed & breakfast £14 – £22
Dinner B & B £26 – £34
Home-made bread and oatcakes. A variety of interesting menus, including traditional Scottish dishes using local salmon, venison and seafoods. Vegetarian by request. Freshly ground coffee.
No credit cards
Proprietors: Pat & Madeline Macphail

Loch Lomond

Map 3

CAMERON HOUSE HOTEL

Loch Lomond, Alexandria
Dunbartonshire G83 8QZ
Tel: 0389 55565
Fax: 0389 59522

Prestige Award Winner 1991

On A82 near Balloch, on the banks of Loch Lomond.

This most impressive location has been developed carefully and skilfully with due regard to the aesthetics of the site and is now a superb luxury resort hotel set in 108 wooded acres on the south west shore of Loch Lomond. There are excellent leisure facilities and a choice of three restaurants. You can choose the elegance of the Georgian Room or the Grill Room with its emphasis on local produce and you can enjoy afternoon tea overlooking the loch in the tranquillity of the Drawing Room. The hotel restaurants are open to non-residents but leisure facilities are for members and residents only.

Open all year
Rooms: 68 with private facilities
Bar Lunch (Clubhouse) 12.30 – 3 pm (a)
Lunch (Brasserie) 12 – 2 pm (b)
Lunch (Georgian Room) 12 – 2 pm (c)
Lunch (Grill Room) 12 – 2 pm Sun only (c)
Dinner (Brasserie) 7 – 10 pm (c)
Dinner (Georgian Room) 7 – 10 pm (f)
No dogs
Facilities for the disabled
No smoking area in Brasserie
No smoking in Georgian Room
Bed & breakfast £75 – £147.50
Dinner B & B £94.50 – £177
STB Deluxe 5 Crowns
Credit cards: 1, 2, 3, 6

Lundin Links

Map 4

OLD MANOR HOTEL
Lundin Links, nr St Andrews
Fife KY8 6AJ
Tel: 0333 320368
Fax: 0333 320911

On A915 Kirkcaldy – St Andrews, 1 mile east of Leven, on right overlooking Largo Bay.

The area of course is a golfers' paradise and golfers would especially appreciate staying at the Old Manor Hotel where the proprietors, the Clark family, are a mine of information, advice and assistance on the game of golf. But there is much more to the hotel than that: the food is of a high order and the Prince Charlie Restaurant presents excellent fare of originality and imagination, complemented by an extensive wine list. As an alternative there is informal eating in the Coachman's Grill and Ale House – in the old coachman's cottage in the grounds – specialising in grilled steaks and seafood. Good bedrooms, attractive public rooms and dedicated staff give a special touch to the place.

Open all year
Rooms: 19 with private facilities
Bar Lunch 12 – 2.30 pm (a)
Dining Room/Restaurant Lunch 12 – 2 pm except Sun Mon Sat (b)
Bar Supper 5 – 9.30 pm (a)
Dinner 7 – 9.30 pm (d)
Facilities for the disabled
No smoking in restaurant
Bed & breakfast £30 – £60
Dinner B & B £49.50 – £79.50
Scottish hill lamb roasted with a rosemary and peppercorn sauce, set on a hot redcurrant jelly. Breast of chicken filled with haggis, on a Drambuie sauce. Roasted marinated pheasant with red wine and thyme jus.
STB Commended 4 Crowns
Credit cards: 1, 2, 3, 6
Proprietors: The Clark Family

Lockerbie

Map 1

SOMERTON HOUSE HOTEL
Carlisle Road, Lockerbie
Dumfriesshire DG11 2DR
Tel: 05762 202583
Fax: 05762 202583

Outskirts of Lockerbie about 300 yards from main A74.

A robust red sandstone Victorian mansion, reputedly designed by Alexander (Greek) Thomson, which stands in its own grounds. It retains the original features of Kauri timber panelling, original fireplaces and fine ceilings with plaster cornices. All bedrooms en suite with TV, central heating and direct dial telephone. The new owners who took over the hotel during 1993 have started a programme of upgrading and refurbishment.

Open all year
Rooms: 7 with private facilities
Bar Lunch 12 – 2 pm (b)
Dining Room/Restaurant Lunch 12 – 2 pm (c)
Bar Supper 6 – 9 pm (b)
Dinner 7 – 9 pm (c)
No smoking in restaurant
Bed & breakfast £25.75 – £46
Dinner B & B £60 – £80
Room Rate £41 – £56.50
Mussels topped with garlic butter and parmesan cheese. Roast Barbary duckling with a cranberry and Port sauce.
STB Commended 4 Crowns
Credit cards: 1, 2, 3
Proprietors: Alex & Jean Arthur

Lybster

Map 6

PORTLAND ARMS HOTEL
Lybster
Caithness KW3 6BS
Tel: 059 32 208
Fax: 059 32 208

On A9, 12 miles south of Wick.

The Portland was built to serve as a staging post early last century. There have been many changes since, but the quality of personal service established then has been maintained. The hotel is fully central heated and double glazed. All rooms have private facilities including colour TV, telephone, tea-making facilities. Four-poster beds available. Executive rooms with jacuzzi baths also available. There is a lovely lounge in which to relax with lots of personal touches and there is an excellent choice of local food representing very good value.

Open all year
Rooms: 20 with private facilities
Bar Lunch 12 – 2.30 pm (a)
Dining Room/Restaurant Lunch 12 – 2.30 pm (a)
Bar Supper 5 – 9.30 pm (a)
Dinner 7 – 9.30 pm (c)
Bed & breakfast £27.50 – £46
Dinner B & B £44 – £62.50
Seafood platter. Baked fillet of sole in cream with prawns. Sauté of pheasant breast with cream and apples. Peppered fillet steak with brandy and cream sauce.
STB Commended 4 Crowns
Credit cards: 1, 3
Proprietors: Gerald & Helen Henderson

Mallaig

Map 6

MARINE HOTEL
Station Road, Mallaig
Inverness-shire PH41 4PY
Tel: 0687 2217
Fax: 0687 2821

Adjacent to railway station. First hotel on right off A82, and a 5 minute walk from ferry terminal.

Mallaig marks the end of the famous West Highland Line and the equally famous Road to the Isles. It is also a busy fishing port and a ferry terminal. The Marine Hotel is perched overlooking the harbour where you can see most of the action. It is family run and friendly, and most of the bedrooms are en suite and are well appointed with colour TVs and the usual facilities. The menu, sensibly, takes full advantage of the freshly landed fish and shellfish and specialises in it. Those who live in large cities remote from a fishing port have just no idea how good fresh fish can taste!

Open Christmas + Boxing Days, 1 to 6 Jan
Note: restricted service Nov to Apr
Rooms: 21, 16 with private facilities
Bar Lunch 12 – 2 pm (a)
Dining Room/Restaurant Lunch on request (b)
Bar Supper 6 – 9.30 pm (b)
Dinner 7 – 9 pm (c)
Bed & breakfast £25 – £30
Dinner B & B £36 – £50
Home-made soups and pâté. Local seafood – scallops a speciality. Scottish meats and vegetables. Imaginative desserts. Scottish breakfast with porridge and locally smoked kippers.
STB Commended 3 Crowns
Credit cards: 1, 3
Proprietors: Elliot & Dalla Ironside

by Maybole

Map 1

LADYBURN
by Maybole
Ayrshire KA19 7SG
Tel: 06554 585
Fax: 06554 580

A77 (Glasgow-Stranraer) to Maybole then B7023 to Crosshill. Turn right at War Memorial (Dailly-Girvan). After exactly 2 miles, turn left and follow signs. 5 miles south of Maybole.
A superb away-from-it-all retreat contiguous to the magnificent Kilkerran Estate, the grounds of which are made available for guests of Ladyburn to enjoy. Jane and David Hepburn's gracious house exemplifies life as it used to be lived and ought to be lived. Jane Hepburn is a charming hostess and the moment you arrive, you are made to feel welcome and somewhat special. The accommodation is superb and there are fresh flowers from the garden everywhere. Food is delicious; honest traditional cooking at its best with none of the pretentious frills that are sometimes adopted to disguise inferior cuisine. The whole experience here will send you home with a warm glow of satisfaction. Italian, French, German and

Russian spoken. Children over 12 years welcome.
Open all year
Rooms: 8 with private facilities
Dining Room/Restaurant Lunch 12.30 – 1.30 pm Tue to Sat (b)
Dinner 7.30 – 8.30 pm Tue to Sat (d)
Note: meals served all day to residential guests
Restricted Licence
No dogs
No smoking in dining room
Bed & breakfast £70 – £80
Dinner B & B £93 – £103
Jane Hepburn uses only fresh local produce, garden vegetables and herbs, and old family recipes – Aunt Ella's traditional chicken and mushroom pie, roast sirloin and Yorkshire pudding, vicarage fish pie – to name but a few.
STB Deluxe 3 Crowns
Credit cards: 1, 2, 3
Proprietors: Jane & David Hepburn

Melrose

Map 2

BURTS HOTEL
Market Square, Melrose
Roxburghshire TD6 9PN
Tel: 089 682 2285
Fax: 089 682 2870

B6361, 2 miles from A68, 38 miles south of Edinburgh.
This distinguished family run townhouse hotel, built in 1722, sits in the main square of Melrose. Its situation in the heart of the Borders makes it an ideal centre for touring this beautiful area of the country. The hotel is tastefully furnished and the en suite bedrooms are all modernly equipped with colour TVs, direct dial telephones, tea/coffee-making facilities. The elegant restaurant offers both à la carte and table d'hôte menus where the emphasis is on the abundance of local game and fresh fish, prepared and presented with flair by Chef Gary Moore whose cooking has earned the hotel much recognition in national guides. The lounge bar menu offers light lunches and suppers. The hotel has its own private car park and extensive gardens. There are several golf courses within easy reach. Salmon and trout fishing can be arranged, so too can game shooting on local estates with prior notice.
Open all year except 24 to 26 Dec
Rooms: 21 with private facilities

Bar Lunch 12 – 2 pm (b)
Dining Room/Restaurant Lunch 12.30 – 2 pm (b)
Bar Supper 6 – 9.30 pm Sun to Thu: 6 – 10.30 pm Fri Sat (b)
Dinner 7 – 9 pm Sun to Thu: 7 – 9.30 pm Fri Sat (d)
Bed & breakfast £35 – £45
Dinner B & B £50 – £56
Mini-break terms available (min 2 nights stay)
Potted spiced rabbit. Smoked salmon and Spring onion tart. Quails egg with herb flavoured Hollandaise. Char-grilled fillet of Tweed salmon. Medallion of venison and maigret duck breast. Grouse, pheasant, partridge in season. Scotch beef and lamb from the char-grill.
STB Commended 4 Crowns
Credit cards: 1, 2, 3, 5, 6
Proprietors: Graham & Anne Henderson

MELROSE STATION RESTAURANT
Palma Place, Melrose
Roxburghshire TD6 9PR
Tel: 089 682 2546

Close to Market Square. Follow signposts to Melrose Station, which is up hill to right of dairy.
A friendly and unpretentious restaurant within the historic Melrose Railway Station building which has been restored and converted to include comfortable and attractive surroundings for diners in a peaceful situation. Simple but imaginative blackboard menus offer a choice of light or more substantial lunches and a table d'hôte dinner at weekends, all at very reasonable prices. The proprietors, Claire and Ian Paris, have gained a good reputation for their personal attention and home-style cooking, using only the best of local produce.
Open all year except 5 days Christmas period, 3 wks Feb
Morning coffee 10 am – 12 noon except Mon
Dining Room/Restaurant Lunch 12 – 2 pm except Mon (a)
Dinner 6.45 to 9 pm Thu to Sat only (c)
Closed Mon
Home-made soups and patés. Interesting filled pancakes and quiches, salad bar at lunchtime. Spinach and smoked salmon roulade. Chicken and Cambazola strudel. Mushroom and cashewnut stroganoff. Variety of game and fish dishes. Tempting selection of home-made desserts.
Credit cards: 1, 3
Proprietors: Ian & Claire Paris

Melvich
by Thurso

Map 6

THE SHEILING GUEST HOUSE
Melvich, by Thurso
Caithness KW14 7YJ
Tel: 06413 256
Fax: 06413 356

Melvich on A836, 18 miles west of Thurso.
With its outstanding scenic views over the Halladale River and Melvich Bay, the quiet peaceful Sheiling caters for every comfort within its warm friendly atmosphere. Guests return year after year to enjoy home-cooked meals and the personal service of Joan Campbell. There are two spacious lounges and the bedrooms all have tea/coffee-making facilities and electric blankets. The menus change daily and there is a large selection breakfast menu. The Sheiling is an ideal stop for touring Caithness and Sutherland being midway between Wick and Cape Wrath (Durness) and within daily reach of trips to the Orkney Isles.
Open 1 Apr to 30 Sep
Rooms: 3 with private facilities
Dinner 6 – 7.30 pm except Sat (b)
Residents only
Unlicensed – guests welcome to take own wine
No smoking in dining room
Bed & breakfast £20 – £22
Dinner B & B £32 – £35
Caithness beef, Sutherland lamb, Melvich Bay salmon and local haddock. Fresh fruit, vegetables from kitchen garden. Sweets and traditional puddings with Scottish cream.
STB Highly Commended 3 Crowns
No credit cards
Proprietor: Joan Campbell

Moffat

Map 1

AUCHEN CASTLE HOTEL & RESTAURANT
Beattock, Moffat
Dumfriesshire DG10 9SH
Tel: 06833 407
Fax: 06833 667

Direct access from A74, 1 mile north of Beattock village, 55 miles south of Edinburgh and Glasgow.
Gracious country house spectacularly situated in 50 acres with fine shrubs and trees. It was built by General Johnston in 1849 and became the home of the William Younger family. The hotel is comfortably furnished and decorated to complement the original features which have been retained. Ten of the 25 bedrooms are in a modern wing. Auchen Castle is ideally placed for visiting the Border Country. Located almost mid way between Carlisle and Glasgow or Edinburgh, it has long been a popular place at which to break a journey either for an accommodation stop or meal time break. Children welcome. A little French spoken.
Open 10 Jan to 17 Dec
Rooms: 25 with private facilities
Bar Lunch 12 – 2 pm (a)
Dinner 7 – 9 pm (c)
Bed & breakfast £26 – £49.50
Dinner B & B £36.50 – £58.25
Special rate Sat only mid Oct to end Mar for Dinner-Dance & Accommodation
Local lamb, poultry, beef and pork. Game in season. Salmon and shellfish.
STB Commended 4 Crowns
Credit cards: 1, 2, 3, 5
Proprietors: Bob & Hazel Beckh

WELL VIEW HOTEL
Ballplay Road, Moffat
Dumfriesshire DG10 9JU
Tel: 0683 20184

At south end of Moffat take A708 (Selkirk). At crossroads, left into Ballplay Road – hotel on right.
This 19th century house is set within easy walking distance of the centre of Moffat yet enjoys a quiet and peaceful setting in its own half acre of garden. The rooms are comfortably furnished and supplied with lots of thoughtful little touches; a welcoming glass of sherry, fresh fruit and hand-made biscuits. In the kitchen Janet Schuckardt prepares

really mouth-watering meals and displays high levels of culinary skill and originality. John Schuckardt looks after the front of house and is well versed in the subtleties of his extensive wine list. Well View is deservedly popular and advance reservation is advisable. German spoken, also a little French. Children welcome. Dogs accepted by prior arrangement.
Open all year except first wk Jan
Rooms: 7, 5 with private facilities
Dining Room/Restaurant Lunch 12.30 – 1.15 pm except Sat (a)
Dinner 7 – 8.30 pm (d)
Prior reservation essential for both lunch + dinner
Facilities for the disabled
No smoking in dining room
Bed & breakfast £23 – £40
Dinner B & B £43 – £59
Room Rate £30 – £78
Smoked haddock soufflé, mousseline of turbot, cauliflower and blue cheese soup, fillet of Galloway beef with Kelso mustard sauce, escalope of venison with a blaeberry and mushroom sauce. Carse of Gowrie raspberry and Armagnac brûlée.
STB Deluxe 3 Crowns
Credit cards: 1, 3
Proprietors: Janet & John Schuckardt

Moniaive
nr Thornhill

Map 1

MAXWELTON HOUSE
Moniaive, nr Thornhill
Dumfriesshire DG3 4DX
Tel: 084 82 385

Entrance on B729, off A76 Dumfries-Thornhill, or A702 New Galloway-Thornhill.
The very name is evocative, and anyone with the slightest claim to Scottish ancestry together with many millions more who have heard the well loved ballad will be drawn to Maxwelton House, the birthplace of Annie Laurie. The house has been magnificently restored by Mr and Mrs Hugh Stenhouse and – together with the chapel and an interesting museum of agricultural and domestic tools – is well worth a diversion on a journey and a few hours of anyone's time. The tearoom is in the Pavilion attached to the house and it serves morning coffee, light and inexpensive lunches, and that rarity now

– delicious traditional afternoon teas with freshly made home-baking.
Open daily Easter to end Sep
Tearoom 10.30 am – 5.30 pm (a)
Unlicensed
Variety of home-made items. Afternoon teas.
Credit cards: 1, 3
Proprietors: Maxwelton House Trust

Muir of Ord

Map 6

ORD HOUSE HOTEL
Muir of Ord
Ross-shire
IV6 7UH
Tel: 0463 870492
Fax: 0463 870492

On A832 Ullapool-Marybank, ½ mile west of Muir of Ord.
John and Eliza Allen offer you at Ord House a stay which will be comfortable, relaxed and enjoyable. table d'hôte and à la carte menus are made up from their own garden produce and local meat, game and fish. Fifty acres of woodlands and beautiful formal gardens, combined with a l7th century laird's house, make Ord something special. All bedrooms have private facilities and many have been recently refurbished. Direct dial telephones in all bedrooms. Downstairs, there are log fires in the bar and drawing rooms to enjoy and in the grounds there are croquet and clay-pigeon shooting.

Fluent French spoken. Children and dogs are very welcome.
Open 5 May to 25 Oct
Rooms: 12 with private facilities
Bar Lunch 12 – 2 pm (a)
Dinner 7 – 9 pm (c)
Bed & breakfast £28 – £50
Dinner B & B £47 – £69
Room Rate £33 – £47
Ord pigeon pâté. Pan-fried Scottish quail with grapes in Madeira. Fillet of fresh wild Conon salmon with a whisky and mushroom sauce. Fillet of venison with poivrade sauce. Brandy snap baskets filled with fresh raspberries and cream. Grape crème brulée.
STB Commended 3 Crowns
Credit cards: 1, 2, 3
Proprietors: John & Eliza Allen

Mull
Isle of

Map 7

ARDFENAIG HOUSE
by Bunessàn, Isle of Mull
Argyll PA67 6DX
Tel: 06817 210
Fax: 06817 210

2 miles west of Bunessan on A849, turn right on private road to Ardfenaig House, ½ mile.
Once occupied by the notorious Factor Mor, chamberlain to the Duke of Argyll, and latterly a private shooting lodge, Ardfenaig House stands in a glorious position on the shore of Loch Caol on the Ross of Mull. Surrounded by open moorland and quiet secluded beaches Ardfenaig is perfect for walking, sailing, painting, exploring or simply relaxing. The Island of Iona is a short ferry ride away and Fingals Cave on Staffa is easily reached. The house is set amongst 15 acres of woodland and gardens. It is the home of Malcolm and Jane Davidson who offer warm hospitality, good food and fine wine in a country house setting.
Open 1 Apr to 31 Oct
Open for house parties off season – by prior arrangement
Rooms: 5 with private facilities
Dinner at 8 pm (d)
Restricted Licence
No smoking in dining room
Dinner B & B £69 – £85
Home-made bread, soups and ice creams. Fresh home-grown vegetables. Locally caught wild salmon, prawns and

mussels. Selection of Scottish cheeses.
STB Highly Commended 3 Crowns
Credit cards: 1, 3
Proprietors: Malcolm & Jane Davidson

ARDRIOCH
Ardrioch Farm, Dervaig
Isle of Mull PA75 6QR
Tel: 06884 264

1 mile from Dervaig on Calgary road.
Ardrioch is a traditionally furnished comfortable cedar wood farmhouse. Guests may relax in the mellow wood-panelled sitting room with its peat fire and extensively filled bookshelves, and enjoy the view of the sea-loch and surrounding hills. All bedrooms have tea-making facilities, wash-basins and room heaters; en suite facilities available. The house is a short stroll to the loch side and two miles from the harbour, where Ardrioch's inter-island day-sailing cruises are available. Ideal for walking, bird-watching and fishing. Multi-activity holidays also available. Working farm – sheep, cows, friendly collies, lambs and calves, enjoyed by children.
Open 1 Apr to 31 Oct
Rooms: 4, 1 with private facilities
Dinner 6.30 – 7.30 pm (b)
Unlicensed – guests welcome to take own wine
No dogs
No smoking throughout
Bed & breakfast £17 – £19.50
Dinner B & B £27.50 – £30
Avocado with smoked trout pâté. Freshly caught mackerel stuffed with gooseberries. Fillets of chicken with a whisky and ginger sauce. Crunchy coffee and chocolate ice cream.
STB Commended 2 Crowns
No credit cards
Proprietors: Jenny & Jeremy Matthew

ASSAPOL COUNTRY HOUSE HOTEL

Bunessan, Isle of Mull
Argyll PA67 6DW
Tel: 06817 258
Fax: 06817 445

Follow A849 toward Iona till reach Bunessan. On outskirts of village, turn left after school.

Assapol Country House Hotel is a small unpretentious family run hotel overlooking Loch Assapol, where guests can fish for sea trout and salmon. A former manse and 200 years old, Assapol offers friendly comfortable and attractive accommodation. Traditional cuisine is served using the island's locally produced pork, game, wild salmon, crab etc. Dinner is served in one sitting at 7 pm, but that provides the excuse to spend the rest of the evening trying a dram of the many speciality cask strength malt whiskies whilst relaxing in front of an open log fire. Surrounded by outstanding countryside, this is an ideal base for walking, bird-watching and sightseeing, and convenient for those going on to Staffa for the day.

Open 1 Apr to 31 Oct
Rooms: 7 with private facilities
Dinner at 7 pm (b) – one sitting – booking by 5 pm
Restricted Licence
Non-residents welcome when dining space available
No children under 13 years
No smoking in restaurant + bedrooms
Bed & breakfast £24 – £28
Dinner B & B £38 – £42
Tomato, leek and apple soup. Cream crab and prawn tart. Game pie with Port and herbs. Chocolate and mint mousse cheesecake.
STB Commended 3 Crowns
Credit cards: 1, 3
Proprietors: Harry & Mary Kay

CALGARY FARMHOUSE HOTEL

Calgary, nr Dervaig
Isle of Mull PA75 6QW
Tel: 068 84 256

B8073 just up hill from Calgary beach.
There are few more delightful places along the beautiful west coast of Mull than the white sands beach at Calgary, and just up the hill the Calgary Farmhouse Hotel has been created from some farm steadings. The rustic charm of the place has been retained as has the comfortable homely atmosphere. The Dovecote Restaurant in what was once a barn with an original dovecote serves a

goodly range of the best of Mull's prime produce, particularly local fish and shellfish, and there is an emphasis on genuine home-cooking. Additionally, a stone arched carthouse has been converted to form the Carthouse Gallery and Function Room where you can have teas, light lunches or delicious home-baking throughout the day, or just browse and enjoy the exhibition of paintings by local artists many of which are for sale.

Open 1 Apr to 16 Oct
Rooms: 9 with private facilities
Light Lunch 11 am – 2.30 pm (a)
Dinner 6.30 – 9 pm (b)
No smoking in restaurant
Bed & breakfast £27 – £31
Dinner B & B £39 – £47
Home-made spicy lentil and smoked mussel soup. Fresh Dervaig oysters. Locally dived scallops with Isle of Mull cheese sauce. Lobster baked with garlic. Skate wing poached in white wine, with lemon and fennel sauce.
STB Commended 3 Crowns
Credit cards: 1, 3
Proprietors: Matthew & Julia Reade

DRUIMARD COUNTRY HOUSE

Dervaig, by Tobermory
Isle of Mull PA75 6QW
Tel: 06884 345/291

Situated adjacent to Mull Little Theatre, well signposted from Dervaig village.
Druimard Country House has a pleasing elevated situation just to the outskirts of the pretty little village of Dervaig and only eight miles from Tobermory, the island's capital. A carefully restored and

well maintained Victorian country house, it has extremely comfortable en suite bedrooms, including a two bedroomed suite, and a restaurant which is gaining increasing recognition (and an AA Rosette) since the new owners, Haydn and Wendy Hubbard, took over. Thoughtfully planned menus take full advantage of the excellent raw materials for which Mull is renowned.

Open all year but limited opening Nov to Feb – by arrangement
Rooms: 6, 4 with private facilities
Dinner 6 – 8.30 pm (c)
Restaurant Licence only
No smoking in restaurant
Bed & breakfast £36.30 – £54.45
Dinner B & B £50.25 – £71.45
Salmon stuffed with prawns and wrapped in filo pastry with a seafood sauce. Smoked venison. Home-made desserts.
STB Highly Commended 3 Crowns
Credit cards: 1, 3
Proprietors: Haydn & Wendy Hubbard

DRUIMNACROISH

Dervaig, Isle of Mull
Argyll PA75 6QW
Tel: 06884 274
Fax: 06884 311

Via ferry from Oban to Craignure. On Salen-Dervaig road, 1½ miles south of Dervaig.
Druimnacroish is an interesting place to stay. Donald McLean virtually converted the buildings himself into an unusual country house hotel in this delightful part of Mull. His wife, Wendy, presides in the kitchen and produces a varied selection of dishes, complemented by vegetables and fruit culled from the hotel's own six acre garden. There is a carefully selected wine cellar. To discover the subtle values of tranquillity and perhaps a new slant on life, it can be a most rewarding experience to join the McLeans in their home at Druimnacroish.

Open mid Apr to mid Oct
Rooms: 6 with private facilities
Packed Lunches to order
Dinner at 8 pm (d)
No smoking in restaurant
Dinner B & B from £73
Specialities include roast pheasant, rib of Aberdeen Angus beef carved at table off the bone. Wild salmon.
STB Commended 4 Crowns
Credit cards: 1, 2, 3, 5, 6
Proprietors: Donald & Wendy McLean

THE OLD BYRE HERITAGE CENTRE
by Dervaig
Isle of Mull PA75 6QR
Tel: 068 84 229

1½ miles from Dervaig. Take Calgary road for ¾ mile, turn left along Torloisk road for ¼ mile, then left down private road following signs.

This old stone farm byre with its outside staircase is now one of those fascinating small heritage centres that one loves to discover on holiday when there is all the time in the world to drift round and enjoy the interesting aspects of it. The tearoom is unpretentious but wholesome, with genuine home-baking and fresh Mull produce in season as daily specials. By prior arrangement special meals will be prepared for groups and there are always vegetarian and vegan dishes available. The home-made crofter's soup is especially good.

Open Easter (Palm Sunday) to end Oct
Light Meals served throughout day
10.30 am – 6 pm (a)
Crofter's soup served with warm rolls.
Ploughman's lunch with Mull cheese.
Cloutie dumpling. Selection of home-baking.
No credit cards
Proprietors: Michael & Ursula Bradley

THE PUFFER AGROUND
Main Road
Salen, Aros
Isle of Mull PA72 6JB
Tel: 068 0300 389

On A849 Craignure – Tobermory road.

The quaint name of this restaurant derives from the old days when the 'puffer' – the local steamboat – ran right on to the shore to unload its cargo and went off on the next high tide. The restaurant has a maritime theme and usually features an exhibition of oil paintings during July and August.

Open Easter to mid Oct

Restaurant Lunch 12 – 2.30 pm except Sun Mon until Jul (a)
Dinner 7 – 8.30 pm Easter to Jul: 7 – 9 pm Aug to mid Oct (b-c)
Closed Sun Mon until Jul
Scottish and Mull produce used whenever possible to create 'home-type' cooking in a friendly atmosphere.
Credit cards: 1, 3
Proprietors: Graham & Elizabeth Ellis

STRONGARBH HOUSE & RESTAURANT
Tobermory
Isle of Mull PA75 6PR
Tel: 0688 2328
Fax: 0688 2142

Upper town – well signposted.

A welcome addition to the limited number of quality establishments in Tobermory, Strongarbh has lovely gardens and delightful views over the Bay. It is one of the earliest of the fine Victorian houses built in the 19th century and has recently been completely and comfortably refurbished without detriment to the character of the building. The restaurant, rightly, concentrates on offering the best of the bountiful supply of fresh local seafood and other island specialities.

Open all year
Rooms: 4 with private facilities
Dining Room/Restaurant Lunch – by arrangement
Dinner 7 – 9.45 pm (d)
Restricted Licence
Bed & breakfast £34 – £37.50
Dinner B & B £52 – £55
Room Rate £68 – £75
Grilled fresh Mull lobster with a light prawn sauce. Supreme of wild Mull salmon. Roast stuffed pork tenderloin with cider braised shallots. Home-made chocolate and hazelnut meringues.
STB Highly Commended 3 Crowns
Credit cards: 1, 3
Proprietors: Ian & Mhairi McAdam

TIRORAN HOUSE
Tiroran
Isle of Mull PA69 6ES
Tel: 06815 232

Prestige Award Winner 1988

From Craignure, A849 towards Iona, turn right onto B8035 at head of Loch Scridain until signposted to Tiroran.

A very special country house hotel, beautifully furnished and exuding an aura of elegance and gracious living. It sits above Loch Scridain in 50 acres of grounds with lovely gardens, lawns and shrubberies and a stream, with occasional wildfowl, meandering through. This is a wonderful away-from-it-all retreat with every conceivable comfort; a splendid base from which to explore Mull, Iona and Staffa, or just to relax and enjoy life. And when you have enjoyed the scenery you will take the same pleasure in the food which is highly acclaimed for its orginality and variety. Candlelit dinners in the dining room looking out over the gardens and Loch Scridain are memorable.

Open mid May to early Oct
Rooms: 9 with private facilities
Lunch as required – residents only (b)
Dinner at 7.45 pm (e)
No smoking in dining room
Dinner B & B £90 – £110
Fresh seafood, including scallops and crab, Hebridean smoked trout and own gravadlax are regular starters. Main courses using lamb and beef from the estate and island venison, with fresh vegetables.
No credit cards
Proprietors: Robin & Susan Blockey

Credit Card Code	**Meal Price Code**
1. Access/Mastercard/Eurocard	(a) under £10
2. American Express	(b) £10 – £15
3. Visa	(c) £15 – £20
4. Carte Bleu	(d) £20 – £25
5. Diners Club	(e) £25 – £30
6. Mastercharge	(f) over £30

WESTERN ISLES HOTEL
Tobermory
Isle of Mull PA75 6PR
Tel: 0688 2012
Fax: 0688 2297

Tobermory is a 40 minute drive from Oban/Craignure ferry.

A magnificent Gothic style building enjoying a truly remarkable situation on the cliff overlooking Tobermory Bay. The views from the dining room, terrace lounge and many of the bedrooms are breathtaking and must surely be regarded as some of the best in Scotland. A suite and some of the other master bedrooms have been lavishly and luxuriously equipped and all other bedrooms are furnished to a high standard with private bathrooms, colour TV, tea/coffee-making equipment etc. There has been a marked improvement too in the standard of the food and a leisurely in the spacious dining room looking out over Tobermory Bay can be a very pleasant experience. Dogs are accepted by prior arrangement, at a small charge.

Open Mar to 4 Jan except Christmas wk
Rooms: 28 with private facilities
Bar Lunch 12 – 1.45 pm (a)
Bar Supper 7 – 8 pm (a)
Dinner 7 – 8.30 pm: 7 – 8 pm Winter (d)
No smoking in dining room
Bed & breakfast £34.50 – £70
Dinner B & B £53.50 – £89
Home-made soups. Many specialities using local products including trout, venison, salmon, prawns, scallops and lobster.
Credit cards: 1, 3 + SWITCH
Proprietors: Sue & Michael Fink

Nairn

Map 6

GOLF VIEW HOTEL
Seabank Road
Nairn IV12 4HD
Tel: 0667 52301 • Telex: 75134
Fax: 0667 55267

At west end of Nairn. Seaward side of A96. Turn off at large Parish Church.

A comfortable well run hotel in a commanding position overlooking the Moray Firth to Easter Ross and well known to the many thousands of golfers for whom the nearby championship golf course presents a special challenge. There is a full range of leisure centre facilities and a heated outdoor swimming pool. There is an air of Victorian grandeur in many of the public rooms enlivened by lots of fresh flower arrangements. There are some very interesting items on the menus and food is well prepared and presented.

Open all year
Rooms: 48 with private facilities
Bar Lunch 12 – 2 pm: 12.30 – 2 pm Sun (a)
Dining Room/Restaurant Lunch 12 – 2 pm: 12.30 – 2 pm Sun (a)
Bar Supper 6.30 – 9.15 pm (a)
Dinner 7 – 9.15 pm (c)
Bed & breakfast £29.50 – £65
Dinner B & B £80 – £120 (min 2 nights stay)
Roulade of spinach and watercress, flavoured with smoked Orkney cheese, with a fresh tomato and coriander sauce. Fillet of Aberdeen Angus beef topped with woodland mushrooms, glazed with tarragon butter, served with a Port wine rosemary sauce. Pan-fried Moray Firth scallops on a bed of creamed leek and prawns, with a mild curry and lemon sabayon.
STB Commended 5 Crowns
Credit cards: 1, 2, 3, 5, + SWITCH, DELTA

Newbigging

Map 3

NESTLERS HOTEL
Dunsyre Road, Newbigging
Lanark ML11 8NA
Tel: 0555 840 680

On A721 midway between Edinburgh and Glasgow, 18 miles north of Peebles.

This traditional stone built house has all the character of the old village inn and has a happy and welcoming atmosphere provided by the friendly and attentive staff. It is now an intimate and unpretentious family hotel with lots of character well situated in rural Clydesdale, almost equidistant from Edinburgh and Glasgow. The menu is sensibly planned with good home-cooking the order of the day. The desserts particularly are renowned locally. Elaine and Nick Anderson go to great trouble to ensure their guests enjoy good hospitality as well as good food.

Open all year except 1 Jan
Rooms: 3, 2 with private facilities
Meals available 8 am – 9.30 pm (a-c)
Bar Lunch (a)

Dining Room/Restaurant Lunch (a)
Bar Supper (b)
Dinner (c)
No smoking in restaurant
Bed & breakfast £22.50 – £27.50
Dinner B & B £35 – £40
Home-cooked ham baked in Pentland honey with cloves and served with a fresh parsley sauce.
STB Commended 3 Crowns
Credit cards: 1, 3, 5
Proprietors: Elaine & Nick Anderson

Newburgh
Aberdeenshire

Map 5

UDNY ARMS HOTEL
Main Street, Newburgh
Aberdeenshire AB41 0BL
Tel: 03586 89444
Fax: 03586 89012

On A975, 2½ miles off A92 Aberdeen-Peterhead, 15 minutes from Aberdeen.

A solid Victorian country hotel owned and run by the Craig family who take pains to ensure the comfort of their guests. Bedrooms are furnished with period furniture which blends in well with the building. The bistro is on two levels, the upper one with windows overlooking the Ythan River and local golf course. In addition there is the dining room which has an air of quiet Victorian charm. The à la carte menu which is available in both the bistro and the dining room changes regularly and specialises in local beef, game and seafood, served in

a cheerful, friendly and unobtrusively attentive manner. For more informal eating the cafe bar has its own special menu. The Garden Suite in the grounds of the hotel is much in demand for conferences, weddings, private parties and dinners.
Open all year except nights of 25 + 26 Dec
Rooms: 26 with private facilities
Bar Meals 12 – 9 pm Sun (a)
Bar Lunch 12 – 2 pm (a)
Dining Room/Restaurant Lunch 12 – 2 pm (d)
Bar Supper 5 – 9 pm (a)
Dinner 6.30 – 9.30 pm Mon to Sat: 6 – 9 pm Sun (d)
Bed & breakfast £31 – £58
Dinner B & B £48 – £78
The Udny Creel: salmon, scallops, mussels, squid, king prawn and crab, cooked in fish and lobster stock, finished with cream, brandy, tomato and tarragon. Lamb steak marinated in lemon and garlic, and chargrilled. Sticky toffee pudding.
STB Commended 3 Crowns
Credit cards: 1, 3 + SWITCH
Proprietor: J D Craig

Newtonmore

Map 6

ARD-NA-COILLE HOTEL
Kingussie Road, Newtonmore
Inverness-shire PH20 1AY
Tel: 0540 673214
At northern end of Newtonmore village. An elevated position in two acres of wooded garden gives this Edwardian shooting lodge fine views out over the valley to the Cairngorms. Bedrooms are very tastefully and comfortably furnished and the food is particularly acclaimed. Nancy Ferrier and Barry Cottam maintain an informal and relaxing atmosphere and each year have raised the reputation of Ard-na-Coille and gained new plaudits for the cuisine. Menus are original and interesting and highlight the excellent variety of produce of the region.
Open 29 Dec to 15 Nov except 1 wk Apr + 1 wk Sep
Rooms: 7 with private facilities
Dinner at 7.45 pm (e) – 5 course set menu
No smoking in dining room
Dogs accepted by prior arrangement
Bed & breakfast £45 – £55
Dinner B & B £63 – £75

Salad of Argyll smoked ham and spiced Loch Linnhe scallops. Chargrilled salmon fillet with langoustines and a shellfish and whisky sauce. Spiced cherry strudel.
Credit cards: 1, 3
Proprietors: Nancy Ferrier & Barry Cottam

Newton Stewart

Map 1

CREEBRIDGE HOUSE HOTEL
Minnigaff, Newton Stewart
Wigtownshire DG8 6NP
Tel: 0671 2121
Fax: 0671 3258
From roundabout signposted Newton Stewart on A75, through the town, bear left over the River Cree, 250 yards on left is Minnigaff.
At one time home of the Earl of Galloway this fine old country house has the best of both worlds. Not only is it set peacefully in acres of well kept gardens but it is also just three or four minutes walk from the busy market town of Newton Stewart. The public rooms are gracious, the drawing room with a particularly fine mahogany fireplace, and the cosy atmospheric bar has a fine reputation for its bar meals – and its large range of malt whiskies. Food in the dining room, which overlooks the gardens, is highly acclaimed and personally supervised by proprietor Chris Walker, who was the overall winner of the Taste of Scotland Scotch Lamb Challenge 1993.
Open all year
Rooms: 18 with private facilities
Bar Lunch 12 – 2 pm: Carvery style Sun (a)
Bar Supper 6 – 9 pm Sun to Fri: 6 – 10 pm Sat (b)
Dinner 7 – 8.30 pm (c)
No smoking in dining room
Bed & breakfast £25 – £38
Dinner B & B £40 – £50
Fillet of Scotch lamb in filo pastry. Escalope of veal stuffed with thyme and

basil. Grilled shell-on shrimps in garlic butter. Hot smoked trout tossed in Vermouth and set on a bed of mixed lettuce.*
STB Commended 4 Crowns
Credit cards: 1, 3
Proprietors: Chris & Sue Walker

THE KIRROUGHTREE HOTEL
Newton Stewart
Wigtownshire DG8 6AN
Tel: 0671 2141
Fax: 0671 2425
Signposted 1 mile outside Newton Stewart on A75.
This splendid 18th century mansion has all the attributes of a grand hotel – superb public rooms opulently furnished, well equipped spacious bedrooms and staff who obviously take pride in the establishment and do their best to anticipate your every need and ensure a high standard of service. Allied to this is some of the best food in the region, carefully prepared and presented by Roux-trained Ian Bennett. The hotel grounds are immaculately landscaped and there are concessionary rates on 5 local golf courses and also free use of the leisure facilities in the hotel's sister establishments – the Cally Palace, Gatehouse-of-Fleet, and the North West Castle, Stranraer – entries for which you will find elsewhere in this Guide. Children over 12 years are welcome. The overall experience is one of quality, service and value.
Open 4 Mar to 3 Jan
Rooms: 22 with private facilities
Snack Lunch 12 – 1.30 pm
Dining Room/Restaurant Lunch 12 – 1.30 pm (c)
Dinner 7 – 9.30 pm (e)
No smoking dining room available
Dinner B & B £60 – £85
Special rates for over 60s + special weekly terms.
Warm salad of west coast scallops with toasted pine kernels. Canon of Scotch lamb topped with a truffle mousse served with baby vegetables and a Madeira sauce. Caramelised lemon tart with Armagnac sauce. Selection of Scottish cheeses with home-made bannocks.
STB Highly Commended 5 Crowns
Credit cards: 1, 3
Proprietors: The McMillan Family

North Berwick

Map 4

HARDING'S RESTAURANT
2 Station Road, North Berwick
East Lothian EH39 4AU
Tel: 0620 4737

Prestige Award Winner 1992

Next to railway station.
The building was originally an Edwardian
tea room – slate roofed and white
painted outside and inside with
astragalled windows looking towards
North Berwick Law. Interior is light and
airy with light oak chairs and checked
linen tablecloths. Simple decor of
framed animal prints and oriental rugs.
The restaurant area looks through to the
kitchen where chef/proprietor Chris
Harding can be seen at work. The aim is
to provide a welcoming informal
atmosphere where someone enjoying a
candlelit dinner will feel just as at ease
as someone who has been in for warm
scones with home-made jam. There are
no dress restrictions. The wine list is
almost entirely Australian with over 70
different wines, all personally chosen by
Chris Harding who is an Australian.
*Open all year except 2 wks Dec + 2 wks
Oct*
*Dining Room/Restaurant Lunch 12.15 –
2 pm Wed to Sat (b)*
Dinner 7.30 – 9 pm Wed to Sat (d)
Restaurant closed Sun Mon Tue
Table Licence
Facilities for the disabled
No smoking in restaurant
*Steamed parcel of sole wrapped with
smoked salmon on a saffron and lemon
sauce. Roasted breast of duck in a tangy
plum sauce.*
No credit cards
Proprietor: Christopher Harding

North Middleton

Map 4

BORTHWICK CASTLE HOTEL
Borthwick Castle Road
North Middleton, Gorebridge
Midlothian EH23 4QY
Tel: 0875 820514
Fax: 0875 821702

*A7 to North Middleton, 12 miles south of
Edinburgh, then follow signs for Borthwick.
A private road leads to the Castle.*
Once the refuge of Mary Queen of Scots,
this 15th century castle has 10
bedchambers including four with four
poster beds. All are different in decor but
offer en suite facilities and are in
keeping with their surroundings. Guests
dine in the great hall of the castle from a
four course set menu prepared from
fresh ingredients. The style of cuisine is
described as modern British, with a
strong bias to Scottish produce, and is
equally suited to intimate dinners as it is
to glittering banquets. The cellars offer a
comprehensive wine list and a fine
selection of malt whiskies.
Open 1 Mar to 2 Jan
Rooms: 10 with private facilities
Dinner at 8 pm (e) reservations only
Table Licence
Room Rate £95 – £165
*Nettle soup with smoked salmon.
Mussel and fennel casserole. Braised
knuckle of lamb with root vegetables.
Bread and butter pudding with apricots.*
Credit cards: 1, 2, 3, 5, 6 + SWITCH

North Queensferry

Map 4

SMUGGLERS RESTAURANT
17 Main Street, North Queensferry
Fife KY11 1JT
Tel: 0383 412567

*Take Junction 1 M90, follow B981 into
North Queensferry.*
Set in a spectacular location between
the Forth Rail and Road Bridges,
Smugglers reputation continues to grow
as the repertoire of skilfully created
dishes expands. Seafood is a particular
strength, thanks largely to the insistence
on ultra fresh produce. Beef and lamb
are matured on the premises and
sauces are noteworthy, with liberal use
of fresh herbs. A relaxed informal atmosphere exists in the candlelit dining room
while attention to detail and genuine
warmth of service have drawn praise.
Complete your visit with a walk under the
floodlit span of the Forth Rail Bridge.
Open all year
Dinner 7 – 10.30 pm Thu Fri Sat only (d)
Closed Sun to Wed
No smoking in restaurant
*Squid with chilli and coriander.
Langoustines in sweet dill sauce.
Woodpigeon and wild mushrooms.
Market selection of fish. Hot sticky
toffee pudding. Bread and butter soufflé.*
Credit cards: 1, 2, 3
Proprietors: Ernest Kallus & Judi Short

North Uist

Map 7

LANGASS LODGE HOTEL
Locheport
North Uist PA82 5HA
Tel: 08764 285

6 miles from Lochmaddy ferryport.
Langass Lodge was originally built as a
shooting-fishing estate house and has
not lost any of that character in its
conversion to a small six bedroomed
hotel. It was recently refurbished and all
bedrooms now have en suite facilities. It
overlooks Loch Langass and immediately
in front of the Lodge is sited one of the
few remaining stone circles in the
islands and nearby is a neolithic burial
chamber. Good wholesome food with a
fair touch of imagination in some of the
dishes welcomes guests in the evening
as they return from their round of
sporting activity or sightseeing.
Open 1 Mar to 31 Dec
Rooms: 6 with private facilities
Bar Lunch 12 – 2 pm (a)
*Dining Room/Restaurant Lunch 12 –
1.30 pm (b)*
Bar Supper 5.30 – 9.30 pm (a)
Dinner 7 – 9 pm (c)
Bed & breakfast £30 – £35
Dinner B & B £45 – £50
*Paupiette of lemon sole with scallop
mousseline. 'Flying Scotsman' fillet
steak. Langass Savoury – home-made
oatcake with smoked salmon, cheese
and egg.*
Credit cards: 1, 3, 6
Proprietors: John & Ann Buchanan

Oban

Map 6

ARDS HOUSE
Connel, by Oban
Argyll PA37 1PT
Tel: 0631 71 255

On main A85 Oban – Tyndrum, 4 miles north of Oban.

Ards House sits on the shores of Loch Etive and benefits from panoramic views over the Firth of Lorne and the Morvern Hills. John and Jean Bowman are caring hosts and strive to make their guests' stay as comfortable and homely as possible. Most of the bedrooms have private facilities, with either baths or showers, and are equipped for making tea and coffee. This guest house makes an excellent base for visiting the central Highlands and islands, or for a relaxing break at any time of the year.

Open Mar to Nov
Rooms: 7, 6 with private facilities
Dinner at 7.15 pm – later by arrangement (b)
Dinner for non-residents by arrangement
Restricted Licence
No children
No dogs
No smoking throughout
Bed & breakfast £20 – £32
Dinner B & B £33.50 – £45.50
Home-made bread and soups. Chicken and smoked salmon served with pasta shells. Pork fillet medallions in a cream and brandy sauce. Honey and almond choux buns.
STB Commended 3 Crowns
Credit cards: 1, 3
Proprietors: John & Jean Bowman

DUNGALLAN COUNTRY HOUSE
Gallanach Road, Oban
Argyll PA34 4PD
Tel: 0631 63799
Fax: 0631 66711

On left, ½ mile past entrance to ferry terminal.

This fine old Victorian house is set in five acres of natural woodland and from the site high above Oban Bay there are splendid views of the Isle of Mull and the Morvern Hills. The atmosphere is homely and the surroundings comfortable and relaxing. Appropriately at this prime port on the west coast, the menus take full advantage of the excellent range of fresh fish and shellfish so readily available

and there is a well balanced wine list and a good selection of Scottish malt whiskies.

Open Feb to Dec
Rooms: 14, 9 with private facilities
Dinner: 6.30 – 9 pm (d)
No smoking in restaurant
Bed & breakfast rates on application
Dinner B & B £40 – £56
Local produce especially fish. Loch Etive mussels, Isle of Seil oysters and creel-caught prawns. Game and prime Scottish beef.
STB Award Pending
Credit card: 1
Proprietor: Elspeth Allan

THE GATHERING SCOTTISH RESTAURANT & CEILIDH BAR
Breadalbane Street, Oban
Argyll PA34 5NZ
Tel: 0631 65421/64849/66159

Entering Oban from A85 (Glasgow) into Dunollie Road and one-way system, then first left. On foot from town centre – just past cinema leads to Breadalbane Street.

There is a wealth of character in this unique restaurant built over 100 years ago to cater for guests attending the annual Gathering in the adjacent Gathering Hall, and the historical association and atmosphere have been well maintained. Now one of Oban's premier restaurants, visitors flock to it to absorb the ambience and enjoy the food. While the menu specialises in seafood and steaks, it has lots of imaginative starters, some game dishes and some "lighter bites". Portions are generous, prices are modest and the service is cheerful.

Open Easter to 1 Jan: weekends only Oct to Jan

Bar Lunch (Jul to Sep) 12 – 2.30 pm except Sun (a)
Bar Supper 5 – 11 pm (a)
Dinner 5 – 11 pm (c)
Facilities for the disabled
No smoking area in restaurant
Crofters chowder – seafood soup with scallops and mussels. Easdale prawns sauté in garlic, butter and chives. Chargrilled prime steaks. Oban Bay seafood platter. Roast haunch of venison with Madeira sauce. Poached scallops in Islay cheese sauce.
Credit cards: 1, 3
Proprietor: Elaine Cameron

ISLE OF ERISKA HOTEL
Ledaig, by Oban
Argyll PA37 1SD
Tel: 0631 72 371
Fax: 0631 72 531

A85 towards Oban. At Connel proceed by bridge on A828 for 4 miles to north of Benderloch village, then follow signposts.

This is an exceptional place by whatever standards you care to measure it by, and not only the imposing Baronial home but the whole island of over 250 acres becomes an integral part of your stay and your enjoyment. The Buchanan-Smiths have long had an outstanding reputation for their warmth of welcome to guests and the remarkable way in which they make everyone feel very special. The house is dignified and elegant yet in no way austere; public rooms are impressive and bedrooms are very comfortable, provided with all sorts of thoughtful little extras. Dinner – indeed more of a banquet – is an occasion to remember, beautifully prepared and presented. You will surely want to go back.

Open Mar to Dec
Rooms: 17 with private facilities
Bar Lunch – residents only
Dinner 8 – 9 pm (f)
Open to non-residents for dinner only
Children over 10 years welcome
No dogs in public rooms
Facilities for the disabled
Bed & breakfast £75 – £135
Salad of local prawns with home-marinated salmon. Mousseline of scallops with a white wine sauce. Fillet of halibut with a chive sauce. Scottish rib of beef carved at table.
STB Deluxe 5 Crowns
Credit cards: 1, 3 + SWITCH
Proprietors: The Buchanan-Smith Family

MANOR HOUSE HOTEL
Gallanach Road, Oban
Argyll PA34 4LS
Tel: 0631 62087
Fax: 0631 63053

From south side of Oban follow signs to car ferry. At ferry entrance continue along main road for further ½ mile.
Perched on a commanding promontory above the bay, the Manor House offers a panorama of harbour, town and islands, yet you can walk into the town centre in just five minutes. There is a comforting feel of chintzy, cosy country cottage about it. Some bedrooms are small but all have en suite facilities, television, direct dial telephone and central heating. The dining room is well appointed and the food is of remarkably high standard with lots of interesting and unusual presentations of the wide range of fish and shellfish so readily available in this west coast port.
Open 1 Feb to 25 Dec
Rooms: 11 with private facilities
Bar Lunch 12.30 – 2 pm (a)
Dining Room/Restaurant Lunch 12.30 – 2 pm except Sun (c) booking essential
Dinner 7 – 9 pm (d)
No smoking in restaurant
Dinner B & B £42 – £66
Fresh west coast oysters with fennel and honey. Lobster Hebridean. Parfait 'Flora MacDonald' – an iced parfait with prunes, chocolate and nuts, flavoured with Drambuie.
STB Highly Commended 4 Crowns
Credit cards: 1, 3
Proprietor: J L Leroy

SEA LIFE CENTRE – SHORELINE RESTAURANT
Barcaldine, Oban
Argyll PA37 1SE
Tel: 063 172 386

On A828 Oban-Fort William, 10 miles north of Oban.
The Shoreline Restaurant is within the Sea Life Centre. In this self-service restaurant a full range of meals and snacks is available including a salad table and a small oyster bar. You'll also be enjoying your meal in comfortable surroundings which give you the best possible vantage point to appreciate fully the majestic splendour of the glorious views over Loch Creran to the mountains beyond.
Open mid Feb to Nov + weekends only Dec to mid Feb

Note: closed Christmas Day + 1 Jan
Coffee Shop open 10 am – 5.30 pm
Meals available 10 am – 5.30 pm:
10 am – 6.30 pm Jul Aug (a)
Table Licence only
No smoking area in restaurant
Seafood lasagne, salmon pie, seafood pie. Local seafood – oysters (fresh), smoked salmon and trout. Coffee shop has freshly ground coffee and home-baked fare.
Credit cards: 1, 3

SOROBA HOUSE HOTEL
Soroba Road, Oban
Argyll PA34 4SB
Tel: 0631 62628

A816 to Oban.
Soroba House stands in a dominant and beautiful site of nine acres above the town, yet close enough to the town facilities, ferry terminal etc. The accommodation is in the form of suites and flatlets, some within the gardens around the hotel, so guests have the option of catering for themselves or experiencing the specialities of the hotel's dining room.
Open all year except 20 Dec to 4 Jan
Rooms: 25 with private facilities
Bar Lunch 12 – 2.15 pm (a)
Dining Room/Restaurant Lunch 12 – 2.15 pm (a)
Bar Supper 7 – 9.30 pm (a)
Dinner 7 – 9.30 pm (b)
Bed & breakfast £28 – £48
Dinner B & B £40 – £60
Selection of local produce features on menus – seafood, fish, venison, lamb, Scotch beef etc.
Credit cards: 1, 3, 6
Proprietor: David Hutchison

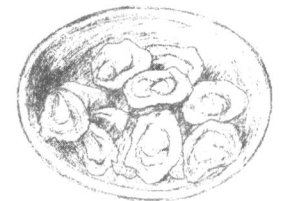

THE WATERFRONT RESTAURANT
No 1 The Waterfront
The Pier, Oban
Argyll PA34
Tel: 0631 63110

The waterfront, Oban.
It would be difficult to get closer to the main source of supply than this. The Waterfront Restaurant has built up its reputation by concentrating on the local seafood arriving at the pier at Oban and likes to boast that it gets it "from the pier to the pan as fast as we can". Lovers of fish and shellfish go here to savour the daily catch at remarkably moderate prices. Part of the same complex but on the ground floor is Creel's Coffee Shop which specialises in home-baking and in a range of sandwiches, including some superb seafood fillings – a very popular rendez-vous for a quick and satisfying snack.
Open all year
Creel's Coffee Shop 8.30 am – 6 pm (a)
Dining Room/Restaurant Lunch 12 – 3 pm (a)
Dinner 6 – 10 pm (b)
Waterfront seafood chowder. Local scallops and prawns in a lobster sauce. Fresh local langoustine cooked in wine and garlic. Specials are selected daily from the fish market landings.
Credit cards: 1, 3
Proprietor: Stuart Walker

WILLOWBURN HOTEL
Clachan Seil, Isle of Seil
by Oban PA34 4TJ
Tel: 08523 276

11 miles south of Oban, via A816 and B844, signposted Easdale, over Atlantic Bridge.
The lovely little Isle of Seil is noted for the wide range of its natural wildlife and if you are lucky you may spot badgers, buzzards, seals, heron and kestrels amongst others. It attracts bird-watchers, photographers, walkers, artists, naturalists and fishermen, almost all of whom get there by crossing the 'only single span bridge to cross the Atlantic' – or a bit of it anyway!

Willowburn is a small modern family run hotel in two acres of ground with the dining room especially having lovely views out over Seil Sound. Both table d'hôte and à la carte menus are available with good use being made of the west coast's excellent seafood in some intriguing combinations of flavours.
Open 1 Apr to 3 Jan, Nov to Dec by arrangement
Rooms: 6 with private facilities
Bar Lunch 12.30 – 2 pm (a)
Bar Supper 6 – 8.30 pm (a)
Dinner 7 – 8 pm (c)
Dinner B & B £37 – £45
Grilled Isle of Seil oysters with a herb crust. Kebab of monkfish with a light Champagne sauce. Roast leg of lamb with spiced apricot and wild rice timbale. Warm blackcurrant and applemint cake. Home grown herbs.
STB Commended 3 Crowns
Credit cards: 1, 3
Proprietors: Archie & Maureen Todd

Onich
by Fort William

Map 6

ALLT-NAN-ROS HOTEL
Onich, by Fort William
Inverness-shire PH33 6RY
Tel: 08553 210
Fax: 08553 462
On A82, 10 miles south of Fort William.
A Highland country house in a magnificent location on a garden knoll on the shores of Loch Linnhe. The elevated position gives spectacular uninterrupted views across the loch. The Macleod family have done much in recent years to improve standards in both accommodation and food. Bedrooms are well equipped and provided with the little essentials that the seasoned traveller has almost come to expect in a well run hotel. The cuisine is an interesting blend of French and Scottish taking full advantage of the wealth of Highland game, salmon and seafood for which the west coast is noted. A good range of malt whiskies and an interesting wine list should add to your enjoyment.
Open all year except mid Nov to mid Dec, mid Jan to mid Feb
Rooms: 21 with private facilities
Dining Room/Restaurant Lunch 12.30 – 2 pm (b)
Dinner 7 – 8.30 pm (c-d)

No dogs
No smoking in dining room
Bed & breakfast £37.50 – £47.50
Dinner B & B £50 – £65
Pan-fried marinated collops of venison, with salad leeks on a juniper and gin sauce. Breast of Guinea fowl with a lentil and coriander sauce. Fillets of lemon sole with a hot mousseline of crab meat and a vegetable fish sauce. Hot chocolate pudding soufflé with a Grand Marnier sauce.
STB Highly Commended 4 Crowns
Credit cards: 1, 2, 3, 5, 6
Proprietor: James Macleod

THE LODGE ON THE LOCH
Onich, by Fort William
Inverness-shire PH33 6RY
Tel: 08553 237/238
Telex: 94013696 • Fax: 08553 463
On A82, 1 mile north of the Ballachulish Bridge.
Everything about The Lodge on The Loch spells good taste and good standards. There is a refined elegance about this acclaimed family run hotel which is immediately apparent and promises to apply to every aspect of it – as indeed it does. The public rooms, the dining room and many of the bedrooms have superb views out over Loch Linnhe to the Morvern mountains beyond. Guests enjoy complimentary use of heated pool nearby. The menus are compiled with the same care and attention as is devoted to the rest of the hotel and meals are of unusually high standard.
Open Christmas + New Year + 1 Mar to 31 Oct
Rooms: 20, 18 with private facilities
Bar Lunch 12.30 – 2.30 pm (a)
Dining Room/Restaurant Lunch 12.30 –

2.30 pm (a)
Dinner 7 – 9.30 pm (d)
Facilities for the disabled
No smoking in restaurant
Dinner B & B £56.50 – £72
Scottish smoked salmon with gravadlax and poached Loch Lochy salmon, served with fresh dill and mustard vinaigrette. Local scampi wrapped in Glen Uig smoked salmon. Medallions of venison with game and rowanberry sauce. Sweet crêpe with Drambuie ice cream and Blairgowrie raspberry sauce.
STB Highly Commended 4 Crowns
Credit cards: 1, 3
Proprietors: Norman & Jessie Young

Orkney
Isles of

Map 7

CREEL RESTAURANT & ROOMS
Front Road, St Margaret's Hope
Orkney KW17 2SL
Tel: 0856 83 311
13 miles south of Kirkwall over Churchill Barriers, at seafront.
A scenic drive which takes you over the famous Churchill Barriers, relics of World War II, brings you to St Margaret's Hope and the Creel Restaurant. The Creel enjoys a reputation to rival the best. It is busy with Orcadians and visitors from all over the world. The restaurant won the Taste of Britain Award in 1986 and was listed in the AA Top 500 Restaurants in Britain 1989. Alan Craigie, the proprietor/chef, works wonders with fish and shellfish and this highly commended restaurant is one at which it is essential to book in advance. The Craigies have recently completed the upgrading of the accommodation to provide comfortable spacious rooms – with sea views – which complement the high standard and reputation of the food.
Open Feb to Dec except Christmas + New Year's Days
Rooms: 3 with private facilities
Dinner 7 – 9 pm Jun to Aug: closed Mon Tue in Apr May + Sep (d)
Note: weekends only Oct to Dec, Feb to Mar
Bed & breakfast £20 – £25
A varied and changing menu using a wide range of local seafood, famous Orkney beef, smoked lamb and local vegetables.
STB Commended 3 Crowns
Credit cards: 1, 3
Proprietors: Alan & Joyce Craigie

FOVERAN HOTEL
nr Kirkwall, St Ola
Orkney KW15 1SF
Tel: 0856 872389

On A964 Orphir road, 2½ miles from Kirkwall.

One of the few purpose built hotels on Orkney, the Foveran is all on one level with a location that provides sweeping views over Scapa Flow. The Scandinavian style dining room is light and airy and bright curtains, china and crystal on shiny pine tables give it a welcoming feel. Foveran does not make the mistake of having an over long menu and concentrates on a few well chosen dishes to represent Orkney produce. Care is taken in presentation and the quality of the food is high, as is the service.

Open all year except Christmas Day + Jan
Rooms: 8 with private facilities
Dinner 7 – 9 pm except Sun (c-d)
Bed & breakfast £42 – £50
Home-made soups and patés; prawns, scallops, lobster, sea trout, fresh Orkney lamb, beef, game, farm-cheese – all as available. New dishes from traditional raw materials.
STB Commended 4 Crowns
Credit cards: 1, 3, 6
Proprietors: Ivy & Bobby Corsie

Peat Inn

Map 4

THE PEAT INN
Peat Inn
Fife KY15 5LH
Tel: 033 484 206

In A Class of Its Own 1989

At junction of B940/941, 6 miles south-west of St Andrews.

They don't come much better than this! The Peat Inn has not just a national, but an international reputation. David Wilson and his wife Patricia have achieved wonders since they acquired this modest looking 18th century village inn situated in the village which bears its name. The Peat Inn is synonymous with good food, bold imaginative cooking of style and distinction. David Wilson was one of the early pioneers who set out to demonstrate to the world at large that not only did Scotland have the prime produce but it also had skilled chefs who could transform it into memorable meals. Recognition and success have

followed and nobody should visit Fife without reserving a lunch or dinner at this special establishment.

Open all year except Christmas Day + 1 Jan
Rooms: 8 with private facilities
Dining Room/Restaurant Lunch 12.30 – 1 pm except Sun Mon (c)
Dinner 7 – 9.30 pm except Sun Mon (e)
Closed Sun Mon
No smoking in dining rooms
Bed & breakfast from £65 – £95
Sauté of scallops, monkfish and pork with spiced apple. Whole local lobster poached in a vegetable and herb broth.
Credit cards: 1, 2, 3, 5 + SWITCH
Proprietors: David & Patricia Wilson

Peebles

Map 2

CRINGLETIE HOUSE HOTEL
nr Peebles EH45 8PL
Tel: 0721 730 233

A703, 2½ miles north of Peebles.

Cringletie is a perennial favourite of its many enthusiastic patrons and continues to demonstrate high standards in all aspects of hotel-keeping. It is a fine old red sandstone baronial mansion in 28 acres of gardens just off the main Peebles-Edinburgh road, in peaceful serene surroundings. Many of the herbs and vegetables for the kitchen come from its own garden. Aileen Maguire exercises a close personal supervision of food preparation and presentation, and meals are imaginative and exemplify home-cooking at its best.

Open 13 Mar to 1 Jan
Rooms: 13 with private facilities
Light Lunch except Sun (a)
Dining Room/Restaurant Lunch 1 – 1.45 pm Mon to Sat (a): Sun (b)
Afternoon tea 3.30 – 4.30 pm
Dinner 7.30 – 8.30 pm (d)
No smoking in restaurant
Bed & breakfast £43 – £60
Smoked fish terrine. Marinated salmon with walnut and tarragon. Iced chocolate hazelnut parfait with Frangelico.
STB Highly Commended 4 Crowns
Credit cards: 1, 3
Proprietors: Stanley & Aileen Maguire

KINGSMUIR HOTEL
Springhill Road
Peebles EH45 9EP
Tel: 0721 720151
Fax: 0721 721795

From High Street, cross the Tweed Bridge (B7062 Traquair) then immediately turn half left into Springhill Road – hotel 400 yards on right.

Kingsmuir is a century-old house standing in its own leafy grounds on the south side of Peebles. It is a family run hotel, specialising in Scottish cooking, using the best of local produce in a wide variety of dishes, served in dining room, lounge or bar, lunchtime and evenings. Smaller portions of most dishes can be served for children and those with smaller appetites. Ideal centre for touring Edinburgh and stately homes of the Borders, golfing and fishing.

Open all year except Christmas + Boxing Days, 1 + 2 Jan
Rooms: 10 with private facilities
Bar Lunch 12 – 2 pm (a)
Dining Room/Restaurant Lunch 12 – 2 pm (a)
Bar Supper 7 – 9.30 pm (a)
Dinner 7 – 9 pm (b)
No smoking in dining room
Bed & breakfast £27 – £40
Dinner B & B £39 – £52
Home-made soups – Cullen skink, Scotch broth etc – and patés. Roast haunch of venison with redcurrant jelly. Kingsmuir steak pie. Tweed kettle of salmon. Roast Border lamb with mint sauce. Fresh selection of home-made sweets daily.
STB Commended 3 Crowns
Credit cards: 1, 2, 3
Proprietors: Elizabeth & Norman Kerr

PEEBLES HOTEL HYDRO

Innerleithen Road
Peebles EH45 8LX
Tel: 0721 720602
Fax: 0721 722999

On A72, eastern outskirts of Peebles on Innerleithen Road.

In a changing world it is always comforting to have the permanence of places like Peebles Hydro, a large imposing chateau style hotel redolent of a grander age. It is set in 30 acres of gardens and grounds overlooking the River Tweed valley and the Border hills, and has grand public rooms with lofty ceilings, wide corridors and well equipped bedrooms all with private bathrooms and all the other facilities to be expected in a resort hotel of this class. Tennis, squash and riding are available and there is a leisure centre with pool, jacuzzi, gymnasium etc. The food is traditional and caters well for the great variety of demand occasioned by a large number of guests. It is a popular conference venue but is equally in demand by families out to enjoy the Borders scenery and a restful holiday.

Open all year
Rooms: 137 with private facilities
Bar Lunch 12.30 – 3 pm (a)
Dining Room/Restaurant Lunch 12.45 – 2 pm (b)
Dinner 7.30 – 9 pm (c)
Bed & breakfast £37 – £59
Dinner B & B £52.50 – £77
Fresh trout from local fish farm. Best of Scottish smoked salmon, Border lamb, beef and other Scottish produce.
STB Commended 4 Crowns
Credit cards: 1, 2, 3, 5, 6

Perth

Map 4

BALLATHIE HOUSE HOTEL

Kinclaven, by Stanley
Perthshire PH1 4QN
Tel: 0250 883268
Fax: 0250 883396

Off A9 north of Perth through Stanley or off A93 south of Blairgowrie to Kinclaven.

There have been management changes at Ballathie during 1993 but Chris Longden, who is now General Manager, is a very experienced and quality conscious hotelier who will assuredly maintain and build on the high standards for which Ballathie is noted. It is a magnificent country house in its own estate and with lawns rolling right down to the bank of the River Tay, famous for its salmon fishing. Graciously proportioned public rooms and splendidly comfortable bedrooms epitomise the leisurely elegance of the place and the food bears evidence of a masterly hand in the kitchen. Menus change daily – always a good sign – and indicate that a chef who knows his job is availing himself of the pick of daily markets. The end result is imaginative meals with an element of excitement to them.

Open all year
Rooms: 27 with private facilities
Bar Lunch 12 – 2 pm (a)
Dining Room/Restaurant Lunch 12 – 2 pm (b)
Dinner 7 – 8.30 pm (e)
No smoking in dining rooms
Bed & breakfast £50 – £85
Dinner B & B £70 – £105
Home-cured Tay salmon. Perthshire lamb and beef. Local game. West coast shellfish. Local asparagus, soft fruits and berries, woodland mushrooms.
STB Deluxe 4 Crowns
Credit cards: 1, 2, 3, 5, 6

THE BEIN INN

Glenfarg, nr Perth
Perthshire PH2 9PY
Tel: 0577 830 216

10 minutes south of Perth. Exit M90, Junction 8 northbound/9 southbound, in the Glen on old A9.

An attractive well maintained traditional coaching inn set in the beautiful Glen of Glenfarg. Character restaurant serving à la carte and vegetarian menus. Cosy lounge bar, "hideaway" snack bar (May to Oct). Well appointed accommodation, most en suite.

Open all year except Boxing Day + 27 Dec
Rooms: 13, 11 with private facilities
Bar Lunch 12 – 2 pm (a)
Dining Room/Restaurant Lunch 12 – 2 pm (b)
Bar Supper 5 – 9 pm (b)
Dinner 7 – 9 pm (c)
Bed & breakfast £22 – £38
Dinner B & B £45 – £66
Cullen skink, Scottish smoked trout and salmon. Highland game soup. Venison casserole, Tayside salmon, local Scottish lamb, beef, pheasant Blairgowrie. Cloutie dumpling.
STB Commended 3 Crowns
Credit cards: 1, 3, 6
Proprietors: Mike & Elsa Thompson

HUNTINGTOWER HOTEL

Crieff Road
Perth PH1 3JT
Tel: 0738 83771
Fax: 0738 83777

Signposted off A85, 1 mile west of Perth, towards Crieff.

There has been a great deal of change at Huntingtower in the last few years and the excellent new range of meeting rooms have made it a prime conference centre for the area. It is set in 3½ acres of beautifully landscaped gardens and the immediate impression is of a peaceful and quiet rural retreat. Situated as it is, just outside the city of Perth, it makes a splendid base from which to explore the region's many attractions. The oak-panelled dining room has a quality feel about it and the standard of food measures up to this in every way.

Open all year
Rooms: 22 with private facilities
Bar Lunch 12 – 2.30 pm (a)
Dining Room/Restaurant Lunch 12 – 2.30 pm (b)
Bar Supper 6 – 9.30 pm (a)
Dinner 7 – 9.30 pm (c)
Bed & breakfast £32 – £46
Dinner B & B £39.50 – £55
Locally caught game and salmon. Fresh local produce prepared carefully and imaginatively.
STB Commended 4 Crowns
Credit cards: 1, 2, 3, 5, 6 + SWITCH

THE LANG BAR & RESTAURANT
Perth Theatre, 185 High Street
Perth PH1 5UW
Tel: 0738 39136
Fax: 0738 24576

Perth city centre in pedestrian zone at middle section of High Street.
The Lang Bar and Restaurant forms an integral part of Perth Theatre and is imbued with the vibrant atmosphere of live entertainment. Built in 1900, the Theatre has been beautifully restored giving a wonderful rich setting for the Restaurant, Coffee Bar and Bar. Enter the front door of the Theatre and pass through the Box Office, and you come to the Coffee Bar where home-baking and light meals are available at lunchtime and in the evening. The Coffee Bar often plays host to art exhibitions by local artists. A short flight of stairs leads to the Restaurant and bar area. Dinner in the Restaurant is dependent on theatre productions and consequently there are occasions when it is not available, so booking or enquiry in advance is recommended.
Open all year except during the day public holidays
Bar Lunch 12 – 2 pm Mon to Sat (a)
Dining Room/Restaurant Lunch 11.45 am – 2.15 pm Mon to Sat (a)
Bar Supper 6 – 7 pm Mon to Sat (a)
Dinner 6 – 10 pm except Sun (b) – booking advised
Closed Sun
Facilities for the disabled
Spinach roulade with mushrooms and walnuts. Beef and artichoke pie. Crusty bread, ham and prawns. Home-made soups.
Credit cards: 1, 2, 3 + SWITCH

MURRAYSHALL COUNTRY HOUSE HOTEL
Scone, nr Perth
Perthshire PH2 7PH
Tel: 0738 51171 • Telex: 76197
Fax: 0738 52595

Prestige Award Winner 1988

4 miles out of Perth, 1 mile off A94.
A grey stone mansion house with corner turret, and the quiet grace and dignity of a bygone age. It is set in its own extensive gardens and parklands and has a golf course with its own club house and facilities for conferences and functions. The Old Masters Restaurant is an elegant room, furnished with good taste and with high quality place settings. The menus changed last year and prices are now more reasonable though not at the sacrifice of standards which remain remarkably good. There are some unusual touches in the menu with interesting combinations of texture and flavour. The hotel has a four acre kitchen garden and grows many of its vegetables and herbs. French and Spanish spoken.
Open all year except 23 to 28 Dec
Note: accommodation closed 23 to 28 Dec
Rooms: 19 with private facilities
Bar Lunch (Club House) 12 – 2.30 pm (a)
Dining Room/Restaurant Lunch (Club House) 12 – 3 pm Sun only (b)
Dinner 7 – 9.30 pm (c)
Gourmet evenings + weekends
No dogs
Bed & breakfast £55 – £65
Dinner B & B £55 – £85
Ballotine of Scottish salmon and sole mousse, centred with monkfish and dill. Roast loin of woodland venison served with a compote of red cabbage and a blackcurrant and Port wine sauce. Delice of pears on a pear purée with blackcurrant sorbet.
STB Highly Commended 5 Crowns
Credit cards: 1, 2, 3, 5, 6

NEWTON HOUSE HOTEL
Glencarse
nr Perth PH2 7LX
Tel: 073 886 250
Fax: 073 886 717

Set back from A85 between Perth and Dundee.
This former Dower House (c. 1840) is set back from the A85, four miles from Perth and 13 miles from Dundee, and is an ideal location from which to explore the dramatic countryside or visit the numerous places of interest such as Glamis Castle, Scone Palace and world famous golf courses. Newton House is now a three star hotel and prides itself on a high standard of "old fashioned hospitality". The ten individually decorated en suite bedrooms overlook the gardens and there are two lounges where guests may relax and enjoy the tranquillity. The hotel offers a range of eating from bar snacks and informal meals in Cawleys to dinners in the Country House Restaurant where the menus, which focus on fresh local produce prepared with a Scottish/French flavour, have earned the hotel an AA Rosette. French, German and Spanish spoken.
Open all year
Rooms: 10 with private facilities
Bar Meals available all day (a)
Restaurant Lunch 12 – 2 pm (b)
Dinner 5 – 9 pm (c) + à la carte
No smoking in restaurant
Bed & breakfast £35.50 – £39
Dinner B & B £46 – £57
Dinner B & B breaks available (min 2 nights stay)
Cream of carrot and courgette soup. Venison cooked slowly in a whisky flavoured sauce with cloves, onions and vegetables. Scottish salmon in a herb filo pastry parcel with tangy lemon sauce. Fillet of rock turbot with a white wine and grape sauce. Prime Scotch steaks.
STB Highly Commended 4 Crowns
Credit cards: 1, 2, 3, 5, 6
Proprietors: Christopher & Carol Tallis

NUMBER THIRTY THREE SEAFOOD RESTAURANT
33 George Street
Perth PH1 5LA
Tel: 0738 33771

Perth city centre.
Number Thirty Three continues to consolidate the sound reputation it has established, and stands out like a beacon in a city in which there is a surprising paucity of good independent restaurants. With its pink and grey art deco theme it looks very smart and stylish yet is remarkably cosy. The principal emphasis of the menu is on fish and shellfish and there are some good speciality soups and sweets. You can enjoy light meals in the Oyster Bar – even just mussels and a coffee – or indulge in a more leisurely and more serious meal in the restaurant. The

attractive ambience of the place combined with this excellent balance of eating styles and the undoubted quality of the food ensures that Number Thirty Three will continue to be a winner.
Open all year except 10 days Christmas/New Year
Bar Lunch 12.30 – 2.30 pm except Sun Mon (b)
Dining Room/Restaurant Lunch 12.30 – 2.30 pm except Sun Mon (c)
Bar Supper 6.30 – 9.30 pm except Sun Mon (b)
Dinner 6.30 – 9.30 pm except Sun Mon (c)
Closed Sun Mon
Mary's seafood soup. Creamy crab and prawn terrine. Monkfish and Spring vegetables parcel. Seafood casserole. Sticky toffee pudding with butterscotch sauce.
Credit cards: 1, 2, 3
Proprietors: Gavin & Mary Billinghurst

PARKLANDS HOTEL & RESTAURANT
St Leonards Bank
Perth PH2 8EB
Tel: 0738 22451
Fax: 0738 22046

Junction of St Leonards Bank and Marshall Place in centre of Perth adjoining South Inch Park.
Parklands has a commanding site overlooking open parkland and, comfortably ensconced with a drink in the conservatory or the outside terrace, it is difficult to believe that you are in the centre of this historic old city and ancient capital of Scotland. It has a good reputation locally and is much used by the local business community though, of course, it makes an excellent base for visitors from which to explore some of the many attractions and historic places in Perthshire and beyond. The restoration of the property has been well done and bedrooms are spacious and comfortably equipped. The quality and presentation of food has been recognised by the award of two AA Rosettes. The table d'hôte menu is good value and has an interesting range of choice.
Open all year except New Year
Rooms: 14 with private facilities
Bar Lunch 12 – 2 pm (a)
Dining Room/Restaurant Lunch 12 – 2 pm (c)
Dinner 7 – 9 pm (e)
Bed & breakfast £40 – £65

Dinner B & B £60 – £80
Room Rate £70 – £130
Special weekend breaks
Warm salad of roasted lamb and citrus segments. Roulade of monkfish mousse centred with scallops and lined with smoked salmon, on a dill butter sauce. Tenderloin of fallow deer with a compote of prunes and a rich Madeira sauce. Poached Scottish salmon with a tarragon and lemon sauce.
STB Highly Commended 4 Crowns
Credit cards: 1, 2, 3, 6 + SWITCH
Proprietors: Pat & Allan Deeson

SCONE PALACE
Perth PH2 6BD
Tel: 0738 52300

On A93 Braemar road, 2 miles out of Perth.
Ancient crowning place of Scotland's kings – now the historic home of the Earl and Countess of Mansfield. See the antique treasures, explore the grounds, enjoy lunch beside the range in the 'Old Kitchen' restaurant, or a snack in the coffee shop. Take home the excellent produce from the shop. To arrange special off-season visits contact the Administrator.
Open 1 Apr to 10 Oct
Food Service 9.30 am – 5 pm Mon to Sat: 1.30 – 5 pm Sun (a)
Dining Room/Restaurant Lunch 11.30 am – 2 pm except Sun (a)
Note: open Sun for Lunch Jul + Aug only
Dinner 7 – 8 pm (f) – by arrangement only
Fresh Tay salmon, home-made soup always available on the lunch menu. Home-baking, chutney and marmalade a speciality.
Credit cards: 1, 2, 3, 6

Peterhead

Map 5

WATERSIDE INN
Fraserburgh Road, Peterhead
Aberdeenshire AB42 7BN
Tel: 0779 71121 • Telex: 739413
Fax: 0779 70670

30 miles north of Aberdeen on A952. 1 mile north of Peterhead.
It comes as a surprise to most people to learn that Peterhead is the most easterly town in mainland Scotland. Another surprise is in store at the Waterside Inn, Peterhead's leading hotel on the northern side of the town but just sufficiently out of it to give a quiet rural setting. The name may suggest a riverside pub but nothing could be further from the truth. The concept is nearer that of a good international chain, with splendid executive and family facilities and extensive conference suites. There is also a leisure complex offering swimming pool, jacuzzi, Turkish steam room, saunas and gymnasium. Ogilvies Restaurant is a sophisticated elegant dining room with a menu to match. Food is imaginative, very well presented and served by courteous well trained staff who seem to take genuine pleasure and pride in their work. The buffet breakfast in the Grill Room is really something!
Open all year
Rooms: 110 with private facilities
Bar Lunch 12 – 2 pm (a)
Dining Room/Restaurant Lunch 12 – 2 pm (b)
Bar Supper 6 – 9 pm (a)
Dinner (Ogilvies) 6 – 10 pm except Sun Mon (c)
(Grill Room open 7 days)
Taste of Scotland applies to Ogilvies Restaurant
Bed & breakfast £27 – £45
Dinner B & B £37 – £39
Lobster and bacon chowder. Skewered king prawns and scallops with a lemon and lime butter. Prime Buchan fillet of beef topped with home-made pâté and a Madeira sauce. Local game cooked with apricots and topped with a light flaky pastry.
STB Commended 5 Crowns
Credit cards: 1, 2, 3, 5, 6

Pitlochry

Map 4

AUCHNAHYLE FARM
Tomcroy, Pitlochry
Perthshire PH16 5JA
Tel: 0796 472318
Fax: 0796 473657

Off East Moulin Road, at end of Tomcroy Terrace.
A delightful little 18th century farmhouse with neat gardens shared by the family's peacocks. It is the home of Penny and Alastair Howman who make their guests feel genuinely welcome and offer them every home comfort and memorable meals. Penny Howman is a cook of distinction and creativity who uses the best of fresh farm and local produce and enhances it with herbs from the herb garden. Dinner is served by candlelight round the family dining table with other guests and conversation flows freely. The four course dinner menu changes daily and is invariably something special. This is a place that is much in demand and not one that you can just expect to drop in to so do 'phone and book in advance. Well behaved dogs and children over 12 years welcome.
Open all year except 22 Dec to 4 Jan
Rooms: 3 with private facilities
Picnic Lunches on request
Pre-theatre supper (two courses + coffee) at 6.45 pm (b)
Dinner at 7.30 pm (c)
Unlicensed – guests welcome to take own wine
No children under 12 years
No smoking in dining room
Bed & breakfast £28 – £32
Dinner B & B £46.50 – £50.50
Smoked cheese soufflé. Chocolate Drambuie marquise. Pan-fried fillet of venison with plums. Chicken breasts in oatmeal with a mustard and cream sauce. Honey glazed duck with grapefruit and ginger sauce. Scottish cheeseboard with home-made oatcakes.
Credit cards: 1, 3
Proprietors: Penny & Alastair Howman

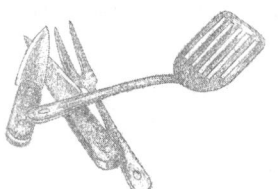

BIRCHWOOD HOTEL
East Moulin Road, Pitlochry
Perthshire PH16 5DW
Tel: 0796 472477
Fax: 0796 473951

200 yards off Atholl Road on Perth side of Pitlochry.
A lovely warm and homely hotel where the proprietors, Brian and Ovidia Harmon, try to maintain a family atmosphere and are committed to making their guests feel welcome and to providing every comfort for them. It is a fine old stone Victorian mansion on a wooded knoll with four acres of attractive grounds, and hospitality is the keynote allied to good food. There is a choice of table d'hôte or à la carte menus with the option to interchange if you prefer and there is sufficient choice available to satisfy most tastes, together with an extensive wine list. All bedrooms have private bathroom, colour TV, telephone and courtesy trays. Dogs are accepted by arrangement.
Open mid Mar to end Oct
Rooms: 16 with private facilities
Dining Room/Restaurant Lunch 12.30 – 1.30 pm (a)
Dinner 6.30 – 8.15 pm (c)
No smoking in restaurant
Bed & breakfast £26 – £37
Dinner B & B £39 – £54
Seafood with horseradish cream. Baked wild salmon with cucumber and yoghurt sauce. Sirloin steak with Drambuie haggis stuffing. Noisettes of lamb with local berries. Chicken supreme stuffed with skirlie in leek sauce.
STB Highly Commended 3 Crowns
Credit cards: 1, 3
Proprietors: Brian & Ovidia Harmon

CASTLEBEIGH HOUSE
Knockard Road, Pitlochry
Perthshire PH16 5HJ
Tel: 0796 472925
Fax: 0796 474068

Just off Pitlochry-West Moulin road.
A fine 19th century house originally built by an English boys' school as a retreat. It sits high on the hillside above Pitlochry with magnificent views of the green hillside across the valley, and is well situated and convenient for the many attractions and places of interest that make the town and the county so popular. All rooms are en suite, and there is a putting green in the garden which is much used. Menus change regularly, concentrate on good Scottish

products, are imaginative and excellent value for money.
Open 1 Feb to 30 Nov
Rooms: 21, 20 with private facilities
Dinner 6 – 7.45 pm (b)
No smoking in restaurant
Bed & breakfast £20 – £35
Dinner B & B £30 – £45
Roast haunch of Scottish venison with a blackberry, cream and tarragon sauce. Deep-fried ice cream in Drambuie batter served with butterscotch sauce.
STB Commended 3 Crowns
Credit cards: 1, 3
Proprietors: Alistair & Diane McMenemie

CRAIGMHOR LODGE, HOTEL & RESTAURANT
27 West Moulin Road, Pitlochry
Perthshire PH16 5EF
Tel: 0796 472123
Fax: 0796 472123

Take A924 Moulin/Braemar road in Pitlochry – 800 yards up hill.
Craigmhor is set in two acres of secluded grounds overlooking the Tummel Valley. This Victorian lodge offers nine beautifully styled en suite bedrooms all of individual character. It also features a relaxing lounge with an Adam fireplace, and an intimate cocktail bar with over 60 malt whiskies. The restaurant specialises in imaginative Scottish cuisine skilfully prepared by the chef/proprietor, Ian Mackenzie.
Open all year
Rooms: 9 with private facilities
Light Lunch 12 – 2 pm (a)
Restaurant Lunch 12 – 2 pm (b) – reservations only
Supper 7 – 9 pm (b)
Dinner 7 – 9 pm: 6.30 – 9 pm during Theatre season (c-d)
Facilities for the disabled
No smoking in restaurant
Bed & breakfast £30 – £35
Dinner B & B £42 – £55
Short breaks available
A galantine of minted tomatoes with west coast prawns in a mint and yoghurt dressing. Fillet of River Tay grilse wrapped in filo pastry, set on a fresh lime sauce. Whole poached peach with fresh peach ice cream, served with a hot white chocolate sauce.
STB Highly Commended 3 Crowns
Credit cards: 1, 2, 3, 6
Proprietors: Ian & Sandra Mackenzie & Jean Hutton

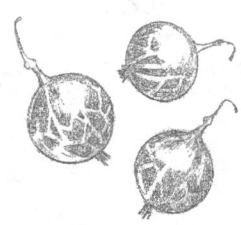

DUNFALLANDY HOUSE
Logierait Road, Pitlochry
Perthshire PH16 5NA
Tel: 0796 472648

On south side of Pitlochry, signposted off road leading to Festival Theatre.
The present house which is the Fergusson Clan seat is built on foundations which date back to the 13th century and was originally built for General Archibald Fergusson in 1790. This Georgian mansion house is now a beautifully refurbished country house hotel. It is magnificently situated within the Dunfallandy Estate and has unrivalled views of the glorious Tummel Valley, with the popular Highland town of Pitlochry nestling below. This characterful house retains its historical features including marble fireplaces, log fires and the 'General's Bath' – the original Georgian ceramic bath of rather alarming depth! The elegant dining room offers imaginative food expertly prepared and presented, enhanced by fresh flowers, silver cutlery, crystal glasses and candlelight. Jane and Michael Bardsley are dedicated to the service of all the good things in Scottish cuisine and are currently increasing the size of new herb gardens to improve standards even further. An extensive wine list features traditional and New World wines.
Open 1 Mar to 31 Oct plus Christmas + New Year
Rooms: 9 with private facilities
Dinner 6.15 – 8 pm (b-c)
No children
No dogs
No smoking in dining room
Bed & breakfast £20 – £35
Dinner B & B £30 – £50
Wild duck breast poached with local chanterelles, fresh garden herbs and claret. Varied selection of vegetarian dishes always available.
STB Highly Commended 3 Crowns
Credit cards: 1, 2, 3
Proprietors: Jane & Michael Bardsley

EAST HAUGH COUNTRY HOUSE HOTEL & RESTAURANT
East Haugh, by Pitlochry
Perthshire PH16 5JS
Tel: 0796 473121
Fax: 0796 472473

On old A9 road, 1 mile south of Pitlochry.
East Haugh House is a beautiful 17th century turreted stone Clan house, set in two acres of lawned gardens, which has been sympathetically refurbished to offer a high standard of accommodation. The restaurant and conservatory bar are complemented by the individually designed and furnished bedrooms, one featuring an antique pine four-poster bed and an open fire. All rooms have direct dial telephone, colour TV and tea/coffee-making facilities. Neil McGown, the proprietor/chef, takes the greatest pride in preparing his dishes which are becoming renowned, and he may even shoot or catch the ingredients for you himself!
Open all year
Rooms: 8 with private facilities
Bar Lunch 12 – 2 pm (b)
Dining Room/Restaurant Lunch – private functions by arrangement
Bar Supper 6 – 10.30 pm (b)
Dinner 7 – 10 pm (d)
No smoking in restaurant
Bed & breakfast £22 – £62
Dinner B & B £42 – £82
Mix of traditional Scottish and classic French. Game in season, an abundance of fresh fish and shellfish. Original vegetarian dishes.
STB Commended 3 Crowns
Credit cards: 1, 3
Proprietors: Neil & Lesley McGown

KNOCKENDARROCH HOUSE HOTEL
Higher Oakfield, Pitlochry
Perthshire PH16 5HT
Tel: 0796 473473
Fax: 0796 474068

High on a hill overlooking village – just off main road in the centre of town, up Bonnethill Road and take first right turn.
Very much a large family home, Knockendarroch is a splendidly confident Victorian house standing squarely on its hill overlooking the Tummel Valley and Pitlochry. John and Mary McMenemie are warm, enthusiastic and attentive to the comfort of their guests and this is evident in the standard of the accommodation. A continuing process of redecoration goes on and family collections of pictures are in the

bedrooms. This is positively a 'no smoking' house and therefore meets what is very much the popular requirement nowadays. The food is described as home-cooking to the highest standard and has recently earned a red Rosette from the Automobile Association. Bookings are advisable and essential for non residents.
Open 12 Apr to 30 Nov
Rooms: 12 with private facilities
Dinner 6.15 – 7.45 pm (b)
Bed & breakfast £26 – £35
Dinner B & B £37 – £48
Good home cooking – vegetarian and special diets catered for. Cream of carrot and cardamom soup. Nut roast provençale. Pan-fried collops of venison with cranberry and Port sauce. Summer pudding. Home-made dairy ice creams.
STB Highly Commended 3 Crowns
Credit cards: 1, 2, 3, 5
Proprietors: John & Mary McMenemie

MILL POND COFFEE SHOP
Burnside Apartment Hotel
19 West Moulin Road
Pitlochry PH16 5EA
Tel: 0796 472203
Fax: 0796 473586

Around 300 yards north of junction of A924 Pitlochry-Braemar (West Moulin Road) and Atholl Road, Pitlochry.
A delightful little coffee shop within an apartment hotel, with 14 serviced studios/apartments, situated in a convenient quiet location. An imaginative menu is served throughout the day, with home-made soups and hot dishes, tasty snacks and sandwiches, vegetarian dishes, home-baking and speciality ices. Selection of teas, coffees and health drinks. Children welcome. There is also a gallery featuring paintings by local/area artists and mixed exhibitions.
Open 1 Apr to 31 Oct
Continuous food service from 10 am – 6.30 pm Mon to Sat: 10 am – 5.30 pm Sun (b)
No smoking in coffee shop
Bed & breakfast from £24
Room Rate from £20.00
Open sandwiches – Tay salmon, smoked gammon; smoked trout, salmon, nut pâté. Ginger cream meringues; carrot, parsnip, banana and apple cakes, and delicious desserts.
Credit cards: 1, 2, 3, 5, 6
Proprietors: Bill & Jessie Falconer

PITLOCHRY FESTIVAL THEATRE RESTAURANT

Port-na-Craig, Pitlochry
Perthshire PH16 5DR
Tel: 0796 473054
Fax: 0796 473054

On south bank of the River Tummel, approx ¼ mile from centre of town. Clearly signposted.

Scotland's 'Theatre in the Hills' is beautifully situated on the banks of the River Tummel and its glass frontage allows wonderful views from the Brown Trout Restaurant and Coffee Bar. Home-baking is a feature of the coffee bar in the foyer, and there is a lunchtime buffet with roasts of the day and local fish. There is always plenty of food but seating can become scarce on a matinee day! Table d'hôte dinners in the evening are served in the spacious modern dining room in one sitting before theatre, normally at 6.30 pm, and booking is essential. French spoken.

Open 11 Apr to 8 Oct
Dining Room/Restaurant Lunch 12 – 2 pm except Sun (a)
Dinner (from 29 Apr) 6.30 pm except Sun (c) – booking essential
Facilities for the disabled
No smoking in restaurant
Smoking area in Coffee Bar
Festival smokie hot pot. Breast of chicken filled with haggis in a cream sauce. Poached fillet of salmon with a cucumber and prawn butter sauce. Casserole of venison in beer with treacle and brown sugar. Oven roast rack of lamb with a lemon, oatmeal and herb crust. Rhubarb gin fool. Speciality Scottish cheeseboard.
Credit cards: 1, 2, 3, 5, 6

TORRDARACH HOTEL

Golf Course Road, Pitlochry
Perthshire PH16 5AU
Tel: 0796 472136

On road signposted to golf course at north end of town.

Torrdarach is a traditional old Scottish house offering a high standard of personal service and traditional home-cooking. The hotel is in a quiet and peaceful woodland setting overlooking Pitlochry, and is maintained in immaculate condition with newly furnished bedrooms. Good value unpretentious home-cooking is complemented by an improved wine list, and menus change regularly. There are few better locations than Pitlochry from

which to set out and explore the myriad attractions of Scotland.

Open 1 Apr to mid Oct
Rooms: 7 with private facilities
Dinner 6.30 – 7 pm (b)
Residents only
No dogs
No smoking throughout
Bed & breakfast £20 – £29
Dinner B & B £30 – £44
Smoked salmon pâté, sweet herring, Angus beef, Perthshire turkey, lamb, salmon.
STB Highly Commended 3 Crowns
No credit cards
Proprietors: Richard & Vivienne Cale

WESTLANDS OF PITLOCHRY

160 Atholl Road, Pitlochry
Perthshire PH16 5AR
Tel: 0796 472266
Fax: 0796 473994

On old A9 north of town centre.

Westlands is situated close to the centre of Pitlochry yet enjoys fine views over the surrounding mountains and Vale of Atholl. The proprietors' policy of continual improvement provides 15 bedrooms (all en suite) with colour TV, tea/coffee tray, radio, hairdryers, direct dial telephones, and central heating throughout. Westlands Restaurant offers distinctive cuisine in tasteful surroundings using the best products Scotland has to offer. 'Taste of Scotland' dishes are a particular feature.

Open all year except Christmas + Boxing Days
Rooms: 15 with private facilities
Bar Lunch 12 – 2 pm (a)
Bar Supper 6.15 – 9.30 pm (b)
Dinner 6.15 – 9 pm (c)
Bed & breakfast £22.50 – £37.25
Dinner B & B £36.50 – £53.75
Reduced rates available for Spring/Autumn, also Winter + Theatre packages
Chunks of tender beef cooked with Scottish beer and onions, topped with a slice of crusty bread spread with grain mustard and Orkney cheese. Tender fillet of pork filled with date and onion stuffing, flavoured with thyme and served with a whisky flavoured sauce.
STB Commended 4 Crowns
Credit cards: 1, 3
Proprietors: Andrew & Sue Mathieson

Plockton

Map 6

Special Merit Award 1993

THE HAVEN HOTEL

Innes Street, Plockton
Ross-shire IV52 8TW
Tel: 059 984 223

In the village of Plockton.

No one should ever be in this part of Scotland without seeing Plockton. With its palm trees along the waterfront and stunning views out over the sea it really is one of the country's loveliest villages. The aptly named Haven Hotel lives up to its name and makes a delightful retreat. It has been carefully converted from a 19th century merchant's house but it is much larger internally than it appears from the outside. It is, in every way, an excellent little hotel which has been furnished and equipped to high standards. The same care goes into the food. It is imaginative and well presented, with an admirable reliance on prime local produce.

Open 1 Feb to 18 Dec
Rooms: 13 with private facilities
Bar Lunch – reservations only (a)
Dining Room/Restaurant Lunch – reservations only (b)
Dinner 7 – 8.30 pm (c)
No smoking in restaurant
Bed & breakfast £32 – £35
Dinner B & B £43 – £51
Plockton prawns, pheasant, local salmon, scallops, venison, haggis, kippers, local black pudding, wild duck, Scottish lamb, beef and pork. Home-made sweets. Scottish cheeses.
STB Highly Commended 4 Crowns
Credit cards: 1, 3, 6
Proprietors: Marjorie Nichols & John Graham

OFF THE RAILS

The Station, Plockton
Ross-shire IV52 8TN
Tel: 059 984 423/306

On platform of Plockton railway station – ½ mile from centre of village and lochside.

Plockton Station is on the famous "Kyle Line" and trains still pass through it regularly. It was built in 1897 and has not changed much since, with the original timber panelling and black iron grates still in position in the converted

waiting rooms. This provided an unusual and interesting location, therefore, for Calum and Jane Mackenzie to have set up their characterful little restaurant in which you can enjoy everything from a morning coffee to a relaxed candlelit dinner. Jenny Moulds' menu takes full advantage of the west coast's bountiful harvest of seafood and there are some very interesting and subtle recipes, flavoured with herbs from the garden created by Calum Mackenzie. There is also an interesting gift shop in the old ticket office, full of specially selected items hand-crafted in Scotland.
Open Easter to Oct
Food service 10.30 am – 9.30 pm over Easter + from late May
Dining Room/Restaurant Lunch 11.30 am – 5 pm (a)
Dinner 6.30 – 9.30 pm (b-c)
Note: Easter to late May open Thu Fri Sat Sun evenings only
No smoking in restaurant
Smoking at outside tables only
Smoked trout and warm tossed salad. King scallops with coconut ginger cream. Roast leg of Scotch lamb with fresh heather shoots. Roast duck breast with orange and Highland sloe liqueur. Whole pigeon en croûte. Celery and hazelnut profiteroles with hazelnut sauce.
Credit card: 1
Proprietor: Jane Mackenzie

Port of Menteith

Map 4

LAKE HOTEL
Port of Menteith
Perthshire FK8 3RA
Tel: 08775 258
Fax: 08775 671

On A81 – at Port of Menteith – 200 yards on road south to Arnprior.
The Lake Hotel stands right on the shore of Scotland's only lake (the others are all lochs). It has been converted from a 19th century manse and has delightful views over the lake to the Trossach hills. The hotel has recently been refurbished to a very high standard of comfort. There is a large conservatory dining room and an elegant lounge. Altogether this is a most attractive establishment in lovely surroundings serving quality fresh food.
Open all year
Rooms: 14 with private facilities
Bistro Lunch 12 – 2 pm (a)

Dining Room/Restaurant Lunch 12 – 2 pm (d) – booking essential
Bistro Supper 6 – 9 pm (a)
Dinner 7 – 9 pm (d)
No smoking in restaurant
Dinner B & B £42 – £66
Sauté smoked prawns and wild mushrooms. Roast local boar with hawthorn jelly. Shortbread cup with lavender mousse.
STB Highly Commended 4 Crowns
Credit cards: 1, 3
Proprietor: J L Leroy

Portpatrick

Map 1

THE FERNHILL HOTEL
Heugh Road, Portpatrick
nr Stranraer DG9 8TD
Tel: 077 681 220
Fax: 077 681 596

Just off main road into Portpatrick.
Portpatrick's leading hotel is spectacularly situated with magnificent views over the Irish Sea and the town. This popular three star hotel is owned and run by Anne and Hugh Harvie who are regularly improving and updating to maintain high standards throughout. The conservatory is especially attractive and is a fashionable eating area for à la carte and bar meals. The restaurant offers a fine selection of food and wine, and the patronage of local people is a pointer to the high quality of the cuisine. Smoking is discouraged in the restaurant and conservatory but permitted in the bar extension. Ample overnight parking is available within the walled grounds.
Open all year except Christmas Day
Rooms: 21 with private facilities
Snacks available all day
Bar Lunch 12 – 2 pm (a)
Dining Room/Restaurant Lunch 12 – 2 pm (a)
Bar Restaurant Meals 6 – 10 pm (a-b)
Dinner 6.30 – 10 pm (c)
No dogs in public rooms
No smoking in restaurant + conservatory
Bed & breakfast £35 – £65
Dinner B & B £46 – £80
Creative dishes using Galloway beef and lamb. Locally cured smoked salmon. Ecclefechan tart.
STB Highly Commended 4 Crowns
Credit cards: 1, 2, 3, 5
Proprietors: Anne & Hugh Harvie

Powmill
by Dollar

Map 4

GARTHWHINZEAN HOTEL & RESTAURANTS
Powmill, by Dollar
Clackmannanshire FK14 7NW
Tel: 0577 840595
Fax: 0577 840595

On A977 Kincardine Bridge-Kinross
This is the latest acquisition of the Brown family whose expertise in hotel management is well demonstrated in the standards they set and maintain at Auchterarder House and the Roman Camp Hotel. Son Paul and his wife Diane have managed the Garthwhinzean for the last year and have a steady programme of refurbishment and improvement ahead of them. Paul's culinary skills at Auchterarder House earned it high praise and recognition, and no doubt he will be determined to establish a similar reputation at Garthwhinzean. Menus have been carefully planned to cater for all tastes and budgets, and the hotel is a popular venue for weddings and conferences.
Open all year
Rooms: 3 with private facilities
Bar Lunch 11.30 am – 3 pm (a)
Dining Room/Restaurant Lunch 11.30 am – 3 pm (b)
Bar Supper 3 – 10 pm (a)
Dinner 5 – 10 pm (a)
Facilities for the disabled
No smoking area in restaurant
Bed & breakfast £22.50 – £35
Dinner B & B £32.50 – £45.50
Best end of lamb coated in a herb crust with a tarragon jus. Sole stuffed with smoked haddock mousse, with a beetroot butter. Roast saddle of venison on a confit of red onion served with a game gravy. Deep fried ice cream with hot butterscotch sauce.
Credit cards: 1, 2, 3
Proprietor: Paul M Brown

Rogart

Map 6

SCIBERSCROSS LODGE
Strath Brora, Rogart
Sutherland IV28 3YQ
Tel: 0408 641 246
Fax: 0408 641 465

A9 over Dornoch Firth Bridge for c. 10 miles, then A836 for 4 miles. In Rogart turn right onto single-track road (Balnacoil) for 7 miles, lodge on left.

A classic Highland sporting lodge built just over a century ago for the Duke of Sutherland and set in spectacular scenery. Peter and Kate Hammond, whose home it is, create a relaxed friendly country house atmosphere, and log fires and the profusion of fresh flowers emphasise that "personal guest" feeling. Bedrooms and public rooms are beautifully furnished and much thought goes into the preparation of interesting five course dinners, drawing on the quality supplies from the locality. The location is such that it appeals to all lovers of outdoor pursuits. A courtesy car service operates to and from Inverness. The Hammonds sum up their philosophy nicely in the phrase – "arrive as strangers, leave as friends."

Open 1 Feb to mid Nov
Rooms: 5 with private facilities
Dinner at 8 pm (or by arrangement) (e)
five course menu
Dinners for non-residents by prior booking only
Bed & breakfast from £40
Dinner B & B from £80
Roast leg of Rogart lamb with orange and rosemary sauce. Salmon in asparagus sauce. Langoustine in garlic sauce. Collops of venison and hedgerow sauce.
No credit cards
Proprietors: Peter & Kate Hammond

Rothes

Map 5

ROTHES GLEN HOTEL
Rothes
Morayshire AB38 7AH
Tel: 034 03 254

About 2-3 miles north of Rothes, on A941 to Elgin.

A very imposing turreted and castle-like mansion in acres of wood and parkland and with an air of Victorian grandeur. Some much photographed hairy Highland

cattle graze contentedly in an adjacent field. The public rooms are lofty and impressive with marble fireplaces and period furniture. There is a 'light choice' lunch menu and a well balanced bar lunch menu both of which are excellent value. Dinner in the evening is served in the dignified ornate dining room and gives due prominence to the extensive range of local game and the fresh fish for which the area is so well known.

Open 1 Feb to 17 Dec
Rooms: 16 with private facilities
Bar Lunch 12.30 – 2 pm (a)
Dining Room/Restaurant Lunch 12.30 – 2 pm (b)
Dinner 7.30 – 9 pm (c-d)
Bed & breakfast £50 – £70
Dinner B & B £78 – £95
Fresh fish and shellfish from the Moray Firth and salmon from the River Spey.
Credit cards: 1, 2, 3, 5
Proprietors: Donald & Elaine Carmichael

Rum
Isle of

Map 7

KINLOCH CASTLE
Isle of Rum
Inverness-shire PH43 4RR
Tel: 0687 2037

The Isle of Rum National Nature Reserve is on the route taken by the small isles ferry service operated from Mallaig by Caledonian MacBrayne.

Kinloch Castle is one of Scotland's most remarkable hotels. Situated on an island nature reserve of spectacular wildness and beauty, the hotel offers guests a chance to experience living history in the Edwardian castle rooms which have changed little since the turn of the century. Over your pre-dinner drink listen to the extraordinary 'orchestrion' – a mechanical organ reputedly built for Queen Victoria. Enjoy the best of fresh local fare served at the original dining

table taken from the owners ocean-going yacht 'Rhouma' during the Boer War. This is a castle with a difference in an island with a difference, and nature lovers will find so much to enjoy.

Open Mar to Oct
Rooms: 9
Dinner at 7.30 pm (d)
Children over 7 years welcome
No dogs
No smoking in dining room
Dinner B & B £68 – £88
The best of Mallaig fish and seafood. Rum venison in season and freshly caught brown trout from the lochs.
No credit cards
Proprietors: Kathleen & Iain MacArthur

St Andrews

Map 4

THE GRANGE INN
Grange Road, St Andrews
Fife KY16 8LJ
Tel: 0334 72670

Grange Road is off A917 to Crail on exit from St Andrews.

Long a favourite rendezvous in St Andrews, the Grange Inn has changed its format somewhat in response to customer demand and now offers a more informal and relaxed style of eating. The dining capacity has been expanded and there are now three separate dining areas, one of which is for non-smokers. All of the charm of this lovely old world inn has been retained and the deft hand of Christopher Trotter, a prominent Scottish chef and now the new partner/chef at the Grange, is evident in the carefully compiled menu, augmented by daily dishes displayed on a blackboard. Whether you are looking for a delicious light lunch or a leisurely gourmet dinner, you will find it here.

Open all year except Boxing Day
Rooms: 2 with private facilities
Restaurant Lunch 12.30 – 2.15 pm (a-b)
Dinner 6.30 – 9.15 pm (a-b)
No smoking dining area available
Bed & breakfast £25 – £30
Mussel and onion stew. Princess scallops with garlic butter. Home-cured gravadlax. Grilled turbot with herb butter. Braised duck with red cabbage. Sticky toffee pudding.
Credit cards: 1, 2, 3, 5 + SWITCH
Proprietors: Ann Russell & Peter Aretz

RUFFLETS COUNTRY HOUSE & GARDEN RESTAURANT

Strathkinness Low Road, St Andrews
Fife KY16 9TX
Tel: 0334 72594
Fax: 0334 78703

On B939, 1½ miles west of St Andrews.
This turreted mansion house is set in beautifully landscaped gardens, 1½ miles west of St Andrews – the mecca of the golfing world – yet only one hour's drive north from Edinburgh. The hotel has been in the same private family ownership since 1952 and is personally managed by proprietor Ann Russell and Peter Aretz, the general manager. Service is friendly and personal within a relaxed ambience. Public rooms are spacious and attractively furnished in contemporary country house style.
The Garden Restaurant is noted for the standard of its cuisine, has gained an RAC merit award for the past three years and now has an AA Rosette. Cooking is light with an emphasis on fresh Scottish produce. Many of the fresh vegetables, herbs and fruits are supplied by the hotel's own gardens.
Open all year
Rooms: 25 with private facilities
Bar Lunch 12.30 – 2 pm (a)
Dining Room/Restaurant Lunch Jan to Apr + Oct to Dec Sun Sat: May to Oct Sun to Sat (b)
Dinner Jan to Dec (d)
Bed & breakfast £40 – £75
Dinner B & B £55 – £99
Layered terrine of local salmon, smoked haddock and monkfish with a lemon and dill sauce. Pan-fried collops of Rannoch venison served on a Port wine sauce with red cabbage and hawthorn jelly. Rufflets raspberries in an almond cup with Drambuie cream on a coulis of Summer fruits.
STB Highly Commended 4 Crowns
Credit cards: 1, 2, 3, 5
Proprietor: Ann Russell

ST ANDREWS GOLF HOTEL

40 The Scores, St Andrews
Fife KY16 9AS
Tel: 0334 72611
Telex: 94013267
Fax: 0334 72188

A91 to St Andrews, turn left for golf course.
Situated on the cliffs with magnificent views over the Links and St Andrews Bay, 200 yards from the world famous "Old Course". The building is Victorian, tastefully modernised with most comfortable bedrooms and elegant public rooms. Quality prints of the best of Scottish artists line the walls. The oak-panelled restaurant offers a fine selection of dishes prepared from the best of local produce and complemented by an extensive and carefully selected wine list. Golf arranging is a speciality, either using one of the hotel's packages or having a holiday tailored to your requirements. The hotel is family owned and run. Children welcome. Dogs accepted – small charge. Italian and some French spoken.
Open all year
Rooms: 23 with private facilities
Bar Lunch 12 – 3 pm (a)
Dining Room/Restaurant Lunch 12.30 – 2.30 pm Sun Sat only (b)
Dinner 7 – 9.30 pm (d)
No smoking in restaurant
Bed & breakfast £52.50 – £67.50
Dinner B & B £66 – £81
Petite eclairs filled with a delicate trout mousse, served with a natural yoghurt and horseradish dressing. Fresh Tay salmon poached in white wine, finished with orange and vermouth sauce. Strips of Perthshire venison sauté with a julienne of fresh vegetables, served with smoked oysters.
STB Highly Commended 4 Crowns
Credit cards: 1, 2, 3, 5, 6
Proprietors: Maureen & Brian Hughes

ST ANDREWS OLD COURSE HOTEL

St Andrews
Fife KY16 9SP
Tel: 0334 74371 • Telex: 76280
Fax: 0334 77668

A91 to St Andrews.
This hotel of international reputation is now hailed as one of Scotland's leading resort hotels. It overlooks the famous 17th Road Hole and the historic Royal & Ancient Clubhouse, and offers superb views of the city, St Andrews Bay and the distant mountains of the Highlands. There is a range of leisure activities including health spa and swimming pool. Both formal and relaxed dining available and the food is of a high standard to match the overall excellence of the establishment.
Open all year
Rooms: 125 with private facilities
Bar Lunch 11 am – 4 pm (a)
Dining Room/Restaurant Lunch 11.30 am – 7 pm (b)
Afternoon tea available
Dinner 7 – 10 pm (e)
Facilities for the disabled
Room Rate £150 – £235
Special short break rates available
Loch Fyne oysters with a cucumber and basil scented sauce. Terrine of lamb fillet studded with provençale vegetables and a rosemary scented dressing. Pinenut crusted supreme of turbot on a bed of artichokes and wheatgerm, with a yellow pepper vinaigrette.
STB Deluxe 5 Crowns
Credit cards: 1, 2, 3, 5

St Boswells

Map 2

DRYBURGH ABBEY HOTEL

St Boswells
Roxburghshire TD6 0RQ
Tel: 0835 22261
Fax: 0835 23945

At St Boswells take B6404 signposted Dryburgh Abbey for 2 miles, then B6356 for just over 1½ miles.
A splendid luxury hotel converted from a magnificent old baronial building on the banks of the River Tweed, and now presenting a desirable venue for fishing, Border sightseeing, conferences and seminars. The public rooms and bedrooms are maintained to high standards and the food shows the originality and imagination to be expected of a good chef. Dryburgh Abbey should go from strength to strength.
Open all year
Rooms: 28 with private facilities
Bar Lunch 12.15 – 2.30 pm except Sun (a)
Dining Room/Restaurant Lunch 12.30 – 2 pm (b)
Dinner 7.30 – 9.15 pm (c-d)
Facilities for the disabled
No smoking in restaurant
Bed & breakfast £40 – £90
Dinner B & B £45 – £110
Chef Patrick Ruse prepares traditional dishes with an imaginative touch using local fresh produce. In addition to daily changing table d'hôte menus, a selection of specialities is offered including chateaubriand and rack of Border lamb carved at table.
STB Highly Commended 5 Crowns
Credit cards: 1, 3, 6
Proprietors: David & Graham Grose

Selkirk

Map 2

PHILIPBURN HOUSE HOTEL
Selkirk TD7 5LS
Tel: 0750 20747
Fax: 0750 21690

A707 Moffat-Peebles, 1 mile from A7.
Philipburn has earned increasingly high ratings for all of the last decade as it has increased the range and scope of its facilities. Basically it is an attractive Georgian house with charming bedrooms but there are also family suites, cottage suites some 50 yards or so from the main building, Pine Lodge, a Finnish log house, and poolside suites. Jim and Anne Hill are energetic progressively minded hoteliers and are constantly seeking to improve standards. There is a distinctly Scandinavian influence in the pine furniture and pine panelling which contributes to the hotel's unique character. The food too has some deft and distinctive differences and there are imaginative bar meals and home-baked afternoon teas. Delightful award winning garden grounds.
Open all year
Rooms: 16 with private facilities
Bar Lunch 12.30 – 2 pm (a)
Dining Room/Restaurant Lunch 12.30 – 2 pm (b)
Bar Supper 7 – 9.30 pm (b)
Dinner 7.30 – 9.30 pm (d)
No smoking in dining room
Bed & breakfast from £45
Dinner B & B from £69.50
Medallions of roe deer with a blueberry sauce and poached pear. Fillet of Border lamb cooked rosy pink on a crisp potato galette with gooseberry and mint sauce.
STB Highly Commended 4 Crowns
Credit cards: 1, 3 + SWITCH
Proprietors: Jim & Anne Hill

Shetland
Isles of

Map 7

BUSTA HOUSE HOTEL
Busta, Brae
Shetland ZE2 9QN
Tel: 080622 506
Fax: 080622 588

On the Muckle Roe road, 1 mile off A970 Hillswick road.
The impressive but slightly severe external appearance of Busta House gives no hint of the charm and elegance of the interior. This is reputedly the oldest continuously inhabited building in Shetland and it enjoys a commanding site overlooking Busta Voe. The public rooms are impressive and have been furnished with good taste while the bedrooms have every thoughtful facility that one would expect from caring hosts. The food lives up to the standard of the rest of the hotel concentrating on the plentiful harvest of good local produce from both land and sea, and there is a well chosen wine list and a stock of over 100 malt whiskies. Peter and Judith Jones can arrange holidays including flights or ferry from the UK mainland, and organise car hire, with a car to meet you at the airport or ferry terminal.
Open 3 Jan to 22 Dec
Rooms: 21 with private facilities
Bar Lunch 12 – 2 pm Mon to Sat: 12.30 – 2 pm Sun (a)
Bar Supper 6.30 – 9 pm (Winter): 6.30 – 9.30 pm (Summer) (a)
Dinner 7 – 9 pm (d)
No smoking in dining room
Bed & breakfast £40 – £60
Dinner B & B £61.50 – £74
Room Rate £60 – £105
Local turbot with white wine and lovage sauce. Shetland salmon and leeks in filo pastry with a fresh oyster sauce. Venison with Port and juniper berries. Shetland lamb with an apricot and orange sauce. Bramble cranachan.
STB Commended 4 Crowns
Credit cards: 1, 2, 3, 5, 6
Proprietors: Peter & Judith Jones

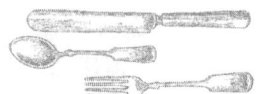

ST MAGNUS BAY HOTEL
Hillswick
Shetland ZE2 9RW
Tel: 080 623 372
Fax: 080 623 373

36 miles north of Lerwick, on north-west branch of A970.
A timber clad hotel erected at the turn of the century with a most unusual history. It was built in Norway and floated across the North Sea for an international exhibition in Glasgow, then brought again by sea to Shetland. It occupies a splendidly dominating position in the village and must rank as one of the most northerly hotels in the British Isles. The original building has been extended over the years, but retaining the impressive stairway and the pine-lined dining room. In addition there is a separate coffee or supper room and a public bar. The chef relies heavily – and rightly – on a copious supply of fresh fish and local shellfish. Children are welcome.
Open all year
Rooms: 26 with private facilities
Bar Lunch 12.30 – 1.45 pm (a)
Dining Room/Restaurant Carvery Lunch 1 – 2 pm Sun only (a)
Bar Supper 6.30 – 8.45 pm (a)
Dinner 7.30 – 8.45 pm (c)
Bed & breakfast £35 – £40
Fresh seafood – lobster, scallops etc. Smoked salmon roulade with a creamy walnut sauce. Shetland lamb pan-fried with juniper berries. Sherry ginger log.
STB Approved 3 Crowns
Credit cards: 1, 3 + SWITCH
Proprietors: Peter & Adrienne Titcomb

Skye
Isle of

Map 7

ARDVASAR HOTEL
Ardvasar, Sleat
Isle of Skye IV45 8AS
Tel: 047 14 223

At roadside A851, close to Armadale pier (Armadale-Mallaig ferry).
Ardvasar was built as a coaching inn in the early 18th century and is an attractive small whitewashed stone building with superb views over the mountains and the Sound of Sleat water to Mallaig. Guests are made very welcome and the atmosphere is cosy and homely with traditional furniture and usually a log fire in the sitting room.

Extremely comfortable attractive bedrooms. Menus highlight a good balance of local produce and most dishes are cooked to order. There is a limited but interesting choice.
Open 1 Mar to 20 Dec
Rooms: 10 with private facilities
Bar Lunch 12 – 2 pm (a)
Bar Supper 5 – 7 pm (a)
Dinner 7.30 – 8.30 pm (c)
Bed & breakfast from £30
Dinner B & B from £50
Fresh lobster, scallops, prawns. Princess scallops. All locally caught – on availability. Beef, venison, game. Daily changing menus.
Credit cards: 1, 3, 6 + DELTA
Proprietors: Bill & Gretta Fowler

FLODIGARRY COUNTRY HOUSE HOTEL & THE WATER HORSE RESTAURANT
Staffin, Isle of Skye
Inverness-shire IV51 9HZ
Tel: 047 052 203
Fax: 047 052 301

A855 north from Portree to Staffin, 4 miles from Staffin to Flodigarry.
Unspoilt by progress, this delightful hotel is a warm sheltered haven amidst the dramatic scenery of northern Skye with views across the sea to the Torridon Mountains and towering pinnacles of the Quiraing providing a remarkable skyline to the views inland. Set in five acres of gardens and mixed woodland, the fine 19th century mansion house is steeped in history and has strong Jacobite associations. Residents and non-residents can enjoy traditional dishes and other specialities which are prepared using fresh, and where possible, local produce. The standard of food is first class and in addition to the full four course table d'hôte menu, there are excellent bar meals available throughout the day and evening. Adjacent to the hotel is the little cottage once owned by the legendary Flora MacDonald planned to become luxurious

period suites for hotel guests.
Open all year
Rooms: 24, 19 with private facilities
Bar Meals 11 am – 10 pm (a)
Dining Room/Restaurant Lunch 12.30 – 2.30 pm Sun only (b)
Dinner 7 – 10 pm (c)
Bed & breakfast £20 – £45
Dinner B & B £38 – £63
Staffin Bay prawns in garlic butter. Local king scallops in a Pernod and cream sauce. Highland venison and pigeon roulade in a blaeberry wine sauce. Flodigarry cured Skye salmon with raspberry vinaigrette. Carageen mousse with cinnamon set in blackcurrant coulis. Selection of fine Scottish cheeses. Vegetarian selection.
STB Award Pending
Credit cards: 1, 3
Proprietors: Andrew & Pamela Butler

HARLOSH HOUSE
by Dunvegan
Isle of Skye IV55 8ZG
Tel: 047 022 367

Off A863, 4 miles south of Dunvegan.
This is one of those cosy friendly small hotels that one loves to come across by chance and then indulge in quiet satisfaction at the discovery. Harlosh has a fine open site on the shores of Loch Caroy with fine views of the Cuillins and the small islands of Loch Bracadale. There are excellent cliff top walks. It is a pleasing and comfortable little hotel to which Lindsey Elford will greet you with great charm and courtesy. Husband Peter masterminds the kitchen and makes imaginative use of the excellent fresh produce, particularly fish and shellfish, for which Skye is renowned. The public rooms are small but this all contributes to the friendly warmth and intimate atmosphere of the place. The master bedroom is superb and, though smaller, other bedrooms are well equipped and comfortable. Harlosh is popular with many visitors to the island so, in the season, do not leave things to chance but book in advance.
Open Easter to mid Oct
Rooms: 6, 5 with private facilities
Dinner 7 – 8.30 pm Tue to Sun (c-d)
Note: Dinner Mon – residents only
No dogs
No smoking area in restaurant
Bed & breakfast from £35
Dinner B & B from £55
Modern restaurant style using fresh Scottish produce – crabmeat parcel;

langoustines with ginger and coriander; brill and scallop ragoût; hazelnut parfait.
STB Highly Commended 3 Crowns
Credit cards: 1, 3
Proprietors: Peter & Lindsey Elford

HOTEL EILEAN IARMAIN
Sleat, Isle of Skye
Inverness-shire IV43 8QR
Tel: 04713 332
Fax: 04713 275

Barely 20 minutes drive on A851 Armadale-Kyleakin.
You do not have to have the Gaelic to enjoy the Hotel Eilean Iarmain (Isle Ornsay Hotel) for though its menus are described in Gaelic there is a very clear English translation underneath. What you will experience is that warmth of welcome and hospitality for which the Highlands and islands are so renowned. This is a traditional hotel with good en suite accommodation, in an idyllic setting overlooking the harbour. A good centre from which to enjoy stalking, shooting, walking, fishing, riding, golf or just laze and lap up the tranquillity. Menus are well balanced and interesting and make full use of the excellent shellfish for which local waters are famous, but there is also lots of other choice for non-shellfish eaters.
Open all year
Rooms: 12 with private facilities
Bar Lunch 12.30 – 2.30 pm (a)
Dining Room/Restaurant Lunch 12.30 – 2 pm (b)
Bar Supper 6.30 – 9.30 pm (a)
Dinner 7.30 – 9 pm (d)
No smoking in restaurant
Bed & breakfast £38 – £49.50
Dinner B & B £62 – £73.50
Fresh scallops in a ginger and cream sauce. Eilean Iarmain fresh oysters. Local wild salmon with fresh chives and cream. Skye lamb and venison. Fresh lobsters as available.
Credit cards: 1, 2, 3
Proprietors: Sir Iain & Lady Noble

LOCHBAY SEAFOOD RESTAURANT
1/2 Macleod's Terrace
Stein, Waternish
Isle of Skye IV55 8GA
Tel: 047083 235

Situated 5 miles down the Waternish Peninsula, in Stein Village. Last house in the village.

Situated in the old fishing village of Stein and located just 30 yards from the jetty and shore with some lovely unspoilt views of the loch and the Outer Isles. It has been converted from two cottages which were built in 1740 and is now a speciality seafood restaurant with accommodation. There is a lot of atmosphere about this friendly little restaurant where you will be made welcome whether formally or informally dressed and enjoy some of its superb fish and shellfish landed by local fishermen practically at the doorstep.

Open Mar to Nov
Rooms: 3
Dining Room/Restaurant Lunch 12 – 3 pm except Sat (a)
Dinner 6 – 9 pm except Sat (b)
Restaurant closed Sat except Easter Sat
Bed & breakfast from £15.50
Starters of squat lobster, princess scallops, oysters, mussels etc. Seafood platter, lobster, king prawns, scallop, various selection of fresh fish. Clootie dumpling etc.
Credit cards: 1, 3
Proprietors: Peter & Margaret
Greenhalgh

ROSEDALE HOTEL
Beaumont Crescent, Portree
Isle of Skye IV51 9DB
Tel: 0478 613131
Fax: 0478 612531

Harbourside location, 100 yards from village square.

The Rosedale sits on the harbourside in the heart of old Portree. From modest beginnings in a row of fishermen's houses which date from the reign of William IV, it has spread its wings in all directions so that it now occupies practically all of one side of the Portree waterfront. Growth was in response to demand and demand was created by satisfied guests returning yet again for another stay. There are many unique and interesting features – not least of which is finding your way to the first floor restaurant! – from which there are splendid views out over the bay. When you get there you will most certainly

enjoy Linda Thomson's creative cooking and excellent presentation of food which contribute so materially to the good standards which prevail throughout this hotel.

Open early May to Sep
Rooms: 23 with private facilities
Dinner 7 – 8.30 pm (d)
No smoking in restaurant
Bed & breakfast £33 – £37
Dinner B & B £54 – £58
Home-made bread. Unusual soups. Raasay scallops with rhubarb. Loin of venison with potato and poppy seed ravioli and a plum sauce, with locally grown huckleberries. Roast spiced saddle of monkfish on a bed of leeks with a saffron sauce. Dark chocolate terrine with glazed apricots.
STB Commended 4 Crowns
Credit cards: 1, 3
Proprietor: Hugh Andrew

SKEABOST HOUSE HOTEL
Skeabost Bridge
Isle of Skye IV51 9NP
Tel: 047 032 202
Fax: 047 032 454

4 miles north of Portree on Dunvegan road.

Built in 1870 this former hunting lodge is now a family run hotel, and turning into the drive to the house is like entering a new world. In direct contrast to the spectacular but stark countryside around it Skeabost is an oasis of cultivated serenity. It is wonderfully positioned on the shore of Loch Snizort and its woodlands and gardens wander down to the waters edge and incorporate a nine hole golf course. The lunchtime buffet menu of fish, salads etc is excellent value for money. The evening table d'hôte menu offers a wide choice, includes some interesting variations, and is served in the splendid panelled dining room. Staff go out of the way to make guests feel welcome and to attend to their needs.

Open 1 Apr to 24 Oct
Rooms: 26 with private facilities
Bar Lunch/Buffet Table 12 – 1.30 pm (a)
Bar Supper 7 – 8.30 except Sun (a)
Dinner 7 – 8.30 pm (c-d)
Bed & breakfast £36 – £49
Dinner B & B £55 – £68
Skye lobster with its own vinaigrette and fresh saffron noodle. Venison saddle with cranberries and oranges in Port with celeriac potato cake and light game sauce. Best end of Skye lamb with

rosemary butter sauce. Prime Scotch beef fillet with a red wine and blackcurrant sauce. Home-made puddings and desserts, ice creams and sorbets.
STB Commended 4 Crowns
Credit cards: 1, 3
Proprietors: Stuart/McNab/Stuart

THREE CHIMNEYS RESTAURANT
Colbost, nr Dunvegan
Isle of Skye IV51 9SY
Tel: 047 081 258 (Glendale)

Prestige Award Winner 1992

4 miles west of Dunvegan on B884 road to Glendale. Look out for Glendale Visitor Route signs.

The road to the Isles may not end here, at this most westerly point in Skye – but it should. This is a gem of a place right down by the shore of Loch Dunvegan. It is an old crofter's cottage with beamed ceilings, interior stone walls, and open fires. It exudes atmosphere and a candlelit dinner here could not fail to be memorable. Eddie and Shirley Spear are a charming couple, and Shirley who presides in the kitchen is much acclaimed by food writers and has earned a high reputation for her cooking. Naturally she specialises in the abundance of delicious shell fish and fresh fish so readily available in the island but she is equally adept in the preparation and presentation of beef, lamb and venison dishes. The piece de resistance in the dessert menu is her special marmalade pudding and local legend has it that people go back to Skye just to have another helping! There

is excellent accommodation in and around the nearby village of Dunvegan and local B & B. No visit to Skye can be really complete without a meal at the Three Chimneys. Macallan/Decanter Restaurant of the Year 1990.
Open 31 Mar to 21 Oct
Dining Room/Restaurant Lunch 12 – 2 pm except Sun (a-e)
Dinner 7 – 9 pm except Sun (e-f)
Closed Sun except Easter Sun + Whitsun
No smoking in restaurant
Local shellfish – fresh Skye oysters, langoustine and lobster. Fresh fish and wild Skye salmon. Fresh Scottish beef, lamb and venison dishes, including steaks. Vegetarian selection.
Credit cards: 1, 3
Proprietors: Eddie & Shirley Spear

UIG HOTEL
Uig, Portree
Isle of Skye IV51 9YE
Tel: 047 042 205
Fax: 047 042 308
Entering Uig from Portree on A856, hotel is halfway down hill on right.
On its dominating site on a hillside overlooking Uig Bay and Loch Snizort, this former coaching inn is a well known and popular stopping-over point to or from the Hebridean ferries or, indeed, as a base from which to explore Skye. The tasteful decor and furnishings of the bedrooms and public rooms owe much to the personal touch and influence of Grace Graham who has owned the hotel since 1946 and now operates it with her son, David Taylor, who supervises the day to day operations. The hotel has some self-catering apartments and its

own pony-trekking centre. This is a hotel where you can expect to find comfort and good standards all round.
Open Apr to mid Oct
Rooms: 17 with private facilities
Dining Room/Restaurant Lunch 12.15 – 1.30 pm (a)
Dinner 7.15 – 8.15 pm (d)
Dogs by arrangement only
No smoking in restaurant
Bed & breakfast £35 – £45
Dinner B & B £53 – £63
Deerstalker venison pie. Peat-smoked salmon from North Uist. Seafood bake with oatmeal topping. Bread and butter pudding. Queen of puddings.
STB Commended 4 Crowns
Credit cards: 1, 2, 3, 5, 6
Proprietors: Grace Graham & David Taylor

ULLINISH LODGE HOTEL
Struan
Isle of Skye IV56 8FD
Tel: 047 072 214
Off A863 between Sligachan and Dunvegan.
Ullinish Lodge is an 18th century country house beautifully set overlooking the Cuillins and the shores of Loch Bracadale. It is ideally situated for walking and climbing, and there is brown trout fishing in the three lochs, salmon fishing in two rivers and rough shooting over 27,500 acres. John and Claudia Mulford are welcoming hosts. There is a large lounge with open fire and a pleasant restaurant where the menu changes daily and features a fine selection of Scottish produce. The hotel has a fine range of malt whiskies and a good selection of wine including a range of Scottish wines and liqueurs. German spoken.
Open Easter to 31 Oct
Rooms: 8 with private facilities
Bar Supper 6 – 8.45 pm (a)
Dinner 7 – 8 pm (or by arrangement) (c)
No smoking area in restaurant
Bed & breakfast £30 – £35
Dinner B & B £48 – £58
Home-made soups and patés. Venison in red wine. Pheasant with cranberries and walnuts. King scallops with Talisker sauce and dressed crab. The house speciality is a seafood dish for two, featuring lobster, local prawns and a range of local shellfish.
STB Commended 3 Crowns
Credit cards: 1, 3
Proprietors: John & Claudia Mulford

South Queensferry

Map 4

THE HAWES INN
Newhalls Road, South Queensferry
West Lothian EH30 9TA
Tel: 031 331 1990
Fax: 031 319 1120
At east end of the village, under the Forth Rail Bridge.
This fine historical building, with its marvellous view across the Firth of Forth, dates from the 16th century. It has literary connections with Sir Walter Scott and was immortalised by Robert Louis Stevenson in 'Kidnapped'. The Hawes Inn is full of character and almost a tourist attraction in its own right. A pleasant 20 minute drive from Edinburgh city centre and only five miles from Edinburgh Airport, it has long been a popular destination restaurant for the city cognoscenti before or after a stroll along the front at South Queensferry. There are eight bedrooms, a quality restaurant, an atmospheric bar with family room attached, and an extensive beer garden.
Open all year except Christmas Day + 1 Jan
Rooms: 8
Food available 12 – 10 pm (a-c)
Bed & breakfast £22.50 – £34
Dinner B & B rates on application
Warm poached salmon with a tarragon mayonnaise. Mussels. Fillet steak Allen Breck – stuffed with haggis and served with a Glayva, syboe and cranberry sauce. Cranachan.
STB Commended 1 Crown
Credit cards: 1, 2, 3, 5

Spean Bridge
by

Map 6

CORRIEGOUR LODGE HOTEL
Loch Lochy, by Spean Bridge
Inverness-shire PH34 4EB
Tel: 0397 712685
Fax: 0397 712696

Follow A82, 17 miles north of Fort William; 47 miles south of Inverness – between Spean Bridge and Invergarry.
Perhaps the finest location in "The Great Glen", with outstanding views over Loch Lochy, this former hunting lodge is the ideal retreat for a well deserved break. This grand old house has been tastefully restored to provide the atmosphere of yesteryear with the comfort of today. All bedrooms have en suite facilities and are individually furnished with antiques. The Loch View Conservatory offers guests a range of high quality cuisine – all home-made, using local produce. While enjoying a meal in this relaxing setting you can watch the boats sailing Loch Lochy on their way through the Caledonian Canal. The hotel has its own pontoon/jetty. A good place from which to explore the Highlands.
Open Mar to Oct
Rooms: 8 with private facilities
Morning coffee + afternoon tea served
Bar Lunch 12 – 2.30 pm (a)
Bar Supper 6 – 9 pm (a)
Dinner 6 – 8.30 pm (c)
No dogs
No smoking in restaurant
Bed & breakfast £28 – £38
Dinner B & B £44 – £54
Salmon en croûte. Seafood platter. All home-made soups, pâtés, pies, desserts and vegetarian dishes.
STB Highly Commended 3 Crowns
Credit cards: 1, 3
Proprietors: Rod & Lorna Bunney

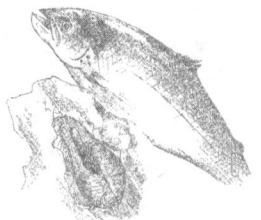

MEHALAH
Lower Tirindrish, Spean Bridge
Inverness-shire PH34 4EU
Tel: 0397 712691

At Spean Bridge take A86 for Roy Bridge/Newtonmore. Turn right at Burnbank sign, house down to left.
Mehalah is a warm friendly little house with lots of pots of flowers around to give it a colourful welcoming look. The bedrooms are delightful and very well equipped, and everywhere the house is tastefully decorated and immaculate. Gillian Rodger likes her guests to share the beauty of the location and sees to it that they both start and end the day with excellent home-cooking, with some really enterprising dishes for such a small establishment.
Open all year except Christmas Day
Rooms: 2 with private facilities
Dinner 7.30 – 8.45 pm (b)
Residents only
Unlicensed
No children
No smoking throughout
Bed & breakfast from £15
Dinner B & B from £30
Wild salmon baked in fresh sorrel and fennel. Lamb marinated in red wine with juniper berries, garlic and rowan jelly, cooked on fresh lavender. Whisky and heather honey creams. Raspberry and walnut shortbread.
STB Highly Commended 1 Crown
No credit cards
Proprietor: Gillian Rodger

OLD PINES
Gairlochy Road, Spean Bridge
Inverness-shire PH34 4EG
Tel: 0397 712324
Fax: 0397 712433

From Spean Bridge take A82 to Inverness. One mile north take B8004 next to Commando Memorial 300 yards on right.
The spectacular Commando Memorial at Spean Bridge is a stopping place for most people, not only for the excellence of the sculpture but for the fabulous views across the Great Glen towards Aonach Mor and Ben Nevis. If you have got this far, you are only 300 yards from the delightful Scandinavian-style home of Niall and Sukie Scott. A really friendly informal atmosphere prevails and guests love it. Much thought goes into the planning of the daily menu and a four course dinner by candlelight in the conservatory dining room is a highlight in most people's day.
Open all year except 2 wks Nov
Rooms: 8 with private facilities
Food available 10 am – 4 pm except Sun (a)
Dining Room/Restaurant Lunch 12 – 2 pm except Sun (b) reservations essential
Dinner 7 – 9 pm – reservations essential for non-residents (c)
Unlicensed – guests welcome to take own wine
No dogs indoors
Facilities for the disabled
No smoking throughout
Bed & breakfast from £25
Dinner B & B from £40
Special rates for 3 nights or more
Fruit and cheese salad. Langoustine and mussel soup. Lochy trout stuffed with leeks and orange. Scotch lamb stuffed with kidney and five fresh herbs. Pheasant with Port, brambles and thyme. Rhubarb and banana brûlée. Lemon feather cake with raspberry sauce. Raspberry and hazelnut meringue. Home-made breads and preserves. Scottish hand-made cheeses.
STB Highly Commended 3 Crowns
Credit cards: 1, 3
Proprietors: Niall & Sukie Scott

Stewarton

Map 3

CHAPELTOUN HOUSE HOTEL
nr Stewarton
Ayrshire KA3 3ED
Tel: 0560 482696
Fax: 0560 485100

From Fenwick exit on A77 (Glasgow to Ayr road), take B778 to Stewarton then join B769 to Irvine. Chapeltoun is two miles along on right hand side.
This beautiful country house retreat in rolling Ayrshire countryside is all the better for being a little off the beaten track. Its secluded position makes it all the more desirable a venue in which to forget the outside world for a time. Built in 1900 it features fine plasterwork and friezes of thistles and roses to celebrate the marriage of a Scottish industrialist and his English wife. The splendid panelled and timbered interior of Chapeltoun induces a sense of comfortable relaxation and that is what this place is all about. Bedrooms are spacious and beautifully appointed, as are the public rooms. Food is varied,

interesting and of high standard relying largely on the excellence of the abundant local produce, from what is one of the richest farming areas in the country. The proprietors are very much in evidence supervising well-trained staff and attending to the comfort and convenience of their guests.
Open all year except first 2 wks Jan
Rooms: 8 with private facilities
Bar Lunch 12 – 2 pm (a)
Dining Room/Restaurant Lunch 12 – 2 pm (c)
Dinner 7 – 9 pm (d)
No smoking in restaurant
Bed & breakfast £45 – £89
Best of local meat, fish, game and vegetables.
STB Highly Commended 4 Crowns
Credit cards: 1, 2, 3
Proprietors: Colin & Graeme McKenzie

Stirling

Map 4

THE TOPPS FARM
Fintry Road, Denny
Stirlingshire FK6 5JF
Tel: 0324 822471

On B818 Denny – Fintry road, off M80.
This much commended working sheep and cashmere goat farm is splendidly sited in central Scotland within easy reach of Edinburgh, Glasgow and Perth. Its huge picture windows give superb views out towards the Fintry and Ochil Hills. A popular restaurant complements the guest house facilities. Jennifer and Alistair Steel's home-cooking is highly praised and covers many traditional favourites as well as really interesting and imaginative dishes. The 'Farmers Breakfast' is quite something, but so too is dinner – as the complimentary comments from satisfied guests confirm.
Open all year
Rooms: 8 with private facilities
Bar Lunch 12.30 – 2 pm Thu to Sat (a)
Dining Room/Restaurant Lunch 12.30 – 2 pm Wed to Sat (a) reservation essential
Dinner 7 – 9.30 pm (b)
Restaurant closed Mon Tue, except pre-Christmas
No smoking throughout
Bed & breakfast £18 – £21
Dinner B & B £32 – 35
Room Rate £36 – £42
Breakfast – trout, porridge, local haggis, black pudding etc. Grumphies and

tatties. Wild garlic lamb. Honey poached salmon. Glenmorangie gâteau. Rosewater meringues. Poached spicy pears.
STB Commended 3 Crowns
Credit cards: 1, 3
Proprietors: Jennifer & Alistair Steel

Stonehaven

Map 5

TOLBOOTH RESTAURANT
Old Pier, Stonehaven Harbour
Stonehaven
Tel: 0569 62287

Off A92, onto A957 to Stonehaven, 10 miles south of Aberdeen.
The Tolbooth – built in the 16th century – is the oldest building in Stonehaven and is set on the harbourside with picturesque views. The restaurant specialises in fresh fish and seafood, but interesting vegetarian and meat dishes are also available. There is a permanent exhibition of Royal Scottish Academy artists on the whitewashed stone walls. Afghan rugs enhance the beautifully polished wooden floors.
Open Apr to Oct: also Nov to Mar for dinner + Sun Lunch only
Dining Room/Restaurant Lunch 12 – 2.30 pm except Mon (b) – Jun to Oct only
Dinner 7 – 9.30 pm except Mon (d)
Closed Mon
Lightly grilled west coast scallops sliced waferthin and served on a watercress salad with tangy lime butter. North Sea bouillabaisse – local fish, mussels and prawns simmered in a saffron and tomato broth. Monkfish cooked with green peppercorns, tomato and cream, served in a puff pastry case. Organic herbs and vegetables.
Credit cards: 1, 3
Proprietor: Moya Bothwell

Strachur

Map 3

THE CREGGANS INN
Strachur
Argyll PA27 8BX
Tel: 0369 86 279
Fax: 0369 86 637

1½ hours from Glasgow on A83 then A815, overlooking Loch Fyne.
A perennial favourite, the Creggans is an old inn set at the roadside on the shore of scenic Loch Linnhe. There have been quite a few changes to it, and the dining room has been refurnished but Lady MacLean's influence on it is still strong and everything is done with the good taste associated with Creggans. The food maintains the high standards which earned the inn its original reputation and dinner at night in the attractive dining room looking across the loch induces a special feeling. Menus still include favourite dishes selected from Lady MacLean's cookbooks. A well designed extension blends well with the original building.
Open all year
Rooms: 21, 17 with private facilities
Bar Lunch 12.30 – 2.30 pm (a)
Bar Supper 6.30 – 7.30 pm (a)
Dinner 7.30 – 9 pm (d)
No smoking in dining room
Bed & breakfast £50 – £60
Dinner B & B £70 – £80
Loch Fyne oysters, smoked salmon, local lobster, mussels, prawns and kippers. Fillet of Argyll hill lamb with Port wine and redcurrant sauce.
STB Commended 3 Crowns
Credit cards: 1, 2, 3, 5, 6
Proprietors: Sir Fitzroy MacLean, The Hon Lady MacLean & Charles E MacLean

Stranraer

Map 1

NORTH WEST CASTLE HOTEL
Portrodie
Stranraer DG9 8EH
Tel: 0776 4413
Fax: 0776 2646

Prestige Award Winner 1989

Seafront – opposite harbour.
Anyone who has ever travelled on the
Stranraer-Larne ferry – and thousands
who have not – will know and love the
North West Castle Hotel. A superbly
managed resort hotel which seems to
incorporate everything that anyone could
possibly want. In its own grounds
overlooking the harbour it has an indoor
swimming pool, jacuzzi, multi-gym,
saunas, sunbeds, bowls, a curling rink,
table tennis, darts, pool, snooker. It
naturally follows that the bedrooms have
colour TVs, radio, trouser press,
hairdryer and coffee-making facilities.
You might like to try one of the new
tastefully decorated suites, with views
over Loch Ryan. A pianist plays in the
Regency Dining Room during dinner.
Open all year
Rooms: 70 with private facilities
Bar Lunch 12 – 2 pm (a)
Dining Room/Restaurant Lunch 12 –
2 pm (a-b)
Dinner 7 – 9 pm (c)
Bed & breakfast £38 – £78
Dinner B & B £55 – £90
Smoked trout mousse wrapped in
smoked salmon with a Scottish whisky
mustard sauce. Halibut steak in pastry
with a warm tomato mousse. Roast
saddle of venison served with a
peppered game sauce. Strawberry
shortcake.
STB Highly Commended 5 Crowns
No credit cards
Proprietor: H C McMillan

Strathlachlan

Map 3

INVER COTTAGE RESTAURANT
Strathlachlan, by Cairndow
Argyll PA27 8BU
Tel: 036 986 396/275
B8000, 7 miles south of Strachur.
Overlooking Castle Lachlan on the
shores of Loch Fyne this cottage exudes

a bistro atmosphere but a coal/log fire
and low ceilings remind you that cottage
is perhaps a more appropriate word. The
overall effect is relaxing and Tony & Gina
Wignell like to keep it this way. The food
is honest and wholesome with a definite
bias towards local dishes.
Open Apr to Oct (7 days)
Note: during Mar Nov + Dec open Fri Sat
Sun only
Bar Lunch 11.30 am – 2.15 pm (a)
Dining Room/Restaurant Lunch
11.30 am – 2.15 pm (b)
Dinner 6 – 9.30 pm (c)
Fresh local produce including shellfish
and fish, lamb, beef etc. Wide selection
of desserts.
Credit cards: 1, 3
Proprietors: Tony & Gina Wignell

Strathyre

Map 4

CREAGAN HOUSE
Restaurant with Accommodation
Strathyre
Perthshire FK18 8ND
Tel: 087 74 638
On A84, ¼ mile north of Strathyre.
In a lovely country setting, Creagan is a
family owned 17th century farmhouse
with five charming bedrooms. The
baronial dining hall with its grand
fireplace provides a unique setting in
which to enjoy good food and fine wines.
A mixture of experience, caring and
friendliness contribute to your
enjoyment.
Open Mar to Jan except 1 wk Oct
Rooms: 5, 3 with private facilities
Dining Room/Restaurant Lunch at 1 pm
Sun only (b)
Lunch parties on other days by
arrangement
Dinner 7.30 – 8.30 pm (c-d)
Booking essential for all meals

No smoking in dining hall + bedrooms
Bed & breakfast £24.50 – £42.50
Dinner B & B £40 – £63.50
Room Rate £49 – £61
Two set price menus available each
evening and may include – smokie in a
pokie, coquilles St Jacques, salmon St
Clements, collops of venison grand
veneur, local raspberry and chocolate
roulade, traditional steam puddings.
STB Highly Commended 3 Crowns
Credit cards: 1, 3
Proprietors: Gordon & Cherry Gunn

Strontian

Map 6

KILCAMB LODGE HOTEL
Strontian
North Argyll PH36 4HY
Tel: 0967 2257
Strontian, south-west of Fort William.
Natural lawns sloping gently down to the
waters edge with the Morvern Hills rising
steeply in the background and 30 acres
of secluded grounds right on the shores
of Loch Sunart make a very pleasing
setting for this charming old country
house hotel. The Blakeway family are as
delightful as is the location and their
natural charm and friendliness makes
guests feel specially welcome. There is a
cosy bar area and an elegant sitting
room and comfortable bedrooms.
Flowers and china and other personal
touches are evident throughout. Food is
first class, and menus are obviously
planned with care and maximise the use
of the area's prime produce. All in all a
very desirable place to tarry and enjoy
the good things of life.
Open 1 Apr to 31 Oct
Rooms: 10 with private facilities
Light Lunch 12 – 2.30 pm
Dinner at 7.30 pm (d)
No smoking in dining room
Bed & breakfast from £40
Dinner B & B from £64
Room Rate £32
Open ravioli of wild mushrooms. Confit of
Barbary duck. Celery, almond and walnut
soup. Roast saddle of venison with Port
and juniper sauce. Baked monkfish tails
with tomato and mushroom sauce.
Caramelised bread and butter pudding.
Home-made profiteroles with
strawberries.
STB Highly Commended 3 Crowns
Credit cards: 1, 3
Proprietors: Gordon & Ann Blakeway

Swinton

Map 2

THE WHEATSHEAF HOTEL & RESTAURANT

Main Street, Swinton
Berwickshire TD11 3NB
Tel: 0890 860 257

12 miles from Berwick-upon-Tweed on B6461 to Kelso.

An attractive country inn in the centre of Swinton, a popular hostelry for locals and one to which people travel from quite some distance to enjoy the good food. There is a lot of old world charm in the quaint bar with its black beams, game birds that have fallen into the hands of the taxidermist, appropriate furniture and considerable ambience. The restaurant menu is extensive and the food is exceptionally good, achieving Julie and Alan Reid's objective of providing the best of fresh local produce in a welcoming but unpretentious atmosphere – and representing excellent value for money. Recent renovation has upgraded the accommodation facilities.

Open all year except Christmas Day + mid 2 wks Feb
Rooms: 4, 2 with private facilities
Bar Lunch 11.45 am – 2 pm Tue to Sat (b)
Bar Supper/Dinner 6 – 9.30 pm Tue to Sat (b-c)
Closed Sun Mon
Facilities for the disabled
No smoking area in restaurant
Bed & breakfast £20 – £30
Medallions of Border lamb in a redcurrant and lemon thyme sauce. Fillets of lemon sole stuffed with a wild salmon mousse in a light vermouth sauce. Wild boar casserole with juniper berries and sloe gin.
STB Commended 2 Crowns
Credit cards: 1, 3
Proprietors: Alan & Julie Reid

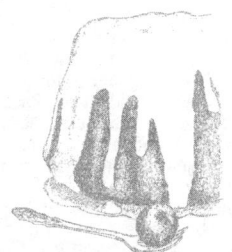

Tain

Map 6

MORANGIE HOUSE HOTEL

Morangie Road, Tain
Ross-shire IV19 1PY
Tel: 0862 892281

Just off A9 Inverness-Wick, on the outskirts of Tain.

Built for a Victorian sweet manufacturer this fine old Victorian mansion is set in its own beautifully kept grounds, close by the shores of the Dornoch Firth, on the northern outskirts of the Highland town of Tain, Scotland's oldest Royal Burgh. The hotel has been extensively modernised but still maintains the character of the building with its superb collection of Victorian stained glass windows. The hotel is very popular and the visitors book bears testimony to their satisfaction. The chefs are proud of their reputation in the district and strive to maintain it in the quality and variety of well presented meals. Efficient and friendly staff also make their contribution to the success of the hotel.

Open all year
Rooms: 13 with private facilities
Bar Lunch 12 – 2.30 pm (a)
Dining Room/Restaurant Lunch 12 – 2.30 pm (b)
Bar Supper 5 – 9.30 pm (a)
Dinner 7 – 9.30 pm (c)
Dogs by arrangement
Bed & breakfast £33 – £50
Dinner B & B £50 – £65
Mussel and onion stew. Salmon steak poached in white wine served with a lobster and prawn sauce. Slices of prime Scottish fillet steak cooked in a Port wine sauce. Local seafood and steaks.
STB Commended 4 Crowns
Credit cards: 1, 2, 3, 5, 6
Proprietor: John Wynne

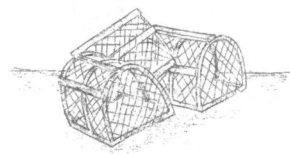

Tarbert

Map 6

THE COLUMBA HOTEL

East Pier Road, Tarbert
Argyll PA29 6UF
Tel: 0880 820808

On East Pier Road, ½ mile to the left around the harbour.

A family-run hotel in a Listed Victorian building splendidly positioned on the loch side at the entrance to Tarbert Harbour where there is always lots of interest on the waterfront. There are fine views over Loch Fyne and the hills start at the back door. There are cosy bars usually with log fires burning and there is a sauna, mini gym and solarium. Restaurant menus place much emphasis on local produce with a leaning towards traditional Scottish dishes and imaginative preparation of other specialities. As the hotel so delightfully puts it "children and other pets are especially welcome".

Open all year
Rooms: 11 with private facilities
Bar Lunch 12 – 2 pm (b)
Dining Room/Restaurant Lunch 12.30 – 2.30 pm Sun only (a)
Bar Supper 6 – 8.30 pm (b)
Dinner 7 – 9 pm (c)
No smoking in restaurant
Bed & breakfast £25.95 – £30.95
Dinner B & B £31.95 – £43.95
Cullen skink. Medallions of Scottish beef with Dunsyre blue cheese and horseradish sauce. Local scallops with gazpacho and turmeric oil.
STB Commended 3 Crowns
Credit cards: 1, 3
Proprietors: Gina & Bob Chicken

Credit Card Code	Meal Price Code	
1. Access/Mastercard/Eurocard	(a)	under £10
2. American Express	(b)	£10 – £15
3. Visa	(c)	£15 – £20
4. Carte Bleu	(d)	£20 – £25
5. Diners Club	(e)	£25 – £30
6. Mastercharge	(f)	over £30

Thornhill

Map 1

TRIGONY HOUSE HOTEL
Closeburn, Thornhill
Dumfriesshire DG3 5EZ
Tel: 0848 31211

*Off A76 south of Thornhill, 13 miles
north of Dumfries.*
Set in tranquil woodland gardens this
attractive house provides a high
standard of comfort, welcome and good
food. There is fine furniture, interesting
ornaments, original woodwork and warm
fires to give character to the building.
The dining room is a lovely bright room
overlooking the garden and it is clear
from the construction of the menu that
food is taken seriously, as indeed it is.
An exacting inspector gave the food high
marks and said "this is a hotel to spend
time in and be pampered". Children over
10 years welcome.
*Open all year except Christmas + New
Year's Days*
Rooms: 9 with private facilities
Bar Lunch 12.30 – 2 pm (a)
Bar Supper 6.30 – 9 pm (a)
Dinner 7 – 8.30 pm (c)
No children under 10 years
Bed & breakfast £28.50 – £40.50
Dinner B & B £45 – £59
*Fine Scots cooking using the best of
Scottish produce available, including
local beef, venison, lamb and Nith
salmon.*
STB Commended 3 Crowns
Credit cards: 1, 3
Proprietors: Frank & Mary Kerr

Tillicoultry

Map 4

HARVIESTOUN INN
Mains Farm, Tillicoultry
Clackmannanshire FK13 6PQ
Tel: 0259 752522
Fax: 0259 752523

*Just off A91 on eastern edge of
Tillicoultry.*
Transformations and restorations
sometimes do not succeed but this one
comes off brilliantly. The original
character of these old farm buildings
form three sides of a spacious courtyard
with a delightful elevated patio by the
front entrance. The warm stone frontage
is inviting but gives no clue to the
luxurious layout of the first floor
restaurant, or the lively informality of the
bistro and bar on the ground floor. For
those with celebrations – or conferences
– in mind, there is also the elegant
Orchid Pavilion. The food is consistently
reliable with a carefully balanced menu
changing to reflect the best the seasons
have to offer, imaginatively presented by
Robert Pew and his team.
Open all year
Bar Lunch 12 – 2.30 pm (a)
*Dining Room/Restaurant Lunch 12 –
2.30 pm Mon to Fri: 12 – 8 pm Sun (b)*
Bar Supper 6 – 10 pm (a)
*Dinner 7 – 10 pm Mon to Sat: 12 –
8 pm Sun (c)*
Facilities for the disabled
No smoking area in restaurant
*Filo parcels of Scottish scallops on a
lemon and chive butter sauce, with deep-
fried vegetable ribbons. Roast rack of
lamb with a herb crust and two
contrasting sauces. Fillet of Scottish
salmon on a bed of crisp mangetout and
hazelnuts with a butter sauce. Glazed
Summer fruits with a Grand Marnier
sabayon sauce and a refreshing sorbet.*
Credit cards: 1, 3
Proprietor: John Lapsley

Tiree
Isle of

Map 7

THE GLASSARY
Sandaig, Isle of Tiree
Argyll PA77 6XQ
Tel: 08792 684

On west coast of island.
A restaurant and guest house situated
on the picturesque west coast with views
of the sandy shoreline and the Atlantic
Ocean. The proprietors Mabel and
Donnie Macarthur genuinely welcome
their guests and strive to ensure their
comfort while their son Iain is chef and
prepares imaginative menus. The
restaurant is a pine-lined converted byre
and the well appointed guest house is all
on one level with residents TV lounge
and tea-coffee making facilities.
Open Easter to Oct
Rooms: 3
*Dining Room/Restaurant Lunch 12 –
2 pm (a)*
Dinner 7 – 8.30 pm (b-d)
Bed & breakfast from £16
Dinner B & B from £26
*Smoked salmon with smoked trout
terrine. Grilled sirloin steak served on a
bed of haggis and coated in whisky
sauce. Traditional bread and butter
pudding laced with Drambuie and served
with cream.*
No credit cards
Proprietors: Mabel & Donnie Macarthur

Tongue

Map 6

THE BEN LOYAL HOTEL
Main Street, Tongue
Sutherland IV27 4XE
Tel: 0847 55 216

*At junction of A838 and A836, midway
between John o' Groats and Cape Wrath.*
Standing in a splendid location
overlooking the Kyle of Tongue, the
peaks of 'The Queen of Scottish
Mountains' and ruined Varrich Castle,
this hotel seems to have been designed
with the sole intention of enabling
guests to enjoy these quite stunning
panoramas from the comfortably
furnished lounge to the beautifully
appointed bedrooms with their pine
furniture, pretty fabrics and four poster

beds. But perhaps the best views can be had from the dining room. However you will find your loyalties torn between relishing the view and savouring the food. Only fresh local produce – much of it home-grown – is used in the preparation of a largely traditional menu.
Open 11 Feb to 31 Dec except 24 to 26 Dec
Rooms: 18, 9 with private facilities
Bar Lunch 12 – 2 pm Mon to Sat: 12.30 – 2 pm Sun (a)
Dining Room/Restaurant Lunch – by prior arrangement only (b)
Bar Supper 6 – 8.30 pm Mon to Sat: 6.30 – 8.30 pm Sun (a)
Dinner 7 – 8 pm (c)
Facilities for the disabled
Bed & breakfast £18 – £32
Dinner B & B £33 – £52
Special rates for 3 or 7 nights available Tartlet of quail eggs. Home-cured salmon with a lemon and shallot oil. Supreme of local salmon with lemon and herb butter. Roast haunch of venison with Madeira and cranberry gravy. Bread and butter pudding. Warm compote of fruit stewed with cinnamon and cloves.
STB Highly Commended 3 Crowns
Credit cards: 1, 3
Proprietors: Mel & Pauline Cook

Torridon

Map 6

LOCH TORRIDON HOTEL
Torridon, by Achnasheen
Ross-shire IV22 2EY
Tel: 0445 791242
Fax: 0445 791296
The only hotel on the A896 (do not turn off to Torridon village).
A stately and impressive country house in a delightful parkland setting extending down to the water's edge of Loch Torridon with pine covered mountain slopes towering up behind. The house is a former shooting lodge built by the first Earl of Lovelace in 1881 and there is much rich wood panelling in the public rooms and lovely ornate ceilings. The food attracts much praise and shows imagination in planning and presentation, earning the hotel two AA Rosettes and designation as the best new AA hotel in Scotland in 1993.
Open to Mar to Jan (restricted service 3 Jan to 22 Feb)
Rooms: 20 with private facilities
Bar Lunch: 12.30 – 2 pm (b)

Bar Supper: 6.30 – 9 pm (b)
Note: Bar meals served in Ben Damph Bar, 100 yds from main hotel
Dinner 7.15 – 8.30 pm (e)
Facilities for the disabled
No smoking in restaurant
Bed & breakfast £45 – £80
Dinner B & B £72 – £120
Gâteaux of smoked mackerel and crab. Panache of local seafood. Fillet of venison with haggis and red wine sauce. Cranachan.
STB Highly Commended 4 Crowns
Credit cards: 1, 3
Proprietors: David & Geraldine Gregory

Troon

Map 1

HIGHGROVE HOUSE
Old Loans Road
Troon KA10 7HL
Tel: 0292 312511
Fax: 0292 318228
Off A759 near Loans.
If there are three key words in Bill Costley's vocabulary they must be quality, freshness and value. His acquisition and transformation of Highgrove House was an immediate success as he introduced his formula of the pick of the market's produce, beautifully prepared and presented and at remarkably modest prices. Success was well earned and the popularity and appeal of Highgrove has continued unabated. Perched high on a hilltop just outside Troon, with fine views out over the Firth of Clyde to Arran, the location could not be better for those who want to play golf at some of the world's premier courses, sail or fish, wander round the country of Rabbie Burns – or just relax and enjoy the excellent food.
Open all year
Rooms: 9 with private facilities
Bar Lunch 12 – 2.30 pm (a)

Dinner 6 – 9.30 pm (c)
Bed & breakfast from £55
Dinner B & B from £90
Warm salad of langoustines and red snapper with dill butter dressing. Steamed turbot with fresh asparagus, crab and orange mousseline.
Credit cards: 1, 2, 3 + SWITCH
Proprietors: William & Catherine Costley

LOCHGREEN HOUSE
Monktonhill Road, Southwood
Troon KA10 7EN
Tel: 0292 313343
Fax: 0292 318661
A79 from Ayr, or A77 from Glasgow to roundabout near Prestwick Airport, take road for Troon (B749). Lochgreen is ½ mile on left.
Lochgreen House in Southwood near Troon is a magnificent mansion built in 1905 surrounded by 15 acres of beautiful woodlands, gardens and private tennis court, and situated in the heart of Ayrshire's Burns Country. The hotel is privately owned and managed by one of Scotland's top chefs, Bill Costley, and his wife Catherine, and it naturally follows that the food is superb, beautifully prepared and presented, and outstanding value for money. It is little wonder that guests come from far and near to sample it and it is therefore always wise to book in advance. This is a hotel with every facility for a relaxing and comfortable stay.
Open all year
Rooms: 7 with private facilities
Dining Room/Restaurant Lunch 12 – 2.30 pm (a)
Dinner 7 – 9.30 pm (d)
No dogs
Facilities for the disabled
No smoking in restaurant
Bed & breakfast £49.50 – £89
Dinner B & B £60 – £75
Roast rack of Ayrshire lamb with creamed leeks and redcurrant sauce. Steamed Doon salmon with a lobster sauce.
Credit cards: 1, 2, 3
Proprietors: William & Catherine Costley

MARINE HIGHLAND HOTEL

Troon
Ayrshire KA10 6HE
Tel: 0292 314444
Fax: 0292 316922

*South end of Troon overlooking golf
course and sea.*

This magnificent four star hotel
overlooks the 18th fairway of Royal
Troon Championship Golf Course with
breathtaking views across the Firth of
Clyde to the Isle of Arran. An atmosphere
of quiet elegance exists throughout the
hotel combined with a standard of
service and hospitality second to none.
There are excellent leisure facilities
within the Marine Leisure and Sports
Club. A very special hotel which has
admirably blended style and tradition
with outstanding facilities, and where the
quality of the food matches in every way
the overall excellence of the hotel.

Open all year
Rooms: 72 with private facilities
*Crosbie's Brasserie open all day for
meals and snacks*
Bar Lunch 12 – 2.30 pm (a)
*Dining Room/Restaurant Lunch 12.30 –
2 pm: buffet Sun 12.30 – 2.30 pm (b)*
Afternoon Tea (Arran Lounge) 3 – 5 pm
*Bar Supper 6 – 10 pm: 5.30 – 10 pm
weekends (a)*
Dinner 7 – 10 pm (d)
Bed & breakfast £69 – £105
Dinner B & B £53 – £85
Room Rate £88 – £138
*Local wild salmon, fresh scallops, prime
Scotch beef and lamb, fresh vegetables.
Scottish cheeses.*
STB Highly Commended 5 Crowns
Credit cards: 1, 2, 3, 5, 6 + SWITCH

PIERSLAND HOUSE HOTEL

Craigend Road, Troon
Ayrshire KA10 6HD
Tel: 0292 314747
Fax: 0292 315613

South corner of Troon.

A very impressive Tudor style building
built at the end of last century for Sir
Alexander Walker grandson of Johnnie
Walker founder of the famous Scotch
whisky firm. It is located in four acres of
garden including a Japanese garden and
croquet lawns. Panelled walls and
splendid beams distinguish the minstrel
hall and reception area as do wood
carvings, fireplaces and tapestry friezes.
Impressive menus offer a wide range of
fine food and the hotel is proud of its

reputation in this field.
Open all year
Rooms: 19 with private facilities
Bar Lunch 12 – 2.30 pm (a)
*Dining Room/Restaurant Lunch 12 –
2.30 pm (b)*
Bar Supper 6 – 10 pm (a)
Dinner 7 – 9.30 pm (c)
Bed & breakfast £44.75 – £57.50
Dinner B & B £61.25 – £74
Room Rate £36 – £59
*Medallions of venison with whisky and
elderflower cordial in a rich game sauce
with oyster mushrooms and blackberries.
Pan-fried scallops and scampi with stem
ginger, pears and chilled muscat grape
in a white wine sauce.*
STB Highly Commended 4 Crowns
Credit cards: 1, 2, 3, 5, 6
Proprietor: J A Brown

Turnberry

Map 1

MALIN COURT HOTEL

Turnberry, Girvan
Ayrshire KA26 9PB
Tel: 0655 31457/8
Fax: 0655 31072

On A719 Ayr-Girvan, south of Maidens.

A near neighbour to the famous
Turnberry Hotel, the comfortably
appointed Malin Court enjoys the same
delightful panoramic views over golf
courses and shoreline. It makes a very
good base from which to tour Burns
country or enjoy the Ayrshire coast. Of
clean low modern construction it has
been very well equipped and offers quiet
relaxation well clear of any bustle. The
dining room has fine views out towards
the Isle of Arran over which there are
sometimes spectacular sunsets.

Open all year
Rooms: 17 with private facilities
Bar Lunch 12 – 2.15 pm (a)
*Dining Room/Restaurant Lunch 12 –
2.15 pm (b)*
Afternoon Tea 2 – 5 pm

Bar Supper 5.30 – 7 pm (a)
Dinner 7.30 – 9.30 pm (c)
Bed & breakfast £55 – £75
Dinner B & B £65 – £85
*Fresh local beef, lamb and pork, salmon
and fresh sea produce.*
STB Highly Commended 4 Crowns
Credit cards: 1, 2, 3, 5, 6 + SWITCH

TURNBERRY HOTEL, GOLF COURSES & SPA

Turnberry
Ayrshire KA26 9LT
Tel: 0655 31000 • Telex: 777779
Fax: 0655 31706

Prestige Award Winner 1990

A77 – 17 miles south of Ayr.

What can one say of a hotel that is
constantly winning awards and
exemplifies in every department the best
of British hotel keeping. Turnberry has it
all. Its unique elevated situation
overlooking the famous Turnberry golf
courses ensures that it starts off on a
pedestal. This is a hotel where elegance
and gracious service are obvious
throughout and especially so in the
superb restaurants renowned for their
food and where a meal looking out over
Ailsa Craig and Arran becomes a
memorable occasion. The magnificent
spa is itself a winner of awards and the
new golf clubhouse incorporates a
special restaurant for hungry hurried
golfers. A superbly well managed hotel of
the highest international standards
offering the ultimate in comfort and
cuisine. Awarded RAC five star Hotel of
the Year 1990, Caterer & Hotelkeeper's
Hotel of the Year 1993 as well as five
red stars from the AA.

Open all year
Rooms: 132 with private facilities
*Bar Meals (Clubhouse Restaurant)
11 am – 4 pm (b)*
*Lunch (Bay at Turnberry Restaurant) 12 –
2.30 pm (c)*
*Dinner (Hotel Restaurant) 7.30 –
10 pm (f)*
Bed & breakfast £72.50 – £200
Dinner B & B £107.50 – £237.50
*West coast scallops and scampi lightly
steamed, served with endive and
spinach leaves, with nantua dressing.
Atlantic sea bass grilled and served on
finely cut bulb fennel with a piquant
sauce. Medallions of Galloway beef with
Madeira, roast shallots, artichokes and
asparagus tips.*
Credit cards: 1, 2, 3, 5, 6

Tyndrum

Map 4

CLIFTON COFFEE HOUSE & CRAFT CENTRE

Tyndrum
Perthshire FK20 8RY
Tel: 08384 271
Fax: 08384 330

On A85 just east of junction with A82.
What started off as a relatively simple self-service restaurant has, over the years, developed to a point where it has almost become a tourist attraction in its own right. A shopping complex selling crafts, books, woollens, gifts and food is augmented next door by the 'green welly' shop specialising in clothing for climbing, hill-walking and outdoor sports. But central to the whole is the self-service restaurant which offers a consistently good standard of home-baking and home-cooking of traditional Scottish meals and snacks with a seemingly endless choice. There are few travelling to, or from, Glencoe who will not stop off at the Clifton for a quick meal or snack.
Open 5 Mar to 5 Jan except Christmas, Boxing + New Year's Days
Meals + snacks served all day 8.30 am – 5.30 pm (a)
No smoking area in restaurant
No dogs except guide dogs
Fresh produce used to advantage, to produce a range of good food at affordable prices.
Credit cards: 1, 2, 3, 5, 6 + SWITCH
Proprietors: L P Gosden,
D D, L V & I L Wilkie

Udny Station

Map 5

MUFFIN & CRUMPET BISTRO

Main Street, Udny Station Village
Aberdeenshire AB41 0QJ
Tel: 0651 842210
Fax: 0651 842965

From Bridge of Don boundary, 8 miles on B999 to Tarves, ½ mile off this road up into village. Or off A92 Aberdeen-Ellon, 4 miles on Culter Cullen Village road.
An interesting conversion of what had been a row of shops, with an equally interesting concept inside. The split level room retains its old pine panelling and has pretty wallpaper on the ceiling and lots of memorabilia on the high shelf. Peter and Marilyn Rattray have created a style of their own with some unusual combinations of food utilising muffins and crumpets in many dishes. Children are made specially welcome and there is special provision and a special menu for them. This is an establishment that will appeal to all tastes and overall an enterprising business that seems likely to expand. Bookings are advisable, especially at weekends.
Open all year except Christmas Day, 1 Jan + last 2 wks Jan
Dining Room/Restaurant Lunch available for group bookings only

Dinner 6.30 – 9 pm except Mon Tue; later Sat (a-b)
Closed Mon
Booking advisable
Table Licence
Trout fillet poached in a whisky and ginger court bouillon served with a little salad. Mussels with wine, onion, garlic and cream, served with crusty bread. Fillet steak with a toasted oatmeal topping, finished in a red wine, black peppercorn and mushroom sauce.
Credit cards: 1, 3
Proprietors: Marilyn & Peter Rattray

Uphall

Map 4

HOUSTOUN HOUSE HOTEL & RESTAURANT

Uphall
West Lothian EH52 6JS
Tel: 0506 853831
Fax: 0506 854220

Just off A89 Edinburgh-Bathgate at Uphall.
The core of this hotel is the old 16th century Tower House, of which the vaulted bar with its great open fireplace is the most striking reminder. Over the years the building has been adapted and extended to provide the comfortable hotel accommodation which is a feature of today. Three adjacent dining rooms on the first floor provide flexibility and create an atmosphere of quietness and intimacy – so much better than one large room. There are 26 acres of grounds, and herbs and vegetables for the kitchen are grown in the garden. Well balanced menus change daily; food is interesting and well presented and there is an extensive and carefully chosen wine list – and a fine range of malt whiskies.
Open all year
Rooms: 30 with private facilities
Bar Lunch 12 – 2 pm except Sun (a)
Dining Room/Restaurant Lunch 12.30 – 2 pm except Sat (c)
Dinner 7.30 – 9.30 pm (e) 4 course menu
No smoking dining room available
Bed & breakfast £25 – £104.50
Dinner B & B £50 – £132
Crayfish and scallops with a leek tartlet on a basil flavoured sauce. Creative desserts.
STB Commended 4 Crowns
Credit cards: 1, 2, 3, 5

Walkerburn

Map 2

TWEED VALLEY HOTEL & RESTAURANT

Walkerburn
nr Peebles EH43 6AA
Tel: 089 687 636
Fax: 089 687 639

A72 at Walkerburn – 8 miles east of Peebles and 10 miles west of Galashiels. 32 miles south of Edinburgh.
The slightly elevated position of the Tweed Valley Hotel gives it pleasing views towards the hills and the River Tweed. There is a lot of character in the building with its oak panelling carvings and an ornate dining room ceiling. It was built in 1906 by Henry Ballantyne as a wedding present for his son and has its own walled garden in which are grown many of the vegetables and fresh herbs used in the hotel kitchen. The hotel also has its own smoker from which it produces some of the succulent home-smoked items which feature on the menus. A convenient base for fishing, bird-watching, golf or other outdoor pursuits and a comfortable place to return to in the evening and enjoy a leisurely dinner.
Open all year except 25 + 26 Dec
Rooms: 15 with private facilities
Bar Lunch 12 – 2 pm (a)
Dining Room/Restaurant Lunch 12 – 2 pm (b-c)
Bar Supper 6.30 – 9.30 pm (a)
Dinner 7 – 9.30 pm (c-d)
No smoking in restaurant
Bed & breakfast £40 – £52
Dinner B & B £48.50 – £71
Trout, salmon, venison and game dishes including grouse, pheasant, duck in season and as available.
STB Commended 4 Crowns
Credit cards: 1, 3 + SWITCH
Proprietors: Charles & Keith Miller

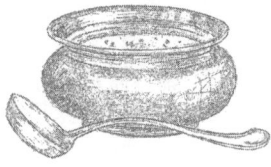

West Linton

Map 2

THE LEADBURN INN

Leadburn, West Linton
Peeblesshire EH46 7BE
Tel: 0968 672952

On the junction of A701, A702 and A720.
Small family run hotel, set in beautiful countryside between Edinburgh and the Borders. One of the oldest inns in Scotland – records date back to August 1777. A menu which is as extensive as any in the Borders is served all day, every day in the lounge, the conservatory or the bar. In the evening dinner is served in the attractive Carriage Restaurant – a luxuriously converted railway carriage. Carefully planned extensive menu includes a selection of traditional Scottish dishes.
Open all year except Christmas + Boxing Days, 1 + 2 Jan
Rooms: 6, 2 with private facilities
Bar Meals 12 – 10 pm (a-b)
Dinner 6 – 10 pm (b)
Bed & breakfast £20 – £25
Dinner B & B £28 – £40
Border game pie. Grilled local rainbow trout. Home-made beef steak pie. Roast rack of Border lamb with a light heather honey and mint glaze. Smoked haddock crumble. Salmon poached in white wine with prawns and mussels.
STB Approved Listed
Credit cards: 1, 2, 3, 5
Proprietors: Linda & Alan Thomson

Whitebridge

Map 6

KNOCKIE LODGE

Whitebridge
Inverness-shire IV1 2UP
Tel: 045 63 276

Prestige Award Winner 1990

On B862, 8 miles north of Fort Augustus. 26 miles south of Inverness.
Most motorists seem to take the road on the north west side of Loch Ness between Inverness and Fort Augustus. Were they to take the route on the south east side of the loch they would have a much better chance of discovering Knockie Lodge, a joy of a country house in idyllic countryside, and for those who like to get away from it all and enjoy real country house living there are few equals to the delightful home of Ian and Brenda Milward. Everything about it spells gracious living at its best; comfortable beautifully appointed bedrooms, elegant public rooms including a billiard room and a reading/writing room – and food to match. The chef has been there for over seven years and knows how to get the best out of the prime raw materials available to him and to present them with panache. In all respects Knockie Lodge is a special experience.
Open 1 May to 23 Oct
Rooms: 10 with private facilities
Bar Lunch 12.30 – 1.45 pm (a) for residents only
Dinner at 8 pm (e)
Note: dinner for non-residents by prior arrangement only
Restricted Licence
No smoking in dining room
Dinner B & B £65 – £95
Brochette of langoustine with a tomato coulis. Gressingham duck breast with apples and a Port wine sauce. Roast lamb fillet with a kidney and mushroom stuffing. Gooseberry ice cream with nutty curls.
STB Deluxe 3 Crowns
Credit cards: 1, 2, 3, 5, 6
Proprietors: Ian & Brenda Milward

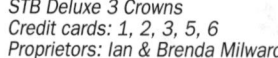

Woodlands

This delightful house has maintained its period decor and antiques and glows with hospitable warmth and a feeling of homeliness.

Its service bells are still in working order and each of the four rooms has one.

There are four bedrooms, one being a twin and the others doubles – one of which is available as a single – and each has a washbasin. Bathroom facilities are shared though one of the doubles has its own shower.

Keeping to period there is no television and the lounge is a great meeting place.

The food is excellent and dinner is of the finest Scottish produce including in season pheasant, salmon, venison, trout, wild mushrooms.

Woodlands is maintained in a genuinely traditional way.

BED & BREAKFAST – £20 • DINNER – £20

WOODLANDS
ST ANDREWS CRESCENT
BLAIR ATHOLL PH18 5SX
YOUR HOST • BIM ATKINSON
TEL • 0796-481 403

see entry page 54

see entry page 143

Coul House Hotel

Our views are breathtaking. The ancient 'Mackenzies of Coul' picked a wonderful situation for their lovely home. Today, Ann and Martyn will give you a warm Highland welcome. You'll enjoy the 'Taste of Scotland' food of chef Bentley, log fires, summer evening piper and 'Skye' and 'Raasay', the hotel's lovable labredors. Why not use our 'Highland Passport' to cruise on Loch Ness, visit Cawdor Castle, sail to the summer Isles... or follow our 'Highland Heritage' trail to Glenfiddich Distillery, the Wildlife Park, Culloden Battlefield... for golfers, there's a 5-course holiday including championship Royal Dornoch... for anglers, we have our own salmon and trout fishing... there's pony trekking too.

Ring or write for our colour brochure.

Coul House Hotel
By Strathpeffer,
Ross-shire
Tel 0997-421487
Fax 0997-421945

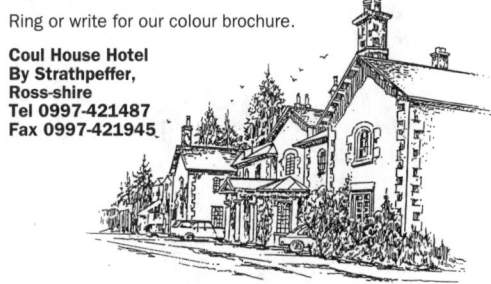

see entry page 60

see entry page 68

THE Columba Hotel

Tranquil Lochside position with stunning views over Loch Fyne.

Log fired bars with local Malt Whiskies.

Local produce imaginatively prepared.

Extensive, but not expensive, Wine List.

STB
♥♥♥♥
Commended

Logis
of
Great Britain

Tarbert, Kintyre,
Argyll PA29 6UF
Tel 0880-820 808

CROMLIX HOUSE

The true traditions of country house hospitality are perfectly exemplified at Cromlix House, set within its own 5,000 acre estate.

Informal and welcoming, the essential feeling is that of a much loved home.

Recently refurbished our 6 unique guest-rooms and 8 spacious suites are furnished throughout with period fabrics and fine antique furniture.

Dining at Cromlix is, quite simply, an experience to be savoured.

Private Chapel, Sportings, Trout Lochs, Golf nearby.

AA ★★★ (red), STB 4 Crown De Luxe
AA 2 Rosettes Cuisine Award
(See Major Guides)
Your Hosts: David and Ailsa Assenti
(4 miles north of Dunblane (Stirling) off A9)
Kinbuck by Dunblane, Perthshire FK15 9JT
Telephone 0786 822125 Facsimile 0786 825450

The Golf Inn Hotel

GULLANE, EAST LOTHIAN

Originally an old Coaching House, the Hotel has been completely refurbished and modernised.

Set in the picturesque 'golfing haven' of Gullane the Hotel has everything to offer the golfer and holiday-maker alike. All bedrooms are en-suite with colour T.V., central heating, direct dial telephone and tea/coffee making facilities.

'Saddlers' Restaurant – for à la carte and table d'Hôte meals.

The Carriage Lounge – for bar meals, steak suppers, tea and coffee etc.

The Public Bar – very popular–offering pool, darts and bar snacks.

All venues open 7 days.

The Bridle Room – for Christenings, Weddings, Conferences etc.

The Hotel is open all the year round
– whether for golf or for a relaxing holiday (there are superb beaches only 5 minutes from the Hotel) our concern is your comfort.

For further details please phone Mrs Saddler or Mrs Marshall on 0620-843259 or Fax 0620-842066

see entry page 94

see entry page 76

KINGSMUIR HOTEL

Charming century-old country house, in leafy grounds, on quiet, south side of Peebles, yet only 5 minutes' walk through parkland to High Street. There are 10 well-appointed bedrooms, all en-suite, with TV, direct-dial phone, tea-maker and hairdrier. The very best of local produce is used in preparing the Restaurant, Bar Lunch and Bar Supper dishes. Winners of several awards for bar meals. Ideal centre for touring Edinburgh and the stately homes of the Borders.

Open all year
Personally run by Elizabeth & Norman Kerr.

Peebles, Borders
Tel 0721-720151 • Fax 0721-721795

STB *Commended* **AA** ★★

see entry page 126

see entry page 134

THE HOWARD HOTEL

The Howard is situated in quiet seclusion amongst the City's elegant Georgian gardens and terraces and was originally three private houses. Its classical facade gives no hint of the welcoming opulence within. Cross the threshold and it is quite clear that this is one hotel quite unlike any other.

The Howard has 16 luxury en suite bedrooms each designed in its own unique style and luxuriously furnished. Our No.36 Restaurant has gained an excellent reputation for its Scottish cuisine which is to the highest international standards and complemented by a club-like intimate atmosphere.

Perfectly located in the centre of the City with its own Private car park, The Howard is close to the business and financial community and within strolling distance of the shops and stores of Princes Street. The ideal base for the Businessman or Leisure Traveller.

 EGON RONAY'S GUIDES   **STB** *Commended*

For brochure and tariff or sample menus please telephone or write to:
The Howard Hotel, 32/36 Great King Street, Edinburgh EH3 6QH
Tel 031-557 3500 Fax 031-557 6515

KINLOCH CASTLE
ISLE OF RUM

NATIONAL NATURE RESERVE

Kinloch Castle is one of Scotland's remarkable hotels. Situated on an island of spectacular wildness and beauty, the hotel offers the guests a chance to experience living history in the Edwardian Castle rooms which have changed little since the turn of the century. Your hosts Kathleen and Iain MacArthur will ensure a warm welcome with good food complemented by fine wines.

The island and castle are owned by Scottish Natural Heritage, which manages Rum as a National Nature Reserve renowned for its wildlife and scenery.

RUM – A UNIQUE EXPERIENCE

If you would prefer a more informal arrangement, why not stay in the hostel accommodation at the back of the Castle? You can opt for self-catering or buy your meals in the Castle Bistro.

For brochure, tariff and reservation please contact:
Kinloch Castle
Isle of Rum PH43 4RR
Tel 0687 2037

ISLE ORNSAY HOTEL
Tigh-Osda Eilean Iarmain

The Gaelic Inn on the Sea

The Taste of Skye
- mostly landed at our own
wharf. Oysters and mussels,
herrings and halibut.
Relish our seafood and relax
in a seaview room. Open all
year. Centrally heated.
Full menus and information
available from:

Effie Kennedy, Isle Ornsay Hotel, Sleibhte, Skye, IV43 8QR.
Telephone: 04713 332 Fax: 04713 275

see entry page 137

see entry page 43

see entry page 108

LOCH DUICH
HOTEL

The Loch Duich Hotel occupies the unique scenic
position of being the only Hotel overlooking the
famous Eilean Donan Castle.
A warm friendly Highland atmosphere is
complemented by fine traditional food prepared by
Chef Carol Macrae.
Proprietors: Iain Fraser & Sonia Moore

 Ardelve,
by Kyle of Lochalsh
Tel 0599-85213
 Fax 0599-85214

The Log Cabin Hotel
& Edelweiss Restaurant

Uniquely built of solid pine logs in a unique setting with
open log fires. Sample the delights of Scotland's larder
in our Edelweiss Restaurant complemented by a superb
wine cellar. Relax in the well-stocked Maltings Bar with
over 100 malt whiskies. Enjoy Bar Suppers and Bar
Lunches each day. For Sunday Lunch choose from our
Scandinavian style cold table. All cuisine is prepared in
our kitchens using the freshest of local produce. Non-
residents always welcome. Open all day for coffees and
teas with homemade shortbread. Visit our craft gallery
specialising in turned wood.

 STB *Commended*

KIRKMICHAEL PERTHSHIRE PH10 7NB
TEL 0250-881288 FAX 0250-881402

152

see entry page 83

see entry page 80

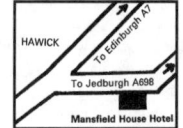
see entry page 95

see entry page 116

SCOTLAND'S COMMENDED

A selection of distinctive Country & Town House Hotels

Scotland's Commended is an Association of Country and Town House Hotels of distinction throughout Scotland, all of which are individually owned and managed. Each must attain high standards of ambience, environment and quality of food and service, set not only by the Association but also by The Scottish Tourist Board's Grading and Classification Scheme. The Hotels listed below have been awarded membership of the Taste of Scotland scheme. For telephone and fax numbers and to find out more about Scotland's Commended Members of the Taste of Scotland scheme refer to the page numbers

To obtain a copy of the Scotland's Commended brochure or to gain free assistance with your itinerary, please telephone 041 221 2300 or fax 041 221 5443

Scottish Salmon

Scottish salmon, well worthy of its title 'King of Fish' is part of the Scottish culinary tradition.

Once, Scottish rivers held such abundant stocks of wild salmon that rich and poor alike could feast on them at will. Poached in vast copper kettles, they graced the Laird's table. The sea captain dined on salmon - pickled, smoked and salted - during his long voyages under sail. So common was it, that historical sources note a clause in Perth apprentices' indentures, limiting the number of salmon meals to not more than three per week!

Wild Scottish salmon have always been a seasonal delicacy, but several factors have caused the numbers landed to decline over the years. With fewer numbers available, the price of Scottish salmon increased. Some 20 years ago, the concept of salmon farming became a reality, offering the potential for salmon to become once more accessible to all.

Scottish salmon, reared in the security of the clear, unpolluted inshore waters of the Scottish lochs, is now available all year round. It is a luxury food at an affordable price and of consistently high quality - a quality now guaranteed by the Scottish Salmon Tartan Quality Mark.

The Quality Mark was launched in March 1991, making it easier to identify premium quality salmon of a true Scottish nature. These assurances come from the fact that all producers supplying Scottish salmon carrying the mark must act in accordance with a comprehensive set of quality standards and their continued adherence to these is regularly checked by independent inspectors.

In early 1992, Tartan Quality Mark Scottish salmon also achieved recognition at the highest level in France with the awarding of the prestigious Label Rouge quality mark - the first time a product outwith France had received such an accolade.

The Label Rouge quality mark is only awarded by the French authorities to products of the highest quality. This was therefore a significant achievement for the Scottish industry and an endorsement of our quality initiatives from a country which prides itself on its gastronomic excellence, particularly as the Label Rouge mark is recognised by 78% of French consumers.

Consumers and chefs alike can therefore be confident that every time they buy salmon carrying the Tartan Quality Mark, they are getting a consistently high quality product.

The nutritional value of salmon is undisputed. A 4 oz portion contains under 200 calories (steamed or poached). It contains protein, calcium and iron, vitamins A and D, riboflavin and thiamin. Its natural oil includes two fatty acids similar to polyunsaturated vegetable oils. Current medical opinion suggests that these may help reduce the risk of heart disease by altering the blood clotting mechanism, reducing the likelihood of arterial blockage.

Scottish salmon is a truly fine example of the taste of Scotland. It is available all year round and is one of life's affordable luxuries. Scottish salmon is delivered fresh, with minimal handling, to fishmongers, market stalls, stores and supermarkets, around the world.

Easy and quick to prepare, Scottish salmon can be served for a family supper or as part of a special celebration meal. It is available fresh or smoked, as whole fish, steaks, fillets or joints, adding variety, quality and flavour to a healthy diet.

In many of the hotels and restaurants recommended in this Taste of Scotland Guide, you will find Scottish salmon featuring as a highlight of the menu. Enjoy Scotland, enjoy Scottish salmon.

SCOTTISH SALMON

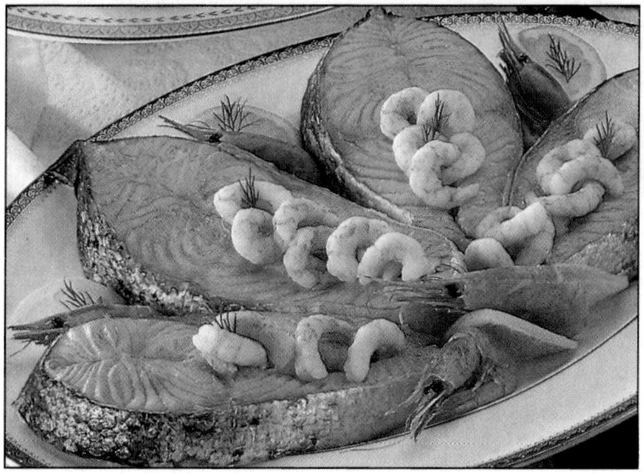

Look for the Tartan Quality Mark when ordering salmon

Only salmon which have met the standards of the Scottish Salmon Quality Assurance Scheme are eligible to carry the mark - providing you with a guarantee that the salmon reaches high standards of freshness, firmness and flavour. This is why it has recently been awarded the prestigious Label Rouge mark in France.

ST ANDREWS & NE FIFE TOURIST BOARD

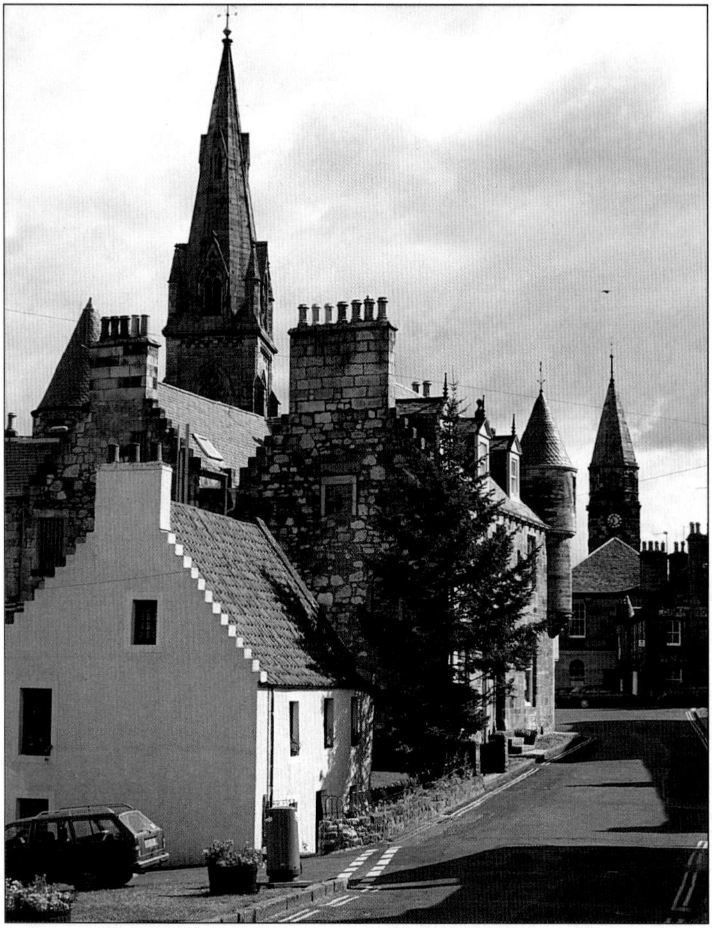

Falkland

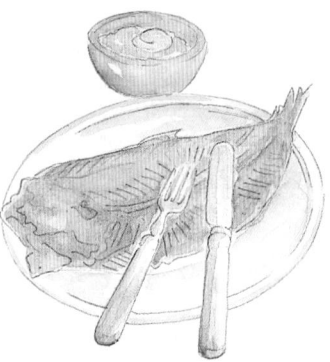

Blair Castle, Blair Atholl

Perthshire Tourist Board

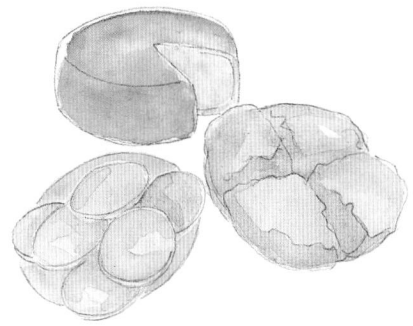

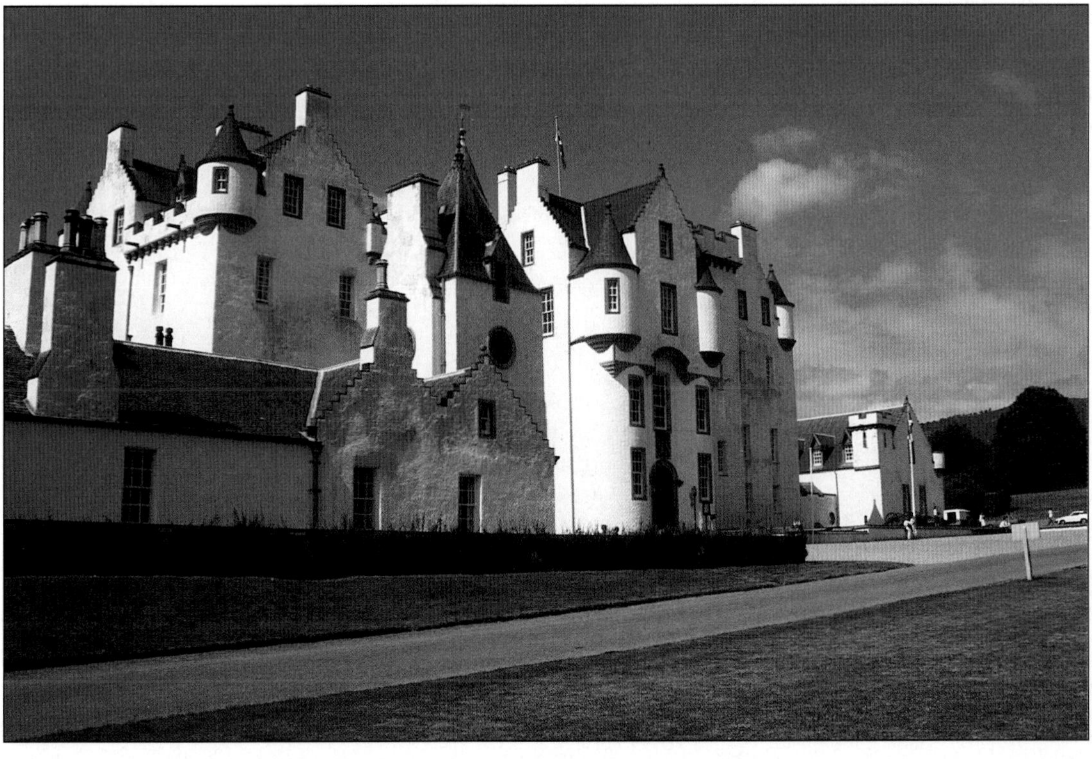

Linlithgow Palace

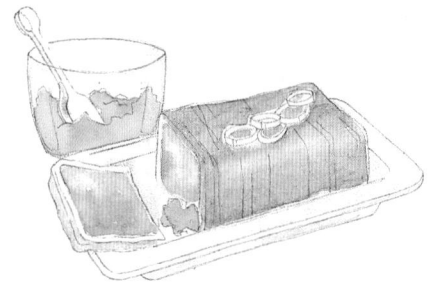

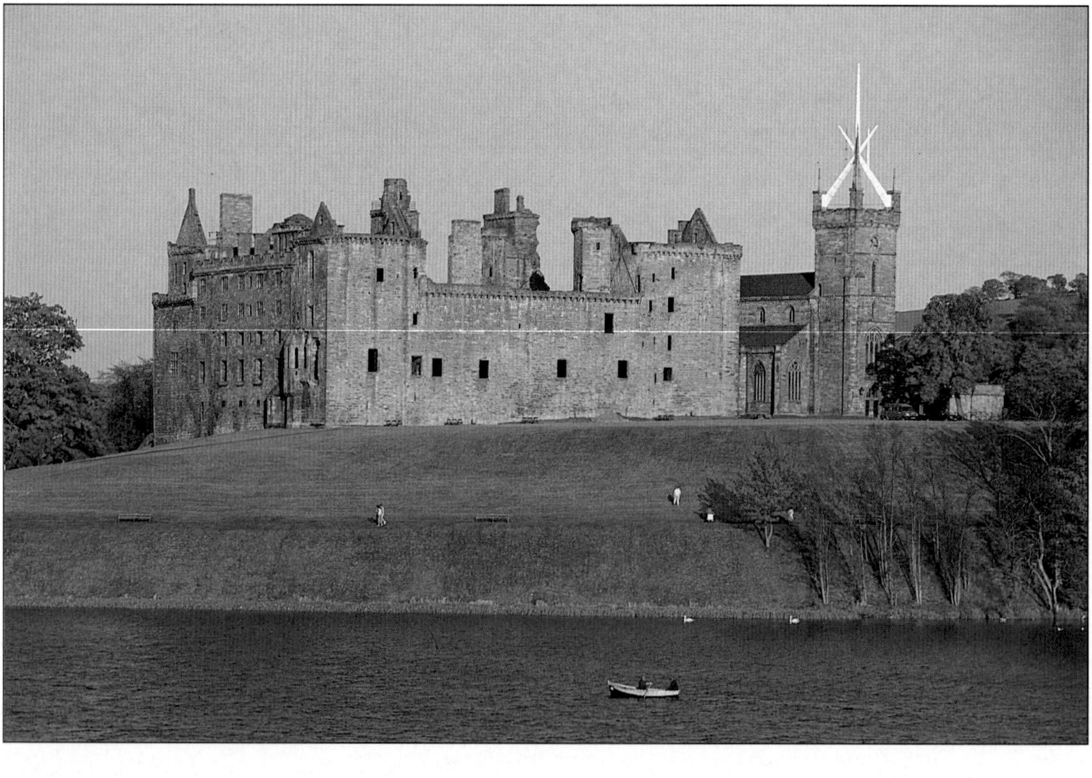

FORTH VALLEY TOURIST BOARD

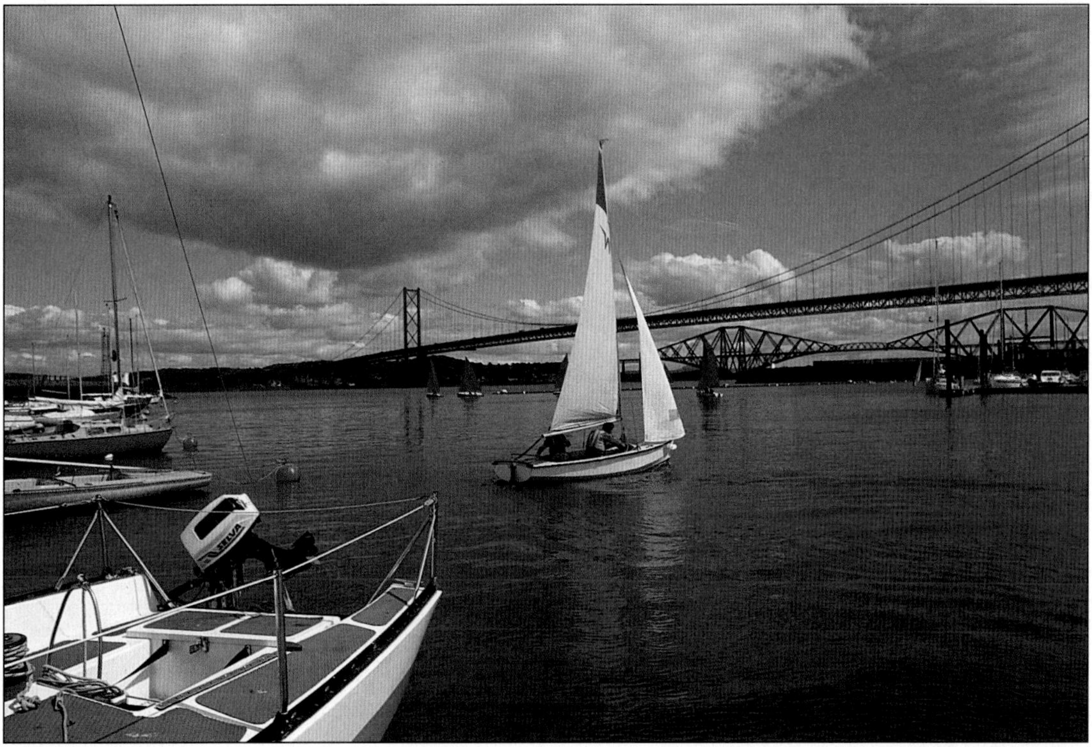

Forth Valley Tourist Board

Forth Bridges

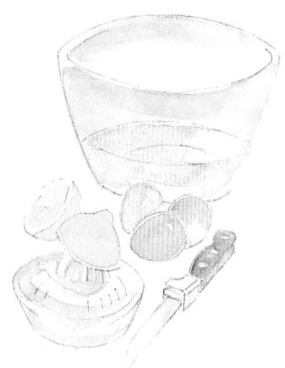

Borthwick

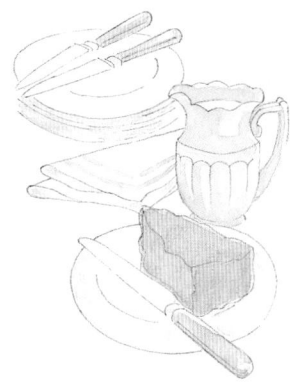

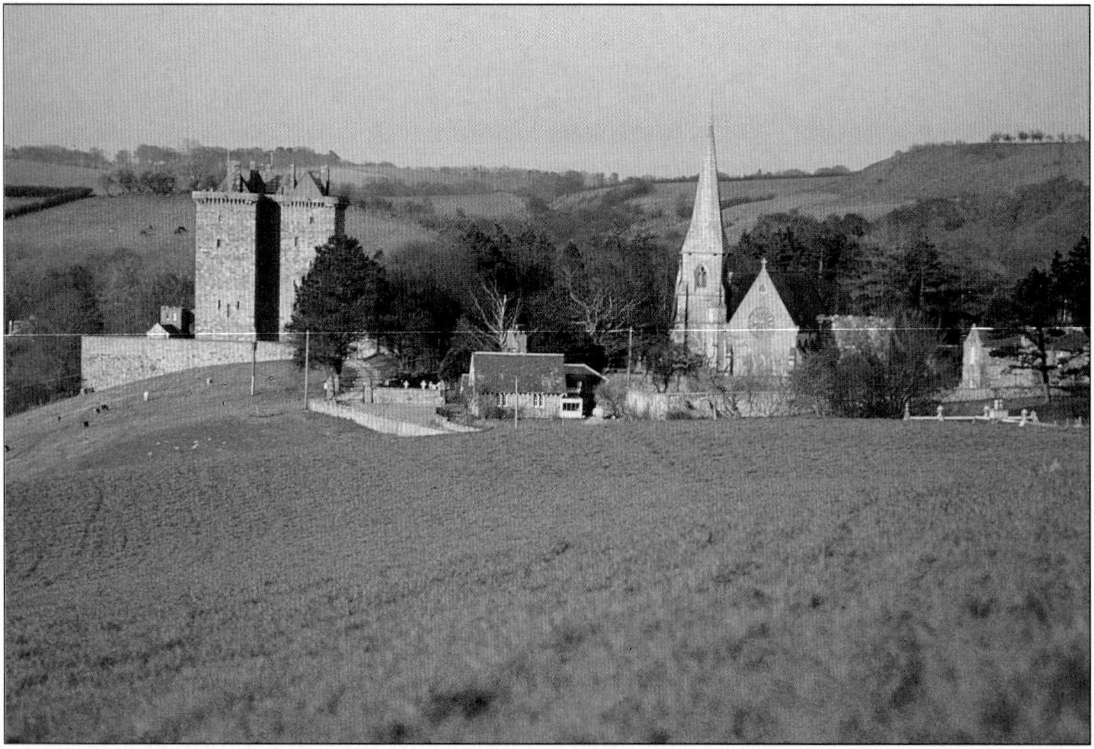

MIDLOTHIAN TOURISM/JAMES GARDINER ASSOCIATES

Brig O'Doon, Alloway

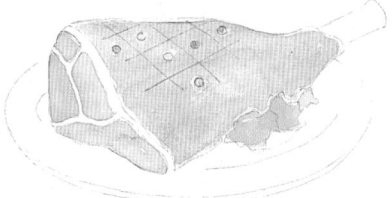

Caerlaverock Castle, nr Dumfries

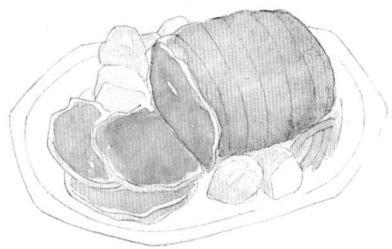

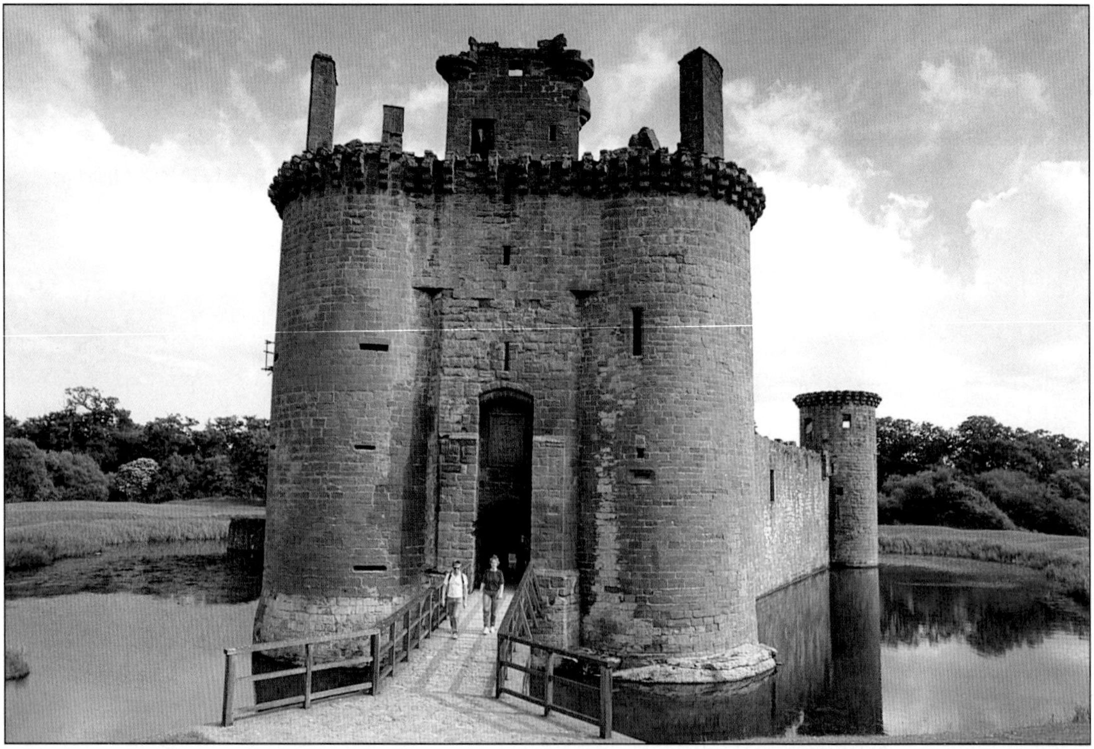

DUMFRIES & GALLOWAY TOURIST BOARD

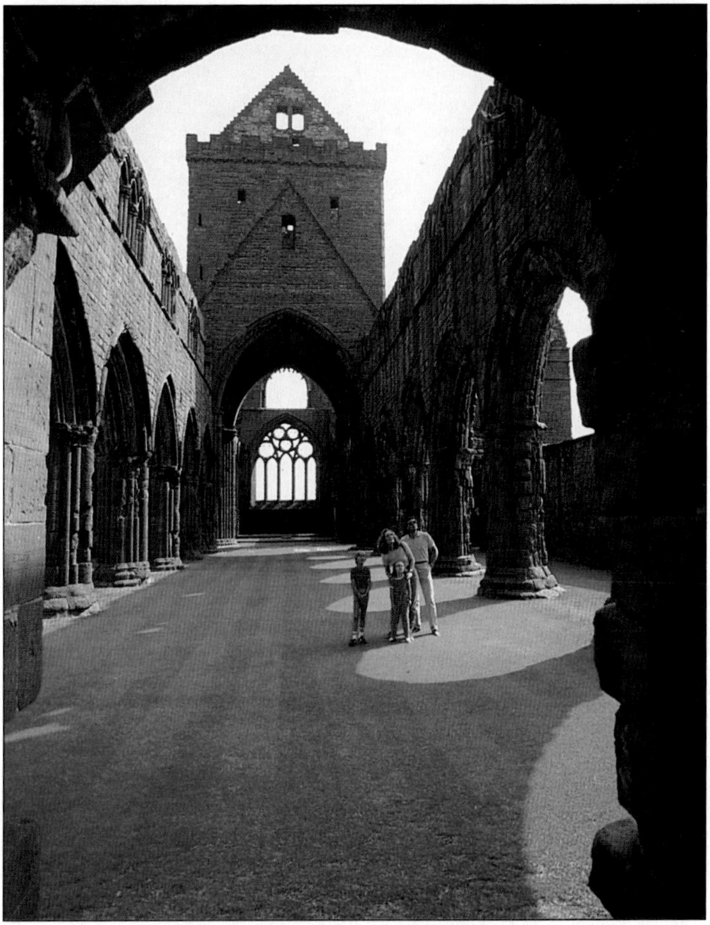
DUMFRIES & GALLOWAY TOURIST BOARD

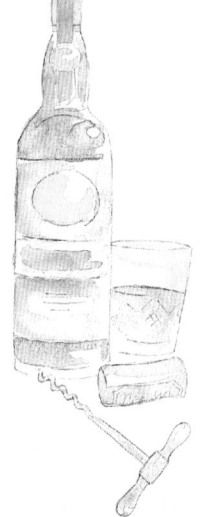

Sweetheart Abbey, nr Dumfries

St Mary's Loch, Borders

SCOTTISH BORDERS TOURIST BOARD

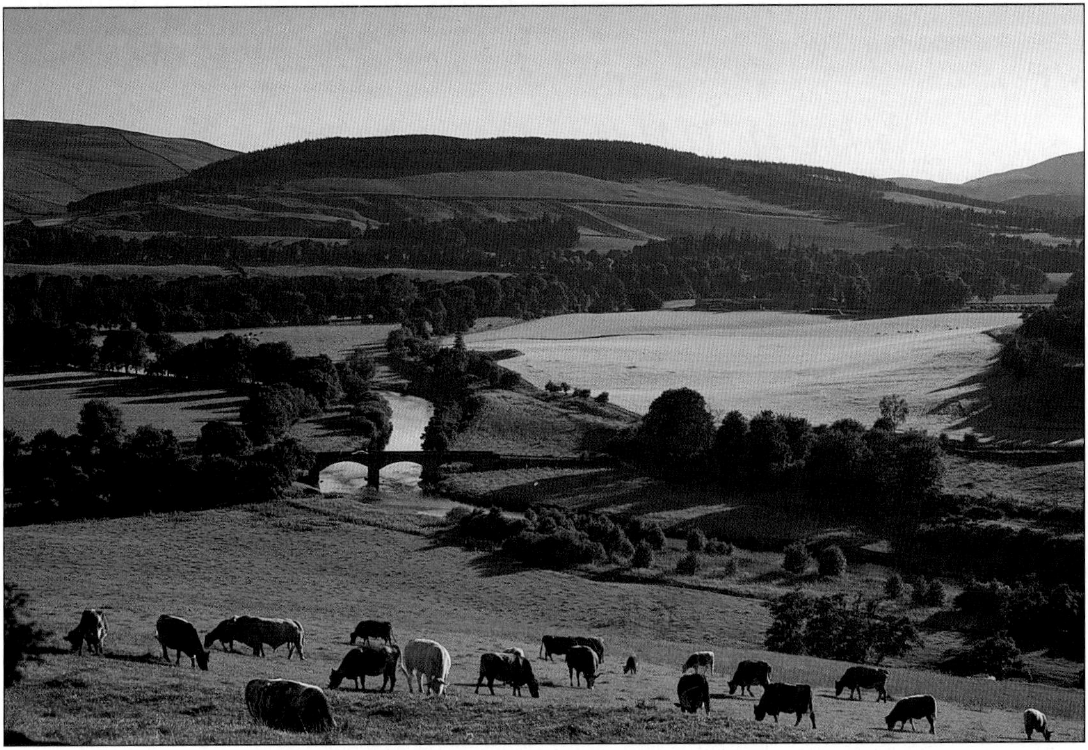

Scottish Borders Tourist Board

Manor Valley, Peeblesshire

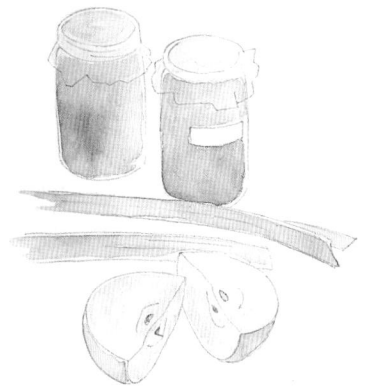

When quality counts - only Scotch Beef and Lamb will do

Prime quality beef and lamb from Scotland

Taste of Scotland
Scotch Lamb Challenge 1993

SCOTCH LAMB
SO CREATIVE AND VERSATILE

Scotch lamb is still a strong favourite with caterers today. Strongly supported by schemes such as Farm Assured Scotch Lamb and Quality Assured Scotch Lamb, you can be guaranteed of 'Quality that Counts'.

THE TASTE OF QUALITY

This was the second year of this prestigious recipe competition, run by the Scotch Quality Beef and Lamb Association in conjunction with the Taste of Scotland Scheme, open to all cooks and chefs employed by Taste of Scotland members.

Entrants were required to devise their own three course meal (starter, main course and dessert) using original recipes, with Scotch lamb as the main course.

The format of the competition was slightly different in 1993 as an additional category was introduced which opened the competition to establishments specialising in the more traditional home-cooked Scottish fare.

The overall winner of the 1993 Taste of Scotland Scotch Lamb Challenge was Chris Walker, chef/proprietor from Creebridge House Hotel, Newton Stewart.

Winner from Category 1	–	Chris Walker
		Creebridge House Hotel
Winner from Category 2	–	Garry Rendall
		Thainstone House Hotel

The standard of entries received from both categories was again extremely high and the use of Scotch lamb cuts in the recipes both innovative and exciting.

In the recipe section that follows, you will find the lamb recipes from the six finalists in the 1993 competition.

Why not try Scotch lamb dishes on the menu next time you visit a Taste of Scotland establishment and experience for yourself the Taste of Quality.

Taste of Scotland Scotch Lamb Challenge
Overall Winner 1993
Chris Walker, Chef/Proprietor
Creebridge House Hotel, Newton Stewart

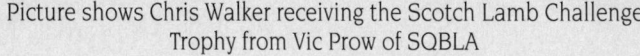

Picture shows Chris Walker receiving the Scotch Lamb Challenge
Trophy from Vic Prow of SQBLA

Oven-Baked Fillet of Scotch Lamb

wrapped in Filo Pastry filled with Arran Mustard Seed and Fresh Garden Rosemary, set on a Port and Redcurrant Sauce.

The Taste of Scotland Scotch Lamb Challenge Overall Winner and Winner, Category 1

Chris Walker Chef/Proprietor Creebridge House Hotel Newton Stewart

INGREDIENTS:

1 rack end of loin of lamb (1 lb 10 oz)
4 sheets filo pastry
4 teaspoons Arran mustard seed
4 sprigs garden rosemary
6 fl oz Port wine
1 tablespoon redcurrant jelly
½ onion, finely diced
6 fl oz jus lie
1 head broccoli
8 small new potatoes
1 old potato
12 baby carrots
mixed lettuce for garnish
4 tomatoes for roses

(Serves four)

METHOD

1. Trim the rack end of a loin of Scotch lamb and bone out the fillet. Cut this into 4 pieces and tenderise with a meat hammer.

2. Spread Arran mustard seed onto the 4 individual pieces and then chop and sprinkle fresh garden rosemary over.

3. Butter a sheet of filo pastry and fold in half. Then place lamb in the centre and bring all four corners to a peak in the centre, hold the pastry then, as if wrapping a parcel, secure the four corners by tying with julienne of carrot and then trimming.

SAUCE

4. To make the Port and redcurrant sauce, melt one tablespoon of redcurrant jelly, add 6 fl oz of Port and 6 fl oz of a good lamb stock. Bring to the boil and thicken with arrowroot to preserve the transparency of the sauce.

5. Bake the parcels on the top shelf at GM7/220°C/425°F for 15 minutes – the lamb should be pink in the middle of a crispy pastry case.

Roast Leg of Scotch Lamb

stuffed with Spinach, Mushrooms, Ginger and Fresh Herbs on a Red Wine Sauce

Second Place, Category 1

*Rita Brown
Chef/Joint
Proprietor
The Hazelton
Guest House
Crail, Fife*

INGREDIENTS:

1½ lb leg of Scotch lamb (trimmed weight)
4 oz washed + trimmed spinach
2 plump cloves of garlic, chopped
8 oz sliced mushrooms
1 teaspoon chopped root ginger
c. ½ oz butter
1 tablespoon single cream
1 tablespoon chopped rosemary
salt & freshly ground pepper

RED WINE SAUCE
10 fl oz lamb stock
5 fl oz strongly flavoured red wine
Crabbies green ginger wine to taste
cornflour
salt & pepper

LAMB STOCK
lamb bones
onions
carrots
parsley stalks
sprig of thyme
black & white peppercorns
bay leaves
water

GARNISH
4 tomatoes
basil
parsley

(Serves four)

METHOD

ADVANCE PREPARATION OF LAMB STOCK

Bring all stock ingredients to boil, skim and simmer for 4 hours.

When cool, strain the stock and chill, remove fat layer from top.

1. Cut 4 thick pieces of the top of the leg and trim off all fat and sinews. Each trimmed piece should weigh 6 oz. To achieve 4 flat escalopes, horizontally cut through each piece a third down almost to the end and open out. Repeat another third down the opposite way. Flatten with rolling pin under cling film until thin and even. Season with salt and pepper.

2. Blanch spinach and cool quickly. Spread out on meat.

3. Gently sauté mushrooms, garlic and ginger in butter. Add cream, salt and pepper, and cook until thick. Spread this mixture on top of spinach to within half an inch of the edges. Roll up into neat even individual portions. Season and sprinkle the rosemary along the top of each piece.

4. Place in a tin and roast on GM5/190°C/ 375°F for about 30 minutes until cooked but still pink. Leave to rest.

SAUCE

5. Put stock and red wine in a saucepan and reduce to almost half. Add a little ginger wine (half teaspoon at a time) and adjust seasoning. Thicken with cornflour as necessary.

PRESENTATION

6. Slice lamb on the slant. Pour sauce onto lower half of plates and place lamb on top in a slight curve. Garnish with baked tomatoes, basil and parsley.

Suggested accompaniments - potatoes roasted with flaked almonds; baton carrots and broccoli florets.

Third Place, Category 1

*Sukie Scott
Chef/Joint
Proprietor
Old Pines
Spean Bridge
Inverness-shire*

Roast Gigot of Scotch Lamb

with a Stuffing of Kidney and Five Herbs, coated with a Herb Crumb, served with Rowan Jelly

INGREDIENTS:

Gigot of Scotch lamb,
    c. 3½ lb tunnel
    boned
Reserved bones for stock
Carrot, onion, celery, leek
    for stock

STUFFING
1 lamb's kidney
Handful of fresh thyme,
    mint, chives,
    marjoram & parsley
2 slices wholemeal bread
2 oz butter
salt & pepper

COATING
Same as stuffing, omitting
    the kidney

(Serves six)

METHOD

STOCK
1. Roast bones and vegetables until well browned.
2. Make a good strong stock and reduce to half a pint.

STUFFING & COATING
3. Make the two quantities of stuffing by liquidising the ingredients. Remove half.
4. Add the kidney and liquidise further, then use to stuff the gigot.
5. Use the reserved quantity to coat, press firmly over the surface of the lamb.
6. Roast for 20 minutes at GM9/240°C/475°F, then turn down to GM4/180°C/350°F for further 50 minutes. Leave to rest for half an hour before carving to allow the meat to become pink right through.
7. Make gravy in roasting tin with one teaspoon of flour and reserved stock then pass through sieve.
8. Serve the lamb with the gravy and a teaspoon of rowan jelly with a bouquet of the five fresh herbs to garnish.

Suggested accompaniments – potatoes baked with cream, garlic and nutmeg; cabbage saute with garlic and juniper berries, and ratatouille.

Roast Spring Lamb
wrapped in Spinach with Girolle Mousse on a Basil Sauce

The Taste of Scotland Scotch Lamb Challenge Winner, Category 2

Garry Rendall Sous Chef Thainstone House Hotel & Country Club Inverurie Aberdeenshire

INGREDIENTS:

1 loin of lamb
1 oz mirepoix of vegetables
8 spinach leaves
¼ oz crepinette/caul fat
garlic
tarragon, rosemary + mint, chopped together

GIROLLE MOUSSE
4 oz chicken breast
1 oz girolles
1 egg
4 fl oz double cream
pinch of seasoning

BASIL SAUCE
1¼ pints brown veal stock
lamb bones
2 oz mirepoix of vegetables
4 fl oz white wine
1 oz clarified butter
mushroom trimmings
sprig of basil
1 oz butter

GARNISH
12 button onions
12 girolles

(Serves four)

METHOD

1. Bone out lamb, remove fat and trim sinews. Rub lamb with garlic and coat with a fine dusting of the herbs, then cut into two. Seal off each piece quickly in olive oil then allow to cool.

2. Chop up bones, brown in oven with mirepoix of vegetables, use to make sauce.

GIROLLE MOUSSE

3. Blend chilled chicken in food processor. Add egg, seasoning and double cream. Pass through sieve into clean bowl over ice. Dice girolles, saute in butter for one minute, cool, then add to chicken mousse.

4. Trim and wash spinach leaves, blanch and refresh, then dry flat in cloth.

5. Clean caul fat in salted water, dry, place on table, then cut into two equal pieces (approx 6 inches x 4 inches long). Line with spinach then spread evenly with girolle mousse. Place lamb loin in centre and roll tightly around. Wrap in greased tin foil then cook lamb in hot oven GM5/190°C/375°F for 8 minutes.

BASIL SAUCE

6. Sweat down chopped onions, mushrooms trimmings and basil. Deglaze with white wine and Madeira, reduce, then add stock and reduce to correct consistency. Pass into clean pan, bring first to boil and finish with butter and cream. Saute button onions and girolles and keep warm.

PRESENTATION

7. Slice lamb loin into 12 pieces and arrange 3 slices down the middle of each plate. Finish with sauce and garnish of button onions and girolles.

Suggested accompaniments: early vegetables – carrot, mangetout; turned celeriac; timbale of carrot

*Michel Nijsten
Head Chef
The Moorings
Hotel
Banavie
Fort William*

Roast Saddle of Scotch Lamb
with Rhubarb and Pickled Onion Chutney and a Lovage Jus

INGREDIENTS:

1 x 3-4 lb saddle of lamb
2 fl oz vegetable oil
salt & black pepper

CHUTNEY
1 lb rhubarb
4 oz onion
pinch of ground ginger
½ oz mixed spice
¼ oz curry powder
salt
8 oz soft brown sugar
¼ pint malt vinegar

SAUCE
2 large sprigs of lovage
7 fl oz lamb jus
2 fl oz red wine
2 oz unsalted butter
salt & pepper

6 large roasting potatoes

4 sheets filo pastry
2 fl oz olive oil

(Serves four)

METHOD

1. Remove top skin from saddle of lamb without losing the fat from the meat. Remove kidneys and fat surrounding fillets. Tie string around the saddle.
2. Season and pre-roast saddle in hot oven GM7/220°C/ 425°F for 15 minutes. Turn heat down to moderate temperature GM4/180°C/ 350°F for a further 25 minutes. Take out and leave to set for 10 minutes before carving.

CHUTNEY
3. Cut rhubarb and clean the onions. Place in a pan and add spices, sugar, salt and half of the vinegar. Simmer for 1½ hours, adding vinegar to prevent sticking. Reduce until thickened.

FILO PASTRY TULIPS
4. Line 4 dariole moulds with 3 small square sheets each brushed with olive oil. Bake in oven at GM6/ 200°C/400°F for 15 minutes until golden brown.

SAUCE
5. Remove saddle out of roasting tray and save remaining fat. Deglaze tray with red wine. When wine boils add lamb jus then leave to simmer until reduced by half.
6. Strain through a fine sieve and season. Add chopped lovage and butter before serving.

POTATOES
7. Turn potatoes in barrel shape and steam for 4 minutes over boiling water.
8. Roast in lamb fat from roasting tin until golden brown and add seasoning.

TO PRESENT
9. Carve the top of the saddle lengthwise giving 2 nice slices per plate. Take off fillets and slice in four equal portions.
10. Set the roast potatoes on top left of plate. Place filo pastry tulip on right side and pour in the warm chutney.
11. Dress the meat in the middle of plate, then add sauce without coating the meat or top of the plate. A nice leaf of lovage between both garnishes to finish.

Roast Loin of Lamb
edged by a Mustard, Pinenut and Mint Coat accompanied by a Filo Pastry Money Bag of Lambs Offal and a Shallot and Port Wine Essence

Third Place, Category 2

Malcolm Warham Senior Sous Chef Westerwood Hotel Cumbernauld

INGREDIENTS:

1 best end of lamb, prepared for noisettes
2 tablespoons Dijon mustard
4 oz crushed pinenuts
1 oz chopped fresh mint

OFFAL
2 oz lambs sweetbreads
2 lambs kidneys
6 shallots
1 garlic clove, crushed
2 filo pastry sheets
20 fl oz lamb stock
Port wine to taste
2½ fl oz double cream
red wine
olive oil
butter

(Serves four)

METHOD

1. Prepare lamb as for noisettes.
2. Spread mustard thinly over fat and roll lamb through a mixture of pinenuts and mint to form a coat.
3. Seal gently in hot saucepan and cook at GM 67/ 200-220°C/400-425°F, approximately 15 minutes until pink. Take out and leave to rest.

MONEY BAG
4. Prepare sweetbreads, removing sinew. Blanch gently and leave to cool.
5. Cut kidney and sweetbreads into quarter inch dice. Cook together with shallots and garlic, binding with cream. Leave to cool.
6. Form money bag with filo pastry and offal filling. Cook in hot oven GM7/220°C/425°F, approximately 15 minutes.

SAUCE
7. Sweat shallots until caramelised. Add Port wine and red wine. Reduce slightly, add lamb stock and reduce until desired consistency. Finish with nuggets of chilled butter.

TO SERVE
8. Cut lamb into noisettes and serve on top of rosti potato. Arrange money bag on plate with accompanying vegetables and pour sauce round.

Jeffrey Purves
Chef/Proprietor
The Green Inn
Restaurant
Ballater

St Andrews Tart
with Apricot Chutney

INGREDIENTS:

1 lb Howgate full fat
    St Andrews Cheese
4 x 4 inch tins of blind-
    baked short paste
4 fl oz double cream
4 teaspoons diced spring
    onions
salt & black pepper

APRICOT CHUTNEY
4 oz dried apricot
small piece of root ginger
8 oz diced onion
½ teaspoon salt
6 oz demerara sugar
¼ pint malt vinegar
½ teaspoon mustard seeds
rind & juice of 1 lemon

(Serves four)

METHOD

APRICOT CHUTNEY

1. Place all ingredients in heavy bottomed pan. Bring to boil and simmer for 1½ hours, stirring occasionally. Mixture when ready should be thick and pulpy. Store in airtight jars in a cool place.

TART

2. Remove rind from cheese. Chop into quarter inch dice.

3. Place into 4 tins containing the already baked short paste.

4. Add diced spring onion, cream, salt and pepper.

5. Bake in oven GM5/190°C/375°F for 15 minutes until cheese is melted but not greasy.

6. Cool slightly then remove tarts from their tins.

7. Serve tarts hot with cold apricot chutney.

Terrine of Scotch Salmon and Scallops

Robert Taylor
Head Chef
Houstoun House
Hotel
Uphall

INGREDIENTS:

6 oz fresh salmon
6 oz scallops
½ pint red Bordeaux
2 oz large leaf spinach
1 sprig rosemary
1 sprig thyme
1 sprig sage
6 tablespoons natural
      yoghurt
2 tablespoons lemon juice
4 shallots
1 sprig dill
2 tablespoons salmon
      caviar
2 tablespoons aspic jelly
salt & pepper
1 pluche chervil

(Serves four)

METHOD

1. Warm and blanch spinach in boiling water. Refresh and dry thoroughly with a tea towel.

2. Into a shallow saucepan place the red wine, finely chopped shallots, rosemary, thyme and sage. Bring to simmering and season.

3. Slice the salmon lengthways 3-4 times then cut into 3 equal pieces crossways.

4. Remove the coral from scallop meat, then trim and wash both. Slice the scallop meat equally into 3-4 pieces.

5. Increase the heat to the cooking liquor and poach the salmon, scallops and coral for 1-2 minutes, then remove from pan and place on a draining rack.

6. While cooking liquor is still simmering, add aspic jelly until dissolved. Remove from heat and pass through a fine strainer into clean bowl. Discard herbs but retain shallots.

7. Line a chilled terrine with the spinach and arrange the salmon, scallop meat and coral in layers liberally spreading cooked shallots onto each layer.

8. When terrine is full, pour strained cooking liquor until covering salmon etc. Place in refrigerator for approximately 30 minutes until set.

9. To make the dressing, roughly chop the fresh dill and place in a clean bowl with the natural yoghurt and lemon juice, then blend together.

10. Remove terrine from mould and slice into 8 equal portions. Arrange the slices onto 4 chilled plates and spoon 3 'pools' of dressing onto each. Top the dressing with salmon caviar and a pluche of chervil.

A Light Leaf Salad of Quail Breasts
with Chanterelles and Shallots

*Edward Peter McGarvey
Chef de Partie
Sunlaws House Hotel
nr Kelso*

INGREDIENTS:

8 quail breasts
1 oz shallots, finely diced
8-10 oz chanterelles
15 fl oz double cream
1 tablespoon parsley & basil
selection of mixed salad leaves
2 oz pine kernels
seasoning

(Serves four)

METHOD

1. Melt butter and cook the shallots and chanterelles. Season to taste. Add basil and parsley.

2. Heat the cream in a separate pan until it thickens, then add the chanterelles and shallots.

3. Arrange the mixed salad leaves on a plate and place in refrigerator to chill the leaves.

4. Pan fry quail breasts and finish in the oven GM6/200°C/400°F for approximately 3-5 minutes. Remove from the oven and let them rest for about 1-2 minutes.

5. Remove the plates from the refrigerator.

6. Flash the quail breasts under the grill.

7. Arrange the quail on the leaves and garnish with the chanterelles and a few sprigs of chervil.

West Coast Lobster

with Poached Smoked Dee Salmon bound in a Champagne and Dill Sauce and presented in a Filo Pastry Basket

*Derek Smith
Head Chef
Raemoir House
Hotel
Banchory*

INGREDIENTS:

1 whole live lobster
3 short lobster heads with feelers
10 oz smoked salmon, cut into ½ inch dice
filo pastry
2 pints double cream
1 oz clarified butter
½ onion, finely chopped
dill
6 fl oz Champagne
4 pints water for fish stock

(Serves four)

METHOD

1. Cut filo pastry into 12 x 4 inch squares. Layer 3 squares brushed with melted butter, so that the corners stick out to form a star shape. Do the same for the other 3 portions and mould into 4 bowls.

2. Cook in a medium oven GM4/180°C/350°F until golden brown. Leave somewhere warm.

3. Plunge lobster into 4 pints of slightly boiling water, bring back to boil and simmer for 15 minutes. Take out and cool.

4. Reduce fish stock by two-thirds.

5. Open up lobster and cut up into even sized pieces.

6. Lightly saute the onion in butter. Add 6 fl oz Champagne and 6 fl oz stock then reduce by two-thirds. Add cream and reduce by half.

7. Add lobster and smoked salmon, dill and seasoning, and simmer for one minute then fill the 4 baskets. Garnish with the 4 lobster heads, legs and parsley.

Parcels of Teviotdale Cheese

Gary Moore
Head Chef
Burts Hotel
Melrose

INGREDIENTS:

4 oranges
5 fl oz white wine vinegar
8 oz brown sugar
2 measures whisky
8 oz Teviotdale cheese
4 oz sliced smoked salmon
4 oz porridge oats
flour
eggwash – 2 eggs beaten
salad to garnish
4 fl oz olive oil

(Serves four)

METHOD

1. Cut the cheese into eight triangles.
2. Cover with sliced smoked salmon.
3. Coat each in flour then eggwash and finally with porridge oats.
4. Heat the oil in pan and brown the oat-coated parcels.
5. Place parcels in moderate oven GM5/190°C/375°F and cook until warm in centre.
6. Make whisky marmalade, thinly pare the rind from the oranges and chop. Remove all the white pith and pips and chop the flesh. Place in pan with sugar vinegar and whisky. Simmer gently until thickened and syrupy.
7. Place cheese on a warm plate with garnish and marmalade.

Sentry of Scallop and Sole

Ralph Porciani
Executive Chef
The Balmoral
Edinburgh

INGREDIENTS:

4 x 3 oz fillet of sole
4 strips of leek
2 courgettes
2 carrots
4 large Western Isles
    scallops
36 spears of asparagus
12 sprigs of chervil
1 oz finely diced red,
    yellow and green
    pepper

TARRAGON BUTTER SAUCE
10 leaves tarragon
½ fl oz Champagne vinegar
4 oz unsalted butter
¼ fl oz Isle of Mull
    vermouth
¼ fl oz double cream
pinch of salt & cayenne
lemon juice to taste

SCALLOP MOUSSE
4 large Western Isles
    scallops
¼ pint double cream
1 egg white
½ fl oz Isle of Mull
    vermouth
pinch of salt & cayenne

(Serves four)

METHOD

SCALLOP MOUSSE
1. Using only the white scallop meat, ensure that it is washed and dried thoroughly then place in a blender and mix to a puree.
2. Remove from blender and rub through a fine sieve. Place into a mixing bowl and set on crushed ice. Add salt and beat.
3. Slowly add three-quarters of the cream, followed by the salt, cayenne and vermouth.
4. Add the remainder of the cream and allow to rest for one hour before use.

SOLE
5. Score the back of the sole to avoid shrinking. If the fillet is too thick then it may be batted out a little.
6. Butter a 3 inch demi-tasse cup, season the sole with salt and cayenne then line the cup. Fill to the top with scallop mousse, cover with cling film and steam for approximately 3-4 minutes.

TRELLIS
7. Top and tail the courgette, slice thinly on a mandolin and trim to ¼ inch x 5 inch strips, keeping an even mix of green skin to white flesh.
8. Top and tail the carrots, peel and square off. Slice on a mandolin and trim to the same size as the courgette. Blanch and refresh in boiling salted water then criss-cross to form a trellis. Cut with a 3 inch cutter.

ASPARAGUS
9. Trim the asparagus into 1 inch spears, turn the bottoms to a spear point then blanch in boiling salted water. Toss in a little seasoned butter before plating.

(Continued on next page)

METHOD (CONTINUED)

SCALLOPS

10. Remove the scallops from the shell and wash through in running water to remove sand and discolouring. Slice the scallops into three even slices and dry well.

11. Heat a pan with a little olive oil, season the scallops with salt and saute. When golden brown on the first side, turn them over. Remove from the pan.

TARRAGON BUTTER SAUCE

12. Roughly chop the tarragon and reduce in the vinegar. Add the vermouth and further reduce before adding the cream.

13. Mount with butter, whisking continuously over a warm heat. Season with salt, cayenne and lemon juice. Pass through a fine sieve and serve.

TO SERVE

14. Place 3 bundles of 3 spears of asparagus around each plate. In between place a small heap of pepper ratatouille steeped in sherry vinaigrette. Top the ratatouille with a slice of scallop.

15. Warm the tarragon butter and pour to form a pool in the centre of the plate.

16. Remove the sole from the cup and top with the trellis. Wrap a blanched strip of leek around each sentry of sole, warm in a steamer then place on top of the sauce.

17. Brush the trellis with butter before serving. Garnish the scallops with chervil.

Carrot and Cashewnut Pie

Carole Harris
Taigh-na-Creag
Isle of Islay

INGREDIENTS:

2 medium onions, chopped
8 oz shredded cabbage
3 oz grated carrots
2 teaspoons cumin seeds
salt & pepper
2 tablespoons oil

PIE CRUST
4 oz crushed cornflakes
2 oz cashew nuts, coarsely
      ground
6 oz strong Islay Dunlop or
      Scottish Cheddar,
      grated
1 teaspoon mixed herbs
2 large eggs
4 oz fresh breadcrumbs
2 oz butter
salt & pepper

(Serves four to six)

METHOD

1. To make the filling, fry onions in oil for 5 minutes then add cumin seeds and fry for 1 minute.

2. Add carrots and cabbage, salt and pepper to taste, and fry for further 4-5 minutes. Leave to cool.

PIE CRUST
3. Mix all ingredients except the butter and 2 oz of cheese in a bowl.

4. Press half the pie crust ingredients into a greased 9-10 inch pie plate and spread with the filling mixture. Then press on the remaining pie crust, press down well, sprinkle with the rest of the cheese and dot with butter.

5. Bake for 25-30 minutes GM6/200°C/400°F, or combination oven 200/low for 15 minutes, until golden brown.

6. Serve with a mixed salad and a raspberry vinaigrette.

Salmon Horns
with Ginger and Spring Onions and a Lime Dip

*Caroline
Hadley-Smith
Chef/Proprietor
Braemar Lodge
Braemar*

INGREDIENTS:

1 lb puff pastry
1 lb salmon fillet cubed
2 oz Chinese preserved
        ginger, chopped
1 bunch spring onions
        (reserve 4 for
        garnish)
1 oz butter
1 beaten egg
sesame seeds
salt & pepper

LIME DIP
3 tablespoons mayonnaise
2 tablespoons crème fraiche
½ teaspoon ginger
½ teaspoon chilli
1 teaspoon soya sauce
juice and zest of 1 lime
salt & pepper
1 lime for garnish

(Serves four)

METHOD

1. Finely slice spring onions and sauté in butter until soft.
2. Mix in a bowl with salmon cubes, chopped ginger and seasoning.
3. Roll out puff pastry and cut into 4 squares, then divide filling between the 4 pieces and fashion each into a horn by rolling the sides up and sealing the end flap.
4. Glaze with beaten egg, decorate with pastry trimmings and sesame seeds.
5. Bake for 25 minutes GM6/200°C/400°F.
6. Mix lime dip ingredients in a bowl and serve alongside the pastries garnished with spring onion and lime.

Suggested accompaniments: salad and new potatoes

Roast Loin of Venison
served with a Gâteau of Chicken and Apricots, presented on an Apricot and Cider Vinegar Sauce

Ian Hornsby
Chef/Proprietor
Strathdon Hotel
Dundee

INGREDIENTS:

1½ lbs loin of venison
    (boned)
1 teaspoon game glaze
6 oz dried apricots
10 fl oz cream
4 oz butter
4 fl oz cider vinegar
1 tablespoon redcurrant
    jelly
2 carrots
1 courgette
salt & pepper
garlic clove
6 oz mirepoix (carrot,
    shallot, celery,
    leek)
1 x 6 oz chicken breast,
    boneless
4 tablespoons crème
    fraiche
2 eggs
ground mace

(Serves four)

METHOD

1. Trim the loin of venison, season and place in refrigerator.

GATEAU

2. Remove any sinew or excess fat from the chicken breast. Place in a processor and purée. Add the crème fraiche, eggs and seasoning.

3. Force the mixture through a fine sieve, cover and chill immediately.

4. Dice half the apricots and add to the chicken mixture.

5. Butter 4 dariole moulds. Divide the mixture between the moulds, cover each mould with buttered greaseproof paper and place back in refrigerator.

6. Prepare the mirepoix.

7. Wash and trim the carrots and courgettes for turning - retain.

8. Cut the remaining apricots into julienne and retain.

9. Melt some of the butter in a frying pan then quickly seal venison all over then place in roasting tin. Add the mirepoix to frying pan. Place the loin on top of the mirepoix and roast quickly in the oven for 15 minutes at GM7/ 220°C/425°F.

10. Steam the gâteaux in a bain marie in the oven for approximately 10-12 minutes until firm to the touch.

11. Glaze the carrots and blanch the courgettes. Keep warm.

12. Remove the gâteaux from the oven and keep warm.

13. Remove the venison from the oven and keep warm.

14. Drain off the excess fat from roasting tin. Deglaze tin with the cider vinegar and reduce by half. Pass through a fine sieve, add the cream and apricots and simmer for 4-5 minutes. Blend in the redcurrant jelly and meat glaze, then add a little butter to the sauce off the heat.

(Continued on next page)

Method (continued)

To Present

15. Slice the venison into 16 slices. Turn out the gâteaux onto 4 warmed plates, cut a section out and draw this section out from the centre of each gâteau.

16. Arrange 4 slices of venison around each gâteau. Coat each gâteau with a little sauce and pour the rest around each plate.

17. Finally, garnish each plate with the turned carrots and courgettes.

Steamed Turbot Fillet
with a Saffron, White Wine and Lemon Thyme Infusion

Christopher Harding Chef/Proprietor Harding's Restaurant North Berwick

Ingredients:

1 x 3 lb turbot, filleted
12 fl oz full bodied
            Chardonnay
pinch of saffron strands
juice of ½ lemon
2 teaspoons fresh lemon
        thyme leaves
4 fl oz fish stock
salt & pepper

Fish Stock

bones from turbot washed
        to remove blood
1 carrot
1 stick celery
1 onion
parsley stalks
1¾ pints water

(Serves four)

Method

1. Prepare fish stock, putting all stock ingredients in a pan and simmer until reduced to 4 fl oz.

2. Steam the turbot fillets for 10-15 minutes approximately or until flesh is firm.

3. Simmer wine with saffron and reduce by one-third.

4. Add stock and lemon juice, then season.

5. Add lemon thyme leaves and simmer for 2 minutes before serving over steamed turbot fillets.

Pan-fried Loin of Woodland Roe Deer

on a bed of Savoury Lentils with a Wild Mushroom, Red Wine, Port and Thyme Essence

*Keith & Nicola Braidwood
Chefs
Shieldhill
Quothquan
Biggar*

INGREDIENTS:

4 x 8 oz portions saddle of roe deer
1 lb venison bones
½ bottle Shiraz red wine
¾ bottle Port
3 oz redcurrant jelly
1 fl oz red wine vinegar
1½ pints brown chicken stock
4 juniper berries
1 bunch thyme
4 dried morels
6 oz butter
8 oz lentil Du Puy
1 clove garlic
2 rashers back bacon
1 pint jellied chicken stock
2 large onions
8 large carrots
6 large potatoes
20 fine mangetout
6 oz mixed wild mushrooms

(Serves four)

METHOD

1. In a large pan brown off venison bones with chopped carrots and onions. Add the redcurrant jelly, vinegar, thyme and morels, then add the Port and half of the wine.

2. Continue cooking then slowly add the rest of the wine and the venison stock. Continue reducing then sieve through a fine strainer.

3. Cook the lentils in chicken stock with chopped garlic, bacon and shallots on a low heat until soft.

4. Boil the potatoes until well cooked. Strain, mash with cream and butter, season and put to one side until serving the dish.

5. Cook the prepared vegetables in boiling water with a little butter. Refresh until needed.

6. Sauté the roe deer until well sealed, then place in a hot oven GM7/220°C/425°F for 4-5 minutes. Use the venison pan to sauté mushrooms.

7. Finish the sauce with butter and thyme leaves and sauté wild mushrooms.

TO PRESENT

8. Place potatoes on top of plate with heated vegetables on top.

   Spoon the lentils into a ring on the centre of plate. Layer the sliced venison round the lentils.

9. Finish sauce with a little butter and adjust seasoning. Sauce the dish and serve.

Peach and Hazelnut Ice-Cream

with Quenelles of Tropical Fruits soaked in Benedictine on a light cream sauce

Paul Bergin
Sous Chef
Ardoe House
Hotel
Aberdeen

INGREDIENTS:

8 peaches
1 lemon
8 eggs
8 oz sugar
1 pint cream
4 oz hazelnuts (crushed)
4 fl oz Benedictine
1 kiwi fruit
1 mango
1 strawberry
1 papaya
4 mint leaves
3 fl oz Grand Marnier

CREAM SAUCE

¼ pint milk
¼ pint cream
1 vanilla pod
4 egg yolks
3 oz caster sugar

(Serves four)

METHOD

1. Purée peaches and lemon juice.
2. Whisk egg whites and half the sugar.
3. Whisk egg yolks and other half of sugar.
4. Whip the cream.
5. Crush the hazelnuts.
6. Combine puréed peaches with egg yolk and sugar mixture, then add the whipped cream and crushed hazelnuts. Lastly fold in the egg whites and sugar mixture.
7. Place mixture into metal rings and set for 1½ hours in freezer.
8. Cut the fruits into small dice at the last minute and soak in Benedictine.

CREAM SAUCE

9. Bring milk, cream and vanilla pod to the boil.
10. Whisk egg yolks and sugar until fluffy.
11. Add boiling milk to mixture.
12. Whisk for 10 seconds.
13. Return to heat and stir with wooden spoon until reaches consistency to coat back of spoon.
14. Strain and cool.
15. Add Grand Marnier.

TO SERVE

16. Remove ice cream from metal rings and set on plate with diced fruit and cream sauce, garnished with mint leaves.

Heather Honey and Bilberry Crème Brulée

Stewart Cameron Executive Chef Turnberry Hotel Turnberry

INGREDIENTS:

¾ pint double cream
3 egg yolks
½ oz sugar
1 oz heather honey
2 oz bilberries

(Serves four)

METHOD

1. Whisk egg yolks, sugar and heather honey in a bowl.
2. Boil the double cream and whisk into egg yolks.
3. Put ingredients back into the pan.
4. In the bottom of the ramekins place the bilberries.
5. Heat the mixture to 82°C very slowly.
6. Pass through a fine sieve and pour over the berries to fill the ramekins.
7. To serve, sprinkle with caster sugar and caramelise under the grill.

Parfait Flora MacDonald
an iced parfait with prunes, chocolate and nuts, flavoured with Drambuie

Patrick Freytag Head Chef/ Manager Manor House Hotel Oban

INGREDIENTS:

1 egg
2 egg yolks
4 oz caster sugar
1 leaf gelatine
8 oz tin of prunes
2 oz plain chocolate
3 oz chopped mixed nuts
      roasted with
      brown sugar
2 measures Drambuie
1 pint whipping cream

(Serves twelve)

METHOD

1. Place eggs, egg yolks and sugar in a stainless steel bowl.
2. Place bowl in hot water and whip contents until hot.
3. Remove from heat, add soaked gelatine and whip until cold.
4. Meanwhile stone prunes and slice them. Retain the liquid for sauce.
5. Grate the chocolate. Roast the nuts with brown sugar. Whip the cream.
6. Add whipped cream to the egg and sugar mixture.
7. Using a wooden spoon, slowly add chocolate, nuts, prunes and Drambuie.
8. Pour into loaf or baking tin and freeze.
9. To serve, cut 2 half inch slices per person and garnish with cream and a little of the liquid from the prunes.

Warm Ginger Pudding
with Heather Honey Almond Ice-Cream and a Toddie Sabayon

David Hunt
Head Chef
Auchterarder
House
Auchterarder

Ingredients:

Ice-Cream
4 egg yolks
3½ oz caster sugar
½ vanilla pod
4 fl oz double cream
8 fl oz milk
3-4 tablespoons heather
     honey
½ oz nibbed almonds

Pudding
3 oz butter
3 oz sugar
2 oz milk
1 teaspoon baking powder
1½ eggs
½ oz candied ginger
¾ teaspoon ginger powder

Sabayon
4 egg yolks
5 oz caster sugar
2 measures Glenturret
     whisky
4 fl oz Moniack Castle White
     Wine

Brandy Snap
8 oz caster sugar
4½ oz salted butter
4 oz plain white flour
pinch of ground ginger
4 oz golden syrup
1 tablespoon brandy

(Serves four)

Method

Ice-Cream
1. Cream 4 egg yolks and 3½ oz caster sugar.
2. Boil 9 fl oz of milk with half a vanilla pod and 4 fl oz double cream until infused.
3. Lightly toast almonds. Cool then add with honey to custard.
   Freeze this mixture.

Pudding
4. Cream sugar and butter, reserving some butter to grease pudding moulds.
5. Add beaten eggs gradually.
6. Add sieved flour, baking powder, powdered ginger and diced candied ginger.
7. Adjust consistency with milk.
8. Butter and sugar moulds then fill to three quarters full and bake in a water bath at GM4/180°C/350°F for 35-40 minutes.

Sabayon
9. Cream 4 egg yolks and 5 oz caster sugar. Add whisky and white wine and whip over bain marie until cooked.

Brandy Snap
10. Cream the sugar and butter in a processor.
11. Add the sieved flour and ginger.
12. Bring together with the syrup and brandy.
13. Roll into small balls and bake on a baking sheet for 5-8 minutes GM6/200°C/400°F. Remove and mould into saucer shapes and cool.
14. Turn out puddings, serve ice-cream in the 'saucers' and nap the sabayon over the puddings.

Summer Peaches
gently caramelised with Nuts and Heather Honey

Gary Bates
Executive Chef
Dalmahoy Hotel
Golf & Country
Club
Kirknewton
nr Edinburgh

INGREDIENTS:

4 tablespoons Heather Honey
2 oz sugar
3 oz butter
juice of ½ lemon
few drops of Grenadine
8 small peaches
2 oz hazelnuts, chopped
1 oz unsalted pistachio nuts

(Serves four)

METHOD

1. Place the sugar and butter in a shallow pan and set over a low heat to gently cook, stirring continuously with a wooden spoon.
2. When the mix becomes golden brown, remove from the heat and stir in the lemon, honey and Grenadine. Keep in a warm place.
3. Pre-heat the oven at GM9/240°C/475°F.
4. Bring a saucepan of water to the boil. Plunge the peaches for a few seconds, then skin them.
5. Place peaches on a roasting tray. Pour over the caramel and scatter over the hazelnuts.
6. Cook in a hot oven for about 10 minutes, basting them from time to time with the caramel.
7. Meanwhile split the pistachios in half and two minutes before the peaches are done, push a few pistachios into the peach flesh.
8. Sprinkle the remaining nuts into the sauce.

TO SERVE
9. Place two peaches on a large flat plate and gently spoon over the nutty caramel sauce.

The 1995 Taste of Scotland Guide

is scheduled to be published in November 1994.

To reserve a copy at a special post inclusive price, just complete the coupon below indicating your method of payment and send it to:

> Taste of Scotland (Guide Sales)
> 33 Melville Street
> Edinburgh EH3 7JF

You will be placed on the priority list to receive the Guide as soon as it is published. For your convenience, we now accept ACCESS and VISA

- ✂

To: Taste of Scotland (Guide Sales), 33 Melville Street, Edinburgh EH3 7JF

Please send ———— copy/copies of
the Taste of Scotland 1995 Guide and debit my ACCESS/MASTERCARD/VISA (please delete as appropriate)

Card No. ☐☐☐☐☐☐☐☐☐☐☐☐☐☐☐☐☐☐☐☐

Expiry Date   Month ———— Year ————

Account Name: ————————————————

Signature ————————————————

Please ✓ appropriate amount:

To addresses   in UK | £5.00 |
                      in Europe | £7.00 |
                      in North America | £8.00 |

Note: cheques in £ sterling also accepted

NAME: ————————————————————

ADDRESS:————————————————————

————————————————————————

————————————————————————

POST CODE: ———————————— COUNTRY: ————————

Block Capitals, Please

• Post inclusive prices to other countries availabile on request •

Taste of Scotland Guide

Taste of Scotland welcomes your recommendations on restaurants and hotels you have visited which you feel merit inclusion but are as yet not listed in the Taste of Scotland Guide.

THE ROMAN CAMP
COUNTRY HOUSE HOTEL

Nestling in the heart of the beautiful Trossachs, the Roman Camp Hotel offers a magical mixture of gracious living and historic atmosphere.

Surrounded by 20 acres of superb gardens on the banks of the River Teith, the hotel's picturesque interior reflects the original charm of this 17th century building.

All bedrooms have private bathrooms, and facilities which make for a welcoming, comfortable stay. Guests can enjoy peace and tranquillity in a truly unique style.

Fresh produce and fine wines will tempt the most discerning diner and friendly personal service creates an atmosphere of leisured living.

The Roman Camp invites you to relax and enjoy the warmest of welcomes and the greatest of pleasure.

For brochure, tariff and reservations write telephone or fax.

**The Roman Camp Hotel
Callander FK17 8BG
Telephone 0877-30003 Fax 0877-31533**

see entry page 57

see entry page 69

Somerton House Hotel

A handsome Victorian mansion, Somerton House is distinguished by unusual Kauri timber panelling from New Zealand and its 'Taste of Scotland' restaurant.

An interesting menu opens with flaked salmon and shrimps in a peppery seafood sauce served with tortilla chips, followed by dishes such as lamb with yoghurt and apricots, and oak-smoked trout with a hot horseradish sauce. Desserts include Ecclefechan Flan and Atholl Brose.

Hours: Open for coffee, lunch, tea and dinner.
Average Prices: A la Carte £10.50; Sunday Lunch £8.25; Snacks £3.40

Proprietors: Mr & Mrs A. Arthur
Somerton House Hotel, Carlisle Road,
Lockerbie, Dumfriesshire DG11 2DR
Tel 0576-202583/202384

RAC★★

AA ★★

see entry page 114

THE SANDFORD
COUNTRY HOUSE HOTEL

The Sandford Hotel, one of the Kingdom of Fife's most picturesque, listed, country house hotels, is renowned for its fine Scottish and European cuisine and comfortable accommodation.

Seasonal dishes in particular, served in the oak beamed restaurant, are the hallmark of Head Chef, Steven Johnstone. An extensive wine list has been carefully chosen in order to complement the variety of dishes on the extensive table d'hôte menu.

The Sandford is located near to both St Andrews and Dundee, and provides an ideal venue for those touring, fishing, golfing or shooting in this region of Scotland.

Bar Lunch 12.00 to 2.00 pm
Bar Supper and Dinner 6.00 to 9.30 pm
Open January to December (inclusive)
Languages: French, German, Italian

**The Sandford Country House Hotel
Newton Hill, Wormit, nr Dundee, Fife DD6 8RG
Tel 0382-541802 • Fax 0382-542136**

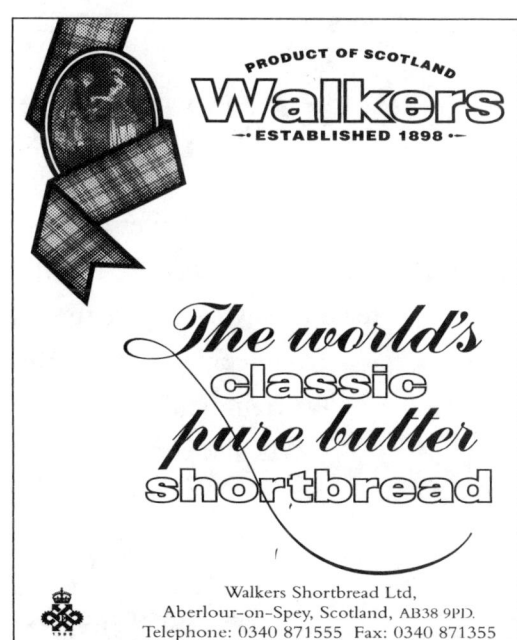

PRODUCT OF SCOTLAND

Walkers
•– ESTABLISHED 1898 •–

The world's classic pure butter shortbread

Walkers Shortbread Ltd,
Aberlour-on-Spey, Scotland, AB38 9PD.
Telephone: 0340 871555 Fax: 0340 871355

TRAQUAIR ARMS HOTEL

A traditional 19th Century Scottish Inn, just 30 minutes from Edinburgh and 10 from Peebles personally run by Hugh and Marian Anderson.

The very best of Scottish produce is used to prepare a wide range of meals served every day, from award winning Breakfasts to imaginative Dinners including Scottish High Teas with all home baked produce.

Borders Real Ales on hand-pumps in our relaxing Lounge complete with open log fires. Offering good value breaks in excellent en-suite accommodation all year round.

INNERLEITHEN, PEEBLESSHIRE EH44 6PD
TEL 0896-830229 • FAX 0896-830260

EGON RONAY "GOOD PUB GUIDE" • CAMRA "GOOD BEER GUIDE"
"BEER, BED & BREAKFAST" GUIDE

♛♛♛
STB Commended

see entry page 97

Send to: Taste of Scotland, 33 Melville Street, Edinburgh EH3 7JF

TASTE OF SCOTLAND PRESTIGE AWARD 1994

I nominate _____ (Establishment)
for a Taste of Scotland Prestige Award for the following category:
(Please tick <u>one</u> category only)

☐ Hotel of the Year   ☐ Country House Hotel of the Year

☐ Restaurant of the Year   ☐ Special Merit

Name _____

Address _____

_____

_____

Date of visit _____

Meal (if appropriate) _____

Closing date for entries: 31 August 1994

- ✄

Send to: Taste of Scotland, 33 Melville Street, Edinburgh EH3 7JF

TASTE OF SCOTLAND PRESTIGE AWARD 1994

I nominate _____ (Establishment)
for a Taste of Scotland Prestige Award for the following category:
(Please tick <u>one</u> category only)

☐ Hotel of the Year   ☐ Country House Hotel of the Year

☐ Restaurant of the Year   ☐ Special Merit

Name _____

Address _____

_____

_____

Date of visit _____

Meal (if appropriate) _____

Closing date for entries: 31 August 1994

Comments on meals in places listed in

The Taste of Scotland Guide are welcomed.

Send to Taste of Scotland, 33 Melville Street, Edinburgh EH3 7JF

94
O
E

Establishment visited

Date   Meal

Comments

Name

Address

✂ -

Comments on meals in places listed in

The Taste of Scotland Guide are welcomed.

Send to Taste of Scotland, 33 Melville Street, Edinburgh EH3 7JF

94
O
E

Establishment visited

Date   Meal

Comments

Name

Address

Send to: Taste of Scotland, 33 Melville Street, Edinburgh EH3 7JF

TASTE OF SCOTLAND PRESTIGE AWARD 1994

I nominate _____ (Establishment)
for a Taste of Scotland Prestige Award for the following category:
(Please tick <u>one</u> category only)

☐ Hotel of the Year   ☐ Country House Hotel of the Year

☐ Restaurant of the Year   ☐ Special Merit

Name _____

Address _____

_____

_____

Date of visit _____

Meal (if appropriate) _____

Closing date for entries: 31 August 1994

- ✂

Send to: Taste of Scotland, 33 Melville Street, Edinburgh EH3 7JF

TASTE OF SCOTLAND PRESTIGE AWARD 1994

I nominate _____ (Establishment)
for a Taste of Scotland Prestige Award for the following category:
(Please tick <u>one</u> category only)

☐ Hotel of the Year   ☐ Country House Hotel of the Year

☐ Restaurant of the Year   ☐ Special Merit

Name _____

Address _____

_____

_____

Date of visit _____

Meal (if appropriate) _____

Closing date for entries: 31 August 1994

Comments on meals in places listed in
The Taste of Scotland Guide are welcomed.
Send to Taste of Scotland, 33 Melville Street, Edinburgh EH3 7JF

94
O
E

Establishment visited

Date   Meal

Comments

Name

Address

✂ --

Comments on meals in places listed in
The Taste of Scotland Guide are welcomed.
Send to Taste of Scotland, 33 Melville Street, Edinburgh EH3 7JF

94
O
E

Establishment visited

Date   Meal

Comments

Name

Address

TIRORAN HOUSE

You will be enchanted by this small remote country house set in beautiful woodland grounds which sweep down to the shores of Loch Scridain. It offers the warmest welcome to those seeking to explore the lovely islands of Mull, Iona and Staffa, or those wishing to enjoy peace and relaxation in the most perfect surroundings. The comfort and cuisine are both traditional and of a very high standard.

 E G O N
RONAY'S
GUIDES

Taste of Scotland 'Good Hotel Guide'
Good Food Guide

Resident Proprietors: Sue & Robin Blockey

ISLE OF MULL, ARGYLL
TEL (TIRORAN) 06815-232

see entry page 119

Index – 1994

Page

EDITOR
NANCY K CAMPBELL BA

PUBLISHED BY
TASTE OF SCOTLAND SCHEME LTD,
A NON-PROFIT MAKING COMPANY LIMITED BY GUARANTEE TRADING AS TASTE OF SCOTLAND

DESIGN, ILLUSTRATION & TYPESETTING
DAVID FRAME CREATIVE
EDINBURGH

PRINTED BY
MACDONALD LINDSAY PINDAR PLC
LOANHEAD

COVER PHOTOGRAPH – LOCHAIN NA H'ACHLAISE & THE BLACK MOUNT, RANNOCH MOOR

COLOUR PHOTOGRAPHY
COURTESY OF

ABERDEEN TOURIST BOARD
AYRSHIRE TOURIST BOARD
CLYDE VALLEY TOURIST BOARD
DUMFRIES AND GALLOWAY TOURIST BOARD
FORTH VALLEY TOURIST BOARD
GREATER GLASGOW TOURIST BOARD
HIGHLANDS & ISLANDS ENTERPRISE
INVERNESS, LOCH NESS & NAIRN TOURIST BOARD

MIDLOTHIAN TOURISM/JAMES GARDINER ASSOCIATES
MORAY TOURIST BOARD/ANNE BURGESS
THE MORGAN PARTNERSHIP
ORKNEY TOURIST BOARD/RICHARD WELSBY
PERTHSHIRE TOURIST BOARD
ST ANDREWS & N.E. FIFE TOURIST BOARD
SCOTTISH BORDERS TOURIST BOARD
SHETLAND ISLANDS TOURIST BOARD

WESTERN ISLES TOURIST BOARD

TASTE OF SCOTLAND SCHEME LTD.
33 MELVILLE STREET
EDINBURGH EH3 7JF
TEL: 031 220 1900
FAX: 031 220 6102

ISBN 1 871445 05 1

YUKON:
PLACES & NAMES

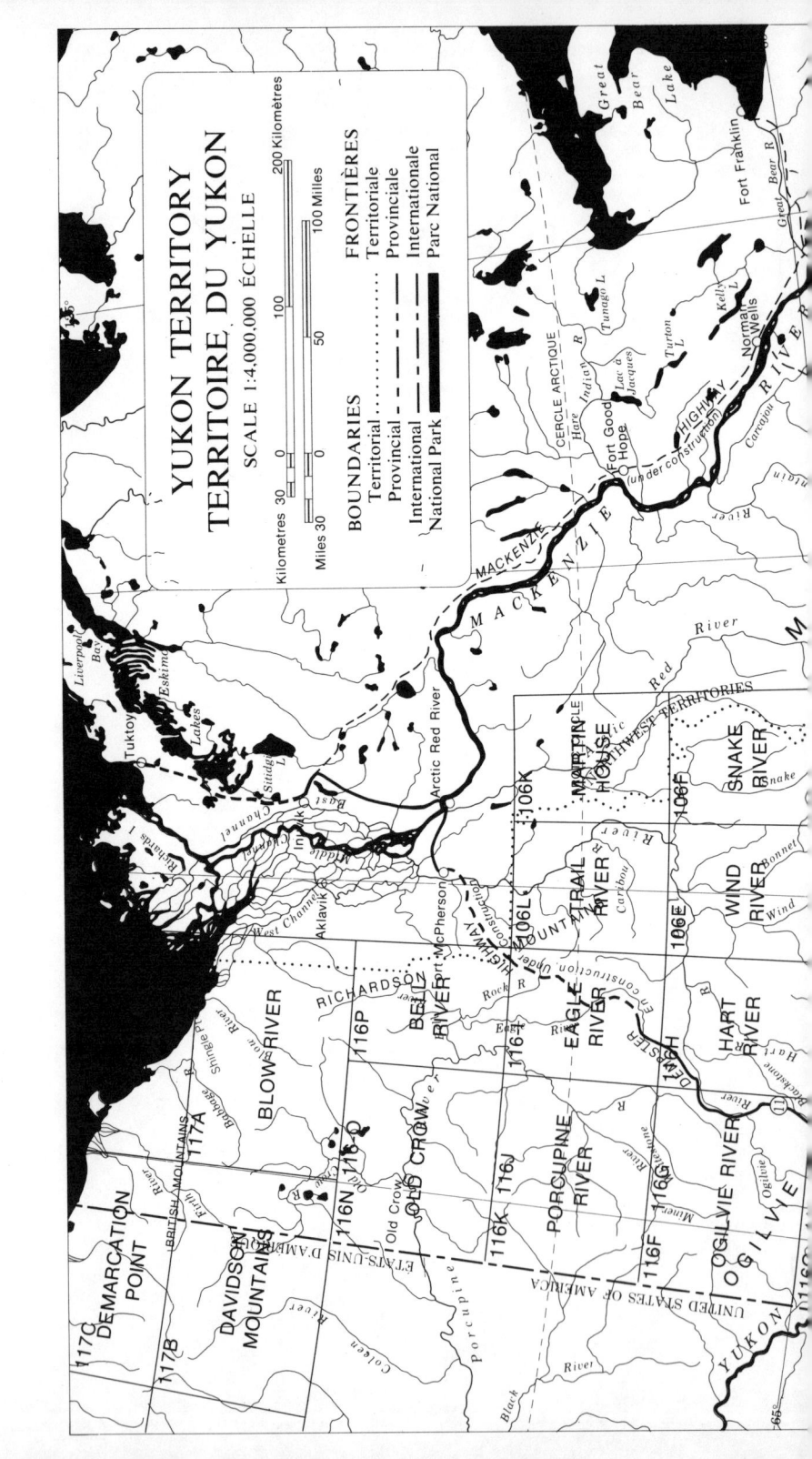

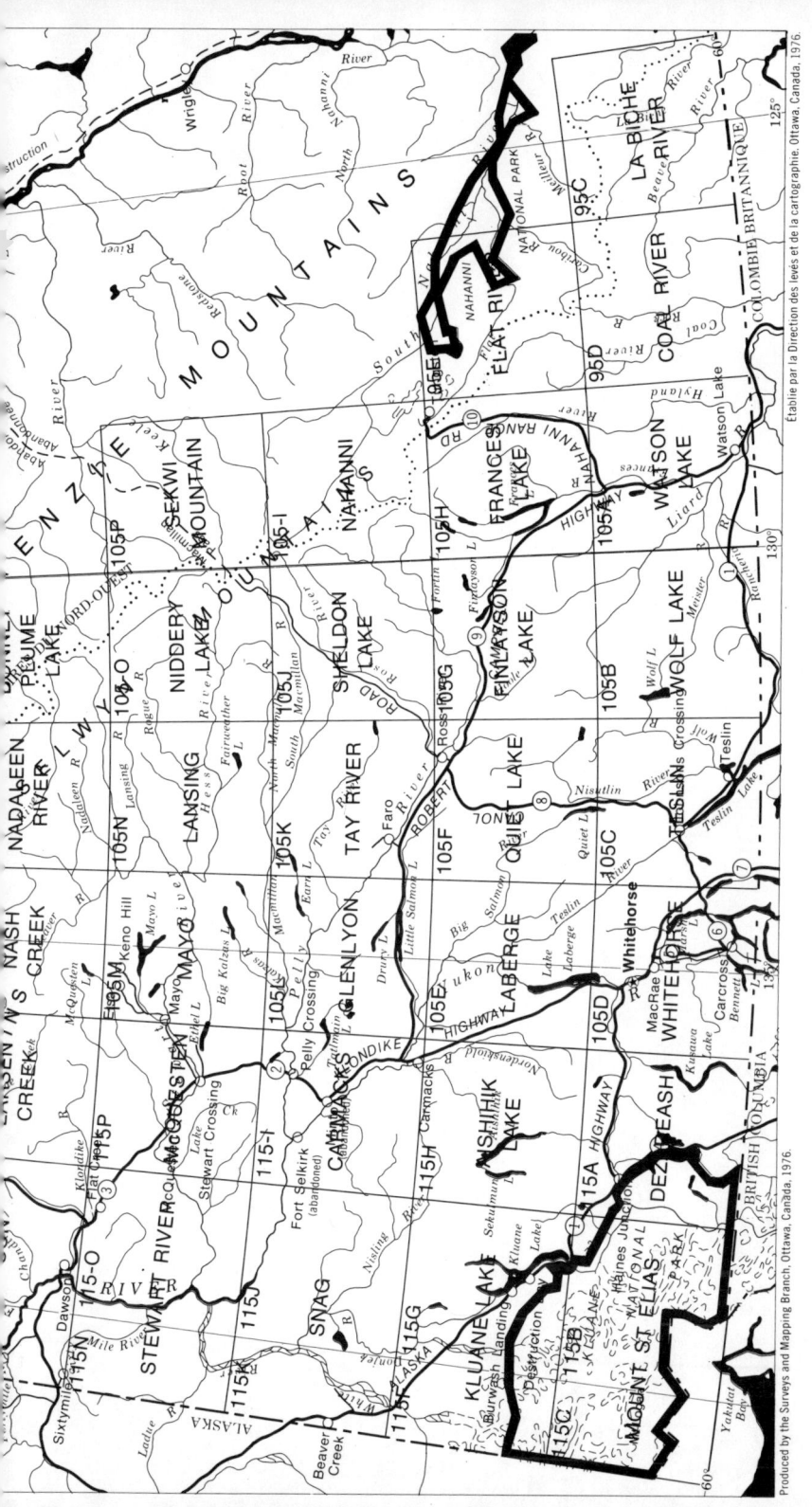

Produced by the Surveys and Mapping Branch, Ottawa, Canada, 1976.

Établie par la Direction des levés et de la cartographie, Ottawa, Canada, 1976.

YUKON:
PLACES & NAMES

R.C. Coutts

 Gray's Publishing Limited,
Sidney, British Columbia,
Canada.

Cover photograph courtesy of Public Affairs Bureau, Yukon Government.

Design and typesetting by The Typeworks, Mayne Island, B.C.

Index map reproduced with permission of the Surveys and Mapping Branch, Department of Energy, Mines and Resources, Ottawa.

Names listed in this book are normally found on maps of the National Topographic Series, scale 1:250,000.

Indexes and ordering instructions can be obtained free of charge from:

> Canada Map Office,
> Surveys and Mapping Branch,
> Department of Energy, Mines & Resources,
> 615 Booth Street,
> Ottawa, Ontario.
> K1A 0E9

Canadian Cataloguing in Publication Data

Coutts, Robert C., 1918–
  Yukon: Places & Names

  ISBN 0-88826-085-7 hardcover
  ISBN 0-88826-082-2 paperback
  1. Names, Geographical — Yukon Territory.
2. Yukon Territory — History, Local. I. Title.
FC4006.C68   917.19′1′0032   C80-091167-9
F1093.C68

FOREWORD

For any country, its names are a part of its history. From the beginning they have been a necessity; they are the means by which inhabitants and particularly explorers tell others where they have been and what they have seen. Indeed, without names, maps, records and books would be unintelligible.

When we see names in books or on maps we often take them for granted, thoughtless of asking ourselves whence they came or whether there is a meaningful story in their origin; but if we are curious, where do we find out? Heretofore, there has been no handy reference for this information on names of the Yukon Territory which, with its growth of population and expanding development, badly needs a published record of the history of its names. In *Yukon: Places & Names*, Robert C. Coutts gives us a book which fills this need admirably.

For him, its compilation has been a labour of love, occupying years of research through old manuscripts, maps, books and all sorts of sources of information including mining records and private diaries. This work has taken him to many parts of Canada and to the United States in his hunt for original sources of names. From this he has produced a convenient alphabetical list of Yukon names, giving the features they apply to, their locations and historical background. In many instances this includes tales of the men who discovered the features, how they chose the names and who or what the names commemorate, in addition to accounts of those whose names the features bear. The author gives historical accounts not only of the well known, established names in common usage but also of lonely creeks and hills, and long-abandoned localities in the hinterlands rarely now remembered, whose stories fade with passing years.

Besides supplying the history of these out-of-the-way places, this volume will make a most useful contribution to resurrecting these old names. When new strikes are made on old ground, where the early names were in obscure records and generally unknown, newcomers are prone to introduce new names. But here is a bulwark against such errors. Throughout its length the book by its very nature supplies a store of historical notes and fills an important place among the historical references for the Yukon Territory.

Five years of experience as representative for the Yukon Territory on the Canadian Board on Geographical Names gave me a very real appreciation of the need for such a work as this book and it gives me great satisfaction that this need has now been so well filled. The author points out that a number of names are omitted for lack of information and almost daily we see more new names established. It is my earnest hope that as time goes on, revised editions, in the same style but containing the missing names and giving the new ones, will follow, keeping the record up to date.

Hugh S. Bostock

Ottawa

INTRODUCTION

"Names are the pegs from which history is hung."
Henry Schoolcraft.

The work contained in this book began about ten years ago as a hobby. When first prospecting in the southwest Yukon and Cassiar country, I was naturally interested in the history of an area about which I had read and been told so much. Becoming curious about the origin or meaning of a Yukon place name, I found that there was often no answer, or conflicting ones. Alone of Canada's provinces and territories almost nothing has been written on this subject. On reading the early literature it often appeared that the modern name was often not that given originally and that in many cases the name and its meaning had been altered or changed. I began to search for the true origins of these names. Gradually, the people and the stories behind the names began to live for me and many were more interesting than much of the fiction written about the territory. As the stories unfolded and extended, my interest became more serious but no less enjoyable. Many newly learned facts revealed other stories and puzzles to be traced and solved.

The stories set down here are almost entirely contained in the written accounts of those who took part in or were close to the events. Little is from hearsay, unless confirmed by other statements or accounts. In cases of conflict the earliest or most obvious story is given; in some cases, two or more equally reliable but differing accounts are recorded and the reader may choose between them.

The stories of most of the early explorers are well known, but those of the common people who opened and developed the country are often remembered only in the name of a feature where they pioneered. As the builders of a country their lives should not be forgotten. This is an attempt to record some of these stories.

This Yukon is a hard and demanding country. For the most part it has always attracted the more self-reliant, individualistic and adventurous types of people. Most asked little of others but gave freely of themselves. They were people worth knowing and people worth remembering.

The first known white man to set foot in the Yukon Territory was John Franklin, the famous English Arctic explorer. During his second expedition, in 1826, he travelled the Arctic coast from the mouth of the Mackenzie River westward into what is now Alaska. Many of the Yukon's coastal features, including Herschel Island, were named by him at that time. However, the first feature in the Yukon to be given a name by white men was Mount St. Elias in the southwest corner of the territory. Seen from the sea on St. Elias Day, 16 July, 1741, it was named by Vitus Bering while he was exploring the coast of Alaska for the Russian government.

The next group of names was given in the period between 1839 and 1850. Robert Campbell of the Hudson's Bay Company entered the central Yukon by way of the Liard, Frances and Pelly Rivers. Campbell established the courses of the Frances, Pelly and Yukon Rivers and built trading posts on or near each of them. He named these rivers and many of their tributaries. Later in the same period John Bell and Alexander Hunter Murray, of the same company, crossed the northern Yukon from the Mackenzie River and established Lapierre's House and later Fort Yukon.

From 1880 on, the early prospector-miners arrived, and in their wanderings gave names to many of the streams where they won gold and to the mountains they used as landmarks. Up to this time the prospectors and explorers retained many of the old native names.

Lieutenant Frederick Schwatka of the United States Army came over the Chilkoot Pass and rafted quickly down the Yukon River in June and July 1883, conducting the first rough survey of its course. Ignoring the names known to the natives, traders and miners he renamed most of the principal streams, lakes and outstanding features along the river after his army superiors and prominent academicians of his day.

Dr. George M. Dawson, Director of the Geological and Natural History Survey of Canada (and one of Canada's outstanding explorer-geologists), in 1887 ascended the Liard and Frances Rivers from the Stikine, and descended the Pelly to its junction with the Yukon, surveying the river and topography as he went. His maps and reports, which included all available information concerning the territory and its inhabitants, were of such high quality that they are still classics of their kind today. He repudiated much of Schwatka's nomenclature, retaining many of the original names.

William Ogilvie, DLS, of the Department of the Interior, ran a precise survey in 1887–88 from Pyramid Harbor near Haines, Alaska, up Chilkoot Inlet to Dyea and over the Chilkoot Pass to Lake Bennett. From Bennett he carried his survey down the Yukon River to the Yukon-Alaska boundary below Fortymile; these were the first accurate surveys made of the route through the central Yukon. He then cut the Yukon-Alaska boundary line from the Yukon River south through the Fortymile and Sixtymile Rivers country, thus settling any disputes as to the national ownership of the rich placer goldfields then being exploited there. He later settled the first disputes as to claim ownership on Bonanza Creek in the Klondike in the fall of 1896. Ogilvie, who was to become the first Commissioner of the Yukon Territory, named a number of prominent peaks after the pioneer prospectors of the Yukon whom he admired, and a number of streams after geological phenomena observed on them.

The Klondike Gold Rush years of 1896–99 saw hundreds of names added to the maps as thousands of gold-seekers overran the country. The custom of the times allowed the first man who found gold and staked the Discovery claim on any creek (the first claim on a stream was double the size of a regular claim) to give it any name he chose. In many cases where the miner was ignorant of this custom the Mining Recorder supplied the name for him.

Other and later mining rushes and stampedes to various parts of the territory added still more names to the maps. Many creeks and lakes were named locally after the trappers, traders and prospectors who made their homes on them. The Geological Survey of Canada has, since Dawson's time, added many names as its geologists mapped the rocks of the region. The Alpine Club of Canada and various institutional mountaineering expeditions have named many of the peaks in the St. Elias Range of the southwestern Yukon. Construction workers of the Alaska Highway and the Canol Pipeline added their share of new names.

The last large group of names was acquired in the 1960–70 period, when the Surveys and Mapping Branch of the Department of Energy, Mines and Resources was preparing its 1:50,000 scale topographical maps. (This project has yet to be completed). As each sheet is titled by the name of a central feature, any that were without such names were given those of early Yukoners. Gordon McIntyre, Yukon Lands Titles Agent and later Member of the Yukon Legislative Assembly was responsible for most of the research. He ensured the perpetuation of the names of many nearly forgotten pioneers.

A continuing class of names is that honouring many Yukoners who died in foreign wars. Individual names have been and are being proposed and adopted with the approval of the Territorial Government and the Canada Permanent Committee on Geographical Names (also known as the Canadian Board on Geographical Names or the Geographical Board).

In no way is this book anything but a beginning. There are still many names for which no information has been found. There are many gaps yet to be filled. Over the years many records have been lost or misplaced and are no longer available. It is my earnest hope that any readers who possess any part of this missing information will share it with the Yukon Archives or with me: it will be received with appreciation. With this help, in time a new and more comprehensive work can be prepared.

R.C. Coutts
Atlin, B.C.

ACKNOWLEDGEMENTS

It is doubtful if any book is solely the work of any one person. Certainly this one is not. Although I have gathered the material together, it would have been a much smaller work without the active help and encouragement of many other people.

My good friend Hugh S. Bostock, Ph.D., gentleman, scientist and bushman, whose 40 years work with the Geological Survey of Canada in the Yukon Territory makes him an authority which he is quick to disclaim, encouraged me steadily. His expert advice and incisive criticism kept me searching for the right answers.

Mrs. Helen Akrigg, herself an authority on such matters, took an interest at the beginning and sponsored my application for a Canada Council grant.

Brian Speirs, the first Archivist of the Yukon Territory and my second sponsor, has encouraged this work from the start and helped in every way to obtain obscure material as well as providing facilities for working. His successor, Linda Johnson, has continued this interest. Diane Johnston, Assistant Archivist, has given much of her own time and thought to finding necessary material over the past four years.

Ron D'Altroy, Curator of Photography at the Vancouver Public Library and an old and valued friend, has contributed much both in ideas and material over the years, for which I thank him.

My gratitude must be expressed to the Explorations Programme of the Canada Council and in particular to Paul-Emile Leblac, Executive Officer, whose patience with amateur writers seems endless. The grant enabled me to do much of the original research for this work.

Appreciation must be expressed to my friends the rare-book dealers, whose advice and assistance in finding almost-unknown material was and is invaluable, particularly to John W. Todd, Jr. of Shorey's in Seattle, David Moon of West Vancouver, Stephen McIntyre and Bill Hoffer of Vancouver and the late R. Hilton Smith of Victoria. Each one has persistently searched for and found material previously unknown to bibliographers.

My gratitude also goes to the many institutions which gave me access to their northern collections, especially to Ann Yandel of UBC and Andy Johnson of the University of Washington, the BC Provincial and the Public Archives of Canada, the people of the Glenbow-Alberta Institute in Calgary and others too numerous to list here.

The foundation for this work was laid at the offices of the Canada Permanent Committee for Geographical Names in Ottawa with the active encouragement and help of Gordon Delaney, the Executive Secretary and his assistant Frank Stevenson who bore with my many questions and requests for many weeks. This interest and help has been continued by Allan Rayburn, the present Executive Secretary.

Mrs. Shirley Connolly, founder and past president of the Atlin Historical Society, aided materially from her own personal knowledge of the Yukon and the people in the Ross River country. Mrs. Sue Morhun, the present president of the society, gave me sound professional advice in putting the material into manuscript form.

To all these friends, thank you.

LOCATING THE FEATURES LISTED

All features named in this work are listed alphabetically. Their positions are based on the National Topographic Series of maps, scale 1:250,000 (1 inch = 4 miles), which gives a complete coverage of the Yukon Territory using 45 separate map sheets. They are available at most territorial government offices. Each of these sheets is known by sheet name and sheet number, e.g. Dawson 116-B&C, Whitehorse 105D.

These maps are plotted in degrees and minutes of latitude and longitude which increase to the north and west from the bottom right-hand corner of the sheet. Using these figures the location of any place is easily and quickly obtained. Settlement locations are pin-pointed. The figures given for a mountain are those of its highest point. Those for lakes are at the centre of the lake; those for rivers and creeks are given at the mouth of the stream.

In this work a rough description of the location is given after the map sheet number.

ABBREVIATIONS USED IN THE TEXT

ACC	The Alaska Commercial Company
CEF	Canadian Expeditionary Forces. (The Canadian Army overseas during the First World War.)
CPCGN	Canada Permanent Committee on Geographical Names.
CIMM	Canadian Institute of Mining and Metallurgy.
CMG	Companion of the Order of St. Michael and St. George. (A British Order of Chivalry.) This is a sort of Long Service and Good Conduct Medal awarded to senior civil servants and their equivalents in the armed forces.
DFC	Distinguished Flying Cross. Awarded for bravery in action by officers of British Air Forces.
DFM	Distinguished Flying Medal. Awarded for bravery in action by non-commissioned officers of British Air Forces.
DLS	Dominion Land Surveyor.
DSM	Distinguished Service Medal. An American decoration for service, both civilian and military.
DSO	Distinguished Service Order. A British award for exceptional leadership by officers against an enemy.

DTS	Dominion Topographical Surveyor. The most highly qualified degree for Canadian surveyors.
FASAS	Fellow of the American Society for the Advancement of Science.
FRGS	Fellow of the Royal Geographical Society.
FRS	Fellow of the Royal Society. This is Britian's most prestigious society for science and scholarship.
FRSC	Fellow of the Royal Society of Canada. (The Canadian equivalent of the Royal Society.)
G&NHSC	Geological and Natural History Survey of Canada.
GSC	The Geological Survey of Canada.
HBC	The Governor and Company of Adventurers of England Trading into Hudson's Bay. As a business title it was more simply called The Hudson's Bay Company: colloquially called "The Bay".
KCMG	Knight Commander of the Order of St. Michael and St. George. A British Order of Chivalry awarded for most distinguished services in any field. It carries a knighthood.
MC	The Military Cross. Awarded to officers of the British armies for bravery in action.
MID	Mentioned in Dispatches. A citation for outstanding conduct during a military operation by any member of the British forces.
MM	The Military Medal. Awarded to non-commissioned officers and men of the British armies for bravery in action.
MP	Member of Parliament.
NAT&TC	North American Transportation and Trading Company. They built Fort Cudahy at Fortymile in 1893.
NCO	Non-Commissioned Officer. (Corporals, Sergeants, Warrant Officers, etc. in any police or armed force.)
NWMP	North-West Mounted Police (1873–1904).
NWT	North West Territories. Before June 1898 the Yukon Territory was part of the NWT.
OBE	Order of the British Empire.
PEng	Professional Engineer. A member of the association of Professional Engineers.
RCMP	Royal Canadian Mounted Police (1920–).
RGS	The Royal Geographical Society. A prestigious British society for the advancement of geographical exploration.

RN	Royal Navy.
RNWMP	The Royal North-West Mounted Police (1904–1920).
RCN	Royal Canadian Navy.
RCAF	Royal Canadian Air Force.
T&D	Taylor and Drury's. A retail store company.
USCGS	The United States Coast and Geodetic Survey.
USGS	United States Geological Survey.
YOOP	The Yukon Order of Pioneers. A society or brotherhood formed by early Yukoners at Fortymile in 1894, of those who had come in the country before 1887. Still active, its membership requirement is now 11 years residence in the Yukon watershed.

HOW TO NAME A FEATURE IN THE YUKON TERRITORY

It is the privilege of any person or organization to ask that a chosen name be given to any feature in the Yukon Territory. There are definite rules of procedure to be followed to make the name official. A booklet prepared by the Committee on Geographical Names, which outlines advice and requirements, may be obtained by writing to:

The Secretary,
Canada Permanent Committee on Geographical Names,
Department of Energy, Mines and Resources,
615 Booth Street,
Ottawa, Ontario, Canada.

Briefly, the requirements for naming a feature are as follows:

1. Names proposed must be for specific geographic features. The committee does not normally select features for naming;

2. The following information should be supplied for all names or name changes proposed:

(a) Location — by latitude and longitude (specify the map you are using), map reference, sketch or photograph;

(b) Feature identification — indicate the extent as precisely as possible by colour, arrows, or description relative to adjoining features;

(c) If new name(s), supply also
    1. origin,
    2. reasons for proposing,
    3. evidence that the feature is unnamed;

(d) If changing existing name(s), supply also
    1. alternate name(s),
    2. reasons for proposed change(s).

ABRAHAM CREEK 63°32'N 139°57'W (115-O).A tributary to the Sixtymile River.

This stream was named after Harry ABRAHAM who mined 27 placer gold claims here from 1913 to 1925 and who had probably prospected in the area much earlier.

ACLAND CREEK 60°18'N 127°29'W (95-D). Flows into the Coal River.

In 1956 G. Rowley named this stream in honour of Sgt. Arthur Edward ACLAND, RNWMP, who was in this area about 1910. He was later in charge of the police post at Kluane in 1912-14.

MOUNT ADAMI 4,158' 63°19'N 138°02'W (115-O).45 miles up the Stewart River on the south side.

F.A. Stretch, Warden at Carmacks, named this hill after Frank ADAMI, long-time Yukoner who had trapped this area from 1936-57. Adami came from a good background, holding three degrees in chemistry and physics from Milwaukee and the Sorbonne but he preferred the solitary life of a trapper to any other. He died in Vancouver, BC, in 1958.

ADAMS CREEK 63°56'N 139°20'W (115-O&N). A small stream entering Bonanza Creek from the west, a short distance above the mouth.

Orginally called ADAMS Gulch, probably by Carlo Tilly who was the first man to stake a claim on it on 31 August, 1896, this little stream was staked immediately after Bonanza and at the same time as Eldorado. The first miners found little gold on it, showing the chanciness of placer mining. However, two years later in 1898 new miners tried again and did find payable gold.

AFE CREEK 62°17'N 135°53'W (105-L). Flows into the Tatchun River.

This was named about 1954 after AFE Brown, pioneer packer, trapper and miner in this area for many years. Acknowledged a superior man by his contemporaries, he was well-liked and respected by all who knew him. He died in 1952 at a sawmill owned by his two sons, at the mouth of the nearby Tatchun River. This creek had been called by his name by the local people long before he died.

AFE PEAK 5,662' 62°15'N 135°22'W (105-L). At the headwaters of Afe Creek.

AFE Brown was further commemorated by the giving of his name to this peak in 1954.

AHVEE MOUNTAIN   3,701' 67°10'N 139°47'W (116-O&N). 28 miles south of Old Crow.

Long known to the people of Old Crow, this is a Vanta Kutchin Indian word meaning "Weasel".

AISHIHIK LAKE   61°25'N 137°07'W (115-H). 100 miles northwest of Whitehorse.

This is an old Indian name meaning "High Place." The lake is 35 miles long and, at an elevation of 3,001' above sea level, is the highest lake of comparable size in all of Canada. A long-time Indian community of the same name on the north shore was abandoned after 1967.

A hydro-electric power dam was recently built at the foot of the lake and, since early 1976, has supplied electricity to the Yukon power grid.

Other sources claim the Indian name means "Big Lake". This is unlikely but if so, it makes the present name redundant.

ALASKA HIGHWAY   1523 miles from Mile "O" at Dawson Creek, BC to Fairbanks, Alaska, of which 1221 miles are in Canada. A paved road in Alaska, the Canadian section is about 90% an all-weather, 30-foot-wide, gravel highway traversing some of the most beautiful scenery in North America.

Since the early 1900's various groups in Canada and the US had pressed for a highway to Alaska. In 1930 the US government established the Alaska International Highway Commission and in 1931 a similar body was set up by the Canadian government to study the location, financing and construction of such a road.

Finally, two major routes were chosen. Route "A" started from Vancouver, BC and went through Prince George, Hazelton, Telegraph Creek and Atlin to Whitehorse: 1275 miles approximately. Route "B" went through Prince George, Fort St. James, Dease Lake, and Atlin to Whitehorse: 1250 miles approximately. Several other routes were proposed for special or local reasons. The major reason advanced for constructing such a road was the advantage of a land link to Alaska in time of war. The major problem was always financing.

In February 1942, the American armed forces, ignoring all previous studies and plans, chose the present and, until then, unconsidered route. The need for an access and service road for the string of airfields being built between Edmonton and Fairbanks to supply Russia with aircraft was immediate; local and future economic needs of the region were of no importance. An agreement with the Canadian government was quickly reached.

Surveys were started the same month and by April 1942 construction had begun. Round-the-clock work by 9,000 US Army Engineers saw a usable truck road pushed through by late November. Following the troops came the civilian contractors, 77 of them; 62 American and 15 Canadian firms employed 12,000 men to bring the road up to standard by late 1943. In all, 7,000 pieces of equipment were used.

The US government paid all construction costs and the cost of maintenance up to 1 April, 1946, when the Canadian section was turned over to the Canadian Army Engineers. The airfields and land communication systems were turned over to the RCAF at the same time. The road was maintained until 1965 by the Canadian Army Engineers and from that date by the Departments of Highways of the Yukon Territory and British Columbia, with federal assistance. The total cost of the highway to April 1946 was never revealed but estimates place it above $138,000,000.

Officially and originally named the "Alaska Military Highway", the men on the job soon shortened this to "The Alcan". Neither name was popular with the public, which had followed the construction with great interest. On 25 March, 1943, Anthony J. Dimond, Congressman from Alaska, proposed the name "The Alaska Highway", which was officially adopted by both governments on 19 July, 1943. (Dimond had been a long-time backer of Route "A").

The speed of construction, the location and climate all make this project one of the great engineering feats of our time. As shorter and more economical routes are being built closer to the Pacific coast, the highway will gradually lose its overall importance but never its history or impact on the Yukon and central Alaska, where its opening heralded the end of an era.

ALBERT CREEK 60°03′N 128°54′W(105-A). A tributary of the Liard River, crossing the Alaska Highway at mile 643 (K1029).

This is a long-known local name after ALBERT Death, an old-time packer and trapper in the area for many years.

MOUNT ALBERTA 10,985′ 60°56′N 140°51′W(115-B&C). In the Centennial Range of the St. Elias Mountains.

This was named in 1967 to celebrate Canada's Centennial year. (See the Centennial Range.)

ALKI CREEK   64°04'N 138°59'W(116-B&C). A small stream entering the Klondike River 20 miles from Dawson.

A.E. Elliott, who had come from Seattle to Skagway in the old steamer *ALKI* found gold, staked the Discovery claim and named this creek on 24 November, 1897.

ALLAN CREEK   60°30'N 129°45'W(105-A). Flows into the Liard River 40 miles northwest of Watson Lake.

This was a long-used local name after Fred ALLAN who trapped here for many years. A striking character, he resembled Buffalo Bill Cody, was a crack shot with pistol or rifle and preferred an isolated life in the bush. In the early 1900's he and George Adsit (reputed to have been a member of Butch Cassidy's Hole-in-the-Wall Gang) drove a herd of horses overland from Montana to Teslin Lake.

ALLGOLD CREEK   63°57'N 136°27'W(115-O&N). A short creek running from King Solomon's Dome to the Klondike River.

Clinton Jones staked and optimistically named this creek on 10 September, 1897. He was mistaken. Although it is in the Klondike and lies between rich placer gold creeks, it produced almost no gold at all.

ALMSTROM CREEK   68°07'N 136°27'W(117-A). A tributary to Cache Creek from the east.

This stream was named in 1973 after Edward ALMSTROM, officer in charge of Water Surveys in the Yukon from 1949 to 52 and Mining Inspector until 1972.

ALSEK RIVER   59°27'N 137°53'W(115-A). Flows from the Kluane Ranges through the St. Elias Mountains and into the Pacific south of Yakutat Bay.

It is a rough and almost impassable stream. The native name "Alsekh" was reported by the Russian Captain Tebenkov in 1825. Earlier, La Pérouse, the French explorer, in 1786 had named it "Rivière du Behring". The New York Times Expedition in 1886 (led by Lt. F. Schwatka) had named it the "Jones" River after one of Schwatka's sponsors. The USCGS called it the "Harrison" River in honour of a president of the US. The US and Canadian governments in 1891 officially gave it back its original and present name.

The first white men to explore the river were the members of the Frank Leslie Illustrated Newspaper Expedition, Edward James Glave and Jack

Dalton, who travelled it by canoe from Neskataheen (near Dalton House) to the sea in 1890, the only men ever to do so.

ALVERSON GULCH 64°06'N 135°02'W(106-D). A small tributary of Scougale Creek in the Davidson Range.

Jack Alverson, who came into the Yukon in 1899, lived and prospected on this creek. Originally from Oregon, he spent most of his life here and about the upper Stewart River country. In 1910 he and his partner, Grant Hoffman, mined 59 tons of high-grade, silver-lead ore, the first ever mined in the Mayo district. The ore body had been found in 1906 by H.W. McWhorter and was the first such ore found in the Mayo area.

MOUNT ALVERSTONE 14,565' 60°22'N 139°02'W(115-B&C). In the St. Elias Range close to the Yukon-Alaska boundary.

This was named in 1908 by the Canadian government after Baron ALVERSTONE, Lord Chief Justice of England and the British member of the Canadian-Alaskan Boundary Tribunal of 1903. He cast the vote which established the present boundary between Canada and Alaska, effectively cutting off the Yukon and the northern half of British Columbia from access to the Pacific except through US territory. He was acting on orders from the British government which had been informed secretly by American President Theodore Roosevelt that if the vote went against the US he would send troops to seize all the disputed areas. Alverstone voted as ordered.

AMERICAN GULCH 63°57'N 139°16'W(115-O & N). Just ¼ mile long, this little brook enters Bonanza Creek on the west side, a mile below Eldorado Creek.

It was staked entirely by American prospectors. B.H. Laughlin and his brother Chester made the discovery and staked the first two claims on 20 August, 1897.

On 15 June, 1904, a gold nugget was found here which, it was claimed, weighed 450 ounces. This would be by far the largest nugget ever found in the Yukon except that a certain amount of quartz was associated with the gold in the nugget and no true weight was ever announced.

AMMERMAN MOUNTAIN 68°23'N 141°00'W(117-B). A high ridge running east-west and centred on the Yukon-Alaska border.

This is a local name, probably after a trapper-prospector in the area, reported in 1911 by the International Boundary Control Survey crew, from the name of a creek which flows along the base of the ridge.

ANDERSON CREEK 61°34'N 129°25'W(105-H). Joins the Thomas River at the head of the east arm of Frances Lake.

Although this area was travelled from the 1840's and smaller streams named, no one found this creek until, in 1949, it was named to honour the memory of First Lt. P.M. ANDERSON RN, DSC, MID, killed in action in the Second World War.

Anderson Lake received its name at the same time.

ANDERSON GLACIER 61°11'N 141°00'W(115-G & F). Straddles the International Boundary in the St. Elias Range.

This was named in 1912–13 by the International Boundary Control Survey party after P. Chandler ANDERSON (1866–1936), of New York; he was arbiter of the Pecuniary Claims Commission of 1910 and a counsel for the US before the Yukon-Alaska Boundary Tribunal in 1903.

MOUNT ANDERSON 60°13'N 135°09'W(105-D). South of the Wheaton River.

John ANDERSON was a well-known prospector in this area for many years. The hill was given his name when he found the first mineral, –gold, silver and others, none in economic quantities – on it in 1910.

ANGEL LAKE 64°49'N 134°39'W(106-D). A very small lake on the Wind River, three miles north of Bond Creek.

It was named by L.H. Green in 1970. About 1960 two prospectors, John Berry O'Neil and John J. O'Neil (not related) crashed here on take-off. Somehow they survived and from this incident the lake was named.

ANIK ISLAND 66°53'N 137°38'W(116-I). An island in the Porcupine River.

The word ANIK means "brother" in the Inuit (Eskimo) language. It was given to the first northern communications satellite, Anik 1, which was launched on 9 November, 1972. Anik 2 was put up in April 1973 and Anik 3 two years later.

The satellites are owned by the Telesat Canada Corporation, a company half owned by the Canadian government and half by ten telephone and communications companies. The purpose of the corporation is to make television and telephone service available throughout Canada's north.

Each satellite can carry 12 colour TV channels (only ten are used — two are spares) or 960 one-way telephone calls at the same time. No direct signals are received except through earth stations which are leased to communities by the corporation.

The name was proposed by Gordon McIntyre, MLA.

ANKER CREEK   68°43′N 137°27′W(117-A). A tributary of the Blow River near the Arctic coast.

This stream was probably named about 1962 by F.G. Young of the Alberta Geological Survey while he was exploring in this area for oil-bearing rock formations.

ANKER Hoidal trapped and prospected for many years on the Arctic slope and was of great service to the geologists mapping the area. (See Mount HOIDAL).

ANN GULCH   64°02′N 135°50′W(106-D). A small tributary to Dublin Gulch, Mayo area.

Fred Taylor mined longer on Dublin Gulch than anyone else. His wife ANN and their two sons lived near here for several years and the name is used locally.

ANNETT CREEK   68°35′N 137°52′W(117-A). Flows into Anker Creek near the Arctic coast.

In 1909 William ANNETT (or ANNET) and David Lord, two trapper-prospectors, claimed to have found placer gold here. In 1916 Annett enlisted with the Black contingent of the Yukon Infantry Company and fought in the First World War.

ANTONE CREEK   60°06′N 128°23′W(105-A). A tributary to the Hyland River, ten miles east of Watson Lake.

A local Indian of this name lived and trapped here for many years.

AQUILA CREEK   66°49′N 137°05′W(116-1). A short tributary to the Eagle River.

This was named during the wilderness study in 1973. The name is a play on words, being Latin for "eagle".

ARCH CREEK   61°30′N 139°43′W(115-G&F). Flows into the Donjek River, ten miles south of the Alaska Highway.

Placer gold was found here during the rush to the Burwash Creek and Kluane goldfields in May 1904, by Henry Flaherty, Morley Bones and Fred Ater. They named the stream because of a peculiar, arch-like opening in the limestone rocks of the canyon.

MOUNT ARCHIBALD   8,400′ 60°47′N 137°52′W(115-A). 15 miles west of Haines Junction.

In 1971 this mountain was named after Dr. E.S. ARCHIBALD, sometime director of the Experimental Farm Service of the Department of Agriculture. He was instrumental in setting up the Pine Creek Experimental Farm near here.

ARK MOUNTAIN   60°14′N 136°10′W(115-A). On the southwest side of Kusawa Lake.

Many years ago local Indians hunting on the mountain found the rotted remains of an old log cabin, built by prospectors far above the timber line. Uneducated except for missionary teachings, and unable to find any reason for anyone to carry logs this far and high, they thought them to be the remains of Noah's ARK.

Dr. E. Kindle, GSC, who explored the mountain in 1950 was told this story and confirmed the name.

ARKELL CREEK   60°48′N 135°43′W(105-D). Flows into the Ibex Creek and to the Takhini River.

In 1890, E.J. Glave and Jack Dalton of the first Frank Leslie Illustrated Newspaper Expedition, after separating from the other two members of the party at Lake Kusawa, travelled in this area and named this creek and also Lake Kusawa after the owner of the paper, W.J. ARKELL of New York. Arkell also owned the humour magazine *Judge* and was secretary and part owner of a patent medicine company. Arkell had organized this expedition to cash in on the publicity value of the recent news of rich gold finds in the Yukon at Fortymile. In 1891 he sent Glave and Dalton back again to explore more of the country.

It was from these two journeys that Dalton conceived the idea of the Dalton Trail to the Yukon. (See Dalton Trail.)

An interesting sequel to these expeditions was that in 1897 when news of the fabulous wealth of the Klondike reached the outside world, Arkell instituted legal claims to the whole of the Klondike, based on these travels. His brother-in-law offered A.B. Schanz, one of the four members of the expedition, $50,000 for any rights he might have to such a claim. So great was the euphoria engendered by the Klondike riches that Schanz turned the offer down. Needless to say, the lawsuit came to nothing.

LAKE ARKELL   (See Kusawa Lake.)

MOUNT ARKELL   7,246′ 60°36′N 135°37′W(105–D). At the head of Arkell Creek, 20 miles southwest of Whitehorse.

This was named in the 1950's in association with the creek.

MOUNT ARMSTRONG   7,083′ 63°12′N 133°15′W(105–N). The highest peak in the Russell Range.

This was named in 1954 under the auspices of the Hon. George Black, MP for the Yukon, after Lt. Col. Neville Alexander Drummond ARMSTRONG, OBE, FRGS, 98'er, prospector, miner, geographer, big-game hunter and conservationist, soldier and gentleman.

Born in England in 1874, Armstrong at the age of 17 spent three years in Texas and New Mexico as a day labourer. In 1898 he came to the Klondike via St. Michaels as assistant manager of the Yukon Goldfields Company. He acquired rich claims for the company on Bonanza Creek and Cheechako Hill and became manager of the company. In 1901 he made a deal with Duncan Gillies, the discoverer, for a placer concession on Russell Creek on the MacMillan River. On 3 August, 1901, together with his crew of six, he took the first steamboat, the *Prospector*, up the MacMillan River to Russell Creek. For this journey he was made a Fellow of the Royal Geographical Society.

In 1904 and 1905 he was appointed Game Warden for the MacMillan River country. Until 1914 he spent almost every summer and several winters on Russell Creek, searching for the elusive gold with little success. In 1914 Armstrong joined the Canadian Expeditionary Forces in France. Given the rank of major he trained scouts and snipers and was awarded the OBE for his outstanding services. Returning to Russell Creek in 1920 he worked until 1926 before giving up the quest. In 1928 he left for England, never to return.

In 1939, at the age of 65 he joined the British army and organized a sniping school. He served in France in early 1940, missing Dunkirk. Transferring to the Canadian First Division he was later retired because of his age. The British army, with better judgment, promoted him to lieutenant-colonel and placed him in command of the Royal Marines Small Arms School.

He died in November 1954. For most of 30 years he was part of the Yukon, believing in its bounty, studying its animals and features and gaining the respect of all who knew him. His two books are Yukon history.

ARMSTRONG'S LANDING   63°05′N 133°25′W(105-N). At the mouth of Russell Creek.

This was a landing place with storage cabins, built by Neville ARMSTRONG in 1901 and later, to service his operations on Russell Creek. No one lived here, and it fell into disuse in 1926 when he abandoned operations.

ARMSTRONG   63°05′N 133°25′W(105-N).

This was a small trading post established in 1919 by Alec Coward and Arthur Zimmerlee of Fort Selkirk, about half a mile downstream from Armstrong's Landing. They were in business here until the 1930's.

MOUNT ARTHUR WHEELER   61°11′N 140°09′W(115-G&F). Above the Steele Glacier in the St. Elias Range.

This was named by the Alpine Club of Canada in memory of their first President, Arthur Oliver WHEELER (1906-1910). Born in Kilkenny, Ireland on 1 May, 1860, he came to Canada in 1876. He became a surveyor and a founder of the Alpine Club in 1906. He died in 1945.

ART LEWIS GLACIER   60°00′N 139°00′W(115-B&C). On the Yukon-Alaska boundary.

This small glacier was named jointly by the US and Canadian governments in 1922 in memory of Arthur LEWIS, a member of the Canadian Boundary Survey parties in 1912 and 1914. He was killed in action in France while serving with the 72nd Highlanders of Canada in the First World War.

ASKIN LAKE   61°56′N 133°14′W(105-F). 25 miles west of Ross River.

In 1951 this little lake was chosen to honour the memory of Gunner C.D. ASKIN, Royal Canadian Artillery, MID. He was killed in action in the Second World War.

MOUNT ATHERTON   62°02′N 133°44′W(105-K). 17 miles southwest of Faro, in the Pelly Mountains.

This was recently named after Charles T. ATHERTON, long-time Yukoner at Whitehorse and a Territorial Councillor in the mid-1930's.

ATLAS CREEK   61°14'N 139°12'W(115-G&F). A short tributary of the Duke River from the south.

This was named in 1973 by the Scenic and Wilderness Study Group for no particular reason.

ATLIN LAKE   60°00'N   133°50'W(105-C).   Straddles   the   BC-Yukon boundary, 20 miles east of Carcross.

With its surrounding mountains, ATLIN Lake is one of the most beautiful in North America. It is 70 miles long and, so far, unpolluted. The Tlinkit Indians who came here for centuries from the Taku River region called it "Ahklen" or "Aht'lah", meaning "Big Water". Dr. G.M. Dawson of the GSC officially adopted the Indian name in 1887.

Probably the first white man to see the lake was Michael Byrne, an explorer working for the Western Union Telegraph Company, who is now believed to have reached the south end of the lake from the Taku River in 1867.

In August 1898, Fritz Miller and Kenneth MacLaren of Juneau found rich placer goldfields on the east side of the lake, second in importance only to the Klondike itself. Of the many people bound to the Klondike via the White and Chilkoot Passes, 10,000 to 15,000 were diverted to this discovery. The White Pass and Yukon Railway, under construction at the time, lost 80% of its workmen almost overnight as they deserted with their tools. Gold has been mined here ever since.

MOUNT AUGUSTA 14,070'   60°19'N 140°27'W (115-B&C). One of the boundary markers in the St. Elias Range.

The mountain was named in 1891 by Professor Israel C. Russell of the USGS after his wife J. AUGUSTA Olmstead Russell. Russell was the first scientist to explore the topography and geology of the St. Elias area with an expedition sponsored jointly by the National Geographical Society and the USGS in 1890–91. Augusta Glacier was named at the same time. (See Russell Col.)

AUSSIE CREEK   64°02'N 137°56'W (116-A). Flows into the Klondike River from the north.

It was originally named Australia Creek in 1897 by Australian miners, of whom there were many in the stampede to the Klondike. The name was changed by W.H. Miller GSC in 1935 to avoid confusion with the earlier-named creek of the same name flowing into the Indian River.

MOUNT AUSTON 64°26′N 136°25′W (116–A). In the south Wernecke Mountains, 12 miles west of Worm Lake.

This was named recently by G.W. Rowley after the late Robert AUSTON, long-time prospector and big-game guide, who discovered and tried to develop copper deposits at nearby Worm Lake.

AUSTRALIA CREEK 63°37′N 138°42′W (115–O&N). A tributary of the Indian River in the south part of the Klondike.

Although Robert Henderson was the first recorded prospector on this stream it is very likely that it was named by other prospectors about 1891–94.

AXEMAN CREEK 64°28′N 138°27′W (116–B). A tributary to the North Klondike River.

In 1968, Dr. Dirk Tempelman-Kluit, GSC, named this creek because of the very old blazed trail he found on it.

BABBAGE RIVER 69°14′N 138°27′W (117–D). Flows north into the Beaufort Sea near Herschel Island.

It was one of the earliest features named in the Yukon Territory when it was found by John Franklin, RN (later Sir), during his second Arctic expedition in 1826. Charles BABBAGE (1792–1871) was a noted British mathematician and a founder of the Astronomical Society.

The Eskimos called it "Cook-Keaktok" or "Rocky River".

BABICHE MOUNTAIN 60°17′N 124°22′W (95–C). In the far south-eastern corner of the territory in a bend of the La Biche River.

This feature was probably named for or by Bobby La Biche, a Mackenzie Indian from Fort Simpson and Fort Liard in the NWT, who trapped in this area for many years.

BABICHE is a northern word used to described raw, or untanned, leather from moose, caribou or deer hides. It is used to string snowshoes and to bind tools, as it shrinks when drying.

MOUNT BACH 61°08′N 136°31′W (115–H). An isolated peak east of the Hutchi Lakes at the head of the Nordenskiold River.

This was named in 1897 after Frank BACH who helped Jack Dalton make a pack trail through here to the Yukon River.

BACK CREEK 62°03′N 137°04′W (115-I). A tributary of Victoria Creek, ten miles southeast of Mount Nansen.

Captain Henry Seymour BACK and his son Frank prospected this creek and named it in 1910. (See Mount Nansen.)

BACKE GLACIER 61°13′N 140°19′W (115-G&F). On the east side of Mount Wood in the St. Elias Range.

In 1971 this mountain was named to honour a pioneer. John BACKE lived and mined for many years in the Mayo district before moving to Haines Junction in 1945 where he built the first lodge. He died in 1970.

BACKHOUSE RIVER 69°36′N 140°32′W (117-C). A small river entering the Beaufort Sea east of Clarence Lagoon.

This was named in 1826 by John Franklin, (later Sir), early British Arctic explorer, after his friend John BACKHOUSE, the Under-Secretary of State for Foreign Affairs of Great Britain at that time.

MOUNT BADHAM 12,625′ 60°52′N 139°52′W (115-B&C). At the head of the Donjek Glacier in the St. Elias Range.

This was named in 1919 to honour the memory of Francis Molyneaux BADHAM, a member of various International Boundary Surveys. Enlisting in the Canadian army in 1914, one of the first, he was killed in action in France in 1915.

MOUNT BAIRD 60°19′N 140°30′W (115-B&C). A high peak five miles northwest of Mount Augusta.

Named by Prof. I.C. Russell, USGS, in 1890 after Prof. Spencer Fullerton BAIRD, Secretary of the Smithsonian Institution.

BAKER CREEK 64°00′N 139°37′W (115-O & N). A small tributary of the Yukon River from the east side, eight miles above Dawson.

J.A. BAKER named this stream in 1897-98. He later prospected for many years in the Livingstone Creek and Boswell River districts.

BAKER LAKE 60°12′N 128°28′W (105-A). 12 miles northeast of Watson Lake.

This was named after Jack W. BAKER, the first weather observer and radio-wireless operator for the Yukon Southern Transport Ltd. at Watson Lake. Baker was an all-round bushman and, in 1941 before the Alaska highway was built, he and his wife and daughters were the only white inhabitants of what is now Watson Lake airport.

MOUNT BAKER   62°34'N   140°09'W   (115-J&K). On the west side of the White River, three miles north of Ten Mile Creek.

William J. Peters and Arthur H. Brooks of the USGS named this peak in early June 1898 while on their expedition up the White River and into the Tanana River basin.

It was named after one of their packers, H.B. BAKER.

BALLARAT CREEK   64°17'N   139°39'W   (116-B&C). A tributary of the Chandindu River.

W.F. Woodward named this stream after the famous goldfields in south-western Australia when he found gold and staked the Discovery claim on 9 March, 1898. The Dawson Mining Recorder allowed another Discovery claim to be recorded on 14 October, 1899 by J.A. Kirkman.

At the time this took place a person staking a claim was allowed 40 days to record it at the Mining Recorder's office for that district. Owing to the lack of maps of the area and to the distance to the recorder's office it sometimes happened that two men found gold on different parts of the same creek at about the same time, unknown to each other. In such a case the Mining Recorder had the option to allow both Discovery claims. Discovery claims were twice the size of regular claims. This happened on Quartz and Dominion Creeks in the Klondike and at several other places in the Yukon. (See Touleary Creek.)

BALLARD CREEK   63°56'N   136°28'W   (115-P). A tributary to the North McQuesten River.

A prospector named BALLARD lived here from the early 1900's to the 1930's   -

MOUNT BARK   61°05'N   137°30'W   (115-H). 15 miles south of Sekulmun Lake.

This mountain was named in 1958 to honour the name of 0-04450 Sub-Lt. Wilfred BARK, RCN, MID. He was born in Toronto, Ontario on 1 March, 1922 and enlisted in the RCN on 13 January, 1942 at Montréal. He served in Canada and at sea and was missing, presumed to have died, on 22 February, 1943.

BARKER CREEK 63°11′N 138°54′W (115-O&N). Tributary to the Stewart River, 20 miles above its mouth.

This was named on 8 November, 1898 by F.M. BARKER who staked the lower half of the Discovery claim that day. Little gold was found and all claims were soon abandoned. In 1903 Louis Marret found good prospects and staked a new Discovery claim. There was another and later stampede on this creek in 1906 but it never lived up to its early promise.

MOUNT BARKER 60°23′N 137°13′W (115-A). Five miles west of Beloud Post.

Edward Herman BARKER was a dredgemaster in the Klondike and Mayo districts as well as for a period in Siberia. He and his partner, Irvine Ray, mined on Haggart Creek in the 1930's and on Shorty Creek about 1946. This mountain was named about 1973.

BARLOW 63°37′N 137°38′W (115-P). At the junction of Clear Creek and the Stewart River.

A small settlement was started here in 1903 when placer mining began on Clear Creek and its tributaries. A steamboat landing, roadhouse and trading post to supply the miners were built. It was abandoned in the 1920's.

BARLOW CITY 63°45′N 137°38′W (115-P). At the junction of Barlow and Clear Creeks.

A small settlement, connected to Barlow by a rough trail, was built here in 1903 with a roadhouse and trading post to supply local miners. It also was abandoned in the 1920's.

MOUNT BARLOW 65°21′N 141°00′W (116-G&F). On the international boundary.

This was named in 1912 by D.D. Cairnes, GSC, after his assistant, F.J. BARLOW, who helped him map the geology along this portion of the Yukon-Alaska boundary that year.

BARNEY CREEK 63°59′N 135°10′W (105-M). A small stream flowing into the Keno Ladue River, north of Keno Hill.

This creek was one of the first to be named in this part of the country when BARNEY Hill found gold in its gravels in 1890.

BARNEY LAKE   60°00′N 127°24′W (95-D). On the Yukon-BC boundary, ten miles west of the Coal River.

Kenneth MacMillan trapped for many years in this area. He made his camp on this lake and named it after his son BARNEY, who was born here.

BARR CREEK   63°04′N 132°48′W (105-N). Tributary to the North MacMillan River.

This was named around 1900 because John BARR had his cabin at the mouth of the stream. Barr came into the country in 1898 and ranged this area for a great many years, trapping and prospecting. Tall, rugged, a supreme bushman, he was known as the "King of the MacMillan Country" by both white and Indian. Courteous and ever-helpful, he was liked and respected by all.

BARWELL LAKE   62°39′N 133°05′W (105-K). 35 miles north of Faro, near the Tay River.

A young Englishman, Charles S.W. BARWELL, became a Dominion Land Surveyor. Coming into the Yukon in the spring of 1897 he worked for the government for several years in many parts of the territory, mostly on claim and route surveys. A friend of his may have given the lake his name.

BATTLE CREEK   62°42′N 138°18′W (155-J & K). A tributary of the Selwyn River.

Pontius Servus Larson and Charles J. Brown found gold here and named the creek on 28 September, 1915. They had just heard the news of heavy fighting in France involving Canadian troops.

BAULTOFF CREEK   62°09′N 140°59′W (115-J & K). A tributary to Beaver Creek.

W.M. BAULTOFF came into the Yukon in 1898 and prospected in the Klondike and western region for many years. He found lode-gold (veins) prospects here in 1903–04. His find led to a minor rush in which other vein deposits were discovered as well as placer gold on some nearby streams in the area.

Baultoff Mountain above the creek was probably named by D.D. Cairnes, GSC, while mapping the geology along the Yukon-Alaska boundary in 1911-12.

BAWN BOY GULCH   64°02'N 135°47'W   (106-D). A very small tributary to Dublin Gulch.

Rich silver-lead ore was found here by Robert Fisher in 1916. He gave his Discovery claim an old Celtic name meaning "Cowherd" or "Cowboy". The name was locally corrupted to "Bum Boy" and was so used for many years in the literature and on mining maps. (See Fisher Creek.)

BEAR CREEK   64°02'N 139°15'W   (116-B & C). A small stream entering the Klondike River from the south about six miles east of Dawson.

On 24 September, 1896, shortly after George Carmack found the Bonanza gold, Salmo Manberg, too late to find a claim on either Bonanza or Eldorado, had prospected this little stream, finding gold and staking a Discovery claim that day. He and his partners, William Corley and Frank Johnson, who staked Nos. 1 and 2 Below Discovery, called the stream BEAR Creek because of the number of black bears that found them and their camp.

The creek gave up considerable wealth although it was not nearly as rich as Bonanza or Eldorado. A settlement was later established at the mouth of the creek by the Yukon Consolidated Gold Corporation Ltd. and was their main headquarters and shops until the cessation of their operations in 1966, when it was abandoned.

Parks Canada has lately taken over the old camps of the YCGC and is developing a complex to house its headquarters as well as a centre to display methods of mining in the Klondike and a museum of mining machinery.

BEAR RIVER   64°55'N 134°43'W   (106-D). A tributary to the Wind River.

This is the translation of an old Loucheaux Indian word meaning "Bear Killed One of Us Here". The full title was shortened over the years.

BEARFEED CREEK   62°11'N 135°08'W   (105-L). Tributary to the Little Salmon River.

In 1925 W.E. Cockfield, GSC, gave this name because of the large number of bears attracted to the stream and the extensive berry patches on its banks.

MOUNT BEATON   60°01'N 137°02'W   (115-A). An isolated peak seven miles south of Dalton Post.

J.N. Wallace, DLS, named this peak after P. BEATON, a member of his International Boundary Survey party in 1908.

BEAUFORT SEA (117-D). The Beaufort Sea is that part of the Arctic Ocean touching the northern shores of Alaska and the Yukon. It is bounded by Cape Barrow on the west and Prince Patrick Island on the east.

1 received its name in 1826 when John Franklin, (later Sir), named it after his friend Captain (later Admiral) Sir Francis BEAUFORT, RN (1774–1857), at that time hydrographer to the British Admiralty. He is best remembered for the scale of wind velocities which he invented, still in general use by all sailors. Several other features on the Arctic slope in Alaska are also named for him.

BEAUVETTE HILL 63°57'N 135°06'W (105-M). The farthest east of the five summits of Keno Hill.

Louis BEAUVETTE (often spelled Bouvette or Bovette) discovered rich silver-lead ore on this hill in 1919. (See Mount Bouvette.)

BEAVER CITY 64°28'N 135°15'W (106-D).At the junction of Carpenter and Settlemier Creeks.

This small settlement was established here in 1923 when silver-lead veins were found in the vicinity. It was a distribution point to supply the prospectors. The ore found was not rich enough to mine in this isolated area and the place was abandoned by 1925. It received its name because many of the prospectors came to the area by way of the BEAVER River. (See Carpenter and Settlemier Creeks.)

BEAVER CREEK 62°27'N 140°38'W (115-J & K). A tributary to Snag Creek.

The whole stream was called Snag Creek until 1902 when this part was renamed BEAVER, leaving the lower part with the original name.

The Beaver Creek area was first prospected by Frederick W. Best, Peter Nelson and William James between 1909 and 1914. Nelson and James went on to discover the rich placer goldfields of the Chisana, Alaska, district just over the boundary, in 1913. This creek was used as a supply route and winter trail between the steamboat landing on the White River and the Chisana diggings.

James B. Hendryx, the western novelist, used this creek as the setting for his series of Yukon short stories and novels concerning Corporal Downey,

Black John Smith, Cushing's Fort and Halfaday Creek which are still read and enjoyed.

The small settlement where the stream crosses the Alaska Highway at mile 1196 (K1914) was started about 1955 and had a post office in 1958. Canada Customs and other businesses have enlarged the community since then. This place is also the scene of the contact point of the northern and southern construction crews building the Alaska Highway. On 20 October, 1942, bulldozer operator Cpl. Refines Sims Jr. of Philadelphia and the 18th US Army Engineers was working south on the section from Fairbanks. He met his opposite number, Pte. Alfred Jalufka of Kennedy, Texas and the 97th Engineers, who was working north from Whitehorse. (See Contact Creek.)

BECKER CREEK 60°14′N 135°10′W (105-D). Tributary to the Wheaton River, 15 miles west of Carcross.

Theodore BECKER was an active prospector for many years in this district and found good mineral showings near this creek in 1906, when he named it. The silver and lead proved uneconomic.

BELIVEAU CREEK 63°48′N 135°29′W (105-M). Tributary to Duncan Creek on the southwest side of Mount Beliveau.

Discovery of good placer gold was made on this stream and the Discovery claim was staked on 7 January, 1902, by Ernest BELIVEAU of Québec, an active prospector who was connected with many of the early finds in the district.

Mount Beliveau was later named for the same man.

MOUNT BELL 6,328′ 60°10′N 135°11′W (105-D). 17 miles west of Carcross.

D.D. Cairnes, GSC, named this feature after his assistant, W.A. BELL of Queen's University, Kingston, Ontario. Bell had done much of the surveying when Cairnes mapped the geology of the Wheaton River district in the summer of 1909.

Dr. Walter Andrew Bell, BSc (Queen's), MA (Cambridge), PhD (Yale) joined the GSC in 1909 and enlisted in the army 1916–19. After the First World War he continued his education and his work with the GSC. He was appointed Chief Palaeontologist in 1938 and Director of the GSC from 1949 to 1953. He was awarded the Logan Medal, the Gold Medal of the Professional Institute of Public Services of Canada, the Inco Medal of the CIMM and the Honorary Degree of LLD from St. Xavier University. He died in 1969.

BELL RIVER   67°17'N 137°46'W (116-P). Flows from the MacDougall Pass to the Porcupine River.

John BELL, Chief Trader of the Hudson's Bay Company, explored this river in 1839 seeking new sources of furs. He was in charge of Fort Good Hope on the Mackenzie River at the time and was married to a daughter of Peter Warren Dease, a famous Arctic explorer of the HBC.

The stream was originally known as the West Rat River and sometimes as Bell's River. R.G. McConnell of the GSC while on his survey of 1887–88, mapped it as the Bell River to avoid confusion with the East Rat River flowing to the Mackenzie from the same source on the Continental Divide. The eastern branch of the Bell is still called the Rat River.

This isolated river was the main trade route into the Yukon for many years, servicing Fort Yukon from 1847 and Rampart House from 1867 to about 1890 when the HBC abandoned the route as uneconomic. Shortly after this time, the company gave up all its business in the territory.

BELOUD CREEK   60°25'N 137°27'W (115-A). Flows into Victoria Creek about 11 miles south of Louise Lake.

B. BELOUD found placer gold here in 1938 and mined till 1939. He found many copper nuggets weighing up to 28 pounds.

BELOUD POST   60°22'N 137°04'W (115-A). 34 miles from Haines Junction at the south end of Dezeadash Lake.

In 1938 B. BELOUD made camp here to explore and mine placer gold. He also began to carry on limited trading. Today it is a resort and lodge.

BENNETT CREEK   63°43'N 136°03'W (115-P). A tributary to Minto Creek from the north.

On 25 May, 1903, Charles E. BENNETT found placer gold and staked the Discovery claim on this stream.

LAKE BENNETT   60°06'N 134°52'W (105-D). Straddles the Yukon – BC boundary below Carcross.

This is "Kusooa"Lake of the Tagish Indians and "Boat" Lake of the early miners, for here it was that they stopped after the back-breaking toil of the Chilkoot Pass. Cutting the spruce trees on the shores of the lake, they laboriously hand-sawed planking and built their boats for the long voyage down the Yukon to the goldfields. Dr. Aurel Krause of the Bremen Geographical Society led an expedition through the Chilkat Pass in 1881 and gave the name "East Kussooa" Lake.

Lt. Frederick Schwatka, US Army, on his expedition in 1883 from Dyea over the Chilkoot Pass and down the length of the Yukon River blithely ignored all previous explorers' and miners' names. He made the first, rough survey of the river's course and named most of the features after superior officers and contemporary and prominent academicians and patrons of exploration. Some of his nomenclature was allowed to remain in use.

He named Lake Bennett after James Gordon BENNETT, editor of the *New York Herald* and a supporter of American exploration. It became one of the best-known names in the north because of its position and part in the stampede to the Klondike in 1897–99. The scene here during that period was one of intense activity as tens of thousands funnelled through the Chilkoot and White Passes, stopping here to organize themselves and build boats for the remainder of the journey to the Klondike. In the winter of 1897–98 the largest tent city in the world was at the head of the lake. Standing now at Carcross bridge it is hard to imagine that over 7,000 craft of all sorts and sizes passed here in 48 hours on 29 and 30 May, 1898, and many more afterwards.

A town was built; sawmills and boat yards sprang up on these shores. Steamboats, their boilers and engines hauled with heart-breaking effort over the passes, were built here in a matter of weeks and, until the White Pass and Yukon Railway was completed to Whitehorse in July 1900, they transported most of the passengers and freight to the territory.

BERNEY CREEK   60°11′N   135°20′W   (105–D). Flows into the Wheaton River near Carbon Hill.

This was named about 1906 after Adam BIRNIE (correct spelling), one of a group of English prospectors who were known as "The Tally-ho Boys". (See Tally-ho Mountain.)

BERTHA CREEK   63°47′N   139°30′W   (115–O & N). A tributary of the Indian River.

On 11 August, 1898, James E. Fairbairn and George B. Perry found placer gold and staked the Discovery claim, naming the stream. A stampede from Dawson saw the whole creek and its main tributaries staked in a few days. Little gold was found and the creek was soon abandoned. In 1902

Fred E. Envoldsen and his partner recorded a new Discovery claim and a new rush ensued. They renamed the stream "Gladstone" Creek but the Mining Recorder refused the name, retaining the original.

BIG CAMPBELL CREEK   61°46'N 131°07'W (105-G). A tributary of the Pelly River at Pelly Banks.

This was named shortly after 1887 by miners who could not distinguish it from Campbell Creek, as they join into a common stream stream a few yards from the Pelly.

BIG CREEK   62°37'N 137°00'W (115-I). Enters the Yukon four miles below Minto.

This stream, quite a large one, entered the Yukon behind an island which has since been eroded and so was missed by William Ogilvie on his survey in 1887.

A soldier named McMartin entered the Yukon with the Yukon Field Force in 1898, served at Fort Selkirk and took his discharge from the army there in 1899. When he took up the first homestead at the mouth of this stream he asked the local Indians for its name. Their reply was that it was a big creek — by which they meant that it was too large for a creek and was really a river. McMartin filed his application for his homestead under this name, which remains.

BIG CREEK   62°53'N 140°11'W (115-J&K). A tributary to the Indian River.

A staking rush took place on this creek in June 1898 from Dawson, when the whole creek was staked and named.

There are five Big Creeks in the Yukon.

BIG GOLD CREEK   64°01'N 140°42'W (116-B&C). Flows into the Sixtymile River.

This was originally named Gold Creek in 1891 during the rush to the newly-found, Sixtymile River goldfields, the second major gold discovery in the Yukon. Although tributaries of this stream produced good gold, little was found on the main stream itself until, in 1905, John Stockton found the pay-streak and the creek was restaked and renamed "BIG GOLD" Creek.

BIG HORN CREEK   61°09'N 139°24'W (115-G&F).Tributary to the Donjek River.

Edward Benson, with W.R. and W.B. Lamb, named this creek when they found and mined gold on it in August 1914.

BIG KALZAS LAKE 63°15'N 134°35'W (105-M). Between the Stewart and MacMillan Rivers.

It is highly probable that this is the lake named "Gauche" Lake by Robert Campbell in 1849–50. It is shown as such on the earliest map of the territory. Gauche was one of Campbell's Indian employees. He was an able and reliable man and was noted, even by Campbell, for his clairvoyant powers.

This was one of the lakes which supplied fish for Fort Selkirk.

BIG SALMON 61°53'N 134°55'W (105-E). At the mouth of Big Salmon River.

This is a now-abandoned settlement on the Yukon. Before the white men came there was an ancient Indian fishing village here. By 1898 it was a steamboat landing, a woodcutter's camp and a supply point for the people up the Big Salmon. For many years it was a station on the Yukon Telegraph.

BIG SALMON LAKE 61°16'N 133°17'W (105-F). Five miles northwest of Quiet Lake on the Big Salmon River.

This was originally called "Island Lake" by John McCormack, prospector, in 1887. The name was forgotten and changed to the present one sometime about 1898.

BIG SALMON RIVER 61°53'N 134°55'W (105-E). A major tributary of the Yukon River.

In 1881 a party of four prospectors, including George G. Langtry and Patrick McGlinchy of Juneau, ascended this river 200 miles above its mouth. They were the first white men to explore the stream. Gold prospects were found along the whole length of the river and two of the party won a fair amount of fine gold from the river bars. These men named the river the "Iyon", from the name of the Indian tribe living near its mouth.

In 1883 Lt. F. Schwatka, US Army, rafting down the Yukon, was told by his Chilkat interpreter that the Indian name meant "Big Salmon". The Tagish or local Indian name was "Ta-Tlin-Hini". Schwatka called it the "d'Abbadie" after M. Antoine d'Abbadie, Membre d'Institut and noted French explorer.

Dr. George M. Dawson, GSC, when reviewing his own notes of the locality and William Ogilvie's survey of the river, disallowed the name and retained the original as used by the natives and the miners. Dawson was given much information on the river by John McCormack, a New Brunswick prospector, who had, with three partners, prospected the river in 1887 and had named several features including Quiet Lake.

H.S. Bostock, GSC, while mapping the area in 1935 applied the name "d'Abbadie" to a small branch of the North Fork of the Big Salmon River.

BIG SITDOWN CREEK 65°41′N 141°00′W (116-G&F). Flows into the Kandik River in Alaska.

In 1910 an International Boundary Survey crew was camp-bound by weather for several days, giving the creek its name.

BIG THING CREEK 60°03′N 134°34′W (105-D). Flows into Windy Arm, Tagish Lake.

In 1905 a large, wide vein of gold-and silver-bearing ore was found on the headwaters of this creek. The finder was extremely proud of his discovery. Payable in the first years, it has been worked unprofitably several times since.

MOUNT BILLINGS 6,909′ 61°14′N 128°54′W (105-D). In the Logan Mountains, southeast of Frances Lake.

This was probably named in 1887 by Dr. G.M. Dawson, GSC, after Elkanah BILLINGS (1820–1876), palaeontologist with the Geological and Natural History Survey of Canada.

MOUNT BISEL 61°37′N 137°07′W (115-H). A small hill northeast of the head of Aishihik Lake.

This was named in 1897, probably by J.J. McArthur, GSC, after a member of Jack Dalton's crew.

MOUNT BLACK 7,044′ 61°12′N 134°04′W (105-E). At the headwaters of the South Big Salmon River in the Livingstone Creek area.

George BLACK was born in Woodstock, New Brunswick in 1872. He qualified as a lawyer but soon was involved in the Klondike Gold Rush. He came into the Yukon in 1897. He had little success in the Klondike area and tried other places. In 1898 he and his partner found good gold on Livingstone Creek. However, in 1901 he was forced to get to Dawson by working as a deckhand on a riverboat.

In Dawson he again engaged in the practice of criminal law. He also became active in politics. He served three terms on the Yukon Council (1905–12) as a member from the Klondike Riding and then represented South Dawson.

In February 1912 he was appointed Commissioner of the Yukon Teritory. He served with distinction, his term being marked by progressive reforms in the civil service, increased road building and better labour and mining laws. He and C.A. Thomas, Manager of the Yukon Gold Company, drove the first automobile from Whitehorse to Dawson in December 1912.

He was given leave of absence in 1916 to enlist for service in the First World War. He formed the Yukon Infantry Company and raised 226 men whom he led to England in January 1917. They were reformed into the 17th Canadian Machine Gun Company and served with distinction. Black was severely wounded in the Battle of Amiens in France during August 1917.

Returning to the Yukon, he was elected in 1921 to sit in parliament as member from the Yukon. He represented the Conservative party. He sat continuously until forced to retire due to ill-health caused by war wounds. His wife, Martha Louise Black, ran in his stead and was elected. He recovered and was again elected in 1940, serving two terms as Speaker of the House of Commons. On his retirement in 1949 he returned to Dawson and his law practice. In August 1951 he was appointed a member for life of the King's Privy Council for Canada, by Prime Minister Louis St. Laurent. He entered politics once more in the election of 1953, losing to J. Aubrey Simmons, a Liberal. He died in Vancouver, BC on 23 September, 1965, at the age of 94.

George Black, BA, LLB, PC was a capable, unassuming, well-liked man. It would be hard to find a more worthy Canadian to honour with a permanent landmark memorial.

The mountain was mapped by H.S. Bostock, GSC, in 1935 and is the highest point in the Big Salmon Range. He also suggested the name, as he was a long-time friend of George Black.

BLACK HILLS CREEK   63°15′N 138°41′W (115-O&N). A tributary to the Stewart River.

One of the earliest miners' names in the territory, this creek was apparently named about 1883–85 by miners who had been in the gold rush to the Black Hills of South Dakota in the late 1870's. Although prospected earlier, payable gold was not found here until July 1898 when a stampede took place and the whole creek was staked in a few days. (See Rosebud Creek.)

BLACKSTONE RIVER 65°51'N 137°15'W (116-H). Tributary to the Peel River.

Indians many years ago named this isolated river because of the deep, extensive seams of coal (lignite) on both sides of a canyon on the stream.

BLANCHARD RIVER 60°02'N 136°53'W (115-A). Crosses the Yukon-BC boundary and joins the Tatshenshini River near Dalton Post.

This was originally called the "Kleheela" River by the NWMP who were here in 1898. They learned the name from the local Indians. It was renamed about 1915 after G. BLANCHARD Dodge, DLS, who was born in Halifax, Nova Scotia, in 1874 and educated at Dalhousie University. He served with the Topographical Survey of Canada from 1900 to 1932. He was in charge of survey parties that delineated much of the Yukon-BC boundary and died in Ottawa in 1945.

BLOOMFIELD LAKE 69°12'N 138°36'W (117-D). A small lake near Phillips Bay on the Arctic coast.

This lake was named in 1958 to honour the memory of B-67396 Pte. George Page BLOOMFIELD, MID. Born in Toronto, Ontario, on 24 August, 1914, he enlisted in the Canadian army at Toronto on 5 March, 1940, and served in Canada, Iceland, Great Britain and France. He was killed in action at Dieppe, France, on 19 August, 1942.

BLUEBERRY CREEK 63°05'N 139°11'W (115-O&N). A small tributary of Thistle Creek.

During the Klondike Gold Rush there were many smaller rushes and stampedes to other areas in the Yukon. One of these was the stampede to Thistle Creek in late 1898. A syndicate of Swedes from Minnesota, who called themselves the "Monitors", staked, named and unsuccessfully worked on this creek that year. (See Monitor Creek.)

MOUNT BOMPAS 10,027' 61°24'N 140°36'W (115-G&F). On the west side of Mount Constantine in the St. Elias Range.

This was named in 1918 to perpetuate the name of the most remarkable churchman in Yukon history, the Right Reverend William Carpenter BOMPAS, DD, first Bishop of Athabaska (1874–1884), first Bishop of the

Mackenzie River (1884–1891), and first Bishop of Selkirk (Yukon) (1891–1906). He was born in London, England, in 1834 and died, still serving at Carcross, in 1906.

His father, Charles Carpenter Bompas, Serjent-at-Law and eminent advocate before the British Bar, was said to be the original of Charles Dickens' Serjent Buzfuz in *Pickwick Papers*.

William Bompas first entered the Yukon in 1873, visiting the Indians at LaPierre House from the Mackenzie River. In 1874 he went to Fort Yukon to encourage and enlarge his Anglican Church missionary services to the natives. He spent 1891 to 1892 at Rampart House on the Porcupine River and having heard of the needs of the miners and natives in the Fortymile district, he set up a mission there. (See Buxton Mission.) He established missions at Fort Selkirk and later at Carcross and, in 1897, erected the original St. Paul's Church in Dawson. His greatest efforts were always for the native people and his school for Indian children at Carcross is still continuing in spirit, although it is neither church-run nor for Indians only.

He served for 43 years in the Mackenzie and Yukon, returning only once to England in all that time.

BONANZA CREEK 64°03′N 139°25′W (115–B&C). A tributary to the Klondike River about three miles east of Dawson.

This is one of the richest and most famous gold-bearing streams in the world. The name was a synonym for immediate and vast wealth. The word BONANZA was in former times used by Spanish miners and *conquistadors* to denote rich ore deposits.

On 16 August, 1896, George Carmack, Skookum Jim Mason and Tagish (later called Dawson) Charlie found rich, coarse gold in the gravels of this stream when they were returning from an inspection of Robert Henderson's diggings on Gold Bottom Creek. On 17 August, 1896, George Carmack staked the Discovery claim, wrote the name "Bonanza" on a piece of bark and nailed it to his discovery post.

On 22 August, on a hillside opposite claim No. 17 Below Discovery, a miners' meeting was held by 25 men, all those who had staked claims on the creek to that time. They agreed to a rough survey to avoid further confusion in claim staking; they elected one of their number, David McKay, to be Mining Recorder and they confirmed the name of the creek as Bonanza. It had previously been called "Rabbit" Creek by the miners and "Tha-Tat-Dik", meaning "Muffler" Creek, by the local Indians.

This is the creek that started a controversy which has never been settled to this day. Did Carmack on this creek or Henderson on Gold Bottom Creek first discover the Klondike gold? Henderson, after 1901, claimed this honour for the rest of his life, backed by local Canadian officials, and was finally awarded a pension and other concessions and proclaimed the discoverer by the Canadian government. Carmack never made any claim other than that he had found the rich gold of Bonanza, but his cause was taken up by the predominant American element in the Yukon and elsewhere. The Canadian government, in 1962, erected a bronze plaque on Carmack's Discovery claim giving the honour to Carmack, Skookum Jim and Tagish Charlie. Oddly enough, it has never been established just who was there at the discovery. Kate Carmack, George's wife, and the boy Patsy Henderson both claimed to have been the first one to find the gold. No matter who found the gold, one thing is certain: the Bonanza Creek find touched off the Klondike stampede.

From 1897 to 1905, as the whole creek was being mined, a number of reports were made of finding older, earlier workings.

Bonanza was phenomenally productive for a length of nearly 12 miles. Counting Eldorado Creek, a tributary, extremely rich gold deposits were mined for nearly 17 miles. A remarkable fact of this discovery was that few of the original claims were staked by experienced miners. The creek had been cursorily prospected by a number of prospectors as early as 1883 and passed by. At the time of Carmack's find nearly all the miners in the Yukon were busy on the productive creeks at the head of the Fortymile River and on the Sixtymile River diggings. As a result, when Carmack made the announcement of his find at Fortymile, only the local tradesmen and lay-abouts had the first news. With newly-arrived prospectors he met travelling up and down the river, these comprised the men who staked Bonanza and Eldorado. Many of them were inexperienced and when the true miners arrived on the scene and evaluated the find they quickly bought claims from the *cheechakos* (newcomers) at low prices.

The first mining on Bonanza was done by hand; pick, shovel and fire were used to thaw and gouge out the frozen gold-bearing gravels that lay above bedrock. This was the period from 1897–1900 that was the hey-day of the Klondike, when the suddenly rich, free-wheeling, big-spending miners made Dawson the "Paris of the North", where gold dust could purchase anything.

Then, as steam-thawing and machinery became available, larger and poorer quantities of gravel were worked, still yielding large profits. Finally, large capital was interested and millions of dollars were invested in large-scale water supply (flumes and ditches stretching in places for over 50 miles), dredges and large hydraulic equipment. In this, the final and longest phase of mining, nearly all the gravel of the valley bottoms was processed. Huge quantities carrying values in gold as low as 40 cents to the cubic yard were handled, still at a profit. This phase lasted until 1966 when the last dredge shut down. Every year since, several people still mine the creek in a small way.

It is impossible to arrive at the correct figure for the total value of the gold taken from this stream but the estimate for the Klondike for 68 years is well over $200,000,000; most of this was mined when gold was valued at $20 per ounce.

BONNET PLUME RIVER 65°56′N 134°57′W (106–E). A large tributary to the Peel River.

Andrew Flett, "BONNET PLUME", was a Loucheaux Indian chief. He had worked for many years as an interpreter for the HBC. He and his band made their home on this river. During the Klondike Gold Rush many of the stampeders from Edmonton made their way through this part of the country. Bonnet Plume gave assistance to many of these unfortunates caught by winter on the trail to Dawson and they named the river after him.

The Loucheaux themselves called it "The Black Sands" River, from the large amounts of black magnetite sand (iron ore) found in its bed.

BONNEVILLE LAKES 60°37′N 135°18′W (105–D). Three small lakes on the west side of Fish Lake, southwest of Whitehorse.

In 1948 these lakes were honoured with the name of A-61080 L/Cpl. Hector BONNEVILLE MM. He was born in Ottawa on 5 June, 1912 and enlisted in the Canadian army at Windsor, Ontario on 10 August 1942. He served in Canada, Great Britain and the Central Mediterranean Theatre. He was killed in action during the attack on the Gothic Line in Italy on 31 August, 1944.

BORDEN CREEK 63°31′N 140°28′W (115–O&N). A small tributary to Matson Creek in the Sixtymile River area.

BORONITE CITY 62°23′N 136°37′W (115–I). A short-lived settlement at the mouth of Williams Creek on the banks of the Yukon River.

This was built in 1907 to service the many prospectors on the new, hardrock copper finds on Williams and adjacent creeks. The WP&YR laid up their steamboat *Whitehorse* here for the winter of 1907–08. About 20 people lived here, running a store, hotel and a blacksmith shop. No commercial copper deposits were found and the settlement was abandoned by 1909.

BORTHWICK LAKE 61°28′N 137°27′W (115-H). Lies between Aishihik and Sekulmun Lakes.

In 1956 this lake was named to perpetuate the memory of A-105676 Pte. George Ross BORTHWICK MID who was born 18 June, 1923 at Thedford, Ontario. He enlisted in the Canadian army at London, Ontario on 6 January, 1943. Serving in Canada, Great Britain and Northwest Europe, he was killed in action on 29 July, 1944.

BOSWELL RIVER 61°03′N 134°13′W (105-E). Tributary to the Teslin River.

This was named by miners in 1887 after the two BOSWELL brothers, Thomas and George, of Peterborough, Ontario, who were the first to prospect the Teslin River. The Boswells were among the first prospectors in the Yukon watershed; records show that Thomas came over the Chilkoot Pass in the spring of 1882 and George came either then or the following year. They were active men and among the first to find the rich bar gold on the Stewart River at Chapman's Bar. A major tributary of the Stewart was given their name at the time. (See Nadaleen River.)

They ranged widely across the Yukon and Alaska for years, always in the forefront of the pioneers. Thomas lost a leg to a grizzly bear in Alaska in 1891 but he and his brother still joined in the Klondike stampede.

BOSSUYT LAKE 66°38′N 135°13′W (106-L). East of Road River.

Charles BOSSUYT was a Yukon Councillor for North Dawson 1912–15. His name is used as the title on the new topographical map of this area, printed in 1973. His name was proposed by Gordon McIntyre.

BOUCHER CREEK 64°01′N 140°20′W (116-B&C). Flows north into Sixtymile River.

Felix BOUCHER, of Québec, had prospected the Sixtymile country in 1891 when the first discoveries were made. At that time this stream was staked and called Larsen Creek and Larsen worked on it with fair results until he was called away in 1896 by news of far richer ground in the Klondike. The creek was abandoned.

In July 1902 Felix Boucher and his partner, James Huot, returned, prospected and staked a new Discovery claim. The Mining Recorder renamed the stream after Boucher. (See Huot Gulch.)

BOUTELLIER CREEK   60°59′N 138°13′W (115–B&C). Tributary to Christmas Creek, southwest of Kluane Lake.

Charles BOUTELLIER, of Québec, prospected and mined on this stream in 1903 when it received its name. He spent many years in the Yukon, prospecting, cutting wood for riverboats, and trapping; in 1914 he owned and operated a roadhouse at Lower Laberge.

MOUNT BOUVETTE   65°17′N 138°37′W (116–G&F). South of the Ogilvie River.

In 1973 this feature was named by the Topographical Surveys Branch as a map sheet title for their new series. Louis BOUVETTE was a pioneer prospector of the district; he found the first of the rich silver-lead ore deposits in 1919 on Keno Hill while hunting mountain sheep. (See Beauvette Hill.)

BOVE ISLAND   60°07′N 134°32′W (105–D). The island in Tagish Lake at the mouth of Windy Arm.

Lt. F. Schwatka, US Army, in 1883 renamed Tagish Lake "Bove" after Lt. BOVE of the Italian navy, who had served with the Austro-Hungarian Expedition of 1872–74.

Dr. G.M. Dawson, GSC, in 1887 gave Tagish Lake its original name and left Bove's name on this island.

BOW CREEK   62°18′N 137°13′W (115–I). Tributary to Seymour Creek near Mt. Freegold.

P.F. Guder of Carmacks assisted the GSC in this area in the summer of 1930. While travelling this stream he commented on its shape, almost a perfect arc, whence its name.

Previously, Captain H.S. Back had named the stream "Rogers" Creek after one of his men in the summer of 1917. They never worked the creek and the name had been forgotten. (See Back, Guder, Nansen and Seymour Creeks.)

BRABAZON GLACIER   61°21′N 140°37′W (115–G&F). Feeds into the huge Klutlan Glacier west of Mt. Bompas.

31

Alfred James BRABAZON, DLS, was in charge of surveys for the International Boundary Survey Commission from 1895–1906 and again in 1909. This glacier was named in his memory in 1925.

BRADEN'S CANYON   62°50'N 136°51'W (115-I). On the Pelly River about 15 miles below Pelly Crossing.

A trapper of this name settled here in 1898 with his native wife and children. They trapped, and for many years supplied cordwood to the riverboats.

BRAEBURN   60°31'N 135°50'W (105-E).

A roadhouse was established here in 1899 on the old winter trail from Whitehorse to Dawson. A small settlement remained here until the 1950's.

MOUNT BRAGG   65°38'N 140°18'W (116-G&F). West of the Porcupine River.

T.G. BRAGG was the principal of the Dawson Public School during 1904–05. In 1973 his name was used to denote the new topographical map sheet of this area.

BRAINE CREEK   64°22'N 134°59'W (106-D). Tributary to the Beaver River in the Wernecke Mountains.

This was named about 1898 after Frank BRAINE who lived in this area at the time. Braine Pass at the head of the creek was discovered and used by Braine in journeys to Fort Good Hope on the Mackenzie River. (See Lansing.)

MOUNT BRATNOBER   6,313'   60°44'N 136°40'W (115-A). In the bend of the Dezeadash River about ten miles southwest of Champagne.

This mountain was named in July 1897 by J.J. McArthur, DLS, a Canadian government surveyor who made an extremely cursory survey of the Dalton Trail that year. He was assisted by Jack Dalton and Henry BRATNOBER, who was one of Dalton's axmen at the time.

Henry Bratnober, of San Francisco, played more than an ordinary part in the Yukon. He was an accredited riverboat captain and had prospected and mined widely in the western United States. He took part in the Klondike rush, was a partner with Dalton during 1901–04 prospecting in the Alsek and White River regions, built and captained the riverboat *Ella* in 1905 and was operating it on the Tanana River in 1910. He was an agent and "mining expert" for the Rothschilds for many years in their mining ventures in the north.

BREFALT CREEK   63°55′N   135°30′W   (105–M). A small creek flowing into Flat Creek from Galena Hill near Elsa.

This was named in the late 1920's after C. BREFALT, who first found high-grade, silver-lead ore here.

MOUNT   BRENNER   64°27′N   138°46′W   (116–B&C).   Five   miles northwest of Tombstone Mountain, in the Klondike district.

This was named after Otto BRENNER, of London, Ontario, pioneer Yukoner and an active and successful prospector and miner.

BREWER   CREEK   63°11′N   138°59′W   (115–O&N).   A   tributary   to Barker Creek.

In June 1906, Charles N. Graham staked a Discovery claim here when he found workable gold. In 1898 a prospector named BREWER had tried but failed.

BREWER   LAKE   60°40′N   133°26′W   (105–C).   12   miles   north   of Johnson's Crossing.

Joseph BREWER, pioneer trapper and prospector, made his home on this lake for many years.

BREWERY CREEK   64°01′N   138°01′W   (116–B). Tributary to the South Klondike River.

Until 1965 this was known as O'Brien Creek. It had been named in 1897–98. The name was changed to avoid conflict with one of a similar name in the White River district which had been named later.

Thomas W. O'Brien came to the Yukon in 1886 and mined in the Fortymile diggings. He gained business interests in Fortymile and in Circle City. He was an early staker in the Klondike and is said to have carried the first news of the find to Circle City. He and J.M. Wilson of the ACC arrived there on 15 December, 1896, and their tidings started a stampede to Dawson which left Circle City virtually deserted. He was one of the founders of the Yukon Order of Pioneers at Fortymile on 1 December, 1894.

Becoming prominent in the business and political life of Dawson and the territory, he built the first brewery in 1898 and, in the same year was instrumental, with Big Alex McDonald, in establishing the first electrical plant and telephone system in Dawson. He owned the first newspaper, the *Yukon Midnight Sun*, a pro-government paper. He was the promoter and financier of the Klondike Mines Railway which ran from Dawson to Sulphur Springs and he sought federal aid to extend it to Fort McLeod in British Columbia.

He served several terms as a Yukon Councillor in the early 1900's. The Liberal Party in the Yukon was known for a number of years as the "Steam Beers" because of O'Brien's prominence in their affairs.

Thomas O'Brien died in Dawson on 24 August, 1916.

MOUNT BRIMSTON 65°33′N 139°06′W (116-G&F). In the Nahoni Range, north of the Ogilvie River.

In 1973 the Topographical Surveys Branch named this feature after George BRIMSTON, former Klondiker and for many years Sheriff of the Yukon. He was also a past president of the YOOP. (See Brimstone Gulch.)

BRIMSTONE GULCH 63°43′N 138°51′W (115-O&N). Flows into Sulphur Creek in the south Klondike district.

This short creek was staked and named in late 1897 by George BRIMSTON. The name was a play on his own and that of Sulphur Creek. By November 1898 he was working his claim and had built and was operating a roadhouse at the mouth of this stream. He worked the stream for a number of years before moving to Dawson.

BRITANNIA CREEK 62°52′N 138°41′W (115-J&K). Tributary to the Yukon River.

This was named by E.L.C. de la Pole and C.M. Printz who staked the Discovery claim on 18 April, 1911.

MOUNT BRITISH COLUMBIA 10,200′ 60°57′N 140°57′W (115-B&C). Near the Yukon-Alaska boundary in the western St. Elias Range.

This is one of the group of mountains named to celebrate Canada's Centennial Year in 1967. (See Centennial Range.)

BRITISH MOUNTAINS 68°50′N 140°20′W (117-C). Range of mountains which crosses the Yukon-Alaska boundary 40 miles south of the Arctic coast.

These were named by John Franklin, (later Sir), the famous English Arctic explorer, in 1826, in honour of his native land.

BRITTON RIDGE 5,286' 62°22'N 138°51'W (115-J&K). The high ridge between the Nisling and Klotassin Rivers.

This hill was named in 1973 after J.C. BRITTON, a pioneer prospector and miner in the region for many years.

MOUNT BROOKE 10,791' 61°30'N 140°57'W (115-G&F). Near the Yukon-Alaska boundary, north of the Klutlan Glacier in the St. Elias Range.

This was dedicated in 1918 to the memory of 8186 Pte. William BROOKE. He was born 15 August, 1893, at Huntingdon, Québec and enlisted in the 2nd Battalion CEF on 13 September, 1914 — one of the very first. He died a prisoner of war in Germany on 13 March, 1917.

BROOKS ARM 61°28'N 139°02'W (115-G&F). A large bay on the north end of Kluane Lake.

This bay received its name in 1945 from Hugh S. Bostock, GSC, when he was mapping the geology of the area that year. Formerly called "Little Arm", he changed it to commemorate Alfred Hulse BROOKS (1871-1924), who served the USGS in Alaska from 1898 to 1923. Brooks travelled this way on an expedition from Pyramid Harbour to Eagle, Alaska, in 1899 and wrote the first geological report about the area. He was appointed chief of the USGS in Alaska in 1903 and later appointed Chief Alaskan Geologist. He was the Chief Geologist for the American Expeditionary Forces in the First World War. He contributed greatly and widely to the knowledge and mapping of Alaskan geology.

Brooks Creek and Brooks Valley were named later.

BROOKS BROOK 60°25'N 133°12'W (105-C). A small stream flowing into Teslin Lake about mile 829 (K1326) of the Alaska Highway.

This little stream was named in 1942 by black troops of the US Army Engineers. They constructed this section of the highway and named the stream after their company officer, Lt. BROOKS.

BROWN LAKE 60°19'N 124°39'W (95-C). In the southeast corner of the Yukon Territory.

In 1963 this lake was given the name of V-19206 Leading Seaman David Henry BROWN, MID. He was born 30 April, 1916, at Perth, Ontario and enlisted in the RCNVR on 20 November, 1940, at Windsor, Ontario. He served in Canada and was missing, presumed to have been killed in action on the high seas, 7 May, 1944.

MOUNT BROWN   60°01′N 135°03′W (105-D). On the east side of Munroe Lake.

This hill was probably used as a survey point by A. St. Cyr, DLS, in 1901 while surveying the Yukon-BC boundary and named after one of his crew.

BROWNS CREEK   64°19′N 140°53′W (116-B&C). A tributary to the Fortymile River.

In late 1886 or early 1887, "Shoemaker" BROWN found and mined gold on this stream, giving it his name. When the rush to the district started in the summer of 1887 he sold his claim for $140.00 and a Winchester rifle, "Because the country is getting too damn crowded."

In the spring of 1893 J.A. Howard and Frank Montgomery rafted logs down the Fortymile River from Sam Patch's Bar to Brown's Creek. They built and ran a roadhouse to service the traffic between Fortymile and the new diggings in the Sixtymile country as the trail between the two ran along this stream. They called it the Brown's Creek Roadhouse.

The Fortymile country lay dormant after 1896, most miners being in the Klondike. By 1906 the old goldfields were again being prospected and in September that year George L. Gates staked a Discovery claim on the abandoned creek. The Mining Recorder thought the claim was on Bear Creek (now Bruin) and decided to change the name, as there were too many Bear Creeks in the country. He named it Gates Creek and the mistake was allowed to stand, although it was referred to by both names on different maps.

In December 1958 the Geographical Board rectified the error and restored the name Browns Creek to the stream.

BRYANT   CREEK   64°01′N 139°32′W (116-B&C). Flows into the Yukon six miles above Dawson.

J.H. Howell of Seattle found gold in the gravels of this stream and staked the Discovery claim on 8 September, 1897. When recording it, he named it after his schoolmate, three-time presidential candidate, William Jennings Bryan. The "t" was added in error by the Mining Recorder.

BUCKLANDS HILLS   69°17′N 139°40′W (117-D). The first range of hills on the Arctic coast facing Herschel Island.

These were originally named the Buckland Range by John Franklin in 1826 after Professor William BUCKLAND (1784–1865), an English geologist and clergyman, and Dean of Westminster in 1845.

BUFFALO MOUNTAIN 5,650' 61°54'N 136°46'W (115–H). 30 miles northeast of Aishihik Lake.

This was named by C.W. Rowley, as some of the last buffalo in the Yukon ranged here one winter. Buffalo have since been re-introduced into the area.

BULL CREEK 61°32'N 140°22'W (115–F). A tributary of St. Clare Creek, east of the Klutlan Glacier.

This was named in the 1900's by Tom Dickson, 98'er, ex-NWMP and noted big-game guide in the area around Kluane and the White River region for many years. He had killed a number of very fine caribou on this stream.

BULLION CITY 60°57'N 138°36'W (115–B&C). On Slim's River, five miles from Kluane Lake.

This was a short-lived mining camp, established in 1903 to serve the local miners. A post office was opened in 1905. The name was changed to Kluane in the following year, and the settlement lasted only a few more years.

BULLION CREEK 60°58'N 138°36'W (115–B&C). A tributary to Slim's River, five miles from Kluane Lake.

On 28 September, 1903, Frank Altemose, Joseph W. Smith, Fred Ater and Morley Bones found rich placer gold on this creek. J.W. Smith made the discovery. They took out 40 ounces of coarse gold in a few hours but never again found as rich a pocket. This discovery in a new area started a major rush to the district which continued to the fall of 1905. As many as 8,000–10,000 people were in the area.

MOUNT BURGESS 66°02'N 139°38'W (116–J&K). In the Ogilvie Mountains near Miner River.

William Ogilvie, DLS, named this peak in April 1888 after A.M. BURGESS, the Deputy Minister of the Interior from 1883–97, who had been extremely helpful in organizing Ogilvie's and Dawson's 1887–88 expedition to the Yukon.

BURKE CREEK   60°52′N 130°36′W (105–B). A tributary to the Liard River south of Wasson Lake.

In February 1936, J.A. Jeckell, Controller of the Yukon Territory and Livingstone Wernecke, of the Treadwell Yukon Mining Co., requested this name. Captain E.J.A. (Paddy) BURKE, formerly of the Royal Flying Corps, died near here.

While flying in to a mining property he crashed on the frozen Liard River. Being uninjured, he and his two companions, Emil Kading and Robert Martin, decided to walk north on the Liard River to Junkers Lake where they had established a food and fuel cache. Deep snow and unseasonably cold weather (it was 11 October, 1930,) together with the lack of snow-shoes made travel extremely difficult. Burke died of exhaustion and exposure on 20 November, the first aircraft pilot to die in the Yukon.

Pilot Everett Wasson found the party after an extensive search. (See Wasson Lake and Junkers Lake)

The oddest part of the story is that although Burke's name has been officially given to a creek in the vicinity near where he landed, the exact creek has not yet been located. Here is an official name with no place.

Burke is buried in Atlin, BC.

BURNHAM CREEK   63°43′N 138°32′W (115–O&N). A tributary to Dominion Creek from the east, eight miles above its mouth.

On 26 January, 1898, John Hafler staked the Discovery claim on this creek. He was probably one of the group which included Major Frederick R. BURNHAM DSO, a noted American scout and frontiersman. Burnham distinguished himself in the American west and in the Matabele Wars in Southern Africa. He came into the Klondike in 1897 and was active in this area. After leaving the Yukon he returned to South Africa as Chief of Scouts for the British Forces and served with great distinction.

BURWASH CREEK   61°30′N 139°16′W (115–G&F). Flows to the Kluane River near Kluane Lake.

This was named on 28 May, 1904, by the well-known team of prospectors, Frank Altemose, Joseph W. Smith, Fred Ater and Morley Bones. On that day they discovered the rich, gold placers of this creek and named the stream after their friend, the Mining Recorder at Silver City, Lachlin Taylor BURWASH. The pay streak of the creek was elusive and sporadic, and consistent deposits were not found until 1909. The creek since then has produced steadily up to the present.

Burwash, born in Coburg, Ontario, was the son of the Rev. J. Burwash, Chancellor of Victoria College in Toronto in 1896. He came to the Yukon in 1897 as a prospector for the NAT&TC — but soon was appointed Mining Recorder at Stewart City in 1900, at Silver City in 1903 and later was named Government Mining Engineer and Mines Inspector for the territory. He served in the First World War in the 1st Pioneer Battalion, CEF from 1915-19, rising to the rank of major. In later years he explored much of Arctic Canada for the Department of the Interior. He died in 1940.

BURWASH LANDING 61°22′N 139°00′W (115-G&F). On the northwestern shore of Kluane Lake at mile 1095 of the Alaska Highway.

This small settlement was started in 1904, shortly after the discovery of Burwash Creek, by the brothers Louis and Eugene Jacquot who were from Alsace-Lorraine. It was a supply centre, serviced by boat, for the miners on the various creeks in the district. The brothers named it after their friend Lachlin Taylor BURWASH. It later became the supply point for the gold rush to the Chisana River placer fields in Alaska during 1913-15.

The Jacquots, who originally were miners, homesteaded here and, after the First World War and for many years, became outstanding big-game guides and outfitters.

MOUNT BUSH 60°19′N 135°05′W (105-D). The ridge between Perkins and Schnabel Creeks.

This was probably named in 1898-99 after Charles J. BUSH, pioneer prospector in the Wheaton River region and a partner of William Schnabel. They discovered and owned the Nevada Mines property on this ridge.

BUTLER GULCH 63°58′N 140°33′W (115-O&N). Tributary to Boucher Creek in the Sixtymile district.

This was named by a man called BUTLER who staked the Discovery claim in July 1902 during the stampede to the new gold discoveries on Boucher Creek. His full name is not known.

BUTTLE CREEK 62°11′N 133°20′W (105-K). Flows into the Pelly River near Faro.

Roy E. BUTTLE was a trapper, prospector and trader who lived on this stream for many years from the early 1900's to the 1920's and had a trading post at Ross River in the 1930's.

BUXTON MISSION 64°26′N 140°33′W (116-B&C). About one-half mile above the town of Fortymile on the Yukon River.

In 1887, Bishop Bompas of the Anglican Church, in response to requests from miners and natives, sent the Rev. J.W. Ellington to Fortymile to start an Anglican mission. The sum of £100 had been contributed for this purpose by T. Fowell BUXTON of Easneye, Ware, England.

Ellington, a young man and the son of missionaries, was evidently humourless and quite incompatible with the rough and ready miners. They found him an easy butt for their practical jokes, many of them crude. His health and his mind gave way and he was soon returned to Winnipeg.

The mission was unoccupied until Bishop Bompas re-opened it in 1892. Its main purpose was always the education of Indian children. He stayed here until 1896 when Fortymile was almost completely abandoned because of the Klondike discovery. He moved to Dawson in early 1897 and built the first church there, St. Paul's.

An attempt was made by Bompas to change the name of Fortymile to Buxton but the miners refused to use the name. The mission is separated from the town by a deep ravine, flooded in high water and crossed by a bridge, which led some to describe it as being on an island in the Yukon.

CABIN CREEK 60°15′N 129°08′W (105-A). Tributary to the Liard River just below the Frances River.

In 1949 the Board on Geographical Names recorded this name, as the cabin and the grave of an old trapper named Stewart are at the mouth of the stream.

CABIN CREEK 60°44′N 130°16′W (105-B). Tributary to the upper Liard River.

In the winter of 1874-75 miners from the Cassiar found and mined gold on this stream, the first payable gold ever found in the Yukon Territory. They built cabins here, giving the stream its name. (See Sayyea and Scurvy Creeks.)

CACHE LAKE 61°13′N 139°04′W (115-G&F). At the headwaters of Halfbreed Creek.

This small lake was named in the summer of 1973 by the personnel of the Yukon Wilderness and Scenic Study Group who left supplies here.

CADZOW LAKE 67°34′N 138°58′W (116-O&N). On the south side of the Porcupine River, 25 miles east of Old Crow.

In 1897 Daniel CADZOW, a Scot, left Edmonton for the Klondike. He took the Mackenzie — Peel River — Rat River route and reached Dawson in the summer of 1899, only to find the Klondike rush was over. Soon afterwards he returned to the northern rivers and settled at Rampart House. He set up as a small trader in 1903 or 04. After the smallpox epidemic of 1911–12 the post was abandoned and Cadzow moved with the Indians and built anew at Old Crow. He married an Indian woman. His trading post, supplied by water from Dawson, was the only base of supplies in the northern Yukon for many years. His family is still in the north.

CAESAR LAKES 61°26′N 127°54′W (95–E). At the headwaters of the Coal River.

On 20 August, 1968, Dr. H. Gabrielse, GSC, gave this name to these small lakes for an Indian family of this name who had lived here for many years.

MOUNT CAIRNES 9,150′ 60°52′N 138°16′W (115–B&C). In the Kluane Range, 15 miles southeast of Kluane Lake.

This mountain was named in the 1920′s for D.D. CAIRNES, GSC, (1879–1917), noted pioneer Yukon geologist who explored and mapped much of this area. His explorations added enormously to the knowledge of the Yukon′s geology.

Cairnes graduated from Queen′s University in Kingston, Ontario. He worked in the Yukon from 1905 to 1917 when he died at the age of 37 in Ottawa.

MOUNT CAIRNES 64°26′N 138°18′W (116–B&C). In the Ogilvie Mountains at the headwaters of the North Klondike River.

This was named in July 1968 by Dr. D. Tempelman-Kluit, GSC, while mapping this area. He greatly admired the work done previously by D.D. CAIRNES, GSC. (See above.)

There is also a Mount Cairnes in BC named for the same man.

CALAMITES CREEK 65°56′N 134°29′W (106–E). Tributary to the Peel River.

About 1944 Dr. Stelck, GSC, found many of these fossil plants in the rock along this stream.

CALDER CREEK 63°47′N 139°07′W (115–O&N). A small tributary to Quartz Creek in the Klondike.

This was named by the first discoverer of gold on the creek, Alex

CALDER, who staked on 21 October, 1897, starting a staking rush to Quartz Creek. He was a partner of "Big Alex" McDonald. From Cape Breton, Nova Scotia, he came into the Yukon in 1896 and was one of the lucky men to stake a claim on Eldorado Creek. He died on 30 March, 1900 at Fort Selkirk.

CALEDONIA CREEK 62°42'N 140°05'W (115-J&K). Tributary to the Donjek River, one mile below Donjek City.

On 1 November, 1913, David Edwards and his partner Burnett Middleton discovered placer gold on this stream, staked the Discovery claim and probably named it after their native Scotland.

CALIFORNIA CREEK 64°01'N 140°21'W (116-B&C). Tributary to the Sixtymile River.

This creek was named in 1892 when coarse gold was first found in the Sixtymile district. In 1905 a Klondiker named Leonard found payable gold on one of the small tributaries which he named after himself. In June 1905 further finds caused another stampede and the whole stream was named Leonard Creek. The new name reverted to California Creek when the excitement died down and most of the stakers abandoned the stream.

CAMERON GULCH 64°06'N 135°03'W (106-D). A small brook running into Scougale Creek, in the Davidson Range.

This was named before 1910 by the prospector, CAMERON, who found and mined gold on this little gulch. This is probably the same Cameron who died one winter in his cabin on the banks of the Stewart River below Russell Creek. His body lay in the cabin for six years before the river changed course and swept both away.

CAMPBELL CREEK 61°46'N 131°07'W (105-G). Tributary to the Pelly River.

Robert CAMPBELL of the HBC, the first explorer of the central Yukon, travelled this creek on his famous journey of exploration in July 1840, when he discovered the Pelly River. Dr. G.M. Dawson, GSC, named this stream when he retraced Campbell's route on the first geological expedition to the Yukon in 1887.

Robert Campbell was born in Perthshire, Scotland on 21 February, 1808, the son of a sheep farmer. At the age of 22, he was hired by the HBC as a sub-manager of their experimental farm at Fort Garry in what is now Manitoba.

In 1833 he left the farm and was sent to Fort Resolution where he traded for the next four years. 1838 saw Campbell starting the series of explorations for which he became noted. The first journey was from Fort Halkett on the Liard River to Dease Lake where he and his Indian companions nearly starved to death the following winter. In early 1840 he ascended the Liard River to the Frances River (which he named), up to Frances Lake, and up the Finlayson River to its lake and then to the Pelly River at Campbell Creek, where he established Pelly Banks Post in 1846.

In 1843 he descended the Pelly River to its junction with the Yukon (the upper part of which he named the Lewes). In 1848 he again made this journey and built Fort Selkirk where the two rivers meet. This first post was moved to the west bank of the Yukon the following year because of flooding problems. It was raided and pillaged by the Chilkat Indians in 1852.

Due to this catastrophe, Campbell made, in the winter of 1852–53, one of the longest snowshoe journeys on record: from Fort Simpson on the Mackenzie River to Crow Wing, Minnesota on the Mississippi River, about 3300 miles, between 30 November, 1852, and 13 March, 1853. (This record stood for 24 years until exceeded by J.S. Camsell, Chief Factor at Fort Simpson, who retraced Campbell's route plus an additional 180 miles from Fort Liard to Fort Simpson.)

Although he was promoted to command the Peace River and Athabaska country, Campbell never was allowed to return to the Yukon. After 41 years service he was abruptly dismissed by the company in 1871. He died and was buried in Winnipeg on 9 May, 1894.

Fort Pelly Banks was built on the Pelly River opposite the mouth of this stream. The stream was first prospected by a man named Theakson who came up from Fort Liard in 1878–79.

MOUNT CAMPBELL 8,200' 64°23'N 138°45'W (116-B&C). 33 miles northeast of Dawson on the headwaters of the Tombstone River.

In 1896 William Ogilvie, DLS, was surveying the Yukon-Alaska boundary near Fortymile and while doing so, named many mountains to the east after Yukon pioneers. He named one, due east about 60 miles, after Robert CAMPBELL of the HBC, the first explorer of the central Yukon Territory. He described it in his report as "the most remarkable peak in the country, a black shaft about 600 feet wide and rising about 1,000 feet above the rest of the mountain ridge."

The early miners of the area and the people of Dawson, knowing nothing of Ogilvie's designation due to the fact that the name Campbell had not appeared on any map available to them, called it "Tombstone Mountain" from its eerie resemblance. In later years some maps showed this name, while others called it Campbell Mountain. A field investigation by the GSC failed to differentiate the two and the name Campbell was dropped and "Tombstone" adopted. Maps are still being printed showing it as Campbell. (See Tombstone Mountain.)

CAMPBELL GULCH 64°02′N 139°24′W (116-B&C). A tributary to Boulder Creek.

This stream was named on 7 September, 1897, when Alex CAMPBELL staked claim No. 6.

CAMPBELL RANGE 61°23′N 130°00′W (105-G&H). On the west side of Frances Lake.

This was named in 1887 by Dr. G.M. Dawson, GSC, after Chief Factor Robert CAMPBELL of the HBC. (See Campbell Creek.)

CANADIAN CREEK 62°48′N 138°43′W (115-J&K). Flows into Britannia Creek.

Named, for obvious reasons, by Joseph Britton and Charles C. Brown on 21 April, 1911 when they discovered gold here. (See Britton Ridge.)

CANALASKA MOUNTAIN 2,260′ 67°22′N 141°00′W (116-O&N). On the Yukon-Alaska boundary.

This composite name was given by J.H. Turner USC&GS, in 1890. It had previously been called Boundary Mountain.

THE CANOL ROAD AND PIPELINE

This road, 513 miles long, was built to provide access for the construction of a wartime emergency oil pipeline from the oil fields at Fort Norman, NWT, on the lower Mackenzie River, to Whitehorse. It ran from Johnson's Crossing past Quiet Lake to Ross River and through the MacMillan Pass to Fort Norman. From Johnson's Crossing the pipeline was built along the Alaska Highway to a refinery at Whitehorse. The gasoline from the Whitehorse refinery was to power the aircraft being flown to Russia and to provide for military needs in Alaska, which was expecting a Japanese invasion at the time. Later, it could help to mount air strikes against Japan.

The line laid was four inches in diameter and supplied about 3,000 gallons of oil per day. The project started in April 1942 and was carried through to completion in April 1944, when the first oil flowed through the line. The road was officially opened to traffic in September 1944 but it and the pipeline were abandoned shortly after the war.

The CANOL Project's total cost was $134,000,000, which includes the road, the pipeline, the refinery and the cost of sinking 26 oil wells at Fort Norman.

In recent years the Yukon government has gradually reopened portions of the road until it is now a good summer road in use by tourists and mining exploration companies searching for minerals.

CANTLIE LAKE 60°40'N 134°49'W (104-D). Eight miles southeast of Whitehorse.

In 1948 this lake was given the name of Lt. Col. Stuart Stephen Tuffnell CANTLIE, MID, CEM. He was born in Winnipeg, Manitoba on 5 October, 1907 and enlisted on 4 September, 1939 at Montréal. He served in Canada, Great Britain and northwest Europe with the Black Watch (the Royal Highland Regiment) of Canada and died of wounds received in action in France on 25 July, 1944.

CANYON 60°52'N 137°03'W (115-A). About mile 996.5 (K1604) on the Alaska Highway, on the east side of the Aishihik River.

During the stampede to the Kluane Lake goldfields in 1903, a wagon road was built from Whitehorse to Kluane Lake. A roadhouse and stores were built here and the small community existed until 1935. It gained its name from the stream beside it; it was called CANYON Creek until the 1940's when it was changed to the Aishihik River. The original bridge across the stream was built by Gilbert Skelly and Sam McGee (of Robert Service fame).

Tourist services were rebuilt here after the opening of the Alaska Highway.

CANYON CITY 61°48'N 140°47'W (115-G&F). On the White River, ten miles east of the Yukon-Alaska boundary.

A now-abandoned mining settlement was started here in 1905 as a supply centre and winter quarters for the prospectors who were developing the new copper finds in the vicinity. It was the head of water transportation and became active when the rich placer gold of the Chisana was found in

1913, which attracted thousands to the area. Much prospecting was done in the area after Solomon Albert found promising deposits of native copper near here in May 1905.

After roads were built in Alaska to serve the Chisana and the deposits themselves were declining, this village lost its reason for being and was abandoned in the 1920's.

CANYON CITY   60°40′N 135°03′W (105-D). On the east side of the Yukon River at the head of Miles Canyon.

This settlement grew up in the summer and fall of 1897 due to the need to portage goods around the dangerous waters of Miles Canyon and the Whitehorse Rapids. Between 1897 and 1899 numerous people were drowned and large quantities of supplies lost in trying to ferry boats through these waters.

In the winter of 1897–98 two tramways were built around these obstructions. The one on the west bank was built by John Hepburn and was 6½ miles long. The one on the east bank was five miles long and was built by Norman MacAuley. The toll on both was three cents per pound and $25 per boat. (Most boats were usually taken through the canyon and rapids by professional pilots for less.) Goods were transported by the tramway by horse-drawn cars which carried about a ton.

MacAuley bought out Hepburn and concentrated his operations on the east bank of the river. Here he built offices, freight sheds and a hotel to serve the travellers. Others built stores and dwellings.

The settlement thrived until July 1900 when the WP&YR arrived in what is now Whitehorse. Canyon City was quickly abandoned and the business men moved their operations to Whitehorse.

CANYON MOUNTAIN   60°41′N 134°54′W (105-D). Four miles east of Miles Canyon and opposite Whitehorse.

This hill was named by the earliest miners travelling down the river in the 1880's. It was a good landmark to warn them of their approach to the dangerous waterway.

Local people now call it Grey Hill or Mountain.

CARBON HILL   60°10′N 135°16′W (105-D). On the south side of the Wheaton River.

In 1893, well before the Klondike rush, two prospectors from Juneau,

Frank Corwin and Thomas Rickman, investigated this area and found veins with rich gold, copper and silver-antimony ore in a number of places.

They found the black, silver-antimony ore on this hill. Returning to Juneau in the fall they both died within a short time and the exact location (there were no maps of the area at that time) of their finds was lost. In August 1906 H.E. Porter (see Porter Creek) rediscovered their old workings and gave the hill its name from the colour of the ore. (See Mount Hodnett and Gold Hill.)

CARCROSS 60°10′N 134°42′W (105-D). At the junction of Bennett and Tagish Lakes.

This was first known as Caribou Crossing, from the time of the earliest miners to come across the Chilkoot Pass, because large herds of caribou crossed the narrows here twice a year on their annual migration. A major way point on the route to the Yukon goldfields and later to the Atlin, BC, goldfields, the townsite was pre-empted by the WP&YR in September 1898. The largest sawmill on the Yukon was near here, owned by Mike King, who also built boats and scows from early 1897. The Caribou Hotel, built in 1898, is still in operation, the oldest continuing hotel in the Yukon Territory.

In 1903 Bishop Bompas, who had established a school here for Indian children in 1901, petitioned the Dominion government to change the name of the community to CARCROSS because of the confusion in mail services due to the duplication of names in Alaska and British Columbia as well as in the Klondike. The post office made the change official the following year but the good bishop had to fight longer with the WP&YR, which retained the name of the station until 1916.

Numerous Yukon pioneers are buried here including Bishop Bompas, Kate Carmack, Skookum Jim Mason, and Tagish Charlie.

CARIBOU CITY 63°50′N 138°44′W (115-O&N). At the junction of Caribou Creek and Dominion Creek in the Klondike.

A settlement sprang up here in early 1897 as a supply point and stopping place for the many miners on the surrounding creeks. Several hotels gave accommodation and amusement to the local miners, among them the Gold Run, the Driard and the Caribou Hotels. A post office was opened in November 1899 but after 1905 the settlement and the post office became known as Dominion.

The place died out during the First World War due to the end of the pick-and-shovel mining and with it the loss of people and business.

CARIBOU CREEK   61°18′N 133°20′W (105–F). Flows into Big Salmon Lake.

This was one of the earliest streams to be named by miners. John McCormack, of New Brunswick, and his partners prospected it for gold and named it in the summer of 1887.

CARLSON CREEK   63°39′N 136°22′W (115–P). A tributary to Bear Creek.

Louis Beauvette and Charles Johnson staked the first placer gold claim on this stream on 10 March, 1911, and named it for a friend.

CARMACKS   62°05′N 136°17′W (115–I). A settlement on the Yukon River at the mouth of the Nordenskiold River.

George Washington CARMACK was born at Port Costa, California, on 24 September, 1860, after his parents had crossed the continent by ox team and Conestoga wagon. In 1885 he went north to Juneau and in April the same year joined a party of seven miners and went over the Chilkoot Pass to prospect the Stewart and other Yukon rivers.

He met and liked the Tagish Indians of the region and, to a certain extent, adopted their life-style. About this time he became associated with Skookum Jim Mason and his sister Kate. In 1887 they worked for William Ogilvie, DLS, packing his supplies over the Chilkoot Pass and travelling from Dyea to Fortymile. In the next few years they prospected the Big Salmon River, the Hootalinqua (Teslin) River and the Stewart.

In 1893 Carmack found a seam of coal near Five Fingers Rapids and another near Tantalus Butte. He built a cabin here while he tried to develop the coal and carried on a certain amount of fur trading with the local Indians. Arthur Harper backed his coal ventures and owned a 50% interest in them. This was the beginning of present day Carmacks.

The settlement grew and became a riverboat stop during the gold rush and later a supply point for various mining operations in the district. After the building of the Dawson—Whitehorse highway it continued to grow.

Carmack, Skookum Jim and Tagish Charlie went on to uncover the golden wealth of Bonanza Creek in August 1896. Carmack died on 5 June, 1922, in Vancouver, BC, a relatively wealthy man. Contrary to the many stories showing him to be renegade white man, he was well-educated and intelligent. His cabin at Carmacks contained an organ which he played and many volumes of classical literature. He subscribed to *Scientific American* and other literate journals and was in the way of being a romantic poet. In all the controversy regarding the discovery of gold in the Klondike he was the only principal who did not attack the stories or characters of the others.

CARMACK'S FORK   63°55′N 139°09′W (115-O&N). The north fork of Bonanza Creek.

This small section of the famous Bonanza Creek is the only feature in the Klondike to perpetuate the name of the discoverer. Very little gold was ever found on it.

CARMACKS – FREEGOLD ROAD

This road was built by the N.A. Timmins mining interests in 1934 to explore and develop the LaForma Gold Mine on Mount Freegold. It was quickly extended by prospectors and the territorial government to other parts of this mineral-rich district.

CARPENTER CREEK   64°23′N 135°11′W (106-D). Flows into Beaver Creek.

Jack CARPENTER was an enterprising prospector who found the first, rich, silver-lead ore in this district. The find sparked a sizeable rush to the area in 1920–23 but, as the mineral finds were not economic at the time, the rush petered out and the country was deserted again. The big ridge to the northwest of the creek was later named Carpenter Ridge.

MOUNT CARTER   4,751′   65°40′N 137°03′W (116-H). Between the Blackstone and Hart Rivers.

In 1973 this mountain was named after Special Constable Sam CARTER, RCMP, a member of the lost Fitzgerald patrol in 1911. (See Dempster Highway.)

CASCADE CREEK   63°38′N 134°51′W (105-M). Flows into the southeast end of Mayo Lake.

Gold was first discovered here by Thomas Heney about August 1903. He was one of a party of four Australians who first prospected the area at that time and found rich gold on this and several adjacent creeks. (See Ledge and Steep Creeks.)

CASINO CREEK 62°38'N 138°52'W (115-J&K). A tributary to Dip Creek in the Dawson Range.

This was named on or shortly before 28 November, 1915, by two prospectors, Jack O'Hara and Frank Farnan, who discovered placer gold on the stream and named it after their favourite card game.

CASSIAR BAR 61°48'N 135°00'W (105-E). One of a group of gravel bars in the Yukon River, six miles above the Big Salmon River and opposite the mouth of Fyfe Creek.

This series of gravel bars was the first and richest found on the Lewes (Yukon) River. Found in the summer of 1884 by Thomas Boswell, Howard Franklin and Michael Hess, it produced the first considerable amount of gold taken out of the upper Yukon region.

In 1886 over $30 (almost two ounces) per man per day were taken from here by many of the miners. The deposits, being shallow, were soon worked out but they gave encouragement to further prospecting in the territory. The miners who found it named it after the country they had come from previously, the CASSIAR, in northern BC.

CASSIAR CREEK 64°20'N 140°10'W (116-B&C). Tributary to the Yukon about 16 miles above the Fortymile River.

This name was applied by miners from the Cassiar country in northern BC when they moved into the Yukon in the 1880's. Although no gold was ever found on this stream in paying quantities, it has another claim to fame. It was the scene of the famous "Nigger Jim" Daugherty stampede of January 1899.

Daugherty, a Virginian, had wagered that he could start a staking stampede at any time he wished. He did, in extremely cold weather in January and several of the duped stampeders were severely frozen. The story, written in many accounts of the Klondike Gold Rush, epitomized the whole spirit and character of the Klondike stampede itself, in miniature.

CASSIAR MOUNTAINS 60°20'N 130°50'W (105-B). On the north side of the Alaskan Highway between mile 690 and 760.

This is a corruption of the Indian name "Kaska" which was applied to two tribes occupying the country to the east of the Stikine River in northern BC.

CATHEDRAL CREEK 65°12'N 141°00'W (116-G&F). Runs across the Yukon-Alaska boundary into Hardluck Creek in Alaska.

In 1909 surveyors on the International Boundary Survey named this creek because of the beautiful, cathedral-like mountains along its course.

CATHEDRAL ROCKS   66°08′N   138°45′W   (116-J&K). On the east side of the Miner River.

In May 1888 William Ogilvie, DLS, passed down this river and thought this feature interesting enough to name. He described it as a large rock exposure extending for a half a mile. It rises 300 to 400 feet from the river and as it is weathered into resemblances to old buildings, he gave it this name.

CENTENNIAL RANGE   60°58′N   140°39′W   (115-B&C).In the northwest corner of the St. Elias Range.

This group of 13 peaks was first selected in 1967 (although the idea was first thought about in 1965) to become the locale for perhaps the most unusual centennial project in Canada's Centennial Year.

It was organized mainly by David R. Fisher of the Alpine Club of Canada, David Judd, Executive Assistant to the Commissioner of the Yukon Territory, and Monty Alford of the Water Resources Board at Whitehorse and a co-ordinator of the Polar Shelf Project. The proposal was accepted by the Centennial Committee and was named the Yukon Alpine Centennial Expedition.

As 1967 also marked the Alaska Purchase Centennial it was decided to have a team of four Americans and four Canadians climb the highest, unclimbed peak on the Yukon-Alaska border. This peak, situated two miles north of Mount Vancouver, was to be named "Good Neighbour" Peak. This was the first part of the project to be carried out on 25 June, 1967.

The second and much more ambitious part of the project was the attempted ascent of the 13 Centennial Peaks in a two-week period. None had been climbed before.

Thirteen teams of four climbers each were organized and, with support personnel, more than 250 people took part in the project. It was the largest effort of its kind known in North America.

The attempt was nearly a total success. Nine peaks were scaled for the first time and climbers came within feet of conquering each of the others. All this was accomplished between 8 July and 13 August. The nine ascents were all made in the period 13–24 July.

CHADBURN LAKE   60°39′N   134°57′W   (105-D). One mile east of Miles Canyon.

This little lake was named in October 1948 to perpetuate the name of a Canadian hero, Wing Commander Lloyd Vernon CHADBURN, DSO and Bar, DFC. He was born on 21 August, 1919, in Montréal. Québec and enlisted in the RCAF on 16 April, 1940, at Toronto, Ontario. He served in Canada and overseas and died of wounds suffered in action on 19 June, 1944.

MOUNT CHAMBERS 5,301' 65°10'N 138°48'W (116-G&F). South of the Ogilvie River.

In 1973 the Topographical Surveys Branch named this hill for Harlow "Shorty" CHAMBERS, who built the first trading post at Champagne and served as postmaster there.

CHAMPAGNE 60°47'N 136°29'W (115-A). At the junction of the Dalton Trail and Dezeadash River near mile 974 (K1658) on the Alaska Highway.

This little settlement, nearly abandoned now, was the centre of activity of the area for many years until the Alaska Highway was built. There are several different stories concerning the origin of the name.

Champagne was originally a camping spot on the Dalton Trail to Rink Rapids. The Klondike Gold Rush brought a great increase in travel and a demand for more horses for a longer part of the year. Jack Dalton wintered stock here as well as at Dalton Post, farther south.

In 1897 Gordon Bounds was taking a herd of 40 cattle to Dawson. He was probably working for Dalton at the time. When this point was reached, the worst of the trail was over and it was said that they opened a case of French champagne from the freight they were carrying to Dawson and celebrated the end of their hardships.

The place assumed some importance in 1902 when Harlow "Shorty" Chambers built his roadhouse and trading post. It became a supply centre the next year when the rush to the Bullion Creek finds started and gained again from the rush to the Burwash Creek diggings in 1904. During these days it was usually called Champagne Landing and, sometimes, Champlain or Champlain's Landing. Chambers' family still owned and ran the roadhouse when it burned in March 1962.

Since the end of placer gold mining in this district and the end of highway construction, the settlement has gradually shrunk to its present size.

CHANDINDU RIVER 64°15'N 139°43'W (116-B&C). Tributary of the Yukon River, 12 miles below Dawson.

This river was named by Lt. F. Schwatka, US Army, in 1883. It is a local Indian name and Schwatka did not obtain the meaning of the word. The early miners however, called it the Twelve Mile River because of its distance from Dawson. After 1900 large ditches were built by the Yukon Gold Company from its headwaters to supply hydraulic mining operations on the Klondike creeks.

CHAPPIE LAKE 65°47′N 134°56′W (106-E). Near the Bonnet Plume River, below its junction with the Peel River.

Ernest CHAPMAN was a trader, trapper and prospector for many years in this area. His home and trading post were on this lake in the 1930-40's. He was killed in an aircraft crash at Dawson on 31 January, 1941.

CHEECHAKO HILL 63°56′N 139°21′W (115-O&N). On the west side of Bonanza Creek between Grand Forks and Adams Creek.

Oliver B. Millet from Lunenburg, Nova Scotia, while working a lay on Eldorado Creek, formed a theory regarding an ancient and different stream channel crossing Bonanza Creek. Acting upon his idea he prospected above Tagish Charlie's claim in the winter of 1897-98 and on 14 April, 1898, he struck the White Channel gravels and their riches. The Bonanza and Eldorado miners, watching his efforts that winter, called the hill "CHEECHAKO Hill", for only a green newcomer, in their estimation, would look for gold on a hill top. Millet, sick with scurvy and nearly penniless, took $20,000 in gold from a small part of his claim (which was only 100 feet square) and then sold it for $60,000. The new owner took a further $500,000 from the ground. (The scoffers still worked for wages on the claims below).

The remainder of the hill, also staked mainly by newly arrived "cheechakos", was almost as rich and many fortunes were dug from its gravels.

CHIEF GULCH 63°52′N 139°14′W (115-O&N). The last tributary to Eldorado Creek.

CHIEF Isaac and men of his Moosehide Band of Indians were in at the beginning of the Klondike discovery. Several of them staked claims on Bonanza and other creeks. Chief Isaac found gold and staked the Discovery claim on this short stream on 4 December, 1896. He and his people were the first to trade with McQuesten when he built Fort Reliance. An able man and a good leader, he was respected by both peoples of that time. The stream was originally named Chief Isaac Creek. (See Mount Chief Isaac.)

MOUNT CHIEF ISAAC 5,280′ 65°27′N 139°25′W (116-G&F). North of the Ogilvie River.

This was named in 1973 after CHIEF ISAAC, Chief of the Moosehide Indian Band at Dawson before and after the Klondike Gold Rush. Much mentioned in the literature of the time, he was helpful and friendly to the early miners. The Moosehide Band received its name from the rockslide on the hill behind Dawson, which resembles a moosehide stretched to dry.

CHITINA GLACIER 61°01′N 141°00′W (115-G&F). Lies across the Yukon-Alaska boundary in the St. Elias Mountains.

The glacier was named in 1912 by the International Boundary Survey team, from its closeness to the Copper River in Alaska. The name CHITINA is an Indian word meaning "Copper", as reported by Dall in 1870. There are variations in spelling such as Chettyna, Chitennah, Chechitna, etc.

CHOHO HILL 67°27′N 138°41′W (116-O&N). A long, low ridge ten miles southeast of Cadzow Lake.

Long known locally, this is a Vanta Kutchin Indian word meaning "Egg".

CHRISTAL CREEK 63°56′N 135°32′W (105-M). A small tributary to the South McQuesten River.

Charles CHRISTAL found and staked the first gold here on 14 November, 1902.

CHRISTIE PASS 63°03′N 129°41′W (105-P). The pass through the Selwyn Mountains, connecting the Gravel (Keele) River in the NWT to the headwaters of the Ross River.

James Murdoch "Jim" CHRISTIE was born on 22 October, 1874, in Perth, Scotland. He came to the prairies as a young man and in early 1898, left Carman, Manitoba to take the Edmonton Trail to the Klondike. He found and used this pass on the way. He prospected the NWT and the Yukon for years, mainly interested in a vast stretch of territory centring on the Rogue River.

In 1907 Joseph Keele, GSC, whom Christie assisted in his geological survey of the area, named the pass and the mountain after him.

It was near here, in late October 1909, that a huge grizzly bear attacked him. With his skull and jaw fractured, his right arm broken and his right thigh terribly bitten, this courageous man made his way, in sub-zero temperatures, seven miles to a temporary camp. His partner, George Crissfield, tended his wounds with the only medicine they had, some Scotch whisky. Crissfield obtained the help of some nearby Indians and their dogs and after four long and terrible days, over rugged mountain country, got Christie to the small settlement of Lansing on the Stewart River. There, the trader, J.E. Ferrell, who had some medical knowledge, tended his injuries and set his arm and jaw. He and his wife nursed Christie for two months. On New Years Day he was taken by dog-sled to Dawson, a journey of 17 days. Later he went to Victoria, BC, where his jaw was re-set and his other injuries given further attention. He was back prospecting in the summer of 1910.

Christie went to Ottawa and enlisted as a private in the famous Princess Patricia's Canadian Light Infantry on 24 August, 1914, one of the very first. He served with great distinction throughout the First World War. He fought in France and was first mentioned in dispatches and then won the DCM. He was commissioned in the field and won the MC and further Allied decorations.

His courage, integrity and good humour were appreciated by all who knew him. As a bushman he was almost without an equal; he once took a party from Dawson to Edmonton by a new route in a remarkably short time, in the dead of winter.

In later life, bothered by his old wounds, he retired with his wife to Saltspring Island, BC, where he died.

MOUNT CHRISTIE 61°01′N 129°41′W (105-P). On the south side of Christie Pass.

This peak was also named by Joseph Keele, GSC, in 1909, after Jim Christie.

CHRISTMAS CREEK 61°03′N 138°21′W (115-G&F). Tributary to Kluane Lake in Christmas Bay.

The Rev. John Pringle was an outstanding figure of the Klondike with his down-to-earth brand of Presbyterianism. He did not believe in turning the other cheek and had a helping hand for every unfortunate. He was active in community life and was a member of the Yukon Council. He was an active prospector when he had time and he and Richard Fullerton found gold and staked the Discovery claim on this creek on Christmas Day 1903. He served as a chaplain with the CEF in the First World War.

CHRISTMAS CREEK 63°31'N 140°30'W (115-O&N). **A tributary of Matson Creek in the Sixtymile River district.**

This creek was discovered, i.e. gold was found, on Christmas Day 1911.

CHUNGKLEE LAKE 67°50'N 139°12'W (116-O&N). **Between the forks of Johnson and Little Flat Creeks.**

This is a Vanta Kutchin Indian word meaning "Open Place".

CHUNGKUCH LAKE 67°57'N 138°55'W (116-O&N). **Near the headwaters of Johnson Creek.**

This is an old Vanta Kutchin Indian name meaning "No Timber".

CHURCHWARD HILL 2,875' 65°34'N 138°12'W (116-G&F). **West of the Ogilvie River.**

This was named in 1973 after Guy S. CHURCHWARD, Dawson's first tinsmith in 1898. He later moved to Mayo in the 1920's. He invented and produced the Yukon Airtight Heater stove.

CLAIRE CREEK 61°59'N 135°25'W (105-E). **A short creek connecting Claire Lake (named later) with the Yukon River.**

This was probably named by or for Thomas CLAIRE, a prospector well known in this district for many years after 1900.

CLARENCE LAGOON 69°38'N 140°49'W (117-C). **On the Arctic coast about five miles east of the Yukon-Alaska border.**

This enclosed, shallow bay was named by John Franklin, (later Sir), in 1826 after Prince William Henry, Duke of CLARENCE, and afterward King William IV of Great Britain. The Clarence River was named at the same time.

CLARK LAKES 64°08'N 134°56'W (106-D). **Four small lakes on Scougale Creek.**

These were named in 1950 to honour the memory of C-19545 Gunner Arthur Raymond CLARK MID, who was born in Brockville, Ontario on 17 December, 1919. He enlisted in the Canadian army on 4 September, 1939, one of the first, at Ottawa, Ontario. He served in Canada, Great Britain and northwest Europe and was killed in action on 31 July, 1944.

CLEAR CREEK 63°37'N 137°38'W (115-P). **A tributary of the Stewart River about ten miles below the McQuesten River.**

This stream was known and named by prospectors in the early 1880's but it was not until 1900 that payable gold was discovered on it.

It was on this creek on 8 January, 1909, that "Big Alex" McDonald, the "King of the Klondike", died alone.

A bear of a man, he was slow moving and slow of speech but his expert knowledge of placer mining, combined with his phenomenal memory for facts and figures and his appetite for mining deals built him the largest fortune in the Klondike in just three years between 1896 and 1899. At his peak he was estimated to be worth in excess of $20,000,000.

Born in Antigonish, Nova Scotia, in November 1854, he went to school and mined there until 1880. For the next 13 years he mined in Colorado, early becoming a mine superintendent. The depression of 1893 broke him, along with most of the mines in the country. He went to Alaska following the stories of gold. After working for a year in the Mexican Mine at Douglas, he went over the Chilkoot Pass in April 1895. He was mining on the headwaters of the Fortymile River when he got word of Carmack's find on Bonanza Creek.

Arriving in Dawson on 22 September he located claim No. 89 Above on Bonanza and No. 11 Below on Hunker Creek. Grasping the potential of the district well before most of the men there he acted quickly to acquire interests in as many claims as possible before development work could disclose their unbelievable riches. His methods were simple: as little cash down as would be acceptable and a further sum to be paid after the spring clean-up, when the gravel mined during the winter would be sluiced and the gold recovered. After making such a deal he then found miners who had been unsuccessful in locating good claims of their own or who were short of money. To these he offered a percentage partnership, or a "lay", as they called such an arrangement. They were to mine the claim, or a portion of it and in the spring would return to him an agreed percentage of the gold they recovered. In this way and by staking, he acquired interests and claims on every gold-bearing stream in the Klondike.

At the same time he quickly bought land in Dawson City at the first, low prices. His ability to persuade others to invest their money and labour with him enabled him to build the McDonald Hotel, the Pioneer Drug Store Block, the Post Office Building and many other business establishments in the town. These he immediately rented to others.

The spring clean-up of 1897 vindicated his judgment and made him a multi-millionaire within weeks. His estimate of the amount of gold in the creeks was proven correct and the value of his holdings, both mining and business, appreciated by hundreds of percent overnight.

Through it all he remained the same man. He continued to buy and acquire more claims. He contributed major financing to build the Dawson Electric Plant, the Telephone Company, an iron works and a brewery among others. He gave $40,000, a large fortune at the time, to build the Roman Catholic Church. He was the largest supporter of the hospital and never refused financial help to any civic cause or needy friends. He was entertained by the highest circles in New York and London, where he met and married his wife.

The depopulation of the Klondike in late 1899 and 1900, caused by the discovery of the rich Nome goldfields, started his downfall. Miners became unavailable to work his claims and further, the richest ground on Bonanza and Eldorado was nearly worked out. His returns dropped and he had to buy extensions of time. His unfaltering belief in the Klondike would not let him sell any of his holdings and kept him acquiring others. By 1900 he was unable to meet some of his commitments and his financial pyramid began to crumble. The population of Dawson had halved and his businesses began to lose money. His efforts to consolidate came too late and by 1904 he had lost almost the whole of his fortune.

He repaid every debt. Nearly penniless, he returned to the simple life of the prospector on the creeks. His wife and son were supported by the income of a small insurance policy he had earlier purchased at the insistence of Belinda Mulroney. (See Grand Forks.)

On this creek, on 8 January, 1909, while chopping wood at his lonely cabin, the King of the Klondike died of a heart attack.

MOUNT CLEMENT 68°26′N 139°24′W (117-A). East of Timber Creek.

This was named in 1973 by the Topographical Surveys Branch after W.H.P. CLEMENT, who was the legal adviser and Registrar of Lands and Titles in Dawson from 1898–1900.

CLINTON CREEK 64°24′N 140°36′W (116-B&C). Tributary to the Fortymile River, three miles above its mouth.

CLINTON Felcht first prospected this stream in late 1886 or early 1887. Having prospected in Africa his friends nicknamed him "The African Hunter". He died of heart disease on 16 August, 1897, the first white man to die in Dawson.

No payable gold was ever found on the creek but it later gave its name to a thriving settlement and an asbestos mine.

CLINTON CREEK 64°27'N 140°37'W (116-B&C). On Clinton Creek, four miles above its mouth.

In 1957, Arthur Anderson, an Indian trapper at Dawson, found the large and valuable asbestos deposits which were worked here. He was born in Fortymile in 1912. This town was built in 1967 to house the employees of the Cassiar Asbestos Corp. Ltd.

This was the most northerly open-pit mine in Canada and the mill had the largest eccentric-jaw crusher ever made at the time. The mine was opened in October 1967 and closed in 1979.

MOUNT CLOSE 68°20'N 137°24'W (117-A). 13 miles northwest of Bonnet Lake in the Richardson Mountains.

This was named in 1973 after Robert CLOSE, born in Mayo and killed in a training accident at Penhold, Alberta, in 1957 while serving in the RCAF.

CLOSELEIGH

In September 1899 the WP&YR proposed this name for the settlement which would be constructed around their railroad terminus at the foot of the Whitehorse Rapids, on the west bank of the Yukon River. The only settlement at the time was on the east bank of the river and was already known as Whitehorse.

W.B. CLOSE, of Close Brothers, financiers of London, England, had raised the majority of the capital to build the railway. The name was used from September 1899 to April 1900 when the WP&YR bowed to public pressure and changed the name to Whitehorse. The east bank settlement was abandoned by then. (See Whitehorse.)

CLOUTIER CREEK 61°43'N 132°10'W (105-F). A small creek emptying into the Ketza River in the St. Cyr Range.

This perpetuates the memory of D-61181 Fusilier Gerard Ludger CLOUTIER MID who was born 1 January, 1917, in Montréal, Québec. He served in Canada, Iceland, Great Britain and France and was killed in action at Dieppe on 19 August, 1942.

CLUETT CREEK 61°16'N 138°47'W (115-G&F). This creek flows into the west side of Kluane Lake at Destruction Bay.

Albert CLUETT was born in the county of Dorset, England in 1875. He came to Canada in 1895 and joined the stampede to the Klondike in 1897.

He met the Jacquot brothers on the trail to the Kluane Lake goldfields on

Christmas Day, 1903, and helped them build their trading post at Burwash Landing the following spring. He worked there for many years when he was not prospecting or trapping. He cooked in a US Army Engineers camp nearby during the construction of the Alaska Highway and was instrumental in having the memorial plaque erected at Destruction Bay.

In 1954, when conflict arose over the name of a water feature in the area, his name was suggested. Everyone knew Bert but few knew or could spell his last name. He was away prospecting at the time and could not be reached, so another name was adopted. However, in 1957 it was decided to name this stream in Bert's territory and after some investigation it was called Klewitt Creek. In 1959 Dr. J.E. Muller, GSC, saw Bert and found the correct spelling. In 1960 the name was officially changed to Cluett Creek.

Bert died at Burwash on 15 December, 1972, a cheerful, friendly and energetic little man.

MOUNT CLUETT 65°36′N 138°46′W (116-G&F). East of the Whitestone River.

This was named in September 1973 after Hubert CLUETT. This was the same man as above except that a different government department checked the name and came up with this variation. However, Bert was never in this part of the country.

CLUM CREEK 64°04′N 137°28′W (116-A). A tributary to the Klondike River.

This was named in 1897 by four brothers who first prospected the creek. They were Peter, Charles, Joseph and Phillip CLUM (or Coulombe) from Massachusetts. They went on after the Klondike to mine in Alaska.

COAL CREEK 64°29′N 140°25′W (116-B&C). A tributary to the Yukon River about six miles below the Fortymile.

This creek was named by William Ogilvie, DLS, in 1887–88 for the coal seams previously found there by prospectors, which he examined.

The first workable coal deposits were found here by Henry Seimer in 1900. By 1904 English capital had formed a company to mine the coal and produce thermal electricity for the large gold dredges in the Klondike. They built a plant here and a 38-mile power line to Dawson. They also built a 12-mile-long, narrow-gauge railway along the creek from the mine to the Yukon River to supply coal to the riverboats.

The company ceased business in 1908 when cheaper hydro-electric power was developed nearer Dawson.

COAL GULCH 63°39'N 139°15'W (116-O&N). Flows into Ruby Creek.

The MacKinnon brothers, Archibald and Donald, who were trying to develop huge tonnages of low-grade gold ore in the Indian River conglomerates near here (see MacKinnon Creek), attempted to develop the coal seams on this gulch as a source of cheap power. Their gold property failing to produce, they also shut down work on the coal, although they had worked from 1910–15.

COAL LAKE 60°30'N 135°10'W (105-D). 15 miles southwest of Whitehorse at the foot of Mount Granger.

Several seams of anthracite coal from three to ten feet thick are located in this area. They were developed for some years after 1905 to supply the copper mines at Whitehorse.

The lake was given its name in 1900 by R.G. McConnell, GSC, when he mapped the area.

COARSE GOLD PUP 63°50'N 138°47'W (115-O&N). A very short valley entering Eldorado Creek from Cheechako Hill.

J.J. Rutledge staked the first claim here on 23 September, 1897, and optimistically named it at that time.

COBALT HILL 63°59'N 134°57'W (105-M). Just east of Keno Hill.

This hill was named by Jim MacDonald when he found rich, silver-lead ore here in 1922. He named it after COBALT, Ontario, a silver-mining camp which flourished from 1905 to 1927. He had prospected and mined there before he came to the Yukon.

MOUNT COCKFIELD 62°39'N 138°27'W (115-J&K). In the Selwyn River area of the Dawson Range.

This was named in 1915 after William E. COCKFIELD by D.D. Cairnes, GSC. He was a long-time member of the GSC and especially active in the Yukon. In 1915 he started as an assistant packer with Cairnes on a geological survey party in this area. He became senior assistant to Cairnes and later, in charge of his own operations, mapped and explored many parts of the Yukon.

COFFEE CREEK 62°55'N 139°03'W (115-J&K). A tributary of the Yukon River from the west.

"COFFEE Jack" was an Indian trapper well-known in this country at the turn of the century. Noted for his dry humour he was once accused of allowing his dogs to rob a white trapper's supplies. The trapper informed Jack that at the next offense he would poison Jack's dogs. Jack replied, "In that case I might shoot you and tell the Mountie I thought you were a moose!"

The creek was mined for gold intermittently over the years, giving reasonable returns but no bonanzas.

COFFEE CREEK POST 62°55'N 139°05'W (115-J&K). At the mouth of Coffee Creek.

Jim Derry ran a small trading post here in the 1920's and 1930's to serve the local miners and trappers.

COGHLAN LAKE 61°33'N 135°29'W (105-E). Ten miles north of Lake Laberge, on the old winter trail to Dawson.

Charles COGHLAN lived and trapped here for many years. He came to the Klondike in 1898 and remained. He accompanied F.C. Selous, a "white hunter" of African fame, on his big-game hunting expeditions to the upper MacMillan River in 1904.

MOUNT COLEMAN 61°10'N 140°08'W (115-G). At the head of the Steele Glacier in the St. Elias Mountains.

This was named by the Alpine Club of Canada after Arthur Philomen COLEMAN (1852–1939), geologist and past president of the club.

MOUNT COLLEY 65°05'N 133°12'W (106-F). West of the head of Snake River.

This was named by the Topographical Surveys Branch in 1973 after Howard "Harry" COLLEY, a well-known and successful prospector in the Dawson and Mayo districts from 1920–55.

COLORADO CREEK 63°58'N 139°00'W (115-O&N). One of the larger tributaries to Hunker Creek, from the west.

This creek was staked and named by Max Scanzon on 26 May, 1898. He, like many other Klondikers, had mined in Colorado.

COLUMBUS GLACIER 60°24′N 139°52′W (115-B&C). On the Yukon-Alaska boundary, west of the Seward Glacier in the St. Elias Range.

This glacier was named by H.R.H. Prince Luigi Amadeo, Duke of Abruzzi, on 31 July, 1897, for Christopher COLUMBUS. Prince Luigi led the Italian expedition which first climbed Mount St. Elias.

CONE HILL 64°24′N 140°35′W (116-B&C). On the south side of the Fortymile River, three miles upstream from the Yukon.

This cone-shaped hill was named by Lt. F. Schwatka, US Army, on his trip down the river in 1883. From the hill he also renamed the Fortymile River the "Cone Hill" River. Although the hill is still known locally by his name, it has been officially abandoned by the Board on Geographical Names as there are another Cone Hill and a Cone Mountain in the territory, both named much later.

CONGDON CREEK 61°09′N 138°33′W (115-G&F). Flows into the southwest end of Kluane Lake.

This stream was probably named after Frederick Tennyson CONGDON by a miner whom he had grubstaked, in February 1904.

F.T. Congdon, a lawyer from Nova Scotia, came to the Yukon in early 1898 as Legal Adviser to the Commissioner of the Yukon. This post he held until 1901. He quickly became the leader of the Liberal Party in the Yukon and was appointed Commissioner of the Yukon Territory in March 1903, a post he held until May 1905. He established the newspaper *The Yukon World* as a party mouthpiece. His tenure was marked by political graft and corruption and extreme political patronage, even in a day when this was common everywhere. In 1908 he was elected to parliament, losing the seat in the next election in 1911. He left the Yukon and engaged in law practice in Vancouver. He died in Ottawa on 13 March, 1932.

CONNOLLY LAKE 62°32′N 132°10′W (105-K). Four miles east of Mount Connolly.

Both this lake and the mountain to the west were known locally by this name for a number of years previous to the official designation in June 1978.

MOUNT CONNOLLY 7,018′ 62°32′N 132°20′W (105-K). 35 miles northeast of Faro.

Thomas Osborne CONNOLLY was born in Prince Albert, Saskatchewan, on 4 July, 1918. He was a born bushman and in his late teens went to Goldfields and then to Yellowknife where he earned his living mining and freighting. He and his lifelong friend, John Dewhurst, spent two years trapping in the Nahanni country and worked their way to the Pelly River country.

He enlisted in the Royal Canadian Naval Fishermen's Reserve in 1942 and soon was sent overseas on combined operations. He took part in the invasion of France, landing 3rd Division Canadian troops on the beach on D Day. He was engaged in numerous other landings and was discharged in March 1945.

Returning to the Yukon he took over the Taylor and Drury trading post at Ross River for a year and then set up his own store. Until 1964 he combined this with outfitting and guiding big-game hunters to the area. In 1964 he moved his family to Atlin, BC, and continued to guide in the Taku River region until his death in Vancouver, BC, on 21 July, 1975.

His fearlessness combined with his outgoing personality made him a true example of the northern pioneer.

CONRAD 60°04′N 134°34′W (105-D). On the west side of Windy Arm, Tagish Lake, about eight miles southwest of Carcross.

On 13 July, 1899, Ira Petty and W.R. Young had found and staked the silver-gold deposits that were to spark an intensive mining era in this section of the Yukon.

By 1905 Colonel John Howard CONRAD, an American mining promoter, had acquired control of most of the newly-discovered gold-silver-lead deposits on the west side of Windy Arm. He organized this settlement which at first was intended as a supply base for his operations. By 1909 it was a thriving town with stores, hotels, chuches and a District Mining Recorder. Steamboats ran schedules between here and Carcross.

The ore in the various mines, – The Big Thing, Montana, Joe Petty, Aurora, The Venus, all under Conrad Consolidated Mines Ltd., – was actively being developed but extensive work showed the erratic nature of the deposits. By 1914, with a drop in the world price for silver, the mines closed down and the town was abandoned. Several attempts have been made to reopen the mines but, so far, without success.

White Mountain, across the lake on the east side of Windy Arm, was locally called Mount Conrad at that time but the name was not officially allowed due to the earlier designation.

THE CONSERVATIVE TRAIL (115-F)

According to Hugh Bostock, the "Liberal Trail" was part of the original winter road between Dawson and Mayo and when placer mining developed on the creeks to the north, the government was urged to build a new trail that would serve more miners. In one of the elections, the Conservative candidate supported the financing of this new trail, while the Liberal advocated maintaining the trail as it was. The Conservative won, so the new trail was built. It ran from Minto Lake, along Bear Creek, across the McQuesten River and up Vancouver Creek to Clear Creek, at which point it merged with the old trail. Thus, the two trails were locally known as the "Liberal" and "Conservative" Trails.

The trails are now abandoned as mail routes but the names are still in use and the trails appear clearly in aerial photographs.

MOUNT CONSTANTINE   10,295′ 61°25′N 140°34′W (115-F). Overlooking the huge Klutan Glacier in the St. Elias Range.

This peak was named in July 1900 by J.J. McArthur, DLS, of the International Boundary Survey.

Charles CONSTANTINE was born in Bradford, Yorkshire, in 1849. A short, neat man with a piercing eye and a commanding presence, he joined the army at an early age. He took part in the Red River Expedition of 1870, became Chief of the Provincial Police of Manitoba and held a commission in the Winnipeg Light Infantry (The Little Black Devils). He saw action in the Northwest Rebellion in 1885 and then enlisted in the NWMP with the rank of inspector.

In 1894 there were no government officials of any kind in what was to become the Yukon Territory; the only law was the miners' meeting. When attended by the usual working miner and prospector it was a most democratic procedure. However, as the flow of gold and the population both increased, the settlements became filled with the usual frontier scum and parasites. When a miners' meeting was called, these people attended, while most of the miners were out at work on the creeks. The verdicts of such meetings became more and more frivolous and biased.

By early 1894 Bishop Bompas and Captain J.J. Healy (who had organized the NAT&TC and built Fort Cudahy at Fortymile) had asked the Canadian government for police to bring law, order and justice to the territory.

In June 1894 Insp. Constantine with Staff Sergeant Charles Brown of the NWMP arrived at Fortymile and, after an inspection of conditions in the region, returned to Ottawa and recommended that a force of NWMP and a

Customs Agent be established at Fortymile. S/Sg. Brown remained behind to represent the government.

Constantine returned on the *Porteous B. Weare* (the NAT&TC's riverboat) from St. Michaels on 24 July, 1895, with NCO's and constables, Insp. D'Arcy Strickland, Ass't Surgeon Willis and D.W. Davis, Collector for Customs for the Yukon. Constantine was appointed Magistrate, Mining Recorder, Coroner, Land and Timber Agent and all other necessary government posts not specified. His powers were wide and his instructions were to govern by the spirit rather than the exact letter of the law. They built Fort Constantine just below Fort Cudahy on the west bank of the Yukon, the most northerly military post of the British Empire.

In August 1896, when the Klondike gold was discovered, Constantine was the sole government official with authority, with the exception of William Ogilvie, who ably assisted him.

When the first claims were being recorded Constantine decided to use the local miners' name for the river and district and he settled on "Klondyke" as being nearest their pronunciation of the Indian name. In all the excitement and pressure on him he never lost control and his handling of such a potentially explosive situation, almost alone, still excites admiration.

In 1904, he was given command of the Athabaska District, NWT, and from 1905-07 was engaged in building a road from Fort St. John, BC, to the head of Lake Teslin, via Bear Lake, BC, and the headwaters of the Skeena River. The road was never completed.

Superintendent Charles Constantine died in Long Beach, California, while on leave, on 5 May, 1912.

CONTACT CREEK 60°00'N 127°44'W (95-D). Crosses the Yukon-BC border at mile 588.1 (K947) of the Alaska Highway.

On 24 September, 1942, bulldozers working their way south from Watson Lake met those working north from Fort Nelson, BC. This meeting of the road construction crews of the US Army Engineers marked the breakthrough of the Alaska Highway from Dawson Creek, BC, to Whitehorse and the first road access to the Yukon Territory. (See Beaver Creek.)

MOUNT CONYBEARE 2,062' 69°29'N 140°07'W (117-C). Ten miles south of the Arctic coast.

This was named by John Franklin (later Sir), in 1826, after William Daniel

CONYBEARE (1787–1857), a prominent English clergyman and noted amateur geologist.

COOK LAKE 62°09′N 130°54′W (105–J). 15 miles northwest of the Pelly Lakes.

This was named in September 1971 after Lesley "Les" COOK, who was a bush pilot and trader. He had a cabin on this lake and a trading post at Sheldon Lake. The trading post was run for a short time by his brother Jim, who was killed by a gun-trap he had set for bears.

Cook scouted the route of the Alaska Highway between Watson Lake and Teslin Lake in 1942 for the US Army Engineers, flew supplies to their survey camps and was later posthumously awarded the US Air Medal for several emergency flights he flew at that time.

He crashed in the Yukon River at Whitehorse later in 1942 and was killed.

MOUNT COOK 13,760′ 60°11′N 139°58′W (115–B&C). A boundary peak in the St. Elias Range.

This was named by W.H. Dall, Assistant of the US Coast Survey in 1871 (later the USC&GS) in 1874 after Captain James COOK, RN (1728–1779), the famous English navigator and explorer who carried out much of the first mapping and exploration of the Alaska coast.

MOUNT COOK 61°55′N 132°55′W (105–F). About 15 miles southwest of Ross River.

In 1951 this mountain was named to honour the memory of J-6276 Squadron Leader Robert Geoffrey COOK, DFC, who was born in Toronto, Ontario, on 5 February, 1921. He enlisted in the RCAF at Toronto on 20 September, 1940. He served in Canada and overseas and was missing, presumed killed in action, on 4 December, 1943.

The mountain had previously been mapped and named "Priest" Mountain in the spring of the same year by a GSC party in the area. The population of the area being almost nil, they had been completely surprised one day when a priest, in clerical garb, riding a motorcycle, went by. However, the Board on Geographical Names disallowed this name the same year. Some of the local people still use it.

MOUNT COOPER 61°11′N 136°19′W (115–H). At the headwaters of the Nordenskiold River.

This was named in 1898 after George COOPER, member of GSC survey party in the area that year. He was with J.B. Tyrrell.

CORBETT HILL 2,511' 66°20'N 136°43'W (116-1). West of the Eagle River.

In 1973 this feature was named to commemorate K-73831 Sapper Herbert Logan CORBETT, 2nd Tunnelling Company, Royal Canadian Engineers. He was killed in a blasting accident while constructing underground fortifications at Gibraltar on 28 November, 1942. He had been a placer miner at Dawson and Atlin, BC, before the war.

MOUNT CORCORAN 2,514' 62°48'N 137°27'W (115-1). Two miles northwest of Fort Selkirk.

This was named in November 1971 after Reg. No. 42 Gunner J. CORCORAN, Royal Canadian Artillery. He was a member of the Yukon Field Force and died and was buried at Fort Selkirk on 27 September, 1898. (See Mount Evans.)

MOUNT CORP 65°22'N 133°13'W (106-F). East of the Snake River in the Canyon Range.

This mountain was named by Hugh S. Bostock, GSC, in 1973, after Ernest J. CORP who came to the Klondike in 1897–98, via the Mackenzie and Gravel Rivers, Bonnet Plume Pass and the Stewart River. He was a successful miner in the Klondike and later prospected for silver on Keno Hill. He was elected for several years a member of the Yukon Council for the Mayo riding.

CORWIN VALLEY 60°17'N 134°58'W (105-D). The valley of the Wheaton River from Lake Bennett north to Annie Lake.

Frank Corwin, a pioneer Yukoner and his partner, Tom Rickman, camped in this valley and prospected the area in 1893. They found several, rich-looking deposits of gold and silver-antimony ores. They returned to Juneau in the fall where both died within a few months. Although they had staked claims on their finds, others whom they had told were unable to relocate them. Some were found in 1906 by later prospectors. (See Carbon Hill and Gold Hill.)

MOUNT COUDERT 60°32'N 136°03'W (115-A). On the northeast side of Kusawa Lake.

This hill was named in 1966 in memory of Bishop John Louis COUDERT, the first Roman Catholic Bishop of Whitehorse. He had served in the north for 45 years. He died in November 1965 while attending a Vatican Council in Rome. His body was brought back and buried in Whitehorse.

COWARD CREEK   62°39′N 134°04′W (105-L). A small tributary to the Tay River.

Aleck COWARD came in the Klondike rush and remained to trap and trade. He and his partner Zimmerlee ran a trading post at Armstrong's Landing on the MacMillan River between 1905-10. Coward then set up a trading post at Fork Selkirk where he traded, trapped and prospected until the 1950's. His wife, who had been a missionary teacher at Fort Selkirk since 1916, did not care for her husband's surname and always styled herself Mrs. Cowaret after their marriage in 1929.

CRAIG CREEK   69°37′N 140°55′W (117-C). Flows into Clarence Lagoon on the Arctic coast.

This stream was named in 1912 by the International Boundary Survey party for J.D. CRAIG, DLS, who was in charge of the Canadian survey team. (See Mount Craig.)

MOUNT CRAIG   13,250   61°16′N 140°53′W (115-G&F). In the Icefield Ranges of the St. Elias Mountains.

John Davidson CRAIG (1875-1936), BSc, DLS, a surveyor, joined the International Boundary Commission in 1905. In the following years he surveyed the Yukon-Alaska boundary from Mount St. Elias to the Beaufort Sea. From 1910 he was chief of Canadian survey parties until the task was finished in 1914. He was a member of the International Boundary Commission from 1925-31 and Director General of Surveys for the Department of the Interior from 1924-31.

CRATER CREEK   61°04′N 133°05′W (105-F). Flows into the west side of Quiet Lake.

This was probably named in 1887 by John McCormack and his three companions when they were the first men to find and prospect Quiet Lake. It was so named because of a peculiar, circular basin or valley nearby.

CRAWFORDSVILLE 61°34′N 134°52′W (105-E). On the east bank of the Yukon at the mouth of the Teslin River.

A short-lived but active settlement was built here in early 1898 and abandoned the following year. Captain Jack CRAWFORD, a famous American army scout, Indian fighter, poet and miner, was the Assistant General Manager of the Klondike, Yukon and Copper River Company. He hired large numbers of men and brought in much equipment to start a dredging operation on the Teslin River. Owing to various physical problems and a shortage of cash, the operation failed and Captain Jack went on to other ventures in Dawson City.

MOUNT CREEDEN 7,000' 61°16'N 137°15'W (115-H). On the west side of Aishihik Lake and six miles north of the Three Guardsmen Mountains.

This mountain received its name in 1966 to perpetuate the memory of J-15353 Pilot Officer James Waldron CREEDEN, DFM. He was born 4 February, 1922, at Brantford, Ontario. Enlisting in the RCAF at Hamilton, Ontario, he served in Canada and overseas. He was killed during air operations on 16 May, 1942.

CRIPPLE GULCH 64°00'N 139°22'W (116-B&C). A short brook, flowing into Bonanza Creek from the east, three miles from the Klondike River.

On 5 November, 1897, William Dugan staked the Discovery claim and named the gulch after CRIPPLE Creek, Colorado, one of the richest gold-mining camps in the USA. The hill above the gulch carried extremely rich gold in the White Channel gravels and was very productive. The stream was first named Cripple Creek.

MOUNT CRONIN 66°47'N 136°10'W (116-I). East of the Rock River in the Richardson Mountains.

In 1973 this mountain was chosen to honour the name of Lt. Alfred CRONIN, born 24 March, 1884, in Liverpool, England. He was working in the Yukon at Whitehorse and went to Victoria, BC where he enlisted in the 57th Batalion CEF on 28 October, 1915. He served in Canada and Great Britain, and was killed in action in France on 27 September, 1918.

MOUNT CRONKHITE 65°32'N 137°08'W (116-H). West of the Blackstone River.

Supt. Howard Hooper CRONKHITE, RCMP, served in the Yukon from 1921 to 35 and 1942 to 46. This peak was named in 1973.

CROSBY CREEK   62°50'N   137°06'W   (115-I). A tributary to the Pelly River.

This was named in the early 1900's after George CROSBY who was a trapper and long-time prospector in this area. Crosby came to the Yukon in 1898 and was a partner of John Barr for many years. They lived in cabins 20 miles apart but worked together.

CROUCHER CREEK   60°47'N   135°04'W   (105-D). Enters the Yukon River three miles below Whitehorse from the east side.

This creek was named in 1949 as a memorial to J-26857 Flight Lt. Gordon CROUCHER, MID, who was born 2 January, 1916, at Montréal, Québec. He enlisted there on 7 June, 1942 and served in Canada and overseas. He was missing, presumed to have been killed in action, on 29 July, 1944.

CUB LAKE   60°47'N   135°26'W   (105-D). The smaller of two lakes, five miles south of Takhini.

This was named several years ago when the CUBS and Boy Scouts initiated their annual summer camp there.

CUESTA CREEK   68°45'N   136°54'W   (117-A). A tributary of Rapid Creek.

In the summer of 1970 F.G. Young, GSC, named this creek after an uncommon geological formation found near its mouth. CUESTA is a Spanish term meaning, roughly, a hill. The term is used mostly by geologists in the American southwest to describe a hill in which the rock-bedding is normal to the gentler-sloping side of the hill rather than parallel to it as is mostly the case.

CYR CREEK   61°19'N   138°34'W   (115-G&F). Flows into Gladstone Creek.

This was named about 1903 after Michael CYR of Québec, who mined here. He was a well-known trapper and prospector in the Yukon for many years.

d'ABBADIE RIVER   (See Big Salmon River.)

D'ABBADIE CREEK   61°46'N   134°22'W   (105-E). A tributary to the North Big Salmon River.
(See Big Salmon River.)

MOUNT D'ABBADIE 61°43'N 134°05'W (105-E). **Lies at the head of D'Abbadie Creek.**

This was named because of its position on the creek.

DAIL CREEK 60°16'N 135°04'W (105-D). **A small tributary to the Wheaton River from Gold Hill.**

In the summer of 1906 a stampede of prospectors was caused by the finding of rich lode-gold ore on Gold Hill. George DAIL, a Klondiker, was one of the first to locate claims on this creek. He was a successful prospector and miner and was widely known in the Yukon for many years.

DAIL PEAK 60°01'N 134°40'W (105-D). **A prominent ridge on the southwest side of Windy Arm.**

George DAIL was one of the pioneer prospectors in the area. He found and staked the first mineral claims here in 1905 when the hill received its name from the local prospectors.

DALTON CREEK 60°19'N 137°17'W (115-A). **Flows into Alder Creek, ten miles southwest of Dezeadash Lake.**

This was named in May or June 1898 after Jack DALTON, famous Yukon and Alaska pioneer.

Born in the Oklahoma Territory in 1855, he ran away from home at the age of 15, some say because of a shooting scrape in which he was forced to kill a man. He roamed the American west in its most lawless period until — another shooting is hinted — he reached Juneau in 1887.

In 1890 he was hired by E. Hazard Wells to accompany the Frank Leslie Illustrated Newspaper Expedition into the Yukon along the old Chilkat trade route, which he later transformed into the Dalton Trail. He and E.J. Glave, an English adventurer, explored the Alsek River country and were the first men to descend the Alsek to the sea.

The following year he travelled much the same country, he and Glave bringing in the first horses seen in the Yukon. When the expedition left, Dalton, who had seen the potential of the country, remained. He started to improve the trail and established posts on it. He proposed both to trade with the Indians in the interior and to freight supplies from Pyramid Harbour to the Yukon River for the ever-increasing mining population there. He also saw that this trail was the only feasible way to get sizeable numbers of livestock into the goldfields.

By 1895 he had found and laid out the best trail and had built posts. The first herds of cattle and sheep to enter the Yukon were taken over the trail in the summer of 1896, to the mouth of the Nordenskiold River.

The only man to control a major route into the Yukon and the Klondike, Dalton ran pack trains and drove livestock to the miners. He allowed others to use his trail on payment of a toll and backed his authority with his reputation and a gun. One group which refused to pay was accompanied for the whole journey by Dalton, who kept them well away from his route and in rough country. They lost most of their stock. No one else tried to travel without paying again. He also set up and ran a Pony Express service for a short time in 1898 to speed mail into the diggings.

After the gold fever died down Dalton continued his packing and freighting until the WP&YR. and the riverboats put him out of business. He stayed in the country for many years, engaging in mining activities in the White River and nearby Alaska country. He helped survey the routes of the Alaska and Copper River railroads.

Retiring in the late 1920's, he spent many more years in Seaside, Oregon and died in January 1945 in San Francisco.

Gold-seekers using the Dalton Trail prospected along the way and found good gold on Shorty Creek. Either Dalton himself, or men working for him, found gold on this stream immediately afterward. Over the years he prospected and invested in many mining propositions in this part of the Yukon with some success.

DALTON POST or HOUSE 60°07′N 137°02′W (115-A). About 18 miles south of Dezeadash Lake and two miles west of the Haines highway.

Jack DALTON established a trading post and base camp here in 1893 or 94 to trade with the interior Indians. The climate being good he wintered his pack horses nearby for many years. A NWMP post was built here in 1897 and closed in 1904. In 1898 Dalton brought in an additional 250 head of fine Oregon horses and started the Dalton Pony Express, to give rapid service to passengers and mail between Pyramid Harbour and Fort Selkirk. He could not compete with the riverboats and the venture soon stopped. Most of the livestock brought into the goldfields came this way.

DALTON RANGE 60°29′N 137°10′W (115-A). A short range of mountains facing the west side of Dezeadash Lake.

This was probably named by J.J. McArthur, DLS, in 1897, after Jack DALTON, one of the most colourful of the Yukon and Alaska pioneers.

DALTON TRAIL

This was a major route from the sea to the Klondike goldfields and the only one over which horses, cattle, sheep and other animals could be driven easily and quickly.

The route was originally an ancient Chilkat Indian "Grease Trail" or trade route to the interior. The Chilkats carried fish oil, or grease, along with other trade goods (except guns). The route was, like the Chilkoot Pass, jealously guarded, as it was so lucrative to the Chilkats.

In 1869 Professor George Davidson, senior officer of the USGS in Alaska, persuaded the Chilkat Chief Koh-klux to draw a map of the trail. (See Fort Selkirk.)

In 1882 Dr. Aurel Krause of the Bremen Geographical Society was the first white man known to enter the country by this route, which he mapped to the Tatshenshini river.

In 1890 the Frank Leslie Illustrated Newspaper Expedition, led by E. Hazard Wells and E.J. Glave, with A.B. Schantz and Jack DALTON, went to Kusawa Lake where the party split in two. Wells and Schantz went on to the Tanana country while Glave and Dalton returned down the Alsek River. Glave and Dalton returned the following year. This time Dalton stayed in the country and began building his trail and trading posts.

By 1896 he had his operation organized: a home and a trading post at Pyramid Harbour; a post at Pleasant Camp, (near the Yukon-Alaska border); and his main trading post at Dalton House, where he wintered most of his horses.

The trail was quickly and very roughly mapped by J.J. McArthur, DLS, in 1897. In the winter of 1897–98, following reports of starvation conditions in the Klondike, the American government gathered reindeer and Lapland herders from Scandinavia and sent a herd over this trail to relieve the miners. By the time they arrived (and less than half got there) the famine had been averted and the remainder of the herd was sent on into Alaska.

A railroad was proposed over this route in 1898 and would have provided the best and cheapest access to Dawson. It was forgotten when the WP&YR was begun the same year. The Haines Junction Highway now follows the Dalton Trail for much of its length from Haines to Dalton House.

The first recorded herd of cattle to be taken over the trail was that driven by Willis Thorpe, his two sons, "Long Shorty" Brooks, George Bounds (a butcher) and two other men in 1896. It is not certain whether they were working for Dalton or paid him toll to pass. The herd consisted of about 40 steers which carried packs of freight. They were driven to Carmacks and rafted down-river to Dawson, arriving in early September 1896.

DALZIEL CREEK 60°29′N 127°10′W (95–D). A tributary of Rock River, 60 miles northeast of Watson Lake.

This was named after George Campbell Ford DALZIEL, trapper, bushman, bush pilot and big-game guide. At 18, in 1926, he came to the Yukon from North Vancouver, BC, and spent the first winter alone, trapping on the Coal River in the southeastern Yukon. Soon acquiring an aircraft he quickly became a superb bush pilot. He scouted the location of the Alaska Highway in this area for the US Army Engineers and was instrumental in finding several downed aircraft that had been lost while being ferried from Edmonton to Alaska and Russia during the Second World War.

A pioneer in the Watson Lake and surrounding country, Dalziel is noted for his ability to survive anywhere, in any season, alone.

DANGER CREEK 62°02′N 132°39′W (105–K). Flows into the Pelly River, two miles below the Lapie River.

In the summer of 1905 Charles Sheldon, noted amateur naturalist and big-game hunter, named this stream after his horse "DANGER." The horse was the first one ever seen in the upper Pelly region. Some maps have this creek named "Old Danger" Creek.

DAN MAN CREEK 62°58′N 139°17′W (115–J). A small creek flowing into the Yukon four miles above Kirkman Creek.

This was known for many years as the home and territory of Daniel MAN, a well-known trapper and prospector.

MOUNT DAOUST 62°04′N 136°06′W (115–I). About five miles southeast of Carmacks.

This was named about 1905 after an operator on the Yukon Telegraph Line who was stationed at Carmacks.

DAUGHNEY LAKE 60°10′N 130°55′W (105–B). On the Swift River six miles north of mile 720 (K1159) on the Alaska Highway.

In 1947 this lake was given the name of an outstanding Canadian soldier, Major Ralph Herman DAUGHNEY, DSO. He was born 30 November, 1908, at Dalhousie Junction, New Brunswick and was commissioned in the Canadian army on 5 September, 1940, at Woodstock, New Brunswick.

He served in Canada, Great Britain and northwest Europe and was killed in action on 10 August, 1944.

DAVIDSON CREEK 63°47′N 135°27′W (105-M). Flows into Duncan Creek near Mayo Lake.

About 1901 Jake DAVIDSON was one of the four men who staked the first claims on Duncan Creek. Shortly afterward he found gold on this stream.

DAVIS LAKE 66°11′N 136°25′W (116-I). One half-mile south of Moose Lake.

This quiet lake was named in 1973 to honour the name of Pte. Harry Henry DAVIS, K-76942, who died a prisoner of war in Holland on 15 January, 1945. He was born in Dawson on 9 January, 1921, enlisted at Whitehorse and served in Canada, Great Britain and northwest Europe in the Lake Superior Regiment (Motor).

DAWSON (CITY) 64°04′N 139°25′W (116-B&C). At the junction of the Yukon and Klondike Rivers.

Dawson City, the "Paris of the North", was the capital of the Yukon Territory from 1897 to 1951.

This was the site of an Indian fishing camp for untold years before white men ever saw the territory, as the Klondike River was one of the best salmon streams in the country.

George Carmack camped here with Skookum Jim and Tagish Charlie, fishing for salmon in early August 1896 before they made their journey of discovery up Rabbit (Bonanza) Creek.

Joseph Ladue, who operated the trading post and small sawmill at Ogilvie (Sixtymile River), had for years been a booster of the gold-mining possibilities of the district on the east side of the Yukon River and had grubstaked Robert Henderson who was and had been, with others, prospecting the tributaries of the Indian River.

While Carmack's party found the riches of Bonanza and started the great rush, Henderson and three companions were digging on Gold Bottom Creek with indifferent results. Henderson went down the Indian River to Ogilvie for more supplies and in early August 1896 showed Ladue a small amount of gold dust from his workings. Ladue, confirmed in his belief of the value of the Klondike district, decided to move some lumber and supplies down river to the mouth of the Klondike, stake a townsite and establish a small trading post.

Seldom has a decision been more fortuitous. He arrived on the scene on 28 August to hear for the first time of the Bonanza strike and to find the area alive with excited men. He immediately staked out a 160-acre townsite on the only available ground and, on 1 September, started to build his store, the first building in Dawson. He sent some of his men back to Ogilvie to bring up the sawmill (which ran night and day for the next two years). He built a small log building and opened the Pioneer, the first saloon in town. He sold lots in his townsite and bought rich claims from the cheechako stakers who did not foresee their value. In January 1897 William Ogilvie, DLS, surveyed the townsite and Ladue and his partner, Arthur Harper, had it officially named after Dr. George Mercer DAWSON (1849–1901), Director of the Geological and Natural History Survey of Canada from 1895 to 1901, explorer, scientist and human being extraordinary.

Called the "Little Doctor" by all who knew him, he was born in Pictou, Nova Scotia on 1 August, 1849, a son of Sir John William Dawson, naturalist, geologist and the first principal of McGill University. A severe illness at the age of 12 made him a hunchback and stunted his growth, leaving him in poor health for the remainder of his life. Tutored at home, he had an abounding interest in the natural sciences and carried this into his studies at McGill and at the Royal School of Mines in London, England where he graduated at the head of his class.

In 1873 he was appointed Geologist and Botanist to the British North American International Boundary Commission. His report on the geology and mineral resources along the 49th parallel from the Lake of the Woods to the Pacific Ocean is still a Canadian classic and resulted in his appointment to the G&NHSC in 1875.

Although crippled and frail he carried out some of the most strenuous surveys ever attempted in Canada, and his yearly reports are incredible for both the quality and sheer quantity of the work accomplished. He reported exhaustively on everything and everyone he encountered. In 1887, with William Ogilvie, DLS, of the Department of the Interior, he organized and headed the first geological and lateral survey conducted in the Yukon Territory. It was typical of Dawson that he chose the hardest route for himself. He came from Wrangell up the Stikine River, the Dease River, the Liard and Frances Rivers and into Frances Lake. From there he went down the Pelly River to the Yukon, up that stream and over the Chilkoot Pass to Dyea on the Pacific. His report encompassed almost everything known about the Yukon to that time.

He was an authority on ethnology, archaeology and botany as well as geology and was later to be called "The Father of Canadian Anthropology".

His collections in these fields, made on his surveys, laid the base of the ethnological collection of the National Museum of Canada. He published dozens of technical papers, many of them still standard.

Appointed Director of the Geological Survey of Canada in 1895, he enhanced and continued the work of his towering predecessors, Logan and Selwyn. His honours included the CMG, LLD from both Queen's and McGill Universities, FRS, President and Charter Member of the RSC, the Patron's Gold Medal of the RGS and FASAS.

He died unexpectedly, after a one-day illness, of acute bronchitis, in Ottawa, on 2 March, 1901.

Dawson City's heyday was from 1897 to late 1899, and most of the literature concerning it was written about this period. The exhaustion of the richest, hand-worked, placer gold and the news of more fabulous finds in the beach sands of Nome depleted the population in 1899 and the equally rich finds at Tanana (Fairbanks) in 1903 took many people away from the Klondike. By 1900 many wives and families had arrived. The machine methods of mining attracted a more skilled and settled people and Dawson became a quieter and more stable town.

The population in late 1898 was estimated at greater than 5,000 but the town was a service and social centre for more than 30,000 in the immediate area. In January 1902, Dawson was incorporated to city status but with the drop in population a petition to rescind the charter was accepted and it was cancelled in 1904. The town then had no mayor and affairs were managed by the Office of the Commissioner of the Territory.

The town always had a rich and varied social life, the more so because of its isolation, especially during the eight winter months. However, as the placers were worked out and little new gold found, the population steadily declined. The final blow was the cessation of dredging activities by the Yukon Consolidated Gold Corporation Ltd., in 1966. Owing to the development of the Clinton Creek asbestos mine at Fortymile and to an increase in the tourist trade, Dawson now has about 800–900 persons.

In the last few years the Canadian government has finally realized the importance of the town as an historical site of major importance and is busy saving and restoring many of the old buildings.

DAWSON CHARLIE CREEK   60°14′N   135°10′W   (105–D). A tributary of the Wheaton River, flowing from Gold Hill.

After August 1896, Tagish Charlie, nephew of Skookum Jim and Kate Carmack, became known as "DAWSON CHARLIE". He and Skookum Jim prospected widely in the southern Yukon and grubstaked other Indian friends and relatives. This area was close to his home at Carcross and in 1903 he staked mineral showings on this stream.

Charlie became a wealthy man from his Klondike claim on Bonanza Creek. On 2 July, 1904, a special Act of Parliament enfranchised him, "with all the rights and privileges of a white citizen." He could vote, sue and be sued, buy and drink liquor and hold office.

Returning home from a celebration on 26 January, 1908, he fell from the WP&YR bridge at Carcross and was drowned. (See Bonanza and Fourth of July Creeks.)

DAWSON RANGE 62°40′N 139°00′W (115-J&K). The range of mountains stretching for nearly 40 miles west of the Yukon River, north of its junction with the Pelly.

These hills were named well before the turn of the century after Dr. G.M. DAWSON, GSC.

The area came into prominence about 1969 with the discovery of potentially vast deposits of copper-molybdenite mineralization, which are still being studied.

(See Dawson City.)

DEADMAN'S CREEK 60°20′N 133°04′W (105-C). A small tributary to Teslin Lake, crossing the Alaska Highway at mile 816 (K1314).

Although officially named at the time of the Alaska Highway construction, the local people claim that the name is much older and was given because the stream runs off DEADMAN'S Hill. The hill, named in early times, resembles a reclining man.

DEADWOOD CREEK 64°06′N 139°28′W (116-B&C). A tributary to the Yukon River from the west at Dog Island, three miles below Dawson.

B.B.S. Phillips, who had probably mined at DEADWOOD, in the Black Hills of South Dakota, named this creek when he discovered gold here on 24 September, 1897.

MOUNT DECOELI 60°50′N 137°53′W (115-A). A prominent peak about four miles west of mile 1030 (K1658) on the Alaska Highway.

This was named in 1950 after E.J. DECOELI, a member of the International Boundary Commission Survey party in 1913.

DeCOURCY LAKE   61°29'N 137°08'W (115-H). Five miles east of central Ashihik Lake.

This three-mile-long lake was named in 1956 to honour the memory of J-17641 Squadron Leader Thomas Joseph DeCOURCY, DFC. He was born 2 August, 1921, at Mitchell, Ontario and enlisted in the RCAF on 7 October, 1940, at Windsor, Ontario. He was serving overseas when he was accidentally killed on 7 June, 1945.

DEMPSTER HIGHWAY

The Yukon's newest highway, it was begun in 1959 as Yukon Territorial Road No. 11. Later it was called the Flat Creek Road when it reached that far; then, as it lengthened, it was known as the Eagle Plain Road and lastly the Aklavik Road.

Leaving the Klondike Highway at mile 26, east of Dawson, the road follows the Klondike River valley. Then it turns north through the Ogilvie Mountains to the Blackstone River, crosses the Ogilvie River to the Eagle River, follows it, and then goes east through the Mackenzie Mountains to Fort MacPherson.

The Yukon Order of Pioneers, founded in Fortymile in 1894 and active in honouring early Yukoners, proposed that the highway be named after Inspector W.J.D. DEMPSTER, RNWMP.

The route of the highway follows roughly the track of the NWMP patrols from Dawson to Fort MacPherson, started in 1905. These patrols were always done in the winter with dog teams.

Inspector F.J. Fitzgerald, Constables G.F. Kinney, Taylor and ex-Constable Sam Carter left Fort MacPherson on 21 December, 1910, on the return journey of this annual patrol. They went astray while trying to find the trail between Little Wind River and the Hart River. Running short of food, they decided to return to MacPherson but owing to exhaustion and starvation they were unable to reach it. Kinney and Taylor died about 35 miles from Fort MacPherson while Fitzgerald and Carter died about 25 miles out.

On 20 February, 1911, when the patrol had not arrived in Dawson, Insp. Snyder, the officer in charge, being concerned, ordered Cpl. Dempster with Constable J.F. Fyfe, ex-Constable F. Turner and Charles Stewart, an Indian guide, to search for the missing party. Leaving Dawson on 28 February they covered the route in record time, despite storms and bad weather which cost them valuable time. On 12 March they found a snow-covered trail on the Little Wind River, followed it with great difficulty and found the bodies of Fitzgerald and his companions. In a country of hardy men Dempster and his party earned respect for this journey.

William John Duncan "Jack" Dempster, RNWMP Regt. No. 3193 was born in Wales in 1876. He joined the force in 1897 and went to the Yukon the same year. By 1911 he was famous as a bushman and a musher. He went on to give outstanding service to the Yukon for a total of 37 years, all in the territory. He retired in 1934, with the rank of inspector, to Vancouver, BC, where he died on 25 October, 1964.

MOUNT DEMPSTER 65°08'N 136°05'W (116-H). North of the Little Wind River.

This mountain, near where he travelled many times, was named in 1973 to further honour Inspector W.J.D. DEMPSTER, RCMP.

DENNIS GLACIER 60°53'N 140°22'W (115-C). A small tongue of the Walsh Glacier, just east of the Centennial Range in the far northwest St. Elias Range.

This glacier was named in 1920 after either of two men. T.C. DENNIS, DLS, was assistant in charge of the International Boundary Survey party in 1910 and was in command of the party in 1912.

Colonel John Stoughton DENNIS, (1820–1885), DLS, DTS, PLS was Surveyor-General of Canada 1871–78 and Deputy Minister of the Department of the Interior 1878–81.

DENNIS MOUNTAIN 67°42'N 136°37'W (116-P). On the headwaters of the Bell River near McDougall Pass.

This was named by William Ogilvie in May 1888, after Col. John S. DENNIS, who had earlier been Ogilvie's superior in the Surveys Branch of the Department of the Interior. (See above.)

DESTRUCTION BAY 61°15'N 138°48'W (115-G&F). On the west side of Kluane Lake.

The first settlement here was a US Army Engineers highway construction camp in 1942. Shortly after construction, high winds destroyed most of the buildings, hence the name.

The memorial plaque erected later to commemorate this event was the result of the efforts of Bert Cluett (of Cluett Creek), a long-time pioneer who was annoyed at the false tales told the tourists about the loss of life and boats here during the Klondike rush.

THE DETOUR 62°40'N 134°36'W (105-L). The long, 15-mile "S" bend in the Pelly River, starting just below the Earn River and ending at Harvey Creek.

This was named by miners in the early 1880's or perhaps even earlier by the HBC men in the 1850's. It was so called because this sudden change of direction seemed to take them many miles out of their way.

DEVILHOLE CREEK 60°17'N 136°19'W (115-A). Flows into the west side of Kusawa Lake.

In 1950 Dr. E.D. Kindle, GSC, reported that the creek was named by the Indians of the area. They said sheep that were shot on the mountainsides disappeared into mysterious holes in the mountain and could not be found.

MOUNT DEVILLE 65°13'N 140°24'W (116-G&F). On the headwaters of the Tatonduk River in the Ogilvie Mountains.

William Ogilvie, DLS, named this mountain in March 1888 while making the first survey of the Yukon-Alaska boundary.

Edouard Gaston DEVILLE (1849–1924), DLS, DTS, OLS, QLS, was Surveyor-General of Canada from 1885–1924.

DEWDNEY MOUNTAIN 66°03'N 139°13'W (116-J&K). On the upper Miner River in the Ogilvie Mountains.

William Ogilvie, DLS, named this mountain in March 1888 after his good friend, the Hon. Edgar DEWDNEY.

Dewdney, born 1835 in Devonshire, England, and educated as a civil engineer, came to British Columbia in 1859 as a surveyor. When rich gold placers were found in the Similkameen he was given the contract to build a road from Fort Hope, head of navigation on the Fraser River, to Similkameen. Started in 1860, it was completed in 1863 and was called the "Dewdney Trail". When new gold finds were made farther east he extended his road to Wild Horse Creek in the Big Bend country of the Columbia River in 1865. These roads opened the interior of British Columbia to the coast and lessened the American influence in the interior.

He was elected to the provincial legislature in 1868–69. He represented Yale, BC, in the House of Commons in Ottawa from 1872–79, when he was appointed Lieutenant-Governor of the North West Territories as well as retaining the Indian Commissionership. During this time he is credited with averting major Indian uprisings during the Riel Rebellion by his just treatment of the larger tribes. He served Sir John A. MacDonald as Minister of the Interior and Superintendent of Indian Affairs from 1888 to 1892. In 1892 he was appointed Lieutenant-Governor of British Columbia and served until 1897. He died 8 August, 1916, at Victoria, BC.

DEZEADASH LAKE   60°28′N 136°58′W (115-A). A beautiful, 15-mile-long lake about 25 miles south of Haines Junction.

One of the earliest known features in the Yukon, this lake was described to George Davidson, senior officer of the US Geodetic Survey in Alaska in 1869 by Kho-klux, the great Chief of the Chilkat Indians. They called it "Dasar-dee-Ash" or "Dasa-dee-Arsh", meaning "Lake of the Big Winds".

DIAMAIN LAKE   62°55′N 136°19′W (115-1). Ten miles northeast of Pelly Crossing.

In 1935 Hugh S. Bostock, GSC, was looking for the name of this lake while mapping the area. Mrs. Ira Van Bibber told him the Indian name was DIAMAIN. The generic term "main" itself means "lake", so that the presently-used name is redundant.

DICKSON CREEK   61°07′N 138°56′W (115-G&F). A tributary of the Duke River.

Thomas A. DICKSON, (1856–1952), was one of four brothers, all ex-NWMP. He was with the Tagish Lake detachment in 1898. Leaving the force, he became the first big-game guide in the Yukon. In 1916 he was the Game Warden at Kluane Lake and had his homestead on this creek. Many of his descendants are still in the Yukon.

DICKSON HILL   60°12′N 135°01′W (105-D). Just south of the Wheaton River.

Ole DICKSON staked one of the first copper discoveries in the Whitehorse area, the Rabbit's Foot claim, on 7 July, 1899. He actively prospected in these parts for many years.

MOUNT DINES   65°37′N 140°37′W (116-G&F). North of the Nation River.

John Dawson DINES was born in Dawson City. He served overseas in the Second World War and was later Mining Recorder at Dawson and Yellowknife, NWT. He moved up to Land Administrator at Ottawa with the

Department of Indian and Northern Affairs where he died in 1973.

DION CREEK   64°02'N 139°27'W (116-B). A small creek entering the Yukon from the east about two miles above Dawson.

This creek was named after H. DION, the leader of a prospecting party from Québec. They found gold here in October 1897.

DIP   CREEK   62°32'N 139°23'W (115-J&K).   A   tributary   of   the Klotassin River.

Gold was discovered here by Jens Rude and the creek named on 12 August, 1915. (See Jens and Rude Creeks.)

DISCOVERY   CREEK   62°04'N 137°14'W (115-I).   A   tributary   to Nansen Creek from the west.

Captain H.S. Back made the first discovery of gold in the area on this creek in August 1899, at the point where it joins Nansen Creek. No work was done at the time but he returned to the region in 1907 with a large prospecting party. On 13 June, 1910, his son, Frank H. Back, with Tom Bee staked the first claim on both Nansen Creek and this stream. (See Mount Nansen, and Back and Seymour Creeks.)

DIXIE   CREEK   61°02'N 137°49'W (115-H).   A   small   tributary   to McKinley Creek in the Alsek district.

P. Harvey Hebb created a great deal of excitement in August 1906 when he thought he had found diamonds in the blue clays on this stream. He had not. The creek had been named in July 1903 when it was first staked for placer gold during the stampede to the Ruby Creek finds in the Shakwak valley. (See Monte Cristo Gulch.)

DOGHEAD   POINT   61°21'N 138°47'W (115-G&F).   A   point   on Kluane Lake on the west side of Talbot Arm.

In the summer of 1945 H.S. Bostock, GSC, gave this name because of the remarkable similarity to a husky's head.

DOGPACK LAKE   61°42'N 139°12'W (115-G&F). A small lake about 12 miles north of Brooks Arm, Kluane Lake.

The name has been used for many years by the local Indians who used pack-dogs to take supplies in to the lake for their winter trapping.

DOLLIS CREEK (See Squaw Creek.)

DOLLY CREEK 62°04′N 137°13′W (115-I). A short brook flowing into upper Nansen Creek.

About 1910, George Mack, one of the original discoverers of gold here, named the stream after his daughter DOLLY (Mack) Golter, who lived on the creek with him.

DOLORES CREEK 64°53′N 133°21′W (106-C). 15 miles east of Fairchild Lake, in the Bonnet Plume Range.

Louis Brown, long-time trapper and big-game guide in this area, named this creek in 1964 after his wife and partner, DOLORES Cline Brown. He had found rich copper mineralization here in 1951. Bonnet Plume Copper Mines Ltd., was organized to explore the deposit.

Mrs. Brown wrote a most interesting book about their guiding and living experiences, entitled *Yukon Trophy Trails.*

DOMINION CREEK 63°37′N 138°42′W (115-O&N). Flowing into the Indian River from the north.

One of the richest and most famous of the Klondike creeks. There is good evidence that "Hootch Albert" Fortier found gold here in late 1896 but did nothing more about it until the spring of 1897. He staked the Lower Discovery claim in late May 1897 but did not record it. Instead, he allowed John E. Brannin to stake it on 12 June while he recorded No. 1 Above. At the same time, Frank Biederman was prospecting the upper part of the stream and, thinking he was the first to find gold on it, staked a Discovery claim on 28 May. The Mining Recorder allowed both discoveries and accepted the name DOMINION, proposed by Fortier.

Albert Fortier came to the Yukon in 1887 from Québec and, as his nickname implies, was noted in the Fortymile country for being able to make alcohol out of almost anything.

This stream was the locale for many of the charges of corruption against the Yukon administration in 1898. The action of Commissioner James Walsh in reserving alternate claims on the creek as a government reserve aroused great bitterness among the miners. His action however, in opening the claims to staking shortly afterwards aroused an even greater outcry when it was found that friends and relatives of government officials had staked claims the day before the general public was informed that the creek was open to staking. These, and other complaints, soon led to Walsh's recall to Ottawa and to the appointment of William Ogilvie, whose integrity was accepted by all.

The major settlement on the creek was at its junction with Caribou Creek and was called Caribou City until 1905. From that date it was called Dominion. The village died during the First World War.

DONJEK CITY 62°40'N 140°05'W (115-J&K). On the west side of the White River, one mile below Caledonia Creek.

A roadhouse was built here in 1913 on the trail from Stewart to the Chisana goldfields. Some gold was found on creeks nearby and a smaller settlement grew here for a number of years to service the miners. The place was abandoned in the 1920's.

DONJEK RIVER 62°36'N 140°00'W (115-J&K). A major tributary to the White River.

This large river was apparently named by Charles Willard Hayes on his 1891 expedition to the district. He took the name from the Indian word "Donyak" or "Donchek", it being the name of a type of pea-vine which grows profusely in the valley. It is extremely nutritious and makes excellent winter feed for game and stock animals.

DONOVAN CREEK 63°32'N 139°56'W (115-O&N). Flows into Abraham Creek in the Sixtymile district.

This name has been used locally since 1911 after Daniel DONOVAN who found the first gold and staked the first claim at Discovery Pup in that year.

MOUNT DOOSHKA 7,156' 61°20'N 127°10'W (95-E). Almost on the Yukon-NWT border near the head of the Coal River.

This name was submitted in 1971 under the auspices of the Commissioner of the Yukon Territory, James Smith. It was adopted in 1972.

DOOSHKA is the Kutchin Indian word for "Love"; as noted in a popular song entitled "The Squaws Along The Yukon". One line says "Dooshka, Dooshka, Dooshka, which means, I love you."

DOUGLAS CREEK 60°53'N 138°38'W (115-B&C). A tributary of Slim's River, about ten miles above Kluane Lake.

Gold was found and this creek named by J. Kay in March 1904 during the rush to the Kluane Lake goldfields.

DRAPEAU CREEK 63°59′N 136°53′W (115-P). A short tributary of Hobo Creek.

Gerrard "Jerry" DRAPEAU prospected in these hills and the Mayo district for many years.

DRURY SPIRE 62°22′N 134°16′W (105-L). At the south end of Drury Lake.

H.S. Bostock, GSC, proposed this name in 1954 to honour William S. DRURY of Yorkshire, England. Coming to the Yukon in early 1898, Drury met Isaac Taylor while working on the Discovery claim on Pine Creek, Atlin, BC. They became partners and over the years built a thriving merchandising business all over the Yukon. (See Tadru Lake.)

DRY CREEK 62°20′N 140°23′W (115-J&K). A tributary of the White River near Snag.

Prospectors working on this creek about 1913 gave it the name because it froze to bottom in the winter. This is not remarkable as it runs through Snag, the coldest spot in Canada.

DUBLIN GULCH 64°03′N 135°51′W (106-D). A small valley off Haggart Creek in the Mayo district.

This is one of the best known and most famous names in the Mayo area. Thomas Haggart, one of the area's first and longtime prospectors, found coarse gold here in 1889. In 1896 he built the first cabin on the gulch and gave it its name. When the influx of Klondikers invaded the country Haggart and others decided to record their claims to protect them against claim-jumpers. John J. Suttles recorded claim No. 1 and continued to work it until 1910.

DUKE RIVER 61°26′N 139°06′W (115-G&F). Flows into the Kluane River a few miles above Kluane Lake.

George DUKE was one of the first prospectors in the Kluane Lake country before 1900. This river was then named for him.

DUNCAN CREEK 63°47′N 135°31′W (105-M). A tributary of the Mayo River just above Mayo Lake.

In 1898, three Norwegians, Gustavus Gustavusen and his two sons, alone in this part of the Yukon, discovered rich placer gold in the canyon on this stream. Because they wished to keep their find secret and because the Mining Recorder was so far away, they did not record any claims on their find. They went to great lengths to prevent anyone else from finding out about it, so much so that they were known on the lower Stewart River as the "Mysterious Three." By September 1901 they had recovered more than $30,000 in gold.

A party of four Scottish Klondikers began prospecting in the area that summer and found the Gustavusen workings. The four, Duncan Patterson, Colin Hamilton, Allen McIntosh and Jake Davidson, found that the claims were not recorded and promptly jumped them while the Gustavusens were down river for supplies. They staked on 12 September, 1901, and named the creek after DUNCAN Patterson. The remainder of the creek was quickly staked by others.

The Gustavusens left the country; the creek was one of the richest ever found in the Yukon outside the Klondike.

The "Code of the North" became badly bent after the Klondike Gold Rush. (See Gustavus Range.)

EAGLE CREEK 64°47′N 141°00′W (116-B&C). A tributary of the Yukon River, north of Fortymile.

E.C. Barnard of the USGS, gave this creek its name in 1898 because the bluffs near its mouth (which is in Alaska) are a favourite nesting place for the bald eagles of the area.

EAGLES NEST BLUFF 2,445′ 62°02′N 135°49′W (105-L). On the north bank of the Yukon River, five miles below the mouth of the Little Salmon River.

This was formerly called Eagle Rock by early miners and riverboat men, from the Indian name meaning the same.

It was here that the worst riverboat disaster ever to happen in the Yukon took place. On 25 September, 1906, the riverboat *Columbian* was destroyed by an explosion and fire which killed six men and wrecked the ship. A crew member, shooting at some wild fowl, accidentally hit a shipment of gunpowder and explosives placed on the forward deck, setting it off. The efforts of the survivors to help the injured were heroic. A monument in the Whitehorse Cemetery is the only record of this disaster.

EAGLE RIVER 67°18′N 137°09′W (116–P). This large stream flows into the Porcupine River from the south, a few miles below Lapierre House.

John Bell, Chief Factor at Fort MacPherson, was probably the first white man to see this river and record the Indian name when he first crossed into the Yukon in 1839.

This lonely river was, in January and February 1932, the scene of the first aircraft-assisted man hunt in Canada. From a fort-like cabin on the Rat River, NWT, Albert Johnson, the "Mad Trapper of Rat River", for 48 days, in temperatures averaging – 40°F., fought a series of four gun battles with the RCMP. He crossed the continental divide and, but for the use of an aircraft piloted by the famous bush pilot "Wop" May, might have escaped. He killed Constable Edgar "Spike" Millen (see Mount Millen) and wounded two other constables. He was killed on 17 February in a small ravine about 15 miles upstream from the mouth of this river.

Little was ever found out about who he was, his past, or his motives.

EAR LAKE 60°40′N 135°02′W (105–D). A small lake on the south side of the Yukon River at the foot of Miles Canyon.

Originally the site of a construction camp of the WP&YR, this pleasant little lake became a favourite camping spot for the people of Whitehorse. It was the scene of the worst mass murder in Yukon history when Alexander Gagoff, a Cossack, shot and killed the section foreman and three workers of the WP&YR here on 30 September, 1915. He was executed in Whitehorse jail on 10 March, 1916.

EARN RIVER 62°45′N 134°45′W (105–L). Enters the Pelly River near the start of the Detour.

Robert Campbell of the HBC, the famous explorer of the Pelly and Yukon Rivers, named this stream after a river of the same name near his home in Perthshire, Scotland. The date was the summer of 1840 when he made his momentous journey down the Pelly to the Yukon.

EDMONTON CREEK 63°47′N 134°48′W (105–M). Flows into the southeast side of Mayo Lake.

On 13 June, 1904, gold was discovered here by P. Beliveau and his partner, Desutel. Beliveau had come to the Yukon via the Edmonton Trail. Before his discovery the creek had been known locally as "Fan" or "Old Fan" Creek.

EIKLAND MOUNTAIN 4,773′ 62°15′N 140°50′W (115-J&K). Five miles west of mile 1185 (K1908) on the Alaska Highway.

In 1967 the name of this mountain, then known as "Nigger Head" Mountain, was changed to that of Peter EIKLAND, a long-time prospector in the area. The change was made by the Board on Geographic Names, owing to complaints that the original name might offend people.

The original name was probably given by stampeders going this way to the Chisana goldfields in 1913–14. It describes the large clumps of grass growing in the muskeg swamps which make walking difficult. They are unstable and if a person trying to step from one to the other slips, he or she is precipitated into the swamp mud. The name is an old one, common across northern Canada. Earlier, they were given the name "Têtes des Femmes" by the French-Canadian voyageurs of the HBC.

EINARSON LAKE 63°52′N 131°35′W (105-O). A small lake on Einarson Creek, a tributary of the Rogue River.

This was named in 1946 to immortalize a hero, J-17276 Flight Lt. Johann Walter EINARSON, DFC, DFM, RCAF. He was born in Wynyard, Saskatchewan on 20 November, 1920, and enlisted in the RCAF on 10 February, 1941 at Saskatoon. He served in Canada and overseas and was missing, presumed killed in action, on 25 February, 1944.

ELDORADO CREEK 63°55′N 139°19′W (115-O&N). The main tributary of Bonanza Creek.

On 1 September, 1896, a party of five, Anton Stander, Frank Kellar, James Clements, Jay "Old Man" Whipple and Frank Phiscator, who had just staked Nos. 32 to 36 Above on Bonanza Creek, decided to prospect this stream on their way back to the Klondike River. Clements and Kellar had panned gravel here in late August on their way up Bonanza and had recovered some gold. A number of others had passed it up and a story persists that someone blazed a tree at the mouth of the creek and wrote "Reserved for Swedes and cheechakos."

They discovered rich gold on No. 3 claim. Whipple claimed discovery and named the creek after himself. They staked their claims on 1 September. Another party of four arrived on 5 September and found dissension among the original five over claim ownership. They reached agreement and that evening Knut Halstead, a Fortymiler, suggested the name ELDORADO. Whipple's name was overruled because he was trying to hog too many claims and had also jumped claims in the Fortymile district.

Because of a rule newly passed by Inspector Constantine, NWMP, limiting the number of Discovery claims on a creek and the number of claims to be held by any one man in a district, further claim-jumping took place. F.W. Cobb, a famous Harvard University football star, jumped Frank Phiscator's No. 2 claim on 6 September but Constantine disallowed his claim. He later claimed to have discovered and named Eldorado Creek.

It has been claimed by various authorities that Eldorado Creek was the richest placer gold stream ever found anywhere in the world. The first 40 claims (about three and one half miles) on the creek produced well over half a million dollars each, with gold then valued at $20 per ounce. Some of the claims gave up over a million and a half dollars in a length of 500 feet. Gold is still being taken from the gravels of this small stream, 80 years later.

ELLEN CREEK 66°41′N 137°55′W (116-I). A small tributary of the Porcupine River.

A local name after an Indian woman "Elentsie" who was buried near the mouth of the stream many years ago.

ELLIOTT CREEK 64°36′N 135°49′W (106-D). A tributary of the Beaver River, in the Wernecke Mountains.

This stream was named in 1945 after Frederick ELLIOTT who prospected in this area in the 1920's. He was associated with Charles Settlemier, another well-known prospector. Elliott Ridge, a mountain north of the creek, was named later.

ELSA 63°55′N 135°29′W (105-M).

This small village, on Galena Hill in the Mayo district, was established in 1929 to house miners at the newly discovered Calumet silver-lead mine; it is not known after whom the settlement was named. Production at the mine did not start until 1937. A post office was started in 1949 and a little later the first oil exploration winter road, called "The Wind River Trail", was built from here north 300 miles to drilling sites in the Bell River area.

ENGER LAKES 62°15′N 140°40′W (115-J&K). Four small lakes near mile 1185 (K1908) on the Alaska Highway.

These were named during the rush to the Chisana goldfields in 1913 as the

"Niggerhead" Lakes by those who had the misfortune to have to backpack across this country. The territorial government in 1967 requested the name be changed as it might offend people.

Harry ENGER was a long-time prospector in the area. (See Eikland Mountain.)

ENGINEER CREEK   65°21′N 138°19′W (116-G&F). A tributary to the Ogilvie River.

This name replaced Big Creek in 1971 at the request of Commissioner James Smith. It was renamed to commemorate the work of the Department of Public Works engineers in the district during the location of the Dempster Highway.

ENSLEY CREEK   63°54′N 139°43′W (115-O&N). A tributary to the Yukon River below Indian River.

The lower Discovery claim was staked on 29 November, 1897 by S. ENSLEY.

ERICKSON GULCH   63°56′N 135°20′W (105-M). A small tributary of Christal Creek on Galena Hill in the Mayo district.

L.B. ERICKSON, a pioneer miner in the Mayo area, made one of his first discoveries of silver-lead ore on this gulch.

ERVIN CREEK   64°28′N 135°15′W (106-D). Flows into Carpenter Creek in the Wernecke Mountains.

E.ERVIN found silver-lead ore on the banks of this stream in 1923 during the rush to the Grey Copper Hill finds. (See Beaver City.)

ESAU HILL   65°42′N 136°51′W (116-H). Eight miles southwest of Pothole Lake and north of the Hart River.

ESAU was an Indian guide whose report to Inspector Snyder at Dawson resulted in Cpl. Dempster being sent to search for the lost Fitzgerald patrol in 1911. (See Dempster Highway.)

ESCAPE REEF   69°00′N 137°15′W (117-A). A long, low, narrow island or reef about three miles east of Shingle Point in Mackenzie Bay on the Arctic coast.

In 1826 John Franklin, (later Sir), named this reef after a touchy meeting with a band of Eskimos at Shingle Point.

ETHEL LAKE 63°22′N 136°06′W (115-P). About 12 miles east of Stewart Crossing.

This large lake was named after his daughter by J.J. McArthur, DLS, in 1898, while he was surveying in the vicinity. He was one of the first government surveyors in the territory and was active in tracing new routes and in claim surveys in the early days of the Klondike.

ETTRAIN CREEK 65°27′N 141°00′W (116-G&F). A tributary to the Nation River.

Thomas Riggs, American member of the International Boundary Survey team, named this creek in 1910. An Indian family in this area at the time had the family name "Yetran". The word was said to mean "Mosquito" in the local dialect.

EUREKA CREEK 63°36′N 138°49′W (115-O&N). A tributary to the Indian River from the south.

Gold was found here and a Discovery claim staked on 28 August, 1897, by J.C. Brown from EUREKA, California. His discovery did not lead to payable gold until February 1905 when a newer and richer discovery led to a stampede in which the whole creek and its tributaries were staked.

EUREKA LANDING 61°15′N 134°36′W (105-E). On the Teslin River.

This was a riverboat landing and supply point for the miners of the Livingstone Creek area, to which a wagon road was built in the summer of 1902. It was abandoned when a shorter route was made from Mason's Landing.

MOUNT EVANS 4,232′ 62°57′N 137°04′W (115-I). 15 miles northeast of Fort Selkirk.

Lt. Col T.D.B. EVANS was the first commander of the Yukon Field Force (1898–1900). Evans marched his 280 men and four women from Telegraph Creek on the Stikine River, to the head of Teslin Lake in the spring of 1898. They built boats and sailed to Fort Selkirk. There they built quarters and half the detachment remained here while the other half went on to Dawson to assist the NWMP.

Three of his group were buried at Fort Selkirk.

Lt. Col. Evans accepted a reduction in rank to lieutenant in order to go overseas during the First World War. This mountain was given his name in 1971. Four others, Hansen, Watson, Walters and Corcoran were named at the same time after the men of his command who died while on service in the Yukon.

EVERETT CREEK   60°51′N 130°35′W (105-B). Flows from near Wasson Lake southwest to the Liard River.

This was named after EVERETT Wasson, a pioneer bush pilot of the Yukon and northern BC. This stream was near the scene of the first air search and rescue mission attempted in the Yukon. The creek had previously carried the name Quartz Creek and is so named on many maps. (See Wasson Lake.)

EXAMINER GULCH   64°02′N 139°23′W (115-B&C). The first valley on the right side above the mouth of Bonanza Creek.

This small valley was given the name of W.R. Hearst's newspaper, the San Francisco *EXAMINER* by W.H. Campbell, a former employee. He discovered gold and staked the first claim on the gulch on 28 October, 1897.

EXCELSIOR CREEK   62°53′N 138°58′W (115-J&K). A tributary to the Yukon River just above Coffee Creek.

This was named in July 1898 by Mrs. Martha Munger Black, MP, probably the most noted woman in Yukon history. Camping here while on her way to Dawson, she met a group of New Zealand miners prospecting the stream. They had found gold and their leader, William J. Beaven, asked Mrs. Black to name the stream. They then staked claims for all, including Mrs. Black, and her claim was later profitable.

MOUNT FAIRBORN   65°06′N 139°52′W (116-G&F). 19 miles east of Sheep Mountain.

In 1973 this mountain was named after James FAIRBORN who was a pioneer transportation man and was agent for the WP&YR at several locations for many years.

FALSE TEETH CREEK   62°12′N 137°49′W (115-I). Tributary to the Klaza River.

In the summer of 1937, W.H. Miller and H.S. Bostock of the GSC were camped here. Their packer, J.V. White, a man of 43 and exceptionally athletic, left his ill-fitting false teeth here when they moved camp to a high ridge seven miles to the west. Arising early the next morning he discovered his loss. He ran back down to the camp here and returned in time for breakfast.

FANGO LAKE   63°40′N 131°42′W (115-O). A small lake which drains into Old Cabin Creek and Rogue River.

This was named by Dr. Aro Aho, President of Dynasty Exploration Co. Ltd., about 1971. It is a Spanish word meaning "Swamp".

FARO   62°14′N 133°20′W (105-K). 25 miles west of the junction of the Ross and Pelly Rivers.

The newest town in the Yukon was built in 1969 to house the people from the nearby Anvil Mine. This is a large, open-pit mine producing lead, zinc and silver. On 13 June, 1969, a forest fire destroyed most of the newly-built town but it was rebuilt in three months.

The game of FARO was an old and simple gambling game of cards, popular throughout the early west. It was probably given to the town by Dr. Aro Aho from the name of the first claims staked on the orebody.

FAT CREEK   60°11′N 132°55′W (105-C). Flows into Fat Lake and then Teslin Lake on the west side.

Arthur St. Cyr, DLS, in 1897, recorded the local name of this stream as "Hall River", probably after Hall Williams, an ex-HBC man who trapped around Teslin Lake in the 1890's and early 1900's.

By 1903 the stream was being called the "North River" on maps of the area. In 1931 the GSC, when mapping the geology, reported that the local people were calling it "Flat Creek" and they so marked it. Somehow, when their maps were issued, the name appeared as FAT Creek and so it remains. (See Hall Creek.)

FENWICK CREEK   60°11′N 135°19′W (105-D). Flows into the Wheaton River.

In 1910 one of the Yukon's early geologists, D.D. Cairnes, GSC, gave this creek his wife's maiden name while he was mapping the geology of the region.

MOUNT FERRELL   64°05′N 133°12′W (106-C). Just south of the Nadaleen River.

James E. FERRELL was a Yukon Councillor for the Dawson District in

1922–28. He also ran a trading post at Lansing from 1908–15. This hill was named for him in 1973. (See Christie Pass.)

FIDO CREEK 63°32′N 132°15′W (105-N). A tributary to the Rogue River from the north.

This was named in 1973 by Dr. Aro Aho, President of Dynasty Exploration Co., Ltd. after Norman Niddery's lead sled dog. The name is a common one for dogs and comes from the Latin *"fidus"* meaning "faithful". (See Niddery Lake.)

FIELD CREEK 63°47′N 135°42′W (105-M). A tributary to the Mayo River from the north.

Fred FIELD, of Gordon Landing, went out hunting before the close of navigation in the fall of 1902, and did not return when he was expected. In February 1903 he was reported lost and search parties went out. On 25 May, 1903, his body, surrounded by all his belongings, was found on a raft in the ice on the Stewart River near Lansing Creek. He had apparently died of exposure and starvation. He had probably got lost on land and was floating down the river, hoping to find a settlement, before the river froze. His body was perfectly preserved.

A terse and chilling report to this effect was made by the NWMP constable in the district and was the epitaph of a hardy Klondiker, one of the first men to prospect in the Mayo region. It is believed that Field found gold prospects on and staked the first claim on this creek that bears his name.

FIELD LAKE 62°40′N 131°03′W (105-J). One of the four lakes near the junction of the Ross and Prevost Rivers.

This was named in 1907 by Joseph Keele, GSC, after Poole FIELD, who kept the trading post at nearby Ross River.

Field was born at Fort Garry, Manitoba, where his father was the HBC trader. He had worked his way west, across the territories and eventually was caught up in the stampede to the Klondike. He spent some time in the NWMP. He and his partner, Clement Lewis, liked the Pelly and Ross River country and bought out Tom Smith's trading post at Ross River in 1905. They named it "Nahanni House".

A third associate, Martin Jorgenson, was one of the mystery men of the Nahanni country. In 1910 he went in to the Nahanni in search of the rich gold supposed to be there and later sent a message to Field by some wandering Indians; it said that he had found rich diggings and requested his assistance and supplies. The message had taken two years to deliver. Field made the journey and found Jorgenson's skeleton, minus the skull, his cabin burned and no gold or signs of workings. Field was convinced enough by his partner's story to return many times to the Nahanni in later years.

FINLAYSON LAKE 61°41′N 130°38′W (105-G). At the height of land between Frances Lake and the Pelly River.

This lake and river were named by Robert Campbell of the HBC in July 1840 while he was on his famous journey of exploration of the central Yukon. It was named after Chief Factor Duncan FINLAYSON, his friend and sponsor, who later became a director of the HBC. The stream and lake were on the main supply route, — Fort Liard, Fort Frances, Fort Pelly Banks — to Fort Selkirk.

Placer gold was mined from the bars at the mouth of the river in 1875, the miners taking $8-$9 per day. This was among the first gold mined in the Yukon Territory.

FIRTH RIVER 69°32′N 139°32′W (117-D). A large river which flows to the Beaufort Sea southwest of Herschel Island.

This was first named "Mountain Indian" River by John Franklin (later Sir) in July 1826. He encamped on the Arctic shore just east of the river and met a group of Eskimos who told him that once a year each spring, a band of Indians came down the river from the interior to trade with them.

J.H. Turner, USC&GS, in 1890 renamed the river after John FIRTH, HBC Agent at Rampart House, who had accompanied him to the Arctic coast that year.

Firth lived in the country as an HBC Factor for over 50 years. A Klondiker who met Firth at Fort MacPherson in 1898 was much impressed, saying that he looked like a man of granite. He was a square, quiet and powerful man with tremendous effect on the Indians and Eskimos. They felt that he could look right into their thoughts, and were careful to mind their manners. John Firth had a large family and one of his grandsons has been twice elected as Member of Parliament for the Northwest Territories.

Gold was found on High Cache Creek, a small tributary of the river, in 1908 by Jujira Wada, a famous Japanese traveller and prospector and his partner, Ben Smith. This led to a small rush to the area.

There have been several rushes to stake the stream about every ten to 15 years but no paying gold has yet been found. (See High Cache Creek.)

FISHER CREEK   61°02′N 138°38′W (115-G&P). A small creek flowing into Sheep Creek from the west.

Two brothers, Bruce and A.C. FISHER, were early and continuing prospectors and trappers in the Kluane country. They found gold and named this creek during the stampede of 1903–04 to the Bullion Creek finds.

The grave of A.C. Fisher had to be removed from the right-of-way of the Alaska Highway in 1943 and was placed just south of the marker on Soldier's Summit.

FISHER CREEK   64°12′N 136°12′W (116-A). A tributary to the North McQuesten River.

In September 1898 two unknown prospectors started a fake stampede to this area. So many people took part that a man named FISHER was appointed Mining Recorder for the district.

The rush died quickly and almost everyone left the creek. Fisher remained here, alone, all winter. In Dawson it was reported that he was dead and the fact was accepted officially. His relatives claimed and received his effects and life insurance. All were surprised when he arrived in Stewart in the spring of 1899 and handed in his records.

FISHING BRANCH   66°27′N 138°35′W (116-J&K). Flows into the Porcupine River.

On 28 May, 1888, William Ogilvie, DLS, on his way to Fort MacPherson, stopped here. His report stated that at the mouth of the creek there were old racks for drying fish that had been erected by the Indians. Thus he called the stream the "Fishing Branch" of the Porcupine.

MOUNT FITTON   68°28′N 137°58′W (117-A). In the Richardson Mountains near the Arctic coast.

This was named in 1826 by John Franklin (later Sir) after William Henry FITTON MD (1780–1861), who in 1852 was President of the Geological Society of Great Britain. It was originally named Fitton Peak.

FIVE FINGER RAPIDS   62°16′N 136°21′W (115-I). In the Yukon River about 20 miles north of Carmacks.

Four columns of basalt rock separate the river into five channels of which only the eastern one is passable by riverboats. They were named by one of the earliest miners, W.B. Moore of Tombstone, Arizona, in 1882.

Lt. F. Schwatka, US Army, on his excursion in 1883, changed the name to

"Rink Rapids" but the name was never accepted and later Dr. G.M. Dawson gave it to the rapids a little lower down the river. (See Rink Rapids.)

FLAT CREEK   63°57′N 138°37′W (115-O&N). Flows into the Klondike River from the south.

William Ogilvie, DLS, named this creek in 1896 as it enters the Klondike in a large, flat valley. It was said that this creek was the mythical "Too Much Gold" creek of the early Indians, who told the miners that there was a creek far up the Klondike River in which the gold was so plentiful that they would have to put gravel with it in order to sluice it.

FLET CREEK   63°59′N 136°20′W (115-P). Tributary of the North McQuesten River.

Robert G. FLETT was a well-known trapper and prospector in this area in the early 1900's. He was subject to fits of insanity and frightened others in the district who complained to the authorities. In 1907, two RNWMP constables were sent in to apprehend him. He evaded them easily and they eventually returned to Dawson empty handed. (The Mounties didn't always get their man!)

In the winter of 1907–08 a group of miners captured him and he was taken to Dawson by dog-team and placed in a mental hospital. The name was misspelled by the map-makers.

MOUNT FOLLÉ   60°18′N 135°03′W (105-D). On the north side of the Wheaton River at the Big Bend.

John "Jack" A. FOLLÉ, was a Klondiker and pioneer prospector in the Wheaton River area, with his partner W.F. Schnabel. In 1905 he staked claims on this hill and worked hardrock prospects for many years.

FOREST CREEK   65°09′N 135°44′W (106-E). Tributary to the Little Wind River.

This was named about 1905 when Special Constable A.E. FORREST, RNWMP, made the Dawson to Fort MacPherson patrol most years from 1905–11. He was noted as one of the greatest travellers of the time. He once carried the mail by dog-sled from Fort MacPherson to Dawson in 19 days — a distance of over 500 miles, in January and February. The mouth of this creek is one of his overnight camping places. His name was misspelled by the map-makers.

He enlisted in Joe Boyle's Yukon Motor Machine Gun Battery in November 1914 and was made sergeant major in France in 1917.

FORT CONSTANTINE   64°26'N 140°32'W (116-B&C). On the north side of the Fortymile River at its junction with the Yukon, north of Fort Cudahy.

This was the first NWMP post in the Yukon Territory. From 1895 to 1897 it contained all the law and government in the territory and Inspector Charles CONSTANTINE was just that.

Fort Constantine was abandoned in 1898 when the growth of Dawson City and the abandonment of the Fortymile mining district required NWMP headquarters to be at Dawson. (See Mount Constantine.)

FORT CUDAHY   64°26'N 140°32'W (116-B&C). On the north side of the Fortymile River at its junction with the Yukon, directly across the Fortymile River from the settlement of Fortymile and adjoined by Fort Constantine on the north.

Captain John Jerome Healy was a soldier, Indian fighter, trader and early Alaskan and Yukon pioneer. Engaging in the whisky trade in Montana and what is now Alberta in the 1870's, he built and operated Fort Whoop-Up in Alberta until dispossessed by the newly formed NWMP. He had at one time been Sheriff of Cocteau County, Montana (Fort Benton). He arrived in Alaska in 1882 and operated the first trading post at Dyea.

He was a firm believer in the potential of the interior country and in 1893, with the backing of his old partners, the Cudahy meat-packing interests of Chicago, formed the North American Trading and Transportation Company and began establishing trading posts along the Yukon River. The post at Fortymile was named after John CUDAHY, a Chicago merchant and a director of the NAT&TC.

The first post office in the Yukon Territory was opened here in October 1894 and used American postage stamps.

This fort too was forced to close down in 1898 as business moved to the larger centre of Dawson.

FORT FRANCES   61°17'N 129°16'W (105-H). On the point of the north side of Frances Lake at the junction of the East and West Arms.

In 1840 a rough building called "Glenlyon House" was built here by Robert Campbell of the HBC. Trading with the Indians did not start until

December 1842, when the post was enlarged and named Fort Frances, after Lady Frances Simpson, wife of the Governor of the HBC. It was the first trading post in the Yukon Territory. The post prospered as long as Campbell ran it but in the late 1840's, while he was establishing Fort Pelly Banks and Fort Selkirk, his assistant allowed it to deteriorate and did little trade. By 1851 the post was vacant for periods while personnel were at Pelly Banks. When Campbell came this way in October 1852 after the loss of Fort Selkirk, he found that the natives had burned and destroyed this post. After 12 years the HBC had no posts left in the Yukon.

The post was revived by the HBC for a short time in the early 1900's and rebuilt on the south side of the narrows. It was later sold and operated at various times by independent traders, and again by the HBC from the 1930's until the Alaska Highway was built. The local Indians then moved to Lower Post and Watson Lake and no business remained. In these later years the post was called simply, "Frances Lake", the name used on present day maps. (See Frances River.)

FORT NELSON **(See Stewart River.)**

FORT RELIANCE 64°09'N 139°29'W (116-B&C). Eight miles north of Dawson on the east bank of the Yukon River.

Now obliterated, this was the first trading post built in the Yukon Territory after the HBC's withdrawal. On 20 August, 1874, Jack McQuesten and Alfred Mayo, assisted by a young man named Frank Barnfield (Clarence Andrews, the distinguished Alaska historian, insisted his name was Bernstein), arrived here on the small steamboat *Yukon* and began erecting the post. As was common in the west in those days they called it a fort. Although the intention was mainly to exploit the Indian fur trade, these men were also prospectors and were highly optimistic about the mineral potential of the country.

Their trading was successful. Mayo stayed at his regular job, running the steamboats for the ACC and, in the spring of 1875, Arthur Harper joined McQuesten at the post. The first miners to winter in the territory were here in the winter of 1882–83. Eleven in number, they were led by E.M. Carr who later became a general in the US National Guard and Commissioner at Fairbanks in 1906. This party prospected in the Klondike area that winter and camped on Eldorado Creek; they found gold showings but none rich enough to impress them or bring them back in the spring.

In 1886 many miners had invaded the territory and good gold was being mined on the Stewart River bars so, in the spring of that year, Fort Reliance was abandoned in favour of the new post at the mouth of the Stewart River.

Fort Reliance was the centre of trade on the upper Yukon between the years 1874 and 1886. It was the Mile "O" of the Yukon River; all distances along the river were calculated from this point, e.g. the Fortymile and Sixtymile Rivers.

The abandoned buildings were soon removed for boiler wood by the riverboats.

FORT SELKIRK   62°46′N   137°24′W   (115-1). On the west side of the Yukon River, just above its confluence with the Pelly.

This spot was selected by Robert Campbell in 1848 to control the fur trade of the central Yukon for the HBC. On 1 June that year he built the first post on the east bank of the Yukon, on the point between it and the Pelly. He named it after Thomas Douglas, fifth Earl of SELKIRK (1771-1820) and also after the post of the HBC at Fort Selkirk in Manitoba. It was abandoned in April 1852 because of flooding problems and the next post was built across the Yukon.

Fort Selkirk broke the trade monopoly of the Chilkat Indians of the coast with the interior Indians. They determined to rectify this situation and on 19 August, 1852, led by their Chief Kho-klux, they attacked and pillaged the post. They were careful not to hurt any of the white men there but took or destroyed almost all the trade goods, supplies and furnishings. Campbell sent some of his people to Fort Yukon and took the rest to Pelly Banks while he continued on to Fort Simpson. The local natives later burned the fort buildings to get the iron fittings for tools.

Robert Campbell then made his famous journey that winter, over 3,000 miles on showshoes, on his way to Lachine, Québec seeking permission to re-establish the post. His request was denied and, except for Rampart House and sometimes Lapierre House, the HBC left the Yukon for nearly 50 years. Campbell never saw the territory again.

On 1 September, 1889, Arthur Harper, who had split up with Ladue, landed on the site of the original fort (on the east bank) with his wife and several children. He had a large stock of trade goods and started a post here, independent of the ACC. It was known locally as "Campbell's Fort". He hired "Buffalo" Pitts to assist him and Pitts was still here when the gold rush was on.

Bishop Bompas built a mission here in 1892 and put the Rev. T.H.

Canham in charge. Canham was then needed elsewhere and the mission was closed in 1895.

The place assumed some importance in late 1898 when it became the headquarters of the Yukon Field Force of the Canadian army. There was a vague intention by Sir Wilfrid Laurier's Liberal government to make Selkirk the capital of the Yukon Territory. Owing to the loss of population caused by the Nome Gold Rush in 1899 and to the Yukon Field Force being recalled because of the South African war, nothing became of the idea. The Yukon Field Force left three of its number behind, buried at the fort. Nearby mountains are named in their memory, as well as one for their commanding officer.

Independent traders and missionaries kept the place alive for many years. In 1938 the HBC returned but remained only until 1950. With the halting of riverboat traffic due to the completion of the Alaska Highway and an allweather road from Whitehorse to Dawson and Mayo, by 1950 the settlement lost all reason for being and, with the exception of one family, was abandoned. (See Mount Pitts.)

FORTYMILE RIVER 64°26′N 140°32′W (116-B&C). A large tributary to the Yukon River about 48 miles below Dawson.

Originally called the "Shitando" or "Chittondeg" by the Tena Indians, meaning "Creek of the Leaves", this is also probably the river that Robert Campbell, on his way to Fort Yukon in 1851, called "Ayonie's River" after the chief of the Indians he found there. Even before gold was found on it in 1886, the miners called it Fortymile River, from its location that distance below Fort Reliance, which was their only supply point. Lt. F. Schwatka, US Army, in 1883 named it the "Cone Hill River" from the isolated hill a short distance above its mouth but the name was not accepted.

Arthur Harper, the pioneer prospector of the central Yukon, found gold showings on the lower part of the river a short time after 1875 but did not pursue them after being told stories of dangerous canyons and rapids upstream by the local natives. Acting on his advice, George McCue and Dick Poplin, in the summer of 1886, found the first payable gold on a gravel bar (Discovery Bar) at the mouth of Moose Creek (on the Alaska side). This again was fine or flour gold and, as usual in river bars, was of limited extent. Shortly afterward Howard Franklin and Harry Madison on 7 September, 1886, found the first coarse gold in the Yukon watershed at Franklin Gulch, about 85 miles up the Fortymile River and well into American territory.

Coarse gold was the goal of all miners and this find established the credibility of the Yukon Territory as a major mining district. The real rush to the Yukon started at this time.

Michael "Mickey" O'Brien found coarse gold on a nearby creek, also a tributary of the Fortymile, a short time after Franklin and Madison, which reinforced the impact of the first discovery.

Harper, McQuesten and Mayo realized the importance of the finds. Harper immediately went from the Stewart River post to the mouth of the Fortymile and in June 1887 started the erection of a trading post there for the ACC. It quickly grew into a thriving town as more of the Fortymile creeks gave up their gold and by 1893 it was serving several thousand miners in the area.

The settlement was almost completely abandoned in weeks after 17 August, 1896, with the discovery of the Bonanza gold and never again regained any importance.

49 GULCH   63°59'N   139°21'W   (115-O&N).   A tributary to Bonanza Creek from the west, five miles from the Klondike River.

The Discovery claim was located on 29 May, 1897, by Louis Hansen who named it because the mouth of the gulch was on claim No. 49 Below Discovery on Bonanza.

MOUNT   FOSTER   61°09'N   140°03'W   (115-F).   East   of   the   Steele Glacier in the St. Elias Range.

This was named in 1970 by the Alpine Club of Canada after Col. William Wasborough FOSTER (1875-1954), a past president (1920-1924) of the club.

FOURTH OF JULY CREEK   61°07'N   138°02'W   (115-G). A tributary of the Jarvis River in the Kluane region.

On 4 July, 1903, gold was found and the Discovery claim staked by "Dawson" Charlie of Carcross, (better known as "Tagish" Charlie). Dawson Charlie, with George Carmack and Skookum Jim Mason had found the rich gold of Bonanza Creek in 1896 which started the Klondike Gold Rush. The 1903 find was the first payable gold found in the Kluane district. This started a large rush to the Kluane which lasted for the next few years.

MOUNT FOWLIE   65°47'N   139°11'W   (116-G&F).On the east side of the East Porcupine River.

Gavin FOWLIE was a Yukon Councillor from 1920 to 23 and this hill was named for him in 1973.

FOX CREEK 60°11'N 132°48'W (105-C). A tributary to Teslin Lake on the east side.

This creek and Fox Point were named many years ago by the Teslin Indians. A legend of theirs tells of a supernatural warning to the tribe against returning to this area. It told of a great disaster to come, on a point in the lake where they would see a fox. Disregarding the warning, the tribe returned and a fox entered their camp. Shortly afterwards, the Tahltan Indians attacked and destroyed their camp, killing everyone except one young woman who escaped to tell the story.

FOX LAKE 60°39'N 134°04'W (105-D). 12 miles northeast of Marsh Lake.

In 1943 Major FOX of the US Air Force made a forced landing on this lake and it has been the local name since.

FRANCES LAKE 61°23'N 129°30'W (105-H), and

FRANCES RIVER 60°16'N 129°10'W (105-A). The river is a tributary to the Liard River. The lake is about 90 miles north of Watson Lake, between the Campbell and Logan Mountains.

In the summer of 1840 Robert Campbell of the HBC made his famous journey of exploration from Dease Lake into the central Yukon, the first white man to do so. He ascended the Liard River to the Frances River and then to Frances Lake and on to the Pelly River.

The local Indians called the Frances River the "Too-Tsho-Tooa", meaning "Big Lake River". Campbell named both river and lake after Lady FRANCES Simpson, wife of Sir George Simpson, for nearly 40 years the Governor of the HBC.

For a number of years this river was part of the HBC's route to the central Yukon but it was finally abandoned because of the loss of life in the dangerous waters both here and on the Liard.

FRANKLIN LAKE 60°41'N 135°18'W (105-D). The southernmost of the two small Jackson Lakes.

This local name has been used since the early 1900's when a copper mining company camped and operated here.

MOUNT FRANK RAY   64°28'N 138°33'W (116–B). At the headwaters of the Tombstone River.

This was named in 1968 by Dr. Dirk Tempelman-Kluit, GSC, after FRANK RAY, a pioneer trapper and hunter in this area. It is the highest mountain in the Tombstone River area.

FRASER CREEK   60°19'N 137°20'W (115–A). A tributary to Alder Creek and Mush Lake.

Gold was found here and the Discovery claim staked by J.W. Smith and Fred Altemose in the summer of 1902. They named the creek after Assistant Surgeon S.M. FRASER of the NWMP who was Mining Recorder and Customs Officer at Dalton Post, 1901–03.

FRASER FALLS 63°31'N 135°09'W (105–M). On the Stewart River, ten miles above Gordon Landing.

The falls were named in 1885 when the first prospectors, a party of FRASER, Chapman, Thomas Boswell and others, were exploring the upper reaches of the Stewart.

Robert Levac operated a trading post here for some time in the 1920's and 30's.

FREDERICK LAKE   60°23'N 136°40'W (115–A). Between Kusawa and Dezeadash Lakes.

This was named by the English explorer Edward James Glave in 1890 when, with Jack Dalton, he made the first entry into this part of the country. He made camp at the head of the lake and named it FREDERICK in remembrance of his brother, who had died a few years earlier.

FREEGOLD   MOUNTAIN 4,772' 62°17'N 137°06'W (115–I).   30 miles northwest of Carmacks.

Lode gold was discovered here in June 1930 by P.F. "Fred" Guder on his Augusta claim. A rush immediately developed in the area, resulting in many other mineral discoveries. (See Guder Creek.)

FRENCH GULCH   63°54'N 139°18'W (115–O&N). A small tributary of Eldorado Creek.

In December 1896, George Lamarre of Québec, found rich gold on this gulch and, because of his origin, named it FRENCH Gulch. Claim No. 17 on Eldorado Creek, at the mouth of this gulch, was reported to be the richest claim ever found in the Klondike, yielding nearly 100,000 ounces of gold in a length of 500 feet.

FRENCH HILL 63°54′N 139°19′W (115-O&N). On the west side of Eldorado Creek above French Gulch.

One of the famous "Hill" or "Bench" deposits of the fabulously rich "White Channel" gravels whose existence went unsuspected for the first year and a half of the gold rush. (See Cheechako Hill.)

On 20 October, 1897, William "Cariboo Bill" Dettering, an old Cariboo miner from Illinois and his partner, Joseph Stacey, staked the first bench claim. They were acting on a theory formed by Dettering and sank a prospect shaft on the hill. It was reported that they recovered 11 ounces of gold from the first pan of gravel taken from bedrock. They took out $13,000 and sold the claim (100 feet by 100 feet square) in July 1898 for $40,000. J.N. Demers staked a bench claim on 9 September, 1897, but did not work it until Dettering and Stacey made their find. He then found rich gold on bedrock.

FRESNO CREEK 64°16′N 139°48′W (116-B&C). A tributary to the Yukon River from the west, 25 miles below Dawson.

F.R. Chandler found some gold here on 14 April, 1898. He staked a claim and probably named the stream after the city of the same name in California.

FRISCO CREEK 63°13′N 139°32′W (115-O&N). A tributary of Thistle Creek.

Gold was found and the Discovery claim staked on 10 November, 1897, by a California miner.

FRYING PAN CREEK 62°00′N 140°55′W (115-F). A tributary of Beaver Creek about 12 miles south of Dry Creek.

This was discovered and named in November 1913 during the rush to the Chisana goldfields. The prospector who found the first gold washed it from the gravels with his frying pan. (See Pan Creek.)

FULLER LAKE 62°58′N 130°15′W (105-J). At the headwaters of the South MacMillan River.

This lake was named on 1 April, 1943, by Herman Peterson, of Atlin, a northern bush pilot well-known for many years in the Yukon and northern BC. He landed Kent FULLER, surveyor who was laying out the Canol Pipeline, here on that day. To keep his log in order he asked Fuller what to call the lake. Fuller told him to choose any name he wished.

MOUNT FYFE   4,793'   65°17'N 136°52'W   (116-H). On the east side of the Hart River.

Near the route of the Dawson-MacPherson Patrol, this mountain was named in 1973 after Rgt. No. 4937 Constable J.F. FYFE, RNWMP. He was one of Cpl. Dempster's party who searched for and found the lost Fitzgerald Patrol in February and March 1911.

FYSH CREEK   64°09'N 139°11'W   (116-B&C).   Flows   into   Lepine Creek, 15 miles northeast of Dawson.

This was named by miners about 1905 after a popular public official in the Gold Commissioner's Office in Dawson, Frederick A.H. FYSH, of London, Ontario.

Fysh, a young accountant, and his brother-in-law Charles Williams made one of the most incredible and least known journeys of the Klondike Gold Rush. In the fall of 1897 they were prospecting on the northwest coast of Alaska with little success. After the first snowfall their companions decided to return to St. Michaels for the winter. Fysh and Williams however, decided to go overland to Fort Yukon and Dawson.

In the dead of an Alaskan winter, with only a small toboggan to haul their supplies and a map torn from a high school atlas to guide them, this amazing pair crossed nearly 600 miles of almost unknown country, including several unmapped mountain ranges. They reached Dawson in early January 1898.

Fysh secured a position in the Gold Commissioner's Office which he kept until he moved his family to the Okanagan valley in British Columbia in September 1909. He was a modest man who was very well liked and respected, especially by the prospectors who appreciated his hardihood.

GALENA   63°47'N 139°46'W   (115-O&N).   On   the   Yukon   River opposite the mouth of Indian River.

This was a trading post at the mouth of Galena Creek, owned by Wy Spees, to serve miners nearby and travellers on the river. It burned down in April 1954 and was never rebuilt.

GALENA CREEK   63°55'N 135°35'W   (105-M). Flows into Flat Creek about three miles west of Elsa.

H.W. McWhorter named this creek in 1906 when he and his partner found a rich vein of silver-lead ore in a canyon on the stream. Their first shipment of high-grade ore was the start of silver-lead mining in the Mayo district.

GARDEN CREEK   60°07′N 128°22′W (105-A). Flows into the Hyland River east of Watson Lake.

A prospector-trapper kept a good garden for many years on the banks of this stream. In the early years both people and gardens were rare in this part of the Yukon.

GATES CREEK   (See Brown's Creek.)

GAUCHE LAKE   (See Big Kalzas Lake.)

GAUVIN GULCH   63°55′N 139°16′W (115-O&N). A short creek flowing into Bonanza Creek.

Alfred and Wilfred GAUVIN of St. Simon, Québec, came into the Yukon in 1895. On 20 May, 1897, they found this small, rich valley and made their fortunes.

GAY CREEK   63°14′N 139°04′W (115-C). Flows into the Stewart River from the north, about 12 miles above the mouth.

About 1886–87 Emil Meriguet (known in the Yukon as Emil GAY) prospected and named this creek. It is now known locally as "Three Kings Creek", after three partners who worked it later. (See Gay Gulch.)

GAY GULCH   63°52′N 139°13′W (115-O&N).A very short gulch off Eldorado Creek on the east, four miles from the mouth.

Emil GAY (Meriguet) discovered the wealth of this tiny valley on 4 January, 1897, when he staked the first claim and named it. An old-time Yukoner, he had come into the country in 1886 and became wealthy from this and other Klondike claims and mining ventures. He returned to France, to his birthplace, where he retired.

His Discovery claim on this gulch yielded over $3,000 to the running foot for a distance of 500 feet.

In 1962 Gay's grandson, Henri Meriguet, of Annecy, France, came to the Yukon during the Dawson Festival, hitchhiking across Canada. He wished to visit the claim that had made his grandfather wealthy and to see the wonderful country he had talked about. He was murdered and his body buried in a gravel pit at mile 693 (K1123) on the Alaska Highway. His suspected murderer, Karoli Marsi, hung himself in the Don Jail in Toronto, Ontario, in August 1967.

GEM CREEK   63°57′N 136°49′W (115–P). Tributary to Sprague Creek.

In the late 1930's George Retter, Jack Alverstone and Cecil Poli found and mined placer gold on this creek.

GEORGE CREEK   63°10′N 133°28′W (105–N). A tributary of Russell Creek.

This was named in 1901 by Major Neville A.D. Armstrong after his partner GEORGE Leith of England. They worked the Gillis, or Armstrong Concession for placer gold on Russell Creek in 1901–02. (See Mount Armstrong.)

GHECHUCK CREEK   63°27′N 136°17′W (115–P). A short creek flowing into the Stewart River, east of the Crossing.

The name was recorded in 1957. It was named after Billy "GHECHUCK" Malcolm, whose Indian name means "Porcupine."

MOUNT GIBBEN   6,500′ 64°43′N 139°11′W (116–B). 45 miles north of Dawson at the head of the Fifteen Mile River.

The highest mountain in the area, it was named for the Honourable Justice J.E. GIBBEN, former Commissioner of the Yukon Territory and Judge of the Territorial Court. In 1970 the name was officially adopted.

MOUNT GIBSON   61°14′N 140°05′W (115–G&F). On the southeast side of the Steele Glacier in the St. Elias Ranges.

This was named in 1970 by the Alpine Club of Canada after a past president of the club, E. Rex GIBSON (1892–1957).

MOUNT GILLIAM   60°18′N 134°55′W (105–D). On the north end of Gray Ridge, ten miles northwest of Carcross.

This name was reported by W.E. Cockfield, GSC, about 1920. Marc H. GILLIAM was a Cornish miner and a pioneer prospector and mine superintendent locally for many years. The mountain had borne his name for a long time locally before it was made official.

GILLIS LAKES   66°26′N 134°45′W (106–L). A large group of small lakes west of the Peel River.

In 1973 these lakes were named after A.J. GILLIS, Speaker of the Yukon Council from 1912–15. He represented South Dawson in the council.

MOUNT GILLIS 5,418′ 62°51′N 133°21′W (105-K). An isolated peak east of Stokes Lake, north of the Tay River.

Duncan GILLIS of Nova Scotia came to the Yukon in 1892. While on a holiday at home he heard the news of the Klondike find. He returned to the Yukon via the Edmonton Trail and the Gravel (Keele) River. He descended the MacMillan River, mistaking it for the Hess. It was on this journey that he discovered the placer gold of Russell Creek. (See Mount Armstrong.)

GIROUARD HILL 1,672′ 68°09′N 138°17′W (117-A). Ten miles west of Bonnet Lake.

This was named in 1973 after J.E. GIROUARD, Registrar of Land Titles in the Yukon from 1898–1908 and appointed Member of the Yukon Council for the same period.

GLACIER CREEK 64°01′N 140°43′W (116-B&C). A tributary to Big Gold Creek in the Sixtymile district.

Gold found on this creek in 1891 started the rush to the Sixtymile district. The creek received its name because glacial ice had to be removed on the upper reaches of the stream to work the gold-bearing gravels.

MOUNT GLADMAN 64°43′N 140°49′W (116-B&C). Near the International Boundary and the Yukon River.

William Ogilvie, DLS, had four assistants with him in 1887–88 when he established the first part of the Yukon-Alaska boundary, from the Yukon River south to the Sixtymile River country.

In March 1888 he named this mountain after one of them, Charles GLADMAN, of Peterborough, Ontario. It was first called Gladman Peak. Gladman accompanied Ogilvie on many other surveys in other parts of Canada. He died in Peterborough in July 1947.

He had also accompanied Warburton Pike, the English explorer of the Frances Lake country, to Lower Post in 1893 but had to leave him there as Ogilvie wanted him for another task.

GLADSTONE CREEK (See Bertha Creek.)

GLADSTONE CREEK 61°19′N 138°40′W (115-G&F). Flows into Kluane Lake.

Although this creek was named during the original stampede to the Silver Creek country of the Kluane in 1903, it was not until 1911 that T.T. Murray and Axel Swanson found the first payable gold on it.

GLENLYON HOUSE 61°17′N 129°18′W (105-H). On a point on the north side of the channel between the east and west arms of Frances Lake.

The first trading post in the Yukon Territory was built here. Robert Campbell of the HBC, in the summer of 1840 left some of his crew here to construct a small building while he continued his exploration to the Pelly River.

He decided to make this a permanent trading post and named it after GLENLYON HOUSE, the seat of the Campbell clan in Scotland. In 1842 he changed the name of the post to Fort Frances.

The post was destroyed by fire in the spring of 1852. (See Fort Frances.)

GLENLYON PEAK 7,184′ 62°32′N 134°28′W (105-L). The northernmost peak in the Glenlyon Range.

A.C. Tuttle, topographer, in 1946-47 gave this peak the name Mount Hodder, from the creek flowing at its base. This was soon changed to honour Robert Campbell but the name Hodder appears on some old maps.

GODDARD POINT 61°21′N 135°14′W (105-E). A point on the northeast side of Lake Laberge.

This was named in 1899 after the little steamboat *A.J. GODDARD* in turn named after her builder, owner and captain. The hull was built in San Francisco and, with the engine, was hauled over the White Pass in the winter of 1897-98 and assembled at Lake Bennett. It was 40 feet long and displaced 15 tons. The *A.J. Goddard* was the first steamboat to make the run from Lake Bennett to Dawson; she left Lake Bennett on 29 May, 1898, ran Miles Canyon and the Whitehorse Rapids and arrived in Dawson on 21 June.

The boat was wrecked in a storm near this point in September 1899 with the loss of the captain (not Captain Goddard), the fireman, cook and a waiter. Their bodies were not recovered until 3 May, 1902. The boat was never raised; its remains may still be seen in calm weather.

GOLD BOTTOM CREEK 63°58′N 138°58′W (115-O&N). The west branch of Hunker Creek.

Robert Douglas Henderson, born in 1857 in Pictou County, Nova Scotia, came to the Yukon over Chilkoot Pass in June 1894. Grubstaked by Joe Ladue, the trader at Ogilvie (Sixtymile), and by some small earnings gained on Quartz Creek, he spent the next two years prospecting the tributaries of the Indian River.

In April 1896 he crossed the divide between Quartz Creek and the west branch of what was later Hunker Creek. On this branch he found low gold values but better than any others he had seen. In his imagination he saw the bedrock of this stream paved with gold nuggets and named it GOLD BOTTOM. Needing supplies and wishing to explore a little more of the country, he went down Hunker to the Klondike River where, at its mouth, he met George Carmack and his party who were fishing for salmon.

He extolled his new find to Carmack and invited him to visit his creek. However, he stipulated that he did not wish Carmack's Indian relatives and friends to stake claims. (The Indians of the Yukon had always had the same right to stake mineral claims as the whites.)

Henderson continued on to Ogilvie and obtained supplies. He returned to Gold Bottom by way of Quartz Creek where he induced 18 miners working there to accompany him to his new find. Arriving at Gold Bottom 14 of the men, after investigating the gravel, immediately returned to Quartz, unimpressed with Henderson's find. Henderson, with the remaining three (one man had turned back), set to work on his claim. In a period of about three months they recovered $720 worth of gold. This was not enough to buy food at that time.

In early August, George Carmack, Skookum Jim and Tagish Charlie travelled up Rabbit Creek (later Bonanza) to visit Henderson. On the way they found encouraging showings of gold.

On Gold Bottom they examined Henderson's showings and were not greatly impressed. Carmack staked a claim beside Henderson's. They then returned to the mouth of the Klondike along Rabbit Creek. It was on this journey that they found rich, coarse gold on the stream that Carmack now renamed Bonanza. Skookum Jim remained on the claim, Tagish Charlie stayed at the fishing camp at the mouth of the Klondike and Carmack went to Fortymile to obtain more supplies. (Some accounts claim that he and Tagish Charlie took saw-logs to Fortymile to sell for supplies). No one went back to Gold Bottom to tell Henderson.

The rush started and Andrew Hunker, after staking on upper Bonanza, looked east. With his partner, Charles M. Johnson, he went up Hunker Creek from the Klondike River. Panning as they went, they soon discovered rich gold showings and staked a Discovery claim and two others, on 6 September, 1896. They went back down to Fortymile and recorded their claims and named the creek Hunker. On their return Hunker went farther up the creek and found Henderson and his three companions at work. They had heard nothing. He persuaded them to come downstream to his discovery. When Henderson saw Hunker's showings he and his companions immediately staked beside Hunker's claims. Henderson staked No. 3 Above Discovery. Henderson then set out for Fortymile where he tried to record a Discovery claim on Gold Bottom. This was disallowed by Constantine as being part of Hunker Creek. Faced with a choice he recorded No. 3 Above rather than his original claim. On his way down he had also staked No. 12 on Bear Creek. This also was not allowed as rules had been made allowing only one claim per man in a mining district. In September 1897 Henderson sold No 3 A to Big Alex McDonald for $3,000, a very respectable sum in those days. McDonald recovered over $800,000 from the claim. Timothy Crowley staked Henderson's original claim on Gold Bottom on 18 September, 1896. There is no record of any appreciable amount of gold being taken from it or any other claim on Gold Bottom. Crowley sold his claim to Big Alex in December 1897.

GOLD HILL   63°55′N   139°22′W   (115-O&N). The hill on the west side of Bonanza Creek at its junction with Eldorado Creek.

On 3 July, 1897, according to O. Finnie, the government historian, G.A. Lancaster located a bench claim at claim No. 2 on Eldorado Creek. (A bench claim is the first claim uphill from a creek claim — the bottom of the hillside.) The claim was part of what later was called Gold Hill. A Dr. P.D. Carper, who had possibly grubstaked Lancaster, gave the hill its name. Lancaster's was the first claim on, and produced the first gold mined from the White Channel gravels.

On 23 July, 1897, Nathan Kresky (he later changed it to Kresge) and Nils Peterson staked the Discovery hill claim. (A hill claim was one hundred feet square and was not connected to any creek claim). In ten days, using a rocker and re-circulated water, they won $6,375 from a piece of ground 11 feet by 17 and three feet deep. This is a little better than $300 per cubic yard — rich indeed! Nils Peterson moved a little farther up the hill, sank a shaft 63 feet deep to bedrock and found far richer gold at the bottom. The hill was well named.

By 14 September every possible claim on the hill had been staked. This find led to the discovery of similar deposits on the Hunker Creek hills a few days later. (See Cheechako Hill.)

GOLD HILL 60°17'N 135°08'W (105-D). On the north side of the Wheaton River, 17 miles northwest of Carcross.

In 1893 Frank Corwin and Thomas Rickman of Juneau prospected this area and found extremely rich gold in a quartz vein on this hill. Both men died shortly after their return to Juneau and as the area was unmapped at the time, the exact location of their find was lost.

Many others searched for the vein and although some of their claim posts were found, it was not until 25 June, 1906, that David Hodnett and Jack Stagar found and staked the Gold Reef claim, believing that they had found the lost lode. Within 90 days over 700 claims had been staked surrounding them. (See Mt. Hodnett, Carbon Hill and Corwin Valley.)

GOLDEN HORN MOUNTAIN 5,610' 60°34'N 135°03'W (105-D). The solitary peak 12 miles south of Whitehorse.

Used as a landmark by the miners boating down the Yukon River, this beautiful hill was named by the earliest white men to see it, about 1881–82.

MOUNT GOOD 6,556' 64°20'N 134°26'W (106-D). In the Wernecke Mountains north of the Beaver River.

In 1973 this peak was named to honour the memory of J-88030 Pilot Officer Ralph Edward GOOD who was born at Carcross on 1 May, 1919. He enlisted in the RCAF at Vancouver, BC on 24 August 1942 and served in Canada and overseas. He was killed during air operations over Germany on 19 August, 1944.

GOODE CREEK 60°33'N 133°52'W (105-C). Flows northeast into Jackfish Lake.

Bob GOODE and his two brothers trapped in this area for many years.

GOOD NEIGHBOUR PEAK 15,700' 60°22'N 139°42'W (115-B&C). Two miles north of Mount Vancouver.

This peak is supposed to be the second highest in the Yukon, Mount St. Elias being the highest. It was climbed as part of the Canadian Centennial Celebration in 1967 by eight members of the Yukon Alpine Centennial Expedition, four American and four Canadian climbers. Monty Alford, of the Water Resources Branch, Department of Northern Affairs, Whitehorse, was Canadian co-leader and Vin Hoeman the American co-leader of the climbing party. They made the ascent on 25 June, 1967. (See Centennial Range.)

GORDON LANDING 63°37'N 135°27'W (105-M). A former settlement on the Stewart River above Mayo, near the mouth of Janet Creek.

This little settlement was established about 1902 to serve the new placer goldfields on Duncan Creek. A trader by this name built the post. Roads were pushed out to Duncan, Highet and Haggart Creeks. The place was abandoned as Mayo and Keno assumed importance.

GRAND FORKS 63°55'N 139°18'W (115-O&N).

This was the largest settlement in the Klondike after Dawson City. Forming naturally at the junction of Bonanza and Eldorado Creeks, one day's journey from Dawson, the settlement began to grow in early 1897. Belinda Mulroney built the first roadhouse, the Magnet, in September 1897. Surrounded by the richest gravels in the world, the town expanded; hotels, stores and services of all kinds flourished. By 1903 the population was over 3,000 and the town was incorporated with Peter Coutts, of Grey North, Ontario, the first mayor. As long as the gravels were rich enough to sustain hand work the town prospered but as these dwindled so did the people and business died down. By 1921 dredging operations encompassing the whole valley had destroyed the town and dug up the ground underneath.

It was the last remaining chartered town in the Yukon Territory until that was revoked on 9 December, 1905.

MOUNT GRANGER 6,675' 60°32'N 135°15'W (105-D). 16 miles southwest of Whitehorse.

William P. GRANGER came from Kentucky to the Yukon in 1895. He was one of the first to find and develop the copper deposits at Whitehorse and the gold-quartz ores of the Wheaton Valley country.

He was killed by carbon monoxide poisoning in a prospect shaft at the Copper King Mine at Whitehorse on 10 May, 1907. This hill was named shortly after.

GRANVILLE 63°40'N 138°37'W (115-O&N). On Sulphur Creek just above its junction with Dominion Creek.

The Granville Mining Company was established in 1911. It was the first large attempt by English capital to consolidate the Klondike placer deposits and mine them by large-scale, mechanical means. A.N.C. Treadgold, an Oxford don and one of the most colourful figures of the Klondike for many years, was the leading figure in this enterprise.

The company was named after Lord GRANVILLE, a backer and the British Secretary of State for the Colonies in the late 19th century. This settlement, started by Treadgold and named by him, was the headquarters of his operations from 1903 for many years and was later used by the Yukon Consolidated Gold Corporation Ltd. It was abandoned about 1965.

MOUNT GRAY 6,085′ 60°09′N 134°51′W (105-D). Six miles west of Carcross on the north shore of Lake Bennett.

This was named by William Ogilvie, DLS, in 1887 or possibly by miners a few years earlier. The name was much later applied to the whole ridge north to Needle Mountain.

GREAVES CREEK 66°29′N 137°39′W (116-1). A tributary to Canoe Creek.

Robert Bruce GREAVES was a well-known figure in early Dawson as the proprietor of the Red Feather Saloon. He later was in business in Mayo. This creek was named in 1973.

GREEN CREEK 63°04′N 139°25′W (115-O&N). A tributary of Thistle Creek.

Gold was first found and the creek named in October 1898. The finder named the stream after the Mining Recorder at Stewart River, a man named GREEN. It is now called Green Gulch.

MOUNT GREEN 6,669′ 61°44′N 132°26′W (105-F). In the St. Cyr Range.

In 1951 this mountain was named to honour the memory of Lt. A.D. GREEN, MID, of the Canadian army, who was killed in action during World War Two.

GREW CREEK 62°04′N 132°56′W (105-K). Flows into the Peel River from the south.

This name was known before 1905. James "Jim" GREW was an old HBC man who lived and trapped this area for a long time. He was about 70 years of age when he died here, alone in 1906.

GREY COPPER HILL 5,254 64°26′N 135°15′W (106-D). East of Carpenter Creek in the Wernecke Mountains.

This was named by Robert Fisher, a pioneer prospector who found rich tetrahedrite (a silver-copper mineral of a rich, grey colour) float here in the autumn of 1923, which led to a stampede to the area in the winter of 1923-24. Several hundred men took part in this rush.

GREY HUNTER PEAK 7,265′ 63°10′N 135°40′W (105-M). In the McArthur Group of mountains.

This was named by H.S. Bostock, GSC, in 1940, from its dark, grey, forbidding appearance.

GROUSE CREEK 60°03′N 132°51′W (105-C). A tributary to Fat Creek from the west.

This was named McCleary Creek by the GSC in 1946-47 after the trader and Justice of the Peace at Teslin, Robert McCleery. The Forest Warden at Teslin protested in 1955 that the common name for this stream was GROUSE Creek, that no one used McCleary, that the spelling was wrong and that McCleery should be commemorated by a mountain north of Teslin. (See Mount McCleery.)

GUDER CREEK 62°19′N 137°12′W (115-I). A tributary to Seymour Creek in the Mt. Freegold area.

Paul Fritz "Fred" GUDER was born in June 1895 in Middle Waldenburgh, Silesia, Germany. As a young man he took ship to Panama and walked across the isthmus. Working his way north by ship he arrived in the Yukon in 1912, walking from Skagway to Whitehorse. He worked for a number of years for the noted Captain H.S. Back in the Mount Nansen area and independently for many more years in the Mount Freegold district which he pioneered and named.

This creek was named in 1929 by his friend, "Happy" Lepage of Carmacks. Fred had found lead ore and was living on the creek at the time.

Among other exploits, Fred once spent a winter alone, trapping in the Nahanni Valley. In the winter of 1918-19 he came and went, hauling supplies from Ross River with a hand-sled up the Pelly River and across the mountains. Still actively prospecting in his late 70's, this quiet, hardworking man is liked and respected by all who know him. (See Mount Freegold.)

GULL LAKE 62°15′N 129°52′W (105-I). Northeast of the Pelly Lakes and near Mt. Pike.

This small lake was named in 1893 by Warburton Pike, the English sportsman, explorer and later, trader at Dease Lake, 1898–99. He found enormous numbers of black-headed gulls (Arctic tern) breeding here. (See Narchilla Brook.)

GUSTAVUS RANGE 63°52′N 135°15′W (105–M). The range of hills lying north of Mayo Lake.

This was named in 1904 by Joseph Keele, GSC, while he was mapping the geology of the district. Known as the "Mysterious Three", GUSTAVUS Gustavusen, a Norwegian, and his two sons found the first gold in the district on Duncan Creek in 1898.

The name has been variously reported as Gustavus, Gustavessen, Gustavuson and Gustavusen, which seems to be the correct spelling from most contemporary accounts. (See Duncan Creek.)

HAECKEL HILL 60°47′N 135°16′W (105–D). Eight miles northwest of Whitehorse.

This hill was named Haeckel Butte by Lt. F. Schwatka, US Army, on his excursion down the Yukon River in the summer of 1883, after Professor Ernst Heinrich HAECKEL, a distinguished German naturalist of Jena.

Because Haeckel was a noted scientist and also because the mountain had no previous name, Dr. G.M. Dawson, GSC, allowed his name to stand in 1887.

HAGGART CREEK 63°54′N 136°01′W (115–P). A tributary to the South McQuesten River.

Thomas Nelson prospected this stream in 1895 and in 1896 found good gold in the canyon about four miles upstream from the mouth. At that time it was locally called "Nelson" Creek. At the same time Thomas Haggart built a cabin on the creek and one on Dublin Gulch. No claims were recorded in the area at that time.

Taking part unsuccessfully in the Klondike rush, they returned to the creek in 1898. Thomas Haggart and his brother, Peter, Thomas Nelson and Warren Hiatt left Dawson but *en route* they quarrelled and split into two parties. Peter HAGGART and Warren Hiatt reached Nelson Creek first and staked a Discovery claim. When they recorded their claims they renamed the stream after Peter Haggart.
(See Highet Creek.)

HAINES JUNCTION 60°45′N 137°30′W (115-A). Situated at the junction of the Haines Highway and the Alaska Highway.

Begun in late 1942 and starting at mile 1016 on the Alaska Highway, a road was built south to Haines, Alaska on the Pacific coast. It was a wartime measure to increase the shipment of materials and supplies from the US to Alaska. It was constructed by the US Army Engineers and follows quite closely the old Dalton Trail.

The first buildings at the junction were US Army Engineers barracks and shops. Because of its position the settlement has continued to grow.

It was named after Haines, Alaska, a town which was originally located in 1879 by the famous pioneer missionary, S. Hall Young, as the site of a Presbyterian mission. It was given the name of the first Secretary of the Committee of Home Missions, Mrs. Francine E. HAINES.

MOUNT HALDANE 6,015′ 63°55′N 135°55′W (105-M). About 15 miles west of Mayo Lake.

This was named about 1920 for an early prospector of that name who lived and mined on HALDANE Creek at the foot of the mountain. Up to that time and to most of the local people since, it was "Lookout" Mountain.

HALL CREEK 60°30′N 133°41′W (105-C). Flows into the west end of Squanga Lake.

This name seems to have been applied for no particular reason in the 1940′s. HALL Williams was an old HBC man who lived on Teslin Lake about the turn of the century, trapping for a living. Fat Creek, on the west side of Teslin Lake was called the Hall River for a time in the 1900′s. Also, just south of Fat Creek in BC, there is a Hall Lake named after the same man about 1898.

HANCOCK HILLS 61°10′N 135°00′W (105-E). On the east side of Lake Laberge.

This was named by Lt. F. Schwatka, US Army, in 1883, after one of his superiors, General Winfield Scott HANCOCK (1824–1886).

MOUNT HANSEN 3,127′ 62°47′N 137°15′W (115-I). A low hill two miles east of Fort Selkirk.

This hill was named in 1971 after Corporal G. HANSEN, Rgt. No. 63 of the Royal Regiment of Canada, a member of the Yukon Field Force. He died while serving at Fort Selkirk, on 18 February, 1899.

HAPPY VALLEY   60°00′N   133°30′W   (105–C). A large valley crossing the Yukon-BC border between Atlin and Teslin Lakes.

On 12 May, 1899, George White-Fraser, DTS, was setting survey monuments on the Yukon-BC boundary between Teslin and Bennett Lakes. This valley, with its chain of small lakes, was so pleasant after the rugged, mountainous terrain he had just encountered that he rested his crew and horses here and gave the valley its name.

MOUNT HARBOTTLE   65°48′N   138°20′W   (116–G&F). South of the Whitestone River.

This was named in 1973 after Francis E. HARBOTTLE. He was a member of the NWMP in the Yukon from 1901–05 and was afterward with the Canadian Customs Service.

HARDLUCK CREEK   65°05′N   141°00′W   (116–G&F). A tributary to Harrington Creek in Alaska.

An International Boundary Survey party lost some of its supplies here in 1910. The name originally applied to the whole creek, including Harrington.

MOUNT HARE   4,073′   66°38′N   136°11′W   (116–I). In the Richardson Mountains.

This was named in honour of a soldier named HARE who was killed in action in the Second World War.

MOUNT HARPER   6,149′   64°41′N   139°52′W   (116–B&C). A high peak in the Ogilvie Mountains, north of Dawson.

This was named by William Ogilvie, DLS, while he was surveying the International Boundary in 1887–88, after one of the Yukon's earliest pioneers and the first recorded prospector.

Arthur "Cariboo" HARPER was born in County Antrim, Ireland, in 1835. As a young man he mined in California and moved north in the search for gold, always in the advance guard. From the Fraser River goldfields he went on to the Cariboo and then opened the Omineca diggings of northern BC. In 1872 with Frederick Hart and others he went down the Liard River and up the Mackenzie, crossed the Rocky Mountains to the Porcupine River and arrived at Fort Yukon on 15 August, 1873, about the same time as McQuesten, Mayo and their party.

In the fall and winter of 1873–74 Harper, Fred Hart and George Fitch went up to the headwaters of the White River, following an Indian tale of gold. They found prospects of placer gold and also of copper deposits but nothing they could mine at a profit. They were the first white men to explore the stream and the first to prospect what is now the Yukon Territory.

Harper alternated prospecting with trading and for many years, in a loose association, ran the ACC's posts at Fort Reliance, Sixtymile (Ogilvie), Stewart River, Fort Selkirk and other locations. He married an Indian woman and had several children.

Although he pioneered most of the major goldfields that were found in the Yukon and his experience and advice led other men to fortune, he never found the riches he sought. He left the Yukon in 1897, a poor man, broken in health from his privations and hardships, and died of tuberculosis in Yuma, Arizona, in November 1898.

HARRISON CREEK 60°55'N 136°14'W (115-A). A small creek, tributary to Cranberry Creek, which in turn flows into the Mendenhall River.

This was named in 1951 to perpetuate the memory of Cpl. E. HARRISON MID, killed in action with the Canadian army in the Second World War.

HART RIVER 65°51'N 136°23'W (116-H). Flows north to the Peel River from the Wernecke Mountains.

This was named very early, after Howard Hamilton HART of Montana, who came to the Yukon in 1884 over the Chilkoot Pass, one of the earliest prospectors in the Yukon. He was an active man and was constantly pushing farther afield than most. He prospected and mined gold on most of the tributaries of the Yukon. In the fall of 1886, acting on advice from Arthur Harper, he discovered and mined gold on "Hamilton Bar" on the Fortymile River.

From 1896 to 98 he had a lay (lease) on Tagish Charlie's No. 1 Above claim on Bonanza Creek, from which he took a fortune. Most of it was lost when the steamer *Islander* was wrecked near Juneau, Alaska in 1905. He died in Dawson in 1908 after falling into the freezing waters of Bonanza Creek. He sometimes called himself Howard Hamilton.

HARVEY GULCH 63°46'N 136°13'W. (115-P). A short creek, flowing into Highet Creek from Scheelite Dome.

This was locally named for HARVEY Ray, a prospector-trapper who lived here in the 1930's.

HASSELBERG CREEK   60°38'N 129°56'W (105-A). A tributary to the upper Liard River.

This stream was named in 1959 after Frederick HASSELBERG who mined and trapped in the upper Liard country for many years from 1910. His cabin is at the mouth of the creek.

When first mapped it was wrongly spelled Heigelberg.

HASSELL CREEK   60°18'N 132°16'W (105-C). A small lake and creek ten miles north of Morley Lake.

This creek and lake were named in the summer of 1951 to honour the name of Sgt. D.B.L. HASSELL, MID, of the Canadian army who was killed in action in the Second World War.

HATCH'S ISLAND   64°02'N 139°27'W (116-B&C). A large island a mile long and a half mile wide, in the Yukon River, a mile and a half above Dawson.

George A. HATCH bought this island in 1901. He cut off the cottonwood trees and sold them for firewood in Dawson. In 1902 he planted potatoes on the ground he had cleared and by 1909 he was producing more than 60 tons per year as well as large crops of oats and other grains and vegetables. He also raised hogs and chickens. He was probably the most successful farmer in the Yukon. He died at his home in Morrill, Maine, in 1917.

HAUNKA CREEK   60°14'N 133°54'W (105-C). Flows into Little Atlin Lake from the east side.

This is a very old name probably dating back to the 1880's. Locally it is said to be the Tagish Indian pronunciation of the name of an old HBC trapper, Hall Williams, who roamed this region in those days. (See Hall Creek.)

HAYDEN LAKE   61°02'N 138°08'W (115-G&F). Ten miles east of the south end of Kluane Lake.

Named after Jack HAYDEN, Klondiker, trapper and noted guide who lived and worked in this area from the earliest years. An American, Hayden was a colourful character who had driven stage coaches in Colorado, punched cattle in Texas and mined in the Klondike. He married a native woman and lived here for many years.

HAYES CREEK   62°43'N 138°15'W (115-J&K). A tributary to the Selwyn River.

This was named for Dr. Charles Willard HAYES who made the first map of this area in his exploration report for the American Geographical Society in 1891. Hayes was later made Director of the United States Geological Survey. (See Hayes Peak.)

HAYES PEAK 6,067′ 60°24′N 133°18′W (105-C). On the west side of Teslin Lake, seven miles south of Johnson's Crossing.

This beautiful, lone hill was named by Arthur St. Cyr, DLS, in 1897, when he was searching for and surveying a possible route from Telegraph Creek to the head of Teslin Lake and on to the goldfields. It was named after Dr. Charles Willard HAYES, USC&GS. Hayes, together with Mark Russell and Lt. F. Schwatka, US Army, in 1891 came this way while travelling from the Taku River to the upper White River country. Hayes later published the first notes on the geology and topography of this region. St. Cyr also named a river entering Teslin Lake at the southwest end for Hayes.

HAYSTACK MOUNTAIN 3,751′ 63°39′N 139°10′W (115-O&N). On the headwaters of Ruby Creek, south of the Indian River.

The mountain was named about 1897 by the first miners in the Klondike because of its shape. It is notable as the site of one of the most unusual funerals in the Klondike.

In one June in the early 1920's Carl Hafstead died. He had mined on Quartz Creek and had looked at this mountain from his claim for all the years he was there. He had expressed the desire to be buried on the summit of this hill and left instructions in his will to that end, including money for a barrel of beer for his pall-bearers and mourners.

Upon his death a simple service was held in a roadhouse at the base of the mountain, conducted by one of his fellow miners. A party of 30 miners then set off carrying the coffin and a barrel of beer. It was a 12-mile journey and a climb of 1000 feet by wagon and foot, on a hot day. An advance party of miners went ahead and dug and blasted a grave on the top of the hill overlooking the Indian River valley. By late evening the burial party had arrived and Carl was laid to rest in his favourite place.

HAZARD CREEK 61°16′N 140°12′W (115-G). A small creek flowing into the Steele Glacier from the north side.

I. Peace HAZARD was a sponsor and member of the American Geographical Society Expedition of 1935 which was the first to explore the upper reaches of the phenomenal Steele Glacier. This stream was given his name in 1966.

HEADLESS CREEK   61°48′N 134°41′W (105–E). A tributary to the Big Salmon River immediately above Illusion Creek.

Not a murder mystery! This was named by H.S. Bostock, GSC, in the summer of 1934. Glaciation had turned the headwaters of this stream into nearby Lokken Creek, leaving this stream headless, or shorter.

HEIGELBERG CREEK   (See Hasselberg Creek.)

HELL CREEK   64°12′N 133°46′W (106–C). A tributary of the east Rackla River.

This creek got its name in 1898 from the men who tried to travel its rough course on the way from Edmonton to the Klondike. The name was originally given to the whole Rackla River.

HENDERSON CREEK   63°21′N 139°29′W (115–O&N). A large creek entering the Yukon River about two and a half miles below the Stewart River.

Robert HENDERSON of Klondike fame, with John Collins and Underwood, found gold and staked the Discovery claim on 9 June, 1897. They wrote on their No. 1 Post "This creek shall be known as Henderson Creek."

A stampede of considerable proportions took place but little payable gold was found. Henderson was so convinced of the stream's potential that he staked a 160-acre townsite on the west side of the Yukon River, opposite the mouth of the creek. Nothing came of it.

HERSCHEL ISLAND   69°35′N 139°05′W (117–D). The only major island on the Arctic coast of the Yukon.

The most northerly place in the Yukon, this historic island was first sighted and named by John Franklin, RN, (later Sir), in 1826 but he did not land there. He gave it the name of Sir William HERSCHEL (1738–1822), the famous English astronomer.

The USS *Thetis* surveyed the island in 1889 and named many of its features. This was also the year the first whaler wintered at the island. It was the only safe winter anchorage from Point Barrow to the Mackenzie delta. As the riches of the Beaufort Sea whaling grounds became known, more whalers wintered here. Being remote from authority of any kind, they began a period of unlicensed debauchery and murder. As many as 100 ships lay here at one time and took full advantage of the unsophisticated Eskimo population. It was the only time and place in western Canada's history that complete and unbridled lawlessness ran amok.

In 1896 the Canadian Church Missionary Society learned of conditions on the island and Isaac O. Stringer (later Bishop of the Yukon), a fearless and indomitable man, was sent to erect a mission and attempt to alleviate the lot of the natives. He pressed Ottawa for help but it was not until 1903 that the RNWMP set up a detachment here. By that time the whaling industry had recessed and conditions on the island had bettered.

The island continued to be a trading centre and a little whaling by both natives and whites was carried on. In 1925 a post office (run by the RCMP) was opened. As population lessened and trade decreased, the settlement dwindled. In September 1938 the post office was closed. By 1968 all had ceased and no one remained.

HESS RIVER   63°33′N 133°56′W (105–N). A major tributary of the Stewart River.

Michael HESS was one of the earliest miners in both the Canadian and Alaskan Yukon. He entered the country over the Chilkoot Pass in 1884 and prospected most of the major Yukon River tributaries. He was one of the discoverers of Cassiar Bar in the Yukon River, the first rich diggings found on the Yukon. It is probable that he prospected and named this stream before 1886. Although well known and prominent in the literature of the time, little is known of the man himself. He died and was buried at Fortymile in 1892.

The range of mountains between the Rogue and Hess Rivers was later given his name.

HESTER CREEK   63°59′N 139°02′W (115–O&N). Flows into Hunker Creek from the southwest, two miles above Last Chance Creek.

John Huntington staked the Discovery claim on this stream on 28 October, 1897 and probably named it after someone in his family.

MOUNT   HICKSON   61°11′N 140°04′W (115–F).   Beside   Mount Gibson in the St. Elias Range.

This was named in 1970 by the Alpine Club of Canada after J.W.A. HICKSON (1873–1956), a past president (1924–1926) of the club.

MOUNT HIGGINS 2,973' 66°09'N 136°33'W (116-1). At the head of Eagle River.

In 1973 this hill was named in remembrance of K-49920 Trooper Struan Alexander HIGGINS who was born on 12 July, 1918, in Vancouver, BC. He enlisted at Dawson and served in Canada, Great Britain and northwest Europe. He was reported missing in action and presumed killed on 9 August, 1944, in France.

HIGH CACHE CREEK 69°09'N 140°09'W (117-C). A tributary of the Firth River about 75 miles from the mouth.

Jujira Wada found placer gold on the Firth River at this point on 1 March, 1908, and named this stream. A cache is a small, log building, usually built on high posts, used to store dry supplies out of the reach of animals.

Wada was an exceptional musher (dog team driver) and made many extraordinary journeys to the far corners of the Yukon and Alaska. He took part in all major and many minor gold rushes and stampedes in both countries from 1898 to 1925. He went from Fairbanks (before it had that name) to Dawson with the news of a new, rich (and mainly imaginary) gold strike. About 1,000 men followed him back and, when they assessed the new camp, held a miners' meeting in which they discussed hanging him. As it happened, they really did not mean it and by summer gold had been found in large amounts. He once mushed, in 1923, from central northern Alaska to Herschel Island, down the Mackenzie and on to Winnipeg, Manitoba, a distance of 2,500 miles.

His find here sparked a stampede but results were uneconomic. Every ten or 15 years another rush takes place to the same prospects. (See Firth River.)

HIGHET CREEK 63°43'N 136°04'W (115-P). Flows into the Minto River.

Warren HIATT discovered the first gold here in May 1903. When he was recording the Discovery claim, his name was spelled phonetically by the Mining Recorder. It was the richest creek in the Mayo area; by 1915 over $500,000 in gold had been won from it. Native bismuth, a mineralogical rarity, was common in its gravels.

William Ogilvie, DLS, when connected with the Stewart River dredging operations of the Yukon Basin Gold Dredging Company in 1908, called it Hyatt Creek.

MOUNT HINTON 6,755' 63°54'N 135°08'W (105-M). Six miles north of Mayo Lake in the Gustavus Range.

This was named in 1904 after Thomas HINTON, a well-liked Mining Recorder at Dawson and Mayo in the early 1900's.

HOBO CREEK 63°56'N 136°57'W (115-P). Flows into the Little Klondike River.

This was named by the famous Captain H.S. Back on 13 November, 1897, when he prospected this creek. (See Back and Nansen Creeks.)

HODDER CREEK 62°34'N 134°26'W (105-L). Flows into the Pelly River from the Glenlyon Range.

HODDER, a Swede, was a ne'er-do-well who existed on a little trapping and the charity of the local Indians. He died on the Pelly River in the winter of 1940 when he drunkenly locked himself outside his cabin in sub-zero weather and froze to death. Mount Hodder is now Glenlyon Peak.

HODGSON GLACIER 61°11'N 140°19'W (115-G). A western branch of the Steele Glacier.

In 1966 Walter Wood named this feature in memory of Forest A. HODGSON Wood, a member of four scientific expeditions (1935, 39, 1941, 47) to the area of the Steele Glacier.

Wood on 27 July, 1957, left the Seward Glacier in a Norseman aircraft with the pilot and his daughter, Valerie. They were never seen again. In 1957, Mount Forest in Alaska was given his name.

MOUNT HODNETT 6,540' 60°19'N 135°12'W (105-D). Between the Watson and Wheaton Rivers.

This was named in 1906 after David HODNETT, the discoverer of lode gold in this area that same year. Hodnett Lakes were also named for him at a later date. (See Gold Hill.)

MOUNT HOFFMAN 64°28'N 136°20'W (116-A). In the south Wernecke Mountains.

Fred HOFFMAN was a pioneer prospector and trapper in this area and a partner of Frank Rae.

HOGAN LAKE 66°21'N 134°03'W (106-L). Between the Caribou and Peel Rivers.

This was named in 1973 for Eugene A. HOGAN who was a Yukon Councillor for the Klondike District, 1912–15.

MOUNT HOGE 61°14'N 139°23'W (115–G&F). In the Donjek Range, west of Kluane Lake.

This peak was named in 1945 by Allan Jeckell, Comptroller of the Yukon Territory and H.S. Bostock, GSC, after Brigadier General William A. HOGE, US Army. Hoge was the Officer Commanding the Northern Command of the Army Engineers during the construction of the Yukon section of the Alaska Highway, March to August 1942. It was his drive and leadership which led to this section of the highway being built in so short a time.

A native of Booneville, Missouri, and a career soldier, he was awarded the DSM in the First World War.

A creek flowing from the mountain was also given his name at a later date.

MOUNT HOGG 6,774' 61°20'N 132°14'W (105–F). East of the McConnell River.

This mountain was named in 1951 to perpetuate the name of another Canadian hero, Squadron Leader J.E. HOGG, DFC, of the RCAF who was killed in action during the Second World War.

HOIDAL MOUNTAIN 2,969' 68°17'N 137°49'W (117–A). Seven miles north of Bonnet Lake.

Anker HOIDAL was a noted northern prospector who headquartered in Dawson and Aklavik. He spent many years from 1920 to 60 prospecting the Arctic slope of the Yukon Territory. This mountain was named for him in 1973. (See Anker Creek.)

HOLMANS LAKE 60°21'N 134°20'W (105–D). A small lake three miles northwest of Tagish.

Although not officially named until after his death in 1952, this lake was the home of HOLMON Good. He settled here shortly after the Klondike rush and remained, trapping and prospecting, for many years. Holmon is the correct spelling.

HOMESTAKE GULCH 63°55'N 139°15'W (115–O&N). Flows into upper Bonanza Creek, two miles from Grand Forks.

James H. Sullivan staked the Discovery claim here on 28 June, 1897, and was working the claim when it was "jumped" (staked illegally by another person) on 13 July. He was able to confirm his ownership and carried on earning a homestake.

A "homestake" is the term used among miners to denote enough money to go home, as opposed to a "grubstake" which is enough money to go prospecting.

HOOLE RIVER   61°45′N 131°42′W (105–G). A tributary to the Pelly River.

Francis HOOLE, half Iroquois and half French-Canadian, was a lifelong employee of the HBC and for a number of years interpreter for Robert Campbell and his companions on their journeys of exploration in northern BC and the Yukon.

This river and the major rapids on the Pelly River, Hoole Canyon, were named for him by Campbell in the summer of 1843 when they made their first trip down the Pelly.

HOOTALINQUA   61°35′N 134°54′W (105–E).

This spot was from ancient times an Indian fishing camp. Situated at the junction of the Teslin (earlier called the HOOTALINQUA) River and the Yukon it soon became in early days, a steamboat landing and supply point for the miners in the Teslin River country. A roadhouse here catered to the travellers on the river. The settlement, except for a telegraph operator, was nearly abandoned by 1910.

The name was sometimes spelled "Hootalinka."

HOPE GULCH   63°55′N 135°12′W (105–M). A tributary to Lightning Creek from Keno Hill.

The Rev. George Pringle, the noted Klondike minister and active prospector, staked the first claim and named this small stream on 3 March, 1902.

There is a Faith Gulch next to the west and a Charity Gulch immediately to the east.

HORNET CREEK   68°45′N 136°35′W (117–A). Flows into Rapid Creek, a tributary of the Blow River, near the Arctic coast.

In 1972 F.G. Young, GSC, was working on this stream when his party ran into trouble due to the excessive numbers of these pesky insects.

HORSFALL CREEK 62°55′N 135°00′W (105–L). A tributary to the MacMillan River.

Joseph S. HOSFALL (to give his correct name) was an Englishman who came into the country during the Klondike stampede, overland from Edmonton. The country and the life suited him so well that he married one of Jack McQuesten's daughters and stayed. He earned a living trapping and prospecting. He accompanied F.C. Selous, Charles Sheldon and other noted big-game hunters into the MacMillan River country and, in their writings, was well-spoken-of by them. He spent a good deal of his time searching for the Lost McHenry Gold Mine, a legendary stream supposedly located in the headwaters of the Pelly River. Remarkably, he was a poor bushman and was often lost. The Hosfalls started a farm on the east bank of the Yukon about five miles below Fort Selkirk and grew good crops of vegetables for several years. He died on or near this stream about 1935.

No account of Hosfall would be complete without particular mention of his wife. In almost every written account which mentions her, she is invariably spoken of in superlatives. She was educated at the mission school at Fort MacPherson and at 20 she married Hosfall. She evidently inherited the best characteristics of both her Indian mother and her New Englander father. She could hunt and shoot, handle boats and canoes, trap, and build cabins as well as most men; in addition, she was as well educated, well-spoken, modest and graceful as any woman might aspire to be. Her knowledge of woodcraft and animal life was superior to that of most people. She did all the traditional tasks of Indian women — tanning skins, catching and drying fish, making clothes, doing beadwork — and she was an excellent cook. The Hosfalls had four daughters, the two youngest of whom were born in the middle of winters, when Mrs. Hosfall was alone with her other children in their cabin on the Pelly. Her husband was away on his trapline, so Mrs. Hosfall kept the house warm, looked after her little daughters and gave birth, entirely unaided, with the temperature outside far below zero. She was liked and respected by everyone who knew her.

HORTON CREEK 61°49′N 132°01′W (105–F). A small creek joining the Pelly River from the south above Hoole Canyon.

This was named in 1909 after an early prospector of this name who lived here.

HOTSPRING CREEK 63°02′N 135°52′W (105–M). A tributary to Woodburn Creek in the McArthur Mountains.

One of the few, true, hot springs located in the Yukon is on the headwaters of this creek.

HOUGHTON LAKE   61°22′N   137°20′W   (115-H). A small lake about six miles west of Aishihik Lake.

In 1956 this lake was chosen to honour the memory of Pte. Donald HOUGHTON of the Canadian army, who was killed in action during the Second World War.

HOWARD LAKE   60°14′N   136°49′W   (115-A). At the head of the Takhanne River.

In March 1898 ex-Lt. Adair, US Cavalry, came from Haines, Alaska, and arrived at the new gold finds on Shorty Creek, just north of Dalton Post, with 36 men and large amounts of equipment and supplies. His party, run on military lines, was sworn to secrecy, so much so that the other prospectors and the NWMP called them the "Mysterious 36". It was thought that Adair was backed by the Standard Oil Company and eastern Canadian capital. They built large camps on Shorty Creek and prospected widely in the area for both placer gold and lode minerals. HOWARD S. Scott was Adair's second-in-command and highly regarded by the local NWMP. It is thought that this lake was named after him by his prospectors.

MOUNT HUBBARD   15,015′   60°19′N   139°04′W   (115-B&C). In the St. Elias Range.

In 1890 Professor Israel C. Russell, USGS named this high peak in honour of Gardiner Green HUBBARD (1822–1897), Massachusetts lawyer and educator, regent of the Smithsonian Institution, founder and first president of the National Geographic Society, which office he held from 1888 to his death. Interested in the exploration of Alaska, he helped to organize Russell's 1890 and 1891 expeditions, which were sponsored jointly by the National Geographic Society and the USGS.

In 1960, because of continued support of exploration in the St. Elias region by the National Geographic Society, the Canadian government also gave his name to a large glacier on the northwest side of the mountain.

MOUNT HULEY   65°54′N   138°40′W   (116-G). On the east side of the East Porcupine River.

In 1973 this mountain was named after Peter HULEY who spent 50 years in the Dawson area. Known as the "Charlie Chaplin" of the Yukon, he had been a silent film comedian who was exact in his imitation of Charlie Chaplin.

HULSE LAKE 60°31′N 127°52′W (95-D). West of the Coal River.

In 1969 James A. Harquail, president of Fort Reliance Minerals Ltd., requested that the name of this small lake be changed to perpetuate the name of John HULSE. He was a geophysicist who spent the last three months of his life in this area and was killed in an aircraft crash on 2 September, 1968. The name was formerly Quartz Lake.

HUNGRY CREEK 65°35′N 135°27′W (106-E). A tributary to the Wind River from the west.

This was named in the winter of 1897–98 by stampeders from Edmonton who were caught here by winter with short supplies of food.

HUNKER CREEK 64°02′N 139°13′W (116-B&C). Flows into the Klondike River from King Solomon's Dome.

Andrew "Old Man" HUNKER, a native of Wittenberg, Germany, and an old Cariboo miner who had come into the Yukon in 1886 or 87, was on the upper Fortymile diggings when he heard the news of Carmack's find. When he and his partner, Charles Mathew Johnson, a Swedish farmer and logger from Ohio, reached Bonanza they were in time to find ground open for staking. Hunker staked No. 31 Below Discovery and Johnson No. 43 Below, a few days after the discovery. Not bothering to record these claims immediately (miners had 60 days in which to record their claims after staking) they decided to prospect some of the creeks farther up the Klondike River.

They reached this stream about 1 September and spent four days prospecting upstream, finding better colours (fine gold) as they went. About 12 miles from the mouth they found a location which gave them $22.75 in gold in two hours panning. This was extremely rich. Hunker and Johnson staked the Discovery claim, Hunker staked No. 1 Below and Johnson No. 1 Above. They then went up to Henderson's workings on Gold Bottom and informed the men there of their find. Henderson and his three men came down immediately and staked claims above Hunker's. It is doubtful that they knew of the finds on Bonanza or Eldorado until told by Hunker. Henderson, Swanson and Munson soon sold their claims to Big Alex McDonald or his agents, without testing the ground. They got about $3000 each. Dalton kept and worked his claim and became fairly wealthy. None of them recorded a claim on Gold Bottom.

Hunker married a Swedish woman whom he had financed to operate a roadhouse near his claim. A man of sober habits, he was never ostentatious and remained active in mining and prospecting. In 1907 he was in Fort MacPherson, NWT, after spending some time investigating reports of gold-quartz deposits on the upper Peel River discovered by H.F. Waugh, whom he had backed.

Hunker Creek was one of the richest placer gold creeks in the world. In the Klondike it ranked next to Eldorado and Bonanza.

MOUNT HUNT 61°29′N 129°12′W (105-H). On the east side of Frances Lake in the Logan Range.

This mountain was originally named Mount Logan by Dr. G.M. Dawson, GSC, in 1887, after Sir William Edmond Logan (1798–1875), founder and director of the Geological and Natural History Survey of Canada.

In 1916 the name was changed as it was in conflict with the later-named Mount Logan in the St. Elias Range, (a more appropriate mountain, being the highest in Canada and the second highest in North America).

This mountain was then renamed after Thomas Sterry HUNT (1826–1892), a chemist with the Geological and Natural History Survey of Canada.

HUOT GULCH 63°59′N 140°29′W (115-O&N). A short stream running into Boucher Creek in the Sixtymile district.

On 12 August, 1902, W.M. Richardson, I.A. Jackson and James HUOT filed locations on the Discovery claim and others on what they named Huot Gulch, a tributary of Boucher on which they had just previously also made the discovery. James Huot was a son of Napoleon Huot of Québec, an early staker in the Klondike.

HYLAND RIVER 59°52′N 128°12′W (105-A). A major tributary of the Liard River at Lower Post, BC.

Robert HYLAND, an Englishman, shipped around Cape Horn in the 1860's and was one of the first men in the rush to the Stikine River and Dease Lake (or Cassiar) goldfields. He was always in the vanguard and though primarily a trader was an adventurous prospector. He was the first man to ascend the river which bears his name, in the summer of 1874 or perhaps as early as 1873. Near Stewart Lake he staked the first lode mineral claim in the territory on a deposit of silver-lead ore which he discovered there. He lived the remainder of his life in this area, owning and operating trading posts at Spatzi River, Dease Lake, Cassiar and Lower Post. He was always in competition with the HBC and other traders and at one time printed and circulated his own money, which was accepted by natives and miners.

In 1834 Peter McLeod of the HBC was the first white man to see this stream which he named the "MacPherson" but by 1873 this name had been forgotten.

The Indians in this region were afraid to go to the headwaters of the Hyland as they believed that something evil lived there. One of their legends tells of a party of hunters who ascended the river and, while passing through a canyon, met with a sudden darkness during which an evil monster rose from the depths of the river and dragged the unlucky hunters into a whirlpool. Since then the Indians dislike the rivers in the district and turn back whenever they see the bones of huge animals (fossil remains) on the bars.

ICE CHEST MOUNTAIN 3,895′ 63°30′N 137°35′W (115-P). Five miles southwest of McQuesten.

H.S. Bostock, GSC, named this mountain in the summer of 1949 to preserve the name of ICE CHEST Reef, a bad rock in the channel of the Stewart River just to the west. Named by the early steamboat captains and pilots, the rock had caused a number of accidents.

ILLES BROOK (See Money Creek.)

ILLUSION CREEK 61°49′N 134°40′W (105-E). A tributary of the Big Salmon River.

This was named in the summer of 1934 by H.S. Bostock, GSC, when some of his party missed a rendezvous, mistaking this stream for Lokken Creek.

MOUNT INA 5,261′ 64°25′N 139°34′W (116-B&C). 30 miles north of Dawson.

This was named in 1970 after the wife of the Hon. Justice H.E. Gibben, a long-time Yukoner, Justice of the Territorial Court and one-time Commissioner of the Yukon Territory.

INDEPENDENCE CREEK 63°31′N 137°49′W (115-P). A tributary to the Stewart River.

Fine gold was found here about 4 July, 1893, by Hugh and A.H. Day. They were among the first miners to enter the Yukon, coming over the Chilkoot Pass in the spring of 1884. They were successful miners on the Stewart River bars.

Later, in the summer of 1896, Jack McQuesten and Dick Poplin (another old-timer who had been here since 1883) found coarse gold on this creek but the find was over-shadowed by the Klondike discoveries.

INDEPENDENCE CREEK   63°59'N 139°01'W (116–O&N). Flows into Hunker Creek between Hester and Colorado Creeks.

Sam Abramson was optimistic when he found enough gold here to stake a Discovery claim and name the stream on 6 December, 1897.

INDIAN   RIVER   63°47'N 139°44'W (116–O&N).   Flows   into   the Yukon River.

This river and the Klondike River enclose what is now called the Klondike area. All the rich placer creeks are between these two streams.

The earliest travellers on the Yukon River noted an Indian community at the mouth of the stream from which it received its name. As was the case in those times, the Indians moved from here and settled closer to the trading posts as they were established.

When Robert Campbell, HBC, made his first journey from Fort Selkirk to Fort Yukon in 1851 it was probably this river that he named "Forcier" River, after one of his French-Canadian voyageurs, Baptiste Forcier.

INGERSOLL ISLANDS   62°41'N 137°11'W (115–I). Ten miles above Fort Selkirk in the Yukon River.

This group of small islands was named by Lt. F. Schwatka, US Army, in 1883 after Col. INGERSOLL, US Army, of Washington, DC.

MOUNT INGRAM   7,080'   60°44'N 135°37'W (105–D).   20   miles west of Whitehorse and south of the Ibex River.

This peak was named in August 1897 by J.J. McArthur, DLS. He was making a hurried trip over the Dalton Trail for the Department of the Interior and mapped it roughly as he went.

On the bank of the Takhini he had found a grave, with a headboard saying INGRAM. Ingram and his partner had come up the Yukon from its mouth, and, after a few years of prospecting, they headed upstream for the coast. They were told to take the righthand stream at the first fork above the Pelly but mistakenly ended up on the Takhini. The ten miles of rapids were evidently too much for them. Ingram's body was buried by William Dickenson, a half-breed Tlinkit trader.

INGS RIVER 61°04′N 131°00′W (105-G). Joins the upper Liard River from the north, in the St. Cyr Range.

It was named in 1947 in memory of Wing Commander R.R. INGS, RCAF, who was killed in action in the Second World War.

INNISSIAG HILL 69°22′N 139°31′W (117-D).On the bank of the Firth River, near the Arctic coast.

This is an Eskimo word meaning "the useful flintstone." In earlier years the Eskimos gathered flint rock from here to make stone tools and weapons.

In the summer of 1956 Dr. R.S. McNeish, an archaeologist with the National Museum of Canada, found the remnants of nine prehistoric cultures near this place. The lower remains may be some of the oldest found on the continent, up to 10,000 years old. This find filled in several gaps in the knowledge of Canadian prehistory. Dr. McNeish noted the old Eskimo name for the hill at that time.

IRON CREEK 60°51′N 133°19′W (105-C). A tributary of Sydney Creek, about ten miles west of the Canol Road.

Gold was found here and the creek staked and named in June 1905 by W. Mooreside, Joe Brewer, Jim Thompson and Charles Anderson. The Mining Recorder, R.C. Miller, gave it the name IRON Creek, because he claimed that there were too many Willow Creeks in the country already. Many attempts were made to mine the creek profitably up to 1936 but with little success, as the values were too erratic.

IRVINE CREEK 60°35′N 131°35′W (105-B). A large stream which flows into the east side of Wolf Lake.

Formerly known as Murray Creek, this name was changed in 1947. W.T. IRVINE lived here in the 1920's and 30's, trapping and prospecting. His cabin was near the mouth of the stream. He made the first sketch map of the area to assist the GSC.

ISAAC CREEK 61°27′N 137°35′W (115-H). Flows into the west side of Sekulmun Lake.

This was named many years ago after Chief ISAAC of the Aishihik band of Tutchone Indians. Chief Isaac guided the first white men, Jack Dalton and E.J. Glave when they entered this part of the country in 1890 and 1891.

A small, short-lived settlement was established at the mouth of this creek in 1913 during the stampede to the Chisana goldfields in Alaska. The settlement was on the winter trail and catered to the miners passing through.

ITSI LAKES 62°48′N 130°15′W (105-J). On the headwaters of the Ross River.

This is an old Indian name meaning "wind". Some years ago the small range of mountains north of the lakes was given the same name.

IYON RIVER (See Big Salmon River.)

JACKSON POINT 61°03′N 138°30′W (115-G&F). On the shore of Kluane Lake about mile 1063 (K1722) of the Alaska Highway.

This point was named in 1960 after Rex JACKSON, the first Forestry Engineer in the Yukon Territory.

JACQUOT ISLAND 61°20′N 138°46′W (115-G&F). The largest island in Kluane Lake, opposite mile 1086 (K1759) of the Alaska Highway.

This was named in 1945 by H.S. Bostock, GSC, after two brothers, Eugene and Louis JACQUOT of Alsace-Lorraine. They came over the Chilkoot Pass in 1898. They were not successful in the Klondike but decided to stay and trap in the Yukon.

Taking part in the rush to the Burwash Creek gold finds, they instead established a trading post and a settlement at Burwash Landing in 1903. Here they remained, trading, homesteading, guiding and successfully mining on Burwash Creek in 1909.

JAKE'S CORNER 60°20′N 133°58′W (105-C). At mile 865.5 (K1402) on the Alaska Highway.

In 1942 the US Army Engineers set up a construction camp here under the command of Captain Jacoby (or Jackobsen) to build this section of the Alaska Highway and a cut-off to Tagish and Carcross for the Canol Pipeline. In 1949-50 a highway south to Atlin, BC, was built from here.

JAMES TRAIL 62°20'N 140°32'W (115-J&K). The road from Snag Junction to Snag.

William JAMES was one of the first prospectors in this area and laid out the trail which the government later followed to make this road. He spent most of his life in the district. (See Beaver Creek.)

JANET LAKE 63°40'N 135°30'W (105-M). 12 miles northeast of Mayo Landing.

In 1898, J.J. McArthur, DLS, was surveying in the area and named this lake after his daughter.

JARVIS CREEK 63°42'N 136°08'W (115-P). A tributary to Minto Creek at its mouth.

Archie McIntyre staked the Discovery claim and named this creek when he found placer gold here on 14 May, 1903.

JARVIS RIVER 60°46'N 138°08'W (115-B&C). A tributary to the Kaskawulsh River.

The river was named by the first prospectors in the area about 1899–1900, after Major Arthur Murray JARVIS, Inspector in the NWMP, who established the police post and Customs on the Dalton Trail in the first days of the gold rush.

MOUNT JECKELL 6,400' 64°19'N 138°50'W (116-B&C). 25 miles northeast of Dawson.

This mountain was named about 1957 to commemorate George Allan JECKELL, a school teacher who was appointed Comptroller of the Yukon Territory from 30 June, 1932 to 18 September, 1947. During the Depression, the federal government did away with the office of Commissioner of the Yukon Territory in an attempt to reduce expenses in the territorial government. Jeckell proved to be an outstanding administrator and performed an exceptional job.

JENS CREEK 62°40'N 138°40'W (115-J&K). A small brook or valley on Rude Creek.

When JENS Rude discovered the gold of Rude Creek in March 1915, he and his partner built their cabin at the mouth of this small stream. The other miners called it Jens Creek. However, the gold on it was found by Otto F.

Kastner and John A. Ross, who staked and officially named it on 16 September, 1915. (See Rude and Dip Creeks.)

JESSICA CREEK 63°08'N 133°25'W (105-N). Enters Russell Creek from the east, one mile above Limestone Creek.

Major Neville A.D. Armstrong, who worked for many years in this area, named this stream after the wife of his partner, Mrs. George Leith of England. The Leiths spent 18 months on Russell Creek with Armstrong and his wife in 1904-05.

MOUNT JESUS 64°02'N 132°59'W (106-C). Three miles southwest of Ortell Lake.

A landmark on the Stewart River from the time of the earliest miners, it was named and known about 1885. It is a beautiful, solitary peak; William Ogilvie, DLS, described it as a very high peak that resembled Mount Hood in Oregon. Somehow, about 1900, it disappeared from all maps, – a curious happening, as it had been so well known up to that time.

MOUNT JETTÉ 8,460' 60°00'N 139°03'W (115-B&C). On the corner of the International boundary where the Yukon, Alaska and British Columbia meet.

It was named in 1905 after Sir Louis JETTÉ, KCMG, Lt. Governor of Québec and Member of the Canadian-Alaskan Boundary Tribunal in 1903.

JOHN LAKE 62°49'N 130°23'W (105-J). On the upper Ross River.

In 1909 when Joseph Keele, GSC, was mapping the geology of this area, he named this little lake after his favourite sled dog, JOHN.

JOHNSON CREEK 66°58'N 138°09'W (116-J&K). A small stream flowing into Pine Creek.

This was named by Otto Heist in 1958 after Andrew JOHNSON, a trapper from Fort Yukon who married a woman from Old Crow and settled in this extremely isolated country for many years. He died at Fort Yukon about 1955.

JOHNSON CREEK 63°49'N 136°27'W (115-P). Enters the McQuesten River just below Ortell's Crossing.

In 1894 the two Garrison brothers found gold on this creek but did not mine it. In the autumn of 1898, F. JOHNSON, who had been unlucky in the Klondike and had prospected this stream previously, returned and staked a Discovery claim, naming the creek.

JOHNSONS CROSSING 60°29'N 133°18'W (105-C). On the Alaska Highway where it crosses the Teslin River.

During 1942 the Teslin River was bridged here to carry the Alaska Highway and the Canol Pipeline. An army construction camp first occupied the site. The US Army Engineers, building the bridge and the highway, named the camp after their Commanding Officer, Col. Frank M.S. JOHNSON, 93rd Engineers.

Local people claim that the crossing was named after George JOHNSTON, a Teslin Indian who ferried the army men and their supplies across the Teslin River at this point, when the bridge was being built.

JONES RIDGE 65°06'N 140°59'W (116-G&F). Crosses the Yukon-Alaska boundary.

About 1914 D.D. Cairnes, GSC, named this ridge after Charles JONES who had been a member of his geological survey parties in this area for a number of years.

MOUNT JOY 7,333' 63°45'N 132°55'W (105-N). The highest peak in the Lansing Range.

While mapping the geology of this region in 1909, Joseph Keele, GSC, named this peak after Sergeant G.B. JOY, Rgt.No. 3045, of the RNWMP.

MOUNT JOYAL 3,055' 66°37'N 136°48'W (116-I). East of the Eagle River.

This mountain was chosen in 1973 to honour 2140278 Pte. Eli Felix JOYAL who was born in Merril, Wisconsin on 13 January, 1887. He enlisted in Victoria, BC on 2 July, 1918, and succumbed to the dreaded "Spanish Flu", which was epidemic around the world at that time, on 19 October, 1918, before leaving Canada.

JUBILEE MOUNTAIN 5,950' 60°12'N 134°07'W (105-D). On the east side of Tagish Lake.

Dr. G.M. Dawson, GSC, named this prominent hill in 1887 in honour of Queen Victoria's Jubilee. In that year she had reigned on the throne of the British Empire for 50 years.

JUDAS CREEK 60°25′N 134°14′W (105–D). Flows into the east side of Marsh Lake.

A stampede took place here from Whitehorse in August 1911, to stake claims near a find made earlier in the month by Benjamin Miller. Some of the stampeders wanted to call it "All-In" Creek because they were exhausted when they reached it. When they found there was almost no gold whatsoever on the stream they gave it this name.

This is wrongly attributed by some to a name given by highway construction crews in 1942.

JUNGLE CREEK 65°29′N 141°00′W (116–G&F). Flows across the Yukon-Alaska boundary to the Nation River in Alaska.

The International Boundary Survey party of 1910 named this creek because of the exceptionally luxuriant growth of vegetation in its valley, which made travel exceedingly difficult.

JUNKERS LAKE 61°02′N 131°21′W (105–G). At the headwaters of the Liard River.

This lake was named in the summer of 1930 by bush pilot Captain E.J.A. "Paddy" Burke and mechanic Emil Kading. They set up a food and fuel cache here to service prospecting activity in the area, from Atlin, BC. They were flying a low-wing JUNKERS aircraft, serial CF-AMX.

On 11 October, 1930, Burke, Kading and prospector Robert Martin left Lower Post, BC, to return to Atlin. Blinded by a blizzard, they were forced down on the ice of the Liard River a short distance north of the present upper Liard River bridge, damaging the aircraft on the second landing. They set out on foot, without snowshoes, to reach this lake and its store of food and fuel. Burke died of exhaustion and exposure after 27 days. Martin and Kading were rescued on 6 December by Everett Wasson and one of the Yukon's best bushmen, Joe Walsh.

This was the first air search and rescue mission ever carried out in the Yukon, and perhaps BC.
(See Wasson Lake and Burke Creek.)

KALZAS LAKE 62°56′N 135°35′W (105–L). On the Little Kalzas River.

This lake was named by Robert Campbell of the HBC, or one of his men, about 1849–52 while establishing Fort Selkirk. It was named after one of his Indian employees. Fish, needed for the fort, were plentiful here. The lake is noted on the earliest map of the territory. It is sometimes called Little Kalzas Lake. (See Big Kalzas Lake.)

KANDIK RIVER 65°51'N 141°00'W (116-G&F). Crosses the Yukon-Alaska boundary and flows to the Yukon River.

This is an Indian name recorded by Lt. F. Schwatka, US Army, on his 1883 excursion. He did not report the translation. It was called "Charlie's River" by the miners and traders of that time, after the chief of the Indian band who had a village at the mouth of the river.

KASKAWULSH RIVER 60°39'N 137°49'W (115-A). The east fork of the Alsek River.

The river names in this area have been much confused and mistaken since the first exploration. This name was first recorded by E.J. Glave in 1891. Later it was applied to what is now the Dezeadash River and at one time was applied to the whole upper Alsek River. For many years this stream was locally called the "O'Connor" River, after a rather mysterious Captain M.J. O'Connor, who prospected and mined in this part of the country, it was said, even before Glave and Dalton explored it. A river in Alaska, farther west, is also named for him.

KATHLEEN LAKES 64°14'N 134°11'W (106-D). Empty into the Rackla River.

This was named on 4 July, 1945, by Bernard J. Woodruff, DTS, of the Geodetic Survey of Canada, after KATHLEEN Emery, the wife of the CPA pilot with their survey party. The name was originally applied only to the largest of the three lakes.

(These are not to be confused with the Kathleen Lakes west of the Haines Highway.)

KATRINA CREEK 62°53'N 140°13'W (115-J&K). Tributary to the White River.

Although the origin of the name has been lost, this creek was known by this name to the miners long before the Klondike Gold Rush.

KAY POINT 69°18'N 138°22'W (117-D). At Phillips Bay on the Arctic coast.

This was named by John Franklin, (later Sir), in 1826, while on his second expedition, after an esteemed nephew.

MOUNT KEARNEY   3,923′ 66°22′N 135°49′W (106-L). On the head-waters of the Trail River in the Richardson Mountains.

This was named in 1973 after Thomas J. KEARNEY who was a Yukon Councillor for the Bonanza District, 1907–09.

KEELE PEAK   63°26′N 130°19′W (105-O). In the Hess Mountains north of the Canol Road.

Joseph KEELE was a noted northern explorer-geologist who was hired in 1898 by the GSC as a topographical surveyor. He spent much of his time from 1901 on in the Yukon and NWT. He mapped much previously unexplored country and added greatly to the knowledge of these areas. He was an expert bushman, canoeman and above all, a scientist. His traverse from the Pelly and up the Ross River, over Christie Pass and down the Gravel River to the Mackenzie in the winter of 1907–08 is among the great Canadian explorations.

He died of throat cancer in 1923, at the height of his career. This large mountain was named in his honour in 1909 by R.G. McConnell, GSC, whose assistant he was that season. Keele Creek and Lake were named much later.

KEELE RANGE   66°55′N 140°20′W (116-J&K). The range of mountains crossing the Yukon-Alaska boundary south of the Porcupine River.

D.D. Cairnes, GSC, named this range in 1911 in honour of his compatriot, Joseph KEELE. (See Keele Peak.)

KELLY CREEK   62°15′N 136°00′W (105-L). A tributary to the Tatchun River.

This was probably named after Gerry KELLY, a trapper and prospector for many years in this area. He married Rose Hosfall, a granddaughter of Jack McQuesten. He was for a number of years an operator of the Yukon Telegraph at the Stewart River station.

MOUNT KELVIN   60°40′N 136°32′W (115-A). Eight miles south of Champagne.

This was named before 1909 after William Thomson, Lord KELVIN, the celebrated British mathematician and physicist.

KENNEBEC CREEK   62°47′N 140°06′W (115-J&K). A tributary to the White River.

The KENNEBEC is a river in the state of Maine and the name was an Indian one, known long before the Revolutionary War. The river was noted during much of the 19th century for its immense stands of white pine and the evolution of modern lumbering methods.

The name was carried by lumberjacks and used again in Québec and Ontario in the late 1880–90's. This stream was probably named by one of these lumberjacks turned miner during the rush to the upper White River copper deposits in 1903.

MOUNT KENNEDY 13,905' 60°20'N 138°58'W (115–B&C). Four miles east of Mount Alverstone in the St. Elias Range.

This was named for the late President of the United States of America, John Fitzgerald KENNEDY at the request of Prime Minister Lester B. Pearson of Canada, on the anniversary of the assassination of President Kennedy. The feature was chosen by Dr. Bradford Washburn, a world-famous mountaineer and a friend of the president.

It was first climbed on 24 March, 1965, and Senator Robert Kennedy, the president's brother, was one of the three to attain the summit.

KENO HILL 6,065' 63°57'N 135°10'W (105–M). 12 miles north of Mayo Lake.

KENO is a gambling game that was popular for many years in western mining camps. Originally this mountain was known as "Sheep Hill" by the first miners; the name was changed in 1919. In July of that year Louis Bouvette (or Beauvette) found the first of the very rich silver-lead ore deposits which started this enormously productive camp. Beauvette had named his claim "The Keno."

KENO LADUE RIVER 63°54'N 134°03'W (105–M). Flows north of Keno Hill to the Stewart River.

Before 1897 this stream was known as Ladue Creek, after Joseph Ladue, a pioneer Yukoner, who had prospected its lower reaches in the 1880's. Later, it was given its present name to avoid confusion with the river and creek of the same name in the Sixtymile district.

KENTUCKY CREEK 64°18'N 139°21'W (116–B&C). A tributary to Twelve Mile Creek.

A stampede from Dawson to this creek took place in early October 1898 and the first man to stake a claim named it after his home state.

KETZA RIVER 61°53'N 132°15'W (105-F). Enters the Pelly River about ten miles upstream from Ross River.

This river was named by Robert Campbell of the HBC on his initial journey down the Pelly River in 1843, after his Iroquois canoeman and companion, KITZA. The name was subsequently misspelled by map-makers.

KILLERMUN LAKE 61°10'N 137°41'W (115-H). In the Ruby Range, this lake empties into the West Aishihik River.

Recorded in 1962, this name is an old Indian word meaning "flint rock". It is believed that the ancient Indians obtained a type of chert (flint) here to make tools and weapons.

KIMBERLEY CREEK 60°52'N 138°04'W (115-B&C). Tributary to the Jarvis River.

During the rush to the Alsek goldfields in January 1904, Tom Laird discovered gold on this creek and named it.

MOUNT KING 65°13'N 140°18'W (116-G&F). At the head of the Tatonduc River near Mount Deville.

In March 1888 William Ogilvie, DLS, named this peak after William Frederick KING (1854-1916), DLS, DTS, Chief Astronomer of Canada from 1890-1905, Director of the Dominion Observatory from 1905-1916, and member of the International Boundary Commission (Canada-U.S.) 1892-1916. (See King Peak.)

MOUNT KING GEORGE 12,250' 60°32'N 139°44'W (115-B&C). 25 miles north of Mount Vancouver in the St. Elias Range.

In February-May 1935 a National Geographic Society Yukon Expedition explored the central part of the St. Elias Range. They named this peak in honour of the Silver Jubilee year of KING GEORGE V of Great Britain. The twin peak about 12 miles to the north they named after Queen Mary. The two peaks they called the Jubilee Peaks.

The party, led by Bradford Washburn, was the first to cross the St. Elias Range on foot from the Yukon to Alaska. They were assisted by Jack Haydon of Carcross whose dog-team moved most of their supplies.

KING PEAK 16,971' 60°35'N 140°39'W (115-B&C). Ten miles west of Mount Logan.

This was named about 1918 after Dr. W.F. KING, one-time International

Boundary Commissioner. The peak was first climbed on 6 July 1966. (See Mount King.)

KING POINT 69°07'N 137°52'W (117–D). 15 miles southeast of Phillips Bay on the Arctic coast.

This was named by John Franklin, (later Sir), in 1826 after Captain Phillip P. KING RN (1793–1856), who made the first survey of the coast of Australia.

Roald Amundsen, the famous Arctic explorer, wintered here in 1905–06 in the *Gjoa*, studying and collecting Arctic bird life.

KING SOLOMON'S DOME 4,048' 63°52'N 138°57'W (115–O&N). The highest and most central hill in the Klondike District.

From it radiate the six richest creeks in one of the richest placer goldfields ever found in the world. Before 1896 miners in the area called it simply, the "Dome", because of its shape. When the riches of the surrounding ground became apparent the present fanciful name was applied, in reference to KING SOLOMON'S riches and to his mythical lost gold mines. From the summit the whole Klondike country, and more, are visible.

MOUNT KINNEY 5,674' 65°02'N 137°04'W (116–H). East of the Hart River.

Constable G.F. KINNEY, RNWMP, died on the Peel River 35 miles from Fort MacPherson, a member of the lost Fitzgerald Patrol in 1911. This mountain lies just east of their route to Dawson and was named in his memory in May 1973.

KIRKLAND CREEK 61°45'N 136°02'W (115–H). The west branch of the Nordenskiold River.

J.B. Tyrrell, GSC, named this creek in 1898 while mapping the geology of the area, after Professor R. Ramsay Wright of the University of Toronto. The creek was abandoned and the name forgotten. In 1915 a new discovery was made here and the first staker renamed it.

KIRKMAN CREEK 62°59'N 139°25'W (115–J&K). Flows into the Yukon about 15 miles above the White River.

On 13 October, 1898, Grant and Albert KIRKMAN of Tulare, California, discovered the first gold here. Their claim did not pay and the creek was soon abandoned. However, in April 1914 a new discovery was staked by

Joseph C. Britton and William Heas. They found the pay streak and prospered. The creek was a good producer for many years and a small settlement grew up at its mouth.

(See Touleary Creek and Britton Ridge.)

KLETSAN HILL 4,698' 61°43'N 140°58'W (115-G&F). An isolated hill south of the White River and near the boundary.

The hill takes its name from the creek on the Alaska side, a Tanana Indian name "Klet-San-Dek", meaning Copper Creek or stream. The name of the creek was first reported by C.Willard Hayes, USGS, in 1891 and D.D. Cairnes GSC, applied the name to the hill in 1913–14 when he was mapping the geology of the international boundary.

It was sometimes locally called "Klutson" or Copper Creek because from ancient times the Yukon Indians came here to obtain nuggets of native (pure) copper for tools, weapons and ornaments.

KLINES GULCH 62°38'N 137°59'W (115-I). Tributary to Hayes Creek which flows into the Selwyn River.

About 1904 a prospector of this name found coarse gold, some nuggets up to two ounces, on this stream. It was said to be the only place where gold was found on the Selwyn River or its tributaries.

KLINE later committed suicide in a most efficient manner. Using dynamite, he arranged two charges so that the first blast killed him inside his cabin while the second blast destroyed the cabin walls, allowing the three feet of soil on the roof to effectively bury him.

KLONDIKE RIVER 64°03'N 139°26'W (116-B&C). A large stream entering the Yukon River from the east.

The earliest reports of this river were given by Frank E. Ketchum and Michael Laberge of the Western Union Telegraph Company in 1867, although this may also be the "Deer River" noted by Robert Campbell in 1851. Ketchum and Laberge were exploring a route for an overland telegraph line through BC, the Yukon and Alaska to the Bering Sea near Nome. They reported its name as the "Deer River", from the Indian word "Chandik". In 1883 Schwatka called it the "Reindeer River". These names were not used by the early miners who were trying to twist their tongues around the then-Indian name "Thron-Duick" or "Tron-Deg", these words meaning, as far as can be determined, "Hammer-water". It derived from the Indian practice of driving stakes in the bed of the stream to form fish traps to catch the salmon migrating upstream. The miners finally settled on the pronunciation, "Clunedik", "Clundyke" or "Clondyke". Insp. Charles Constantine NWMP, and Mining Recorder at Fortymile, on the discovery of Bonanza Creek, made the name "Klondyke" official. Most of the miners were Americans and their usage substituted an "i" for the "y". British and some Canadian publications continued to use the word Klondyke for some time afterward but with the issue of the first report of the Canadian Board on Geographical Names, the name Klondike was made official in 1898.

It was one of the finest salmon streams in the Yukon and the local Indians maintained drying racks at the mouth of the river. George Carmack and his party were here to catch salmon in early August 1896. It was only because of the poor run of fish that they decided to prospect up Bonanza.

KLOO LAKE CITY   60°58′N 137°52′W (115–A). On the north side of Kloo Lake.

A small sawmill settlement was built here in 1905 to supply lumber for the Alsek diggings. It was abandoned a few years later.

MOUNT   KLOTZ   5,903′   65°23′N 134°06′W (116–G&F).   In   the Ogilvie Mountains.

This was named by the Board on Geographical Names in 1945 after Dr. Otto Julius KLOTZ (1852–1923), Assistant Chief Astronomer of Canada, who carried out several geodetic surveys in western Canada. He had earlier named a mountain in southern BC after himself but his superiors had disallowed it.

KLUANE   61°02′N 138°23′W (115–G&F). On the south end of Kluane Lake, near mile 1054 (K1707) of the Alaska Highway.

This old settlement started in 1903 with the discovery of good placer gold in the streams nearby. The name at first was "Silver City" but the next year was changed to Kluane as there was another Silver City in the White River country. This was the main supply point for the area for many years but it was gradually abandoned as the Burwash Creek placer fields assumed importance and the local creeks were worked out. The wagon road from Whitehorse was extended to the west in later years, which did away with steamboat landings here.

The first post office was opened in October 1904 with the name "Bullion Creek", altered four months later to Kluane. It was finally closed in 1921.

Originally an Indian fishing village, its name was Tlinkit Indian, meaning, "Whitefish Place" or "Big Fish Place."

The lake name was first reported by Professor Aurel Krause of the Bremen Geographical Society on his expedition in 1882. Kluane Lake is the largest in the Yukon with an area of about 154 square miles. The name Kluane has since been given to a glacier, river, hills, ranges and a plateau.

KLUKSHU LAKE 60°19'N 136°59'W (115-A). Three miles south of Dezeadash Lake.

This name was recorded by E.J. Glave on 22 November, 1890, on his first expedition into the region. He did not find out the meaning of the word. Later reports say the word is Tlinkit Indian, meaning "Last Lake".

KLUTLAN GLACIER 61°27'N 140°37'W (115-G&F). In the St. Elias Range.

This large glacier is the source of the Generc River, and a major source of the White River. The native name was recorded without translation by C. Willard Hayes, USGS, in 1891.

KNORR CREEK 65°22'N 134°40'W (106-E). A tributary to the Bonnet Plume River.

A.N. KNORR came into the Klondike in 1898. He later married a woman from Old Crow and raised sums of money in Dawson to prospect the Bonnet Plume River country. He and his wife lived here for a number of years between 1905-10 in complete isolation and seem to have disappeared without trace after that time. (See Margaret Lake.)

KOIDERN RIVER 62°03'N 140°27'W (115-J&K). Flows into the White River.

This is from an Indian word meaning "Water Lily". Miners in the area before 1915 called it "Lake Creek" because of the number of ponds along its valley but the name was not adopted. The name was first noted by C. Willard Hayes, USGS, in 1890, on his expedition to the White and Copper Rivers.

KOHSE CREEK 64°32'N 133°26'W (106-C). A tributary of the Bonnet Plume River.

In the sumer of 1952 E. and F. KOHSE were packers for the GSC party surveying the region, led by J.O. Wheeler. He named this creek to show his high regard for their work.

KUSAWA LAKE 60°20′N 136°22′W (115-A). Empties into the Takhini River.

This lake was known and described to Dr. George Davidson in 1869 by the Chilkat chief, Kho-klux. (He led the raid on Fort Selkirk in 1852). In June 1882 the lake was visited by Dr. Arthur Krause, the first white man to see the lake. He was a geographer of the Bremen Geographical Society and brother of Aurel Krause. In 1890 it was again seen by E. Hazard Wells, Chief of the Frank Leslie Illustrated Newspaper Expedition, who renamed it "Arkell Lake" after W.J. Arkell, sponsor of the expedition.

In 1898 the Board on Geographical Names restored the original name. (See Arkell Creek.)

LAKE LABERGE 61°11′N 135°12′W (105-E). On the Yukon River about 15 miles north of Whitehorse.

In the summer of 1867 Frank E. Ketchum of Saint John, New Brunswick and Michael LABERGE of Chateaugay, Québec, explorers for the Western Union Telegraph Company, came up the Yukon River from Fort Yukon to Fort Selkirk. They were looking for a possible route for the Collins Overland Telegraph line being built from New York to Paris. It was never clear if Laberge did visit the lake but he had it described to him by the local Indians. Returning to Fort Yukon they found the project had been stopped. William H. Dall, Director of the Scientific Corps of the Western Union Telegraph Expedition, wrote a massive report on Alaska in 1870 and gave Laberge's name to the lake.

In 1883 Schwatka reported the Tagish Indian named "Kluk-tas-si" and in 1882 Dr. Aurel Krause had recorded the Tlinkit name "Tahini-wud", both without translation.

LACELLE LAKE 61°23′N 137°01′W (115-H). A small lake just east of central Aishihik Lake.

In 1956 this lake was named to perpetuate the memory of Pte. Henri LACELLE, Canadian army, who was killed in action in the Second World War.

LADUE RIVER 63°10′N 140°20′W (115-O&N). A tributary to the White River.

This river was prospected and named in the early 1880's by Joseph LADUE who found some gold on it, as well as on the small creek of the same name which enters the river near its mouth.

Ladue, who came from New York State, was one of the first prospector-entrepreneurs to come to the Yukon, arriving over the Chilkoot Pass in the spring of 1882. Combining prospecting with trading and other enterprises, he was early convinced that a major goldfield would be found in the general area of the Indian and Klondike Rivers. This belief led him to encourage and grubstake prospectors to work there. He grubstaked Robert Henderson in 1894–95 and sent him up Quartz Creek to visit William Redford who was successfully mining there. He himself was one of the first to prospect the Sixtymile and Fortymile districts, although with limited success. He and Jack McQuesten prospected Bonanza Creek in early 1886 but missed the rich gold there. Loosely associated with the ACC, he and Arthur Harper opened a trading post and brought in the first sawmill to the Yukon, at the mouth of the Sixtymile River in 1894. At first called Sixtymile Post, they soon changed the name to that of their friend, William Ogilvie.

In early August 1896 Ladue had, by a remarkable coincidence, decided to remove his sawmill from Ogilvie to the flat at the mouth of the Klondike River, where he intended to set up a small trading post. He arrived there on 28 August and realizing the potential of the new finds, staked the flat land, 160 acres, as a townsite. He set up his sawmill and trading post and quickly built a fortune, becoming a millionaire in the next two years.

He returned to Schuyler Falls, New York in 1897 and married his childhood sweetheart. On 27 June, 1901, suffering from tuberculosis, he died at his home there.

(See Dawson City.)

LAFORCE LAKE 62°41′N 132°18′W (105-K). This lake drains to the Riddell River.

In 1946 this lake received the name of a brave man, Pte. Alphonse LAFORCE MM, of the Canadian army. He was killed in action on 12 May, 1945.

LAHCHAH MOUNTAIN 67°36′N 140°56′W (116-O&N). A long, low ridge 20 miles west of Old Crow.

This is an old name, a Vanta Kutchin Indian word meaning "Low Hill".

LAKE CREEK 62°26′N 140°05′W (115-J&K). A tributary to the White River.

Alyre Morin and Wilfred Grenier prospected this stream and in the summer of 1913 had found enough gold to warrant staking the Discovery claim. They named the stream, "Lake Creek" for the number of ponds and small lakes along its course in the wide valley. On 2 March, 1914, the Gold Commissioner changed the name to "Pond Creek" as the miners in the White River area were already calling the Koidern River and the Tchawsahmon Creek by that name. A number of years later, when names were being sorted out in the area, the name reverted to the original Lake Creek.

LAKE CREEK 64°38′N 137°10′W (116-A). The west fork of Rae Creek.

This is the only "Lake" feature in the Yukon in which it is not a descriptive name. In 1956 this creek was named after Frederick LAKE who, with his partners Frank Rae and Afe Brown, trapped and prospected in the Hart River region during World War One and did a little mining on this stream.

MOUNT LAMBART 10,725′ 61°31′N 140°59′W (115-G&F). In the St. Elias Range, just north of the Klutlan Glacier.

This was named after Howard Frederick John LAMBART, DLS, (1880–1946), one of Canada's best mountaineers. He was born and died in Ottawa, Ontario. He graduated in Civil Engineering from McGill University in 1904. He spent most of his working life with the Geodetic Survey of Canada. He was a pioneer of the development and use of aerial photography for mapping. He was the Canadian leader of the joint Canadian-American Expedition which made the first ascent of Mount Logan in 1925.

He surveyed the Yukon-Alaska boundary from 1906–17, including the position and altitude of this mountain.

MOUNT LANDREVILLE 65°09′N 132°52′W (106-F). East of the Snake River in the Backbone Range.

Max LANDREVILLE was a journalist who came to the Yukon in 1898. He was active politically and was chosen as one of the group to carry the miners' complaints of government inefficiency and corruption to Ottawa that same year. He was also a Yukon Councillor for the Klondike District in 1903. This hill was given his name in 1973.

MOUNT LANSDOWNE   5,875′ 60°22′N 134°31′W (105-D).   15 miles northeast of Carcross on the west side of Marsh Lake.

William Ogilvie, DLS, in 1887 named this feature after Henry Charles K. Petty Fitz-Maurice, fifth Marquis of LANSDOWNE, who was Governor-General of Canada from 1883–1888.

LANSING   63°45′N 133°32′W (105-N).

This was named because of its location at the confluence of the Stewart and Lansing Rivers. In 1897–98 Frank Braine, who had been a trader in northern Saskatchewan, and Percival Nash travelled through this country on their way to the Klondike from Edmonton. Disappointed in their search for gold, they returned to the vicinity of Fort Norman in the NWT to trap and trade. In 1902 they decided to return to this area to reap the fur harvest. They brought several families of Mackenzie River Indians with them and built a trading post here. James Mervyn took over the post in 1912. The post prospered until many of the Indians died during an epidemic of influenza in the late 1920′s. The post gradually lost its importance and with the coming of roads and the cessation of riverboat travel, it faded into oblivion in the 1950′s.

LANSING RIVER   63°45′N 133°28′W (105-N). A tributary of the Stewart River.

Samuel LANSING was one of the first prospectors in the Yukon Territory and mined the bars of the Stewart River in 1883. He prospected this stream that year, when it received his name. He prospected widely in the Yukon and was one of the first at the Fortymile finds in 1886. He was moderately successful in the Klondike and was, for a number of years, the manager of the Harper and Ladue Co.'s mining operations there. He retired in 1926 to Sumner, Washington.

LAPIE RIVER   62°02′N 132°36′W (105-K). A tributary of the Pelly River, west of Ross River.

Dr. G.M. Dawson, GSC, named this river in 1887 after one of Robert Campbell's Iroquois Indian canoemen, who had accompanied him on his explorations on the Pelly in 1843.

LAPIERRE HOUSE   67°24′N 137°00′W (116-P). On the Bell River near the mouth of the Rat River.

Lapierre House was established in 1843–44 by Chief Factor John Bell,

HBC, of Fort MacPherson, as an outlier of that place, to facilitate trade with the tribes west of the Richardson Mountains.

LAPIERRE, the man who built and ran the post for the first few years, was half Iroquois and half French-Canadian. The first post was probably at the junction of what is now the Little Bell and the Bell Rivers, about 35 miles upstream from the present site.

After Alexander Hunter Murray built Fort Yukon in 1847, the post became a way point between there and Fort MacPherson, used to transfer goods and furs. After the building of the second Rampart House on the Porcupine and the supply of that place by steamboat up the Yukon, at much lower cost, Lapierre House fell into disuse and was abandoned by 1890.

For many years the post supplied much of the meat and fish consumed at Forts MacPherson and Yukon. Caribou were killed by the thousands and fantastic numbers of fish were caught and dried.

In the fall of 1847 Anne Murray, wife of A.H. Murray, gave birth to a daughter, Helen, while staying here. Helen Murray was the first white child born in the Yukon Territory. Robert Kennicott, the brilliant young American naturalist and explorer, at that time Director of the Scientific Corps of the Collins Overland Telegraph, spent about a month here in the winter of 1862, studying the natural history of the region.

Sometimes spelled LaPierre's, Lapierre's, or Lapiers, it was also known to HBC employees as "The Small House", and to the Indians as "Koahze" meaning "Little House".

MOUNT LAPORTE 7,050′ 61°13′N 127°42′W (95–E). In the southeast corner of the Yukon Territory.

In 1972 at the request of the Commissioner of the Yukon, James Smith, this mountain was named after the Hon. Pierre LAPORTE, journalist and Minister of Labour in the Québec government. He was kidnapped and murdered by FLQ terrorists in Montréal in 1971.

LARSEN CREEK 60°10′N 125°01′W (95–C). Flows into the Beaver River.

In 1958 the long-known local name was officially adopted for this creek and lake, where L. LARSEN, the first white trapper in the area, lived and died in his cabin at the head of the lake.

LASKA GULCH 63°49′N 136°19′W (115–P). A small stream off Johnson Creek.

Joe Laska placer mined on Johnson Creek for many years in the 1930's and 40's. George Ortell lived about a mile and a half away and though the two men had frequent disputes and times when they hardly spoke, they were partners in a way. When one saw no smoke from the other's chimney, he investigated. Ortell admitted that Laska was a great help in time of trouble. (See Ortell's Crossing.)

LAST CHANCE CREEK 64°01′N 139°06′W (116-B&C). A tributary to Hunker Creek two miles from its mouth.

The Discovery claim was staked on 2 October, 1896, by Fred Belanger who may have named it, although a miner on the creek later wrote that a native, "Indian Sam" first found gold on the creek and staked a claim.

LAST MOUNTAIN 4,407′ 60°46′N 126°37′W (95-D). On the Yukon-NWT boundary.

This was named in the 1940's by G.C.F. Dalziel, big-game guide of Watson Lake, and at one time owner-operator of Northern British Columbia Air Services. The hill was used by bush pilots as a landmark. (See Dalziel Creek.)

LAST PEAK 6,062′ 61°36′N 134°14′W (105-E). East of the Big Salmon River and south of Teraktu Creek.

In 1898 Arthur St. Cyr, DLS, surveyed the Quiet Lake-Big Salmon country. He occupied ten triangulation stations on various mountain peaks within the area. This was the last one he used.

MOUNT LAURIER 5,838′ 61°02′N 134°52′W (105-E). Ten miles east of the head of Lake Laberge.

Originally named Mount Dawson by William Ogilvie in 1888, the name was changed in 1890 by Dr. G.M. Dawson, GSC, to honour the then Prime Minister of Canada, Sir Wilfrid LAURIER.

MOUNT LEACOCK 10,200′ 60°38′N 138°43′W (115-C). In the St. Elias Range, five miles east of Kaskawulsh Mountain.

This beautiful peak was named in 1970 in remembrance of Stephen LEA-COCK (1876-1944), Professor of Economics at McGill University and Canada's beloved humourist and author.

LECKIE LAKE 61°33′N 129°38′W (105-H). Located between the arms of Frances lake, at the north end.

In 1962 this lake was named to honour another of Canada's war dead, Sergeant J.C. LECKIE, Canadian Infantry Corps, who was killed in action in the Second World War.

LEDGE CREEK   63°40′N 134°52′W (105–M). Flows into Mayo Lake.

Gold was first discovered here and in several nearby creeks about August 1903 by a party of four Australian prospectors. They named the creeks when they were recording their claims in Dawson. The creeks were rich, for the discoverers brought with them 175 ounces of coarse gold.

LEGAR LAKE   62°39′N 136°33′W (115–I). About ten miles northeast of Minto.

In 1936 Dan Van Bibber reported that this name had been in local use for many years. Because of the number of pike in the lake, the name may have been given by a French-Canadian prospector or trapper who fished them.

MOUNT LEOTTA 3,156′   63°58′N 138°50′W (115–O&N). Between Hunker Creek and the Klondike River.

John Scott named this hill during the Klondike rush in 1897, after his sister. He had been in the Yukon for many years.

LEPINE CREEK   64°05′N 139°05′W (116–B&C). The west fork of Rock Creek, ten miles east of Dawson.

W. LEPINE was working for the HBC when R.G. McConnell GSC, met him on the Liard River in 1887. He had spent many years in the Yukon and NWT. Before the '98 rush he went to Fortymile and it is believed that he prospected and lived on this stream in 1897–98.

LESLIE RIDGE   62°38′N 138°45′W (115–J&K). Between Dip Creek and the Klotassin River, northeast of Stevenson Ridge.

H.S. Bostock, GSC, gave this name in 1941 after the junior partner of a mining company on Rude Creek. They were successful miners and prospectors for many years in the district. At the start of the Second World War in 1939, LESLIE and his partner Stevenson bought an expensive radio in Dawson. They laboriously packed it and the heavy batteries used at the time into their camp and set up an elaborate aerial. Switching on the set, the first station they received was a German short-wave propaganda station. They instantly chopped the radio to bits and threw it outside the cabin, their patriotism outraged. They never bought another. (See Stevenson Ridge.)

LEWES RIVER   The old name for the Yukon River above its junction with the Pelly River.

On 16 June, 1843, Robert Campbell of the HBC arrived at this junction. He called the river below this point the Pelly and considered the river above it to be a tributary of the Pelly and named it after John Lee LEWES, Chief Factor of the HBC. The local Indians told him that the headwaters of this stream formed a trade route to the coast, which undoubtedly influenced his selection of this place as the site of Fort Selkirk. By the 1880's the miners were using this name for the river as far as Lake Laberge.

In 1883, Lt. F. Schwatka, US Army, ignoring Campbell and the miners, named it the Yukon River. It was not until May 1945 that the Canadian government officially changed the name Lewes to the Yukon River.

In the early years the section of the Yukon from Lake Laberge to Marsh Lake was called the Thirtymile River. This was later dropped and included in the Lewes and then, the Yukon.

LEWIS LAKE   60°22'N 134°50'W (105-D). On the west side of the WP&YR tracks, about 15 miles north of Carcross.

Although often misspelled Lewes (after the old name for the Yukon River at this point), this lake received its name in the summer of 1898 from an engineering error during the construction of the railway. A.B. LEWIS, the locating and construction engineer, while carrying out his grade survey, found that the surface of this lake was somewhat above the railway grade. A ditch was dug from the south end of the lake to drain away the excess water. The plug was removed in the evening and during the night the force of the out-flow washed the ditch much deeper in the loose gravel than was anticipated and the lake was quickly drained by a depth of 50 or more feet. The flood washed out a considerable length of newly constructed roadbed below the lake, holding up construction and embarrassing the engineer. The name was early mistaken with that of the Lewes River and has been so printed on maps since then.

LEWIS LAKE   62°35'N 131°05'W (105-J). Part of the upper Ross River.

Joseph Keele, GSC, named this lake in 1907 during his explorations, after Clement S. LEWIS, son of Archbishop Lewis of Ottawa. Lewis came into the Yukon in 1898. After various prospecting and mining ventures of limited success, he and Poole Field bought the trading post at the mouth of Ross River in 1902. Tom Smith, the owner, had built it a few years earlier. They named it "Nahanni House." About 1906 or later they sold out to

Taylor and Drury, Whitehorse merchants, and Lewis managed it for them for a number of years, until about 1910. He was Justice of the Peace for the area and collected specimens of the local flora and fauna for the National Museum of Canada at Ottawa.

He then managed the Taylor and Drury post at Teslin until about 1915 and during this time he accumulated an important collection of birds of the area which was purchased by the museum.

LIARD RIVER   60°00′N 128°35′W (105-A).

The headwaters of the mighty Liard River are in the St. Cyr Range of mountains of the south central Yukon. The river flows southeast to cross the Yukon-BC border a few miles below Watson Lake. From there it flows east and north to join the Mackenzie River at Fort Simpson.

The early HBC traders on the Mackenzie called this stream the "West Branch", the "Mountain River" and the "Great Current River". The Mackenzie Indians called it the "Erett-Chichie" and "Thattadesse" and the Yukon Indians, the "Too-Ti", words expressing its size and force.

The Liard was first explored by John McLeod of the HBC when the company began expanding its empire across the Rocky Mountains and westward. He traversed the river at least as far as what is now Lower Post in 1834. It was his French-Canadian voyageurs who gave it the name "Rivière aux Liards", "liard" being the French name for the cottonwood (poplar) trees which still line the banks of the lower river in profusion.

The next white man on the river was Robert Campbell, also of the HBC who, from 1838 to 1852, opened up the route from the Mackenzie to the central Yukon. Campbell explored the Yukon Territory by way of the Liard and its tributary, the Frances River, leading to the Pelly River and the Yukon proper. While travelling the Liard in 1838 Campbell did not realize that it was the same river McLeod had explored, and named it the "Bell River" after Chief Trader John Bell. The name was used on some maps but when its course was determined the old name "Liard" was kept.

In 1874 a party of Cassiar miners ascended the headwaters of the river where they found and mined placer gold on a number of its tributaries. This was the first production of gold in what is now the Yukon Territory. These miners corrupted the name of the river to "Deloire" and for at least the next 15 years they prospected its upper reaches with indifferent results.

The river is dangerous and in 1852 the HBC abandoned the route because of the number of men lost while trying to supply the posts at Frances Lake and Pelly Banks from Fort Simpson on the Mackenzie. Numerous prospectors were drowned in the river, especially in the Great Canyon, below Watson Lake. A number of Klondikers tried to reach the goldfields in 1897–98 by this route but few were successful, the recorded tragedies of that time only emphasizing those of earlier years.

Of scholarly interest is the number of variations of the names used for the river. Deloire, Deliore, Delyare, d'Eloir, D'Liard, Delaird, Del'Liard, Liard, Rivière des Liards, Lizzard and the Ure. Confusion in the early history also arises from the fact that the Fort Nelson River (not Nelson River) and the Dease River, both tributaries of the Liard, were sometimes called the Deloire River and that Delure Creek, a tributary of the Dease River, was sometimes called Deloire Creek. (See Cabin and Sayyea Creeks.)

LIBERTY CREEK 62°19'N 137°06'W (115-I). A tributary of Stoddard Creek in the Mount Freegold area.

This has been a local name since 1929 when Fred Guder staked his Liberty claim on the creek, the first mineral find there.

LIBERAL TRAIL (See Conservative Trail.)

LIGHTNING CREEK 63°53'N 135°21'W (105-M). Tributary to Duncan Creek in the Mayo district.

In 1907, the discoverers of gold on the creek gave it the name of the riverboat *LIGHTNING*, which brought miners and supplies up the Stewart River to Duncan Creek in the early 1900's.

LISTER CREEK 61°27'N 137°12'W (115-H). Flows from Houghton Lake into the west centre of Aishihik Lake.

In 1956 this stream was selected to honour the name of Flying Officer J.E. LISTER, RCAF, who was killed in action during the Second World War.

LITTLE BLANCHE CREEK 63°49'N 139°04'W (115-O&N). A tributary to Quartz Creek from the west.

Bob Ensley staked and named this creek in October 1897. He was in love with a Dawson dance-hall girl and named the stream after her. Later in 1898 when his claim proved to be rich he induced LITTLE BLANCHE to marry him, by giving her her weight in raw gold.

This little creek is notable as the scene of one of the tantalizing stories of gold found in the Klondike before 1896. It is claimed that in the spring of 1894, Andrew Hart and his partner Hansen prospected the creek and found payable gold. They mined it for a couple of months before running short of supplies and recovered over $2,000 in gold. They went out to Fortymile and, because no one had seen them all summer, decided to keep their find a secret. For unknown reasons they did not return and Ensley and Little Blanche profited from the gold they left.

LITTLE GEM CREEK   63°48′N 138°55′W (116-B&C).   A tributary to Hunker Creek.

In October 1898 Frank Criderman was so pleased with his initial find of gold that he applied this name. The Little Gem Mining Company was later formed and operated in several localities in the Yukon.

LITTLE JIMMY LAKE   60°54′N 129°43′W (105-A). About 20 miles northwest of Simpson Lake.

In 1949 LITTLE JIMMY, a local Indian, had erected a sign at his cabin here proclaiming his ownership. He had trapped from here to the east arm of Frances Lake for many years. Named by the trader at Lower Post, Jimmy was something of a prospector. In 1937 he brought samples of high grade silver-lead ore to Anton Money at McDame Creek in the Cassiar. The samples came from the east side of Frances Lake. Money made arrangements with a Vancouver, BC, firm to finance the search for the vein and others like it. The search was carried out over the next few years with some success. (The property has not yet made a mine but it has been investigated several times again in the past few years.) (See Money Creek.)

LITTLE RIDGE   4,482′   61°03′N 135°54′W (105-E). On the east side of Thirty Seven Mile Creek.

H.S. Bostock, GSC, named this small hill after the old LITTLE River Roadhouse, on the old Dawson Trail five miles to the southeast.

LITTLE SALMON RIVER   62°03′N 135°40′W (105-L). A tributary of the Yukon above Carmacks.

Miners in 1882 translated the Indian name for the stream and used it. In 1883 Schwatka ignored both the Indians and miners and named it after the Hon. Charles P. Daly, President of the American Geographical Society. Dr. G.M. Dawson, GSC, disallowed the name and it was forgotten.

LITTLE VIOLET CREEK 61°25'N 134°23'W (105-E). A tributary to the South Big Salmon River.

The prospector who first found gold here about 1903 was a widower who had his small daughter with him. A mining company was later formed using the same name.

LIVINGSTONE 61°20'N 134°21'W (105-E).

A small settlement near the mouth of Livingstone Creek came into being in the summer of 1898 to serve the miners in the newly found goldfields of the area. It was connected to Lake Laberge by a 40-mile-long winter trail and a little later by a 16-mile wagon road to Mason's Landing on the Teslin River. The settlement flourished for many years. It contained a dance hall and a red light section in addition to roadhouses and stores. It decayed with the goldfields as they were worked out and died in the 1930's.

LIVINGSTONE CREEK 61°22'N 134°23'W (105-E). A tributary of the South Big Salmon River.

Joseph E. Peters prospected this area before the gold rush and, it is claimed, sank a prospect shaft on this creek in 1894. In any event he and George Black (later to be the Member of Parliament and Commissioner of the Yukon Territory), were partners when they discovered the rich, coarse gold of this stream. They named it after Black's friend and fellow lawyer, M.D. LIVINGSTONE of Whitehorse and Dawson. He may have contributed to their grubstake. In the four weeks preceding freeze-up the two took out $3,600 in gold.

Peters worked in this area until the First World War. It is claimed that over a million dollars in gold was taken from the creek by 1920. Placer mining is still carried on sporadically in the area.

MOUNT LOGAN 19,850' 60°34'N 140°24'W (115-B&C). In the St. Elias Range.

This is the highest mountain in Canada and the second highest in North America. It was named by Professor Israel Cook Russell, USGS, in 1890. He first saw it when he was on a National Geographic Society Expedition in southeast Alaska and southwest Yukon, in the foothills of the St. Elias Range.

He named it in honour of Sir William E. LOGAN, founder and for many years director of the Geological Survey of Canada.

Sir William Edmond Logan, KB, LLD, FGS, FRS, was born in Montréal, Québec, on 20 April, 1798. Taken to Scotland at 14 by his father, he attended Edinburgh High School. His work in geology in Wales (a spare time project) was so good that it was accepted *in toto* by the Geological Survey of Great Britain. When the Canadian government decided to set up such a department in Canada Logan was so highly recommended that he was chosen over others more academically qualified. He served 27 years and, mostly by his own work in the field, laid the basis of eastern Canadian geology. He received most of the scientific honours of his day. He died in Llechryd, Wales, in 1875. His monument, erected in Ottawa reads:

The Father of Canadian Geology
Founder and First Director of the Geological
Survey of Canada. 1841–1869.

His name is on several other features in Canada.

This mountain was first climbed on 23 June, 1925, by a joint Canadian-American Expedition, led by H.F. Lambart, Canadian, and A.H. McCarthy, American. (See Mount Hunt.)

LOGAN MOUNTAINS 61°30′N 120°00′W (105-H). The mountain range on the east side of Frances Lake.

In 1887 Dr. G.M. Dawson, GSC, gave this range the local name "Too-Tsho", which is their name for Frances Lake, meaning "Big Lake". This was changed in 1929 to the Logan Mountains. (See Mount Logan.)

LOKKEN CREEK 61°50′N 134°38′W (105-E). Flows into Walsh Creek.

This was named in 1936 after H.O. LOKKEN, a long-time pioneer from gold rush days. He was for many years the head linesman on the Yukon Telegraph. He was always an active prospector, especially in this area.

The mountain at the headwaters of the creek was given the name first by W.H. Miller, GSC, while he was mapping the area, and the creek was named later.

LOMBARD GULCH 63°52′N 138°53′W (115-O&N). The last small stream entering the headwaters of Dominion Creek from the north.

L.H. LOMBARD found the first gold and staked the Discovery claim here on 13 July, 1897. It was never very productive.

LONELY DOME   63°35'N 134°28'W (105–M). Ten miles east of the south end of Mayo Lake.

H.S. Bostock, GSC, named this isolated hill while mapping the area in 1940.

LONER MOUNTAIN   63°32'N 131°58'W (105–O). Between the Rogue and Hess Rivers on the west end of the Rogue Range.

This was named in 1973 by Dr. Aro Aho of the Dynasty Exploration Company, while he was working in the area.

LONG'S CREEK   61°54'N 140°14'W (115–G&F). Flows into the Koidern River.

This brook was given its name in 1953 to perpetuate the name of Pilot Officer R.W. LONG, RCAF, who was killed in action in the Second World War.

LOOTZ LAKE   60°11'N 126°53'W (95–D). Lootz Lake and Creek flow into the Rock River.

Clem LOOTZ, a trapper, lived on the north shore of the lake for a number of years and both the lake and the creek were officially given his name in 1949. His family still resides at Lower Post, BC.

LORD CREEK   67°33'N 139°09'W (116–O&N). A tributary to the Porcupine River near Old Crow.

David LORD, a French-Canadian, was a grand old man in his 80's when he died in Dawson in 1954. A Klondiker, he had lived and trapped with his family in this region for many years. He had lived at New Rampart House and Old Crow since 1900. He was respected and well-liked by all who knew him.

MOUNT LORNE   60°28'N 134°42'W (105–D). On the west side of Marsh Lake.

In 1887 William Ogilvie, DLS, named this landmark after the Right Honourable Sir John Douglas Sutherland Campbell, Marquis of LORNE, who had been Governor-General of Canada from 1878-1883.

The section stop on the WP&YR was named from its proximity to the mountain in 1899.

LOST HORSES CREEK   63°56'N 137°08'W (115–P). A tributary to the Little South Klondike River.

In 1947 H.S. Bostock's GSC party lost half their pack horses here. The search time for the animals upset their schedule.

LOUISE LAKE   60°32′N 137°27′W (115-A). The westernmost of the Kathleen Lakes.

In 1938 George Chambers named this beautiful lake after LOUISE Davis, (Mrs. Alex Dickson) who lived alone in this area for some years. The lake tends to be calm and serene and reminded Chambers of Mrs. Davis' disposition. In 1959 she was living in Champagne and had 12 living children, 45 grandchildren and 17 great grandchildren.

LOVETT GULCH   64°01′N 139°22′W (116-B&C). The first small tributary from the east on Bonanza Creek, a mile above the mouth.

B.F. LOVETT was very active in the Klondike and had many mining interests. He probably staked this gulch in late 1896. He accumulated much ground on the hill between this short stream and the Klondike River. It was known as Lovett Hill and proved very rich, with wide stretches of the White Channel gravels. (See Mint Gulch.)

LOWELL GLACIER   60°17′N 138°30′W (115-B&C). Just north of Mount Kennedy.

Bradford Washburn named this feature in 1908 for a former and famous president of Harvard University, Abbott Lawrence LOWELL.

MOUNT LUCANIA   17,150′   61°01′N 140°28′W (115-G&F). In the Icefield Ranges of the St. Elias Mountains.

On 31 July, 1897, the Duke of Abruzzi saw this huge mountain and named it after the Cunard liner in which he and his party had crossed the Atlantic Ocean. It was first climbed on 9 July, 1937, by Bradford Washburn and Robert H. Bates.

LUCKY LAKE   60°02′N 128°35′W (105-A). A small lake at mile 626 (K1014) of the Alaska Highway, just south of Watson Lake.

This pond was named by American Army Engineer troops in 1942 during the construction of the highway and is still so called. At that time a young woman set up a tent business and clients there referred to transactions as "a change of luck". The lake is shallow and protected and warms quickly in the summer. It is one of the few lakes in the area where swimming is possible and comfortable.

LUCKY LAKE 61°30'N 127°22'W (95-E). A narrow lake almost on the Yukon-NWT border, on the headwaters of the Coal River.

On 20 August, 1968, Dr. E.J. Roots GSC, was in a small float plane when the engine failed. Their glide barely reached this lake where they made a safe landing.

LUSK LAKE 66°21'N 135°15'W (106-L). At the headwaters of the Caribou River.

Isaac LUSK was a freighter who carried the mail between Dawson and Minto Bridge for many years. He was also a Yukon Councillor for South Dawson from 1912-15. This lake was given his name in 1973.

LYNX CREEK 63°59'N 135°52'W (105-M). Flows into Haggart Creek.

Originally named "Lick Creek" after a salt lick nearby, the name was corrupted to "Link" and finally to Lynx. H.S. Bostock, GSC, was told of this by old miners in the area.

MOUNT MACAULAY 61°13'N 135°15'W (115-F). Just south of Mount Wood in the Icefield Ranges of the St. Elias Range.

In 1958 this mountain was named after Judge Charles Daniel MACAULAY who served for many years with distinction on the Territorial Bench.

MacAULEY CREEK 60°03'N 135°15'W (105-D). Flows into the west end of the west arm of Lake Bennett.

A good gold prospect was found here in the spring of 1900 by Dr. L.S. Sugden and "Red" Rogers. They were grubstaked by Norman MacAULEY and Thomas O'Brien. MacAuley was the builder and owner of the Miles Canyon Tramway and the proprietor of the Whitehorse Hotel as well as many mining interests.

The mountain at the headwaters of the creek, on the Yukon-BC border, was given his name at a later date.

MOUNT MacDONALD 6,750' 63°09'N 135°50'W (105-M). In the McArthur Group of mountains.

James MacDonald, a pioneer prospector, spent his later years (he was in his 70's and 80's) searching for a lost copper mine in this area. The mountain received his name in 1972.

MOUNT MacDONALD 64°43′N 132°47′W (106-C). On the head-waters of Corn Creek, west of the Snake River.

This was named officially in 1973 after a well-known prospector, Allan John "Hardrock" MacDONALD, who explored much of the northern territory from 1920 to 1960.

"Hardrock John" was noted as a musher, and once travelled alone in the dead of winter from Mayo to Aklavik in 17 days, a journey seldom equalled. In 1961, while he was still alive, there were requests to give his name to a tributary of the Boswell River where he had prospected. (See McDonald Creek.)

MACK'S FORK 63°49′N 139°03′W (115-O&N). A small tributary of Quartz Creek from the east, above Little Blanche Creek.

On 20 August, 1897, A. MACK staked a normal-sized claim on Quartz Creek at the mouth of this stream. The stream received his name but for some reason his claim was known afterward as Mack's Discovery. It was not, for he gave Stewart's discovery higher up Quartz Creek as a reference point when recording his own claim. (See Quartz Creek.)

MacKINNON CREEK 62°05′N 139°50′W (115-J). A tributary to the Donjek River south of Wellesley Lake.

Andrew MacKINNON was a prospector who lived here while he mined and trapped in the area. The name was locally used for many years and was made official in 1953.

MACKINTOSH CREEK 61°57′N 137°17′W (115-H). Flows into the Nisling River.

In 1965 G.W. Rowley requested this name after George Whitfield Cameron MACKINTOSH. He joined the NWMP in 1900 and served until 1902 when he took his discharge in Whitehorse. He lived for many years at the Bear Creek trading post and died 29 November, 1939, a respected man.

MacMILLAN RIVER 62°50′N 135°56′W (105-L). A major tributary of the Pelly River.

Robert Campbell of the HBC, while on his first journey down the Pelly River in June 1843, named this stream after Chief Factor James McMILLAN, who had sponsored his employment with the HBC.

Correct spelling is McMillan; sometimes spelled Macmillan, M'Millan.

McARTHUR PEAK 14,253' 60°37'N 140°11'W (115-B&C). About seven miles northeast of Mount Logan.

This was named in 1918 after James Joseph McARTHUR DLS, (1856-1925). He was in charge of survey parties of the International Boundary Commission from 1901-24 and in 1917 was appointed a commissioner and served until 1924.

McArthur was one of the surveyors sent to the Yukon by the Department of the Interior in May 1897 to survey the routes to the Klondike. He travelled the Dalton Trail from Pyramid Harbor to the Yukon River and with a minimum of instrument work produced a very rough map. He approved the route as being suitable for either a wagon road or a railroad. It is probable that a railway would have been built on this easier route if the WP&YR had not been begun first.

He did further work in the Yukon of a much better quality. Some years after his death a small range of mountains, in the south Mayo area where he had also worked, was named the McArthur Group.

McCABE CREEK 62°32'N 136°46'W (115-I). Five miles south of Minto.

After the business establishments and other services in Fort Selkirk had closed their doors, the post office closed in December 1952. The few remaining people moved up the river to where the old Whitehorse-Dawson winter stage road leaves the river near Minto. Here, near the mouth of McCabe Creek, they settled and another post office was opened on 5 December, 1953, by Mrs. Alec Cowaret under the name McCabe Creek. In October 1970 this too was closed as the last remaining people had left.

McCABE had been a trader here in the 1920's and 30's and was noted for his highly successful potato crops.

McCANN HILL 64°55'N 141°00'W (116-B&C). A boundary peak, south of the Tatonduc River.

Named by D.D. Cairnes, GSC, after his assistant, W.S. McCANN while they were mapping the geology of the boundary country in 1912.

MOUNT McCLEERY 60°19'N 132°02'W (105-C). At the south end of Englishman's Range.

F.S. Bailey, Forest Warden at Teslin, requested this name in 1954 after Robert McCLEERY, his late admired friend. McLeery came in with the

Klondike rush, was a veteran of the First World War and, in 1926, built a trading post at Teslin which he operated until 1951. He was also a Justice of the Peace and postmaster at the same time. A creek, tributary to Fat Creek across Teslin Lake, carried his name for a few years in the 1920's but was changed to Grouse Creek. This is a better monument to a fine man.

M'CLINTOCK LAKES 60°55′N 134°31′W (105-D). A series of small lakes on the headwaters of M'Clintock River.

These were named by Arthur St. Cyr, DLS, in November 1897 while he was surveying a route to the Klondike from Telegraph Creek in BC to the south end of Teslin Lake. He had finished his survey and had decided to cross overland from Teslin to Marsh Lake and determine if a trail this way would be feasible. (See M'Clintock River.)

M'CLINTOCK RIVER 60°33′N 134°29′W (105-D). This stream flows into the northeast end of Marsh Lake.

Lt. F. Schwatka, US Army, named this river in 1883 after one of the most famous of the early Arctic explorers, Admiral Sir Francis Leopold M'CLINTOCK, RN, (1819-1907). It is one of Schwatka's names that Dr. G.M. Dawson, GSC, allowed to stand.

McCONNELL LAKE 60°27′N 134°55′W (105-D). About 25 miles north of Carcross.

This was the last feature to be named after this famous explorer and geologist. In 1956 the Geographical Board gave this lake his name as he had based some of his surveys from here. (See McConnell Peak.)

McCONNELL PEAK 6,182′ 61°18′N 132°21′W (105-F). At the mouth of the McConnell River.

This was named about 1945 after one of Canada's foremost geological explorers, Richard George McCONNELL (1857-1942). Born in Chatham, Québec, he graduated with a B.A. from McGill University. He joined the Geological Survey of Canada in 1880. He made an exploratory circuit of the Yukon Territory in 1887-88 which, while more difficult, was over-shadowed by that of Dawson at the same time. He spent ten years mapping the geology of the Yukon, especially making the first authoritative study (1901) of the Klondike goldfields and the Whitehorse copper belt. His great work was the solution of the foundation of the Rocky Mountain system. He was the author of many geological reports and maps, many still in use. In 1914 he became Deputy Minister of Mines in the federal government and filled the post with distinction throughout the war years and until 1920. He died in Ottawa on 1 April, 1942.

McCONNELL RIVER 61°16′N 132°30′W (105-F). A tributary of the Nisutlin River.

This was the first feature to be named after R.G. McCONNELL, GSC, and was probably designated by Morley Ogilvie, son of William Ogilvie and at the time assistant to Arthur St. Cyr, while they were surveying the east side of Teslin Lake in 1897.

MOUNT McCOUBREY 10,250′ 61°13′N 140°04′W (115-G&F). To the east of the Steele Glacier.

This was named in 1970 after Alexander Addison McCOUBREY (1885-1942), surveyor and past president of the Alpine Club of Canada (1932-1934).

MOUNT McCULLUM 5,559′ 65°28′N 137°34′W (116-H). West of the Blackstone River.

In 1973 this peak was named after the Rev. Creighton McCULLUM, Anglican Minister at Mayo and Dawson in the 1920 and 30's. He served as a private soldier in the First World War and as a chaplain in the Second World War.

MOUNT McDADE 4,918′ 62°07′N 136°58′W (115-I). About 23 miles west of Carmacks.

This was first called McDade Hill in 1931 when George McDADE discovered rich silver-lead ore and precipitated a staking rush which uncovered many more potential ore bodies. He and Afe Brown made the first finds on Victoria Creek. The hill was officially named Mount McDade in 1958.

McDONALD CREEK 61°02′N 133°47′W (105-F). A tributary to the Boswell River.

This creek has been known locally by this name for a number of years. On it was the home of Allan John "Hardrock" MacDONALD, an old-time prospector in this area who was noted for his stamina and hardihood.

In 1961 G.W. Rowley, Forest Warden, suggested the name be made official. As "Hardrock" was still alive the request was denied. (See Mount MacDonald.)

McDOUGALL PASS 67°43'N 136°27'W (116-P). Through the Continental Divide between the Bell and Rat Rivers.

In May 1888 William Ogilvie, DLS, named this pass after Junior Chief Trader James McDOUGALL of the HBC. Travelling out of Fort MacPherson in 1872, McDougall was the first white man to discover and map the pass, although his clerk Thomas Scott was the first white man to actually cross it. It was used by a number of Klondike stampeders in 1897-98 on their way from Edmonton to Dawson.

McEVOY LAKE 61°48'N 130°14'W (105-G). Northwest of Frances Lake.

Dr. G.M. Dawson, GSC, while on his survey up Frances Lake and on to the Pelly, explored the area at the head of the lake and named this lake after his assistant, James McEVOY, BS, ME.

MOUNT McGUIRE 5,116' 67°56'N 137°22'W (116-P). West of the Bell River.

Mr. Justice T.H. McGUIRE, the first Judge of the Court of the Provisional District of the Yukon in 1897 and for a number of years after, was commemorated by this designation in 1973.

McINNES HILL 64°07'N 139°24'W (115-B&C). The hill between Examiner Gulch and Klondike City (South Dawson).

William Oscar Smith, on 16 September, 1906, found gold enough to stake a Discovery hill claim here. He named the hill after the then Commissioner of the Yukon Territory, William Wallace Burns McINNES, who was born in Dresden, Ontario, on 10 April, 1871, the son of the Hon. T.B. McInnes, Lt. Governor of British Columbia. Graduating in law, he was appointed Commissioner of the Yukon on 27 May, 1905, and served till 31 December, 1906. He instituted an unpopular regime of government economies, cutting down the number of both civil servants and the RNWMP in the territory. His short term was noted for controversy.

He served eight years as a County Court Judge in Vancouver, BC; he unsuccessfully tried for political office but died in obscurity.

McINTYRE CREEK 60°46'N 135°05'W (105-D). A tributary to the Yukon River, northwest of Whitehorse.

On 6 July, 1898, John McINTYRE of San Bernardino, California, found the first of the high grade copper ore bodies of the Whitehorse Copper Belt on this creek, which received his name at that time. His first claim was named the "Copper King". The first shipment of ore from the claim was made in 1900 and contained nine tons of bornite grading 46.40% copper.

In the winter of 1902–03 McIntyre was in Atlin, BC and had contracted to carry the mail from there to Log Cabin on the WP&YR. He and Joseph Abbey left Atlin with the mail carried by dog sled, on 25 November, 1902. They never arrived at Log Cabin. A long search was made and the dogs, sled and mail were found beneath the ice of Windy Arm by George Coutts and John Fountain. Abbey's body was found in the lake on the 28 April and that of McIntyre was recovered on 14 May, 1903.

McINTYRE MOUNTAIN 5,200′ 60°37′N 135°08′W (105-D). Seven miles southwest of Whitehorse.

Shortly after his death in 1902, this mountain was named after John McINTYRE. (See McIntyre Creek.)

MOUNT McINTYRE 64°21′N 138°41′W (116-B). 27 miles northeast of Dawson and south of Tombstone Mountain.

This was after Angus McINTYRE who came to the Yukon in 1898 and remained until 1942. He was "Foreman of the Ditch" during the construction of the immense 70-mile-long flume and ditch built to bring large quantities of water to the hydraulic workings in the Klondike before the First World War. He died in Kelowna, BC, in 1950 at the age of 90.

McKAY HILL 64°21′N 135°25′W (106-D). In the eastern Ogilvie Mountains.

This was named after Thomas McKAY who prospected in this area in the 1920's. He was a Yukon Councillor for the Mayo District about 1929–30.

McKINNON CREEK 63°44′N 139°05′W (115-O&N). Flows into the Indian River from the south.

Donald and Archibald McKINNON were brothers who found and tried for many years to develop a huge gold deposit they had found in widespread conglomerate rocks here in 1910–15. They had earlier, in 1898–1900, worked a placer gold claim on the same creek.

McKINNON LAKE 60°02′N 129°19′W (105-A). On Albert Creek, 25 miles west of Watson Lake.

Dan McKINNON trapped and prospected for many years in a wide area around here. He died near Toobally Lakes.

McLAGAN CREEK 63°41'N 136°12'W (115-P). Tributary to Minto Lake.

Miners on this creek in 1902 named it after Jack McLAGAN who was Mining Recorder for the Mayo district at that time.

McLEAN CREEK 64°25'N 135°19'W (106-D). A tributary of Carpenter Creek.

John McLEAN was one of a group who first prospected and found silver-lead ore on Silver Hill, part of Settlemier Ridge, in late 1923.

McLEOD CREEK 63°55'N 135°20'W (105-M). A tributary to Lightning Creek, off Galena Hill in the Mayo district.

About 1915 A. McLEOD found a vein of silver-lead ore on the banks of this creek.

McMILLAN LAKE 60°31'N 127°55'W (95-D). A mile west of Hulse (Quartz) Lake.

This was named by James Harquail, president of Fort Reliance Minerals Ltd., after a trapper named McMILLAN of Lower Post, whose cabin still stands at the west end of the lake.

MOUNT McNEIL 60°08'N 135°27'W (105-D). Two miles northeast of Mount Skookum, north of the Wheaton River.

This was named in 1911 after Hector McNEIL, a prospector well-known in this district for many years.

McPARLAND CREEK 66°05'N 137°56'W (116-I). A tributary of the East Porcupine River.

This stream was chosen in 1973 to commemorate K-98595 Cpl. George Lynn McPARLON, MM, who was killed in action at the storming of Ortona, Italy, on 23 December, 1943. Lynn McParlon was born at Waldo, BC, on 29 June, 1912. He enlisted in and served with the Seaforth Highlanders of Canada at Vancouver, BC, on 18, July, 1940.

Through some error his name was written as McParland.

McPARLON CREEK (See McParland Creek.)

McPHERSON LAKE 61°53'N 129°32'W (105-H). 20 miles north of Frances Lake.

In August 1840 Robert Campbell of the HBC, while exploring the Frances

Lake country and upper Pelly River region, named this lake after Murdoch McPHERSON, Chief Factor of the Mackenzie District at that time.

McQUESTEN RIVER 63°33'N 137°27'W (115–P). A major tributary of the Stewart River.

Leroy Napoleon "Jack" McQUESTEN, was born in 1836 at Litchfield, New Hampshire, USA. As a young man attracted to life in the wilds, he entered the employ of the HBC at Fort Garry in what is now Manitoba. For about two years he worked in the area between Minnesota and Hudson Bay. Although he was six feet tall and weighed 200 pounds he was disappointed that he could not handle the standard, 200-pound packs over the portages as easily as could the much smaller French-Canadian voyageurs.

Leaving, he went on to California in the early years of that gold rush and found prospecting for gold attractive. Working north, he was on the Fraser River in BC when gold was first found there in 1858. He worked at the Gamble Lumber Mill near what is now Vancouver for a short period. Always moving north, he next mined in the Cariboo country. In 1863 he left Quesnel, BC, for the Peace River basin and for the next ten years prospected and traded with the Indians in northeastern BC and into Hay River and Lake Athabaska.

In 1871, while wintering with Alfred Mayo at the mouth of the Nelson River, he met Arthur Harper and Frederick Hart. There they learned from the Hudson's Bay men of the American purchase of Alaska and decided to go there.

The parties split up in the spring of 1873 and McQuesten and Mayo went down the Mackenzie to the Peel, which they followed to its headwaters, and traversed McDougall Pass to the Rat River and the Porcupine to Fort Yukon. They arrived there on 15 August, 1873. Arthur Harper and Hart arrived shortly afterwards.

After spending the winter on the lower Yukon River and at St. Michaels, they came to a loose working arrangement with the ACC and purchased a trading outfit from that company. On 20 August, 1874 McQuesten, Mayo and Barnfield (Bernstein) landed at the site of Fort Reliance (six miles down river from Dawson) on the little steamboat *Arctic*. Here they built their first trading post.

McQuesten and Mayo spent the next eight years setting up and operating trading posts along the Yukon River for the ACC, but always prospecting when the opportunity arose. In the winter of 1882–83 11 miners wintered at Fort Reliance, the first to do so in the territory. The first miners' meeting to be held in the territory took place and McQuesten was elected the first Mining Recorder.

He alternated trading and prospecting and was up the Stewart River in 1885 shortly after the first rich bar gold was found. The miners there at the time gave his name to the first north branch of the river.

Although he was running his trading post at Circle City when the Klondike goldfields were found, he grubstaked others and purchased interests in claims on Eldorado and Bonanza and so participated in the new-found wealth.

He left the Yukon in late 1898 with over $200,000, and built a large home in Berkeley, California, for his wife and children. He invested widely in mining interests in California and the west without losing his fortune. When the Alaska-Yukon Pacific Exposition was held in Seattle, in 1909, he was appointed the official representing the Yukon. While in that city he underwent an operation for bunions, contracted blood poisoning and in a few days the "Father of the Yukon" was dead.

That title had been bestowed on him by the miners in the Yukon while he was still alive and in business in the territory. His name was a byword for integrity and honesty. His trust in his fellow man was unbounded and seldom wrong. Nowhere in the literature of the Yukon is it possible to find a critical or unkind word about him. It is rare anywhere to find a man as highly regarded during his own lifetime as was Jack McQuesten.

McQUESTEN 63°33′N 137°25′W (115-P).

Shortly after the discovery of gold on the Stewart River bars the miners chose this spot to winter over and a small settlement sprang up. It later became a roadhouse on the winter trail from Whitehorse to Dawson. It was abandoned in the 1950's.

McRAE CREEK 63°46′N 136°11′W (115-P). A small tributary to Highet Creek.

J.D. McRAE found placer gold and staked the Discovery claim on this little stream on 24 June, 1903, during the rush to the Mayo and Minto finds.

McTAVISH LAKE 60°00′N 128°24′W (105-A). A small lake crossing the Yukon-BC border, 17 miles southeast of Watson Lake.

It was officially named in 1943 to confirm a long-established local name after the trapper from Lower Post whose base camp was here for many years.

MAGNET HILL   63°57′N 139°21′W (115-O&N). The hill on the west side of Bonanza Creek, one mile below Adams Gulch.

This was one of the early high level diggings. Gold was discovered here in the White Channel gravels by J.E. McKenzie in early 1897. He named the hill because of its resemblance to a horseshoe magnet.

Magnet City, a small community of dwellings, stores, shops and a roadhouse was begun here in early 1897. Mrs. M.P Rothweiler started for the Klondike by herself in the spring of 1897 but was caught by weather and spent the winter of 1897–98 in the ice at the mouth of the Stewart River. Arriving in Dawson in the spring, she bought a dug-out called "Mary's Place" near No. 17 Below Discovery on Bonanza Creek, rebuilt it and called it the Magnet Hotel. Magnet City was the largest settlement between Dawson and Grand Forks.

The gulch below the hill was discovered and staked on 10 July, 1897, by Peter Erussard de Ville.

MAGUNDY RIVER   62°12′N 134°26′W (105-L). Flowing into the east end of Little Salmon Lake.

This area has been the trapping grounds of the MAGUNDY family for many years.

MAIDEN CREEK   64°23′N 140°38′W (116-B&C). A tributary to the Fortymile River.

Andrew Jackson MAIDEN was one of the hardy prospectors who followed the trail of gold up the west coast of North America from California to the Yukon. He crossed the Chilkoot Pass in 1884 and in 1886–87 found gold on this creek during the rush to the new, coarse gold finds on the Fortymile River.

Being middle-aged in a country where young men were the rule, he was nick-named "Old Maiden". He carried a stack of about 50 old newspapers with him on his travels, claiming that they not only improved his mind but were useful in settling arguments. His good character and open heartedness were remarked upon by his peers in a country where these qualities were taken for granted.

George Carmack claimed that Andrew Maiden had prospected in the Klondike in 1889 and that he had reported this to the YOOP in Fortymile.

He had found gold but not in what was then considered paying quantities. He returned here in 1896 and being too late to stake on Bonanza or Eldorado creeks, found good ground elsewhere. He mined here until 1906-07 when he went to Fairbanks. He died there, a respected pioneer, in 1913, at the age of 76.

MAISY MAY CREEK 63°14′N 138°48′W (115-O&N). Flows into the Stewart River from the north.

In 1897 Samuel Henry took up a homestead at the mouth of this stream and started the MAISIE MAE ranch. He grew 26 tons of hay that year and successfully continued farming for a number of years afterward. He specialized in feed for the horses in Dawson and the mines. In 1906 he had over 100 acres under cultivation.

The name was first spelled Maisie Mae, then Maizy May.

MOUNT MALASPINA 60°19′N 140°34′W (115-B&C). 11 miles east of Mount St. Elias.

A peak in this range was given this name in 1874 by W.H. Dall, USC&GS, after Captain Don Alessandro MALASPINA, Italian navigator and explorer who, while in the service of Spain, explored the northwest coast of North America in 1791.

Professor Israel C. Russell, who led an expedition to Mount St. Elias in 1890, wrote that it was impossible to decide to which peak Dall had applied the name of the great navigator, so they gave his name to a peak about 11 miles east of Mount St. Elias.

MALCOLM RIVER 69°33′N 139°37′W (117-D). Flows into the Beaufort Sea about five miles west of Herschel Island.

John Franklin (later Sir) during his exploration of the Arctic coast in 1826, named this river after Admiral Sir Pulteney MALCOLM (1768-1838), on 23 July.

MOUNT MALONEY 6,375′ 61°41′N 137°44′W (115-H). 30 miles northwest of Aishihik Lake in the Nisling Range.

This was named in 1897 after J.F. MALONEY who was one of Jack Dalton's freighters between Pyramid Harbour and the Yukon River during the gold rush years.

MOUNT MANITOBA 11,150′ 60°58′N 140°48′W (115-B&C). In the Centennial Range of the St. Elias Mountains.

This was one of the 13 previously un-named and unclimbed peaks in this locality chosen to celebrate Canada's centennial year of 1967. (See Centennial Range.)

MARGARET LAKE 65°21′N 134°30′W (106–E). Near the junction of Knorr Creek and the Bonnet Plume River.

It is believed that the cabin on this lake was built by A.N. Knorr and his wife MARGARET about 1907. (See Knorr Creek.)

MARION CREEK 63°10′N 133°28′W (105–N). A tributary to Russell Creek.

In 1901 N.A.B. Armstrong named this stream after his wife. (He spelled her name Marian and sometimes, MARION). She spent 18 months here in 1905–06 with her husband and their friends George and Jessica Leith. Neither woman had ever spent any time outside England; they were completely isolated here for most of the time. (See Jessica Creek and Mount Armstrong.)

MARSH LAKE 60°25′N 134°18′W (105–D). Part of the Yukon River system, this 20-mile-long lake is about 25 miles southeast of Whitehorse.

Originally called "Mud Lake" by the first miners, this lake was renamed by Lt. F. Schwatka, US Army, in 1883 after Professor Othniel Charles MARSH (1831–1899), palaeontologist at Yale University from 1866 to 99. He was a founder and first president of the National Academy of Sciences for 12 years and was the Chief of Vertebrate Palaeontology for the USGS from 1881 to 99. A wealthy man, he served Yale with no salary and left his entire estate to the university after his death.

This is one of Schwatka's names that Dawson did not consider changing.

MARSHALL CREEK 60°48′N 137°20′W (115–A). A tributary to the Dezeadash River from the north.

Antoine and Mac Cyr were on their way to the newly found Ruby Creek goldfield in the Shakwak valley when they stopped to examine this stream. On 6 August they found enough gold to stake a Discovery claim. It is thought that they named the creek after one of their party.

MOUNT MARTHA BLACK 60°40′N 137°37′W (115–A). In the Auriol Range about seven miles south of Haines Junction.

This was named about 1945 by H.S. Bostock, GSC, for Martha Munger

BLACK, wife of George Black, MP and one-time Commissioner of the Yukon Territory. When her husband was forced to retire from politics for a period, due to ill health, Martha Black ran for Parliament and was elected. She was a pioneer Klondiker, who came to the Yukon in 1898, and was a leading personality there for the rest of her life. She was probably the most outstanding woman in the history of the Yukon.

MOUNT MARTIN 4,460' 60°08'N 124°09'W (95-C). In the extreme southeast corner of the territory, just west of the Labiche River.

In 1963 this mountain was given the name of Major Ivan Harold MARTIN, MID. He was born at Sterling, Ontario on 2 August, 1912 and enlisted in the Canadian army at Chatham, Ontario on 7 December, 1949. He served in Canada, Great Britain and Northwest Europe and died of wounds sustained in action on 21 August, 1944.

MASCOT CREEK 62°47'N 138°25'W (115-J&K). A tributary to the Yukon River, six miles below the Selwyn River.

Gold was found on this stream in the late fall of 1900 by two French-Canadian prospectors, Archill Massicotte and Albert Leboeuf. When they came to Dawson on 16 February, 1901, and recorded their claims it was a Monday. The news got out and the whole creek was staked from end to end by Tuesday night. Massicotte's name was shortened by the recorder.

MASON HILL 67°19'N 137°40'W (116-P). West of Lapierre House.

This was named in 1973 after the brothers, Willoughby and Reuben MASON. (See Mason Lake.)

MASON LAKE 66°24'N 138°59'W (116-J&K). Near the junction of the Fishing and Miners Rivers.

This was named by Professor Otto W. Geist of the University of Alaska on 27 November, 1958, after the MASON brothers, Willoughby "Bill" and Reuben. The Masons trapped and prospected in this general area from 1900 to the 1930's.

Due to a vague location the name was given to the central of the three small lakes shown. The creek beside the lakes and a few hundred yards to the south is probably Mason Creek.

MASON LANDING 61°26'N 134°39'W (105-E). On the Teslin River about 20 miles south of Hootalinqua.

This now-abandoned settlement was a steamboat landing and stopping place for miners on their way to and from the Livingstone Creek goldfields from 1901 to 14. A wagon road led from here to Livingstone.

MOUNT MATHESON 7,515′ 60°02′N 134°43′W (105-D). One and one half miles south of Montana Mountain.

This peak is the highest point in the Conrad district. It was named by D.D. Cairnes, GSC, in 1907 after H. MATHESON, who was his assistant and topographer in the area in 1907–08.

MATSON CREEK 63°43′N 140°12′W (115-O&N). A tributary to the Sixtymile River.

John MATSON, a Swedish prospector, came into the Yukon in 1898. Discovering gold on this creek in the early years, he remained to mine it until he died and was buried on the claim in 1947.

Matson's one claim to fame was his marriage on 14 July, 1933, to "Klondike Kate" Rockwell, a dance-hall entertainer in Dawson in 1898–99 and self-styled "Queen of the Klondike".

The *Whitehorse Star* of 19 January, 1912, stated "The Gold Commissioner has changed the name of the South Fork of the Sixtymile River on which the discovery was made, to Matson Creek, after John Matson, who first prospected it and discovered gold on it fourteen years ago."

MAUNOIR BUTTE 61°31′N 135°04′W (105-E). A prominent hill on the east bank of the Yukon (Thirty Mile River), about ten miles below Lake Laberge.

This landmark was named in 1883 by Lt. F. Schwatka, US Army, after M. Charles MAUNOIR, secretary of the Geographical Society of France.

MAY CREEK 61°16′N 134°11′W (105-E). A tributary to the South Big Salmon River in the Livingstone area.

This is a long-known local name after Samuel MAY who prospected this area for many years after 1903.

MAYO 63°35′N 135°54′W (105-M).

This village at the mouth of the Mayo River was started in the winter of 1902–03 after gold was discovered on Duncan, Minto and Hyatt Creeks. As steamboats could navigate the Stewart from the Yukon, this was a close supply point for the miners. It grew fast enough to have the townsite surveyed in March 1903. The Keno Hill silver mines increased the traffic by their large ore shipments and the town was an important centre for many years. A road was opened in 1949 to connect the town with the Dawson road. In a few years the riverboats stopped and the population dwindled to its present small size.

It was also called Mayo Landing.

MAYO LAKE 63°43′N 135°04′W (105-M). The largest lake in the Mayo District.

Alexander MacDonald of New Brunswick was the first man to prospect the Mayo region. In 1887 he found this lake and named it after Captain Alfred S. MAYO, a partner of Harper and McQuesten. Together with Frederick Hart, these men were the first to realize the prospecting potential of the upper Yukon. The first three utilized trading as a means to support themselves while prospecting and, because the region was rich in fur, they prospered. They built every trading post from Rampart (Alaska) to Fort Selkirk. McQuesten and Harper were the traders; Mayo captained the small steamboat *New Racket* which they had bought from Ed Scheiffelin in 1883.

Mayo was born in Maine and in his younger days had been a circus acrobat. He often astounded the natives with displays of his agility. Marrying a native woman, he alone of all the partners spent the rest of his life in the country, dying at Rampart on 17 July, 1924.

MacDonald, the first explorer of this country, left his name nowhere. A solitary traveller, he was the first man to ascend the Beaver (McQuesten) River and enter the watersheds of the Wind and Peel Rivers from the south. He was found dead of natural causes in his lone camp on the banks of the Yukon in 1894.

MAYO RIVER 63°36′N 135°57′W (105-M). A tributary of the Stewart River.

This was named by William Ogilvie, DLS, after talking to Alex MacDonald in 1887. He also knew Alfred MAYO well as he was in charge of the trading post at the mouth of the Stewart at the time.

MEANDER CREEK (See Miller Creek.)

MEISTER RIVER 60°19′N 129°28′W (105-A). A tributary to the upper Liard River from the west.

This stream was known in the 1880's and later as the "Rondeau" River. After 1898 the name was forgotten and in 1947 it was renamed. The name of Pte. L. MEISTER, MM, was perpetuated here. He was from Nova Scotia and was killed in action during the Second World War.

MELOY CREEK 62°42′N 138°48′W (115-J&K). Flows into Casino Creek in the Dawson Range.

In 1970, C.D.N. "Red" Taylor, P. Eng. named this creek after Jack MELOY, a Yukon prospector for nearly 50 years and discoverer, among other things, of the porphyry-copper deposits in the Dawson Range. He was born in 1894 in the state of Washington and lived in Dawson most of his life.

MENDENHALL RIVER 60°45′N 136°03′W (115-A). A tributary to the Takhini River.

This stream was probably named in 1890 by E.J. Glave, the English explorer and member of the Frank Leslie Illustrated Newspaper Expedition. The name honours Professor Thomas Corwin MENDENHALL, (1841–1924) Superintendent of the USC&GS.

MERRICE CREEK 62°23′N 136°35′W (115-I). A tributary to the Yukon River below Yukon Crossing.

This creek was named in 1898 after Homer MERRICE, who first discovered gold on the stream. In 1908 the name was changed, by mistake, to "Merritt Creek" which it remained for a number of years until corrected by the Geographical Board.

MERRITT CREEK (See Merrice Creek.)

MICHELLE CREEK 64°59′N 137°09′W (116-A). A tributary of the Hart River.

This was named on 29 June, 1956, by Forest Warden C.J. Shattuck, after a half-breed Indian who had trapped and prospected on this creek about 1910. Not much is known about him.

MOUNT MICHIE 5,830′ 60°30′N 134°06′W (105-D). About eight miles east of Marsh Lake.

Lt. F. Schwatka, US Army, named this hill in 1883 during his excursion down the Yukon, after one of his teachers, Professor MICHIE of West Point.

Michie Creek, named many years later, flows from the mountain to the M'Clintock River.

MICKEY CREEK 64°24'N 140°37'W (116–B&C). Flows into the Fortymile River, just above its mouth.

This was named in late 1886 by or after "MICKEY" O'Brien who was said to be one of the first discoverers of gold on the upper Fortymile River that year, supposedly on Franklin Bar. He is credited by others with finding O'Brien Creek on the Alaska side, the first find of coarse gold in that region.

MIDNIGHT DOME 64°04'N 139°24'W (116–B). The mountain behind Dawson.

From the earliest days this was called "Moosehide Hill" or Dome and sometimes "Mooseskin Mountain," from the peculiar shape and colour of a rock slide on the slope facing the Yukon River. About 1900 the custom began of picnicking on the summit on the evening and night of 21 June to observe the sun barely setting before it arose again. The event became a yearly custom and people began to call the hill "The Midnight Dome".

MILES CANYON 60°40'N 135°02'W (105–D). On the Yukon River two miles south of Whitehorse.

First called the "Grand Canyon" by the early miners, this constriction was renamed by Lt. F. Schwatka, US Army, after his superior officer, Brigadier General Nelson A. MILES, Commander of the Department of the Columbia (which included Alaska) of the US Army, on 1 July, 1883.

Although Miles Canyon was most awesome in appearance, and was approached with apprehension by miners and stampeders, it was the Whitehorse Rapids immediately below which were the more dangerous. Such records as there are show only a dozen deaths by drowning up to 1896 and about the same in the following three years. Most of these were in the rapids.

John McKenzie in 1883 is the first man known to have run a boat through Miles Canyon and the Whitehorse Rapids. The narrowness of the channel and the velocity of the current together with the whirlpool halfway through the canyon gave a real spice of danger which made this the highlight of the whole journey to the stampeders.

The canyon and rapids were the one major obstruction to navigation on the whole Yukon River, from the head of Lake Bennett to the Bering Sea. Without them, the largest steamboats could have run freely from Carcross to St. Michaels. The WP&YR would have ended at Carcross, making it the main freight terminal of the region and obviously making the city of Whitehorse unnecessary.

Several small to medium riverboats ran the canyon and rapids both ways; in July 1907 Fred R. Alley took a raft 132 feet long through safely.

Since the building of the power dam below, the rapids have disappeared and Miles Canyon can be navigated in safety by the smallest craft.

MILES CREEK 61°57′N 140°33′W (115-G&F). A tributary of the White River.

Frank R. MILES came into the Yukon in 1898. In 1900 he found native copper on this stream and gave it his name. He died in Kalispell, Montana, in 1912. The ridge along the north side of the creek was given this name many years later.

MOUNT MILLEN 67°28′N 136°25′W (116-P). Northeast of Lapierre House.

Constable Edgar "Spike" MILLEN RCMP, was born in Belfast, Ireland in 1901 and joined the force in 1920, volunteering for northern service. He was stationed at Aklavik and in the Mackenzie valley, where he was well liked.

He was killed in a gun battle with Albert Johnson, the "Mad Trapper of Rat River" on 30 January, 1932, during the greatest man-hunt in the history of the northwest. This mountain was named for him in 1973.

MILLER CREEK 61°22′N 134°40′W (105-E). A tributary to the Teslin River below Mason's Landing.

Henry "Hank" Summers came from California to the Yukon country in 1885, one of the first miners here. He mined on the Stewart, the Fortymile and the Sixtymile, and made a fortune in the Klondike.

In 1913 he found gold on this creek and when he recorded his claim he named the stream, "Meander Creek". The Mining Recorder, who was Assistant Gold Commissioner R.C. MILLER, changed it to his own name.

Summers died in Whitehorse on 6 December that year.

MILLER CREEK 63°57′N 135°21′W (105-M). Flows from Galena Hill to Cristal Creek.

In 1924–25 Oscar MILLER found silver-lead ore at the head of this stream, on Galena Hill and staked the Dragon claim.

MILLER CREEK 63°59'N 140°48'W (115-N). Tributary to the Sixty-mile River.

Oliver C. "Three Fingered Jack" MILLER came into the Yukon in 1883 among the very first prospectors. He travelled far and wide and was the first, or among the first, in three of the most important goldfields to be found here. In late 1891 he found the first payable gold on this creek, which has, together with nearby creeks, produced for many years. He was also among the first to find the Birch Creek goldfields (in Alaska) in 1893, which established Circle City. In the Minook District another creek was given his name and he was elected the first Mining Recorder there. Like many since, he seemed more interested in looking for than in mining the gold he found. He was noted for his long and arduous journeys in the Yukon and Alaska.

MOUNT MILLER 4,047' 62°11'N 136°25'W (115-I). Ten miles above Carmacks.

This was named in 1911 for the pioneer coal miner and prospector, Captain Charles E. MILLER, who first developed and mined the coal deposits near Carmacks. Miller, who was a coal miner from Mauchunk, Pennsylvania, came to the Klondike in 1897. Although G.W. Carmack of Bonanza fame had first found coal here about 1893, Miller was the first to locate on the deposits and mine them. (Carmack, with Arthur Harper as a silent partner, had made limited attempts to mine coal at Five Finger Rapids about 1893–95 but without success.)

Between 1897 and 1900 Miller built and operated the riverboats *Clara*, *Reindeer*, and *Eldorado* as well as building and running the Yukon Saw-mill at Dawson City.

He located and mined the Five Fingers Mine in 1900 and the Tantalus Mine in 1903 and in two years produced 40,000 tons of coal for the river-boats. In 1905 he located the Tantulus Butte Coal Mine and estimated 5,000,000 tons of coal reserves. This is the mine which is now being worked for the Anvil Mining Corporation at Faro.

MILLER'S RIDGE 5,021' 62°06'N 136°30'W (115-I). About 15 miles west of Carmacks.

In 1960 H.S. Bostock, GSC, and Col. Cyril H. Smith, RCE, named this ridge after the late W.H. MILLER, a former Director of the Surveys and Mapping Branch of the Department of Mines and Technical Surveys.

Miller organized and started the topographical mapping of Canada by Canadians, a task formerly performed by the US Army Engineers. It was on this ridge that he laid out his baseline for the mapping of the Carmacks and Laberge areas.

MILLHAVEN BAY 60°06′N 134°55′W (105–D). The bay on the north shore of Lake Bennett, ten miles west of Carcross.

Here, in the winter and spring of 1897–98, Otto H. Partridge, general manager of the Bennett Lake and Klondyke Navigation Company, erected a sawmill and shipyard on the west side of the bay. They built the river-boats *Ora*, *Flora* and *Nora*. These were all taken through Miles Canyon and the Whitehorse Rapids and worked the Whitehorse-Dawson run until 1903. The mill continued to turn out timbers and railroad ties for the WP&YR as well as lumber to build Whitehorse.

MILLS CREEK 63°26′N 138°49′W (115–O&N). A tributary to Black-hills Creek from the west, seven miles from the mouth.

Joseph Victor MILLS found placer gold here and staked the Discovery claim on 26 January, 1907.

MOUNT MILTON 62°12′N 136°15′W (115–I). Five miles north of Tantalus Butte.

This small hill was named in 1968, probably by H.S. Bostock, GSC, after George H. MILTON, who organized and was general manager of the Five Fingers Coal Company, which owned all the coal deposits known in the district.

MINERS RANGE 61°09′N 135°41′W (105–E). The range of hills ten miles west of and parallel to, Lake Laberge.

Dr. G.M. Dawson, GSC; on his 1887 journey back to the coast, named these hills after the miners in the Yukon whom he admired and who aided him in his work.

MINT GULCH 63°56′N 138°53′W (115–O). A short, half-mile-long stream flowing into the south side of Hunker Creek.

Gold was discovered here, Discovery claim staked and the stream named on 7 August, 1897, by B.F. Lovett.

This gulch is remarkable because of the enormous number of fossil bison and mastodon bones found in the gravels of its bed. The numbers were so great as to suggest that whole herds of these animals had perished here in some prehistoric disaster.

MINTO 62°35′N 136°52′W (115-I). On the east bank of the Yukon River, 15 miles southwest of Pelly Crossing.

Originally an Indian settlement called "Kitl-ah-gon", meaning "The Place Between The High Hills", this village, now almost totally destroyed, was a riverboat stop and a roadhouse on the Whitehorse-Dawson stage road for many years.

Lord MINTO, when Governor General of Canada, visited the Yukon with Lady Minto in 1900 and it was in his honour that the settlement was given its name.

MINTO CREEK 63°43′N 135°55′W (105-M). Empties Minto Lake into Mayo River.

Many discoveries of gold were made in this general area after the finding of rich gold on Duncan Creek. J.G. Scrivener and P.F. Haggart were two of the most active prospectors of the time. This was one of the gold-bearing streams they found, staking the Discovery claim on 19 May, 1903. They named the creek after Lord MINTO, Governor General of Canada, who had visited Dawson in 1900. (See Haggart, Highet and Paradise Creeks.)

MINTON CREEK 63°47′N 136°21′W (115-P). Tributary to Johnson Creek.

This was named in 1957 by H.S. Bostock, GSC, after Peter MINTON who relocated No. 9 Below on 21 May, 1916, and remained here working the claim for many years. The original discovery of gold had been made by Mike Sed in February 1915.

MIRROR CREEK 62°28′N 140°54′W (115-J&K). Flows into the Snag River near mile 1206 on the Alaska Highway.

This creek got its name in 1898 from W.J. Peters and A.H. Brooks of the USGS because of its exceptionally clear water, which is unusual for the region.

MIST LAKE 63°12′N 134°21′W (105-M). Southwest of Big Kalzas Lake.

In 1939, H.S. Bostock, GSC, and his party were on pack horses crossing the country to this location. The topographer had missed this lake when he was mapping and the geological crew had to make a long trip around the lake in a snow storm to get to their camp site. When they suggested the name "Missed Lake", the topographer did not appreciate the irony and compromised on the present name.

MOUNT MOFFAT   61°12′N 140°02′W (115-F). In the Icefield Ranges of the St. Elias Mountains.

This undistinguished peak was named in 1970 by the Alpine Club of Canada after Thomas Black MOFFAT (1870-1939), an engraver and past president (1928-30) of the group (which seems to have named everything in the St. Elias Range that any member has ever seen).

MONEY CREEK   61°24′N 129°36′W (105-H). Flowing into the West Arm of Frances Lake.

This was noted by Dr. G.M. Dawson, GSC, in 1887 as "Illes Brook" and by others as "Il-es-too-a", meaning "Salt Lick". These names were forgotten in time and about 1930 Anton MONEY, an English prospector, found gold on the stream and worked it. The name was given by local people at the time.

One of the few men living who have features in the Yukon bearing their names, Money was born in Albury, Surrey, England on 16 September, 1900. Educated at Cranleigh he served for two years in the British forces in the First World War and then tutored privately as a mining engineer. He engaged with the HBC in 1923 and was sent to their post at Telegraph Creek on the Stikine River. He soon left their employ and started his life of successful prospecting. From 1929 to 46 most of his work was in the Frances Lake region. He was most successful in mining placer gold in "Half Moon Canyon" in the Finlayson River. He recently published an interesting account of his experiences entitled *This Was The North*.

MONITOR CREEK   63°18′N 138°44′W (115-O&N). A tributary of Black Hills Creek.

This was named in July 1898 by a group of Scandinavians from Minnesota who called themselves the "MONITOR Gold Mining and Trading Company". They staked claims here and named the stream but found no payable gold. (See Blueberry Creek.)

MOUNT MONSON   62°08′N 136°24′W (115-I). Six miles northwest of Carmacks.

This was named in April 1911 after Constable MONSON of the NWMP, a long-time Yukoner.

MONSTER RIVER   64°59′N 140°56′W (116-B&C). A tributary of the Tatonduc River.

Although not an official name, this stream has been known by this name locally since 1952, instead of the previous Sheep Creek. Intending to haul supplies northward for the construction of the Distant Early Warning (DEW) Line from Eagle, Alaska, the contractors bought a Letourneau "Snow-Freighter". This immense machine was a 24-wheeled vehicle with five trailer units, capable of hauling 125 tons of freight across country. The machine caught fire on the upper reaches of the river and was abandoned. However, the company managed to salvage it about three years later. In the interval, passing trappers and prospectors had renamed the river after the "MONSTER" lying at its headwaters.

MONTANA CREEK 63°41′N 138°58′W (115-O&N). A tributary to the Indian River.

There was a stampede to this creek in January 1897. The original stakers were working for Captain John Jerome Healy, an old Indian fighter, Montana law officer and manager of the NAT&TC, of Fort Cudahy. Because Captain Healy and most of his men were from MONTANA, they were called "The Montana Boys", and so the creek got its name.

MONTE CRISTO GULCH 63°59′N 139°22′W (115-O&N). A tributary to Bonanza Creek, one half-mile above Boulder Creek.

P.H. Hebb and Edward Monahan had worked at the small, rich MONTE CRISTO Gold Mine west of Everett, Washington, before they came to the Klondike. Too late to stake claims on the main streams they turned to this small feeder. Here they found good gold showings and staked their first claims on 6 July, 1897.

The hill above the gulch was much richer in gold, as the White Channel gravels lay there.

Hebb later prospected many parts of the Yukon and gained the nickname "The Diamond King". (See Dixie Creek.)

MONTREAL CREEK 63°47′N 139°25′W (115-O&N). A tributary to the Indian River.

Robert Picotte (whose father staked and mined No. 17 on Eldorado Creek) found the first gold here and staked the Discovery claim on 3 July, 1901. He named it after his home town in Québec.

MONUMENT ISLAND 60°01′N 134°54′W (105-D). A small island on the east side of Bennett Lake, near the BC border.

Inspector Constantine and Staff Sergeant Charles Brown of the NWMP, the first of the force to enter the Yukon, are said to have built their boat here in 1894. Stories of the time claim that when the first rough survey of the Yukon-BC boundary was made, a temporary boundary marker, or monument, was set on this little island.

MOONEY CREEK   60°10'N 125°03'W (95-C). A tributary to Larsen Creek.

In 1963 this creek was chosen to commemorate the name of Honorary Captain Thomas Edmund MOONEY, MID. He was born on 21 January, 1906, at Westport, Ontario, and was appointed to the Canadian army as a chaplain on 10 January, 1942. He served in Canada, Great Britain and northwest Europe and was killed in action on 14 September, 1944.

MOOSEHORN RANGE   63°06'N 140°58'W (115-O&N). A 14-mile-long ridge extending across the Yukon-Alaska border, south of the Ladue River.

This ridge was originally named "Moosehorn Mountain" by A.H. Brooks and W.J. Peters, USGS, while they were on their expedition up the White River to the Tanana in 1898.

MORLEY RIVER   60°06'N 132°30'W (105-C). Flows into the southeast corner of Teslin Lake.

In the spring of 1897 Arthur St. Cyr, DLS, of the Department of the Interior was given the task of finding and surveying a feasible wagon road or railway route from Telegraph Creek, BC, on the Stikine River, to the head of Teslin Lake. He was also placed in charge of other surveyors engaged in defining the boundary between the Yukon Territory and British Columbia. His assistant on the Telegraph Creek-Lake Teslin survey was W. MORLEY Ogilvie, DLS, the son of William Ogilvie, DLS.

They quickly found and surveyed a trail to the foot of Teslin Lake. St. Cyr then set out for Tagish Lake and Bennett to oversee the boundary survey. Morley Ogilvie was instructed to survey the east shore of Teslin Lake and continue down the Teslin River to its junction with the Yukon (Lewes) River. Ogilvie carried out this task successfully and St. Cyr afterward named this river, near his starting point, after him.

Ogilvie went on to spend some years as a government surveyor in and around Dawson. By 1908 he was associated with his father as field superintendent of the Yukon Basin Gold Dredging Co. on the Stewart River. His father was the president of the company.

The names Morley Bay, Lake and Mount were added in the 1930 to 50's. The settlement, lodge, restaurant and gasoline station were started about 1943-44 by Clyde Wann, one of the first bush pilots in the Yukon. (See Mount Wann.)

MORRIS LAKE   60°27'N 131°40'W (105-B). At the head of Morley River.

Jake MORRIS, an Indian trapper, had his cabin on this lake before 1900 and for many years after.

MORRISON   CREEK   63°50'N 136°06'W (115-P).   A   tributary   to Seattle Creek.

This was named in the early 1900's by Hector MORRISON. Born in Zorra, Ontario, in 1856, he came to the Yukon in 1894. In 1911 he found a rich deposit of silver-lead ore in Gambler's Gulch on Keno Hill. He later sold his holdings to Keno Mines and retired to Vancouver, BC, where he died in 1930.

MOUNT   MORRISON   64°44'N 140°56'W (116-B&C).   Two   miles north of the Yukon River, just east of the Alaska border.

This was called Morison Peak by William Ogilvie, DLS, in 1887 after a member of his boundary survey party. William T. MORISON of Ormiston, Québec, worked for Ogilvie for five or six years in the Yukon and BC, all on exploratory surveys. After leaving Ogilvie's employ he entered theological school and became a Presbyterian minister, serving for many years in Montréal. He died in May 1951, aged 87. The name was later misspelled.

MOSES HILL   67°19'N 136°48'W (116-P). South of Rat River.

This hill was named in 1973 after John MOSES. He was the Indian special constable who drove dog teams for the RCMP in their hunt for Albert Johnson, the "Mad Trapper", in 1932. (See Mount Sittichinli.)

MOSQUITO   GULCH   63°58'N 139°21'W (116-B&C).   Flows   into Bonanza Creek, opposite Boulder Creek.

A Discovery claim was staked here on 1 September, 1897 by L.W. Steele. It had been staked earlier but the claim had been abandoned and never worked.

MOUNTAIN INDIAN RIVER   (See Firth River.)

MUNROE LAKE 60°02'N 135°01'W (105–D). South of the West Arm of Lake Bennett.

Alexander MUNROE was the best axeman on Arthur St. Cyr's boundary survey crew in 1899–1900. He broke his leg near here and St. Cyr named this lake after him in 1901. He named the peak on the east side of the lake Munroe Peak (6,735') at the same time.

MURRAY CREEK 62°09'N 136°22'W (115–I). A tributary to the Yukon River from the west.

Although named before the turn of the century, this stream has been known locally for many years as "Meyer's Creek". Myers was a wood-cutter who provided fuel for the WP&YR riverboats for many years. His cabin is at the mouth of the stream. He came into the country from Cordova, Alaska, during the Chisana rush of 1913.

The name MURRAY probably came from the first man to stake a claim on the creek; he found no gold and quickly left.

MURRAY CREEK 63°46'N 133°22'W (105–N). A tributary to the Stewart River above Lansing.

"Mike" MURRAY prospected this area and the Rogue River country for many years in the early 1900's. For a number of those years he was the only white man in the region, with the exception of Frank Braine and Percy Nash, the traders at Lansing.

MURRAY CREEK 61°36'N 139°40'W (115–G&F). A tributary to the Donjek River.

This was named about 1903–04 after T.T. MURRAY who was a long-time prospector in the area and who worked on this creek.

MOUNT MURRAY 7,093' 60°53'N 128°49'W (105–A). 20 miles northeast of Simpson Lake, in the Logan Mountains.

The old name was "Tent Peak", given by Dr. G.M. Dawson, GSC, in 1887 because of its shape. The name was regarded as redundant by the Geographical Board in 1949. They then changed it to the name of Alexander MURRAY (1810–1884), assistant to Sir William E. Logan, the first director of the Geological and Natural History Survey of Canada.

MUSH CREEK 60°18'N 137°29'W (115–A). Flows into Mush Lake.

The discovery of coarse gold in the summer of 1902 by M.I. Christner led to a staking rush in this area and the naming of this and other nearby streams. Christner had been prospecting this area since early 1900.

MUSSELL GLACIER 60°43'N 140°54'W (115-C). A branch of the Ogilvie Glacier in the St. Elias Range.

This was named in 1966 after H.S. MUSSELL, DLS, who was in charge of the International Boundary Survey party for Canada 1910 to 12.

MOUNT MYE 6,763' 62°20'N 133°08'W (105-K). 12 miles northeast of Faro.

J.R. Johnson, GSC, named this peak in 1935 after his fiancée Myrtle "MYE" Hay. He used her nickname as it resembled that of an old trapper and prospector in the area, years before.

NADALEEN RIVER 63°58'N 133°39'W (105-N). A major tributary to the Stewart River.

In 1885 this stream was named by the first miners to see it, Thomas Boswell and perhaps his brother George, who were from Peterborough, Ontario. About 1905, perhaps because the name had been forgotten or because there was another Boswell River in the Big Salmon country, the name NADALEEN was adopted. It is supposedly a local Indian name. (See Boswell River.)

NAHONI MOUNTAINS 65°30'N 139°30'W (116-G&F). At the headwaters of the Porcupine River.

In April 1888 William Ogilvie, DLS, named these mountains because he believed them to be the home of the NAHONI (Nahanni) Indians.

NANSEN CREEK 61°59'N 137°12'W (115-H). A tributary of the Nisling River.

Captain Henry Seymour Back and his party discovered gold on this creek in July 1899 but did not work it. He returned to the region with a large prospecting party in 1907. Re-examining the creek they found prospects worth working and the Discovery claim was staked by his son, Frank H. Back and Tom E. Bee on 13 June, 1910.

Captain Back named the stream in honour of the famous Norwegian Arctic explorer, Fridtjof NANSEN. (See Mount Nansen.)

MOUNT NANSEN 5,593' 62°06'N 137°18'W (115-I). At the headwaters of Nansen Creek.

Mount Nansen overlooks a richly mineralized area which was discovered by Captain Henry Seymour Back, an outstanding pioneer. He gained his rank in the American Civil War and, moving west, became an Army scout and Indian fighter, later a trader and prospector. He came to the Klondike in 1897 where he was successful. This area came to his attention in 1899. Attracted by stories of richer finds he went on to Alaska. In 1907 he returned with a party of seven or eight men, including his son Frank and prospected the area intensively until about 1920. He was then in his 80's. He and his men found gold and named many of the streams in this area; this mountain is named after Fridtjof NANSEN, the Norwegian explorer.

His son, Frank H. Back, remained in the country after his father died. He continued prospecting and in 1917, owned and operated a black fox fur farm at Carmacks. (See Back, Hobo, Discovery and Seymour Creeks.)

NARCHILLA BROOK 61°52′N 129°45′W (105-H). Flows into the foot of McPherson Lake.

Warburton Pike, the English sportsman and explorer, named this stream in 1893 after his guide and companion, a Frances Lake Indian.

NARES LAKE 60°10′N 134°39′W (105-D). A small lake joining Bennett and Tagish Lakes.

Called "Moose Lake" by the early miners, this lake was renamed by Lt. F. Schwatka, US Army, in 1883, after Vice Admiral Sir George Strong NARES, RN, a famous English Arctic explorer. The mountain immediately to the northeast of the lake was later also named for Nares.

NASH CREEK 64°39′N 134°37′W (106-D). A tributary to the Wind River.

Percival NASH, prospector and trader in this area, was a partner of Frank Braine when they operated the trading post at Lansing on the Stewart River in the early 1900's.

NATAZHAT GLACIER 61°34′N 140°55′W (115-G&F). A small glacier on the northwest of the St. Elias Range.

This was reported in 1912 by Thomas Riggs, Jr., of the US International Boundary Survey. The Indian name was recorded by C.W. Hayes, USGS, in 1890 but no translation was given.

NATION RIVER 65°31′N 141°00′W (116-G&F). A tributary to the Yukon River in Alaska.

This was first mapped in 1883 by Lt. F. Schwatka, US Army, who called it "Tahkandik". J.E. Spurr, USGS, in 1896 reported "Tahkandit". At the same time F.C. Schrader, USGS, noted that the early miners had already named it the "Nation River". The stream had some prominence in 1897–98 because of a coal seam found near its mouth.

NELSON CREEK 63°39'N 134°48'W (115-M). A tributary of Mayo Lake at the east end.

Rich placer gold was found here in 1916 by two prospectors known only as "Big Steve" and "Little Steve". One of them was surnamed NELSON.

NESHAM GLACIER 61°23'N 140°50'W (115-F). A branch of the huge Klutlan Glacier.

In 1916 this name was given after E.W. NESHAM, DLS, a British member of the International Boundary Survey party of 1915.

NESKATEHEEN LAKE 60°10'N 137°04'W (115-A). Three miles north of Dalton Post.

It was near here that the old Indian village of the same name was occupied long before any white man recorded it. It was an important meeting place where the coast tribes came to trade with the interior Indians.

The first white men known to have visited the lake and village were E.J. Glave and Jack Dalton of the Frank Leslie Illustrated Newspaper Expedition in 1891. Dalton later established his headquarters a short distance below here. Klondikers called the place "Neskatahin" and J.J. McArthur, DLS, while travelling the Dalton Trail, called it "Weskatahin". No one gave a translation. (See Weskatahin.)

MOUNT NEVIN 60°00'N 136°10'W (115-A). Marks the boundary between the Yukon and British Columbia.

James NEVIN Wallace, DLS (1870–1941), surveyed this mountain in 1908. It was the highest peak he had crossed in two survey seasons and he had personally made more ascents than any other boundary surveyor up to that time. He was engaged in such surveys from 1907 to 24.

NEWBAUER CREEK 62°02'N 137°12'W (115-I). A small tributary of Nansen Creek.

A long-known local name after the prospector who worked here and in the general area from about 1910–15, it was made official in 1968.

MOUNT NEW BRUNSWICK 11,115' 60°55'N 140°38'W (115-B-&C). In the Centennial Range of the St. Elias Mountains.

This mountain was named to celebrate Canada's Centennial Year. (See Centennial Range.)

MOUNT NEWFOUNDLAND 12,040' 60°57'N 140°33'W (115-B&C). In the Centennial Range of the St. Elias Mountains.

This mountain was named in 1967 to celebrate Canada's Centennial Year. (See Centennial Range.)

MOUNT NEWTON 13,811' 60°19'N 140°53'W (115-B&C). In the southwest corner of the St. Elias Range.

Professor I.C. Russell named this mountain when he mapped it with the National Geographic Society and USGS Expedition in 1890, after Professor Henry NEWTON of the Columbia School of Mines and the USGS.

Until 1964 this was the highest unclimbed peak in North America. In that year it was climbed by the Blanchard-Eichorn party.

NEW ZEALAND CREEK (See Printers Creek.)

NIDDERY LAKE 63°18'N 131°20'W (105-O). A small lake south of the Hess River.

Norman NIDDERY was a trapper and prospector in this area for many years. In 1946 Bernard J. Woodruff of the Geodetic Survey of Canada proposed this name in gratitude for Niddery's help and information about the region. (See Fido Creek.)

NIGGERHEAD LAKES (See Enger Lakes.)

NIGGERHEAD MOUNTAIN (See Eikland Mountain.)

NIGGER JIM'S GULCH 63°55'N 139°15'W (115-O&N). A tributary to Bonanza Creek, two miles above Grand Forks.

James "Nigger Jim" Daugherty was from Virginia and gained his nickname from his accent. He was a famous figure in the Klondike and many stories were written about him. He was especially noted as a stampeder. He discovered gold on and staked this little stream on 4 December, 1897.

NISUTLIN RIVER   60°14'N   132°34'W   (105-C). The major tributary to Teslin Lake from the northeast.

This name was known from the earliest times. It is a Tlinkit Indian word meaning "Quiet Water" and was probably first applied to the large and beautiful Nisutlin Bay.

NOBLE CREEK   64°10'N   139°15'W   (116-B). Tributary to Lepine Creek, ten miles northeast of Dawson.

George NOBLE, an early Yukoner, staked the first claim on this creek about 1897. His brother, who worked in the Gold Office in Dawson, was known as "Colonel Bill".

NOGOLD CREEK   63°27'N   135°05'W   (105-M). Tributary to the Stewart River at Horseshoe Slough.

This was named by miners in 1895 who found gold colours here but no payable gold.

MOUNT NOLAN   4,566'   63°59'N   140°36'W   (115-O&N). South of the Sixtymile River.

This was called "Dog Tooth Mountain" by the early miners on the Sixtymile creeks in the 1890's. The name was changed by the GSC in 1920. They named it after the manager of the NAT&TC at the time.

NORDENSKIOLD RIVER   62°06'N   136°18'W   (115-I). Flows into the Yukon River at Carmacks.

This was called "Thuch-en-Dituh" meaning "Meeting Place" by the Indians who lived there. The Chilkat Indians met the interior Indians here to trade every year. The route the Chilkats used from the coast became the Dalton Trail and Carmacks was one of its terminals.

In 1883 Lt. F. Schwatka, US Army, named this river after Baron Nils Adolf Erik NORDENSKIOLD, 1832–1901, the famous Swedish Arctic explorer and geologist. Nordenskiold made the first passage northeast of the European and Asian continent in his ship, the *Vega*, in 1878–79.

NORTH CROOKED CREEK   63°16'N   136°30'W   (115-P). Crooked Creek flows into the Stewart at Stewart Crossing.

Named by the Geographical Board in 1941, the only claim to distinction held by this stream is that neither of the local names was officially adopted. "Hardrock" MacDonald and "Hotstove" Douglas lived and worked here and no one called the creek Crooked. Both of these old-timers were alive when it was proposed to make the name(s) official. (See Mount MacDonald.)

NORTHERN LAKE   61°45'N 133°45'W (105–F). Between the Big Salmon and Salmon Rivers.

Although this appears to be a descriptive name, in fact it is the name of a brave Canadian, J-14566 Flight Lt. Edward NORTHERN, DFC, who was born 7 December, 1917, in Sheffield, England and enlisted in the RCAF at Toronto, Ontario, on 10 September, 1941. He was missing on air operations on 1 May, 1944, and was presumed killed in action.

MOUNT NORTHWEST   10,550'   60°59'N 140°58'W (115–B&C). In the Centennial Range of the St. Elias Mountains.

This was named in 1967 after the NORTHWEST Territories to celebrate Canada's Centennial Year. (See Centennial Range.)

MOUNT NOVA SCOTIA   10,800'   60°56'N 140°29'W (115–B&C). In the Centennial Range of the St. Elias Mountains.

This was named during Canada's Centennial Year of 1967. (See Centennial Range.)

NUTZOTIN MOUNTAINS 62°00'N 140°45'W (115–J&K). Straddling the Yukon-Alaska boundary in the north Kluane district.

In 1898 W.J. Peters and A.H. Brooks, USGS, first mapped this area and named these mountains after the NUTZOTIN Indians of the region. A.H. Brooks later became Alaska's foremost geologist and Chief Alaskan Geologist of the USGS. The huge Brooks Range in northern Alaska was named for him.

O'BRIEN CREEK   62°38'N 140°04'W (115–J&K). A tributary of the White River, four miles above Donjek City.

This creek was named when Antoine Boulay staked the Discovery claim on 1 November, 1913. He was working for, or grubstaked by, Thomas O'BRIEN, the old Fortymiler and Klondike millionaire. Boulay found the gold on this stream when he prospected it on his way to the new gold finds in the Chisana District in Alaska. (See Brewery Creek.)

OBSERVATION MOUNTAIN   60°49'N 138°42'W (115-B&C). At the junction of Slim's River and the Kaskawulsh Glacier.

In June 1952, J.O. Wheeler, GSC, mapped this area using bearings from this hill to place other features nearby. A. Cameron Ogilvy, of Whitehorse, a student engineer assisting Wheeler at the time, carried the transit to the summit and suggested the name.

O'CONNOR RIVER   (See Kaskawulsh River.)

OGILVIE   63°34'N 139°44'W (115-O&N).

In the summer of 1894 Arthur Harper and Joseph Ladue set up a trading post on this large island in the Yukon River, opposite the mouth of the Sixtymile River. They were taking advantage of the increased activity in the Sixtymile gold fields.

At first it was called the Sixtymile Post but Harper and Ladue shortly renamed it after William OGILVIE, DLS, of the Department of the Interior, who had surveyed the Yukon-Alaska boundary line in the Fortymile district, settled the miners' disputes and was the only government official visible at the time.

Ladue built and ran the first sawmill in the Yukon at this place. It was abandoned shortly after the discovery of gold in the Klondike. (See Ogilvie Mountains.)

OGILVIE MOUNTAINS   65°21'N 138°15'W (116-G). North of Dawson and encompassing the headwaters of the Ogilvie and Porcupine Rivers.

In 1966 this range of mountains was named by the Government of Canada to honour one of Canada's outstanding men.

William OGILVIE was born in Ottawa, Upper Canada, on 7 April, 1846, the son of James Ogilvie and Margaret Halliday. He was educated in Ottawa and in 1869 was admitted to practice as a Provincial and Dominion Land Surveyor. He later became a Dominion Topographical Surveyor, passing one of the most exacting survey examinations in the world.

Between 1875 and 1898 he carried out many surveys and explorations in the Canadian west, the most notable of these being the first survey of the Yukon-Alaska boundary in the Fortymile area in 1887–88, and his initial surveys in the Klondike goldfields and the Dawson townsite in 1896. At this time he was the only representative of the Canadian government, with the exception of Insp. Constantine, in the territory and his reputation for honesty, integrity and impartiality was such that his unofficial decisions were accepted by all.

In September 1898 he was made Commissioner of the Yukon Territory, replacing Major James Walsh and in April 1901 he resigned. He was later made a Fellow of the Royal Geographical Society for his survey explorations in the Yukon.

Ogilvie, in June 1901, after his resignation, went up the Yukon in the riverboat *Susie*. Leaving Skagway, Alaska, he visited Nome on his way home and while he was there, he rescued a young lady, a Miss Richardson, from drowning. A short time later he married her at her home in Paris, Texas. She was his second wife.

Ogilvie died on 13 November, 1912, in Winnipeg, Manitoba.

OGILVIE RIVER 65°52'N 137°15'W (116-H). The north branch of the Peel River.

This river was named by the Dominion Geographer, J. Johnston, in 1888 to honour William OGILVIE'S great exploratory work.

OGILVIE VALLEY 61°25'N 135°16'W (105-E). The valley extending northwest from the foot of Lake Laberge to Coghlan Lake.

In 1887 Dr. G.M. Dawson, GSC, named this feature after William OGILVIE, DLS, of the Department of the Interior who carried the first accurate survey from the Lynn Canal into the interior of the Yukon Territory and gave the GSC its accurate base for geological mapping.

O.K. CREEK 64°02'N 139°31'W (116-B&C). Flows into the Yukon from the northeast, five miles above the town of Dawson.

Joseph Pellerin found the first gold and staked a Discovery claim here on 19 January, 1898. He renamed it "O.K.;" it had formerly been called Six Mile Creek.

OLD CROW 67°34'N 139°50'W (116-O&N). On the Porcupine River.

This settlement of Loucheaux Indians has been in existence since 1911. Their forebears had lived around old Fort Yukon, established in 1847 by Alexander Hunter Murray of the HBC, at the confluence of the Porcupine and Yukon Rivers. When the HBC was driven from American territory in 1869 the Indians, priding themselves on being "King George Men" and not

"Boston Men", moved with the company to Old Rampart House, farther up the Porcupine River and thought to be on Canadian soil. Again the post was found to be in American territory and again it was moved. The new site was called New Rampart House. In 1911 the population was devastated by an epidemic of smallpox. The survivors burned the post and moved again, this time to the junction of the Porcupine with the Crow River.

The new settlement took its name from a noted chief of the old days, "Te-Tshim-Gevtik", meaning "Walking Crow". He died in the 1870's, leaving his people a legacy of high standards and moral principles which have persisted to the present time. The settlement is in the centre of the most prolific muskrat-breeding grounds in the entire northwest, if not in all of Canada. In 1955 Father J.M. Mouchet, of the Oblate Fathers, introduced skiing to the native people and in 20 years, some of Canada's finest young cross-country skiers have developed here.

Edith Josie has for many years, as a reporter for the *Whitehorse Star*, contributed one of the most colourful newspaper columns written in Canada.

The Old Crow Mountains north of the town and the river, were all named after the same chief, "Walking Crow". The word "crow" here refers to the northern raven, as true crows are unknown this far north.

OLD DANGER CREEK   (See Danger Creek.)

OLD TRAIL CREEK   63°26'N 137°49'W (115-P). A tributary to Lake Creek.

This name was suggested by the GSC in 1949 as the old trail from Stevens Roadhouse to Stewart Crossing followed this stream.

OLD WOMAN ROCK   64°31'N 140°29'W (116-B&C). On the Yukon River, 15 miles below Fortymile.

This is an Indian name known to the early miners. Old Woman Rock is on the east side of the river and Old Man Rock is on the west side. The names are from an old Indian legend.

Lt. F. Schwatka, US Army, on his raft voyage down the Yukon in 1883, renamed these the "Rocquette Rocks" after M. Alexandre de la Rocquette of the Paris Geographical Society. The name was never accepted or used.

MOUNT OLIVER WHEELER   61°12'N 140°09'W (115-F). East of the Steele Glacier in the St. Elias Range.

In November 1970, the Alpine Club of Canada named this mountain after Sir Edward OLIVER WHEELER, KB, MC, Leg. H., RE (1890–1962), engineer and surveyor. He was president of the club from 1950 to 54.

O'NEIL'S GULCH 63°55'N 139°14'W (115-O&N). A tributary to Bonanza Creek about three miles above Grand Forks.

John King staked the first claim here and recorded it on 7 July, 1897. It had previously been staked by a prospector named O'NEIL but he did not regard it highly enough to record his claim; however, his name stuck to the creek.

MOUNT ONTARIO 12,200 60°58'N 140°44'W (115-B&C). In the Centennial Range of the St. Elias Mountains.

This mountain was named in honour of the province of ONTARIO during Canada's Centennial Year, 1967. (See Centennial Range.)

OPHIR CREEK 63°47'N 139°20'W (115-O&N). A small stream flowing into the Indian River from the north.

Alexander MacDonald, Scottish mining engineer and author, named this creek in the winter of 1897 when he found good prospects of gold on it. The name "Ophir" is that of the legendary place in Africa where the Queen of Sheba got her gold and is synonymous with the idea of untold wealth.

MacDonald (not to be confused with "Big Alex" McDonald) returned to Scotland in early 1898 and wrote some vivid and highly coloured accounts of his adventures in the Klondike, including gun fights and battles with the Indians, for various newspapers. He prospected in Africa and Australia and wrote several fictionalized accounts of his travels and adventures.

ORA GRANDE GULCH 63°53'N 139°17'W (115-O&N). A short stream entering Eldorado from the northeast, opposite Nugget Gulch.

Ransom Noblett named this gulch in Spanish for "Big Gold", on 27 September, 1897. It did not live up to its name.

ORCA COVE 69°34'N 139°15'W (117-D). On the west side of Herschel Island.

This bay was named by Lt. Commander Stockton of the USS *Thetis*, when he surveyed the coast of Herschel Island in 1889. He named it after the whaler *ORCA* which was in the bay at the time.

ORCHAY RIVER   62°08′N 132°58′W (105-K). A tributary of the Pelly River.

In June 1843 this stream was named by Robert Campbell of the HBC, during his major journey of exploration down the Pelly River. It was named after a river of the same name in his native Perthshire, Scotland.

ORTELL'S CROSSING   63°49′N 136°23′W (115-P). On the Stewart River at Johnson Creek.

Ortell's Crossing was on the trail from the Stewart River, along Johnson Creek and down Highet Creek to Minto Creek and Mayo. It was used by miners in the early 1900's to carry supplies to the new diggings on Highet and surrounding creeks. It was so named because George L. ORTELL had lived for many years near the head of Johnson Creek, at one time the only person in this area.

He came into this part of the country shortly after 1900 and spent the rest of his life near here. Well known and highly respected for his abilities as a bushman and trapper, he assisted Joseph Keele, GSC, with his exploration and mapping of the upper Stewart country.

He died 3 April, 1943 in St. Mary's Hospital in Dawson. The manner of his death was a display of stark courage and endurance. About the end of February 1943 he froze his hands on a trip to Highet Creek, the temperature at the time being –61°F. He stopped at the cabin of a friend, Joe Laska, who persuaded him to remain there while Laska went to Mayo for help. Laska, himself in his early 70's, was persuaded when he reached Minto Bridge to rest while the roadhouse keeper arranged for someone else to go for Ortell. Contacting the RCMP it was found that every dog team in Mayo was out on a job for the US Army. On the third day a dog team was found and the rescue mission began.

In the meantime, Ortell had begun to worry about Laska and his safety in the intense cold. He decided to walk to Mayo to see if Laska was alive.

Twelve miles down the trail a snowshoe strap broke. With his frozen hands he was unable to repair it so he discarded the snowshoes and struggled on in the deep snow. Fatigue and the Arctic night overtook him. He was unable to light a fire. His only hope was to remain erect and to keep moving, in the hope that someone would happen by.

Too tired to walk, he stood beside the trail and banked snow around his legs up to his knees and steeled his mind to keep standing. He knew that if he sat or lay down he would die. All through the night and into the following afternoon he stood, slowly freezing to death, only his indomitable will keeping him erect.

Dick Kimbel and Corporal d'Easum were stunned when they found him. They lifted him from the snow and rushed him to the nurse at Mayo who did everything possible to relieve his suffering. A plane took him to Dawson the next day.

Both feet had to be amputated and he appealed to the doctor to save as much as he could: "I got to hobble around some way. Figure to get me a fine catch of beaver on the McQuesten River this spring."

When he realized that he could never return to his beloved wilderness he lost heart. He gave up, for the first and last time in his life.

MOUNT ORTELL 6,769' 63°58′N 132°49′W (105-N). In the Tasin Range, south of the Stewart River.

Joseph Keele, GSC, named this peak in 1907 after George L. ORTELL, whose help and knowledge of the region greatly aided him in his geological mapping of the area.

MOUNT OSBORNE 65°46′N 140°50′W (116-F). South of the Kandik River.

Harriet C. OSBORNE, OBE, wife of Franklin Osborne of Dawson, was active in the Anglican Church, IODE and St. John's Ambulance. She organized the first Girl Guides in the Yukon in 1914 at Dawson. She was made an Officer of the Order of the British Empire for public service and in 1973 this mountain was named for her.

OSCAR CREEK 60°39′N 128°51′W (105-A). Flows south to False Canyon Creek, a few miles north of Stewart Lake.

The creek and lake were named in 1943 after OSCAR Stewart, a trapper and the son of a trapper, both of whom had spent many years in this area. The name had been in local use for a long time.

MOUNT OSGOODE 63°02′N 132°29′W (105-N). North of Mount Selous.

This mountain was named in 1909 after Wilfred Hudson OSGOODE (1875-1947), a member of the US Biological Survey. Osgoode came into the Yukon in 1899 on an expedition for the US Department of Agriculture, over the White Pass and down the Yukon. He was with F.C. Selous, the famed African white hunter and naturalist, in this area in 1904 and camped on the mountain while he studied the local flora and fauna.

OTTER FALLS   61°05'N 137°00'W (115–H). On the Aishihik River at the foot of Canyon Lake.

This falls is sometimes called "Five Dollar" Falls because its picture appeared for many years on the reverse side of the five-dollar Canadian banknotes.

PACKARD POINT   60°58'N 133°04'W (105–C). The large point at the southeast end of Quiet Lake.

During the 1920 and 30's a wealthy American construction man by this name came yearly to hunt in this area. His companies had built many of the New York City docks. A large, impressive and friendly man, he claimed that he could build anything. He died here and his body was sent to the northeastern United States for burial.

PACKERS MOUNTAIN   4,743'   61°50'N 135°32'W (105–E). On the east side of the Chain Lakes.

A.E. Pattison was head packer for D.D. Cairnes, GSC, from 1905 to 17. He was a master horseman and an exceptional bushman. Possessed of a fine singing voice, he and Cairnes often gave impromptu concerts when they came to town. In 1930 he died and W.D. Cockfield, GSC, who had also worked with him, named this mountain to commemorate him and the other packers who had served the GSC in the Yukon. (See Mount Pattison.)

MOUNT PAGE   4,198 69°20'N 140°53'W (117–C). On the headwaters of the Malcolm River, 25 miles south of the Arctic coast.

In June 1958 this mountain was chosen to perpetuate the memory of Lt. Pierre Roger Joseph PAGE, MID. He was born on 2 February, 1918, at Knowlton, Québec and enlisted in the Canadian army on 10 September, 1940, at Sherbrooke, Québec, He served in Canada, Great Britain, Newfoundland and northwest Europe and died of wounds received in action on 13 August, 1944.

PAN CREEK 62°00'N 140°55'W (115–J&K). A tributary of Tchawsahmon Creek, which flows into the White River.

In the winter of 1912–13, William E. James, Peter Nelson and Frederick Best discovered good placer gold on this stream. One of them used a frying pan to wash the first colours (gold) from the gravel. They claimed to have good values but an inrush of water to their workings forced them to stop.

In the spring of 1913 James and Nelson prospected farther west over the Alaska border. There they found the rich and famous Chisana goldfields.

On 23 August, 1913, Paul Jacobs recorded a new Discovery claim on the creek and at this time the Gold Commissioner for some reason changed the name from the original "Frying Pan" Creek to Pan Creek. In 1915 it was again changed to Frying Pan Creek.

PARADISE CREEK 63°42′N 136°08′W (115-P). A tributary to the southeast corner of Minto Lake.

On 19 May, 1903, J.G. Scrivener staked the Discovery claim on this stream and named it for its beautiful setting.

PARENT CREEK 63°50′N 135°27′W (105-M). A tributary to Duncan Creek from the east.

During the rush to this area Dennis PARENT and G. Beaudet prospected this stream and found placer gold. They staked the Discovery claim and named the creek on 20 June, 1902.

PARIS 63°49′N 138°40′W (115-O).

This was a small mining camp and settlement at the junction of Dominion and Portland Creeks in the southwest Klondike district. It had a post office from 1904 to 43 but was abandoned after that date.

PARTRIDGE CREEK 60°14′N 135°08′W (105-D). Flows into the Wheaton River.

Officially named in May 1911 but locally known for at least ten years before that, this creek bears the name of Otto H. PARTRIDGE, a prominent but lesser known figure of the Klondike Gold Rush.

In 1897 Partridge, as general manager of the Bennett Lake and Klondyke Navigation Company, brought the boilers and fittings for three small steamboats over the White Pass. That winter he built a sawmill and shipyard at Millhaven Bay on the west arm of Bennett Lake. Early in the spring of 1898 the three boats went down to Whitehorse. Although there is some argument, it is likely that one of these boats was the first to navigate through Miles Canyon and the Whitehorse Rapids.

His mill and shipyard prospered and he cut timber on this and other nearby creeks. Partridge was early interested in the development of the

Engineer Gold Mine (hard rock) on Windy Arm of Tagish Lake. The locale suited him and he and his wife settled on the west side of the arm. Their home "Ben-My Chree", (Manx for "Girl of my Heart") was a showplace for tourists on the WP&YR until the early 1930's.

PAT LAKE   65°06′N 136°40′W (116-H). About 15 miles east of the Hart River.

This lake was named by bush pilot I.A. Reid for the convenience of himself and other pilots assisting mining exploration in the area. It was probably named after E.P. "PAT" Callison, noted pioneer Yukon bush pilot who landed the first aircraft on the lake. It is the only lake within a very large area that is large enough on which to land a fixed-wing aircraft.

MOUNT PATTERSON   11,300′   61°09′N 140°07′W (115-F). On the east side of the Steele Glacier in the St. Elias Range.

It was named in November 1970 after John Duncan PATTERSON (1864-1940), business man and past president of the Alpine Club of Canada.

MOUNT PATTERSON   6,819′   61°56′N 133°51′W (105-F). North of the North Big Salmon River in the Pelly Mountains.

This beautiful mountain was chosen in November 1951 to honour the memory of a Canadian hero, Lt. William Clark PATTERSON, MID. He was born on 22 August, 1915, in Toronto, Ontario and enlisted in the Canadian army on 27 May, 1940, at Toronto. He served in Canada and Great Britain and was killed in action during the attack on Dieppe in France on 19 August, 1942.

MOUNT PATTISON   62°28′N 138°34′W (115-J&K). East of the Klotassin River in the southeast Dawson Range.

A.E. PATTISON trapped and prospected this country for many years. He worked as a packer for GSC parties from 1905 to 30. An excellent horseman and packer, he was liked for his cheerful disposition and ability as a bushman.

In the summer of 1930 he was as usual packing for the GSC. It was a bad year for flies and Pattison, worried about his horses, stayed up at night and kept smudge fires burning to protect them from the insects. He carried on with his normal work during the day but it was too much for his health and he suffered a stroke. He was taken to Vancouver where he died shortly afterward at the age of 64.

D.D. Cairnes, GSC, had named this peak for him about 1916. (See Packers Mountain.)

PATTON GULCH   62°45'N 138°51'W (115-J&K). On the north side of Patton Hill at the head of Canadian Creek.

This gulch and the mountain above it were named in 1911 by Jack Meloy, a well-known Yukon prospector. His old friend James "Jim" PATTON had found and worked the first placer gold in the area at a much earlier date. Patton spent many years prospecting in the Dawson Range. The name was made official in 1970. (See Meloy Creek.)

PATULLO LAKE   68°03'N 139°20'W (117-A). A small lake east of Old Crow Flats.

This name was proposed by Gordon McIntyre in June 1973 as a sheet designation for the new series of topographical maps.

Dufferin PATULLO was a lawyer, prominent in Dawson and Yukon politics during the gold rush era. He later became premier of British Columbia.

PAULINE COVE   69°34'N 138°55'W (117-D). On the east side of Herschel Island.

It was named by Lt. Commander Stockton of the USS *Thetis*, when he surveyed the coast of Herschel Island in 1889. He used the name of a whaling ship that was in the bay at the time.

PEASOUP   CREEK 64°17'N 138°29'W (116-B&C).   Crosses   the Dempster Highway and flows into the North Klondike River.

This was named in 1969 by highway construction crews when one of their number, a French Canadian, fell into the stream. The blunt sense of humour of his companions supplied the name.

PEEL RIVER   67°00'N 134°59'W (106-L). A tributary of the Mackenzie River.

In 1826, John Franklin (later Sir) on his second overland expedition to the Arctic, named this large river after Sir Robert PEEL (1788-1850), Home Secretary and later, Prime Minister of Great Britain. Peel organized and established the first police force of the modern type. (Hence, British police were and are called "peelers" or "bobbies").

The Peel River was first explored by Chief Factor John Bell of the HBC in

1839, when he ascended it as far as the Snake River. He explored the Snake thinking it was the Peel. In 1840–41 it was explored farther by Alexander Kennedy Isbister, also of the HBC, and still farther in 1893 by Count V.E. de Sainville. Charles Camsell, GSC, made the first complete survey of the river in 1905.

The river was most important for many years as the only route to the lucrative fur trade of the upper Yukon Territory and the Yukon River.

PELLY BANKS 61°46′N 131°07′W (105–G). On the north side of the Pelly River opposite the mouth of Big Campbell Creek.

On 25 July, 1840, Robert Campbell of the HBC arrived here, while establishing the true course and location of the Yukon River. That day he named the Pelly River and the high bluffs across the stream after Sir John Henry PELLY (1777–1852), Governor of the HBC. Later, when Campbell wrote his report informing Pelly of his discoveries, Pelly replied calling the river and banks, "Campbell" River and Banks. Campbell declined the honour but regretted his decision in later life.

In 1846 he built a trading post here, on the east bank of Campbell Creek on the Pelly, supplied from Fort Frances. It never did well. In the early winter of 1849, while Campbell was at Fort Selkirk, the post burned down, leaving the staff destitute. Two of his men died of starvation that winter and some of the Indians resorted to cannibalism to save themselves.

The post was never re-established by the HBC. Independent traders operated here for many years after 1900.

PELLY CROSSING 62°49′N 136°34′W (115–I). About 25 miles east of Fort Selkirk on the Pelly River.

Situated on the Whitehorse-Dawson road, this small settlement had two roadhouses and a trading post run by Ira Van Bibber and his partner Woolen. In 1958 the ferry across the Pelly River was replaced by a modern bridge but the settlement still persists and grows.

PELLY LAKES 62°05′N 130°17′W (105–J). Two long narrow lakes at the head of the Pelly River.

These lakes were named about 1840 by Robert Campbell of the HBC, while he was exploring the country, after the Governor of the company, Sir John Henry PELLY (1777–1852).

PELLY MOUNTAINS 61°40′N 132°30′W (105–F). The huge range of mountains that lies south of nearly the total length of the Pelly River.

These hills were named in 1887 by Dr. G.M. Dawson, GSC, while he was mapping this country for the first time.

In 1947 his nomenclature was expanded so that the Pelly Mountains now include the Big Salmon, the St. Cyr, the Glenlyon, Campbell and Simpson Ranges. (See Pelly Banks.)

PELLY POST OFFICE 62°47′N 137°24′W (115-I). At the junction of the Pelly and Yukon Rivers.

Although the settlement here was always called Fort Selkirk, the government established a post office in September 1899 and named it Pelly Post Office. It was closed in 1939.

PELLY RIVER 62°47′N 137°20′W (115-I). A major tributary of the Yukon River and one of the longest.

The early Indian name for this river was the "Ayan" or "Iyon", after the native tribes who lived near its mouth. The latter name was used on the USC&GS maps of the late 1880's.

Robert Campbell named the river in 1840 after Sir John Henry PELLY, Governor of the HBC.

The Pelly was one of the first streams to be prospected in the Yukon; men panned its gravels as early as 1883.

MOUNT PERKINS 6,665′ 60°20′N 135°06′W (105-D). In the upper Corwin Valley.

In 1905 J. PERKINS found and staked the first gold-quartz lode claims found on the mountain.

PERTHES POINT 60°09′N 134°27′W (105-D). On the north side of Tagish Lake, at the foot of Nares Mountain.

In 1883 Lt. F. Schwatka, as he was passing, named this point after Justus PERTHES of Gotha, Germany, a famous geographer.

MOUNT PHELPS 65°03′N 133°56′W (106-F). South of Rapitan Creek.

This is a map designation name given in 1973 for Willard PHELPS, a longtime Whitehorse lawyer and a Yukon Councillor for the Whitehorse District for many years in the 1930's.

PHILLIPS BAY 69°17′N 138°30′W (117-D). At the mouth of the Babbage River on the Arctic coast.

John Franklin, (later Sir) on his second Arctic expedition in 1826, named this bay after Thomas PHILLIPS (1770-1845), professor of painting at the Royal Academy in London.

PILLAGE POINT 68°52'N 136°43'W (117-A). The point of land immediately south of Tent Island in Shoalwater Bay.

On Friday, 7 July, 1826, John Franklin and his two small boats *Lion* and *Reliance* were seized in the shallow waters of this point and forced to land. The Eskimos robbed the boats of stores and supplies and owing only to the coolness of Franklin and Lt. Back, there was no loss of life. The Eskimos, after listening to another chief from Hudson Bay who was accompanying Franklin, restored the goods and thereafter traded.

PILOT MOUNTAIN 6,739' 61°01'N 135°33'W (105-E). West of Lake Laberge in the Miners Range.

This peak was named in honour of the first riverboat pilots who ran the Lewes (Yukon) River, by H.S. Bostock, GSC, in 1935. The pilots used it as a landmark.

PINGUICULA LAKE 64°41'N 133°24'W (106-C). East of the Bonnet Plume River.

In the summer of 1940, Mr. and Mrs. George Black, accompanied by Livingstone Wernecke, flew into this lake on a camping trip to the area. The large number of butterwort plants (*Pinguicula vulgaris*) growing around the shores of the lake suggested the name to Mrs. Black. She was an acknowledged authority on the wildflowers of the Yukon. (See Mount Black.)

PIRATE CREEK 60°04'N 137°08'W (115-A). A tributary of the Tatshenshini River just south of Dalton Post.

In 1949 H.S. Bostock, GSC, mapped this area. He gave this name because the stream features had altered in the area. This creek had captured the headwaters of Robbed Creek and other small streams in the neighbourhood.

MOUNT PITTS 5,214' 62°35'N 137°35'W (115-J). 25 miles west of Minto.

In June 1899, J.J. McArthur, DLS, named this after Harold PITTS, a member of his boundary survey party in the area that year. He was nick-named "Buffalo" Pitts.

Pitts came into the Yukon over the Chilkoot Pass in 1895. He lived at Fort Selkirk almost continously till late 1909 when he went outside and saw Whitehorse for the first time. He made his living trading with the Indians.

In a letter to E.G. DeVille, Surveyor General of Canada, on 24 September, 1909, at Fort Selkirk, Pitts asked that this peak be officially named for him, giving as a reason that he was "somewhat like a mule, without pride of ancestry or hope of posterity."

Pitts was on the riverboat which made the first successful trip up the White and Donjek Rivers in 1909. (See Fort Selkirk.)

PLATINUM GULCH   64°01'N 135°51'W (106-D). A small tributary to Haggart Creek.

This small stream was named by early miners because of the amount of platinum found with the gold in the 1920's.

POLICE CREEK   64°25'N 135°22'W (106-D). The north fork of the Beaver River.

This stream was probably named about 1905 or a little later. One of the trails used by the RNWMP MacPherson Patrol ran along it. This route was from Dawson to Fort MacPherson via the Little Wind River.

POLLEY HILL   66°51'N 136°40'W (116-I). West of Rock River.

43176 Bombardier Frank POLLEY was born on 31 July, 1874, at Benson, Oxfordshire, England. He enlisted in the Royal Canadian Artillery at Valcartier, Québec on 24 September, 1914, one of the first Canadians. He served in Canada, Great Britain and France and was discharged as medically unfit, from wounds received, on 30 November, 1917.

He died later from the effects of his wounds. In June 1973 this mountain was named in his memory.

POOLY CANYON   60°02'N 134°37'W (105-D). On the south side of Montana Mountain on the west side of Windy Arm.

The canyon below the forks of Pooly Creek was named in 1905 after the existing Pooly Creek.

POOLY CREEK   60°02'N 134°37'W (105-D). Flows into Windy Arm from the south side of Montana Mountain.

This was named in early 1905 after John M. POOLY, one of the first hardrock prospectors in the Windy Arm district. Pooly gave the creek the name Uranus Creek, after the first claim he staked there but the GSC soon changed it to the present one.

PORCUPINE RIVER 67°25′N 141°00′W (116-O&N). A major tributary to the Yukon River, which leaves Canada at this point.

This river was explored by John Bell, Chief Trader for the HBC at Fort MacPherson in 1842 and 44. Bell first saw the Yukon River on his second trip in 1844. Shortly afterward, in 1847, he sent Alexander Hunter Murray to establish Fort Yukon at the junction of the two streams. The Porcupine remained a regular trade route until the transfer of Alaska to the United States in 1867, when Fort Yukon was abandoned. It remained in limited use until 1894 when the HBC abandoned the territory.

The river was first surveyed and mapped by R.G. McConnell, GSC, in 1888. F.F. Sparks, a member of William Ogilvie's party in 1888, travelling from Fortymile to Fort MacPherson, found the source of the Porcupine to be a small hot spring.

PORTER CREEK 60°47′N 135°09′W (105-D). A tributary to the Lewes (Yukon) River.

This creek was named by H.E. PORTER in July 1899 when he found a rich copper ore body on the seventh of the month, which he called the "Pueblo" claim. Porter lived and prospected in the district for many years. He died while prospecting on the headwaters of the Stewart River in early June 1907. Porter Creek subdivision of the City of Whitehorse was given this name.

PORTLAND CREEK 63°49′N 138°41′W (115-O&N). A tributary to Dominion Creek, four miles above Jensen Creek.

John Salme named this stream after his home town in Oregon when he discovered gold and staked the first claim on 27 December, 1897.

POTATO CREEK 68°09′N 140°23′W (117-B). A tributary to Surprise Creek and the Old Crow River.

This name was reported by Cpl. E.A. Kirk, RCMP, in 1949. The name "Schaefer Creek" had been applied mistakenly by the International Boundary survey crew of 1911 and was shown as such on maps until 1950.

POVOAS MOUNTAIN 61°22′N 135°06′W (105-E). At the northeast corner of Lake Laberge.

This was named about 1908 by D.D. Cairnes, GSC, after an early prospector and miner of this name who lived in the area.

PREJEVALSKY POINT   60°05′N   134°53′W   (105-D). The point on the south side between Lake Bennett and the West Arm.

This was named by Lt. F. Schwatka, US Army, in 1883 after a well-known Russian explorer of the time.

PREVOST   RIVER   62°36′N   131°10′W   (105-J).   A   tributary   of   Ross River.

PREVOST, a French Canadian, was probably the first white man to travel this river. He and a partner trapped and prospected here in 1900 and at Prevost Canyon on the Ross River in the early 1900's.

PRIMROSE   LAKE   60°06′N   135°41′W   (105-D).   A   long   (12   miles) narrow lake east of the Takhini River.

This was probably named by George White-Fraser, DLS, of the Department of the Interior, while setting out monuments on the Yukon-BC boundary in 1900. He named it after Captain, later Inspector, P.C.H. PRIMROSE, NWMP, who was in charge of the Tagish Post and this district that year. The river was named later. Rose Lake, farther up the river was derived from this name. The mountain was named last of all.

MOUNT   PRINCE   EDWARD   ISLAND   12,260′   60°57′N   140°39′W (115-B&C). In the Centennial Range of the St. Elias Mountains.

This peak was named in honour of the province during Canada's Centennial Year, 1967. (See Centennial Range.)

PRINGLE LAKE   60°08′N   136°59′W   (115-A). On the west side of the Haines Junction Road near Dalton Post.

Sgt. J.A. PRINGLE, NWMP, served at Dalton Post in the early 1900's and after being discharged, continued to live here for many years. He was a brother of John and George Pringle, the famous Presbyterian ministers of the Klondike and Atlin goldfields and the First World War.

PRINTERS CREEK   61°10′N   138°24′W   (115-G&F). Flows into Cultus Creek on the east side of Kluane Lake.

Named "New Zealand Creek" by the first men to find gold and stake claims during the rush to the Kluane goldfields in 1903–04, by 1914 the creek was abandoned. A new find was made and another stampede to stake claims took place. The new stakers named it Printers Creek. To many of the local people it was known as "Buck-Off Creek", after an incident concerning pack horses.

MOUNT PROFIET 64°47′N 133°04′W (106–C). West of the Snare River.

This was named in January 1973 by Gordon McIntyre, Territorial Land Titles Agent, for the Topographical Branch's new series of 1:50,000 maps, after Alexander PROFIET, the first school teacher in the Mayo district, in 1914.

PROSPECTOR MOUNTAIN 62°27′N 137°48′W (115–I). In the Dawson Range.

This was proposed by H.S. Bostock, GSC, in 1934, to commemorate the prospectors of the Yukon whom he admired and respected. His liking for the working prospectors was only equalled by their respect and liking for him.

PTARMIGAN CREEK 62°07′N 130°07′W (105–J). Flows into the east end of Pelly Lake.

In 1893 Warburton Pike, an English gentleman-explorer, travelled the Liard River, Frances River and Frances Lake and examined this area. He named this creek because of the numbers of these birds he found upon it. (See Narchilla Brook.)

QUARTZ CREEK 63°45′N 139°07′W (115–O&N). Flows from King Solomon's Dome to the Indian River in the Klondike district.

Although the mouth of Quartz Creek was seen by prospectors working on the Indian River as early as 1887, it was probably named by William "Billy" Redford who found and mined the first gold in 1894. The creek gained its name as about 80% of the gravels are composed of quartz pebbles.

William Redford was born in Devon, England in 1861 and became a sailor. While on a whaling voyage, he reached the mouth of the Mackenzie River in 1891. The following year he went to southwestern Alaska and in 1893 crossed the Chilkoot Pass and went down to Fortymile.

In late 1893 or early 1894 he was the first to find and mine the gold of this stream, first on the bars and then in the deeper gravels. He staked a

Discovery claim near the mouth of Calder Creek (unnamed at the time). This was the first payable gold recorded on the east side of the Yukon River below the Stewart. Previous to this it had been the consensus of opinion among the miners of the region that none would be found in this part of the territory.

Joe Ladue, who had a trading post at the mouth of the Sixtymile River (Ogilvie), used Redford's find to encourage others, including Robert Henderson, to prospect in the area the following year. Thus, in the summer of 1896 about 20 men worked for Redford and others mining on the stream. A number of pre-1896 miners claimed that Henderson worked for Redford in the winter of 1895–96. The men who accompanied Henderson to Gold Bottom Creek that spring all came from Quartz Creek.

Because he obtained his supplies at Sixtymile Post which was only 45 miles away and the Mining Recorder was at Fortymile, 85 miles downstream, Redford did not bother to record his claim. It was safe in those days as long as he was working it. When Bonanza and Eldorado Creeks were discovered, Quartz was deserted except for Redford. The overflow of men from the Klondike in the summer of 1897 threatened his claim and he went to Dawson and recorded it in September. He was not allowed a Discovery claim as one had been filed on 11 August by D.D. Stewart, evidently on Redford's own claim. Also, another Discovery claim had been allowed to A. Mack, higher up the stream, on 20 August. However, the recorder seems to have reversed his decision sometime later and evidently returned Redford's claim to him.

Redford also found when recording his claim that the district had been divided into two mining divisions; the Klondike comprised all streams entering the Klondike River and the new Indian River division contained those streams running into the Indian River. This new partition was later used effectively to ignore Redford's claim to being the first to find payable gold in the Klondike, which enhanced Henderson's claims to that honour.

His priority was acknowledged by most of the pre-1896 miners and by R.G. McConnell, GSC, the noted explorer-geologist who made the first study of the Klondike goldfields and who included the south-flowing tributaries of the Indian River as part of the Klondike district.

Redford was a shy, self-effacing man who made few public claims. He mined on his Discovery claim continuously every year from 1894 to 1937, never making better than good wages. He died in St. Mary's Hospital in Dawson on 18 October, 1944, sadly neglected by history. A settlement grew up on his claim and lasted until the 1940's. (See Readford).

QUARTZ LAKE (See Hulse Lake.)

QUEBEC CREEK 64°10′N 139°33′W (116-B&C). A tributary to the Yukon from the west, about two miles below Fort Reliance.

S. Villeneuve, of Québec, named this stream when he and his partners first found gold and staked the creek.

MOUNT QUEBEC 12,300′ 60°56′N 140°42′W (115-B&C). In the Centennial Range of the St. Elias Mountains.

This was named in honour of the province of Québec during Canada's Centennial Year of 1967. (See Centennial Range.)

MOUNT QUEEN MARY 12,750′ 60°39′N 139°42′W (115-B&C). In the centre of the St. Elias Icefield Ranges.

This peak was named in 1935 by Bradford Washburn in honour of King George V and QUEEN MARY's Silver Jubilee Year. (See Mount King George.)

QUIET LAKE 61°05′N 133°05′W (105-F). About 40 miles north of Johnson's Crossing, west of the Canol Road.

John McCormack and three companions prospected up the Big Salmon River in the summer of 1887, as far as this lake. They named the lake, which almost always lives up to its name, when they prospected and named many of the streams which flow into it. McCormack gave Dr. G.M. Dawson, GSC, a good description of the river, the lake and the surrounding country when he met him later in the year.

QUILL CREEK 61°32′N 139°19′W (115-G&F). A tributary of the Kluane River at mile 1112 (K1801) on the Alaska Highway.

The creek probably received its name in the stampede to the Burwash Creek diggings in late 1904.

About 1952 Wellington Green, who had come into the Yukon in 1944 after prospecting in eastern Canada, California and BC, discovered a deposit of nickel-cobalt ore. The Hudson Bay Mining and Smelting Company developed the mine, naming it the Wellgreen, and brought it into production in June 1972. However, costs were high and the ore body proved limited, so they were forced to close in August 1973.

QUINN GULCH 63°46′N 138°53′W (115-O&N). A small tributary to Sulphur Creek, one mile below the settlement of Sulphur.

William QUINN found the first gold here and named the stream on 28 August, 1897.

QUINTINO SELLA GLACIER   60°35'N 140°53'W (115-B&C). North of the Columbia Glacier in the St. Elias Range.

This was named by His Royal Highness, Prince Luigi Amadeo of Savoy, Duke of the Abruzzi, on his expedition to Mount St. Elias in 1887, after an illustrious pioneer of Italian mountain climbing.

RAABE'S HILLS   62°10'N 136°09'W (115-I). A low range of hills a few miles northeast of Tantalus Butte.

These hills were named in 1968 after Captain George RAABE of Portland, Oregon. He had piloted riverboats between Whitehorse and Dawson from 1900 to 20. Raabe's Slough, three miles above Tantalus Butte, although misspelled on some maps, is the backwater of the Yukon River in which he laid up his boats in the winter.

RACKLA RIVER   64°07'N 134°23'W (106-D). Tributary to the Beaver River. (North branch of the McQuesten River).

From 1897 this stream was called "Hell River" by the stampeders who came this way from Edmonton. The GSC, however, applied the local Indian name, without translation. It is swift and shallow, making for extremely difficult boating.

RADER LAKE   62°20'N 130°45'W (105-J). 20 miles northwest of Traffic Mountain.

Louis Thomas "Slim" RADER in his earlier years was an employee of the HBC in the NWT. It is said that he accompanied Peary's North Pole Expedition in 1909 as far as the Arctic coast. In the 1920 and 30's he trapped on the Mackenzie and Liard Rivers and moved into this part of the Yukon. He once spent a winter in the Nahanni Valley without supplies, living by his rifle. He managed the T&D trading post at Pelly Lakes from 1938 to 50. In the early 1960's he was caretaker of the Hudson Bay Quill Creek Mine after its closure.

Retiring to Haney, BC, he died on 31 July, 1967, liked and respected.

RAE CREEK   64°53'N 137°01'W (116-A). Flows north into the Hart River.

Frank RAE was an old-time trapper and prospector in this region. He had his cabin on Rae Lake (Worm Lake). He and his partner, Fred Hoffman, worked here in the 1930 and 40's.

RAILWAY SURVEY CREEK 62°10'N 134°00'W (105-L). A small creek flowing north into the Magundy River.

In 1942 Col. James J. Truitt, US Corps of Engineers, headed a survey group on a proposed railway location through this country, naming this creek on the way. (See Truitt Creek and Truitt Peak.)

RAMPART HOUSE 67°25'N 140°59'W (116-O&N). Just east of the Yukon-Alaska boundary, on the Porcupine River.

When Fort Yukon, the HBC post at the confluence of the Porcupine and Yukon Rivers, was closed after the American purchase of Alaska in 1867, it was moved to a site up the Porcupine River thought to be in Canadian territory. The new location was called "Rampart House" because of the steep banks of the river at that place. Turner's survey of 1889 showed that this post was also on American soil. They burned the post and moved farther upstream to this location where they were sure of being on Canadian ground.

For a time it was called "New Rampart House." The HBC abandoned this post and all others in the territory in 1894.

Dan Cadzow, a Scot and early Klondiker, opened a new trading post in the summer of 1905 and traded until 1911. In that year the settlement was again abandoned and burned, due to an outbreak of smallpox in the community. The people moved to a new community farther up the river at Old Crow.

RANCHERIA RIVER 60°13'N 129°07'W (105-A). A tributary to the Liard River, west of Watson Lake.

This is an old Californian or Mexican miners' term from the Spanish, meaning a native village or settlement.

When Dr. G.M. Dawson, GSC, passed this river in 1887 he found that the Cassiar miners had named the creek during the Sayyea Creek excitement in 1875–76.

RANKIN CREEK 64°01'N 134°55'W (106-D). Flows into the Keno Ladue River in the Mayo district.

This stream was named on 21 April, 1945, to honour the memory of

Captain Robert Lowe James RANKIN who was born on 29 May, 1910, in London, England. He enlisted in Toronto, Ontario on 3 June, 1941, and served in the Canadian army in Canada, Great Britain and northwest Europe. He was killed in action in France on 18 July, 1944.

RAY CREEK 62°40′N 138°38′W (115-J&K). A tributary to Rude Creek.

During the rush to the new placer gold finds on Dip and Rude Creeks in the fall of 1915, Peter Anderson and David RAY found the first gold on this stream and named it on 16 September, 1915.

RAY LAKE 60°21′N 137°11′W (115-A). West of Dezeadash Lake.

Irvine RAY was a well-known miner in the Whitehorse and Mayo districts. He mined on Shorty Creek in 1946. This creek was known locally by his name for many years and the name was made official in September 1973.

MOUNT RAYMOND 66°24′N 136°10′W (116-I). In the Richardson Mountains.

Born in Digby, Nova Scotia on 22 February, 1896, George Vail RAYMOND enlisted in the Canadian army at Dawson, YT, as a private in the Yukon Infantry Company on 2 October, 1916. He was appointed a second lieutenant in the RAF on 20 December, 1917 and was killed in action on 24 July, 1918. This mountain was named in his memory in 1973.

READFORD 63°47′N 139°07′W (115-O&N).

The postal department opened an office on Redford's Discovery claim on Quartz Creek on 19 August, 1905. There was a small settlement here at the time. The authorities called this first post office "Radford". It was closed from April 1934 to September 1934. On 16 November they changed the name to "Readford" when they re-opened. The office was closed permanently on 31 December, 1952; two tries in 47 years and the name was misspelled both times. (See Quartz Creek.)

READY BULLION CREEK 63°53′N 139°08′W (115-O&N). A tributary to Bonanza Creek.

This was named on 6 November, 1897, by the first staker, Peter Farrell, after the READY BULLION Mine at Juneau, Alaska in which he had been employed. This small stream produced good gold, almost the only stream on upper Bonanza Creek to do so.

REID HOUSE   63°32'N 137°25'W (115-P). Supposedly on the south bank of the Stewart River, near the mouth of the creek emptying the Reid Lakes.

All the above is supposition. The existence and location of Reid House is a genuine Yukon mystery. The first map to show any of the interior features of the Yukon Territory was John Arrowsmith's map, drawn in 1854 in London, England. Arrowsmith gained all his information about the central Yukon from Robert Campbell of the HBC, the first explorer, in 1853. This place was shown on Arrowsmith's map. Campbell, when interviewed later by Dr. G.M. Dawson, GSC, stated that no such place existed although he had had a John REID with him at Pelly Banks and Fort Selkirk in the years 1846 to 51. John Reid was also questioned by Dawson and denied any knowledge of such a settlement although he did state that there were a number of small lakes near this location where they obtained good numbers of fish and that a small hut or shelter had been built there while fishing.

Both Reid House and Reid Lakes were shown on almost every map of the territory until 1899. Reid Lakes are still there, sometimes spelled Reed.

MOUNT REID   60°10'N 135°28'W (105-D). On the north side of the Wheaton River between Skukum and Barney Creeks.

This feature was named in May 1911 after Percy REID, the Mining Recorder of the Conrad Mining Division which included this area. He was well regarded by the miners of that day.

REMINGTON PUP   63°52'N 138°51'W (115-O & N). A very short stream entering Dominion Creek one half-mile below Upper Discovery.

On 13 August, 1897, Edward REMINGTON found gold in this little gulch and staked the first claim.

REVENUE CREEK   62°21'N 137°17'W (115-I). Flows into Big Creek three miles above Seymour Creek, from the south.

This creek was named about 1940 by Fred Guder, who has sporadically worked placer gold here since then, because he said he could always win enough gold from the creek to get a grubstake. The present Yukon Revenue Mining Company bases its name on mineral deposits owned near the stream.

REVERSE CREEK 63°33'N 136°48'W (115-P). Tributary to Moose Creek.

Because this stream turns 180° to reverse its flow, H.S. Bostock, GSC, gave it the name in 1949 while mapping the geology of the area.

RICE CREEK 63°15'N 140°51'W (115-N). A tributary to the Ladue River from the north.

This stream was named in May 1920 by a GSC party after an old trapper of the name who was living here.

MOUNT RICHARDS 66°04'N 136°05'W (116-I). East of Canyon Creek.

This hill was named on 22 June, 1973 to honour the name and memory of R-252 612 Flight Sgt. Edward Gordon Coke RICHARDS. Born 10 October, 1916, at Strathmore, Alberta, he enlisted in the RCAF on 25 March, 1943. He was missing, presumed killed in action on 14 March, 1945.

RICHARDSON MOUNTAINS 67°55'N 136°40'W (116-P). This range parallels the Yukon-NWT boundary.

In 1825 John Franklin, RN, (later Sir,) named these mountains after Sir John RICHARDSON (1787-1865). An Arctic explorer in his own right, Richardson was the surgeon and naturalist on Franklin's land expeditions of 1819-20 and 1825-27 and later commanded a boat expedition in search of Franklin in 1848.

RICHTHOFEN ISLAND 61°06'N 135°10'W (105-E). On the west side of Lake Laberge.

In 1883 Lt. F. Schwatka, US Army, thought this was a peninsula and gave it the name "Richthofen Rocks". Dr. G. M. Dawson, GSC, corrected the error in 1887 but allowed the name to stand in honour of Freiherr von RICHTHOFEN of Leipzig, Germany, a famous geographer of the time.

The stream behind this island was called the "Red River" by the early miners because of the red rocks along its banks but the name was changed about 1930 or 40 to Richthofen Creek.

MOUNT RIDDELL 6,101' 62°43'N 131°18'W (105-J). South of the MacMillan River.

In 1907 Joseph Keele, GSC, hired Robert B. RIDDELL to accompany him while he mapped the geology of the headwaters of the Pelly, Ross and Gravel Rivers, the first exploration of much of this area. Riddell had been the first white man to explore and trap in a great part of this region from about 1898 on.

Keele named this mountain in recognition of Riddell's character and services.

RIDDELL RIVER   62°50′N   132°24′W   (105-K). A tributary of the upper MacMillan River.

In 1904 Captain Frederick C. Selous, the famed African white hunter and naturalist was assisted by Robert B. RIDDELL to obtain big game specimens for various museums. He admired Riddell for his hardihood in exploring this great tract of wilderness by himself, following no other white man. He noted the name of the river, which was the site of Riddell's home.

RIGHTHOOK CREEK   63°41′N   137°03′W   (115-P). Flows into Vancouver Creek.

The outline of this creek when it was mapped suggested this boxing term to H.S. Bostock, GSC and his men in 1949.

RIGHT ON MOUNTAIN   61°06′N   138°47′W   (115-G). Near the head of Congdon Creek.

This was named in October 1973 by junior members of the Yukon Scenic and Wilderness Study Project, from a then-current slang expression, "Right on... wow", which is intended to express approval.

RINK RAPIDS   62°19′N   136°23′W   (115-I). Five miles downstream from Five Finger Rapids.

This name, after Dr. Henry RINK of Christiana, Denmark, an authority on Greenland and Director of the Royal Greenland Trade at Copenhagen, was originally applied to what is now Five Finger Rapids by Lt. F. Schwatka, US Army, in 1883. It was never used by travellers on the river and the name was transferred to this minor obstruction by Dr. G.M. Dawson, GSC, in 1887.

In the winter of 1902–03 most of the dangerous rocks were blasted from the channel by P.E. Mercier, Territorial Engineer.

ROAL CREEK   64°19′N   140°00′W   (116-B&C). Enters the Yukon River from the west about five miles above Cassiar Creek.

This creek was named after Louis ROAL who prospected this area and found lead-zinc ore near here in the 1920's.

ROBBED CREEK 60°07'N 137°02'W (115-A). A tributary to the Tatshenshini River at Dalton Post.

H.S. Bostock, GSC, named this creek in 1949 while mapping the area. The headwaters of this stream were diverted by glacial action and now flow into Pirate Creek.

ROBERT SERVICE CREEK 64°27'N 138°13'W (116-B&C). A tributary to the North Klondike River. (See below.)

MOUNT ROBERT SERVICE 62°25'N 138°11'W (116-B&C). At the headwaters of the North Klondike River.

These names were proposed in 1968 by Dr. Dirk Tempelman-Kluit, GSC, to commemorate the Bard of the Yukon, author of "The Cremation of Sam McGee" and other verses.

ROBINSON 60°27'N 134°51'W (105-D). A way station on the WP&YR about 22 miles south of Whitehorse.

In late 1899 the WP&YR built a way station here while constructing the railway. It was given the name of their labour foreman and construction man *extraordinare*, "Stikine Bill" ROBINSON.

William C. ROBINSON was from North Anson, Maine. He had followed railroad construction across the continent. In early 1898 he was general foreman during the short-lived MacKenzie and Mann attempt to build a railroad from Glenora, on the Stikine River, to the foot of Teslin Lake. He acquired his nickname on that job.

Mike Heney, the contractor who built the WP&YR, hired him in the same capacity. In addition, he was put in charge of the early freighting from the Summit to Bennett and Whitehorse, using both horse-teams and boats.

From 1908 to 12 he assisted Heney in building the 136-mile-long Copper River and Northwestern Railway from Cordova to Chitina and on to the enormously rich Kennecott Copper Mines. He continued to engage in prospecting and mining ventures in Alaska until he died on 29 September, 1926.

W.P. Grainger and H.W. Vance, prominent miners of Whitehorse, surveyed a townsite here in 1906 when the mineral wealth of the Wheaton River area to the west appeared capable of major production. A post office was open here from 1909 to 15.

ROCK RIVER 67°17′N 137°06′W (116–P). A tributary to the Bell River.

On 19 June, 1847, Alexander Hunter Murray of the HBC found and named this stream the "Blue Fish River". This name was later changed to avoid redundancy with the "Blue Fish River" near Ramparts on the Porcupine, in Alaska.

ROCQUETTE ROCKS (See Old Woman Rock.)

RODIN CREEK 63°51′N 136°18′W (115–P). A tributary of the South McQuesten River.

A prospector named RODIN (or Roden) found and mined gold on this creek in 1907.

ROLAND CREEK 69°22′N 138°57′W (117–D). Flows into the Spring River on the Arctic coast.

Anker Hoidal, who spent his lifetime trapping and prospecting in the Arctic Yukon, said that this stream had been known by this name after an Eskimo who lived on it for more than 30 years, beginning in the 1920's. (See Anker and Hoidal Creeks.)

ROSE CREEK 62°25′N 132°41′W (105–K). A tributary of Anvil Creek on the north side of Rose Mountain.

Oliver ROSE came into the Yukon over the Edmonton Trail in 1897–98. He came up the Pelly to prospect and settled here for the remainder of his life. The RNWMP reports of the time indicate that his name was probably Olivier LaRose and that his birthplace was in Québec. They also note that he was a solitary, hard-working and well-regarded man.

On 17 September, 1905, Charles Sheldon, noted big-game hunter and naturalist, while collecting specimens for American museums in the region, met Rose and named this stream where he lived. (See below.)

ROSE MOUNTAIN 6,513′ 62°20′N 133°35′W (105–K). On the north side of the Pelly River about 12 miles west of Faro.

Oliver ROSE had his home and a small trading post at the foot of this mountain on the Pelly River. It was known as Rose's Cabin. Charles Sheldon, the American naturalist, gave the mountain its name on 13 September, 1905. (See above.)

ROSE RIVER 61°10′N 132°59′W (105–F). A tributary of the Nisutlin River near the foot of Quiet Lake.

In the early 1900's Oliver ROSE prospected extensively in the area between here and the Pelly. Lapie Creek and Rose River give an almost complete waterway from the Pelly to Quiet Lake. (See Rose Creek and Mountain.)

ROSEBUD CREEK 63°17′N 138°26′W (115-O&N). A tributary of the Stewart River.

Alexander MacDonald (not "Big Alex") from New Brunswick, explored and prospected the Stewart River in 1887 or even earlier. He found some gold showings on this stream and named it, probably after the Battle of the ROSEBUD River in the Sioux Wars in the American west during the 1870's, in which it was thought he took part. (It is believed that he also named Black Hills Creek in the same vicinity.)

ROSS CREEK 63°53′N 136°02′W (115-P). A tributary of the South McQuesten River.

An early prospector named ROSS found placer gold here and named the creek about 1898-99. He remained in the country for many years. (See the other Ross Creek.)

ROSS CREEK 64°00′N 137°33′W (115-P). A tributary to the Little South Klondike River.

ROSS came into the country during the gold rush. He prospected and lived in the area until the 1930's. He was the first to find gold on this stream but there was not enough to pay. (See the other Ross Creek; both were named by or for the same man.)

ROSS RIVER 61°59′N 132°26′W (105-F). At the junction of the Ross and Pelly Rivers.

This settlement was first established by Tom Smith about 1903 but was soon sold to Poole Field and Clement Lewis who named it "Nahanni House", because a number of Indians from the Nahanni country in the NWT had followed them to this area to trap and trade.
The post was later taken over by the Whitehorse firm of Taylor and Drury. It continued under various owners until 1945.

ROSS RIVER 61°59′N 132°26′W (105-F). A major tributary of the Pelly River.

In 1843 Robert Campbell of the HBC made his famous first journey down the Pelly River to its junction with the Yukon. During this journey he named most of the tributaries of the Pelly. This was named after Chief Factor Donald ROSS of the HBC.

ROWLINSON CREEK 62°03′N 136°17′W (115-I). Flows into the Nordenskiold River three miles south of Carmacks.

D.D. Cairnes, GSC, while mapping this part of the country in 1911, recorded this name from Seymour ROWLINSON who was living and mining on the stream. He had been the first to find the gold and had then been here for a number of years.

ROY LAKE 60°32′N 127°49′W (95-D). A small lake immediately east of Hulse (Quartz) Lake.

In February 1970 this lake was named by James Harquail, President of Fort Reliance Minerals Ltd., to commemorate Andrew ROY. In the summer of 1968 Roy had been camp cook for the company's exploration crew and had lost his life in an aircraft crash on the lake on 2 September, 1968.

ROYAL MOUNTAIN 6,567′ 65°02′N 135°04′W (106-E). East of Wind River in the Wernecke Mountains.

In September 1897 George Mitchell of Montréal and his party were trapped here by winter. They were on their way to the Klondike via Edmonton, the Mackenzie, Peel and Wind Rivers. They established a small community near the mouth of the Wind River called "Wind City". Mitchell named this peak that winter because it reminded him of the shape of MOUNT ROYAL.

He later published an account of his experiences under the title, *The Golden Grindstone.*

RUBE CREEK 66°36′N 138°14′W (116-J&K). Tributary to the Porcupine River.

This name was officially proposed on 27 November, 1958, by Professor Otto William Geist of the University of Alaska after RUBE Mason. Geist stated in the application that Rube and his brother Bill were noted trappers and "highly esteemed individuals". This area was their trapping grounds and this stream was locally known as "Mason" and "Rube Mason" Creek. (See Mason Lake.)

RUBY CREEK 61°05′N 137°56′W (115-H). A small stream joining Lake Creek to flow south into Jarvis River.

The Discovery claim on this stream was staked and the creek named by

W.H. Weisdepp on 6 July, 1903, and the stampede to the Shakwak Valley goldfields was on.

The *Whitehorse Star*, on July 27, 1903, reported, "The arrival of an Indian in the town of Whitehorse in July last, with a small quantity of gold, which he said he obtained near the surface on a creek in the Shakwak district, brought this part of the Yukon into greater prominence. The Indian who made the discovery informed several other Indians who immediately started for that part. They returned after ten days and several claims were recorded on a creek they called 'Ruby'. A general stampede then took place, close upon five hundred persons went out and staked, returned and recorded. (Skookum Jim Mason and Dawson Charlie were among the first)."

The creek was worked out within a few years. During this period a small settlement of the same name grew up at the mouth of the stream, with a post office, roadhouse and stores. It died with the decline of the stream.

RUDE CREEK 62°40'N 138°43'W (115-J&K). A tributary to Dip Creek in the Dawson Range.

Jens RUDE and his partner were extremely active prospectors in this area. They found good gold on this stream and staked the Discovery claim on it on 12 March, 1915. They worked the gravels here for several years.

RUNT CREEK 66°16'N 141°00'W (116-J&K). A small tributary to the Salmon Fork, across the Yukon-Alaska boundary.

This little stream got its name from surveyors of the International Boundary Commission, in 1908.

RUSSELL COL 60°19'N 140°55'W (115-B&C). The connecting ridge between Mount St. Elias and Mount Newton.

This feature was named to honour Professor Israel C. RUSSELL, USGS, who first mapped this area and named Mount Logan. He made three expeditions to the Yukon. On the first, in 1889, he went by boat from St. Michaels to Fort Selkirk, continued up the Yukon River with a group of miners and emerged at Dyea, after exploring in the White River area. In 1890 and '91 he crossed the Chilkoot Pass and again ascended the White River to the Mount St. Elias region where he continued his mapping and explorations. He added greatly to the knowledge of this part of the territory. It was probably named in 1891 by the USGS.

RUSSELL CREEK   63°03'N 133°26'W (105-N). Tributary to the Mac-Millan River, just below the forks.

Thomas Duncan Gillies (or Gillis) prospected in the Yukon from 1892. In the winter of 1896–97 he was at his home in Nova Scotia when he received news of the Klondike discovery. He returned via Edmonton and the Mackenzie River, thence up the Gravel (Keele) River, across the continental divide and down the MacMillan River, mistaking it for the Hess. Prospecting along the way, he panned good gold at the mouth of this creek, which he named "Slate Creek" from the rocks thereon. He spent several weeks prospecting the stream and was caught by winter. Having few supplies and being unable to raft because of the ice, he was forced to walk overland to Fort Selkirk. He suffered great hardships and privations but arrived safely.

Returning the next year with partners he was encouraged to obtain a concession which was granted to him in 1900, when he changed the name of the stream to Russell Creek. The reason for the change is not known.

N.A.D. Armstrong, acting for an English company, bought out the concession and worked it unprofitably for many years. (See Mount Armstrong.)

MOUNT RUSSELL   67°44'N 136°30'W (116-P). On the north side of MacDougall Pass on the Yukon-NWT border.

This peak was named by William Ogilvie, DLS, on his journey from Fortymile to Fort MacPherson in May 1888.

RUSSELL RANGE   63°13'N 133°10'W (105-N). North of the upper MacMillan River near the forks.

This was named about the turn of the century, or slightly earlier, after Mark RUSSELL, a noted pioneer Yukon prospector. He ranged far and wide in Alaska and the Yukon. He accompanied Dr. C.W. Hayes, USGS, and Lt. F. Schwatka, US Army, in 1891 from Juneau up the Taku to Teslin Lake and on into the White River country, probably the first to make the journey.

SABBATH CREEK   63°47'N 136°21'W (115-P). A tributary to Johnson Creek from the west.

Rudolph Rasmussen found the first gold on this stream on a Sunday and staked the Discovery claim on 8 August, 1909.

SABINE POINT   69°04′N 137°44′W (117-D). On the Arctic coast.

John Franklin, RN, named this in 1825 after Major General Sir Edward SABINE, RA, (1788-1883), a celebrated British astronomer and physicist. He was astronomer to the first John Ross expedition of 1818 and to the Parry expedition of 1819-20. He was President of the British Association in 1853 and of the Royal Society from 1861 to 71.

MOUNT ST. CYR   6,725′   61°21′N 133°10′W (105-F). Ten miles north of Quiet Lake.

This mountain was named about 1901 after Arthur ST. CYR, DLS, QLS. He was sent by the Department of the Interior of the Dominion government in May 1897 to find and survey a possible wagon or railway route from Telegraph Creek on the Stikine River to the head of Teslin Lake for the expected hordes of gold-seekers. The government wished it to be an all-Canadian route. This task he accomplished that summer, exploring several alternate routes and carrying his surveys not only to Teslin Lake but also along the lake and up the Teslin River to the Lewes.

He continued this work through 1898, and in 1899 to 1901 he was engaged in surveying the boundary between the Yukon and BC.

The St. Cyr Range was named later.

MOUNT ST. ELIAS   18,008′ 60°17′N 140°56′W (115-B&C). At the southwest corner of the Yukon Territory.

This mountain, sometimes called "the corner post of Alaska", was first seen by Vitus Bering on ST. ELIAS Day, 16 July, 1741. Bering, a Dane employed by the Russian government to explore the coast of Alaska, commanded the ship *St. Peter*. This mountain was the first feature in the Yukon Territory to be named by white men.

The first attempt to climb it was made by Lt.F. Schwatka, US Army, in 1886. His expedition was a fiasco which barely got off the beach and turned back in a few days. The peak was first climbed by Prince Luigi Amadeo of Savoy, nephew of King Humbert of Italy, and his party in the summer of 1897.

ST. GERMAIN CREEK   61°25′N 134°24′W (105-E). A tributary to the Big Salmon River.

Joseph ST. GERMAIN of Québec, discovered payable gold and named this stream in the fall of 1900.

SALTER HILL 66°09′N 134°49′W (106-L). West of Peel River.

A map-designation name, this peak was given the name of Maxwell Charles SALTER, a Yukon Councillor for South Dawson from 1917 to 20.

SAMBO CREEK 60°25′N 129°33′W (105-A). Flows into the upper Liard River, east of Frances Lake.

"Old SAMBO" or "Old Sam" lived and trapped on this creek, and the lake of the same name at its head, for many years. Interviewed in 1942 shortly before he died, he could remember white men and former black slaves (from the underground railway between the southern United States and Canada) searching for gold along the Dease River in the 1870's.

MOUNT SAMPSON 11,000′ 61°12′N 140°03′W (115-F). East of the Steele Glacier in the St. Elias Range.

This was named in 1970 by the Alpine Club of Canada after Herbert E. SAMPSON (1871-1962), a lawyer and past president of the club (1930-32).

SAMUELSON HILL 2,057′ 66°19′N 137°11′W (116-I). East of the Canoe River.

In June 1973 this hill was named in memory of Helmer SAMUELSON. Born in Dawson, he served in the Second World War. He was owner, editor and printer of the *Dawson News* and, later, of the *Whitehorse Star*.

SANPETE CREEK 62°14′N 140°24′W (115-J&K). Crosses the Alaska Highway at mile 1175 (K1903).

This stream was named about the turn of the century by a prospector from SANPETE County, Utah.

SAPPER HILL 65°21′N 138°16′W (116-G). On the east side of the Ogilvie River.

James Smith, Commissioner of the Yukon Territory, in 1971 requested this name to honour the Royal Canadian Engineers for their work. In the summer of that year they had built the George Allan Jeckell Bridge over the Ogilvie River near here.

The name "Sapper" is a nickname given to all army engineers and dates from medieval days when they were employed mostly to dig "saps" or tunnels under enemy fortifications.

**MOUNT SASKATCHEWAN   11,390′ 60°57′N 140°51′W (115-B&C).
In the Centennial Range of the St. Elias Mountains.**

This peak was named for the province of Saskatchewan in Canada's Centennial Year of 1967. (See Centennial Range.)

SATAH RIVER   67°00′N 134°34′W (106-L). A tributary to the Peel River.

The Compte V.E. de Sainville, French sportsman and explorer, named this river in 1893. He was exploring this portion of the North West Territories and the Yukon and met here a band of Indians whose chief was SATAH.

SAVAGE GULCH 63°47′N 136°19′W (115-P). A small stream flowing into Johnson Creek from Scheelite Dome.

A prospector of this name found and worked a placer gold deposit here in the early 1900's.

SAYYEA CREEK   60°45′N 130°21′W (105-B). A tributary of the upper Liard River.

This small, little-known creek is the location of the first gold mined in the Yukon Territory.

Historical writings on the Yukon usually concentrate on the miners who entered the territory by way of the Chilkoot Pass and up the Yukon River. They begin with Harper and Mayo unsuccessfully prospecting the upper reaches of the White River in the fall and winter of 1873–74 from the lower Yukon, and with George Holt who was the first known white man to cross the Chilkoot Pass, finding little but prospects in the summer of 1875.

The first known payable gold mined in the watershed of the Yukon River was obtained by a miner named Cummins and his three partners from a small stream about 15 miles above Miles Canyon, in 1880.

However, in 1874 John SAYYEA and three companions came from Dease Lake up the Liard River, discovered gold on this stream and remained to mine it during the winter of 1874–75. From 115 days work they recovered 77 $^3/_{16}$ ounces of coarse gold, including nuggets of over an ounce in weight. Their find started a rush from the Cassiar goldfields in the spring of 1875 and gold was found on several nearby creeks. After Sayyea's first find no other payable deposits were worked, due mostly to problems of water in the deeper gravels. There was enough encouragement to keep prospectors active in this part of the Yukon until the time of the Klondike rush. The drawback to prospecting the Yukon Territory from this direction was the extreme difficulty of the route from either the Cassiar country or the Mackenzie valley. Either way was much more difficult and longer than by way of the Chilkoot Pass and the upper Liard Canyon was itself a much greater hazard than Miles Canyon. In fact, it was mainly the dangers of this route that had influenced the HBC to abandon its posts in the region in 1852. (See Cabin, Scurvy and Squaw Creeks, also Finlayson and Hyland Rivers.)

SCHAEFFER CREEK   67°50'N 139°51'W (116-O&N). A tributary of the Old Crow River.

Albert E. SCHAEFFER, a German trapper, married into the Old Crow Band. With his family he trapped the numerous muskrats in this part of the Old Crow Flats and the creek has been known locally by this name for many years. Schaeffer died of scurvy in Dawson in 1940.

The mountain in the bend of the river was named much later.

MOUNT SCHELLINGER   65°29'N 132°39'W (106-F). East of the Snake River.

In February 1973 this mountain was named after Arthur K. SCHELLINGER who was a mining engineer with the Yukon Consolidated Gold Co. of Dawson for many years, and then from 1920 to 30 worked for Keno Hill Mines Ltd., and the Treadwell Yukon Mining Company at Mayo. He was a well-known and well-regarded man.

SCHNABEL CREEK   60°19'N 134°59'W (105-D). Flows into Annie Lake at the big bend of the Wheaton River.

William F. SCHNABEL came into the Yukon in 1897. In 1898 he was the first man known to prospect Gray Ridge and that summer he found a coal seam on this creek. His wife was the first white woman in this part of the country; they lived in the district until they moved to Oregon in 1914.

Schnabel was nicknamed "Cowboy", as he never walked anywhere that he could ride a horse.

SCHWATKA LAKE   60°41'N 135°02'W (105-D). Above the power dam on the Yukon River at Whitehorse.

This lake was formed behind the hydro-electric power plant and dam on the Yukon River at Whitehorse. The lake covers the dreaded Whitehorse Rapids and Squaw Rapids and has eliminated the swift currents through Miles Canyon. This was accomplished and the plant put into operation in 1959.

Lt. Frederick SCHWATKA was born 29 September, 1849, in Galena, Illinois. His family moved west and he attended Willamette University in Oregon until he was accepted at West Point Military Academy from which he was graduated in 1871. Studying while serving at various western army posts, he acquired degrees in law and medicine.

In 1879–80 he led an expedition to the Canadian Arctic in search of the lost Franklin Expedition, which established his reputation as an Arctic explorer.

In 1883, under orders from General Nelson A. Miles, Commander of the Department of the Columbia (which included Alaska) and without notice to the Canadian authorities, he crossed the Chilkoot Pass and rafted down the Yukon River. Pte. Charles A. Homan, his topographer, made a rough but fairly accurate survey of the course of the river, the first to that time. Schwatka ignored all previous and contemporary nomenclature of the region. He seems to have assumed that no one had given names to any feature in the country before him so he named most of the rivers and lakes and some prominent hills along his route after his superior officers and prominent academicians of his day. He discarded Robert Campbell's "Lewes" River and changed it to the Yukon and named Lake Lindeman as the source of the Yukon River without investigating the Teslin or the Pelly. Dr. G.M. Dawson, GSC, disallowed most of Schwatka's names but allowed others to stand because of the international figures they honoured. Another reason was that Schwatka's work was incorporated into a map issued in 1885 by the USCGS. This was the best map of the region until the GSC issued those made by Dawson and Ogilvie in 1888.

Schwatka led an expedition in 1886 to climb Mount St. Elias, sponsored by George Jones of *The New York Times.* Schwatka was accompanied by William Libby of the College of New Jersey and by the only member of the party with any Alpine experience, Heywood W. Seton-Karr, an English sportsman and naturalist. It was remarked that for Seton-Karr to try to guide the 250-pound Schwatka up a 19,000 foot mountain would be a "quixotic enterprise". The party was away from the beach only nine or ten days and Mount St. Elias remained unclimbed.

In 1891, with C. Willard Hayes, USGS, and Mark Russell (a noted pioneer prospector who had made the trip previously), he went from Juneau via the Taku and Teslin Lake to Fort Selkirk and into the basin of the White River.

Schwatka early realized the value of publicity and rapidly published many glowing accounts of his travels, always emphasizing the hardships and dangers encountered. He became a member of many prestigious scientific societies and died in Portland, Oregon, on 2 November, 1892.

SCOTCH CREEK 63°05′N 139°19′W (115-O&N). The first tributary on the left up Thistle Creek.

This was named in late 1898 by someone of the party of eight Scots who first discovered the gold of Thistle Creek.

SCOTTIE CREEK 62°38′N 141°00′W (115-J&K). A tributary to the Chisana River in Alaska.

W.J. Peters and A.H. Brooks, USGS, named this stream for a member of their 1898 geological survey party. Gold was found in the gravels of the creek during the Chisana gold rush of 1913. It was sometimes called "Scotty" or "Big Scotty" Creek.

SCOUGALE CREEK 64°12′N 134°43′W (106-D). A tributary of the Beaver River.

This was named in the early 1900's by James A. SCOUGALE, a pioneer prospector in the Mayo district, who lived and mined here.

SCOUT LAKE 60°47′N 135°25′W (105-D). South of the Takhini River.

This lake was officially named in November 1973. A Boy Scout summer camp has been located here for a number of years.

SCOUTCAR CREEK 64°19′N 138°26′W (116-B&C). Crosses the Dempster Highway into the North Klondike River.

This was probably named in 1969 when highway construction workers bogged down such a vehicle in the stream.

SCROGGIE CREEK 63°12′N 138°51′W (115-O&N). A tributary of the Stewart River.

Ernest R. SCROGGIE of Rawdon, Québec, led a party of nine prospectors into this area in the summer of 1898. On 27 August two of the men, J.G. Stephens of Deadwood, North Dakota and H. LeDuke of Québec, found the first gold and staked the Discovery claim. The remainder of the party staked claims and the creek was named by Wealthy T. SCROGGIE, a brother of Ernest.

The creek has produced gold sporadically up to the present time.

SCURVY CREEK   60°49'N 130°32'W (105-B). A tributary of the upper Liard River.

Gold was found here in the summer of 1874 by Cassiar miners working north from the Dease Lake country. The journey was arduous and some miners wintered on this and neighbouring creeks rather than face the difficult trip back to the Dease Lake country.

In the following winter at least four of these men died of scurvy and were buried near the mouth of the creek, on the banks of the Liard. The remaining men were saved by three of their number who walked to Laketon (on Dease Lake) in March 1875, for help. The Victoria *Colonist* of 21 July, 1875, carried a letter from McDame Creek;

"I think it my duty to notify you of the great suffering of the Deloire (Liard) pioneers from the scurvy. Four have died from the said disease and ten others had a narrow escape. The only thing that saved them was three of their number coming out on the ice and getting to Laketown on 12 March, to report the suffering that four of their number endured at the time of their leaving them, I may mention the date, 12 February. We all subscribed at Laketown, and in two days we dispatched one white man and an Indian with medicine, rum, vegetables, potatoes, lime-juice, vinegar, etc. which the sick men received in sixteen days. Those who got here on the 19th inst. state that only for what was sent from here more than half of the sick men would have perished. The four who died were ailing all winter and were too far gone by the time they received the medicines.... The unfortunate men have died easy deaths. They got frozen in with their boats on 25 October 1874."

SEAFORTH CREEK   60°27'N 133°34'W (105-C). Flows north across the Alaska Highway into Squanga Lake.

This is an early name thought to have been given by a trapper who had seen service in the famous Seaforth Highlanders Regiment. During the construction of the highway the name was changed to "John Creek" by US Army Engineers but the name soon reverted to the original.

SEAGULL CREEK   60°00'N 131°11'W (105-B). Tributary to Swift River at mile 734 (K1189) on the Alaska Highway.

This was named by US Army Engineer troops during highway construction in 1942 because of the vast numbers of these birds that visited the camp's garbage dumps nearby.

On the mountainside east of this creek about 1960, Jack Shields found the only gem quality topaz ever found in the Yukon.

SECRET CREEK 63°57'N 135°58'W (105-M). A tributary of Haggart Creek.

Narcisse A. Lefebvre and Isaac Mallette found gold and named this stream on 7 September, 1911, giving the name because the stream enters Haggart Creek in such a way as to be nearly hidden from view. They mined their claims until August 1914.

MOUNT SEDGEWICK 2,956' 68°53'N 139°09'W (117-A). In the Buckland Mountains near the Arctic coast.

John Franklin, (later Sir) on his second expedition in 1826, named this mountain after Adam SEDGEWICK (1785-1873), the famous British geologist.

SEGUIN LAKES 66°43'N 134°22'W (106-L). East of the Peel River.

In April 1973 this map-designation name was given to commemorate Alavie J. SEGUIN, who was a Yukon Councillor for North Dawson from 1912 to 15.

MOUNT SELOUS 7,138' 62°58'N 132°28'W (105-K). North of the South MacMillan River.

This mountain, the highest peak in the Russell Range, was named about 1907 after Frederick Courtenay SELOUS by Joseph Keele, GSC. Selous had hunted here in 1904 and 1906 for specimens of big game. He was a noted naturalist as well as a famous African white hunter. Most of his hunting was for trophy specimens which were carefully preserved for various museums. From 1870 to 90 he hunted areas in Africa in which no other white man had ever set foot, finding and procuring new species of animals for museums at his own expense.

He died as a captain in the 25th Royal Fusiliers of the British army, decorated for bravery with the DSO, leading his troops in battle against the German army in East Africa. He was 65 years old when he was killed.

The peak had previously been known as "Chang Mountain", a name given it by N.A.D. Armstrong who mined on nearby Russell Creek for many years.

SELWYN MOUNTAINS 65°00'N 135°00'W (105-O). Paralleling the Yukon-NWT boundary.

The Selwyn Mountains comprise three ranges: the Logan, Hess and Wernecke Mountains. They were named in 1901 by Joseph Keele, GSC, after Dr. Alfred Richard Cecil SELWYN (1824-1902). Born in Somerset,

England, he was one of the most distinguished geologists of his time. He was with the Geographical Survey of Great Britain from 1845 to 52. From then until 1869 he was Director of the Geological Survey of Australia and from that date until his retirement in 1895 he was the Director of the Geological Survey of Canada. His contribution to the science was immense in all three countries. In Canada alone, he organized, expanded and directed the Geological and Natural History Survey after Confederation.

SELWYN RIVER   62°48′N 138°17′W (115-J&K). A small tributary to the Yukon River.

Lt. F. Schwatka, US Army, named this stream in 1883 after Dr. A.R.C. SELWYN, Director of the Geological and Natural History Survey of Canada. The name was allowed by Dawson. There was a small settlement at the mouth of the stream from 1900 to about 1950, as a telegraph post and a wood point for riverboats.

The river was prospected in 1885 by a man named Duval, an ex-jailer from Tacoma, Washington. In August 1898 he returned and staked a Discovery claim which he soon sold. Little gold was found on the stream and it was afterwards claimed that he had salted his claim, — i.e. that he had sprinkled gold dust in the gravels to make the claim appear richer than it actually was.

SEMINOF HILLS   61°27′N 134°35′W (105-E). The range of hills on the east side of the Yukon and Teslin Rivers.

Lt. F. Schwatka gave this low range of hills the name of von SEMINOF, President of the Imperial Geographical Society of Russia, in 1883. Sometimes spelled Semenof, or Semenov.

SERGERENT CREEK   61°44′N 140°12′W (115-F). A tributary of the Koidern River.

This was named about 1923 (officially in 1949) after a French big game hunter of this name who hunted here in 1913 and again in 1923. He was outfitted and guided by Gene Jacquot of Burwash. Buck Dixon, a well-known guide in the area, supplied the name to the GSC.

SERPENTHEAD LAKE   61°40′N 138°45′W (115-G&F). At the north end of Talbot Arm of Kluane Lake.

From the hills above, the lake resembles a striking snake head. H.S. Bostock, GSC, thought so in 1945 when he and his men were mapping the geology of the district.

MOUNT SETHER 5,296' 63°20'N 136°13'W (115-P). **On the south side of Ethel Lake.**

Although this mountain was named in June 1967, the creek which flows from it to Ethel Lake was prospected many years before by Ole SETHER, who found and worked on a gold-quartz vein nearby.

SETTLEMIER CREEK 64°28'N 135°14'W (106-D). **A tributary to the Beaver River in the Wernecke Mountains.**

Charles SETTLEMIER was an editor of the Dawson *Daily News* in the 1920's. He prospected widely in the Mayo area then and in the 1930's. This creek was named when he found silver-lead ore near it in 1923. The hill on the east side of the creek was later given the name Settlemier Ridge.

SEVENTEEN MILE 63°28'N 136°18'W (115-P). **On the south bank of the Stewart River.**

This was the location of an old riverboat wood camp. Louis Brown's roadhouse on the old Mayo winter trail was nearby. It has been long abandoned.

SEYMOUR CREEK 62°21'N 137°10'W (115-I). **A tributary to Big Creek in the Mount Freegold area.**

In 1899 Captain Henry SEYMOUR Back prospected in this area. He returned in 1910 with a party of men to re-prospect the region. In 1916 he developed gold prospects on this creek and gave it his name. His party found gold not only here but on many nearby streams. Back originally named the main stream after the famous British First World War Commander in Chief, Field Marshall Lord Kitchener of Sudan. The east fork he named Seymour. The name Kitchener was never adopted. (See Back Creek.)

SHATLAH MOUNTAIN 4,166' 67°37'N 140°05'W (116-O&N). **Eight miles northwest of Old Crow village.**

Named in 1973 to confirm a long-known local name, the Vanta Kutchin Indian word means "Long Hair."

SHAW CREEK 64°02'N 139°33'W (116-B&C). **A very short creek on the south side of the Yukon River about five miles above Dawson.**

This creek, really a gulch about one quarter-mile long, saw an exciting stampede in September 1903. Fred SHAW and Fred Jorgenson found good coarse gold and half the town of Dawson ran all the way to stake claims. The Mining Recorder named the creek.

SHEEP CREEK   60°58'N 138°34'W (115-B&C). A tributary of Slim's River.

The creek was named when placer gold was discovered and staked in October 1903 by the well known prospectors, Ater, Altemose, Smith and Bones.

SHELDON LAKE   62°42'N 131°03'W (105-J). On the Ross River near the south MacMillan, east of the Canol Road.

This lake was named "Rudyard Lake" in 1900 by Poole Field and Clement Lewis, early traders and sometime prospectors in the area. The name was common locally until Joseph Keele, GSC, mapped the region in 1907. He named it for Charles SHELDON, wealthy American sportsman and amateur naturalist who had hunted and camped in the area in 1905.

MOUNT SHELDON   6,937' 62°44'N 131°05'W (105-J). Three miles north of Sheldon Lake.

In 1900 Poole Field and Clement Lewis of the Ross River trading post "Nahanni House", named this peak "Kipling Mountain" in conjunction with Rudyard Lake at its base. Joseph Keele, GSC, however, renamed them both after Charles SHELDON in 1907.

SHELL CREEK   64°31'N 140°26'W (116-B&C). Flows into the Yukon River about five miles below Fortymile, from the east.

William Ogilvie, DLS, named this stream in the summer of 1896 when he found fossil shells in the rocks along its banks.

SHOALWATER BAY   68°53'N 136°43'W (117-A). An arm of Mackenzie Bay on the Arctic coast.

John Franklin sailed into this bay in 1826 and named it after running aground several times. (See Pillage Point.)

SHOOTAMOOK CREEK   60°49'N 131°00'W (105-B). A tributary to Scurvy Creek.

Billy Smith, Chief of the Tagish Band and a trapper and prospector, found gold on this creek in 1936 and named it "Shomdenook" which means "Rising Up" and probably relates to an Indian legend of a mythical golden man.

SHORTY CREEK 60°24'N 137°10'W (115-A). Flows to Alder Creek.

The man who found gold here in May or June 1896 and named the stream was an extraordinary character. "Long SHORTY" Bigelow was a pioneer in the Haines-Kluane country before 1894. He helped drive the first herd of cattle over the Dalton Trail in 1895. In 1903 he was sentenced to 15 years at hard labour in San Quentin Penitentiary in California by a St. Michaels judge after committing armed robbery on the Lower Yukon River. In 1909 he was granted a pardon when friends brought to the attention of the government the fact that he had once, in the dead of winter, hauled a crippled woman in a hand sled from the Big Salmon River to Skagway.

Returning to the country he married an Indian woman and afterward lived a quieter life.

SHUTDUNMUN LAKE 61°07'N 137°45'W (115-H). On upper Lake Creek.

This small lake which lies on the old Indian trail between Sekulmun Lake and the Jarvis River is called, in the local Indian dialect, "The Rest Place." The name was officially adopted in July 1962.

MOUNT SIBBALD 10,050' 61°14'N 140°01'W (115-G&F). On the east side of the Steele Glacier.

This was named in November 1970 after Andrew S. SIBBALD (1888-1945), lawyer and past president of the Alpine Club of Canada (1934-1938). The name was proposed by the club.

SIDNEY CREEK 60°46'N 132°57'W (105-C). A tributary to the Nisutlin River below Quiet Lake.

Gold was discovered on this stream in 1902 by Jim Thompson. News of the find started a rush to the district in June and July 1905 when he first thought he had found payable gold. He also found the first gold prospects and named Willow and Marble Creeks in the same area.

SIFTON RANGE 60°58'N 136°15'W (115-A). Small range of hills about 15 miles northeast of Champagne.

These hills were named before 1898 after the Hon. Clifford SIFTON, Minister of the Interior, 1896-1906, who had the unprecedented task of setting up the government apparatus of the Yukon Territory in 1897–98 under the most difficult conditions. This he did with outstanding ability and competence.

SIMPSON LAKE 60°44'N 129°15'W (105–A). On the west side of the Frances River, 50 miles north of Watson Lake.

In the summer of 1834, Chief Factor John McLeod of the HBC ascended the Liard River from the Mackenzie to the Frances River (which he called the Liard). He travelled the Frances as far north as this lake which he named after Sir George SIMPSON, the Governor of the HBC. This was the first lake in the Yukon Territory to be named by a white man.

SIMPSON RANGE 60°46'N 129°33'W (105–A). The mountains on the west side of Simpson Lake.

These were named about 1956 when the Campbell Highway (the Cantung Road at that time) was laid out.

SIMPSON TOWER 61°24'N 129°22'W (105–H). The lone peak sitting midway between the arms of Frances Lake.

On 19 July, 1840, Robert Campbell of the HBC first saw this peak and named it after Sir George SIMPSON, the Governor of the company. He named the lake the same day after Sir George's wife, Frances. (See Frances Lake.)

MOUNT SITTICHINLI 67°11'N 136°15'W (116–P). South of the Rat River.

Lazarus SITTICHINLI was a Special Constable of the RCMP. He drove dog teams for the RCMP patrol in the famous search for Albert Johnson, the "Mad Trapper of Rat River", in 1932. (See Moses Hill.)

SIXTYMILE RIVER 63°34'N 139°46'W (115–O&N). A tributary of the Yukon River, 50 miles above Dawson.

In 1876 Arthur Harper, sometime partner of McQuesten and Mayo, found good showings of gold on this river. Returning to Fort Reliance which had just been established and was the only trading post in the territory, he gave this river its name because it was 60 miles upriver from the fort. Although Harper made little from his prospects, others followed him and in 1891 rich placer gold was found on tributaries of this river. (See Ogilvie.)

SKOOKUM GULCH 63°56'N 139°20'W (115–O&N). A tributary to Bonanza Creek, just below its junction with Eldorado Creek.

Joseph Goldsmith had been in the Yukon for several years and was mining on American Creek, in Alaska, when he heard the news of the Klondike find. Too late to stake a claim on one of the major creeks he prospected the feeders and found extremely rich gold on this one. He staked the first claim and named the stream on 22 March, 1897. He and his partner panned $2,800 in four days and sluiced $40,000 in four months from claims 1 and 2.

SKOOKUM is a Chinook or coast trade word meaning "Strong".

MOUNT SKOOKUM JIM 65°11′N 139°03′W (116-G&F). South of the Ogilvie River.

In September 1973, the 75th anniversary of the Klondike Gold Rush, this mountain was named to commemorate one of the discoverers, SKOOKUM JIM Mason.

He and George Carmack assisted William Ogilvie over the Chilkoot Pass in 1887. In 1896, with Tagish (later Dawson) Charlie, they discovered not the first but the richest gold in the Klondike and on the east side of the Yukon River. Although there were many arguments as to which of the three actually panned the first gold on Bonanza Creek, Jim took little or no part in them. He worked and handled his claim wisely and remained a dedicated prospector until he died. He was instrumental in finding other placer goldfields in the Yukon, such as the Kluane fields.

He died in Carcross on 23 July, 1916. He left his estate not only to his family but also to help his people. He was always generous and respected by all who knew him.

SKULL RIDGE 3,106′ 68°32′N 137°26′W (117-A). 15 miles west of Mount Gilbert Davies.

This is a very old native name and was given because of the numerous animal bones and skulls they found there many years ago.

MOUNT SLAGGARD 61°11′N 140°34′W (115-G&F). In the St. Elias Mountains.

In July 1958 this mountain was given the name of Joseph R. SLAGGARD, a pioneer prospector in this area of the Yukon from the early 1900's. With his partners M.C. Harris and Solomon Albert (who made the original discovery) he staked the first claims containing significant amounts of copper ore at the headwaters of the White River near here in May 1905. Slaggard himself found the largest slab of pure native copper ever found in the territory. This specimen now stands at the McBride Museum in Whitehorse. They tried for many years to develop a mine on their discoveries but never found enough ore to be of economic value.

SLAGGARD RIDGE   61°45'N 140°45'W (115-G&F). At the headwaters of the White River.

This name was given by prospectors about 1906 after Joseph R. SLAGGARD, who was instrumental in locating copper deposits in this area. (See above.)

SLEEP CREEK   61°24'N 132°32'W (105-F). Flows into Seagull Creek and then into the McConnell River.

This was named in May 1962 to honour the memory of a gallant man, J-9483 Flight Lt. Kenneth Stephen SLEEP, MID. Born on 19 November, 1922, at Lindsay, Ontario, he enlisted at Toronto in the RCAF on 10 April, 1941. He served in Canada and overseas and was killed during air operations on 1 December, 1945.

SLEEPY MOUNTAIN   68°41'N 138°20'W (117-A). In the Barn Mountains.

Anker Hoidal, a long-time prospector and trapper on the North Slope, reported in 1961, according to the CPCGN records, that the name originated from an old Eskimo legend about a woman who took refuge on this mountain from a group of men. The woman had supernatural powers and put the men to sleep, thus eluding them.

MOUNT SLIM   60°56'N 134°52'W (105-D). South of Joe Creek.

Frank SLIM, an old-time riverboat pilot, died in 1973. This mountain was very shortly afterward named in his memory.

SLIM'S RIVER   60°59'N 138°33'W (115-B&C). Flows into the southwest end of Kluane Lake.

In the early part of 1903, during the rush to the Bullion Creek (or Kluane) goldfields, SLIM was drowned while crossing this river. He was a prospector's packhorse and his owner honoured him in this way.

MOUNT SLIPPER   5,583'   65°16'N 140°55'W (116-F). On the Yukon -Alaska border.

On 4 July, 1914, D.D. Cairnes, GSC, named this point after his assistant, E.S. SLIPPER. He had aided Cairnes in 1912 in mapping the geology along the boundary. This is the highest point on the boundary between the Yukon and Porcupine Rivers.

SMARCH RIVER (See Smart River.)

SMART RIVER 60°00′N 131°45′W (105-B). Flows south into British Columbia in the Cassiar Mountains.

This name is misspelled. The river was originally and for many years the homesite and trapping area of the SMARCH family, a well-known Indian family in the southern Yukon. They lived near where the river crosses the Alaska Highway.

SNAFU CREEK 60°08′N 133°53′W (105-C). A tributary to the Lubbock River.

In 1949-50 the Canadian Army Engineers located and built the road from Jake's Corner to Atlin, BC, a distance of 61 miles.

The name they gave this creek (the lake at its head was named later) was a catch-word widely used in the British and Commonwealth Armed Forces during the Second World War. It originated before the war, probably in the RAF. The term means "Situation Normal—All Fouled Up". Anyone who served in the armed forces will recognize this. (See Tarfu Creek.)

SNAG 62°24′N 140°22′W (115-J&K). A tributary to the White River.

In 1899 A.H. Brooks and W.J. Peters, USGS, named this river because of the obstacles they met while travelling along it.

The Dominion Department of Transport established a weather station and an emergency flight strip near the mouth of the stream in 1942, in conjunction with the air-lift to Russia. The coldest temperature ever officially recorded in Canada was measured here on 3 February, 1947. It was −81°F. The station was closed in September 1966.

SNAKE RIVER 65°58′N 134°12′W (106-E). A tributary to the Peel River.

When John Bell, Chief Trader of the HBC at Fort MacPherson, explored the lower part of this river in 1839 he named it the "Good Hope" River, after Fort Good Hope on the Mackenzie River. Charles Camsell, GSC, noted in 1905 that although the name had long been changed some of the local people still referred to it as the "Good Hope".

The name was probably changed by A.K. Isbister of the HBC in the winter of 1840-41 when he explored farther up the river. The stream is an unending series of bends and oxbows, which could account for the name. Oddly enough, although there are no snakes in the Yukon, the Loucheaux

Indian name for the river translates as "Hairy Worm River", perhaps in memory of an infestation of some sort of caterpillars.

SOLDIER'S SUMMIT 61°02′N 138°31′W (115–G&F). On the southwest shore of Kluane Lake at the foot of Sheep Mountain.

At this spot on 20 November, 1942, the Alaska Military Highway was officially opened by E.L. Bartlett of Alaska and Ian MacKenzie of Canada, eight months after the start of construction. A monument marks the spot.

SOMME CREEK 62°24′N 138°40′W (115–J&K). Flows into the Klotassin River.

D.D. Cairnes, GSC, named this creek in 1916 after the Battle of the Somme in France in which he lost some of his friends.

SONORA GULCH 62°40′N 138°02′W (115–J&K). A tributary to Hayes Creek.

George Beal found gold and staked the Discovery claim on this creek in September 1898. He named the creek after the Mexican state of SONORA, where he had previously prospected.

SOUCH CREEK 61°37′N 133°45′W (105–F). A tributary to the Big Salmon River.

On 1 November this stream was honoured by the name of a Canadian hero, J-16825 Flying Officer George Allan SOUCH, DFC. He was born in Toronto, Ontario on 13 August, 1916, and enlisted in the RCAF there on 7 March, 1941. While serving overseas he was killed during air operations on 29 July, 1943.

SOURDOUGH GULCH 63°59′N 139°22′W (115–O&N). A tributary to Bonanza Creek from the west, four miles above the mouth.

Fred E. Envoldsen and his partner, John P. Hering, found the first payable gold on this stream on 5 June, 1901, and renamed it. It had been staked by others in 1897 who had named it 67 Pup, from its location, but were unable to find enough gold and abandoned it. (See Strathcona Creek.)

SPRAGUE CREEK 63°55′N 136°28′W (115–P). Flows into the North McQuesten River.

Gold was found and the creek named by a miner-prospector of this name. He continued to live here for many years.

SQUANGA LAKE 60°29′N 133°38′W (105-C). At mile 850 (K1377) on the Alaska Highway.

This small, pleasant lake received its name from the Indians long ago. The name is that of a small, rounded type of whitefish of superior flavour, which abounds in the lake.

SQUAW CREEK 60°02′N 137°10′W (115-A). Flows into the Tatshenshini River below Dalton Post.

In 1927 Paddy Duncan of Champagne and Klukshu found the gold of this stream and named the creek. In 1936 he was sentenced to life imprisonment for murder.

The creek had been called "Dollis" Creek by miners around 1898 but had been long abandoned when Duncan renamed it. The name "Dollis" is still found on some maps.

SQUAW CREEK 63°47′N 137°28′W (115-P). A tributary of Clear Creek.

About 5 May, 1901, this creek was staked and named by W.A. MacDonald, Dan MacDonald, Edward Carroll and George Kennedy. They were too late to stake claims in the stampede to the Clear Creek gold finds but found enough on this stream to stake it and name it.

THE SQUAW TITS 5,900′ 60°29′N 136°44′W (115-A). On the northeast side of Dezeadash Lake.

These rounded twin buttes beside the Dalton Trail were named by Dalton or his men before the Klondike Gold Rush and were used as landmarks by those travelling the trail. They were first reported and mapped by J.J. McArthur, DLS, who examined the trail for the Department of the Interior in 1897.

STAN LAKE 65°10′N 140°05′W (116-G&F). Southwest of Mount Deville.

This was named in September 1973 after STANLEY Rivers, a long-time prospector in the area.

STARR CREEK 61°47′N 131°51′W (105-G). A tributary to the Pelly River.

Gilmore and Elsie STARR came into the Yukon in May 1898. They had arrived in Skagway in 1897 but Gilmore contracted spinal meningitis while packing supplies over the White Pass. They had financed their journey to the Klondike by the sale of their North Dakota homestead after it had been laid waste by a cyclone.

Arriving in Dawson in the spring of 1898, they prospected up the Klondike River and then on Eureka Creek. Elsie owned and ran the Hillside roadhouse on Hunker Creek in 1899. They later prospected up the Pelly River and it is believed that they lived here about 1905 to 10, after finding some gold in the stream.

STEAMBOAT BAR 63°36′N 137°33′W (115-P). A large gravel island in the Stewart River about 14 miles below the mouth of the McQuesten River.

This is the richest bar ever found on the Stewart River and was reported in 1885 to have yielded for some time at the rate of 8½ ounces of gold per day per man. The deposits, being shallow and about two feet in thickness, were quickly exhausted.

In 1885 a group of miners hired the ACC's small steamboat the *New Racket*. It had been brought up the river from St. Michaels by the Schieffelin brothers of Arizona and was the second steam vessel on the Yukon. The boat was hauled up on the bar and her engines were detached from the paddlewheel. They were made to drive a set of pumps manufactured on the spot, which supplied water for the set of sluice boxes. With this crude machinery, the miners cleared $1,000 each and paid an equal amount to the owners of the boat. This was the first use of powered machinery to mine in the Yukon.

STEAMBOAT MOUNTAIN 6,376′ 64°15′N 135°38′W (106-D). In the Ogilvie Mountains.

This was named by Tony Hollenback, an early prospector in the region, because of its appearance. The name was confirmed in 1955.

MOUNT STEELE 16,640′ 61°06′N 140°19′W (115-G&F). In the Icefield Ranges of the St. Elias Mountains.

J.J. McArthur, DLS, while surveying the international boundary in July 1909, named this peak after one of the most outstanding men in the history of the Yukon.

Major General Sir Samuel Benfield STEELE, KCMG, CB, MVO, was born in Purbrook, county of Simcoe, Ontario, in Upper Canada, on 5 January, 1849. His father was Captain Elmes Steele, RN, and an uncle, Colonel Samuel Steele, had served at the capture of Québec.

He was commissioned an ensign in the 35th Simcoe Foresters at the age of 15, after serving as a private. He took part in the repulse of the Fenian Raids in 1866. To see action, he reverted to corporal in the Ontario Rifles during the Red River Rebellion of 1870.

He and his two brothers enlisted at the formation of the North-West Mounted Police in August 1874, when he was immediately appointed Sergeant Major of "A" Division. He took part in the Great March of 1874 and by 1878 he had reached the rank of inspector. During the Northwest Rebellion of 1885 he commanded the cavalry composed of the NWMP and Steele's Scouts of the Alberta Field Force.

1887 saw him in command of the NWMP expedition to the Kootenays in eastern BC, the establishment of Fort Steele and the settling of the Indian troubles in that country. During this period he maintained law and order during the construction of the Canadian Pacific Railway through the Rocky Mountains.

He commanded the NWMP posts on the White and the Chilkoot Passes from February to July 1898, the height of the Klondike Gold Rush. At this time he was also magistrate and in charge of Canada Customs for the area. In July 1898 he was prompted to lieutenant-colonel, made a Member of the Council of the Yukon Territory and commander of all NWMP forces in the territory. He held all these positions with honour, distinction and efficiency until September 1899. The tradition of NWMP efficiency and incorruptibility was upheld and strongly reinforced by him and his men during this time.

He raised and commanded the Lord Strathcona's Horse and again served with more than ordinary ability and distinction in the South African War from 1899 to 1901, winning many honours and decorations. He commanded the Transvaal Division of the South African Constabulary, 1901–1906. On 1 March, 1903, he resigned from the NWMP.

In 1907 he returned to Canada and, promoted to colonel, was placed in command of Military District No. 13 (Calgary) until 1909, and of Military District No. 10 (Winnipeg) until 1914. During this period he greatly increased and developed the Canadian militia on the prairies.

In 1914 at the outbreak of the First World War, he was promoted to major general and made Inspector General of Western Canada. At this time he published his autobiography, *Forty Years in Canada*. He organized, commanded and trained the 2nd Canadian Division from May to August 1915 and from then to July 1918 commanded Shornecliff Military District which contained nearly all the Canadian troops in England. At the same time he was Chairman of the Canadian Militia Council in Great Britain, 1915–16, which made him nearly equivalent to commander-in-chief of the Canadian forces in the United Kingdom. Again he won high honours, finally being made Knight Commander of the Order of St. Michael and St. George, one of the most distinguished honours of the British Empire.

Owing to failing health he retired in July 1918. He died on 30 January, 1919, at Putney, England and was buried at Winnipeg.

STEEP CREEK   63°42′N   134°57′W   (105-M). Flows into the south arm of Mayo Lake.

This was one of several rich, gold-bearing creeks found by a party of four Australian prospectors in August 1903. They named the creeks and brought 15 ounces of coarse gold from this stream into Dawson where it assayed a value of $19.57 to the ounce, probably the purest placer gold ever found in the Yukon.

MOUNT STENBRATEN   6,466′   64°05′N   132°08′W   (106-C). Near the headwaters of the Stewart River.

In May 1973 this mountain was named after John O. "Stampede John" STENBRATEN, a noted Yukon prospector from 1904 to 1960. It is said that Stampede John took part in nearly every mining rush in the Yukon, Alaska and into Siberia in these years.

STEVENS CREEK   60°15′N   134°58′W   (105-D). A tributary to the Wheaton River.

In 1905 George STEVENS found the first quartz-gold lode on the hill above this creek. Later, about 1908, it was named after him. He lived beside the creek here which already had his name.

STEVENSON RIDGE   4,493′   62°34′N   138°50′W   (115-J&K). Between Dip Creek and the Klotassin River.

Hugh S. Bostock, GSC, named this ridge in 1941 after a man named STEVENSON, who was a senior partner in a placer mining company on Rude Creek for many years and an active prospector in the area at the same time. (See Leslie Ridge.)

STEWART GULCH   64°02′N   135°49′W   (106-D). A small valley on the left side of Dublin Gulch.

This was named after J.S. STEWART who found and worked on a lode quartz gold vein here in 1917.

STEWART LAKE 60°38′N 128°42′W (105-A). 40 miles north of Watson Lake.

An old trapper, half-Indian, half-black, of that name, lived here and trapped in the general area toward the Frances River for many years. He and his family were still here in 1941 and some of them are buried here.

STEWART RIVER 63°19′N 139°26′W (115-O&N). A major tributary of the Yukon River from the east.

In the winter of 1849 Robert Campbell of the HBC at Fort Selkirk, sent his "dear and gallant friend" James G. STEWART, who was also his assistant clerk, northeast of the fort to find some Indians believed to be hunting in that area. Stewart travelled farther than anyone had before and crossed this stream on the ice. He reported it to Campbell on his return and Campbell named it after him. Stewart was the son of the Hon. James Stewart of Montréal.

The Indians of the district reported in 1883 to Lt. F. Schwatka, US Army, that the river's native name was "Na-Chon-De" which was also the name of the tribe living upon it. Schwatka did not change the name of this large river.

Prospecting started on the Stewart in 1884 with a few men who found encouraging signs of good, payable, fine gold on the river bars. In the spring of 1885 Frank Moffatt recovered the first of this rich bar gold. In the late summer of the same year "Slim Jim" Wynn, who had first come over the Chilkoot Pass in 1879, found a rich bar 100 miles upstream. Called "Wynn's Bar" it paid at $6,000 to the man for less than 50 days work. In 1886 fully 100 men were working on the bars of the Stewart and some had prospected nearly to its headwaters.

One group of miners made a deal with Mayo and McQuesten to rent the little steamer *New Racket* and used its engines to mine the gravels of Steamboat Bar. (See Steamboat Bar.)

Some of the bars worked were Wynn's (Winn's), Dutch John's, Lac de Bar, Halfmoon, Chapman's, Joe Jay Bar, Low Water and Black Mike's Bar. These and other bars were worked until the Klondike Gold Rush, although they were deserted for a time after the discovery of the Fortymile goldfields in late 1886. The miners in the Yukon referred to the Stewart as the "Grubstake River", because enough gold could always be won on it to provide money for supplies for another season of prospecting.

In the summer of 1886 Frederick Harper, of Harper, McQuesten and Mayo, established a trading post at the mouth of the river to serve the miners upstream. Some of the miners called the post "Fort Nelson" after Pte. Edward William Nelson of the Signal Service of the US Army, who was said to have been there at the time, collecting specimens of the flora and fauna of the region. (He went on to make invaluable collections of the Yukon and Alaska and later became one of America's most famous naturalists.) In late 1886, coarse gold was found on the Fortymile River and the miners abandoned the Stewart for a few years. Harper moved his trading post to Fortymile in June 1887.

In Klondike days the settlement of the same name at the mouth of the river was revived as a wood point for riverboats, a NWMP post and a wintering place for miners unable to reach Dawson before winter. Many of these men prospected the tributaries of the river in 1897–98 and later. In July 1897 Robert Henderson staked a 40-acre townsite on the banks of the Yukon opposite the mouth of the Stewart but it never succeeded.

William Ogilvie, who had been Commissioner of the Yukon from 1898–1901, became the President of the Yukon Basin Gold Dredging Co. Ltd., of Missouri, which held extensive leases on the Stewart and operated with limited success, 1908–12.

David and Mary Shand ran the Hotel Stewart, a roadhouse here, from 1900 until it burned in 1918. They rebuilt it and operated it as Johnson's Roadhouse until 1930. They wrote a book about their experiences there entitled *The Summit and Beyond.*

STOKES POINT 69°21'N 138°42'W (117–D). Southeast of Herschel Island on the Arctic coast.

On 16 July, 1826, John Franklin named this feature after his friend Capt. John L. STOKES RN, commander of the *Acheron.*

STONY CREEK 60°47'N 135°59'W (105–D). A tributary to the Takhini River.

This is notable only because an American Army Engineers maintenance camp was established here in 1942–43 during the construction of the Alaska Highway.

STOWE CREEK 63°37'N 138°59'W (115–O&N). A tributary to Montana Creek from the west.

Gold was discovered and the creek named by A.F. STOWE in May 1901. The lower part of this creek was originally called Conglomerate Creek.

STRATHCONA CREEK   63°47'N 139°32'W (115-O&N). A tributary to Indian River from the north.

On 5 January, 1902, Fred Eugene Envoldsen and C.W. Williams found gold, staked and named this stream, probably in honour of the Lord Strathcona's Horse, a Canadian cavalry regiment raised and first commanded by Col. Sam B. Steele of the NWMP. The regiment served with great distinction in the South African War from 1899–1902.

Envoldsen was one of the most active prospectors in the country for many years. He was a participant in the stampede to the Firth River placer gold finds in 1948. (See Sourdough Gulch, Bertha Creek and Firth River.)

MOUNT STRICKLAND   13,818'   61°14'N 140°40'W (115-G&F). In the Icefield Ranges of the St. Elias Mountains.

This was named about 1918 after Inspector D'Arcy STRICKLAND of the NWMP. He had enlisted in 1891 and was one of the first of the force in the Yukon, arriving at Fortymile in July 1895 with Inspector Charles Constantine. He was the first officer in command of the detachment on the White Pass in February 1898 and later at the important Tagish Lake Post where every gold-seeker was registered and passed through Customs.

He died in the service in 1908 in the midst of a distinguished career.

MOUNT STUTZER   4,165'   61°58'N 136°06'W (115-H). On the east side of the Nordenskiold River about ten miles south of Carmacks.

D.D. Cairnes, GSC, named this peak sometime in 1908 after Dr. Otto STUTZER, Assistant Professor of Geology at the Royal School of Mines in Freiberg, Germany. Stutzer had assisted Cairnes in 1908 when he mapped the geology of this area.

SUGDEN CREEK   60°41'N 137°54'W (115-A). A tributary to the Kaskawulsh River from the north. (See Ferguson Creek.)

SUGDEN PUP 61°01'N 138°44'W (115-G&F). A very short tributary of Bullion Creek from the south.

Dr. L.S. SUGDEN, an American physician, was prominent in early Dawson and Yukon politics. He was also an active prospector and mining promoter, in which he was fairly successful. He took part in the first prospecting of the Bullion Creek goldfields and was the first to find gold on this small gulch in the winter of 1907–08.

Dr. Sugden, in the early years of the Klondike, went to Lake Laberge one winter to attend a sick man. Upon arrival he found the man dead. He was unable to bury him, owing to the depth of frost in the ground. The wreck of the riverboat *Olive May* was nearby so Sugden cremated the body in the boiler of the boat. This incident was the basis of Robert W. Service's famous poem "The Cremation of Sam McGee".

SULLIVAN HILL 64°21′N 135°26′W (106-D). At the headwaters of the Beaver River.

This was named after John SULLIVAN, a prospector who was one of the first men into the area during the rush to the silver-lead finds on nearby Carpenter Creek in the early 1920's. He prospected in the Mayo district from 1920–50.

This map location is shown as McKay Hill, which is a few miles farther east.

SULLIVAN ISLAND 63°12′N 139°34′W (115-O&N). A small island at the mouth of the White River.

It was named after an early woodcutter who supplied the riverboats about 1897 and later. David and Mary Shand built and operated a small sawmill here in May 1898 and ran it till 1900.

SULPHUR CREEK 63°38′N 138°40′W (115-O&N). Flows into Dominion Creek in the Klondike.

This creek was named about 1896 or early 1897 for the suphur-bearing mineral water springs found near the headwaters on King Solomon's Dome, claim No. 73 Above Discovery.

There were two Discovery claims filed on this creek; the first was found by a prospector named Stafford on 22 July, 1897. He was mining on nearby Quartz Creek and one night had a dream of finding gold on Sulphur. He told his partner the next morning, set out for Sulphur and did find gold! For some reason this claim was not recorded. However, on 24 August, 1897, W.A. Miller and his partner W.C. "Swiftwater Bill" Gates staked another Discovery claim much lower downstream and found gold in large enough amounts to start a stampede from Dawson in which the whole creek and its tributaries were all staked. Gates' claim been staked by another man in late July but he also did not record it.

Although not nearly as rich in gold as Eldorado, Bonanza or Hunker Creeks, Sulphur Creek paid steadily and well. The pay streak for much of the creek was the widest of any of the Klondike, up to 500 feet of gold-bearing gravels. Andrew Baird, a young Australian farmer, came over the White Pass in the spring of 1898 and staked No. 11 Above Discovery. Later in 1899, when the news of the Nome finds depopulated Dawson, he cannily purchased ten more claims on the creek for a standing price of $1,000 each, from gold won from No. 11. After mining for a number of years he sold out to a large company which wished to set up dredging operations, becoming their accountant at the same time. He eventually became the manager of the Yukon Consolidated Gold Co. from which he retired, a wealthy man, in his late 70's. He had mined for 60 years on the Klondike, the title he gave to his autobiography. He died in Vancouver, BC in April 1975 at the age of 99.

SULPHUR SPRINGS 63°52′N 138°58′W (115-O&N). At the head-waters of Sulphur Creek.

These mineral springs gave Sulphur Creek its name. In the fall of 1906 a 30-mile-long railroad, the Klondike Mines Railway, was completed from Dawson to this spot. Sulphur Springs was the terminus, with waiting rooms, offices, freight sheds and other conveniences.

SUMMIT CREEK 61°23′N 134°22′W (105-E). A tributary of the Big Salmon River near Livingstone Creek.

Gold was discovered here and the stream named by a prospector named Meany in 1901. In August 1905 a nugget of gold weighing 39 ounces, the largest found in the area to that time, was found on the stream.

SUNAGHUN CREEK 67°31′N 141°00′W (116-O&N). Flows into the Porcupine River near Rampart House.

This is a Kutcha-Kutchin Indian name reported by the International Boundary Survey party of 1914. According to Professor O.W. Geist of the University of Alaska, this word means "old woman". The creek was so named because, according to Orth's *Dictionary of Alaska Place Names*, "An old woman at Rampart House could not climb the steep river bank so she used this creek as a route to obtain her firewood. Hence, Old Woman Creek".

SUPER CUB CREEK 60°02′N 137°57′W (115-A). A small tributary to the Alsek River.

In August 1963 Dr. Alex Smith, GSC, named it after a small lake just over the border in BC. The lake was named because a mining company working in the area found that a Piper Super Cub aircraft was the largest that could use the lake.

SURPRISE LAKE   60°33'N 133°20'W (105-C). A very small lake about four miles north of Johnson's Crossing.

This little lake was named by the Chief of the Teslin Indian Band in 1952 while he was guiding a party of the Canadian Army Topographical Survey.

SURVEYS RANGE   63°35'N 132°12'W (105-N). Between Fido Creek and the Rogue River.

Hugh S. Bostock, GSC, named these hills in November 1970 to honour the topographical and geodetic surveyors of Canada who had prepared the maps of the Yukon. They had been uncommemorated to this time. He had originally proposed the name "Surveyors Range."

SWANSON CREEK   61°19'N 138°18'W (115-G&F). A tributary to Gladstone Creek near Kluane Lake.

This was named by Axel SWANSON who, with T.T. Murray, was the discoverer of gold on this stream and on Gladstone Creek in 1911.

SWEDE CREEK   60°58'N 131°18'W (105-B). A tributary of the upper Liard River.

An old prospector, known only as "The SWEDE", lived here between 1900 and 1930. He travelled the Liard River in a beautifully built dug-out canoe, 32 feet long, which he had constructed himself. It would travel lightly through the most dangerous waters and he propelled it with a minimum of effort, the envy of all the Indians and prospectors who saw it.

SWEDE CREEK   64°01'N 139°34'W (116-B&C). A long tributary to the Yukon River, five miles above Dawson.

When C.A. Olafson and his group found gold and staked the Discovery and other claims here on 2 February, 1898, the Mining Recorder at Dawson named the stream after the nationality of the men. A stampede from Dawson resulted in over 600 claims being staked on the creek and its tributaries in the following three weeks. In spite of these efforts little gold was ever mined. For a number of years at the time a small settlement existed at the mouth of the creek. A steamboat wood point, it was also a favourite vacation camping place for Dawson people.

SWEDE JOHNSON CREEK 61°36'N 139°24'W (115-G&F). A tributary to the Kluane River, near the highway.

Ernest "SWEDE" JOHNSON prospected and trapped in this area for many years. He was the discoverer of the first gold found on Tatamagouche Creek.

SWIM LAKES 62°11'N 132°52'W (105-K). A group of small lakes 15 miles east of Faro.

These lakes were given their name in the summer of 1935 by J.R. Johnston, GSC, and his survey party. They were the only lakes found that season which were warm enough for swimming.

TABOR LAKES 66°58'N 134°46'W (106-L). East of the Peel River.

These small lakes were named after Charles William TABOR as a map-designation name in 1973. He had been a Yukon Councillor representing North Dawson from 1912 to 15 and a pioneer lawyer in the territory.

TADRU LAKE 62°28'N 135°42'W (105-L). Ten miles southeast of Tatlmain Lake.

This was named in 1950 by R.B. Campbell, GSC. The word is a contraction of the name Taylor and Drury, a firm of Whitehorse merchants. They operated trading posts in many of the most isolated parts of the Yukon from 1899 on.

Isaac Taylor was born in Thirsk, Yorkshire, England and came to the Yukon with the Klondike rush in 1898 via Australia. He met William S. Drury, from Kirme, Lincolnshire, while working on the Discovery claim on Pine Creek in Atlin, BC. Here they decided to go into business supplying the needs of the miners.

They then opened a tent store in Bennett on 14 August, 1899. They moved their store to Whitehorse when the railroad was completed in July 1900. Their venture succeeded and they expanded by opening posts in various parts of the territory: Pelly Banks in 1905; Teslin in 1906; Mayo, Carmacks and Fort Selkirk in 1919. They built a small riverboat, the *Kluane*, to service these posts. In 1912 they amalgamated with Whitney and Pedlar, Whitehorse merchants who were instrumental in developing the first copper ore bodies at Whitehorse, and built the present large store. They had stores in 18 locations at one time and even had company coins minted in Ottawa which were in use from 1912 to 1950. The business was finally sold by the family in 1974.

TAGISH 60°19′N 134°16′W (105-D). On the narrows between Tagish Lake and Marsh Lake.

The road from Carcross to Jake's Corner on the Alaska Highway was built in late 1942 to lay the gasoline pipeline from Skagway to Watson Lake. The present settlement of Tagish grew up around the bridge built then. The old location during the gold rush years was a TAGISH Indian village about three miles south and on the east side. The NWMP built one of their most important posts in the Yukon at this place, calling it Fort Sifton after the then Minister of the Interior. Every traveller passing this point was required to register his party and his boat was given a registration number. Customs officers, sometimes police, examined all outfits. Opened in early 1897, it brought some order to the mad rush down the river. Inspector D'Arcy Strickland, who had come in with Inspector Constantine in 1895, was in charge. A post office was open from 20 August, 1897, to 1 October, 1901.

TAGISH LAKE 60°10′N 134°20′W (105-D). A large, many-armed lake straddling the Yukon-BC border east of Carcross.

The name is ancient and from the Indian "Ta-Gish-Ai", which is also the name of the native people who lived there. Schwatka ignored the Indian name and designated it Lake Bove after a Lt. Bove of the Italian navy. Dr. G.M. Dawson, GSC, disallowed the name, relegating it to a small island at the entrance of Windy Arm. Dawson retained the old Indian name for the lake.

The early miners called it "Tako" or "Tahko" Lake. Part of the main route to the lower Yukon River and the goldfields, two places on the lake were approached with trepidation by the miners sailing down; the mouths of Windy Arm and Taku Arm were given to sudden and furious winds and these locations were the scenes of many wrecks and drownings.

MOUNT TAGISH CHARLIE 65°53′N 139°48′W (115-G&F). West of the Porcupine River.

This northern peak was named in the Klondike Jubilee year of 1973 to commemorate TAGISH CHARLIE. He, with George Carmack and Skookum Jim Mason, found the fabulous gold of Bonanza Creek on 16 August, 1896, which sparked the greatest gold rush in history. He was afterwards known as "Dawson Charlie."

At and before the gold rush, Indians usually took English Christian names from white associates, with the tribal or band designation added, i.e. "Tagish Charlie", "Tahu Jack", "Stick Jim", etc.

Charlie was the first Indian (and perhaps the only one) of the Yukon Territory to be given the full rights of a Canadian citizen by an Act of Parliament; he was allowed to vote, hold public office, sue and be sued and to buy and drink spirituous liquors.

On 26 January, 1908, he fell from the railway bridge at Carcross and was drowned.

TAHTE CREEK   61°59'N   137°11'W   (115-H). A small tributary to the Nisling River from the south.

When J.J. McArthur, DLS, made his rough survey through this country in 1897 he thought that the Nisling River was the "Tahte" of the local Indians and so mapped it. After the error was corrected this name was given to this small stream. No translation was given.

TAKHINI   60°51'N   135°27'W   (105-D).

This old settlement lay at the crossing of the Takhini River on the old Dawson road. It was the first stop out from Whitehorse and had a NWMP post as well as a roadhouse. The roadhouse was owned and operated by W.A. Puckett. Both it and the police post were closed in May 1907.

TAKHINI HOT SPRINGS   60°53'N   135°22'W   (105-D). About five miles up the present Dawson Highway.

These hot mineral springs were discovered and staked by W. A. Puckett, who owned the nearby Takhini roadhouse, and Stephen Simmons in late April 1907.

The water flow then and now is about 86 gallons per minute at a temperature of 118°F (47°C). The water is sweet and odourless, containing no sulphur. It is said to be beneficial to sufferers of arthritis and rheumatism.

TAKHINI RIVER   60°51'N   135°11'W   (105-D). A large tributary to the Yukon River about 12 miles north of Whitehorse.

This river was first noted by Dr. Aurel Krause of the Bremen Geographical Society in 1882, the first white man to explore the southwestern part of the territory. The name, recorded by Krause, is from the Tagish Indian "Tahk-Heena", "Tahk" meaning "mosquito" and "Heena" meaning "river."

TAKIAH CREEK   67°51'N   137°58'W   (116-P). Flows into Driftwood Creek.

This is a local name which in the Vanta Kutchin language means "Little".

TALBOT ARM   61°30′N 138°37′W (115-G&F). The large bay at the southeast end of Kluane Lake.

This bay was named in the summer of 1945 by H.S. Bostock, GSC, after Albert Charles TALBOT, DLS, who made the first good map of Kluane Lake and the area in 1898 while with the Department of the Interior. He liked this calm bay. He was a member of the International Boundary Commission, 1893–95. The bay had been previously known as "Little Arm".

TALLY-HO MOUNTAIN   60°14′N 135°03′W (105-D). In the big bend of the Wheaton River.

About the year 1906 there was much prospecting activity and a number of promising mineral finds were made in this area. Among the more successful was a group of young English prospectors who worked energetically in this vicinity. In a gulch on the west end of this hill they found good lode showings of gold-silver-lead ore which they called the "TALLY-HO" claims. They explored this ground until about 1916 and were known locally as the Tally-Ho boys. The mountain, which had been known as Big Bend Mountain, was soon given the name of the group. Most of them went to England in 1915–16 to enlist in the British forces for the First World War and it is supposed that most of them were killed in the fighting as they did not return to the Yukon.

TANTALUS BUTTE   2,568′ 62°08′N 136°16′W (115-I). Five miles north of Carmacks.

This lone hill was named in 1883 by Lt. F. Schwatka, US Army. Because of the convolutions of the Yukon River in this area, anyone approaching the place became confused; at one point approaching the hill, and at another going away, repeatedly.

George Carmack, the discoverer of Bonanza Creek, found a seam of coal on this hill in 1893 and made sporadic attempts to develop it. He was backed by Arthur Harper who had a 50% interest in the venture. In 1903, Captain Charles E. Miller, who had been a coal miner in Mauchunk, Pennsylvania, located a claim on this coal and mined 40,000 tons in the next two years to supply the riverboats. He came into the Yukon in 1897 and built the Yukon Sawmill in Dawson, then ran the riverboats *Clara* and *Reindeer*. After the *Reindeer* burned in 1900 he turned to coal mining. In 1905 he located the Tantalus Butte Coal Mine which had an estimated reserve of five million tons of coal. He sold out his holdings soon afterward to the WP&YR.

TARFU CREEK 60°06′N 133°53′W (105–C). A tributary to the Lubbock River, northeast of Atlin Lake.

In 1949–50 the Canadian Army Engineers located and built the road from Jake's Corner to Atlin, BC. While surveying the route they gave this stream a name derived from a common World War Two slang expression. The word TARFU was an extension of the word Snafu: "Situation Normal, All Fouled Up". Tarfu means "Things Are Really Fouled Up". (See Snafu Creek.)

TASIN RANGE 63°55′N 132°45′W (105–N). Between the Stewart and Lansing Rivers.

This was mapped in 1907 by Joseph Keele, GSC, who retained the local name which in the Indian language means "Black" or "Dark". Mount Ortell is the highest peak in the range.

TATAMAGOUCHE CREEK 61°22′N 139°18′W (115–G&F). A tributary to Burwash Creek.

Ernest "Swede" Johnson, a pioneer prospector, discovered gold here and named the creek after the river of the same name in New Brunswick in 1904 during the rush to the Kluane goldfields. It is also spelled Taddemagooch. (See Swede Johnson Creek.)

TATCHUN RIVER 62°17′N 136°19′W (115–I). A tributary to the Yukon River at Five Finger Rapids.

Dr. G.M. Dawson, GSC, retained this Indian name on his survey of 1887 but did not obtain the translation.

TATLMAIN LAKE 62°37′N 135°59′W (105–L). South of the Pelly River.

In the winter of 1848–49 Robert Campbell, while at Fort Selkirk, obtained large quantities of fish for the fort from this lake. The whitefish here are particularly succulent and plentiful. The name is the original Indian one of that time and no translation was given.

TATONDUK RIVER 65°00′N 141°00′W (116–G&F). A tributary to the Yukon River from the Ogilvie Mountains.

It was variously called Tatondu, Tatonduc, Totondu and, by the early miners, Sheep Creek. TATONDUC is an Indian name reported by Lt. F. Schwatka, US Army, in 1883 as "Tatondu" and by J.E. Spurr, USGS, in 1896 as "Tatonduc." The name means "Broken Rock" River because of the numerous rocks in the channel. William Ogilvie, DLS, was the first white man known to traverse this stream when he and his party travelled its length in the spring of 1888, on their way from Fortymile to Fort Mac-Pherson.

TAY RIVER 62°34′N 134°22′W (105–L). A tributary of the Pelly River from the north.

In 1848, Robert Campbell of the HBC, while making his epic journey down the Pelly to the Yukon River, named this stream after the River TAY which flows through the city of Perth in Scotland, near his ancestral home.

Tay Lake was named much later and Tay Mountain, 6,991′, near the mouth of the stream was named because of its proximity.

TAYLOR CREEK 62°44′N 138°48′W (115–J&K). A small tributary to Casino Creek in the Dawson Range.

This creek was named by R.J. Cathro of Whitehorse in May 1970 after C.D.N. "Red" TAYLOR, BSc., P. Eng., a veteran mining engineer for 30 years in the Yukon. He explored this area and its copper deposits very extensively.

TELFORD CREEK 63°11′N 138°58′W (115–O&N). Flows into the Stewart River from the south.

It is likely that this creek was named after Captain TELFORD of the RNWMP, who was officer in charge at Mayo about 1917.

TELLURIDE CREEK 60°52′N 138°05′W (115–B&C). A tributary to the Jarvis River.

Tom Laird found placer gold here and named the stream in January 1904 during the stampede to the newly-found Alsek goldfields.

TELLURIDES are a group of rare minerals formed from tellurium, gold and sometimes sulphur, iron or other elements. None have ever been found in this area and it is likely that Laird named the creek after the gold-mining camp of Telluride, Colorado, where he may have worked earlier.

TEMPEST MOUNTAIN 61°17′N 140°11′W (115–G&F). On the north side of the Steele Glacier in the St. Elias Range.

This peak was officially named in November 1970 by the Alpine Club of Canada. It was first climbed on 26 August, 1941, by Anderson Bakewell. The name describes the weather conditions met on the climb.

TENT ISLAND 68°55′N 136°35′W (117–A). On the Yukon-NWT border of Shoalwater Bay.

On Friday 7 July, 1826, John Franklin with his two boats *Lion* and *Reliance*, sailed close to this island where they discovered several hundred Eskimos camped in tents.

(See Pillage Point.)

TESLIN LAKE 60°15′N 132°57′W (105–C). A large lake in the south central Yukon, straddling the Yukon-BC boundary.

This beautiful lake retains its Indian name although slightly changed: "TES-LIN-TOO" meaning "Long, Narrow Water". The first white men known to have seen the lake were "Ike" Powers, a noted pioneer prospector, and eight or nine companions who came from Juneau and up Taku Inlet and overland to the foot of the lake in either 1876 or 77. They built three boats and did a limited amount of prospecting around the lake. The next white men here were Charles Munroe and his three companions who followed Powers' route in 1880 and also prospected the lake and some of its tributaries. It was long thought that Michael Byrne of the Western Union Telegraph Company had explored north from Telegraph Creek to the foot of the lake in 1869 but opinion now is that he reached Atlin Lake.

As part of an all-Canadian Route to the Klondike, many people travelled from Glenora and Telegraph Creek 160 miles to the foot of the lake. There they built boats and sailed down to the Teslin River, on to the Lewes (Yukon) and down to Dawson. By using this route they missed the dangerous Miles Canyon and Whitehorse Rapids as well as the frightening storms of the Chilkoot Pass. The little steamer *Anglian* was built at the foot of the lake and was launched on 13 June, 1898.

Although there had been temporary settlements at the south end of the lake (in British Columbia) in 1897–98 and a HBC post there until 1903 or 04, the first trading post set up on that part of the lake in Yukon territory was built by Tom Smith in 1903 at the mouth of the Nisutlin River. He came from Dawson in the little steamer *Quick*, piloted by Captain Henry

Henderson (brother of Robert Henderson). The post was operated by Taylor and Drury for many years till about 1955 and a settlement has existed there ever since.

On maps of the 1880's the lake was sometimes called "Aklen", "Ahklen" and "Arklun". Dr. G.M. Dawson officially retained the original Indian name in 1887.

TESLIN RIVER 61°34'N 134°54'W (105–E). A major tributary to the Yukon River.

The Indians of the very early days had several names for this stream. Michael Byrne of the Western Union Telegraph Company, although he did not see the river, was told that it was the "Hootalinkwa" or "Hotaliqu". The first miners to prospect up the river from the Yukon in 1881 called it the "Iyon" after the tribal name of the natives living at its mouth. The USCGS map of 1884 used this name. Lt. F. Schwatka, US Army, while on his 1883 excursion named it the "Newberry" River, after Professor Newberry of New York. This name was never accepted or used. The Tagish Indians called it the "Nas-A-Thane" meaning "No Salmon", although there are such fish in the river and the lake. Some early maps mistakenly named it the "Tahko" River.

This was the first major tributary of the Yukon River to be prospected; fine gold was found in many of the gravel bars, but no coarse gold was ever located.

It was one of the major routes to the Klondike goldfields in 1897–98. After Teslin Lake was reached the river was clear sailing down to Dawson and all major obstacles were by-passed.

TETLIT CREEK 66°43'N 135°23'W (106–L). A tributary to the Road River.

This was named in 1962 by B.S. Norford, GSC, after the TETLIT band of Indians who live in the area.

THATCHELL CREEK 61°33'N 137°35'W (115–H). Flows into the northwest corner of Sekulmun Lake.

Recorded by the GSC field crew in 1956, this is an old Indian name meaning "Hide Scraper". The Indians for untold years came here to obtain a certain type of shale rock from which were fashioned good scrapers to work animal hides.

THETIS BAY 69°34′N 139°05′W (117-D). On the east side of Herschel Island.

Lt. Commander Charles Stockton, USN, in the survey ship USS *THETIS* charted much of the Arctic coast and the shores of Herschel Island in 1889. He named this bay after his ship and many of the island features after the whalers he found there. The bay is one of the very few safe anchorages to be found on the western Arctic coast and was much used by wintering whalers, 1885–1905.

THISTLE CREEK 63°04′N 139°28′W (115-O&N). A tributary of the Yukon River just above the mouth of the Stewart River.

In the summer of 1898 a party of eight Scottish prospectors examined this stream and found good payable gold. The two discoverers, Murdoch McIver and Robert Haddow each staked a Discovery claim on 28 September, 1898. They named the creek after the Scots nation emblem — a THISTLE. Robert Henderson bought or otherwise acquired 50% interest in McIver's Discovery claim. Their party prospected the neighbouring streams and named several of them. Thomas Barton, one of the original party, died in Dawson in 1916.

THISTLETON 63°04′N 139°27′W (115-O&N).

This small settlement and steamboat landing at the mouth of Thistle Creek was built to serve the miners working there. Sometimes called "Thistle Creek", it lasted only a few years after 1898.

THOMAS CREEK 68°11′N 140°39′W (117-B). Flows south into the Old Crow River.

Neil MacDonald, living at Old Crow, a grandson of the first Anglican minister of Fort Yukon, Robert MacDonald, stated that a local Indian named THOMAS had erected a caribou fence on this stream. It was several miles long and was used to trap the caribou to kill them. The remains of the fence still exist.

THOMAS GULCH 64°03′N 139°23′W (116-B&C). A very short stream entering the Klondike River from the south, one mile upstream from Bonanza.

D.W. THOMAS found enough gold here to stake the first claim on 20 November, 1897, but it did not pay when it was dredged in 1912–14.

THOMAS RIVER 61°33′N 129°31′W (105-H). Joins the Anderson River to flow into the north end of the west arm of Frances Lake.

This stream was named in July 1840 by Robert Campbell of the HBC after THOMAS Simpson, a friend of Campbell's in the company.

THOMPSON CREEK 63°55′N 135°42′W (105-M). Flows north into the South McQuesten River.

This was likely named by or for Ogden Pickett THOMPSON, who came into the Yukon in 1898 and spent a number of years in this immediate area. He left here in 1914 and lived at Johnson Creek in the Mayo district where he made a new and profitable discovery which he mined for some further time. He was known as a good, hard-working prospector.

THOROUGHFARE CREEK 63°41′N 137°05′W (115-P). Flows into Vancouver Creek.

H.S. Bostock, GSC, gave this name in the summer of 1949 because the old Conservative Trail to Clear Creek runs along the banks of this stream.

THORPE CREEK 60°02′N 125°37′W (95-C). Flows into the Crow River.

On 2 February, 1966, this small stream was named after William George THORPE (1892-1955) who was for many years in charge of the map collection in the Department of Lands and Forests at Victoria, BC. He was supervisor of map production for BC from 1951 to 55.

THRASHER BAY 69°33′N 139°12′W (117-D). On the southwest side of Herschel Island.

This bay was named by Lt. Commander Charles Stockton, USN, of the survey ship U.S.S. *Thetis*, when he surveyed the coast of Herschel Island in 1889. The name is that of a whaler which was anchored in the bay at the time.

THREE BARREL LAKE 64°56′N 136°06′W (116-A). In the Wernecke Mountains.

This small, one-mile-long lake was named in the early 1960's by "Pat" Callison, member of a pioneer Yukon family and a noted bush pilot. He kept a gasoline cache (storage) on the lake for his aircraft during mining exploration in the area.

THE THREE GUARDSMEN 61°11′N 137°13′W (115-H). **A group of three peaks on the south shore of Ittlemit Lake, southwest of Aishihik Lake.**

These three prominent peaks were named by miners in the 1890's who used them for landmarks. Named after the three musketeers in Alexandre Dumas' famous novel of that name, they are from east to west, Mount Athos, Mount Porthos and Mount Aramis.

MOUNT TIDD 5,563′ 62°04′N 131°19′W (105-J). **About 28 miles west of Pelly Lake.**

This was named in September 1971 to commemorate Sergeant Claude Britoff TIDD, RCMP. He came to the Yukon in 1915 and served at Old Crow, Ross River, Mayo, Dawson and Fortymile until the 1940's. His entire enlistment was spent in the Yukon Territory.

TILLEI LAKE 61°46′N 129°29′W (105-H). **About 12 miles north of the west arm of Frances Lake. Drains into the Thomas River.**

Dr. G.M. Dawson, GSC, although he did not visit the lake, gave it its Indian name "TIL-E-I-TSHO" meaning "Walking Stick River". (Actually, he gave the name to the creek which drains the lake.) In 1887 he traversed this country and spoke to Henry Thibert, the discoverer of the Dease Lake goldfields in the Cassiar, who had been prospecting in this area. Thibert gave him much information on the lakes and streams of the region.

TINDIR CREEK 65°19′N 141°00′W (116-G&F). **Flows across the Yukon-Alaska border to the Nation River.**

This small creek was named in 1910 by a survey team on the international boundary. Thomas Riggs of the US was in charge. The word is an Indian name meaning "Moose".

TINTINA TRENCH 64°25′N 140°00′W (105-K, 115-P).

The GSC gave this name, meaning "Chief" in the native language, to the broad valley north of, and parallel to, the Yukon River between Fortymile and Dawson. The valley occupies one of the largest faults in the Yukon geological system. It was named by R.G. McConnell, GSC, in 1901–02. He spelled it "TIN-TIN-A".

TINY ISLAND LAKE 63°50′N 134°15′W (105-M). **15 miles east of Mayo Lake.**

H.S. Bostock, GSC, named this small lake in 1940 while investigating the area for strategic minerals for Canada's war industries.

TIZRA CREEK   67°03'N 137°30'W (116-P). Drains Whitefish Lake.

A long-known local name, "TIZRA" is a Vanta Kutchin Indian word which describes a certain type of whitefish.

TOM CREEK   60°11'N 129°02'W (105-A). About eight miles west of Watson Lake, flowing into the Liard River.

This is a long-used local name after "Liard TOM", an Indian trapper whose cabin is at the mouth of the stream. He appears in an article written about the district in the National Geographic Magazine of May 1942.

TOMBSTONE MOUNTAIN 8,200' 64°24'N 138°40'W (116-B&C). About 33 miles northeast of Dawson at the head of the Tombstone River.

This was originally named by William Ogilvie, DLS, in 1896 after Robert Campbell (1808-1894), Chief Factor of the HBC, the discoverer of the Pelly, Lewes and upper Yukon Rivers, and builder of Forts Frances, Pelly Banks and Selkirk. It is a shaft of black rock about 600 feet wide, that rises 1,000 feet above the surrounding ridge.

The Klondikers who spread out through these valleys in their search for gold in 1897–98, having no maps of the area and unaware of its name, called it TOMBSTONE Mountain because of its singular resemblance to a grave marker.

Since that time much argument has gone on concerning its exact location. In 1968, Dr. D. Tempelman-Kluit, GSC, determined that they were both the same mountain. The Geographical Board of Canada decided to retain the miners' name. However, both before and after that date many maps, both governmental and others, still call this peak "Mount Campbell."

TOOBALLY LAKES 60°15'N 126°20'W (95-D). Two lakes on the Smith River in the southeastern corner of the Yukon Territory.

These lakes were known and fished in the 1830's to supply food for the HBC trading post at Fort Halkett at the junction of the Smith and Liard Rivers.

TOO-TSHO RANGE (See Logan Mountains.)

TORONTO CREEK 63°46'N 139°07'W (115-O&N). A tributary to Quartz Creek.

Herbert W. Savage of Toronto, Ontario, named this stream when he found enough gold on it to stake the first claim on 3 January, 1898.

TOULEARY CREEK 62°56′N 139°13′W (115-J&K). Flows into the Yukon from the east, just above Kirkman Creek.

Grant and Albert Kirkman found gold here in the summer of 1898, staked the Discovery claim on 26 July and named the creek after their home town of Tulare, California. Someone spelled the name phonetically.

TOWER PEAK 5,672′ 61°17′N 133°14′W (105-F). On the north side of Big Salmon Lake.

Because of its distinctive appearance, Arthur St. Cyr, DLS, gave the peak this name in 1898 while surveying and mapping the Quiet Lake-Big Salmon River area.

TRAFFIC MOUNTAIN 6,739′ 62°07′N 130°18′W (105-J). The lone peak within the junction formed by the Pelly River and Lakes.

This prominent and long-known landmark is another Yukon mystery. Although probably named about 1840 by Robert Campbell of the HBC or one of his men, and shown on a map made in 1849 and nearly all maps since, there has been no record yet found of what or whom the name represents.

TRAIL RIVER 66°40′N 134°40′W (106-L). A tributary to the Peel River.

This is the English version of the local Indian name. It is so called because the Indians ascended this stream on foot on their way across country from the Peel to the Bonnet Plume River. The stream is wild and unnavigable so all must walk the length of the river.

TRESIDDER CREEK 63°29′N 136°14′W (115-P). Enters the Stewart River about ten miles above Stewart Crossing.

In September 1941 the Geographic Board of Canada confirmed this old local name. Charles TRESIDDER was an old-timer who had trapped and lived for many years on this creek.

TRITOP PEAK 6,079′ 62°13′N 137°31′W (115-I). Ten miles north-west of Mount Nansen.

About 1910 the early miners in the Mount Nansen district called this hill "The Haystack". A few years later the name was changed by a GSC survey party, ignorant of its local name and the new name was made official. The name comes from its appearance: it has three summits.

TROMBLEY CREEK 62°40′N 138°36′W (115-J&K). A small tributary to Dip Creek in the Dawson Range.

This brook was named on 16 September, 1915, during the staking rush to Rude Creek. Timothy TROMBLEY was from Québec and an active prospector in many parts of the Yukon.

TROPICAL CREEK 60°05′N 126°19′W (95-D). Flows into the Smith River, south of Toobally Lakes.

This was named by the personnel of an oil exploration company in 1949 because of the luxuriant vegetation along the banks of the stream, caused by the waters of the hot springs found there.

TRUITT CREEK 62°12′N 134°22′W (105-L). Flows into the east end of Little Salmon Lake.

This creek was named by a survey team of the US Army Corps of Engineers in the summer of 1942. Col. James J. TRUITT was in charge of location surveys for a proposed railway from Prince George, BC to Fairbanks, Alaska, which was intended to supplement or replace the Alaska Military Highway then being constructed.

Section "A" of the Trans Canadian, Alaska and Western Railway was between the above points. Section "B" was to be carried from Fairbanks to Nome, Alaska. On section "A" actual field surveys were carried out by 24 teams comprised of 556 men. They started early in May and completed the surveys by October 1942.

It was estimated that the railroad from Prince George to Fairbanks would be by way of Finlay Forks and Lower Post, BC, then to Ross River, the Five Finger Rapids and west to Fairbanks. The line was to have been approximately 1417 miles in length and estimated to cost about $111,000,000.

After the defeat of the Japanese forces in the Aleutian Islands and the successful construction of the Alaska Military Highway, the railroad project was dropped in favour of improving the highway.

The present Ross River—Carmacks Highway used these surveys as a guide to location. (See Railway Survey Creek and Truitt Peak.)

TRUITT PEAK 6,799′ 62°15′N 134°15′W (105-L). In the Glenlyon Range, at the headwaters of Truitt Creek.

Col. James J. TRUITT, US Army Corps of Engineers, was on an inspection flight of survey parties on the routes of the Trans Canadian, Alaska and Western Railway and the Canol Road in the early spring of 1942. He was returning to Whitehorse by aircraft when the pilot of the bomber they were flying allowed him to take over the controls. He had never flown an aircraft before and nearly crashed into this mountain. The pilot flew the rest of the way. After landing, the aircraft crew suggested they name this peak after him as a joking reminder of his only attempt at flying and the survey parties accepted the name. The name was later confirmed on GSC maps and was made official in 1946. The survey parties later used the name for the creek below the peak.

TUMMEL RIVER 62°47′N 135°06′W (105–L). A tributary to the Pelly River from the south.

Robert Campbell of the HBC, on his exploration of the Pelly River in the summer of 1840, named this stream after a river of the same name near his home in Perthshire, Scotland.

TURNER LAKE 66°11′N 134°15′W (106–L). West of the Peel River.

This was named in April 1973 for the new, small-scale topographical maps, after John TURNER who had been a Yukon Councillor for the Bonanza District from 1915–17.

MOUNT TURNER 65°24′N 136°14′W (116–H). East of the Hart River.

This peak was named in May 1973 to commemorate Constable F. TURNER, RNWMP, a member of the Dempster Patrol which searched for and found the lost Fitzgerald Patrol, starved to death in the Peel River country in 1911. He volunteered for this task although he was no longer a member of the force.

TUSTLES LAKE 61°43′N 129°12′W (105–H). 15 miles northeast of the west arm of Frances Lake.

This was named by Dr. G.M. Dawson, GSC, in 1887, from the Indian name "TUSTLES-TO", for which he provided no translation.

TWELFTH OF JULY CREEK 61°10′N 138°03′W (115–G&F). A tributary of Fourth of July Creek.

During the start of the rush to the Kluane Lake goldfields, Charles Racine discovered gold and staked the Discovery claim on this stream on 12 July, 1903, eight days after "Dawson" Charlie staked that of Fourth of July Creek which started the whole rush.

TWO LADDER CREEK   60°01′N 131°44′W (105-B). A tributary to the Smart (Smarch) River.

This name was given to Dorsey Lake about 1939–40. Two local Indians sank a prospect shaft for placer gold near the lake and reported that it was two ladders deep.

Dorsey Lake has regained its name and for some reason this name has been applied to this stream ten miles away.

TWOPETE CREEK   62°42′N 133°56′W (105-K). A tributary to the Tay River from the south.

J.R. Johnson, GSC, in 1935 noted this name in local use after two Swedish prospectors and trappers who lived here. Both had the given name of Peter. The mountain was named later.

TYERS RIVER   61°14′N 129°12′W (105-H). Flows into the south end of Frances Lake.

This river was named by Robert Campbell of the HBC, probably about 1840 when he was building Fort Frances. The original Indian name is not known and this is probably a Scottish name.

MOUNT TYRRELL   4,747′ 63°43′N 140°04′W (115-O&N). Between the Sixtymile and Yukon Rivers.

Joseph Burr TYRRELL (1858–1957) served the GSC from 1880 to 98 and was a noted exploration geologist in the North West Territories and the Yukon. He was born in Weston, Ontario on 1 November, 1858, and educated at Upper Canada College and the University of Toronto, where he won scholarships and graduated with distinction. He took an active part in the militia and served with the Queen's Own Rifles and later in the Governor General's Foot Guards. He was a crack shot with both rifle and pistol.

After resigning from the GSC he practised as a mining engineer in Dawson for seven years. His hobby, for which he became well-known, was researching and writing about the men of the early fur trade and their explorations in Northern Canada. He died in Agincourt, Ontario.

TYRRELL CREEK 61°55′N 138°02′W (115–G&F). A tributary to the Nisling River.

This was officially named in June 1955 after Joseph Burr TYRRELL BSc., GSC, who travelled this stream when he mapped the geology of the area, including the Nisling River, in 1898.

ULU MOUNTAIN 10,160′ 60°13′N 138°46′W (115–B&C). Ten miles southeast of Mount Kennedy.

Named after the "ULU", the Eskimo women's knife which is the symbol of the Arctic Winter Games. The peak was first climbed on 6 March, 1970, by "Monty" Alford, Louis Lambert and Jim Boyde, to celebrate the newly-established Games which embrace people from the NWT, Alaska and the Yukon.

URANUS CREEK (See Pooly Creek.)

MOUNT VAN BIBBER 6,456′ 63°02′N 135°37′W (105–M). In the McArthur Group about 35 miles south of Mayo.

This name was requested by Mrs. D.J. Fulton of Cranbrook, BC in March 1967 to commemorate her father, Ira VAN BIBBER.

Ira Van Bibber with his two brothers Theodore and Patrick, came from West Virginia to the Klondike in 1898. Ira loved the country and married an Indian wife. They trapped for three years in the then almost totally unknown Nahanni country. He became one of the best big game guides in the Yukon. He made his home for most of these years at Pelly Crossing and this mountain is in the midst of the region where he hunted and trapped. After more than 60 years in the Yukon he died, leaving many descendants to carry on his traditions.

VAN CLEAVES HILL 63°49′N 135°32′W (105–M). Six miles west of Mayo Lake.

VAN CLEAVE, prospector and trapper, lived for years at the foot of this mountain.

MOUNT VANCOUVER 15,700′ 60°20′N 139°41′W (115–B&C). A boundary line peak in the St. Elias Range.

In 1874 Professor W.H. Dall, who was with the Western Union Telegraph Company expedition as scientific director, named this peak in honour of Captain George VANCOUVER, RN, (1758–1798).

Captain Vancouver, in command of the sloop *Discovery* and accompanied by Lt. W.R. Broughton, RN, in command of the tender *Chatham*, made an exploring and surveying voyage from England to southeastern Alaska and around the world from 1790–95.

Vancouver's expedition, among other accomplishments, added a wealth of knowledge of and names to the previously ill-defined coastal features of southeastern Alaska. He respected the names he found applied by the inhabitants and traders and the nomenclature of his charts was generally accepted.

This mountain was first climbed by N.E. Odell, A. Bruce, Bill Hainsworth, Bob McCarter and Robertson on 5 July, 1949.

MOUNT VANIER 6,049′ 60°37′N 136°02′W (115–A). At the northeast corner of Kusawa Lake.

Georges VANIER, DSO, MC and Bar, MID, Legion of Honour (France), Order of Merit (US), BA, LLD, was born in Montréal on 23 April, 1888.

Vanier was educated in law at Laval University but found an early aptitude for military life. In 1914 he helped found the 22nd French Canadian Battalion, the famous "Van Doos". (In 1920 the battalion was made the Royal 22nd Regiment).

He served overseas in France from 1915–18 with high distinction, winning many decorations for bravery and losing his right leg in battle in August 1918. He continued as a soldier, attending Staff College at Camberley, England in 1922. In 1925 he was promoted to lieutenant colonel and given command of the Royal 22nd Regiment.

His diplomatic career began about this time; he was chosen as a Canadian delegate to the League of Nations in 1927 and made Minister to France in 1939, holding the post until 1942. He was a part of the highest Allied war councils and a major figure in Canadian diplomacy during the war and after.

On 3 August, 1959, he was made Governor General of Canada. He was the first French Canadian to hold the post and a popular one in all parts of the country. Serving, as always, with distinction, he died on 5 March, 1967.

VAN GORDER CREEK 62°13′N 133°22′W (105–K). A tributary of the Pelly River near Ross River.

Dell Charles VAN GORDER was born in Ord City, Nebraska on 4 March, 1876. He came to the Yukon about the turn of the century, attracted by the stories of gold.

In the early years he gravitated to the upper Pelly River country where he prospected and trapped for many years, often with Ira Van Bibber. About 1910 he became the manager of the Taylor and Drury trading post at Pelly Banks. Leaving there about 1944, he took over their post at Ross River until 1949. He retired to Teslin where he died, a respected pioneer, on 21 November, 1953. That same year Allan Kulan found a large lead-zinc-silver ore body near this creek. In June 1971 the new school at Faro was given Van Gorder's name.

His name was often misspelled "Van Gorda" and as such will be found on most maps.

VEESHRIDLAH MOUNTAIN   67°07'N   139°21'W   (116–O&N). On the headwaters of Lord Creek in the Keele Range.

This is an old Vanta Kutchin Indian word meaning "dark", which describes the appearance of this hill.

VICTOR CREEK   62°38'N   138°50'W   (115–J&K). A tributary to Dip Creek.

Gold was found here and a Discovery claim was staked on 16 September, 1915, by Timothy Trombley and Henry Detraz. They named it Galena Creek but the name was changed by the Mining Recorder in Dawson as there already was a Galena Creek. (See Trombley Creek.)

VICTORIA CREEK   60°32'N   137°26'W   (115–A). Flows into Louise Lake, the westernmost of the Kathleen Lakes.

Peter Ehret found the first placer gold in this creek in the summer of 1902. When he recorded the Discovery claim on 24 May, the Mining Recorder, Insp. A.E.C. McDonnell, NWMP, named the stream for the occasion.

VIRGIN CREEK   60°25'N   137°26'W   (115–A). A tributary to Victoria Creek, ten miles west of Dezeadash Lake.

To quote the *Whitehorse Star* of 19 August, 1905, "Thomas Laird arrived yesterday from Virgin Creek, of which he is the discoverer, in the Kluane district. He has taken out enough gold to pay good wages all summer." Laird made his find in June.

There is some evidence that an earlier prospector in the area, one William Trettin, had prospected and named the stream in 1903 during the rush to the Kluane Lake diggings.

VITTREKWA RIVER   67°00'N   135°35'W   (106-L). Crosses to the NWT in the western Richardson Mountains.

In 1900 and later an Indian of this name lived on this river. The Dawson-MacPherson Patrol of the RNWMP camped at his cabin. They spelled his name "Vitchiquah", which in the Loucheaux language means "No Cry".

VOLCANO   MOUNTAIN   4,063'   62°55'N   137°22'W   (115-I).   11 miles north of Fort Selkirk.

Hugh S. Bostock, GSC, in 1935 reported in GSC Memoir No. 189 that "This is probably the only well preserved volcano and crater of its size in Canada."

VON WILCZEK CREEK   62°36'N   136°54'W   (115-I). Enters the Yukon River north of Rink Rapids from the east.

Lt. F. Schwatka, US Army, named this stream in the summer of 1883 after Graf VON WILCZEK of Vienna, Austria, but called it a river.

The Geographical Board of Canada changed the designation to creek in July 1960 and at the same time gave the same name to the small lakes on the upper reaches of the stream.

VOREEKWA LAKES   67°08'N   138°16'W   (116-O&N). Southeast of the Sharp Mountains.

These were named in 1973 as a map designation. Enquiries of the natives of Old Crow concerning the origins of the name brought the answer that it is a Vanta Kutchin word meaning "no name". (Some field man had his leg pulled on this one.)

MOUNT   VOWLES   61°25'N   136°11'W   (115-H).   East   of   Aishihik Lake.

D.D. Cairnes, GSC, while mapping the geology of the area in 1910, named this landmark on the Dalton Trail after Stanley Tom VOWLES, RNWMP No. 4206. He enlisted in the force in 1904 and resigned in 1908. Most of his service was spent in this area, where Cairnes knew him.

VUNTA CREEK   67°55'N   136°33'W   (116-P). A small tributary to Fish Creek, north of McDougall Pass.

This was named in the summer of 1962 by B.S. Norford, GSC, after the VUNTA Band of Indians whose trapping grounds run from here to the Porcupine River.

WALHALLA CREEK 63°07'N 138°37'W (115-O&N). Flows into Scroggie Creek.

This was known in the earliest days as the left fork of Scroggie Creek until paying gold was found in 1912 by a prospector named LeBouef. It was believed that he had been prospecting in Australia in earlier years and named this creek after the rich goldfields of WALHALLA, in the state of Victoria, Australia, which had been discovered before 1900.

MOUNT WALLACE 7,726' 61°03'N 138°34'W (115-G&F). At the southwest corner of Kluane Lake.

This mountain was named in 1960 to honour Dr. Robert C. WALLACE, past president of the University of Manitoba, former principal of Queen's University at Kingston, Ontario and distinguished scholar and geologist.

WALSH GLACIER 60°53'N 140°37'W (115-B&C). South of the Centennial Range in the St. Elias Mountains.

J.J. McArthur, DLS, of the International Boundary Survey Commission, named this feature after Supt. J.M. WALSH of the NWMP in 1900. (See Mount Walsh.)

MOUNT WALSH 14,780' 61°00'N 140°01'W (115-G&F). A boundary peak in the south St. Elias Mountains.

In July 1900, J.J. McArthur DLS, of the International Boundary Commission, named this mountain after Superintendent James Morrow WALSH of the NWMP.

Born in 1841 at Prescott, Upper Canada, Walsh was one of the original force, enlisting in 1873. After a distinguished career in the west he resigned in 1883. When the Klondike frenzy broke out he was called upon by the Canadian government, with almost unanimous public approval, to administer and govern the newly-formed Yukon Territory. He went to the Yukon in September 1897, armed with almost dictatorial powers. As well as being given the post of the Commissioner (Governor), he was handed sole command of the NWMP in the territory and appointed Supervisor of Customs and Mail Services.

Walsh spent only a year in the Yukon. Although there were many criticisms of his methods and ethics, there is no denying that, under almost intolerable conditions, he skilfully organized order out of chaos. He was ably assisted by some of the great names of the NWMP, such as Steele, Jarvis, Constantine, Wood, Belcher and others. He was hindered by honest but inefficient civil servants whose inability to cope with the huge numbers of persons flooding into the territory led to unproven charges of government graft and corruption.

He died of a stroke on 25 July, 1905 at Brockville, Ontario.

MOUNT WALTERS 3,189′ 62°47′N 137°04′W (115-I). Ten miles east of Fort Selkirk.

This was named in 1971 to commemorate No. 127 Private H. WALTERS of the Royal Regiment of Canada, a member of the Yukon Field Force of 1898. He marched overland from Glenora on the Stikine River, to the foot of Teslin Lake and came by boat (rowing, not steam) to Fort Selkirk. He died here in service on 28 February, 1899, and is buried here.

MOUNT WANN 65°56′N 140°15′W (116-G&F). West of the Porcupine River.

In September 1973, this mountain was named after Clyde Gavin WANN, who organized the first commercial air service in the Yukon. He carried the first air mail between Whitehorse, Mayo, Keno, Dawson, Carcross and Atlin in 1928–30. He assisted the US Army Corps of Engineers in scouting the route for the Alaska Highway and, immediately after it was opened for public travel, built some of the first tourist services on the road at Rancheria, Morley River and Destruction Bay.

WAREHAM LAKE 63°41′N 135°52′W (105-M). On the Mayo River, five miles above Mayo Landing.

The fore-bay, or reservoir of the hydro-electric power plant here has been known locally as Wareham Lake ever since it was created, after the late Rev. G.W.N. WAREHAM, who drowned in Mayo Lake some years ago. The plant was built in 1952 to provide power for the silver-lead mines in the area.

WASSON LAKE 60°52′N 130°27′W (105-B). On the southeast side of the Simpson Range near the headwaters of the Liard River.

This small lake was named in February 1936 after Everett WASSON, the first bush pilot in the Yukon. He flew a Fairchild 71 for the Treadwell Yukon Mining Company, 1928–35. From 1935 until 1940 he was general manager and chief pilot of the WP&YR's Aviation Division.

Wasson flew the first air-search and rescue mission in Yukon history. The Burke party was lost on the upper Liard River and Wasson was called in.

On 3 November, 1930, he and Joe Walsh, an experienced Yukon prospector and guide, started the search. Due to a lack of knowledge of Burke's original destination much time was lost searching in the wrong directions.

Wasson and Walsh found the party on the banks of the upper Liard River on 6 December. After taking care of the survivors Walsh had to repair the aircraft's propellor, which had been damaged on landing. He whittled an axe handle and spliced the propellor. The repaired propellor held and the aircraft was flown to Atlin, BC. Burke had died of exhaustion and exposure shortly before the party was found. This was the first operation of its kind in the Yukon. The Dominion government awarded Wasson $1,500 and Walsh $500 for their hazardous efforts.

Wasson died of a heart attack in Alexander Valley, California in December 1958.

WATERS RIVER 67°28′N 137°01′W (116-P). Flows into the Bell River at Lapierre House.

It is probable that this river was named after Corporal WATERS of the RNWMP, who assisted the GSC in 1917 when they were mapping in this area.

MOUNT WATES 61°14′N 140°04′W (115-G&F). Southeast of the Steele Glacier in the St. Elias Mountains.

This was named by the Alpine Club of Canada in 1970, after Cyril Geoffrey WATES (1884-1946), a telephone engineer and past president of the club (1938-41). This is the south of the twin peaks, the north peak being Mount Gibson.

WATSON CREEK 63°33′N 135°07′W (105-M). A tributary of the Stewart River.

This local name has been in use since 1899, after Robert WATSON.

Watson graduated in mathematics from the University of Toronto and came to the Yukon in 1895, or 96. He was cheated out of a claim on Bonanza Creek in 1896 and was so soured that he formed a revulsion for all other men. He moved to this small stream, at that time almost totally isolated, and trapped for a living. While living here he made an intensive study of the works of Shakespeare as a source of modern slang. He died and was buried on the creek in 1905.

WATSON LAKE 60°07′N 128°48′W (105-A). At mile 635 (K1029) on the Alaska Highway in the southeastern Yukon.

Frank WATSON of Yorkshire, England started for the Klondike in early 1897 from Edmonton. Fighting his way through unmapped country he arrived on the upper Liard River in the spring of 1898. His illusions of easy gold in the Klondike were by this time completely dissipated. The country was appealing and he decided to stay in this region, to prospect and trap. He married an attractive Indian girl from Lower Post and from then on led an unrestricted and unhurried life. The upper Liard and its tributaries were his trapping and prospecting grounds while his home was on the shore of Watson Lake. The lake had been known since the 1870's as "Fish Lake". In 1941 the area become too crowded for him when construction was begun on the airport and the highway. He moved his family a few miles north to Windid Lake.

With the building of the Alaska Highway, most of the activity in the area moved ten miles east to what was then called Watson Lake Wye, the site of the present town.

To quote the *Alaska Highway News*, Special Edition, Summer 1959, "In the spring of 1941 operations for the construction of the airport at Watson Lake were begun. First stage was the shipment of supplies by boat from Vancouver to Wrangel. It was then necessary to tranship them by riverboat and barge some 160 miles up the Stikine River to Telegraph Creek, from there by truck some 76 miles to Dease Lake but only after this section of the road had been made passable. At Dease Lake the equipment was again unloaded into barges and boats and transported down the Dease River to Lower Post on the Liard River. Here a tote road some 26 miles in length had to be built into Watson Lake to the airport site."

Two runways approximately 5,000 feet in length were built, along with administration buildings and staff quarters for both RCAF and Department of Transport personnel. The work was completed in the autumn of 1943. The project was handed over to the government by the General Construction Company Ltd., which had built it all. A post office was opened on 1 July, 1942. Watson Lake being noted for its famous collection of sign posts, it may be of interest that the first post erected was the one put up by Carl L. Lindley of Denville, Illinois, in early 1942. He was a soldier in Company "D", of the 341st Engineers, US Army.

Frank WATSON died here but some of his family still live in the community. (See Baker Lake.)

MOUNT WATSON 62°55′N 137°11′W (115-I). East of Volcano Mountain, about 12 miles northeast of Fort Selkirk.

In November 1971 this mountain was given the name of No. 125 Corporal M. WATSON of the Royal Regiment of Canada. He was a member of the Yukon Field Force of 1898. They marched overland from Glenora on the Stikine River to Teslin Lake and rowed, in boats they had built, to Fort Selkirk.

Known as Cpl. M. Watson of the RRC's, it was found after his death that he was, in reality, the Hon. M.W. St. John Watson Beresford of Creaduff House, Athlone, Ireland, a nephew of Viscount Castlemain. He was 38 years of age and had been in the service for 10 or 11 years before killing himself, accidentally, with a service revolver in the barracks at Dawson on 28 March, 1900. (See Mounts Walters, Evans, Hansen and Corcoran.)

WATSON RIVER 60°11′N 134°44′W (105-D). Flows into the north end of Lake Bennett at Carcross.

This river was named by Lt. F. Schwatka, US Army, in 1883 after Professor Sereno WATSON of Harvard University. As it was previously unnamed, Dr. G.M. Dawson, GSC, allowed the name to stand.

WAUGH CREEK 64°55′N 137°02′W (116-A). A tributary to the Hart River in the Wernecke Mountains.

The Forest Warden for this region, C.J. Shattuck, stated in a letter to the CPCGN in June 1956 that "Waugh Creek is named after a fairly ordinary man. He was a miner and promoter who started a placer mine on this creek in 1906. About $50,000 in equipment was shipped via the Mackenzie and Peel Rivers in 1909. Some doubt exists as to whether the equipment was used or abandoned en-route. At any rate Waugh took his own life by hanging, in a hotel in Chicago in May 1910 rather than admit his failure to his backers."

Harry F. WAUGH was born in New Brunswick and came into the Yukon in the spring of 1896 and was one of the first to stake a claim in the Klondike. He staked the first claim after Carmack and his party, locating No. 14 Below Discovery, while his partner, Burpee, staked No. 15 Below.

Waugh's name appears in many newspaper accounts from 1905–10 in the Yukon, all concerning his efforts to establish a viable mining operation in one of the most inaccessible and inhospitable places on the North American continent. For instance, in 1906 he and "Black" Sullivan (another Klondike original) appeared at Herschel Island with specimens of gold-bearing quartz ore and went out to Dawson on the whaler *Kar-Luk* to record their claims. He searched the country from the Ogilvie Mountains to the Arctic slope in his quest for minerals. His partners in these ventures were almost all well known Yukoners of wealth and experience, such as "Black" Sullivan, Andrew Hunker and Thomas O'Brien, who had enough faith in his ability and integrity to back him financially for years.

Waugh's last action in the Yukon was to assist the RNWMP in a long search for some lost men.

Waugh may have seemed to be of no importance, and suspect because of his willingness to gamble his own and his friends' money on such chancy ventures as looking for mines. However, his actions over the years in choosing a life of hardship in this desolate country, the regard in which he was held by his peers and his eventual suicide, all point to a man with a terrible sense of integrity and responsibility. He was certainly no "ordinary man".

WEBBER CREEK 62°03′N 137°13′W (115-I). A small tributary to Nansen Creek from the east side.

Charles and Jack WEBBER were coal miners at Carmacks before deciding to go prospecting. In 1912 they explored the Mount Nansen area and found gold on this stream.

WELLESLEY LAKE 62°21′N 139°49′W (115-J&K). This large lake is the source of the Nisling River.

Charles Willard Hayes (1859–1916), USGS geologist from 1887–1911, joined Lt. F. Schwatka, US Army, in his last expedition in 1891. The expedition, sponsored by a syndicate of American newspapers, was to explore the region between the Lynn Canal and the Copper River. Mark Russell, a noted prospector of his time, accompanied them as their guide. Their route followed the Taku Inlet trail to Teslin Lake, along the Teslin River to the Lewes, up the White River and over the Skolai Pass into Alaska and then down the Chitina and Copper Rivers.

Hayes made the first classification of the Alaskan physiographic provinces. For much of the area covered he gathered the first scientific information. He named this lake after Wellesley College in Massachusetts. The college, established in the early 1800's, was named after Lord Mornington WELLESLEY, the Duke of Wellington. The "Iron Duke" was the conqueror of Napoleon's armies in the Spanish Peninsular and French Wars.

WERNECKE 63°56′N 135°15′W (105-M). On Keno Hill.

This small mining camp was started in 1921 to serve the newly-found silver-lead mines of Keno Hill. It was named for Livingstone WERNECKE ME, the manager of the Treadwell-Yukon Mining Company Ltd.

Wernecke, an American mining engineer, was working at the Alaska Gatineau Mine at Juneau as a construction engineer in 1914. He was next employed as a geologist at the Alaska Treadwell Gold Mining Co. at the same place. He was the last man out of that huge mine when it caved in and sea water filled it forever in 1917.

His company had followed with interest the new finds of high-grade, silver-lead ore in the Keno Hill area and in 1919 sent Wernecke there to investigate. He bought up several promising properties which were then formed into the Treadwell-Yukon Mining Co.

By 1923 they were shipping high-grade ore to Kellogg, Idaho. In 1925 they had a mill in production. The concentrated ores were shipped by horse and wagon to Mayo Landing, by WP&YR riverboats to Whitehorse and by rail to Skagway. From Skagway the ore went by steamer to Seattle and then again by rail to Idaho. Clearly, this ore had to be very rich to pay for this expensive and costly handling and still yield a profit. Although operations were suspended from 1927–32, Wernecke, as well as managing the mines in an excellent manner, continued to explore and to send out prospectors to find more mines. He had an abiding faith that large and rich mineral deposits would be found in the mountains to the east of the Mayo district and paralleling the Yukon-NWT boundary, a theory that is now being proven correct.

The Treadwell-Yukon Mining Co. suspended operations permanently in 1942 due to the difficulty in obtaining labour and supplies during the war years. The little settlement had been abandoned about 1933 when the ore gave out in the nearby mines.

Livingstone Wernecke was killed in an aircraft crash somewhere between Juneau and Ketchikan in 1941. His death may have influenced the company in their decision to suspend all operations. The Wernecke Mountains, in whose hidden riches he firmly believed, were named at a later date in memory of this exceptional man.

WESKATAHIN 60°08′N 137°03′W (115-A). Near the site of Dalton Post on the Tatshenshini River.

The history of this Indian settlement (now abandoned) begins long before any white man ever saw it. It was the meeting place for the interior Indians and the coastal tribes to trade each year. Jack Dalton, the famous gold-rush packer, came over the old trade trail from the coast in 1890 and '91, saw this sheltered place and made it the site of his main post and head-quarters in 1894. (See Neskataheen Lake.)

WEST LAKE 63°42'N 132°22'W (105–N). Northwest of the Rogue River.

This is a local name after Runer WEST, a Swedish trapper who lived here in the 1940's.

MOUNT WESTMAN 5,905' 64°06'N 134°11'W (106–D). East of the junction of the Beaver and Rackla Rivers.

In November 1964 this mountain was chosen to commemorate R-101306 Warrant Officer Robert Morris WESTMAN. He was born at Regina, Saskatchewan on 21 September, 1915 and enlisted in the RCAF at Van-couver on 8 May, 1941. He served in Canada and overseas and was missing, presumed killed in action, on 29 April, 1943.

WHEATON RIVER 60°07'N 134°53'W (105–D). Flows into the north end of Lake Bennett.

This river was named in 1883 by Lt. F. Schwatka, US Army, after Brevet Major General Frank WHEATON, US Army.

MOUNT WHITE 60°20'N 133°53'W (105–C). Two miles south of Jake's Corner.

William Ogilvie, DLS, during his survey of the Yukon River in 1887, named this bald hill after the then Minister of the Interior, the Hon. Thomas WHITE, who had supported the exploration and survey of the Yukon. Ogilvie had already named the White Pass after the same man.

WHITEHORSE 60°43'N 135°03'W (105–D). The capital of the Yukon Territory.

Situated at the upper limits of feasible steamboat navigation on the Yukon River and at the terminus of the WP&YR, a settlement began here in 1900. As well as controlling the shipping of the territory it became a supply and communications centre for the southern Yukon. The discovery and exploitation of the rich copper ore bodies nearby from 1899 to 1920 also helped to stimulate business and growth in the town.

Many fanciful stories have been and are told about the origin of the name

Whitehorse. It is probable that the first miners in 1880–81 saw a resemblance to white horses' manes in the white waters of the rapids. The name was in common use by 1887. The foot of the rapids made a natural stopping place for those passing through Miles Canyon and the rapids below. Few people dared these hazards with loaded boats, the majority preferring to unload and carry (portage) their goods around the dangerous waters. The boats were either let down on ropes or taken through by professional pilots. In any case this location made a good place to stop and reorganize outfits before proceeding on down the river. Most landed on the east side of the river and it was there that the first townsite of Whitehorse was surveyed in September 1899 by Paul T.C. Dumais, DLS.

The WP&YR had been granted 640 acres of land on the west side of the river for their terminus and in late 1899 laid out and surveyed a townsite which they named "Closeleigh", in honour of the Close brothers, of London England. The brothers had been instrumental in financing the construction of the railroad and the freighting operations of the company. The WP&YR, on 21 April, 1900, announced that "the name of the town is to be the old, known on two continents... Whitehorse."

The building of the Alaska Highway in 1942–43 assured the growth and permanence of the community. At the beginning of 1942 the population was about 500, which had increased to 8,000 by early summer when US Army Engineers and some civilian contractors arrived. This population decreased to about 3,000 by 1955 but the increasing search for oil and minerals in the north reversed this trend and it has grown steadily. The first post office was opened on 1 June, 1900, by F.W. Cane. In March 1951 the city replaced Dawson as the capital of the Yukon Territory.

The name of the town was always spelled as two words until the Geographic Board of Canada combined them on 21 March, 1957.

WHITE RANGE 60°01′N 134°29′W (105–D). On the east side of Windy Arm of Tagish Lake, near the BC boundary.

In the summer of 1899, George William Richard Montague WHITE-FRASER, DLS, DTS, BCLS, was engaged with a crew of two men in setting boundary monuments (cairns) on the Yukon-BC border between Lake Bennett and Teslin Lake. The burst of mining activity in the district had made the immediate delineation of the boundary between the Yukon and BC a necessity.

Arthur St. Cyr, DTS, in charge of the boundary survey, was following White-Fraser and cutting the actual line of the boundary, ten feet wide across country. He named this prominence after White-Fraser but when the maps of the survey were produced in Ottawa the Fraser had been dropped and it was never replaced. For a time in 1905 to 10, the period of intense mining activity, the hill was known locally as Mount Conrad and was so named on a geological map of the district. This name too was eventually dropped.

A few years ago the rest of the mountain group was included and White-Fraser Mountain, changed to White Mountain, then to Mount Conrad, is now the White Range.

WHITE RIVER 63°11′N 139°36′W (115–O&N). A major tributary to the Yukon River from the St. Elias Mountains.

Robert Campbell of the HBC in 1850 was the first white man to see this stream and named it for the colour of its water, caused by the suspension of white, volcanic ash that it carries. The Stick Indians called the river "Yu-Kon-Hini" or "Yu-Ko-Kon-Heena" and the Chilkats called it "Sand River". At the head of the stream the Tanana Indians called it the "Nasina" or "Erk-Heen" meaning Copper River.

This was the first river to be prospected in the Yukon watershed. Arthur Harper, Frederick W. Hart, A. Gestler and George W. Fitch (or Finch) spent the winter of 1873–74 on the upper part of the river. They were searching for the source of native (pure) copper described to them by the Indians. They did not find the deposits but did find placer gold prospects which were not large or rich enough to mine or to induce them back to the region the following summer.

This river is remarkable for the amount of sediment it carries down from its upper reaches. Some of it is silt, fed from the large glaciers of the St. Elias Mountains but most of it comes from an extended layer of volcanic ash through which the river flows.

Great eruptions of ash from volcanoes in the St. Elias Range took place about 900–1100 A.D. covering an area about 220 by 370 miles, reaching from Alaska into the Northwest Territories. It has been estimated that about 165 cubic miles of rock in the form of ash were deposited in some places up to 100 feet in depth. It is this ash which gives the river its colour and name.

WHITESTONE RIVER 60°01′N 137°13′W (115–A). Flows from British Columbia north into the Tatshenshini River.

This river was long known locally as "Tole" Creek after "Old Tole" who headed a prospecting party into the area in 1900 and was active here for many years afterward. When it was found that he was still living, the creek's name was changed. As he is now dead perhaps the maps will revert to the local name.

MOUNT WHITNEY   65°38'N 139°37'W (116-G&F). East of the Porcupine River.

This is a map designation name given in 1973 after Frank A. WHITNEY, who was an early principal of the Dawson Public School in 1917–18.

WILEY CREEK   61°02'N 133°47'W (105-F). A tributary of the Boswell River.

In May 1962 this stream was chosen to commemorate J-7234 Flight Lt. George William WILEY, MID. He was born on 24 January, 1922, at London, Ontario, and enlisted in the RCAF on 4 December, 1940, at Windsor, Ontario. He served in Canada and overseas and died a prisoner of war on 25 March, 1944.

WILKINSON RANGE   62°50'N 134°30'W (105-L). A small range of hills north of the Earn River.

This has been named after the WILKINSON family, two generations of whom have lived and trapped in this area.

WILLIAMS CREEK   62°24'N 136°37'W (115-I). Flows into the Yukon River five miles below Yukon Crossing.

A prospector of this name found the first gold on this stream and gave it his name in 1898. In 1907 other prospectors found quartz veins carrying good copper values on the banks of the stream, which started another rush to the area. A settlement called Boronite City was built at the mouth of the stream.

WILLIAMS CREEK   63°50'N 135°28'W (105-M). A tributary to Duncan Creek in the Mayo area.

This creek was probably named by and after Frank WILLIAMS who prospected and trapped from here east to the Mackenzie Mountains. He came in 1898, one of the first men in the district, and his name occurs often in the early news from the region. (See below.)

WILLIAMS CREEK   64°20'N 134°50'W (106-D). A tributary of the Beaver River.

This creek was also named after Frank WILLIAMS. (See above.) He assisted Charles Camsell, GSC, in his exploration of the Peel and Wind Rivers in the winter of 1904-05. Camsell held him in high regard, naming this stream for him. The mountain at the headwaters of the creek was later given the same name.

MOUNT WILLIAMS 5,585′ 60°46′N 135°23′W (105-D). South of the Takhini River.

J.D. WILLIAMS was a Canada Customs Officer at Whitehorse after the First World War. He was long active as a leader in the Boy Scout movement in the Yukon. This mountain was named in his honour in November 1973.

WILSON CREEK 60°36′N 133°30′W (105-C). Flows into the Thirty-mile River.

In August 1952 this creek was named in memory of George WILSON, a former postmaster at Whitehorse. He was also a prospector; he found gold on this creek and mined it for several years.

WILSON LAKE 62°52′N 130°04′W (105-J). At the headwaters of the Ross River.

This was named by Joseph Keele, GSC, in 1907 when he mapped the geology of this region. Charles WILSON prospected and trapped in this area in 1904-08 and gave Keele much assistance in his work. (See below.)

MOUNT WILSON 7,466′ 62°52′N 129°40′W (105-I). At the headwaters of the Ross and Pelly Rivers on the Yukon-NWT border.

Joseph Keele, GSC, named this peak, as well as the above creek in 1907. Charles WILSON, whom most people called "Old Man" Wilson, came into the Yukon with the Klondike rush. He soon gravitated to this section of the territory where he remained. Keele appreciated his wide knowledge of the country from here to the Mackenzie valley.

He spent the rest of his life, to about 1930, searching for the Lost McHenry Gold Mine. This was a phenomenally rich deposit of placer gold supposed to be somewhere in this general area. According to Keele, McHenry was said to have been an old Dease Lake miner who penetrated this region in the late 1870's or early 1880's. He returned to Dease Lake with about 40 pounds of coarse gold and nuggets. Various reasons were given for his failure to return to his find but he gave certain friends approximate directions to the location. Many prospectors have since searched for it without success. The area of the story overlaps the Nahanni country and may be connected with the lost gold mine stories of that area.

WIND CITY 65°43'N 135°12'W (106-E). On the west bank of the Wind River about eight miles above the Peel.

In the fall of 1898 many of the gold-seekers attempting to reach the Klondike from Edmonton by way of the Mackenzie, Rat, Porcupine, Peel and Wind Rivers were caught by winter and were unable to travel farther as the rivers froze. They gathered in small groups and built cabin communities to pass the winter where they were halted.

About 70 men and women gathered at this spot. Eben McAdam, a leader, quotes in his diary, "20 September 1898. Up at seven a.m. Left for lower cache at 9:20 a.m. Back at 1:23 p.m. with last load. Have named this place Wind City. Expect about 10 shacks and about 40 men to put up in this place this winter." (*The Klondike Rush through Edmonton* by J.G. McGregor)

The settlement existed from September 1898 to March 1899. To overcome the boredom of dark winter days and to avoid friction between themselves, they organized card clubs and tournaments, choirs, lectures, concerts and outdoor sports. Only two men died of scurvy despite a lack of fresh vegetables and meat. Most continued on to Dawson in the early spring although a few returned to Fort MacPherson and on home.

WIND RIVER 65°50'N 135°19'W (106-D&E). A major tributary to the Peel River.

This river has had this name from ancient times. The Loucheaux Indians of the country called it this because of the furious winds which blow down its course almost constantly.

WIND RIVER TRAIL

This was a winter road built for truck haulage of oil-well-drilling equipment and supplies. Beginning at a point just a few miles beyond Mayo it ran north to a point on the Bell River just a few miles short of the Arctic coast.

Leo Proctor of Whitehorse was instrumental in the conception and construction of this trail and it was built by the Arctic Oilfields Transport Ltd., a subsidiary of the WP&YR. Construction was started on 12 October, 1959, and completed on 12 January, 1960, for a distance of 385 miles.

Over 3,000 tons of material moved over the road, the most northerly truck road in North America.

MOUNT WOOD 15,885' 61°14'N 140°30'W (115-G&F). In the St. Elias Range.

J.J. McArthur, DLS, while surveying the International Boundary in July 1900, named this peak after Inspector (later Commissioner) Zachary Taylor WOOD NWMP.

Wood was the grandson of the twelfth president of the United States and a graduate of the Royal Military College of Kingston, Ontario. He joined the NWMP in 1883. By 1897 he had become an outstanding officer and held the rank of inspector. Chosen to go to the Yukon, he was for a period in charge of the Dawson detachment and earned a lasting reputation for his cool, efficient and totally successful maintenance of law and order in those turbulent times. He soon rose to command the RNWMP and died in 1915.

WOODBURN CREEK 63°08'N 136°15'W (115-P). Runs into Crooked Creek, south of Stewart Crossing.

A miner of this name was the first to find gold and to stake a claim on this stream in 1915. A sizeable rush followed with the creek and others around being staked.

WOODSIDE RIVER 62°03'N 139°34'W (105-J). Flows into the Pelly Lakes.

This was named in 1909 after Major Henry WOODSIDE. He came into the Yukon in 1898 and took an active part in Dawson and Yukon political affairs. He was the Yukon Census Commissioner in 1901 and was editor of the *Yukon Midnight Sun* newspaper in the early 1900's. He was active in promoting mining exploration in the territory and spent much time in the bush. He had an anti-American bias and strongly pushed Robert Henderson's claim to be the first man to discover the gold of the Klondike. He was instrumental in having the Canadian government recognize the claim and award Henderson a pension and other benefits.

MOUNT WORTHINGTON 60°35'N 137°23'W (115-A). In the Auriol Range.

This was named in June 1968 after one of Canada's most distinguished professional soldiers, Major General Frederick Frank WORTHINGTON

CB, MC, MM, CD. He was born at Peterhead, Scotland on 17 September, 1889. Enlisting in the Canadian army at Montréal, Québec on 17 March, 1916, as a private, he won a commission in the field in France and several decorations for bravery. He enlisted again on 1 September, 1939, and was instrumental in developing armoured fighting vehicles for the Canadian and Allied armies. He organized and commanded the 5th Canadian Armoured Division until 1943. He served until his retirement on 18 March, 1943, and died on 5 December, 1967.

WOUNDED MOOSE CREEK 63°36′N 138°42′W (115-O&N). Flows north into the Indian River in the Klondike District.

There is some evidence that this stream was named by Robert Henderson when he prospected it in March or April 1895. No payable gold was found on it. The mountain at its headwaters was given the same name at a later date.

YING YANG CREEK 64°18′N 138°28′W (116-B&C). Flows into the North Klondike River from the west.

This was named in 1968 by one of the men surveying the route of the Dempster Highway.

YUKON CROSSING 62°21′N 136°29′W (115-I). On the Lewes (Yukon) River near Rink Rapids.

This little settlement was at the point where the old Whitehorse-Dawson Road crossed the Lewes (Yukon) River. During the summers a ferry operated here. A roadhouse and telegraph station were also located here. The settlement was abandoned with the end of the riverboat era and the building of the new highway to Dawson.

MOUNT YUKON 10,600′ 60°58′N 140°58′W (115-B&C). In the Centennial Range of the St. Elias Mountains.

This peak was named in 1967 to honour the Yukon Territory during Canada's Centennial Year. (See Centennial Range.)

THE YUKON RIVER

The Yukon River is the focal point of Yukon history. It provided the only feasible access by itself and its tributaries to almost 70% of the territory, and for many years was the main route for people and traffic. In those days life in the territory was governed by the periods when the river was open or frozen. The summer was a time of bustling activity and the riverboats carried prospectors and freight to all parts. In the winter men settled in to mine their summer prospects, to trap in their chosen areas and above all, to pass away the long, cold, dark winter. Limited to horse and dog teams, transportation was slow and costly in the winter. The cold brought movement to a minimum.

As well as access, the river provided food. Its magnificent runs of salmon, as well as other fish, formed a major proportion of the diet of the native peoples, most of whom lived along the waterways.

The name Yukon was given by the HBC trader John Bell, who in 1846 descended the Porcupine River from the Mackenzie delta to its junction with the Yukon. He called it the "Youcon", his version of the Loucheaux Indian word"Yuchoo", meaning "the Greatest River" or "Big River". At this junction in 1847 Alexander Hunter Murray established the first HBC post on the river, Fort Yukon.

The estuary of the Yukon had been explored in 1835–38 by the Russian Glasunov, who named it the "Kwikhpak", the Aleut Eskimo word meaning "Great River". The Tanana Indians called it "Niga-to", with the same meaning.

Robert Campbell of the HBC, the first explorer of the south and central Yukon region, reached the headwaters of the Pelly (the main branch of the Yukon) in 1840 by way of the Liard and Frances Rivers. In 1848 he descended the Pelly to the Yukon River, the upper part of which he called the Lewes River and the lower part, below the junction, the Pelly. In the same year he began construction of Fort Selkirk and, floating downstream, arrived at Fort Yukon. This journey established the course and fact of a new and great trade route through the Yukon and Alaska Territories. Although he had named the river the "Pelly", he now adopted that given by John Bell and the river was known as the Yukon from its mouth to Fort Selkirk.

The GSC gives the length of the river from the foot of Marsh Lake to the Bering Sea as 1979 miles. Other authorities, using the Pelly or Teslin branches, argue for total distances of up to 2300 miles. It is navigable by large riverboats from its mouth to Whitehorse (before the bridge was built at Carmacks). It was the last major river to be explored in North America, the fourth longest, and the fifth largest in volume of water flow.

Since the advent of cheaper and more regular transport by road and aircraft the river has reverted to the wilderness and is now much the same as it was a century ago, before the coming of the white man; perhaps more so, as the native Indians who once lived along its banks have now mostly moved to the settlements. The last riverboat to carry freight and passengers stopped in 1956. However, as the main part of the "Trail of 98", the river acquired a glamour that it will never lose.

THE YUKON TERRITORY

In 1670 the Hudson's Bay Company (The Governor and Company of Adventurers Trading into Hudson's Bay) was given its charter by King Charles II of England. This charter gave them, in effect, the outright control of northern Québec, Ontario and all of what is now middle, western and Arctic Canada. To quote the charter, "The true and absolute Lords and Proprietors."

It was not until early in the 19th century that they began to realize just how vast an empire they had been given. They gradually relinquished parts of it to the established governments of eastern Canada as these governments developed and lands became colonized. With the Deed of Surrender in 1869 of Rupert's Land and the old Northwest Territories, the Hudson's Bay Company became a wholly commercial enterprise with no powers of government. After the passing of this act the Yukon was made a provisional district of the NWT, to be governed from the NWT capital at Regina.

This situation lasted until the tremendous influx of people to the Yukon after the discovery of gold on the Fortymile River in late 1886. The Dominion government, in the next few years, decided to assume a more direct role in the affairs of the territory. This was started by sending in Inspector Charles Constantine and 18 men of the NWMP in 1894–95 as well as a Canada Customs Agent. Constantine was appointed Dominion Agent for the territory. The Order-in-Council effecting this action also demarked the Yukon as a separate district of the NWT.

In 1897 the Dominion government was forced into action because of the huge preponderance of American nationals in the population of the Yukon; a figure often set at 75%. They appointed Major James Morrow Walsh as the Chief Executive Officer of the Yukon Territory (which was not yet in existence). Thomas Fawcett was appointed Gold Commissioner, Dominion Agent and Mining Recorder. T.H. McGuire was made Judge of the Court of the Yukon Provisional District.

In June 1898 "An Act to Provide for the Government of the Yukon Territory" was passed, which made the Yukon, for the first time, a separate territory. It also provided a council composed of six senior officials, all taking orders from Ottawa, with all ties to Regina severed.

In 1900 two of the councillors were elected from the general public. In 1902 all five were elected. In later years the total number of councillors was increased to seven and in the last year, to 12. The commissioner has always been appointed by Ottawa.

YUSEZYU RIVER 61°38′N 129°42′W (105-H). Flows into the north end of the west arm of Frances Lake.

Dr. G.M. Dawson GSC, on his exploration of this region in 1887, recorded this local Indian name but gave no translation. Henry Thibert, the discoverer of the Dease Lake goldfields, had explored this area in the 1870's and gave Dawson much of his information.

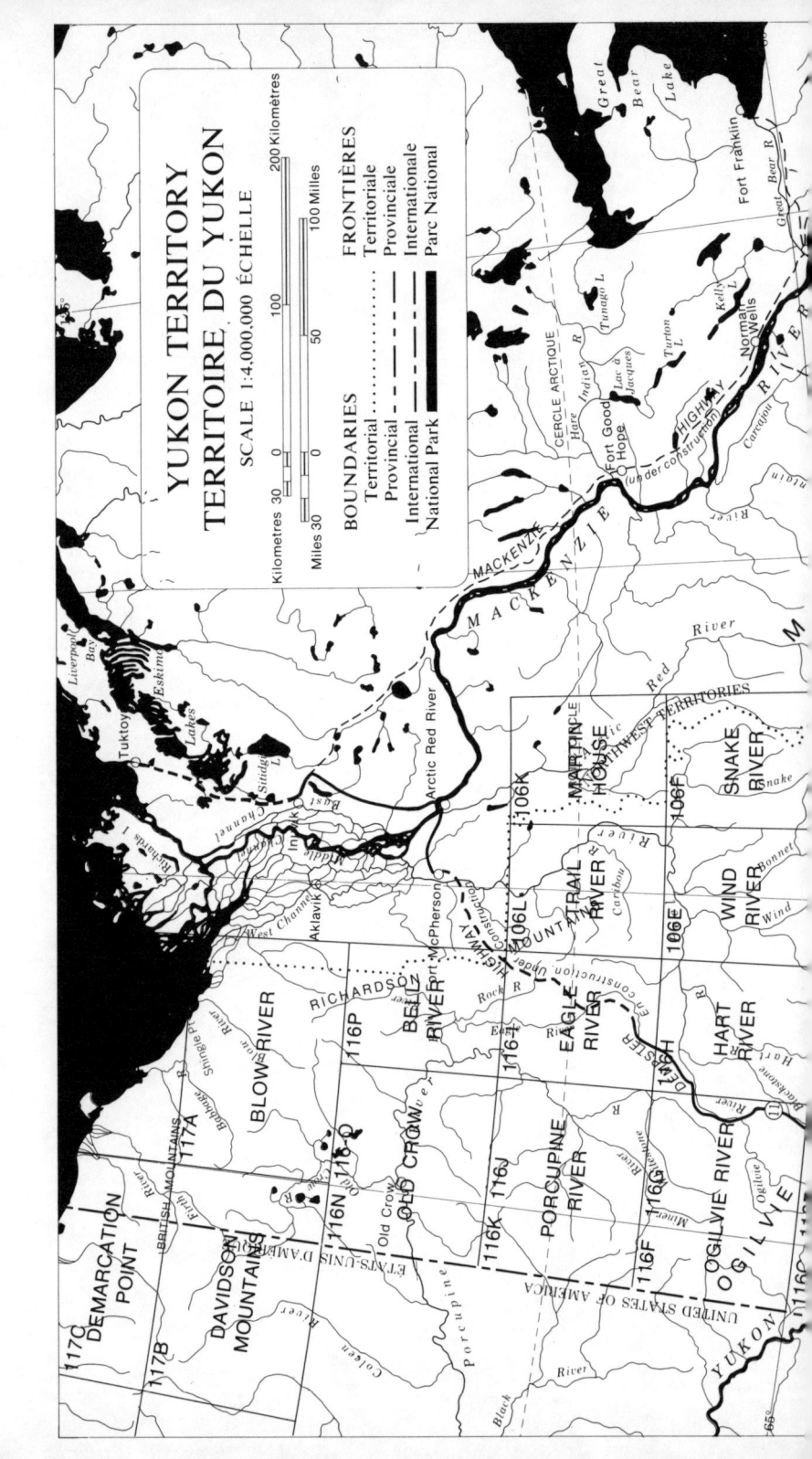

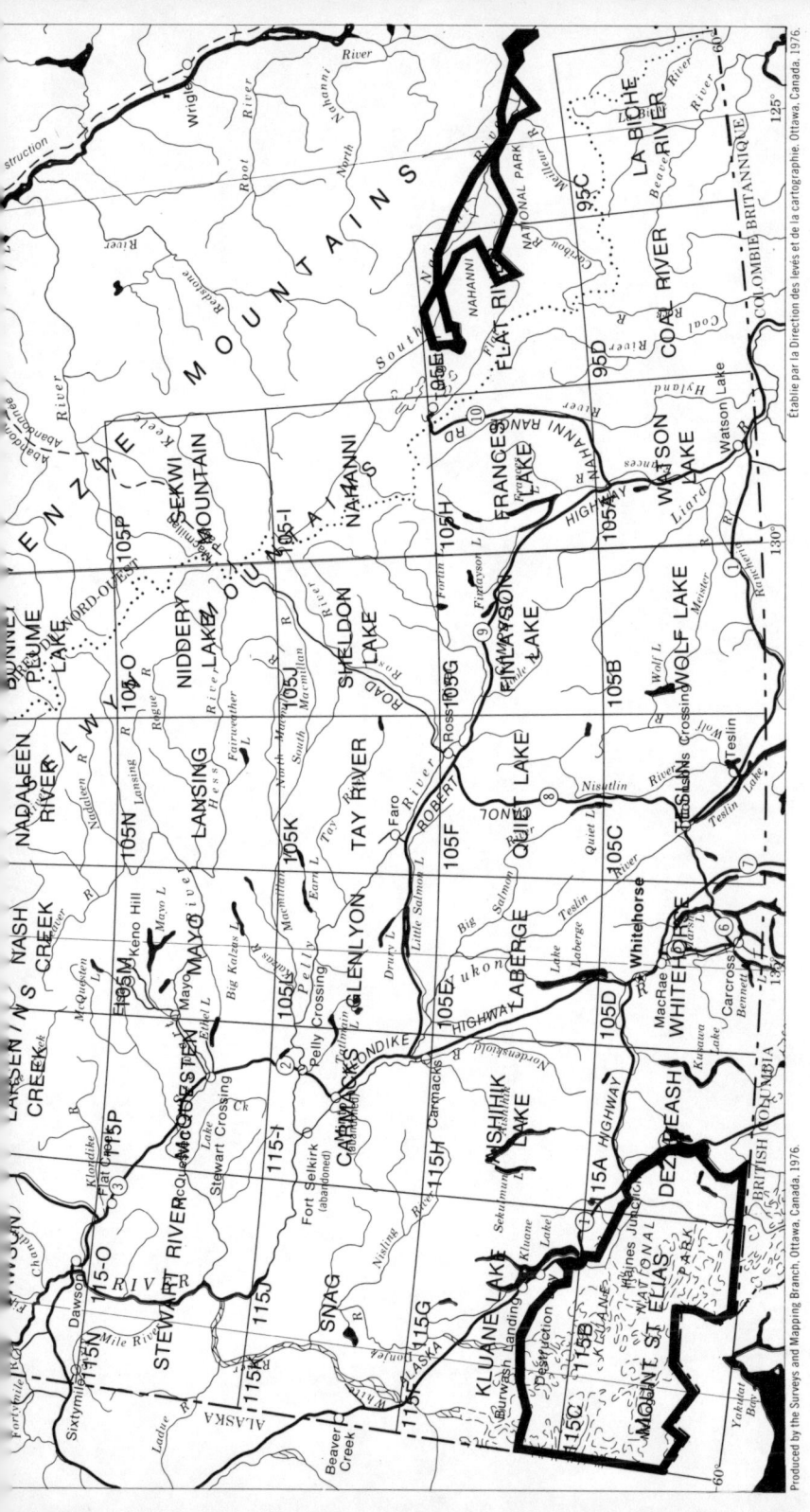

Produced by the Surveys and Mapping Branch, Ottawa, Canada, 1976.

Établie par la Direction des levés et de la cartographie, Ottawa, Canada, 1976.

NOTES

NOTES

NOTES

NOTES